D0685758

MUHAMMAD NAJEM, WAR REPORTER

MUHAMMAD NAJEM, WAR REPORTER

How One Boy Put the Spotlight on Syria

Muhammad Najem and **Nora Neus**
Illustrated by **Julie Robine**

Colors by Shin-Yeon Moon

LITTLE, BROWN AND COMPANY

New York Boston

About This Book

This book was edited by Andrea Colvin and designed by Karina Granda. The production was supervised by Bernadette Flinn, and the production editor was Jake Regier. The text was set in Colby and Brandon, and the display type is Colby.

Text copyright © 2022 by Muhammad Najem and Nora Neus
Illustrations copyright © 2022 by Julie Robine
Colors by Shin-Yeon Moon
Lettering by AndWorld Design

Cover illustration copyright © 2022 by Julie Robine. Cover design by Karina Granda.
Cover copyright © 2022 by Hachette Book Group, Inc.

Hachette Book Group supports the right to free expression and the value of copyright. The purpose of copyright is to encourage writers and artists to produce the creative works that enrich our culture.

The scanning, uploading, and distribution of this book without permission is a theft of the author's intellectual property. If you would like permission to use material from the book (other than for review purposes), please contact permissions@hbgusa.com. Thank you for your support of the author's rights.

Little, Brown and Company
Hachette Book Group
1290 Avenue of the Americas, New York, NY 10104
Visit us at LBYR.com

First Edition: September 2022

Little, Brown and Company is a division of Hachette Book Group, Inc. The Little, Brown name and logo are trademarks of Hachette Book Group, Inc.

The publisher is not responsible for websites (or their content) that are not owned by the publisher.

Photo credits: Pages iv, 302, 310, 311, 312 courtesy of Muhammad Najem. Page 313 (*top*) courtesy of Muhammad Najem. Page 313 (*center*) and page 313 (*bottom*) courtesy of Nora Neus.
Page 314 courtesy of Nora Neus.

Library of Congress Cataloging-in-Publication Data
Names: Najem, Muhammad, author. | Neus, Nora, author. | Robine, Julie, illustrator.
Title: Muhammad Najem, war reporter : how one boy put the spotlight on Syria /
Muhammad Najem with Nora Neus; art by Julie Robine.
Description: New York: Little, Brown and Company, 2022. |
Audience: Ages 8–14 | Summary: "A graphic memoir by young Syrian Muhammad Najem, who rose to international notoriety during the Syrian Civil War due to his on-the-ground reporting using social media." —Provided by publisher.
Identifiers: LCCN 2021027580 | ISBN 9780759556898 (hardcover) |
ISBN 9780759556904 (trade paperback) | ISBN 9780759556911 (ebook)
Subjects: LCSH: Najem, Muhammad—Comic books, strips, etc. | Reporters and reporting—Syria—Comic books, strips, etc. | War correspondents—Syria—Biography—Comic books, strips, etc. | Reporters and reporting—Syria—Juvenile literature. | War correspondents—Syria—Biography—Juvenile literature. | Syria—History—Civil War, 2011—Personal narratives—Comic books, strips, etc. | Syria—History—Civil War, 2011—Personal narratives—Juvenile literature. | LCGFT: Graphic novels.
Classification: LCC DS98.72.N34 A3 2022 | DDC 956.9104/23—dc23
LC record available at https://lccn.loc.gov/2021027580

ISBNs: 978-0-7595-5689-8 (hardcover), 978-0-7595-5690-4 (pbk.), 978-0-7595-5691-1 (ebook),
978-0-316-33219-4 (ebook), 978-0-316-33237-8 (ebook)

PRINTED IN GERMANY

Mohn Media

Hardcover: 10 9 8 7 6 5 4 3 2 1
Paperback: 10 9 8 7 6 5 4 3 2 1

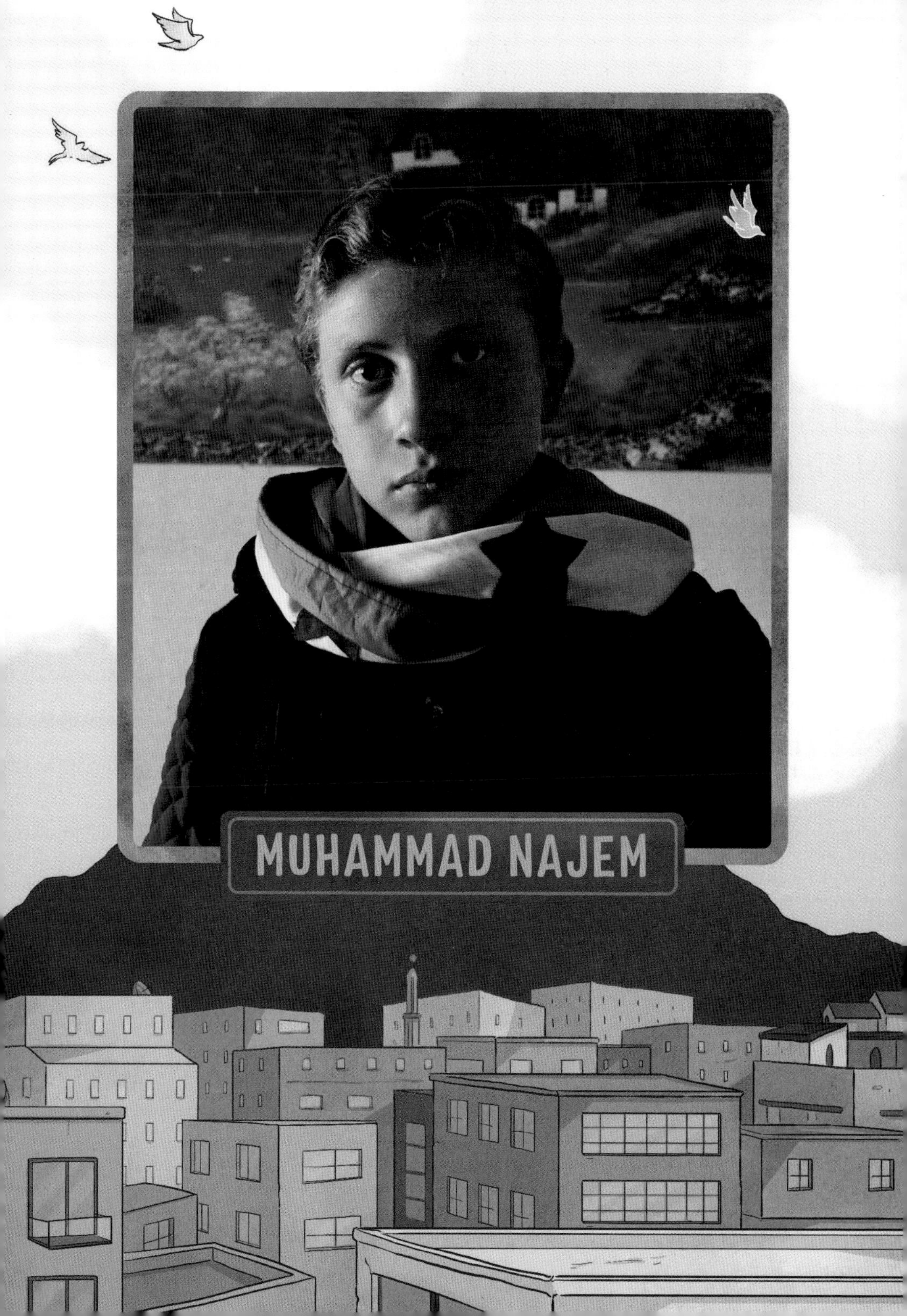
MUHAMMAD NAJEM

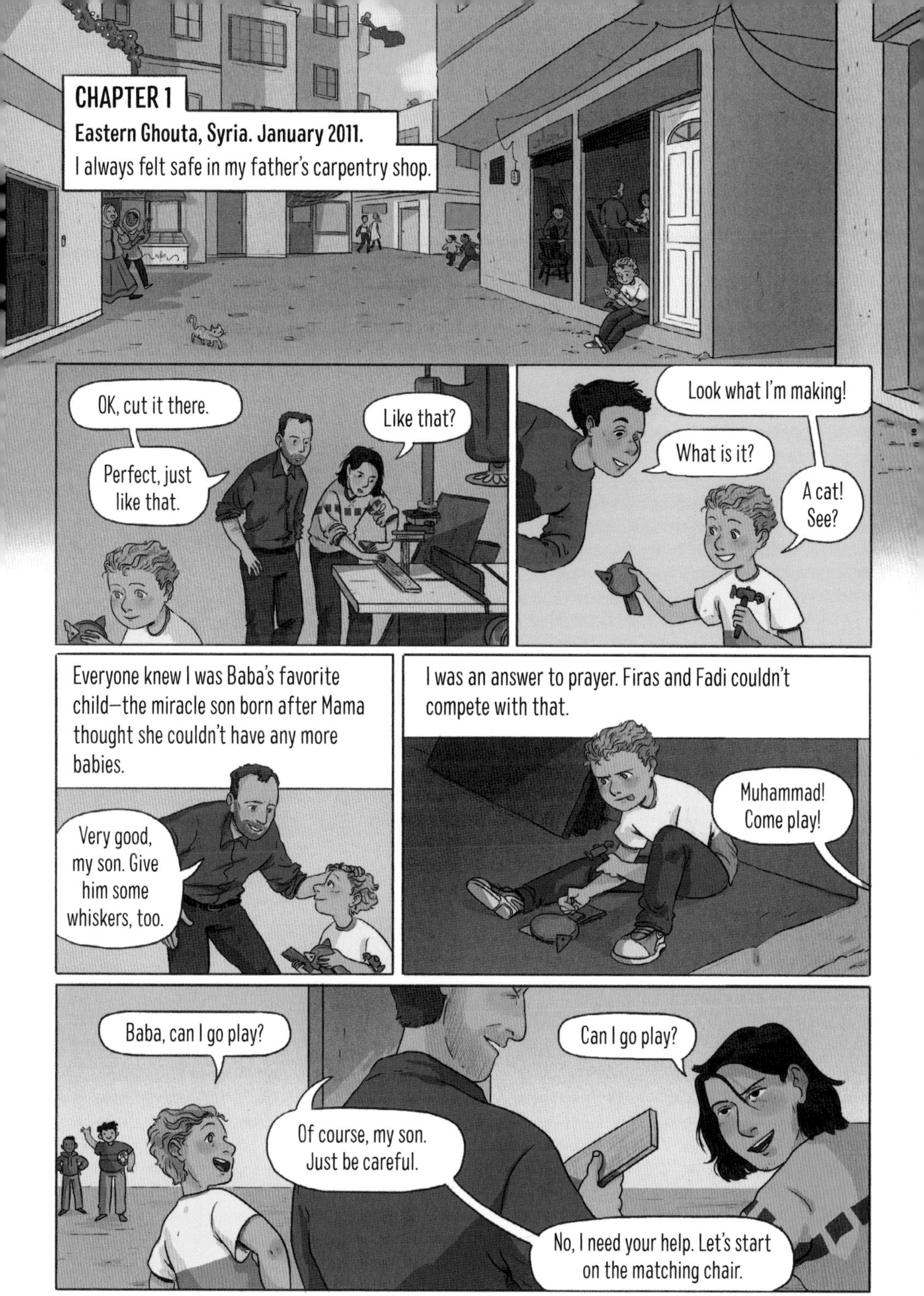
CHAPTER 1
Eastern Ghouta, Syria. January 2011.
I always felt safe in my father's carpentry shop.
OK, cut it there.
Like that?
Perfect, just like that.
Look what I'm making!
What is it?
A cat! See?
Everyone knew I was Baba's favorite child—the miracle son born after Mama thought she couldn't have any more babies.
Very good, my son. Give him some whiskers, too.
I was an answer to prayer. Firas and Fadi couldn't compete with that.
Muhammad! Come play!
Baba, can I go play?
Can I go play?
Of course, my son. Just be careful.
No, I need your help. Let's start on the matching chair.

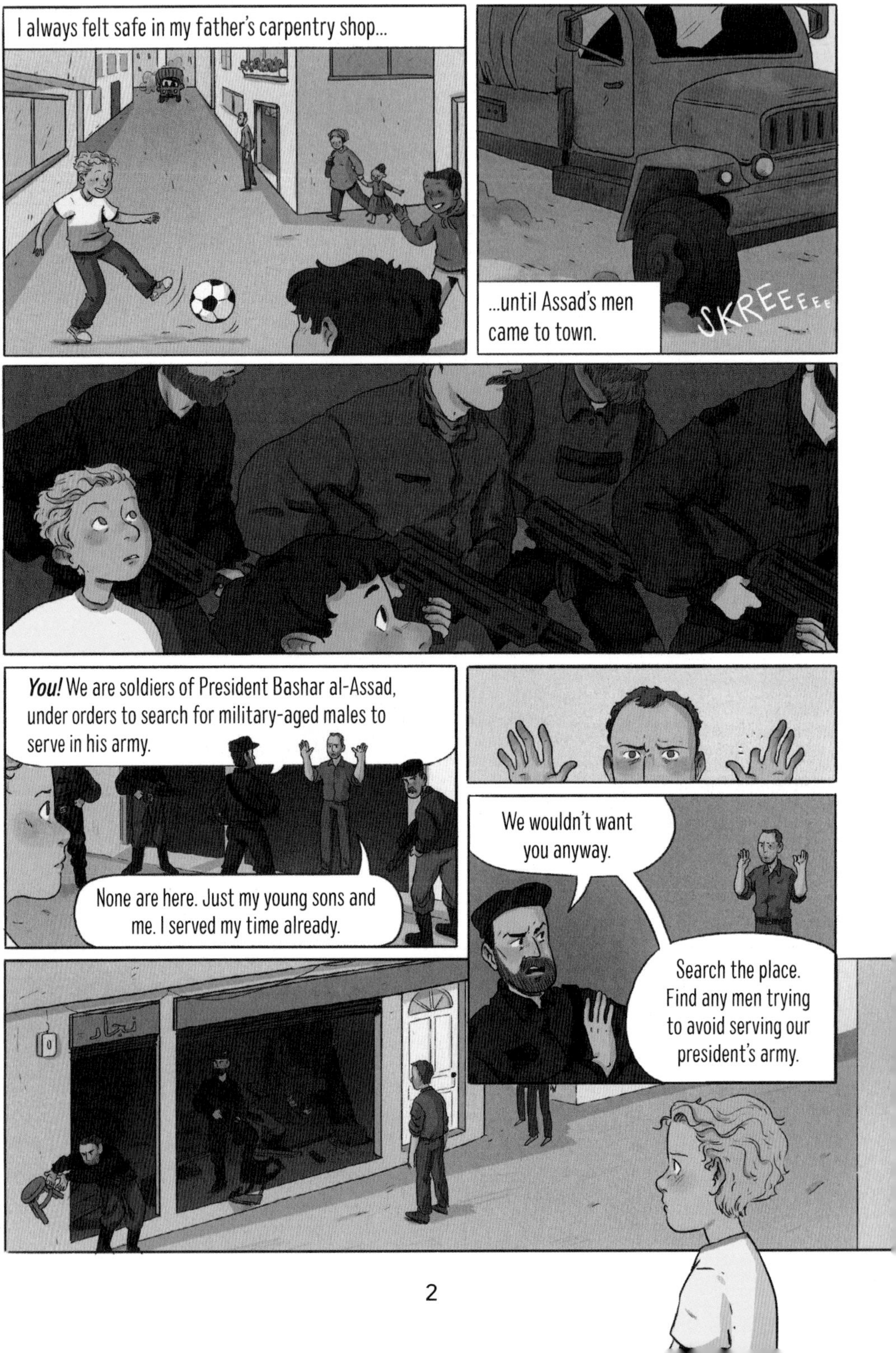
I always felt safe in my father's carpentry shop...
...until Assad's men came to town.
SKREEEEEE
You! We are soldiers of President Bashar al-Assad, under orders to search for military-aged males to serve in his army.
None are here. Just my young sons and me. I served my time already.
We wouldn't want you anyway.
Search the place. Find any men trying to avoid serving our president's army.
نجار

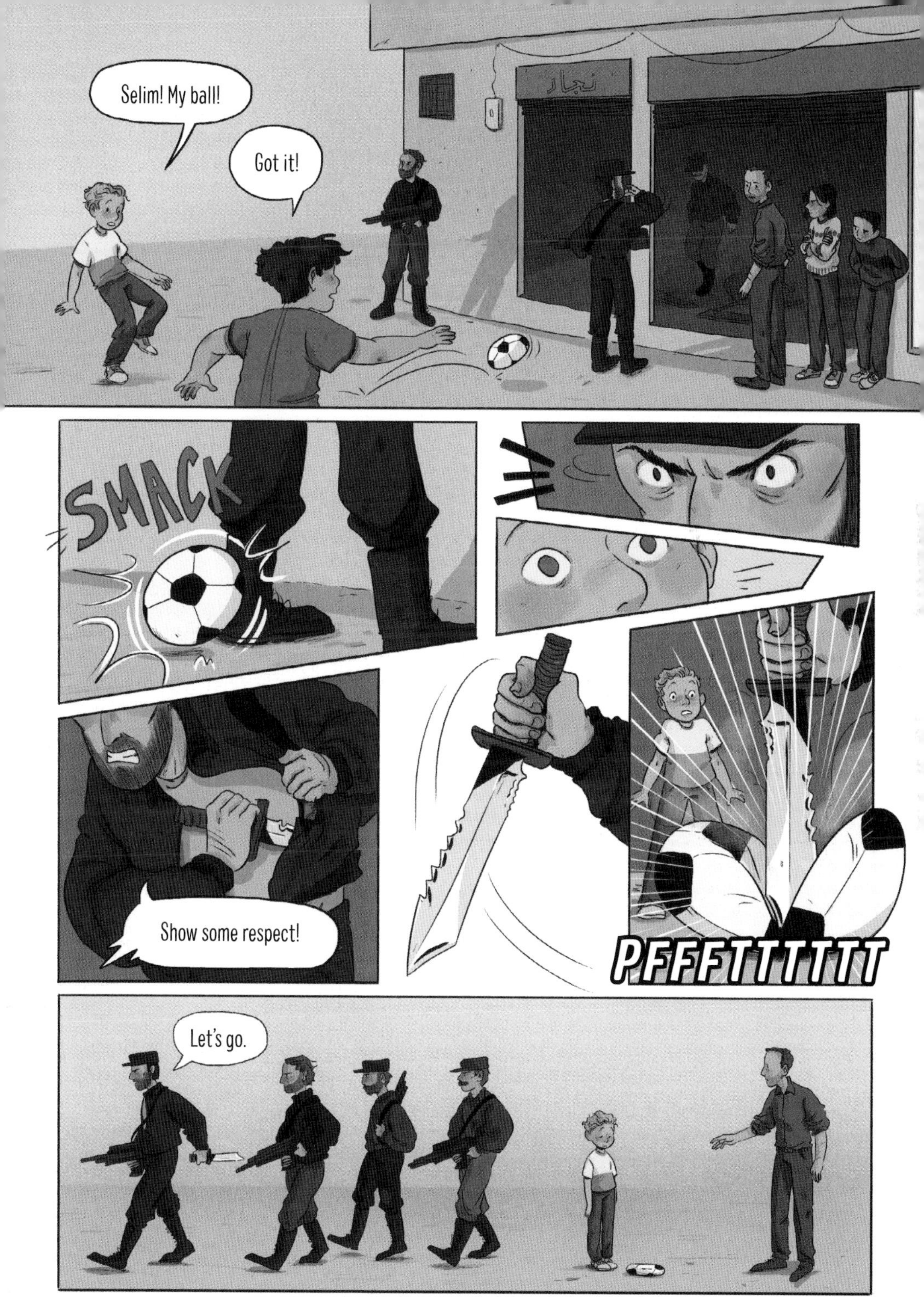
Selim! My ball!
Got it!
SMACK
Show some respect!
PFFFTTTTTT
Let's go.

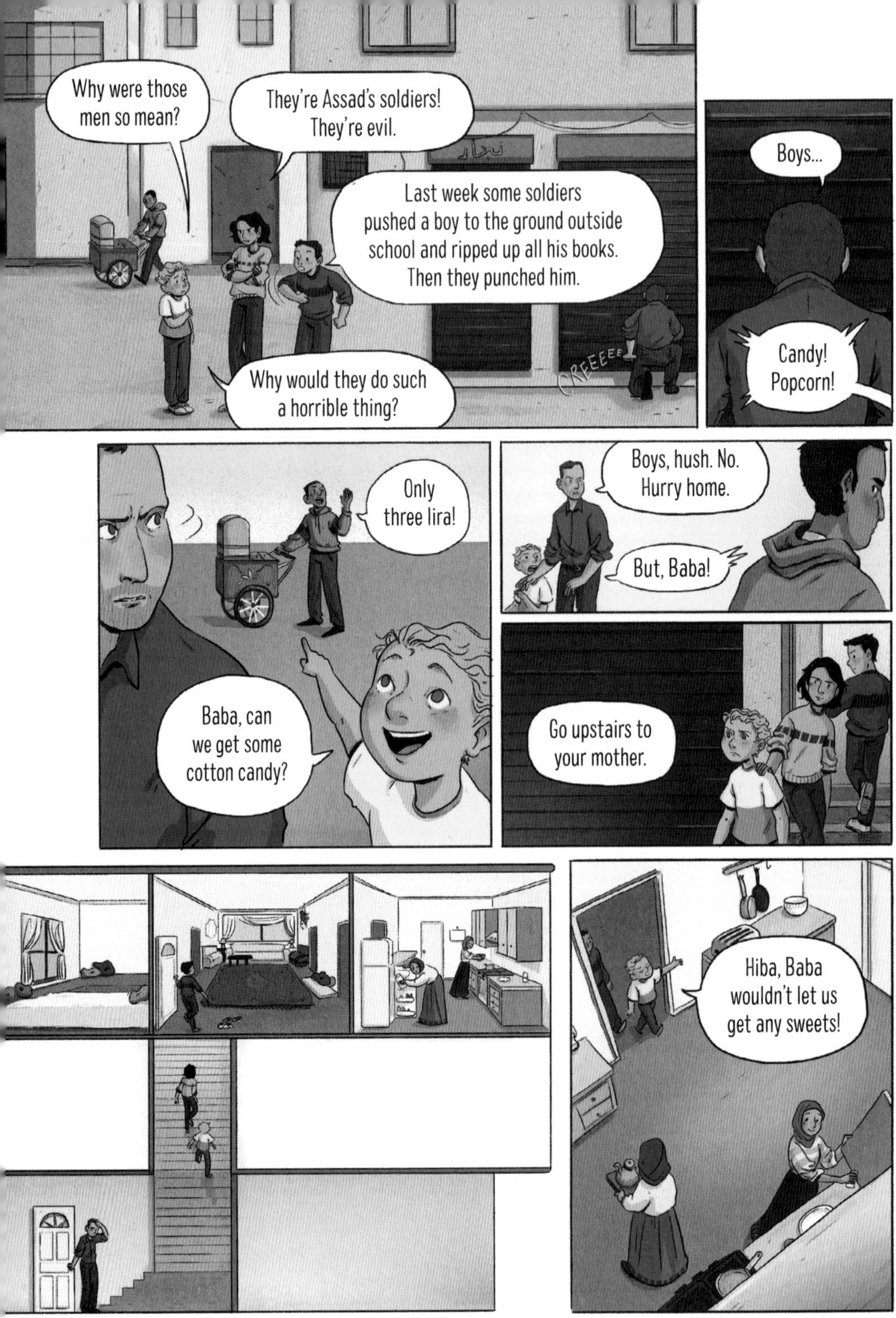
Why were those men so mean?
They're Assad's soldiers! They're evil.
Last week some soldiers pushed a boy to the ground outside school and ripped up all his books. Then they punched him.
Why would they do such a horrible thing?
CREEEEE
Boys...
Candy! Popcorn!
Only three lira!
Baba, can we get some cotton candy?
Boys, hush. No. Hurry home.
But, Baba!
Go upstairs to your mother.
Hiba, Baba wouldn't let us get any sweets!

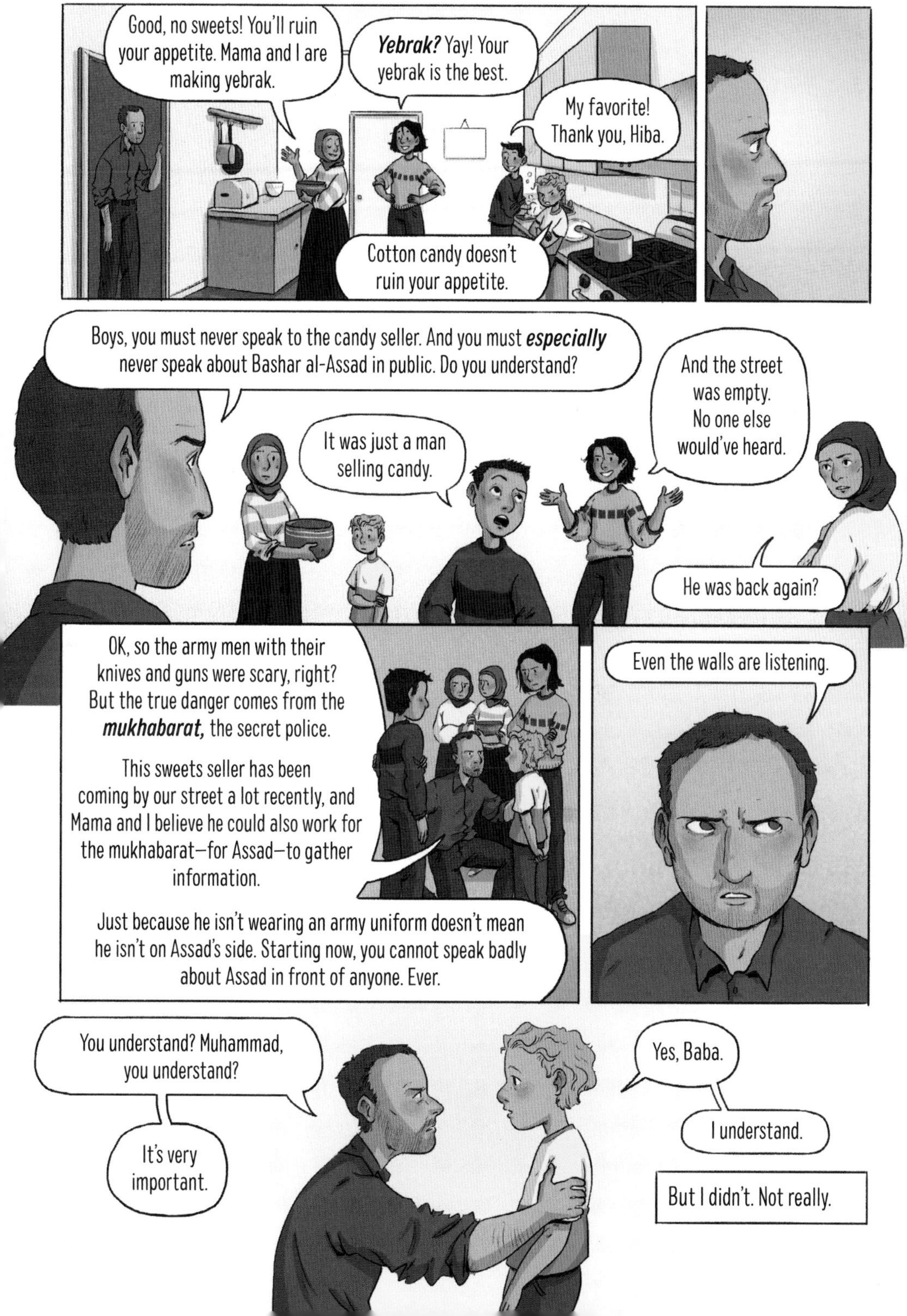
Good, no sweets! You'll ruin your appetite. Mama and I are making yebrak.
Yebrak? Yay! Your yebrak is the best.
My favorite! Thank you, Hiba.
Cotton candy doesn't ruin your appetite.
Boys, you must never speak to the candy seller. And you must ***especially*** never speak about Bashar al-Assad in public. Do you understand?
It was just a man selling candy.
And the street was empty. No one else would've heard.
He was back again?
OK, so the army men with their knives and guns were scary, right? But the true danger comes from the ***mukhabarat,*** the secret police.
This sweets seller has been coming by our street a lot recently, and Mama and I believe he could also work for the mukhabarat—for Assad—to gather information.
Just because he isn't wearing an army uniform doesn't mean he isn't on Assad's side. Starting now, you cannot speak badly about Assad in front of anyone. Ever.
Even the walls are listening.
You understand? Muhammad, you understand?
It's very important.
Yes, Baba.
I understand.
But I didn't. Not really.

Syria is my home. It's a country in the Middle East, near Turkey, Jordan, Lebanon, and Iraq. It only gained its independence from France in 1946. The people who lived in this newly created country of Syria were from different ethnic groups, religions, and races. They spoke different languages and professed different faiths. Everybody argued over what a "real Syrian" was. This led to a lot of fighting within Syria for the next few decades about who would be in control.

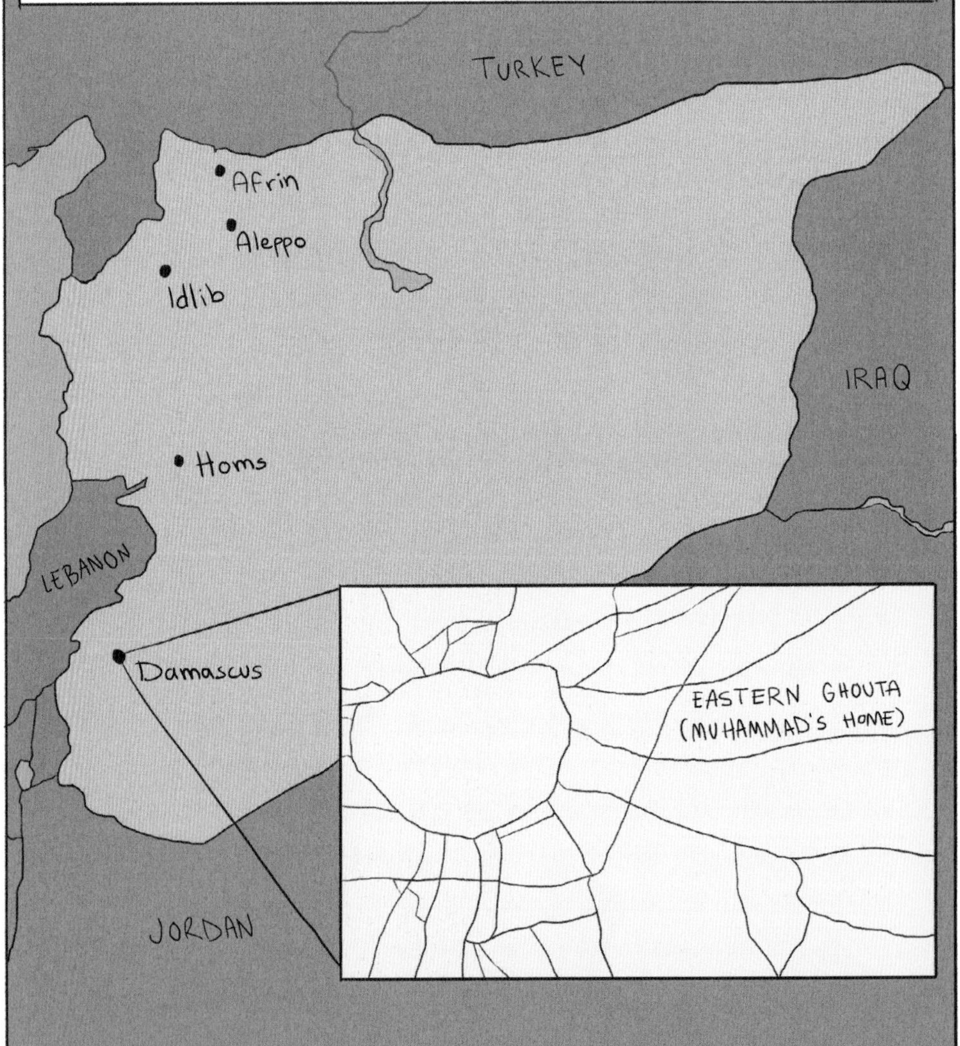
TURKEY
Afrin
Aleppo
Idlib
IRAQ
Homs
LEBANON
Damascus
EASTERN GHOUTA
(MUHAMMAD'S HOME)
JORDAN

Hafez al-Assad

But in November 1970, a new man, who would stay in power for a really long time, took control. Hafez al-Assad used the military to seize power. He ruled until his death in 2000, when his son Bashar took over. (Bashar had been an eye doctor before.) President Bashar al-Assad has been in power ever since. His regime is very powerful, and to keep that power, he is very brutal. The Assad regimes—both the father's and the son's—used torture, intimidation, and even murder to keep people in line.

In 2011, protestors decided they'd had enough of Assad's intense military rule. Revolutions had ushered in new democratic governments in North African and other Middle Eastern countries, such as Egypt and Libya, as part of what would come to be known as the Arab Spring. Why not here?

The protests started that March, when I was eight years old.

President Bashar al-Assad

CHAPTER 2

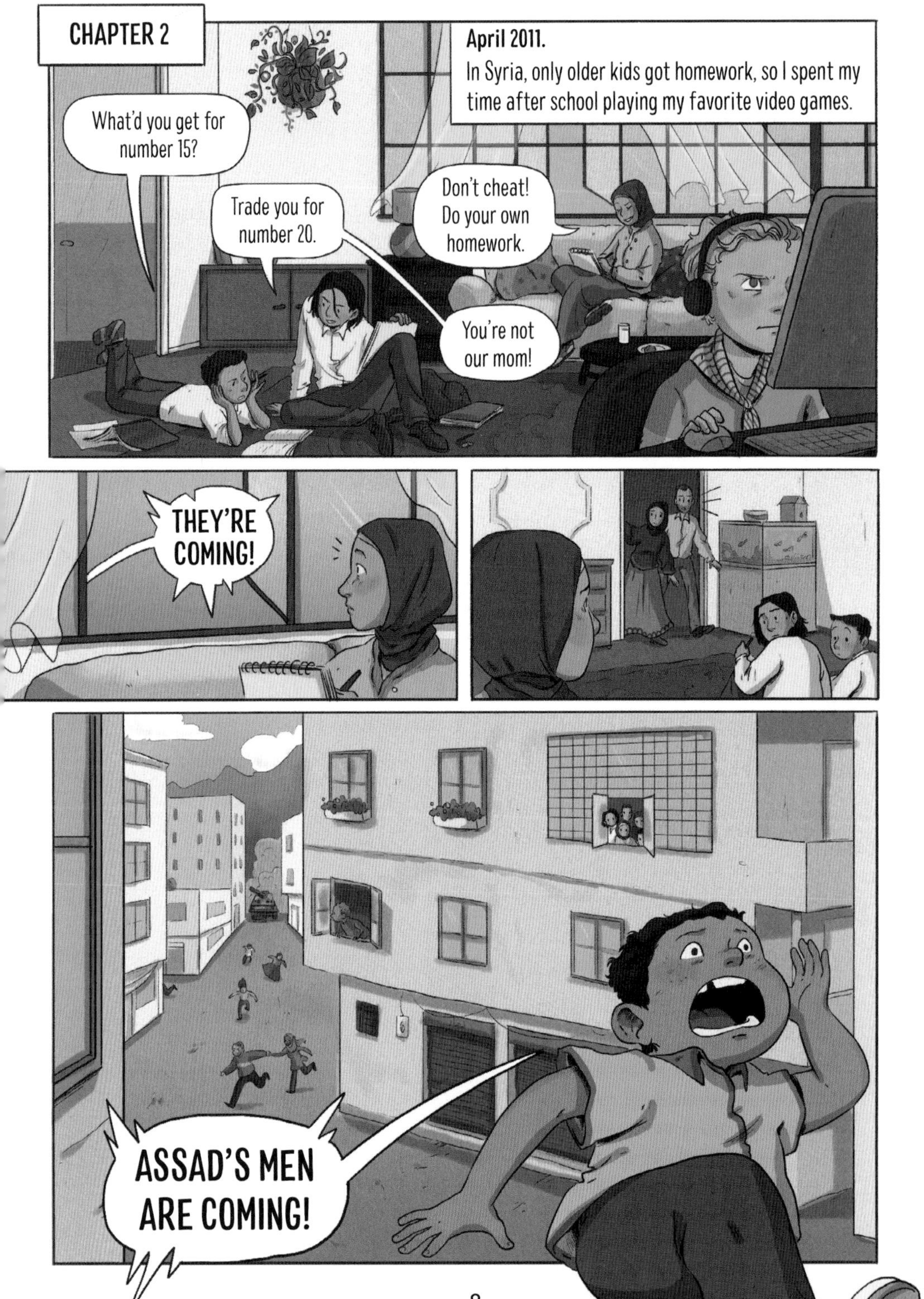
April 2011.
In Syria, only older kids got homework, so I spent my time after school playing my favorite video games.
What'd you get for number 15?
Trade you for number 20.
Don't cheat! Do your own homework.
You're not our mom!
THEY'RE COMING!
ASSAD'S MEN ARE COMING!

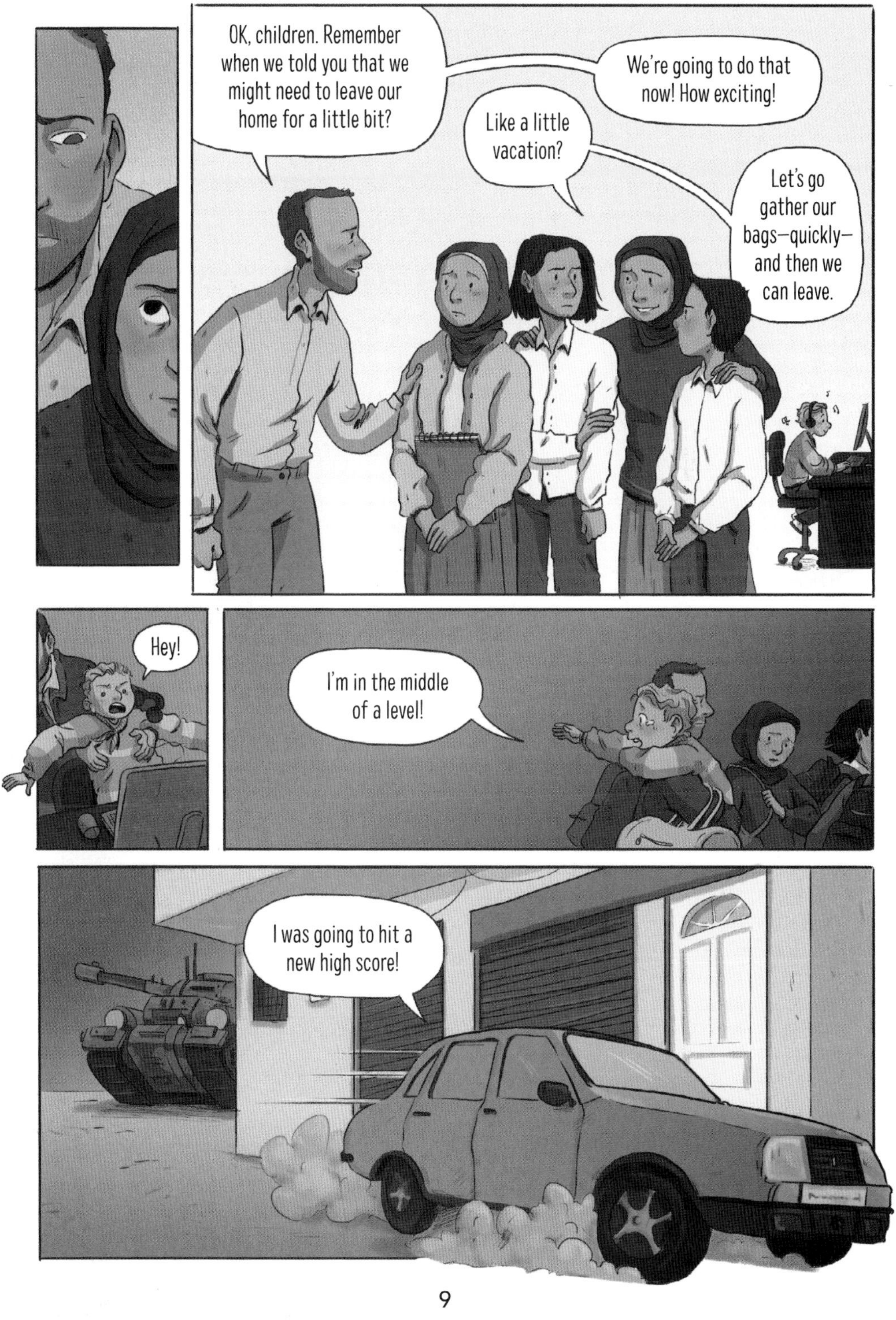
OK, children. Remember when we told you that we might need to leave our home for a little bit?
Like a little vacation?
We're going to do that now! How exciting!
Let's go gather our bags—quickly—and then we can leave.
Hey!
I'm in the middle of a level!
I was going to hit a new high score!

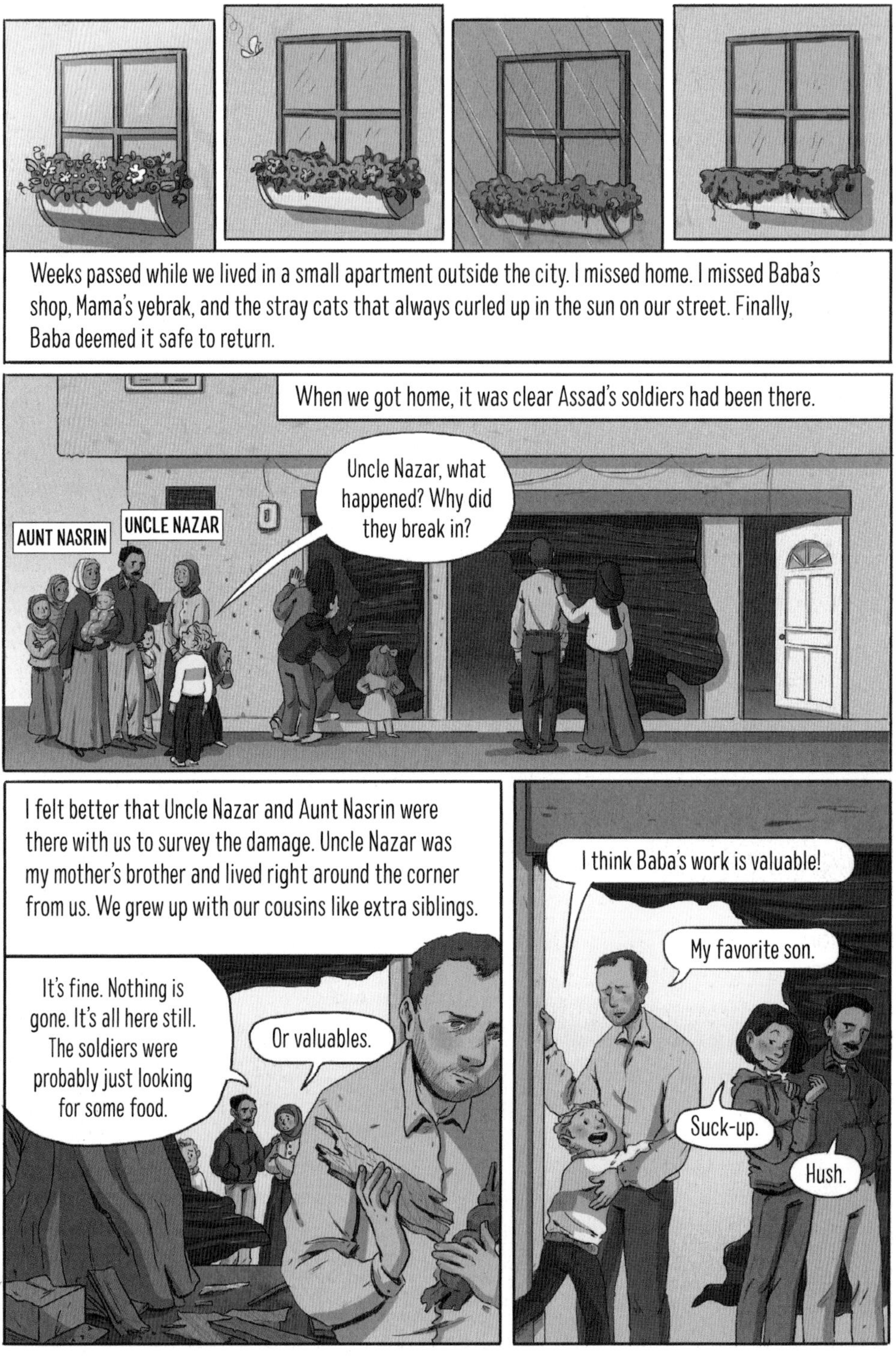
Weeks passed while we lived in a small apartment outside the city. I missed home. I missed Baba's shop, Mama's yebrak, and the stray cats that always curled up in the sun on our street. Finally, Baba deemed it safe to return.
When we got home, it was clear Assad's soldiers had been there.
AUNT NASRIN
UNCLE NAZAR
Uncle Nazar, what happened? Why did they break in?
I felt better that Uncle Nazar and Aunt Nasrin were there with us to survey the damage. Uncle Nazar was my mother's brother and lived right around the corner from us. We grew up with our cousins like extra siblings.
It's fine. Nothing is gone. It's all here still. The soldiers were probably just looking for some food.
Or valuables.
I think Baba's work is valuable!
My favorite son.
Suck-up.
Hush.

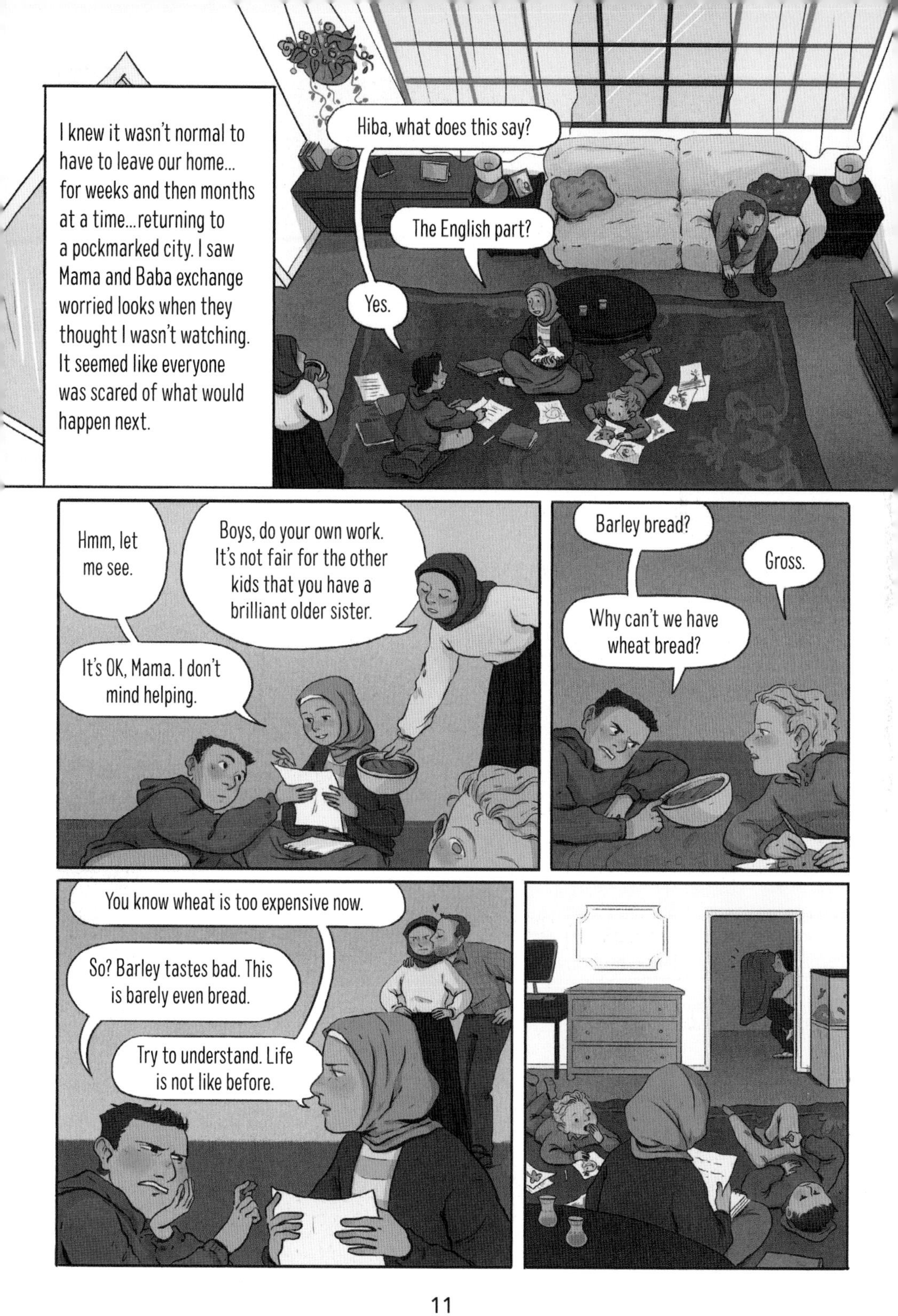
I knew it wasn't normal to have to leave our home... for weeks and then months at a time...returning to a pockmarked city. I saw Mama and Baba exchange worried looks when they thought I wasn't watching. It seemed like everyone was scared of what would happen next.
Hiba, what does this say?
The English part?
Yes.
Hmm, let me see.
Boys, do your own work. It's not fair for the other kids that you have a brilliant older sister.
It's OK, Mama. I don't mind helping.
Barley bread?
Why can't we have wheat bread?
Gross.
You know wheat is too expensive now.
So? Barley tastes bad. This is barely even bread.
Try to understand. Life is not like before.

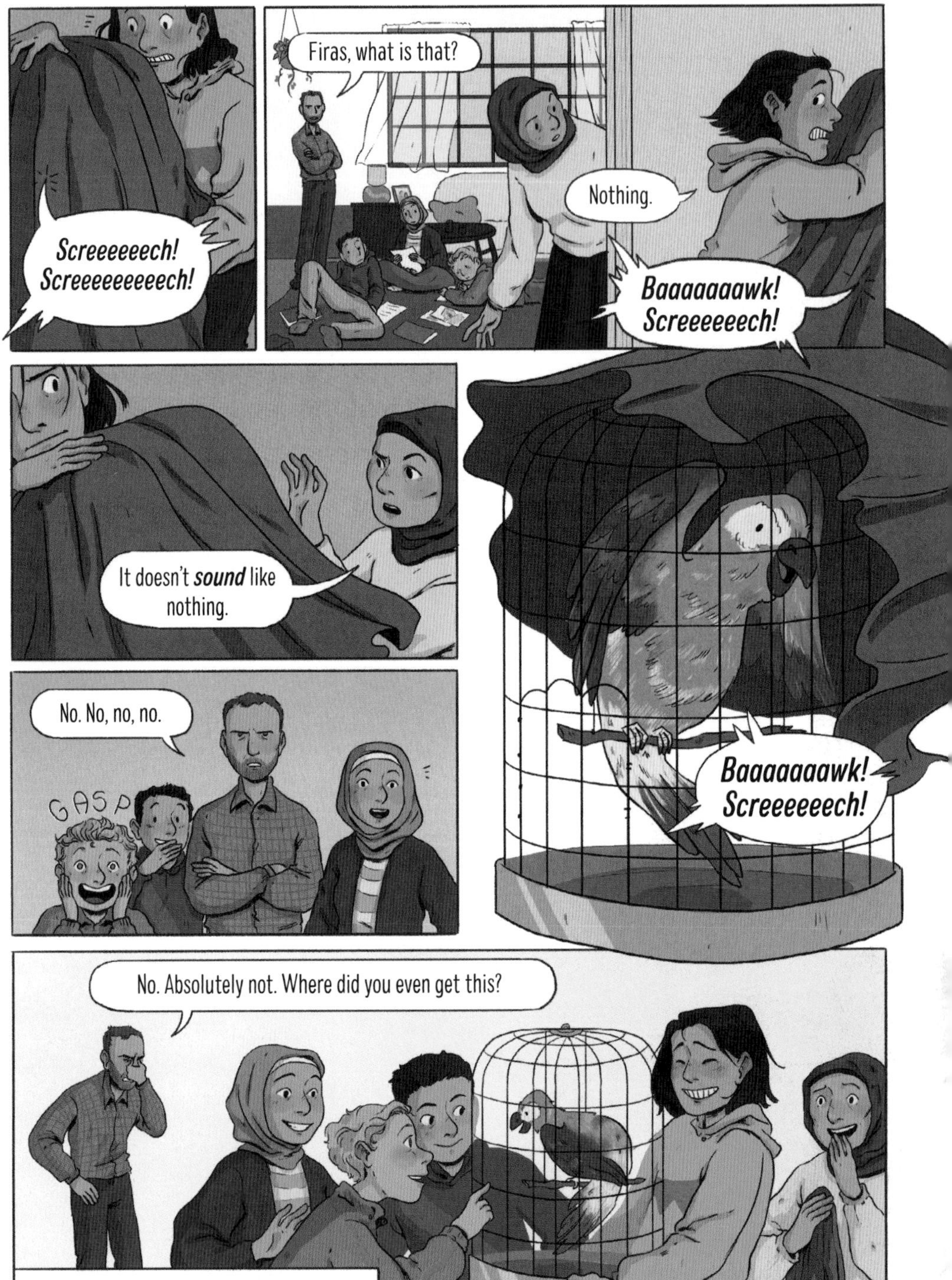
Screeeeeech!
Screeeeeeeeech!
Firas, what is that?
Nothing.
Baaaaaaawk!
Screeeeeech!
It doesn't **sound** like nothing.
Baaaaaaawk!
Screeeeeech!
No. No, no, no.
GASP
No. Absolutely not. Where did you even get this?
This is one of my strongest memories.

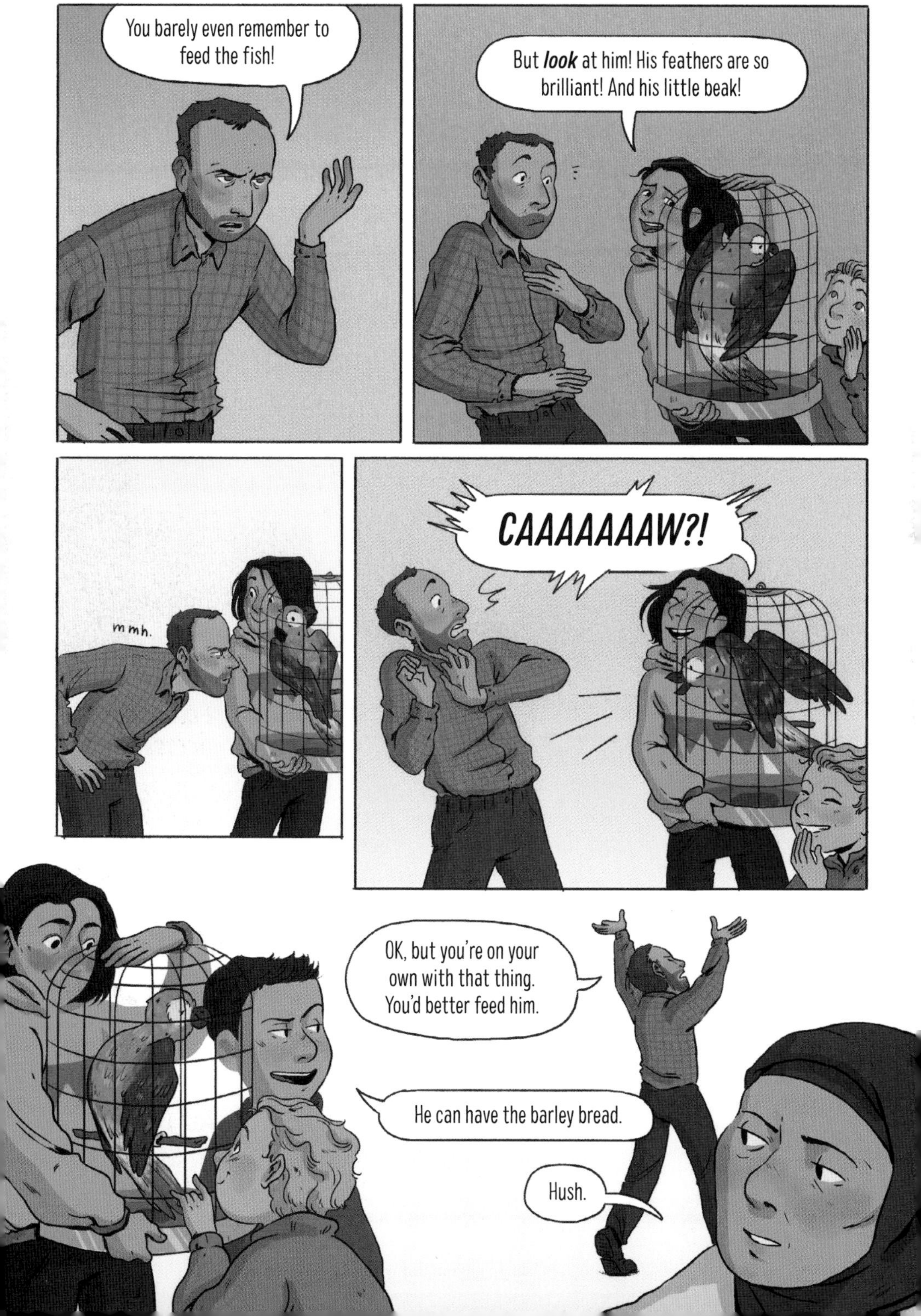

You barely even remember to feed the fish!
But *look* at him! His feathers are so brilliant! And his little beak!
mmh.
CAAAAAAAW?!
OK, but you're on your own with that thing. You'd better feed him.
He can have the barley bread.
Hush.

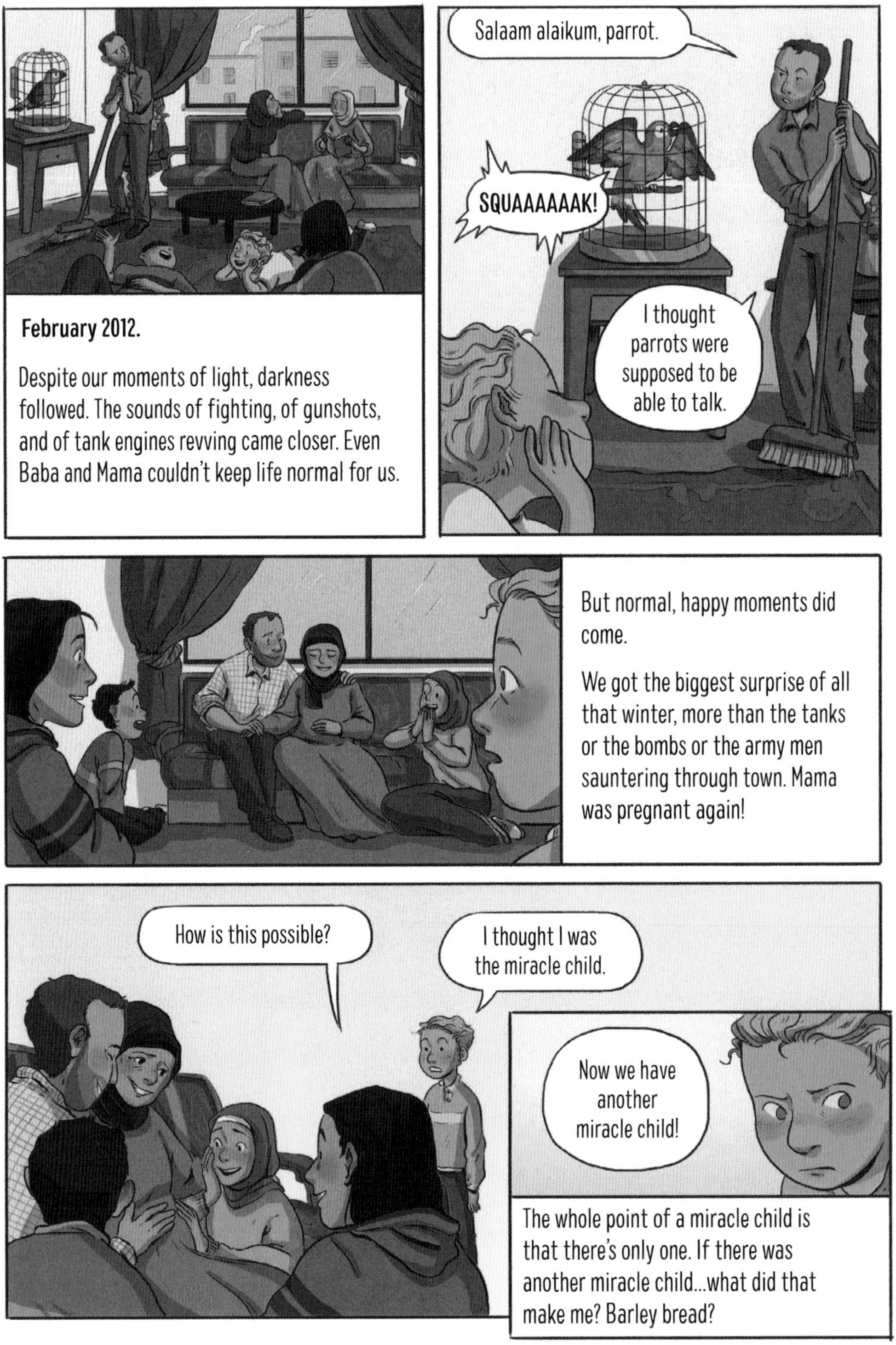
February 2012.
Despite our moments of light, darkness followed. The sounds of fighting, of gunshots, and of tank engines revving came closer. Even Baba and Mama couldn't keep life normal for us.
Salaam alaikum, parrot.
SQUAAAAAAK!
I thought parrots were supposed to be able to talk.
But normal, happy moments did come.
We got the biggest surprise of all that winter, more than the tanks or the bombs or the army men sauntering through town. Mama was pregnant again!
How is this possible?
I thought I was the miracle child.
Now we have another miracle child!
The whole point of a miracle child is that there's only one. If there was another miracle child...what did that make me? Barley bread?

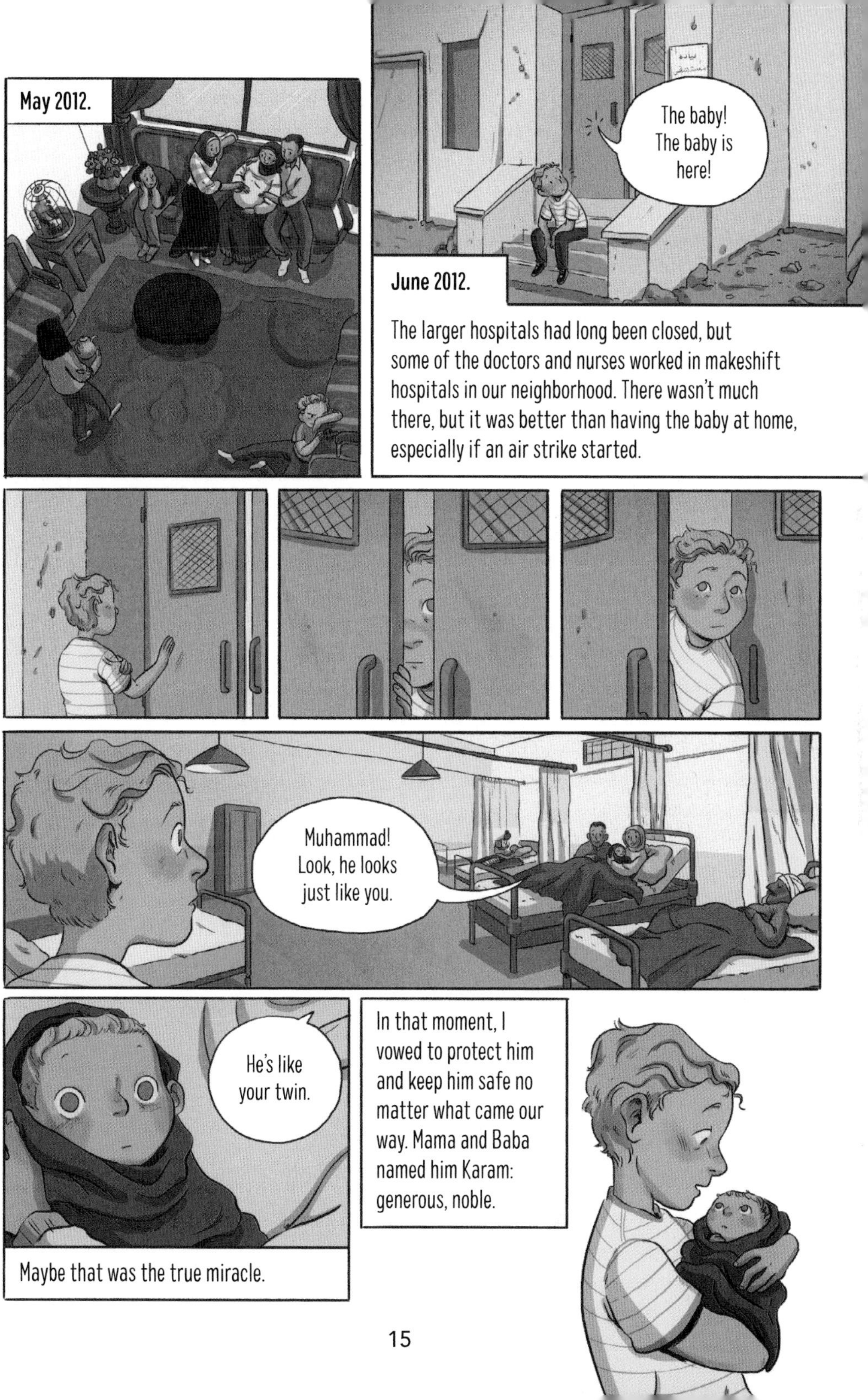
May 2012.
The baby! The baby is here!
June 2012.
The larger hospitals had long been closed, but some of the doctors and nurses worked in makeshift hospitals in our neighborhood. There wasn't much there, but it was better than having the baby at home, especially if an air strike started.
Muhammad! Look, he looks just like you.
He's like your twin.
Maybe that was the true miracle.
In that moment, I vowed to protect him and keep him safe no matter what came our way. Mama and Baba named him Karam: generous, noble.

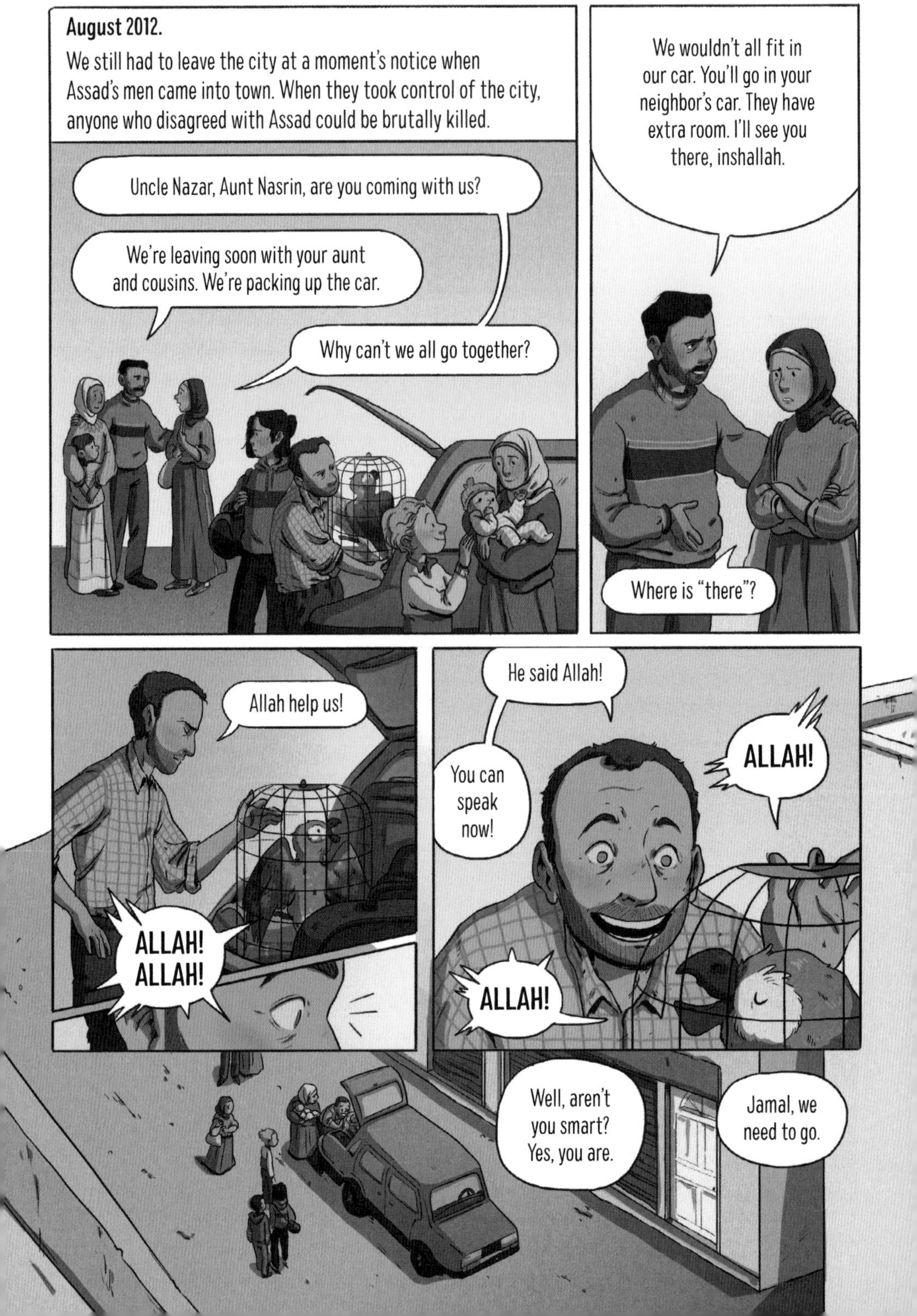
August 2012.
We still had to leave the city at a moment's notice when Assad's men came into town. When they took control of the city, anyone who disagreed with Assad could be brutally killed.
Uncle Nazar, Aunt Nasrin, are you coming with us?
We're leaving soon with your aunt and cousins. We're packing up the car.
Why can't we all go together?
We wouldn't all fit in our car. You'll go in your neighbor's car. They have extra room. I'll see you there, inshallah.
Where is "there"?
Allah help us!
ALLAH! ALLAH!
He said Allah!
You can speak now!
ALLAH!
ALLAH!
Well, aren't you smart? Yes, you are.
Jamal, we need to go.

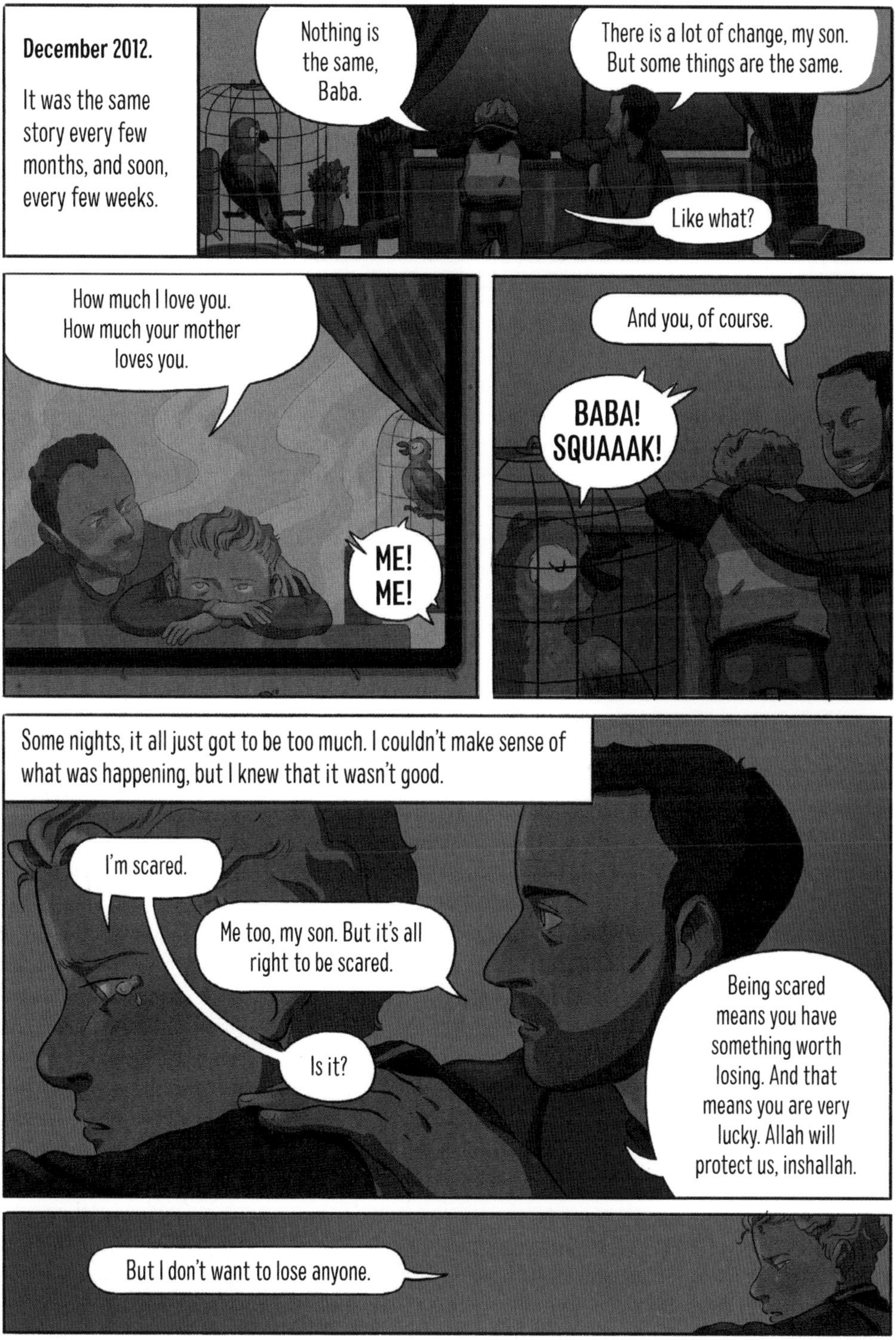

December 2012.
It was the same story every few months, and soon, every few weeks.
Nothing is the same, Baba.
There is a lot of change, my son. But some things are the same.
Like what?
How much I love you. How much your mother loves you.
ME! ME!
And you, of course.
BABA! SQUAAAK!
Some nights, it all just got to be too much. I couldn't make sense of what was happening, but I knew that it wasn't good.
I'm scared.
Me too, my son. But it's all right to be scared.
Is it?
Being scared means you have something worth losing. And that means you are very lucky. Allah will protect us, inshallah.
But I don't want to lose anyone.

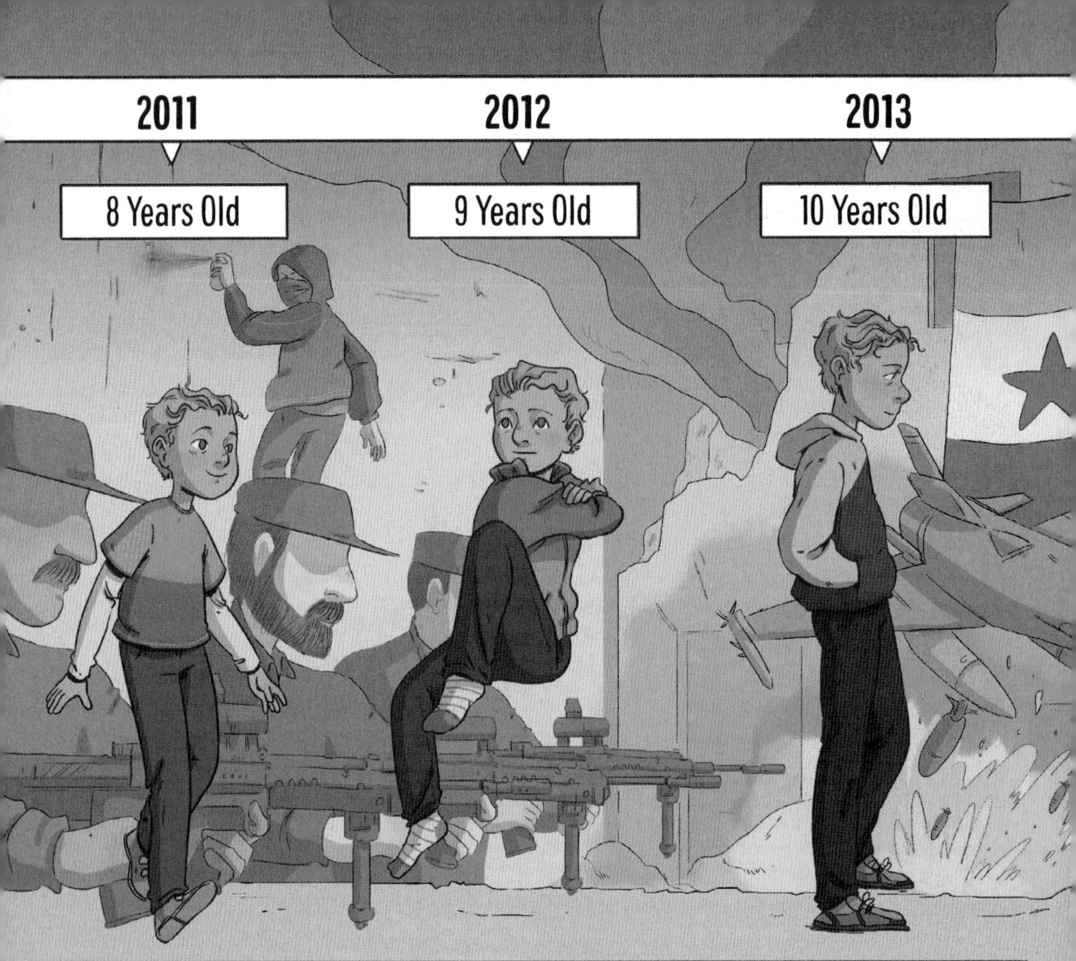
2011
8 Years Old
2012
9 Years Old
2013
10 Years Old

Pro-democracy protests in Daraa, about an hour and a half drive south from our town, begin when teen boys scrawl pro-freedom graffiti on a wall. As protests grow across the country, President Assad tries to control the protestors by sending in the military, who kill hundreds.

The conflict's violence escalates. Assad's government bombs its own citizens in an attempt to stop the revolution. The Free Syria Army launches bombs in response. Thousands of people are killed, and hundreds of thousands have to move away from their homes. By the end of the year, many other countries, including the US, the UK, France, and Turkey, officially recognize the opposition as the legitimate government of our country.

By 2013, the conflict appears to be reaching a violent stalemate, as both sides refuse to give up, yet neither is winning. Soon, countries such as Turkey, Saudi Arabia, and the US get involved, each backing different sides, sending weapons and other support. Another group joins the fight, too: the Islamic State in Iraq and Syria, also known as ISIS. This radical group of terrorists takes advantage of the chaos already in our country to gain more power and take more land.

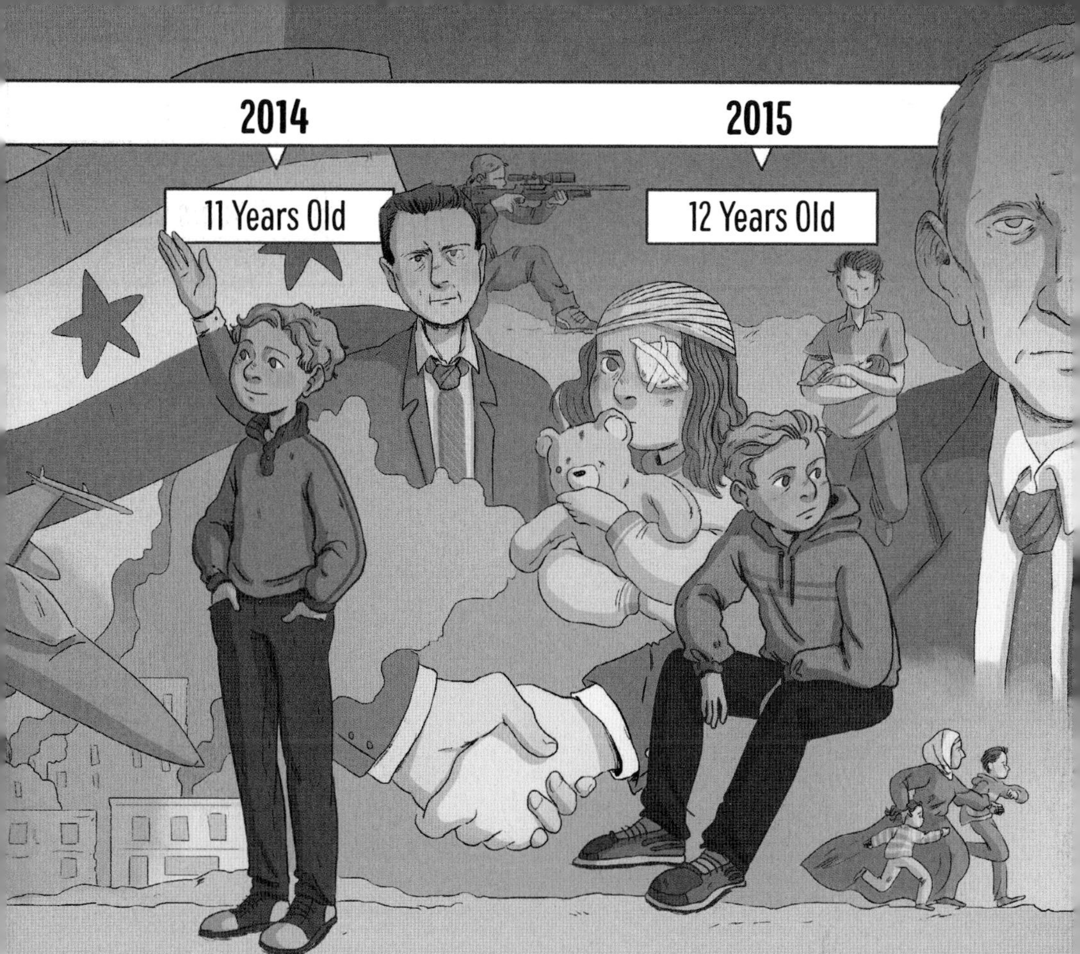

2014
11 Years Old
2015
12 Years Old

Peace talks in Geneva, Switzerland, fail without helping us at all. The United Nations votes to send us more humanitarian aid. Assad is reelected in June in the first election since the conflict started, but the opposition says it isn't really a free election. Then ISIS declares they will create a ***caliphate,*** kind of like a kingdom, in Syria and Iraq. As ISIS takes hold in Syria, especially in Raqqa, the US and its allies start launching air strikes against ISIS targets. Millions of refugees leave Syria.

Kurdish fighters help US forces and their allies fight ISIS. More peace talks fail. By September 2015, more than four million Syrians escape the violence in our country in one of the largest refugee crises in history. This is when a lot of foreigners actually start paying attention. This year also sees way more international involvement in our domestic fight, including Iranian troops under the leadership of Ayatollah Ali Khamenei. They help Assad's government.

The US now agrees to send special operations troops to fight in Syria, and Russian President Vladimir Putin announces Russia will support Assad's government. Russia launches its first air strikes in Syria. President Assad even flies to Moscow to thank President Putin for his support.

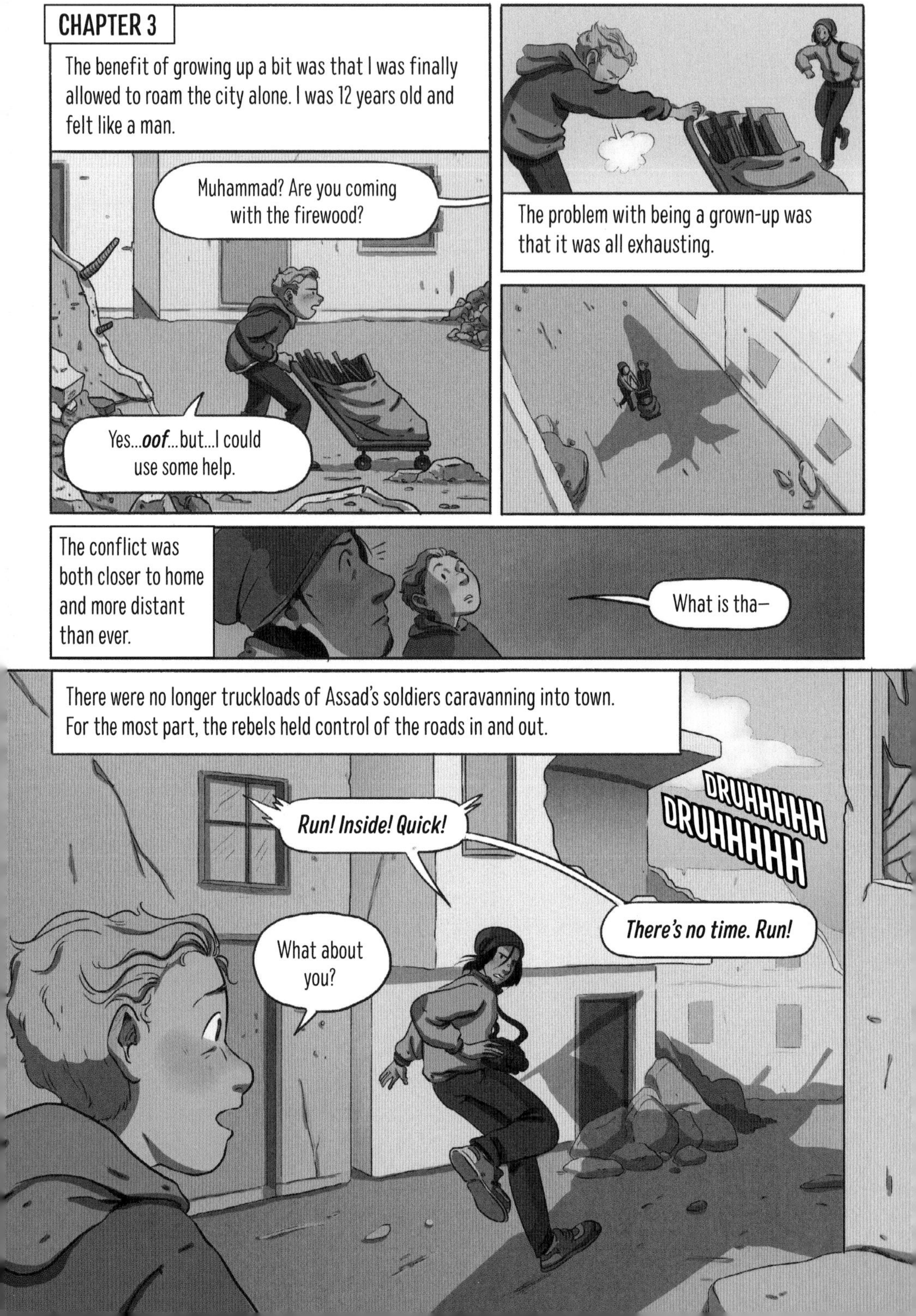
CHAPTER 3
The benefit of growing up a bit was that I was finally allowed to roam the city alone. I was 12 years old and felt like a man.
Muhammad? Are you coming with the firewood?
Yes...*oof*...but...I could use some help.
The problem with being a grown-up was that it was all exhausting.
The conflict was both closer to home and more distant than ever.
What is tha—
There were no longer truckloads of Assad's soldiers caravanning into town. For the most part, the rebels held control of the roads in and out.
DRUHHHHH
DRUHHHHH
Run! Inside! Quick!
What about you?
There's no time. Run!

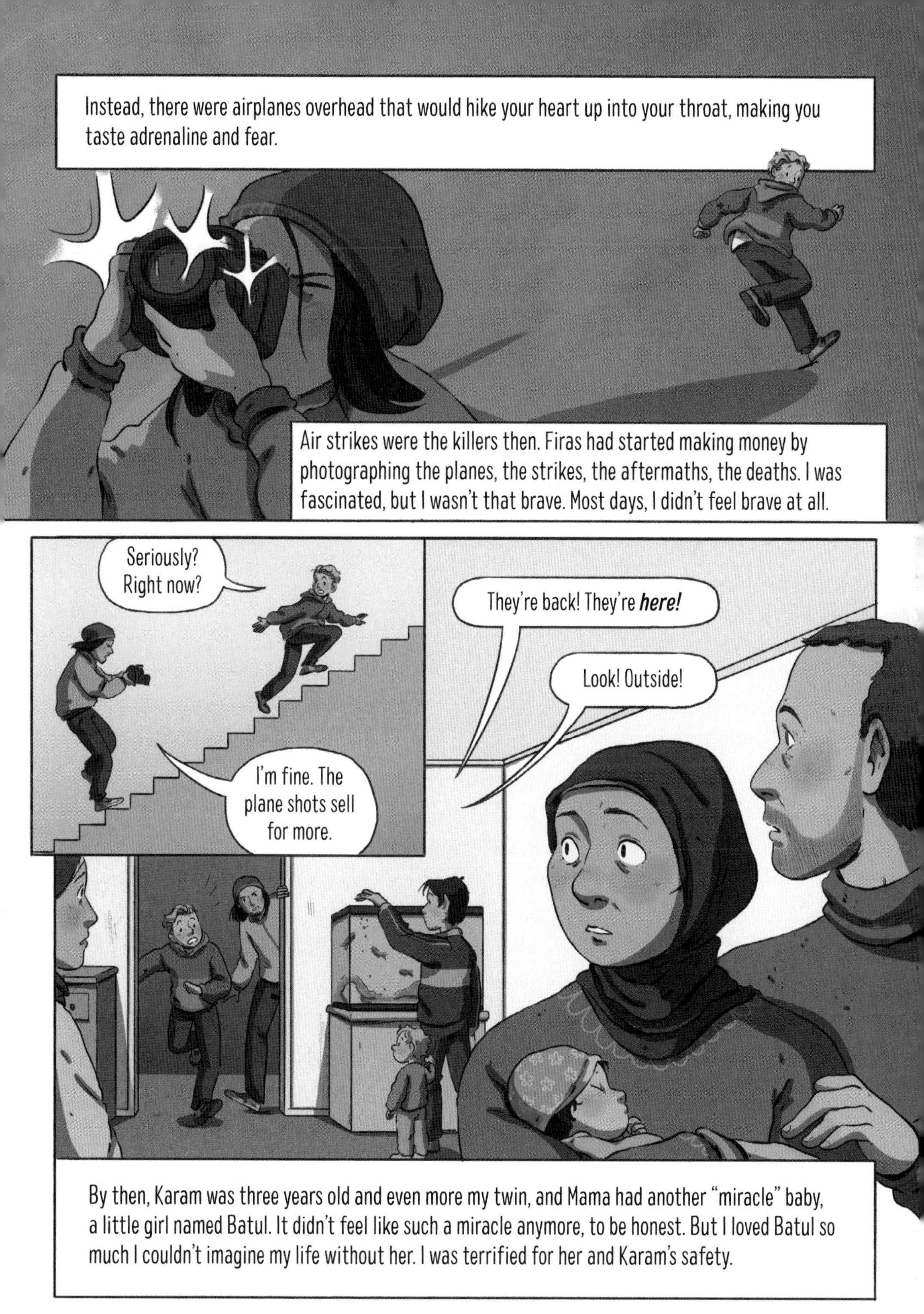
Instead, there were airplanes overhead that would hike your heart up into your throat, making you taste adrenaline and fear.
Air strikes were the killers then. Firas had started making money by photographing the planes, the strikes, the aftermaths, the deaths. I was fascinated, but I wasn't that brave. Most days, I didn't feel brave at all.
Seriously? Right now?
I'm fine. The plane shots sell for more.
They're back! They're ***here!***
Look! Outside!
By then, Karam was three years old and even more my twin, and Mama had another "miracle" baby, a little girl named Batul. It didn't feel like such a miracle anymore, to be honest. But I loved Batul so much I couldn't imagine my life without her. I was terrified for her and Karam's safety.

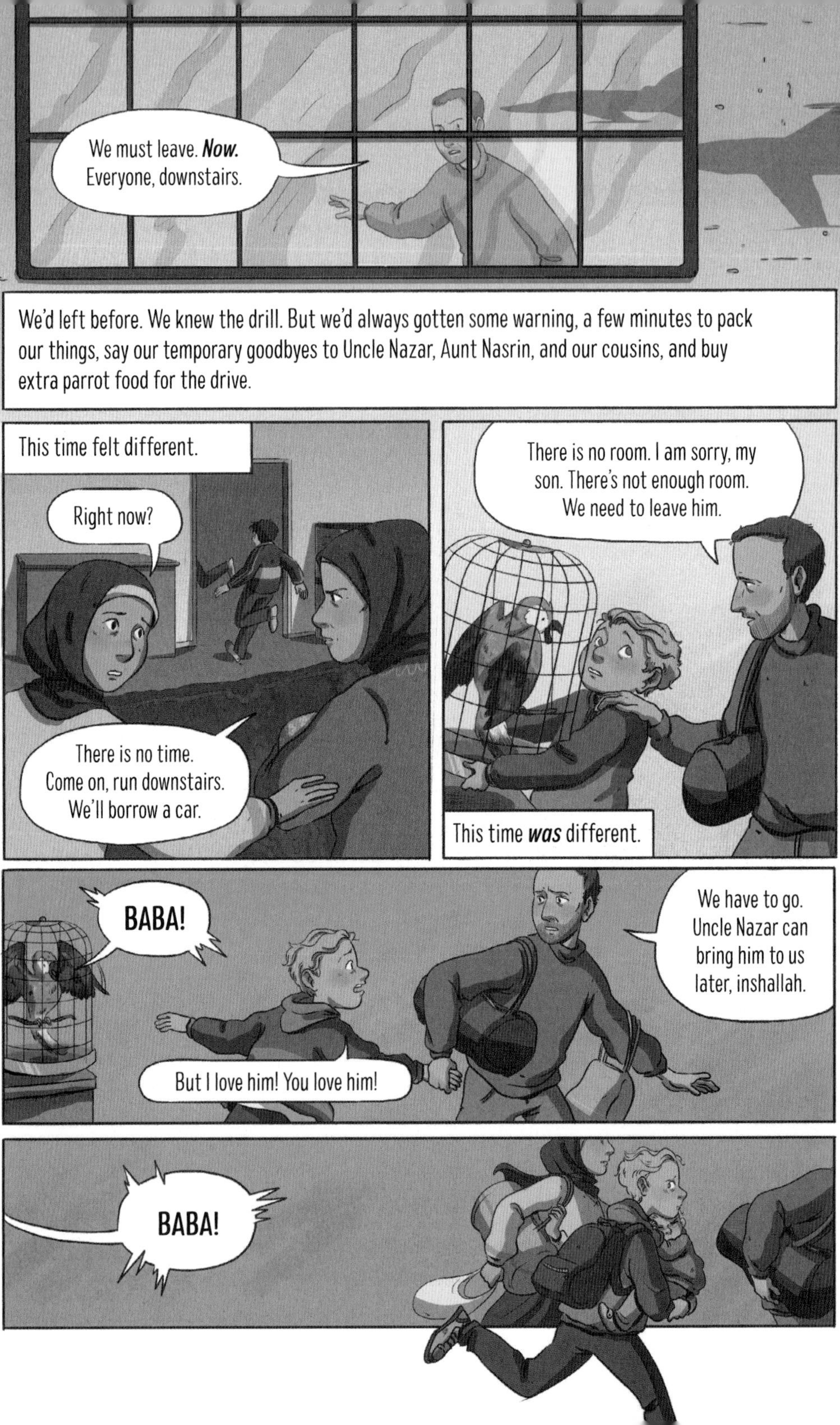
We must leave. ***Now.*** Everyone, downstairs.
We'd left before. We knew the drill. But we'd always gotten some warning, a few minutes to pack our things, say our temporary goodbyes to Uncle Nazar, Aunt Nasrin, and our cousins, and buy extra parrot food for the drive.
This time felt different.
Right now?
There is no time. Come on, run downstairs. We'll borrow a car.
There is no room. I am sorry, my son. There's not enough room. We need to leave him.
This time ***was*** different.
BABA!
We have to go. Uncle Nazar can bring him to us later, inshallah.
But I love him! You love him!
BABA!

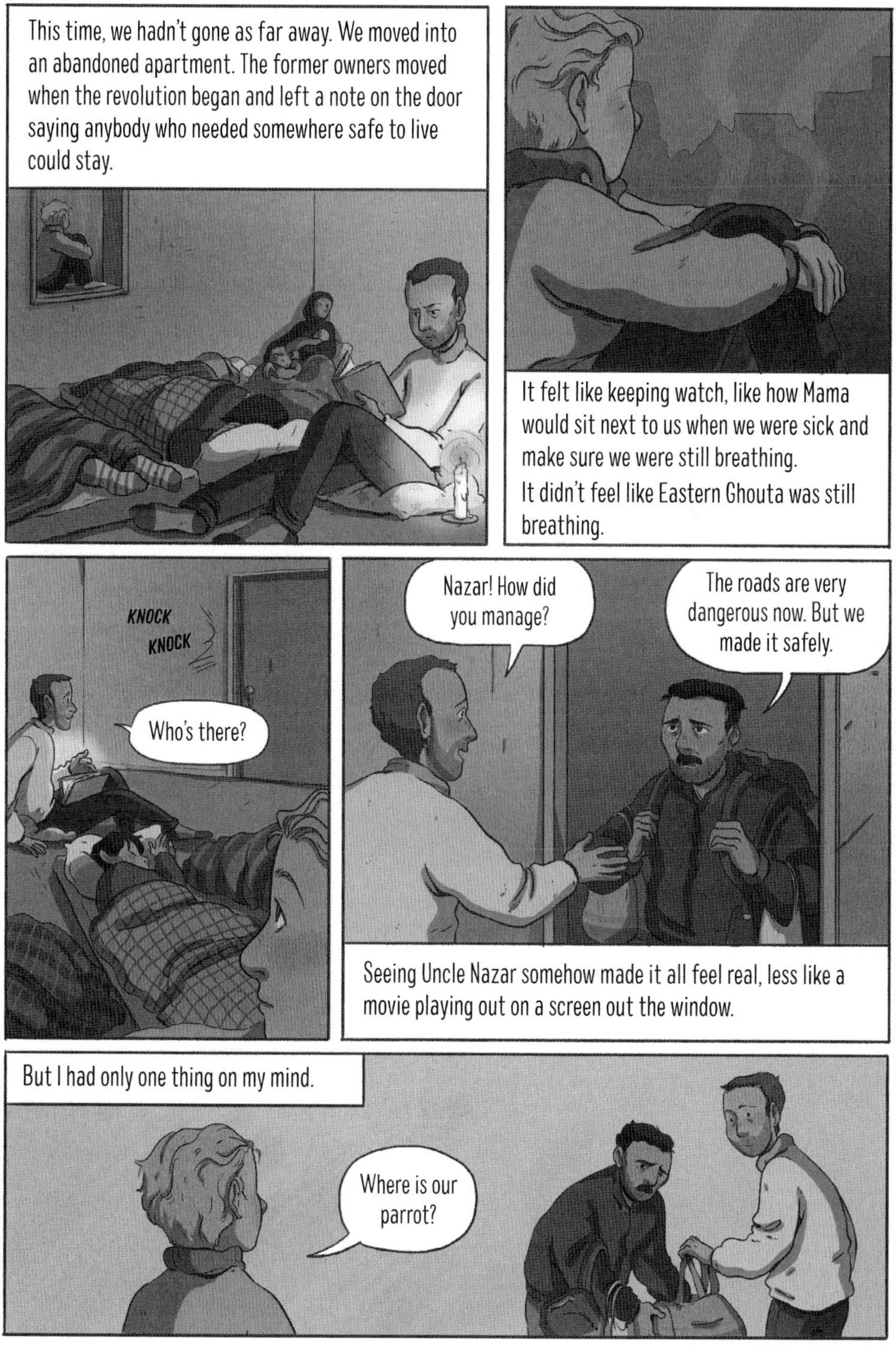
This time, we hadn't gone as far away. We moved into an abandoned apartment. The former owners moved when the revolution began and left a note on the door saying anybody who needed somewhere safe to live could stay.
It felt like keeping watch, like how Mama would sit next to us when we were sick and make sure we were still breathing.
It didn't feel like Eastern Ghouta was still breathing.
KNOCK
KNOCK
Who's there?
Nazar! How did you manage?
The roads are very dangerous now. But we made it safely.
Seeing Uncle Nazar somehow made it all feel real, less like a movie playing out on a screen out the window.
But I had only one thing on my mind.
Where is our parrot?

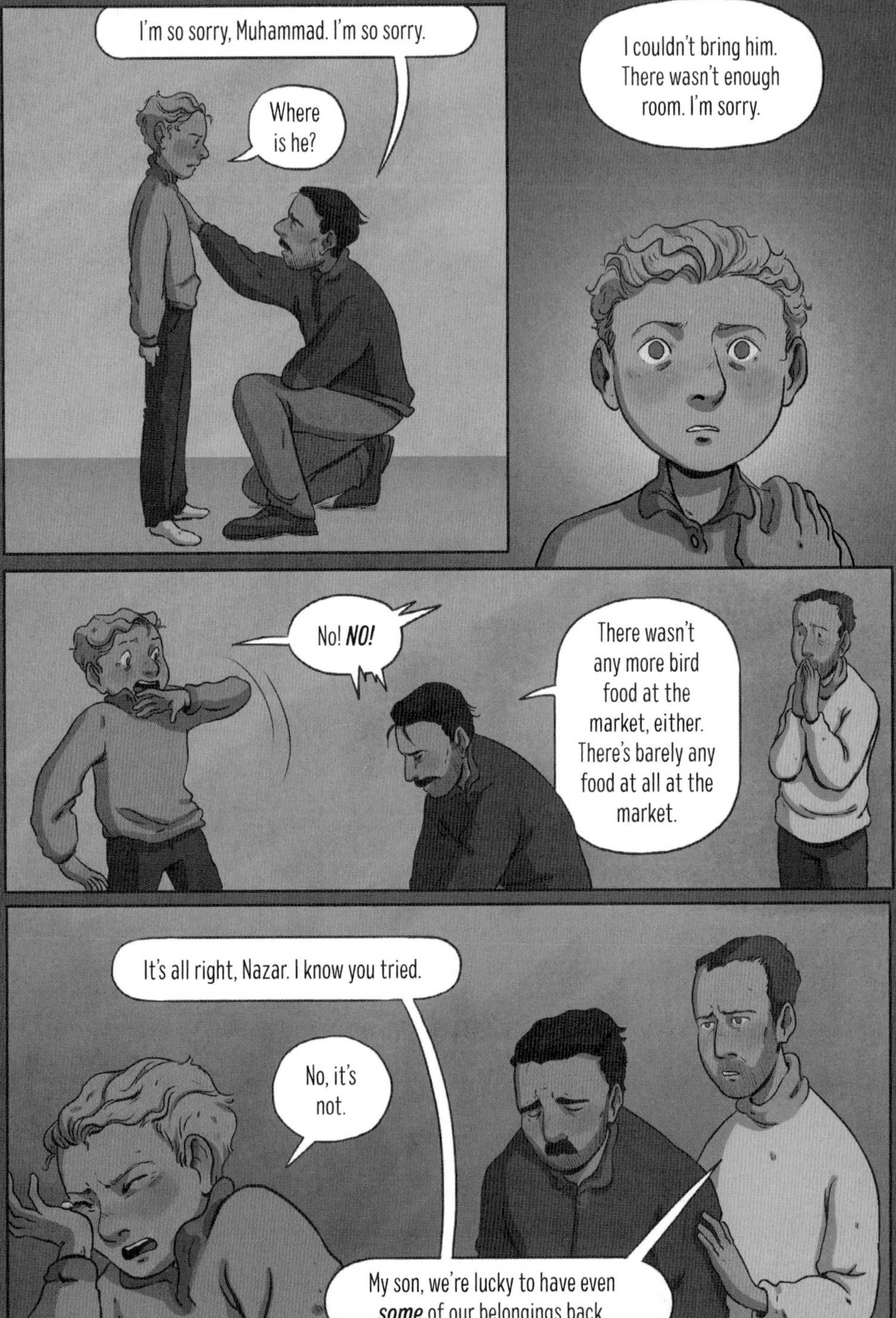

I'm so sorry, Muhammad. I'm so sorry.
Where is he?
I couldn't bring him. There wasn't enough room. I'm sorry.
No! ***NO!***
There wasn't any more bird food at the market, either. There's barely any food at all at the market.
It's all right, Nazar. I know you tried.
No, it's not.
My son, we're lucky to have even ***some*** of our belongings back.

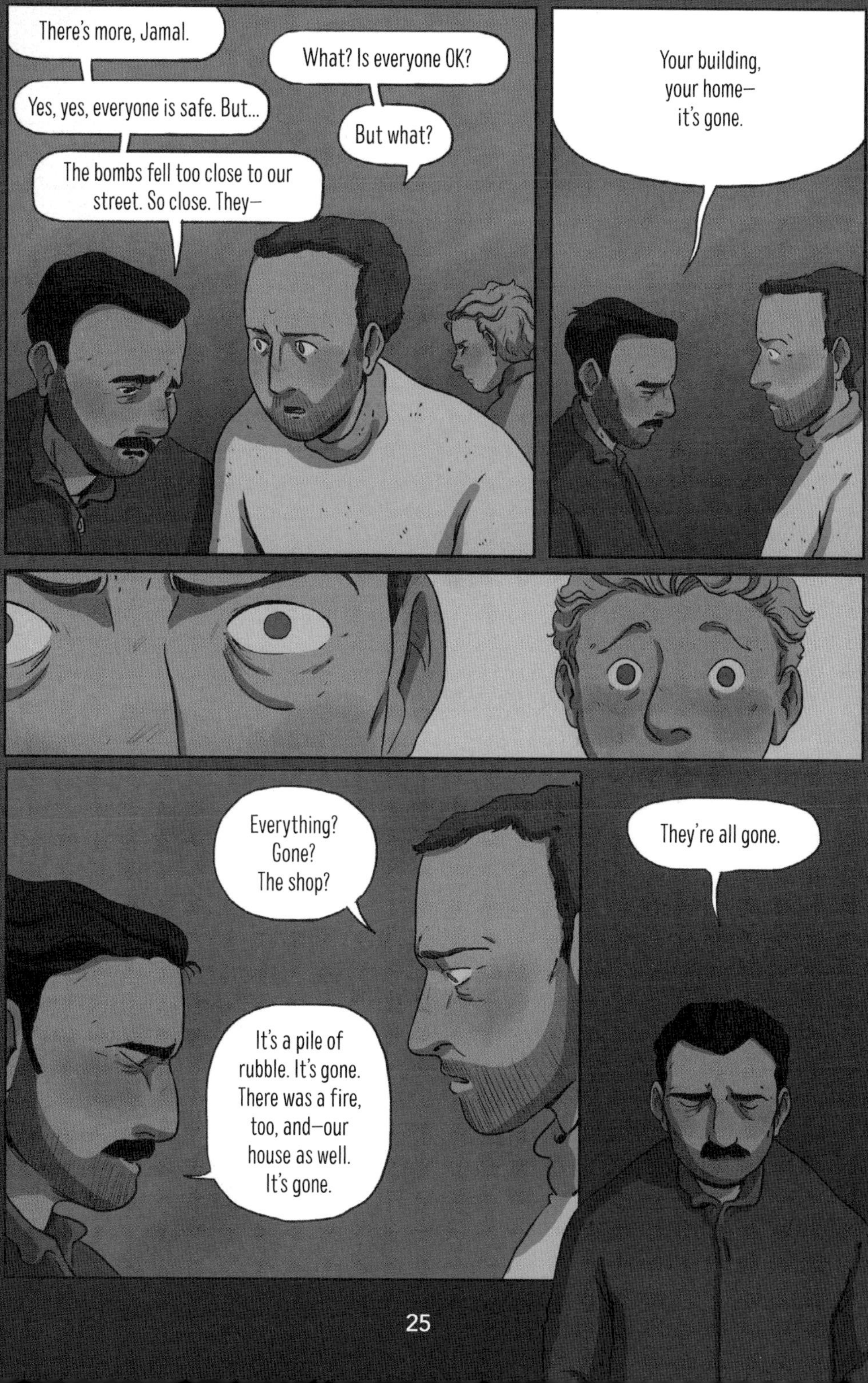

There's more, Jamal.
Yes, yes, everyone is safe. But...
The bombs fell too close to our street. So close. They—
What? Is everyone OK?
But what?
Your building, your home— it's gone.
Everything? Gone? The shop?
It's a pile of rubble. It's gone. There was a fire, too, and—our house as well. It's gone.
They're all gone.

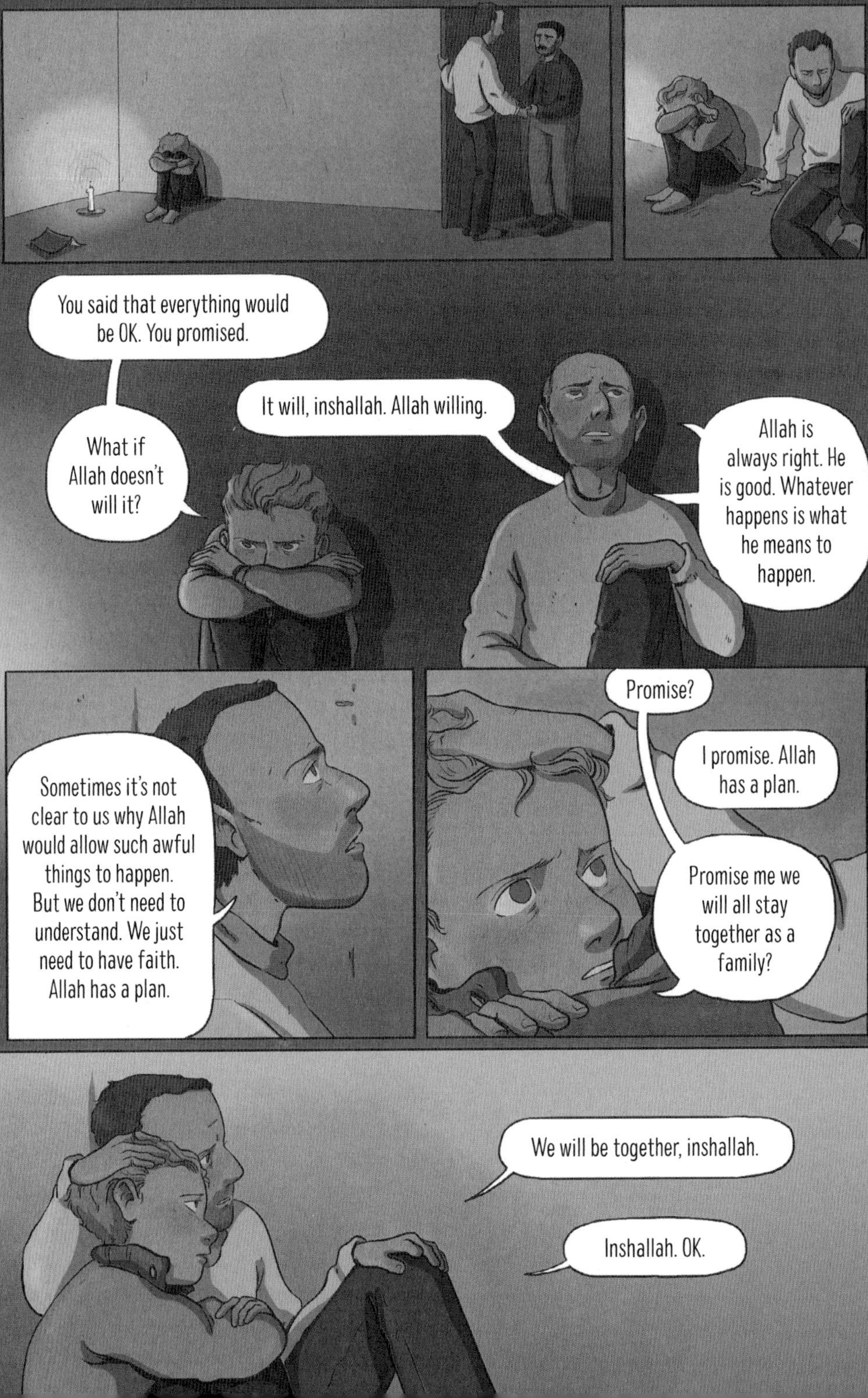
You said that everything would be OK. You promised.
It will, inshallah. Allah willing.
What if Allah doesn't will it?
Allah is always right. He is good. Whatever happens is what he means to happen.
Sometimes it's not clear to us why Allah would allow such awful things to happen. But we don't need to understand. We just need to have faith. Allah has a plan.
Promise?
I promise. Allah has a plan.
Promise me we will all stay together as a family?
We will be together, inshallah.
Inshallah. OK.

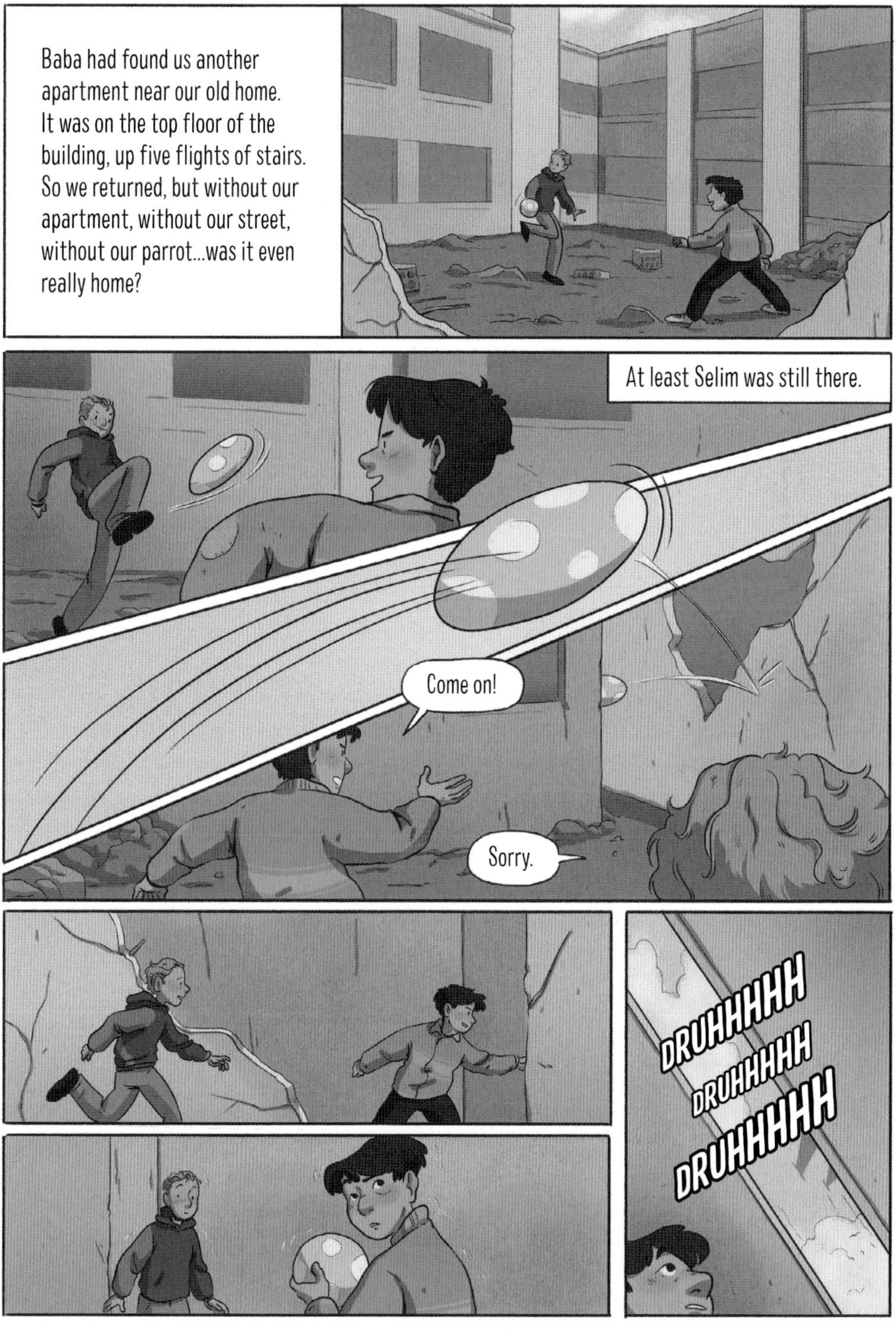
Baba had found us another apartment near our old home. It was on the top floor of the building, up five flights of stairs. So we returned, but without our apartment, without our street, without our parrot...was it even really home?
At least Selim was still there.
Come on!
Sorry.
DRUHHHHH
DRUHHHHH
DRUHHHHH

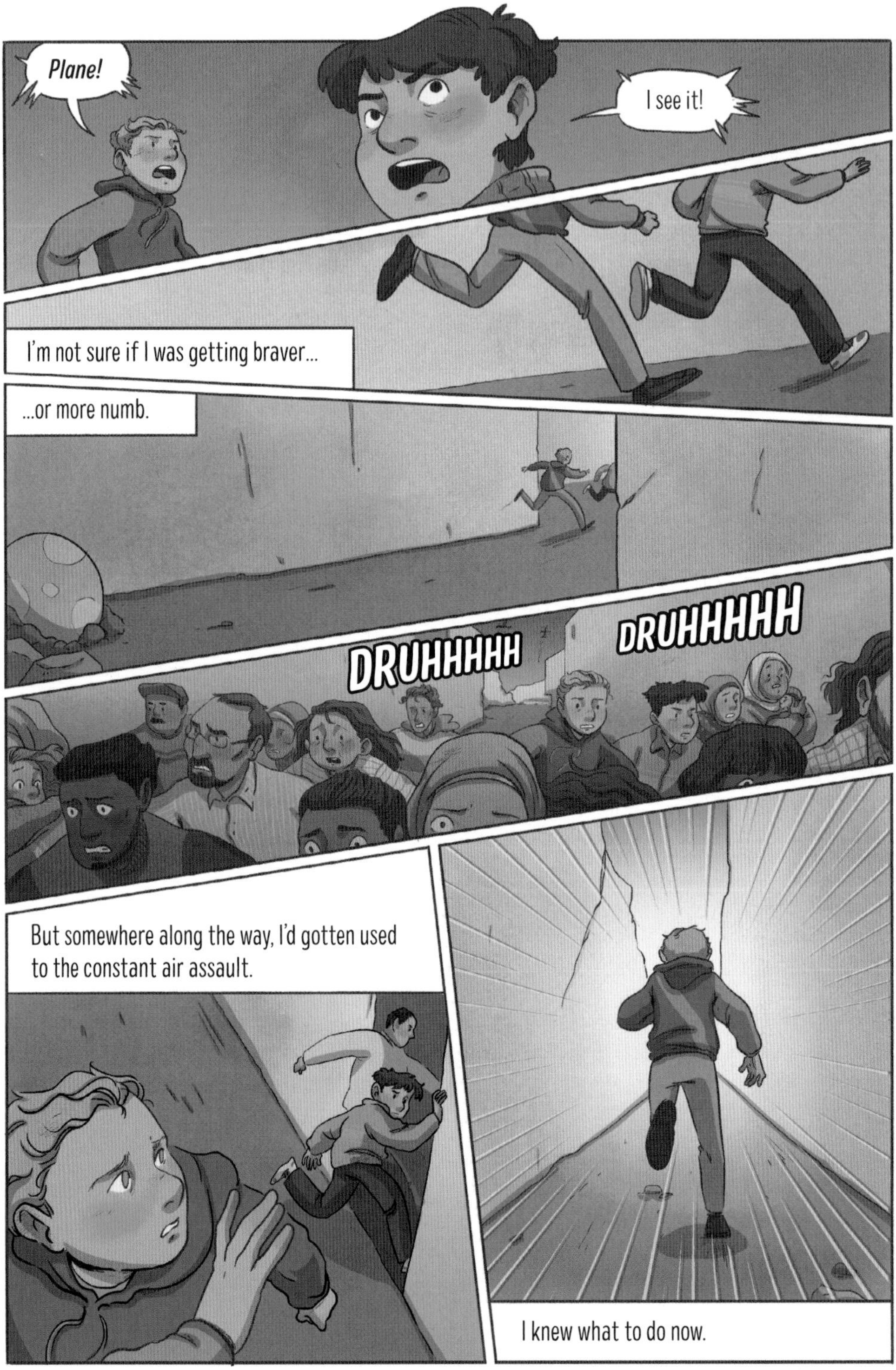
Plane!
I see it!
I'm not sure if I was getting braver...
...or more numb.
DRUHHHHH
DRUHHHHHH
But somewhere along the way, I'd gotten used to the constant air assault.
I knew what to do now.

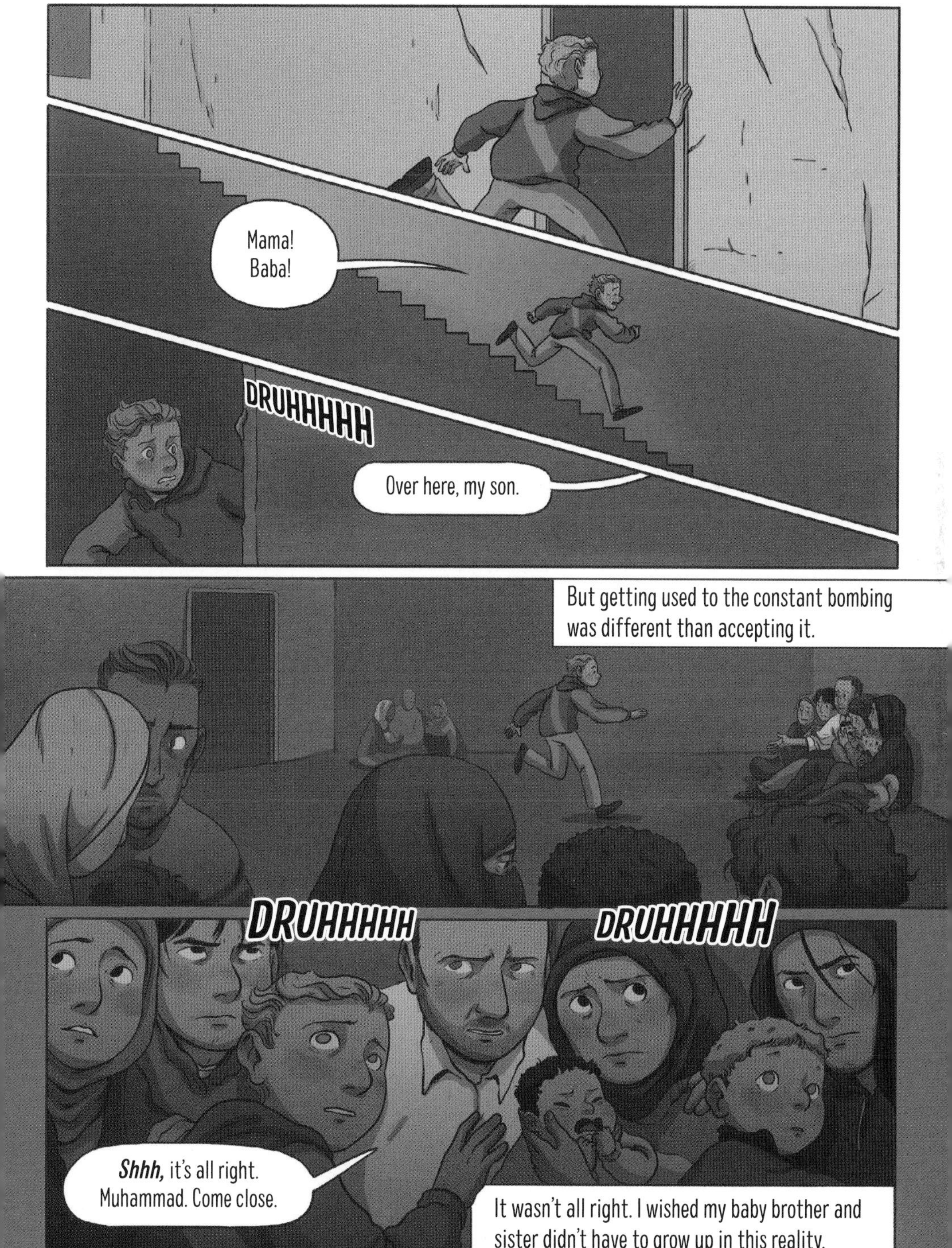
Mama!
Baba!
DRUHHHHH
Over here, my son.
But getting used to the constant bombing was different than accepting it.
DRUHHHHH
DRUHHHHH
Shhh, it's all right. Muhammad. Come close.
It wasn't all right. I wished my baby brother and sister didn't have to grow up in this reality.

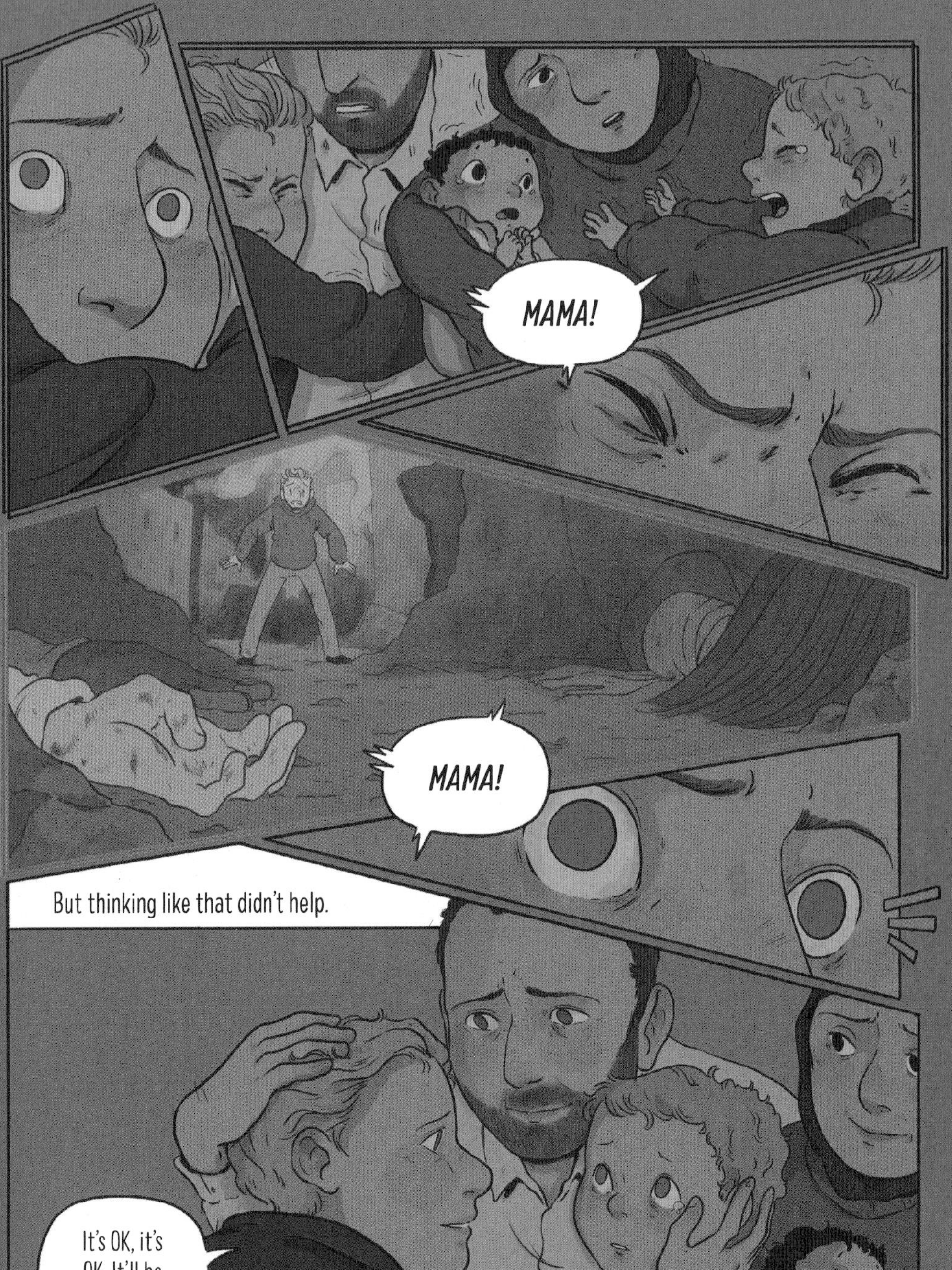
MAMA!
MAMA!
But thinking like that didn't help.
It's OK, it's OK. It'll be over soon, inshallah.

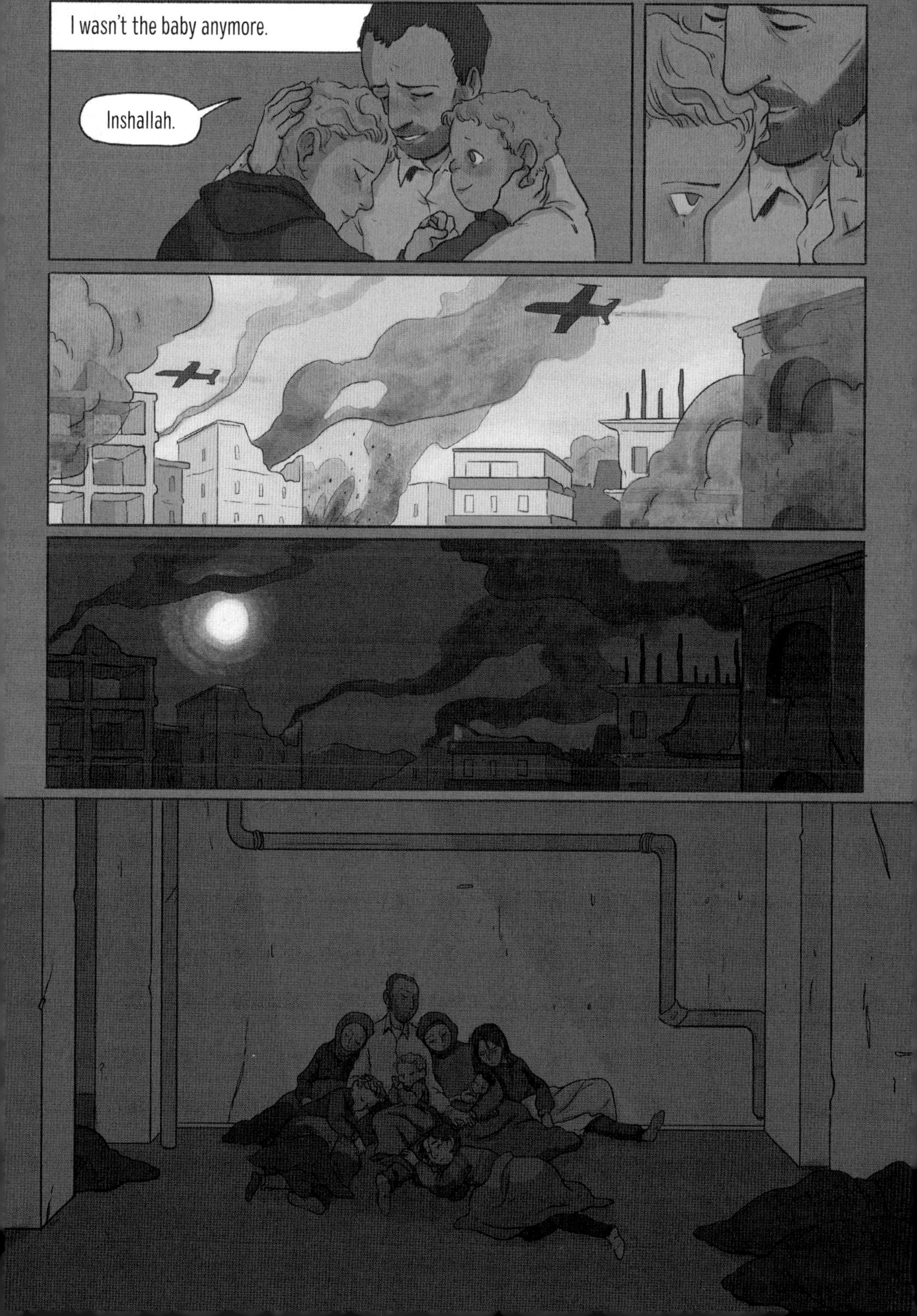
I wasn't the baby anymore.
Inshallah.

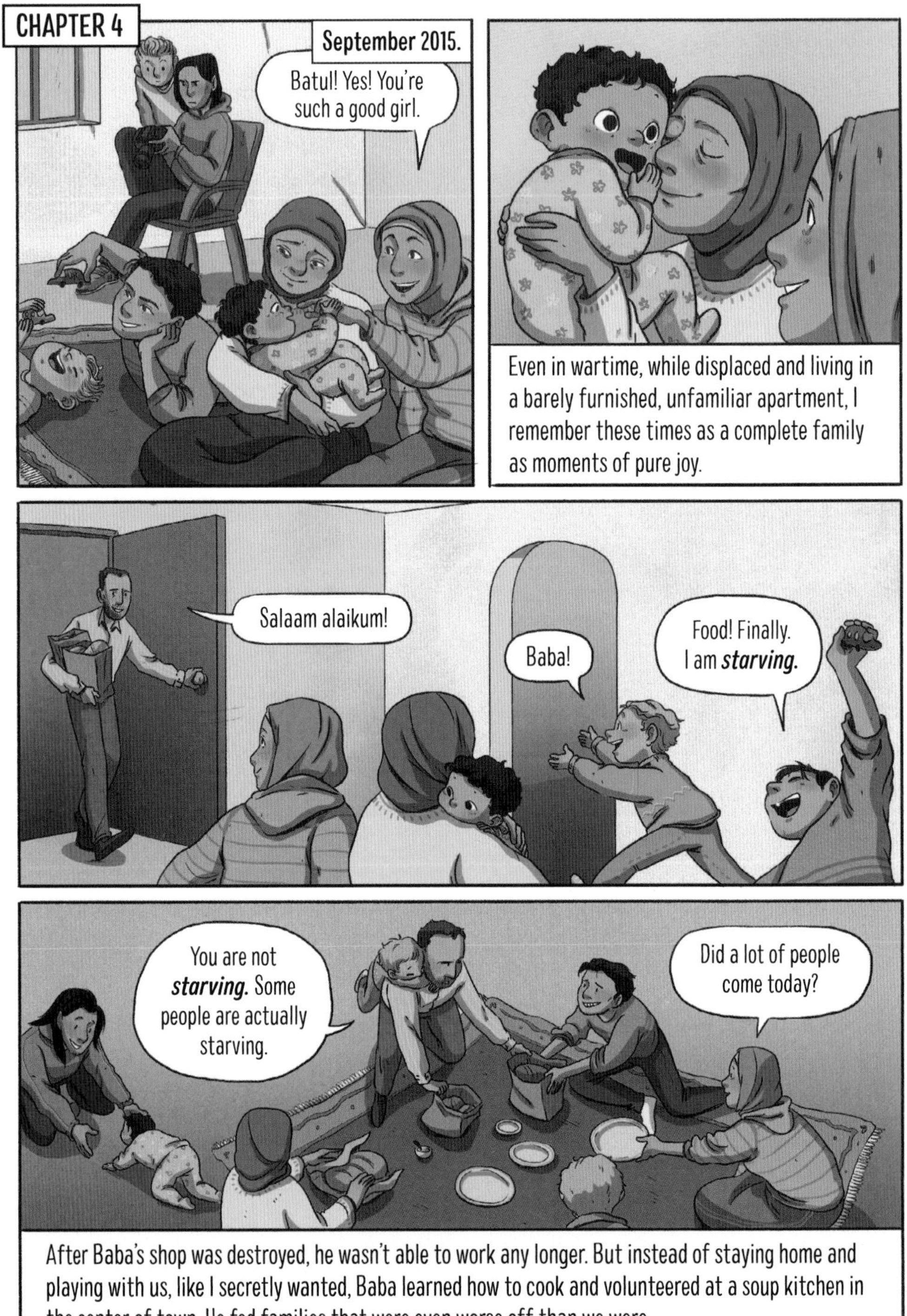
CHAPTER 4
September 2015.
Batul! Yes! You're such a good girl.
Even in wartime, while displaced and living in a barely furnished, unfamiliar apartment, I remember these times as a complete family as moments of pure joy.
Salaam alaikum!
Baba!
Food! Finally. I am ***starving.***
You are not ***starving.*** Some people are actually starving.
Did a lot of people come today?
After Baba's shop was destroyed, he wasn't able to work any longer. But instead of staying home and playing with us, like I secretly wanted, Baba learned how to cook and volunteered at a soup kitchen in the center of town. He fed families that were even worse off than we were.

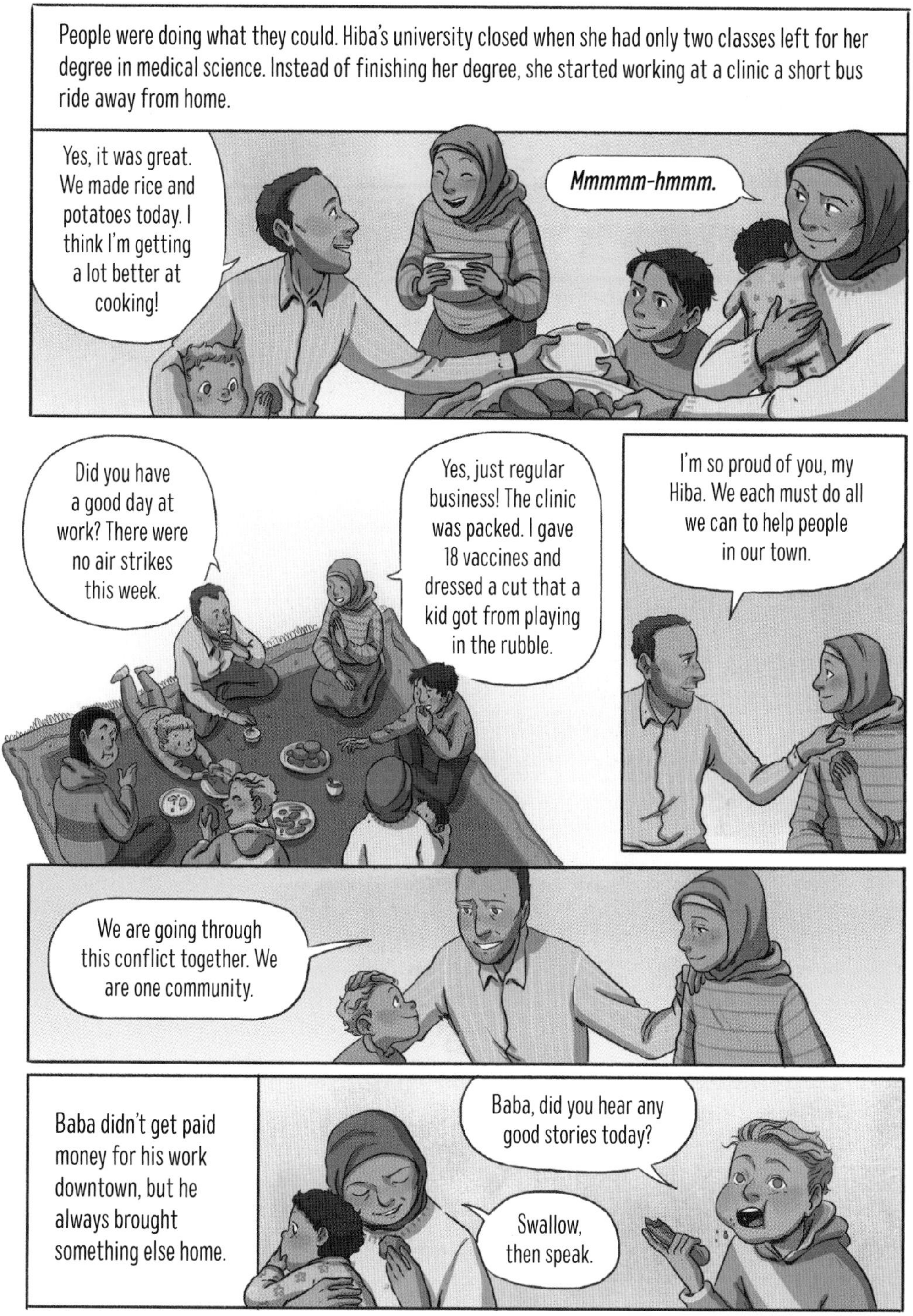
People were doing what they could. Hiba's university closed when she had only two classes left for her degree in medical science. Instead of finishing her degree, she started working at a clinic a short bus ride away from home.
Yes, it was great. We made rice and potatoes today. I think I'm getting a lot better at cooking!
Mmmmm-hmmm.
Did you have a good day at work? There were no air strikes this week.
Yes, just regular business! The clinic was packed. I gave 18 vaccines and dressed a cut that a kid got from playing in the rubble.
I'm so proud of you, my Hiba. We each must do all we can to help people in our town.
We are going through this conflict together. We are one community.
Baba didn't get paid money for his work downtown, but he always brought something else home.
Baba, did you hear any good stories today?
Swallow, then speak.

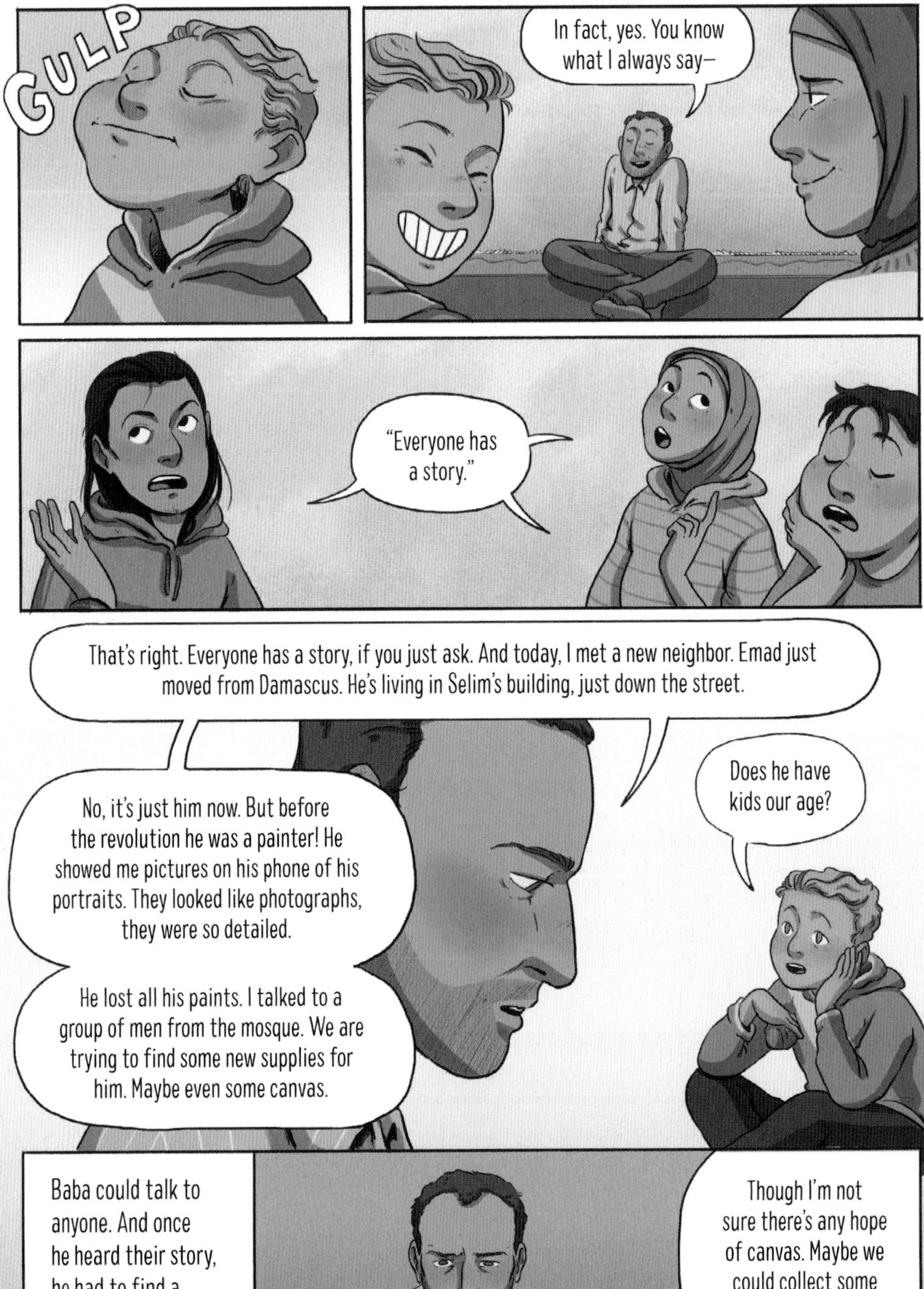
GULP
In fact, yes. You know what I always say—
"Everyone has a story."
That's right. Everyone has a story, if you just ask. And today, I met a new neighbor. Emad just moved from Damascus. He's living in Selim's building, just down the street.
Does he have kids our age?
No, it's just him now. But before the revolution he was a painter! He showed me pictures on his phone of his portraits. They looked like photographs, they were so detailed.
He lost all his paints. I talked to a group of men from the mosque. We are trying to find some new supplies for him. Maybe even some canvas.
Baba could talk to anyone. And once he heard their story, he had to find a way to help.
Though I'm not sure there's any hope of canvas. Maybe we could collect some cardboard.

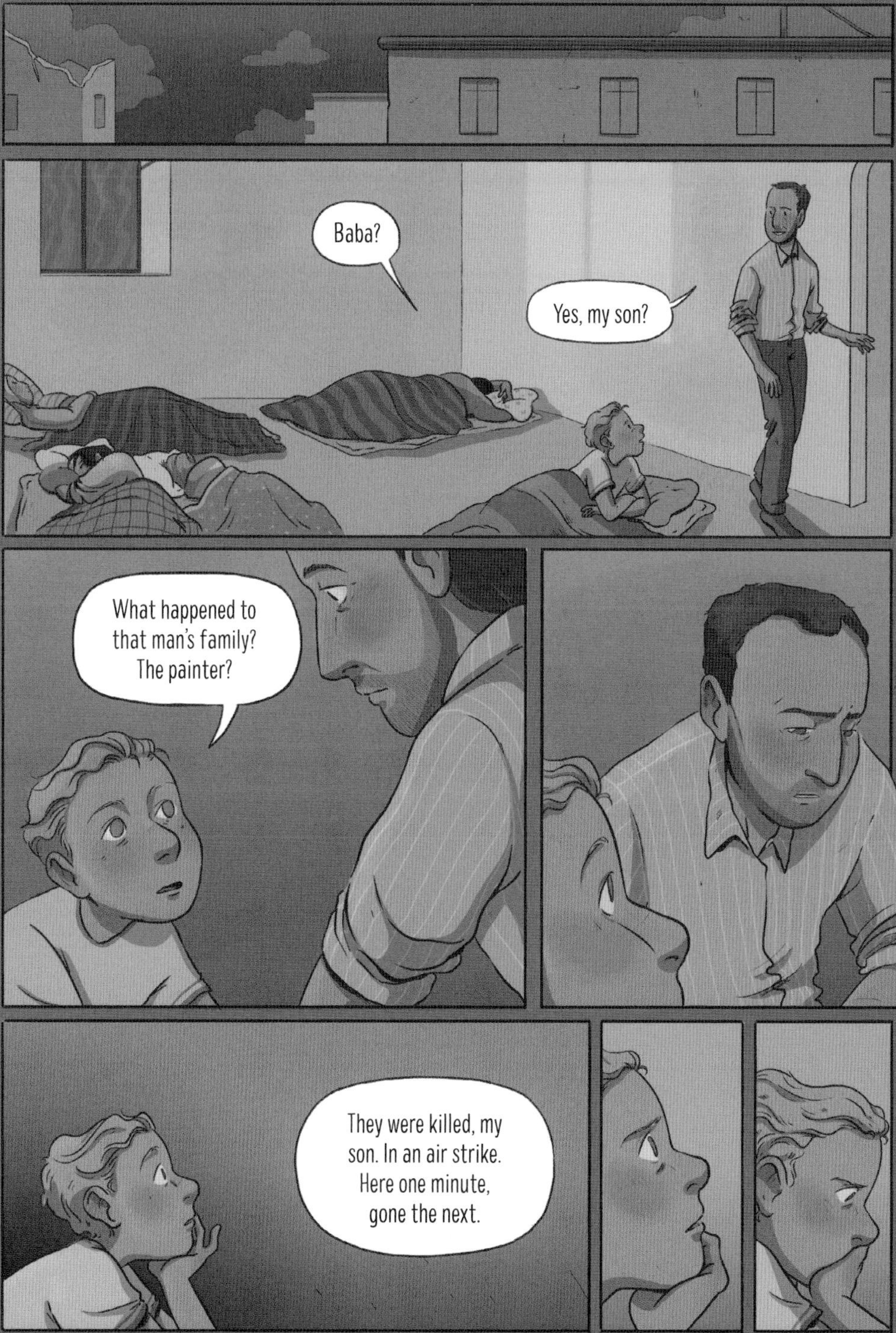
Baba?
Yes, my son?
What happened to that man's family? The painter?
They were killed, my son. In an air strike. Here one minute, gone the next.

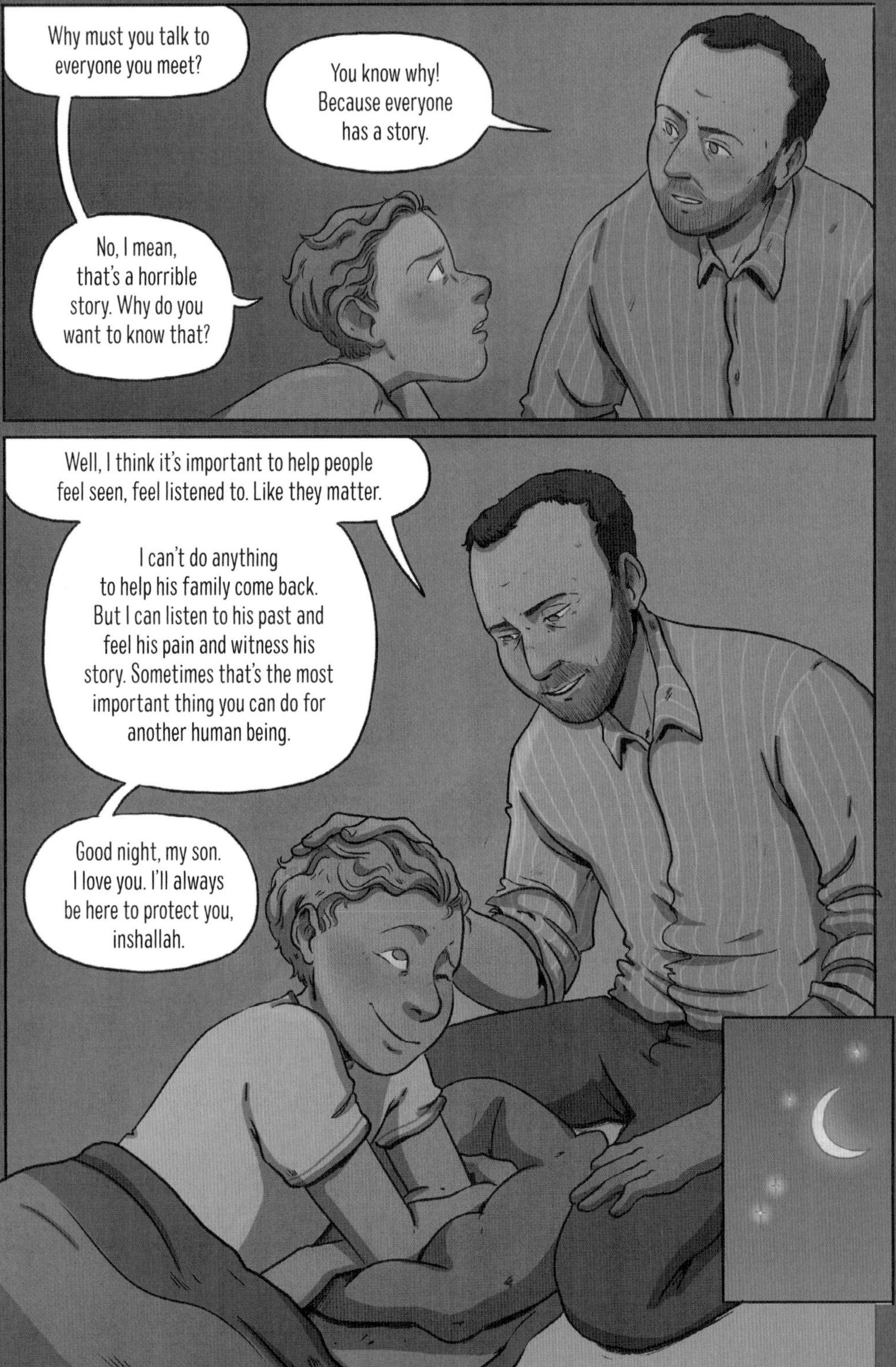
Why must you talk to everyone you meet?
You know why! Because everyone has a story.
No, I mean, that's a horrible story. Why do you want to know that?
Well, I think it's important to help people feel seen, feel listened to. Like they matter.
I can't do anything to help his family come back. But I can listen to his past and feel his pain and witness his story. Sometimes that's the most important thing you can do for another human being.
Good night, my son. I love you. I'll always be here to protect you, inshallah.

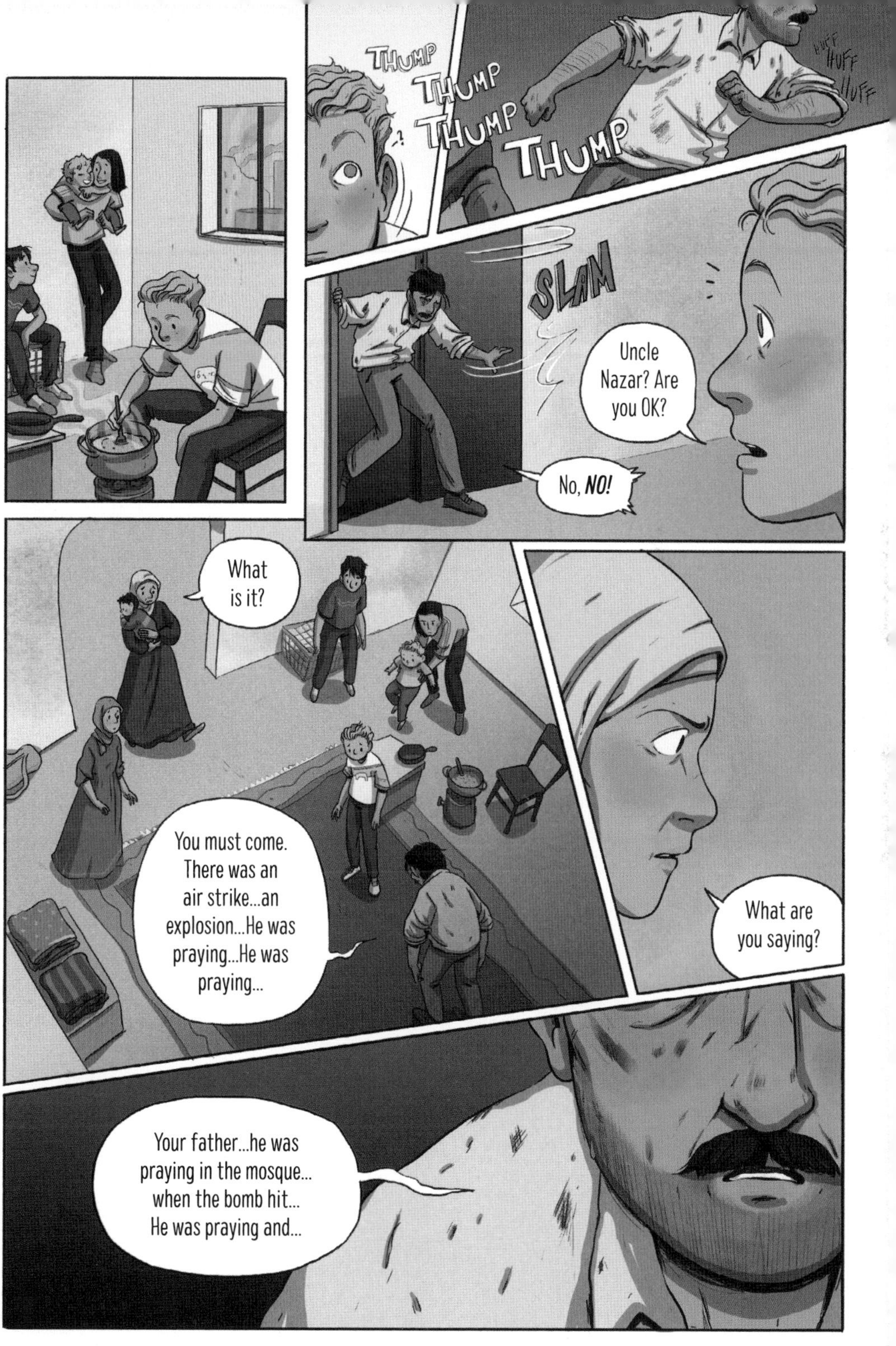
THUMP
THUMP
THUMP
THUMP
HUFF
HUFF
HUFF
SLAM
Uncle Nazar? Are you OK?
No, NO!
What is it?
You must come. There was an air strike...an explosion...He was praying...He was praying...
What are you saying?
Your father...he was praying in the mosque... when the bomb hit... He was praying and...

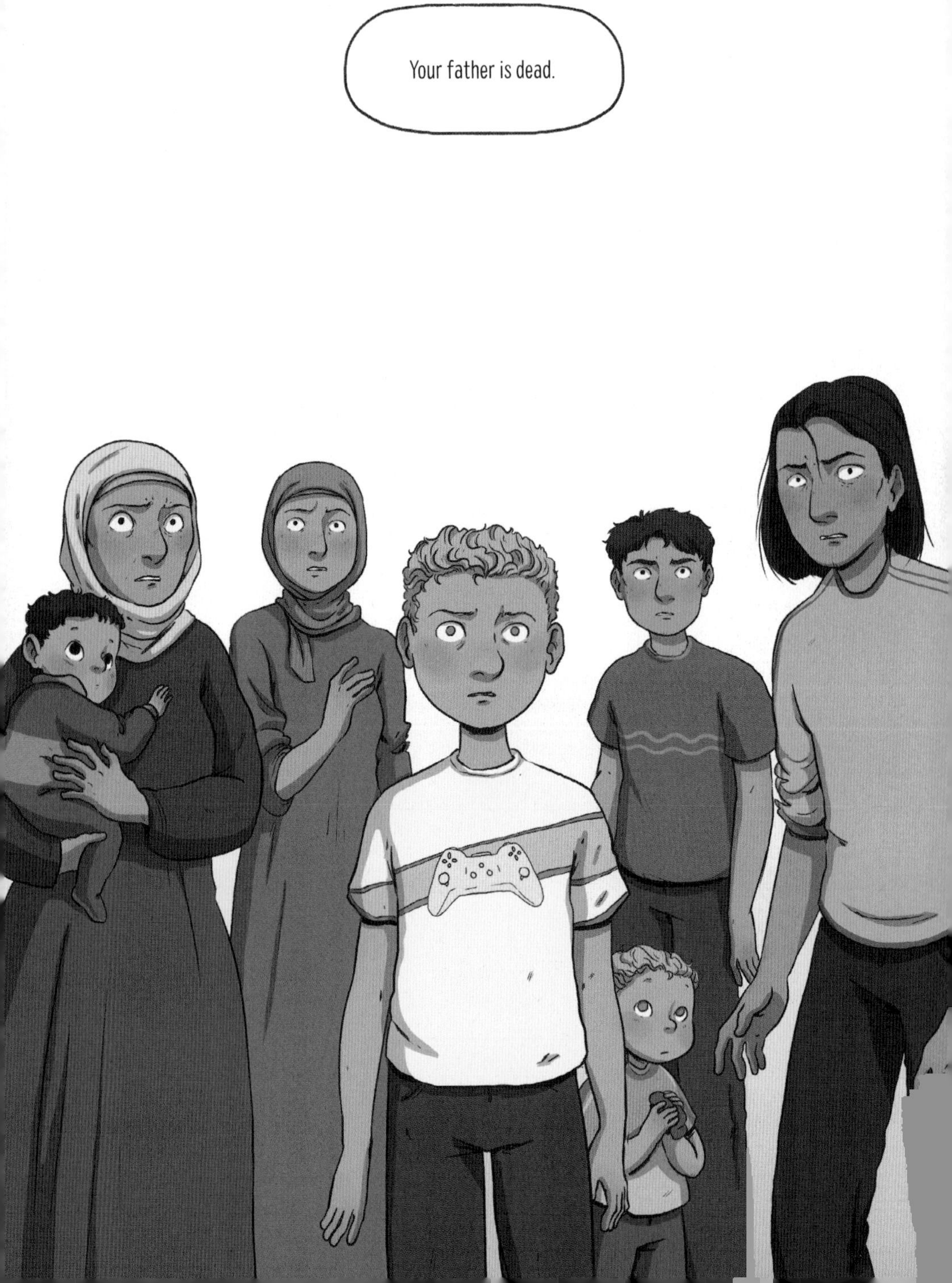
Your father is dead.

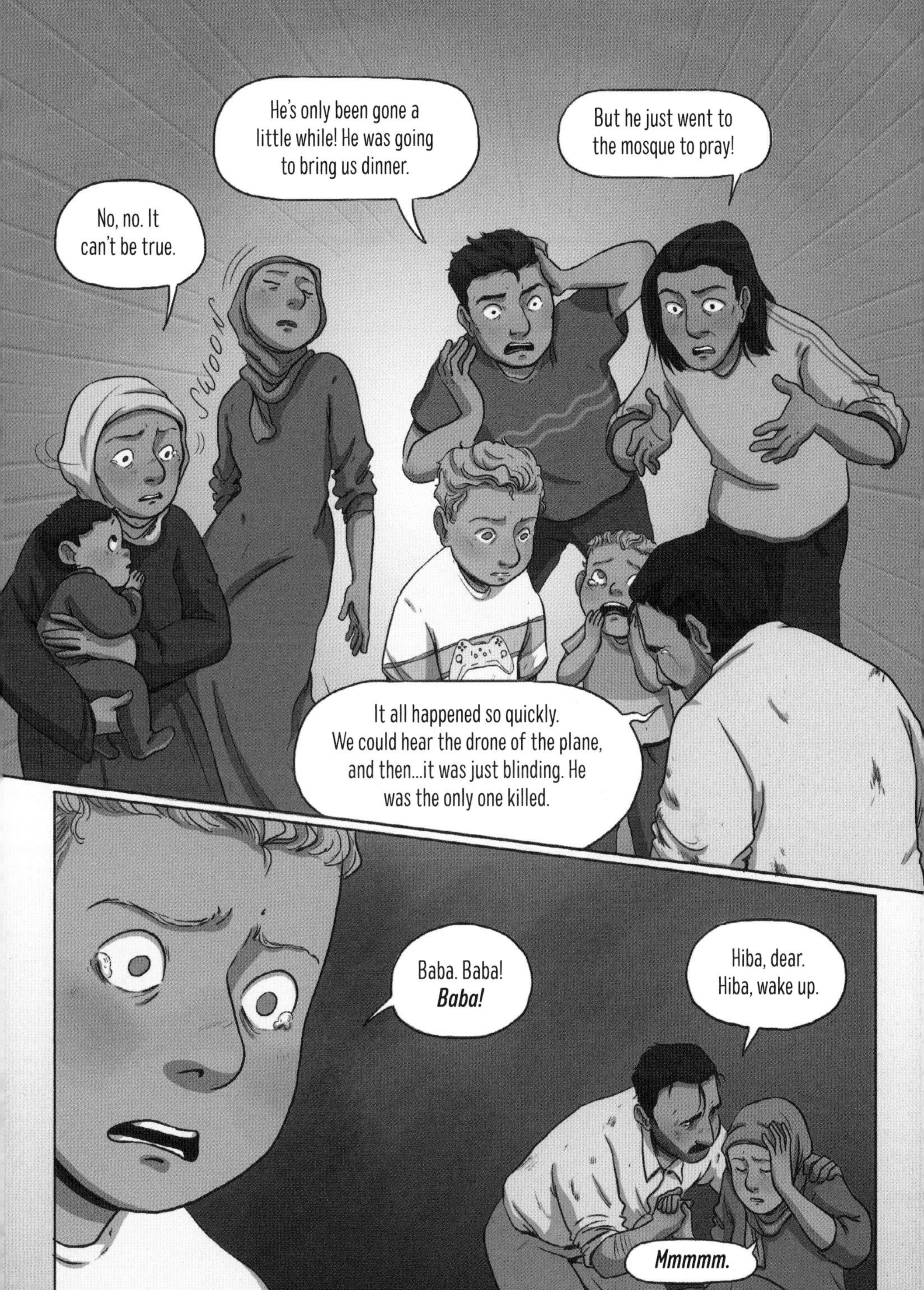

No, no. It can't be true.
He's only been gone a little while! He was going to bring us dinner.
But he just went to the mosque to pray!
It all happened so quickly. We could hear the drone of the plane, and then...it was just blinding. He was the only one killed.
Baba. Baba! ***Baba!***
Hiba, dear. Hiba, wake up.
Mmmmm.

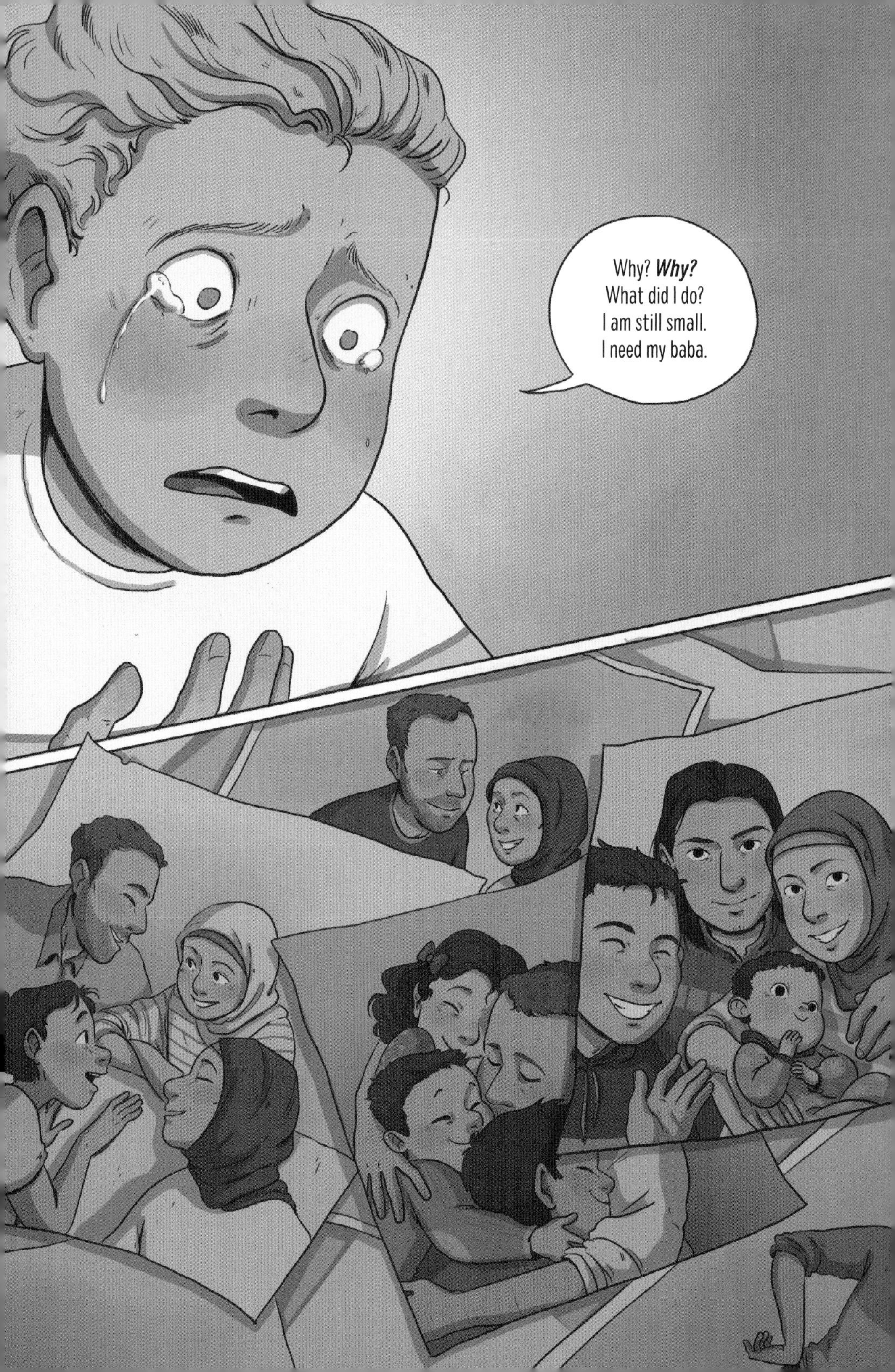
Why? **Why?** What did I do? I am still small. I need my baba.

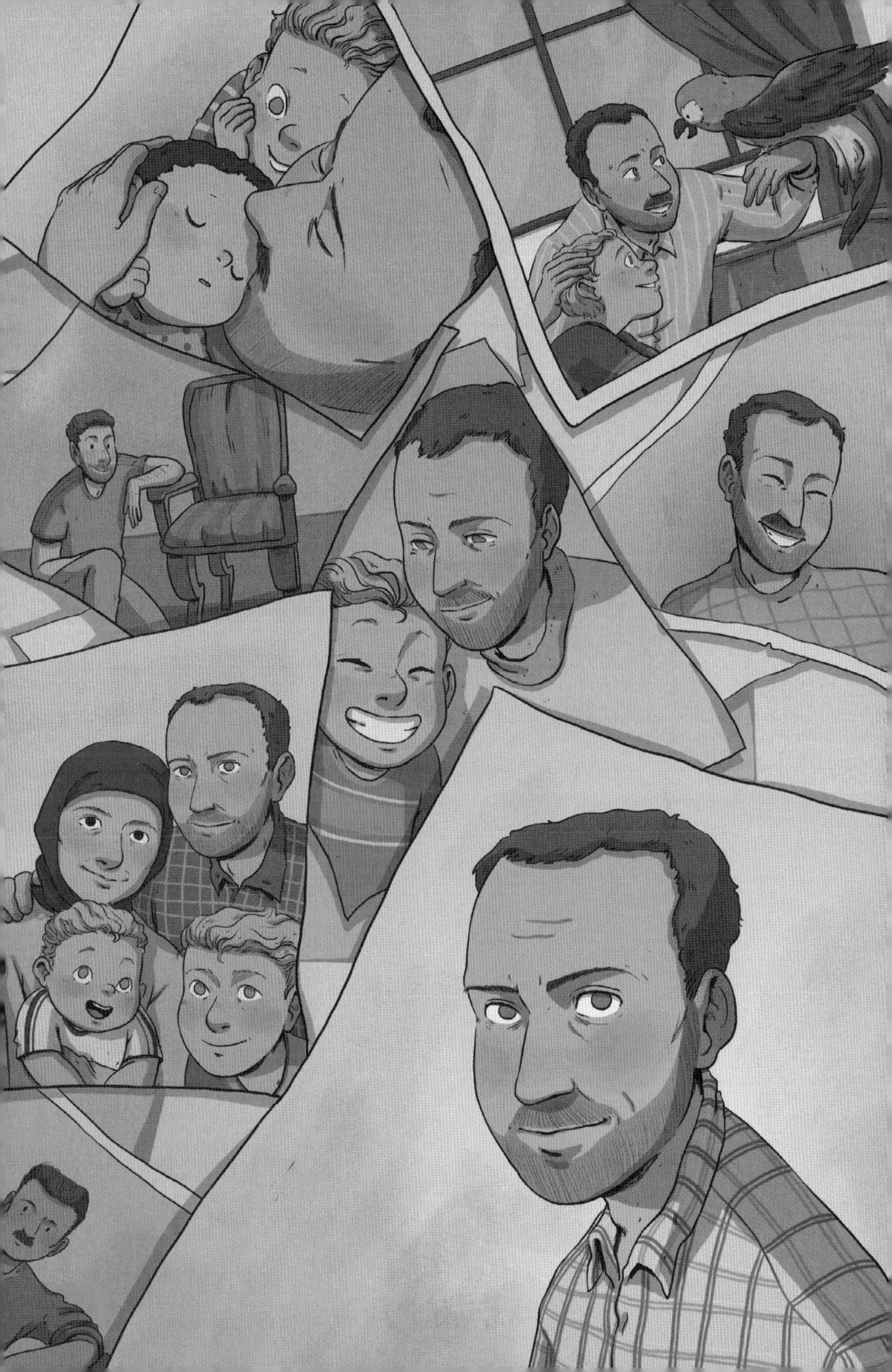

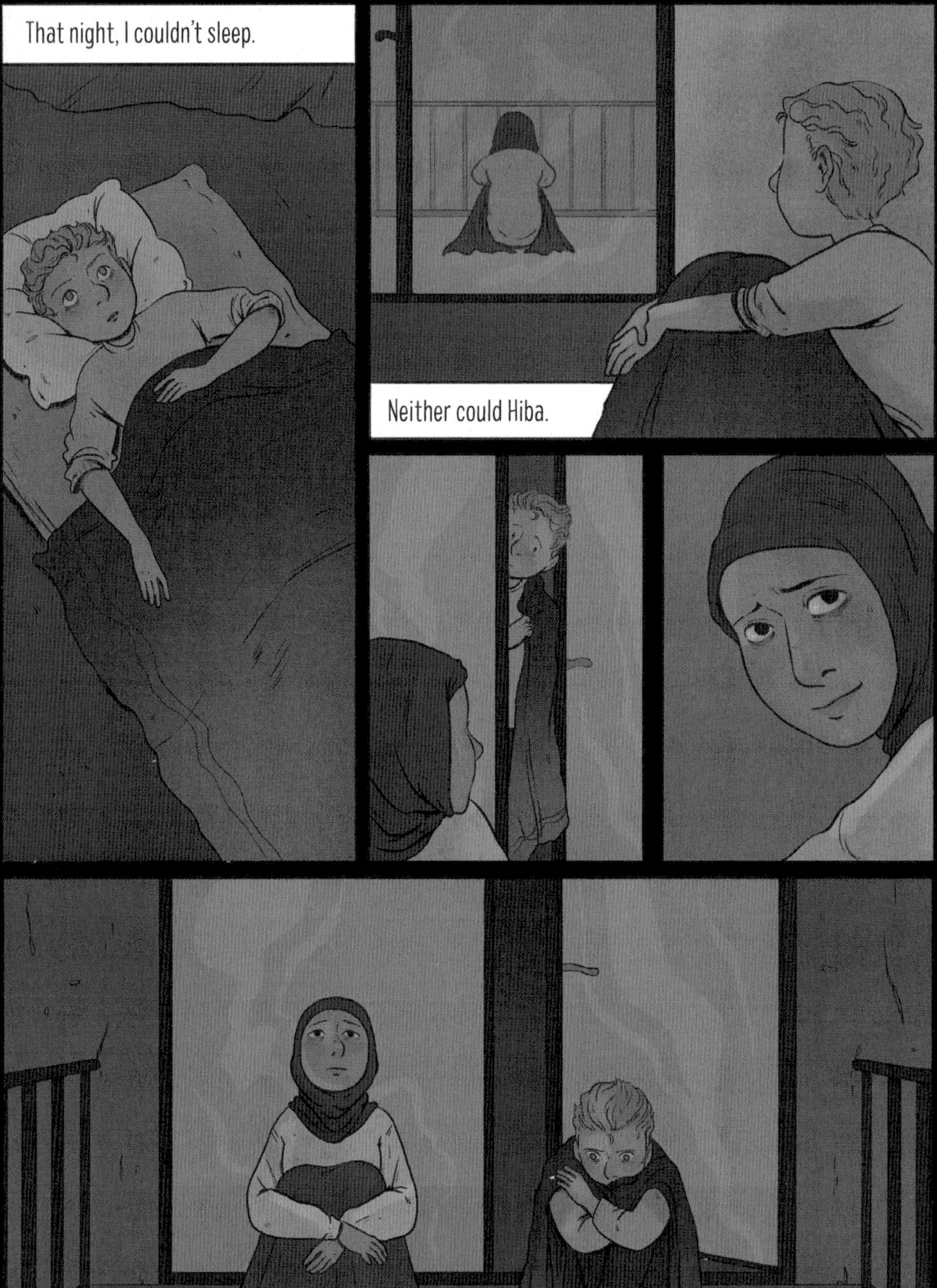
That night, I couldn't sleep.
Neither could Hiba.

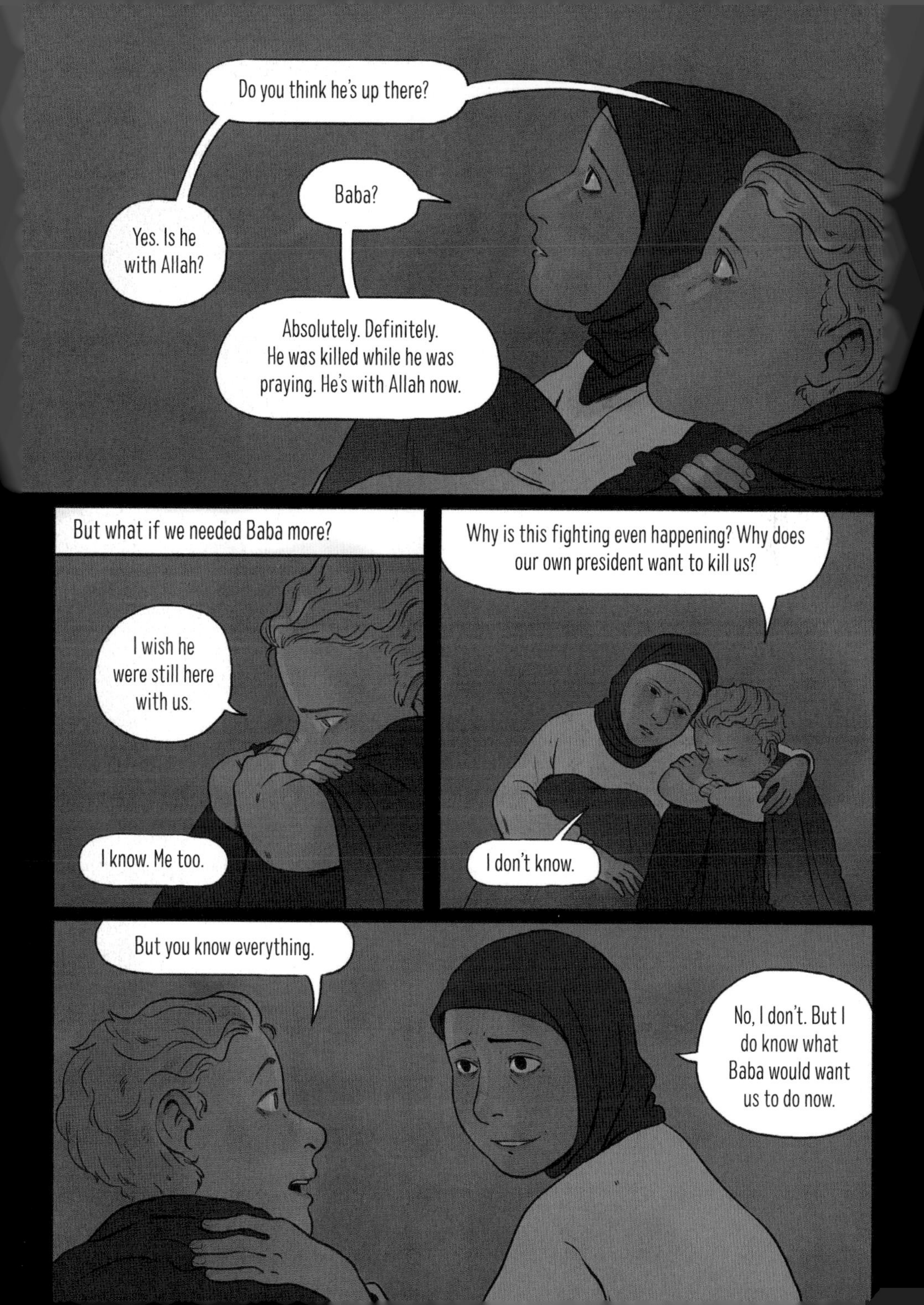
Do you think he's up there?
Baba?
Yes. Is he with Allah?
Absolutely. Definitely. He was killed while he was praying. He's with Allah now.
But what if we needed Baba more?
I wish he were still here with us.
I know. Me too.
Why is this fighting even happening? Why does our own president want to kill us?
I don't know.
But you know everything.
No, I don't. But I do know what Baba would want us to do now.

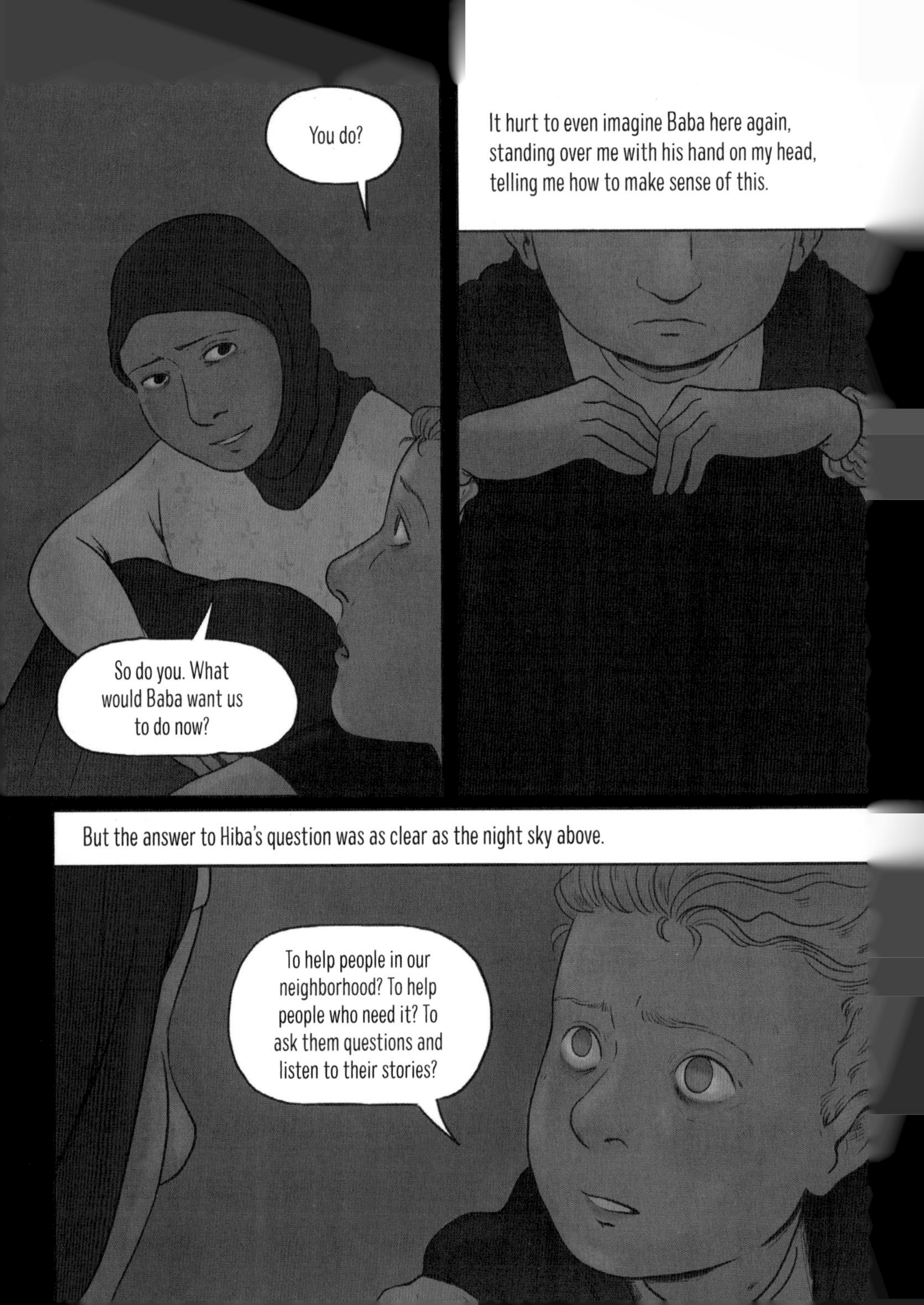
You do?
So do you. What would Baba want us to do now?
It hurt to even imagine Baba here again, standing over me with his hand on my head, telling me how to make sense of this.
But the answer to Hiba's question was as clear as the night sky above.
To help people in our neighborhood? To help people who need it? To ask them questions and listen to their stories?

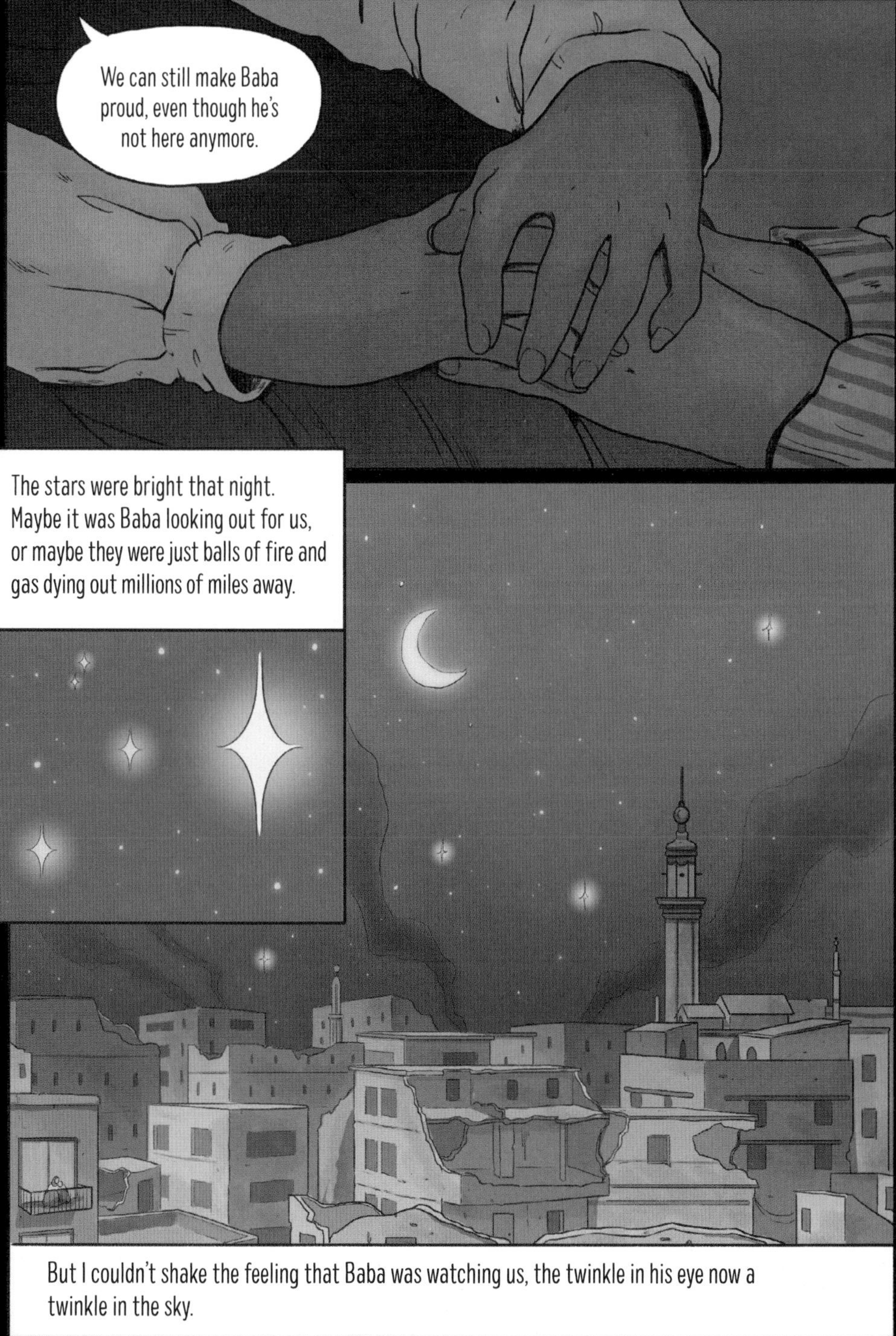
We can still make Baba proud, even though he's not here anymore.
The stars were bright that night. Maybe it was Baba looking out for us, or maybe they were just balls of fire and gas dying out millions of miles away.
But I couldn't shake the feeling that Baba was watching us, the twinkle in his eye now a twinkle in the sky.

CHAPTER 5

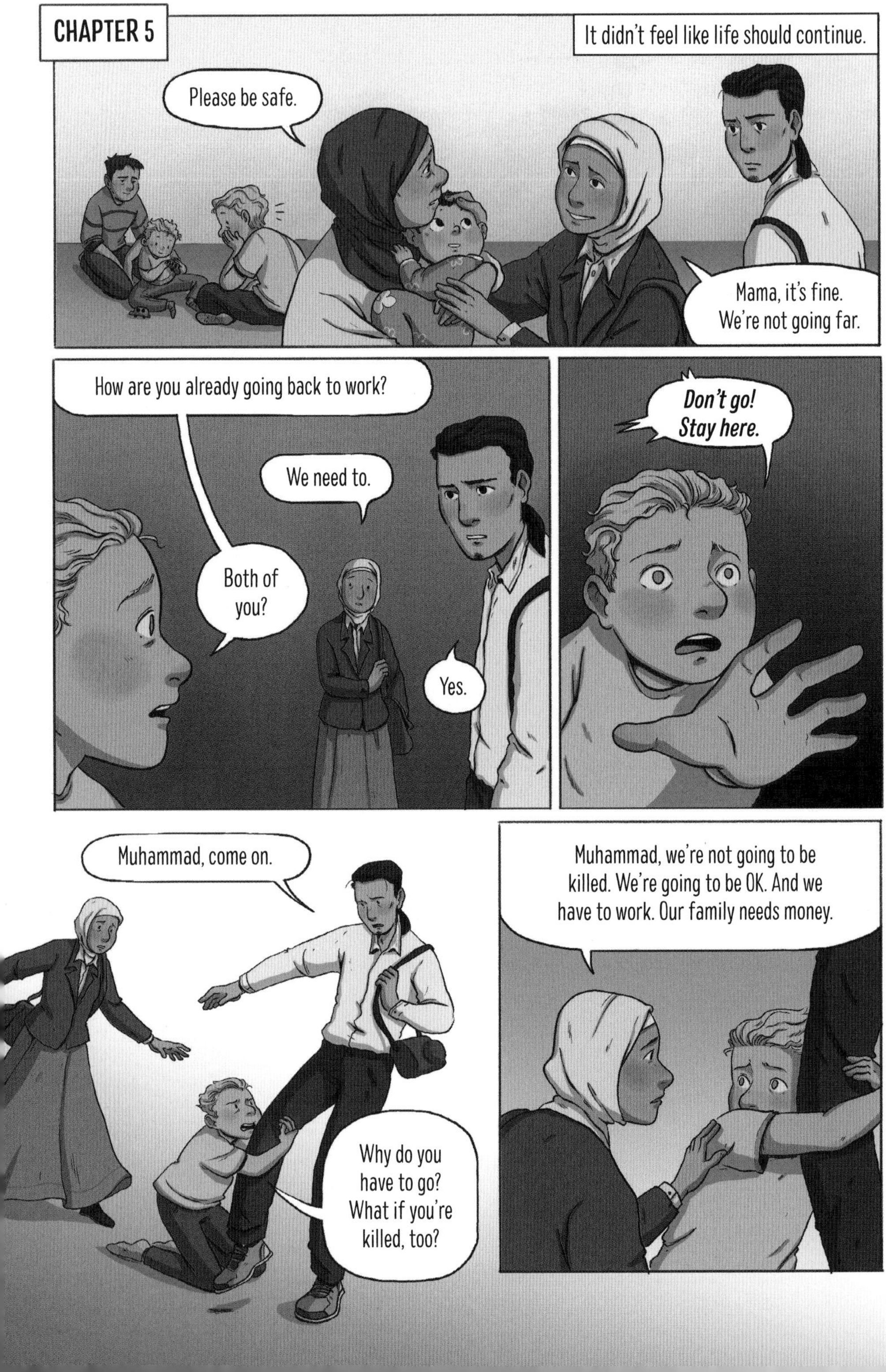
It didn't feel like life should continue.
Please be safe.
Mama, it's fine. We're not going far.
How are you already going back to work?
We need to.
Both of you?
Yes.
Don't go! Stay here.
Muhammad, come on.
Why do you have to go? What if you're killed, too?
Muhammad, we're not going to be killed. We're going to be OK. And we have to work. Our family needs money.

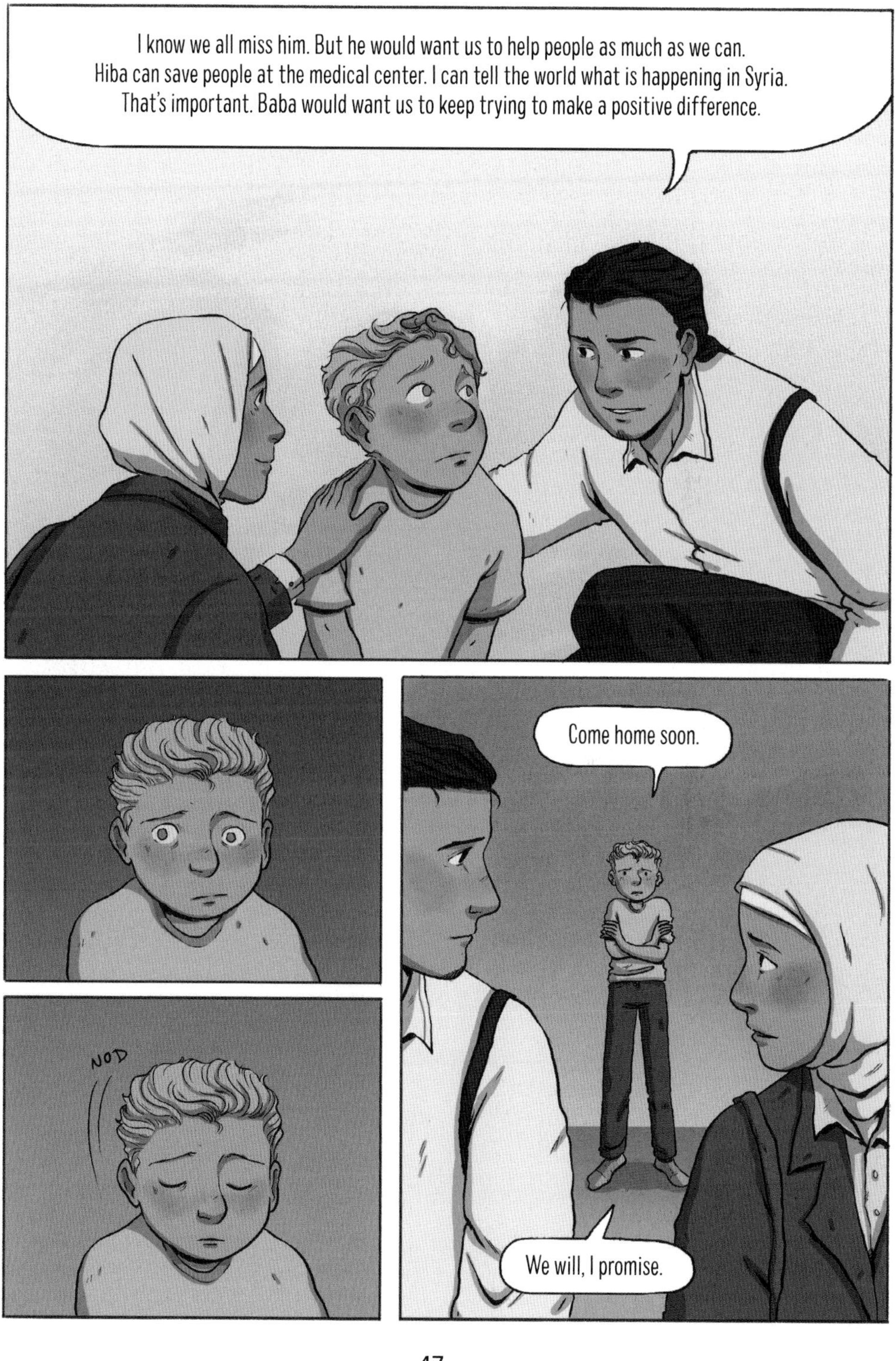
I know we all miss him. But he would want us to help people as much as we can.
Hiba can save people at the medical center. I can tell the world what is happening in Syria.
That's important. Baba would want us to keep trying to make a positive difference.
NOD
Come home soon.
We will, I promise.

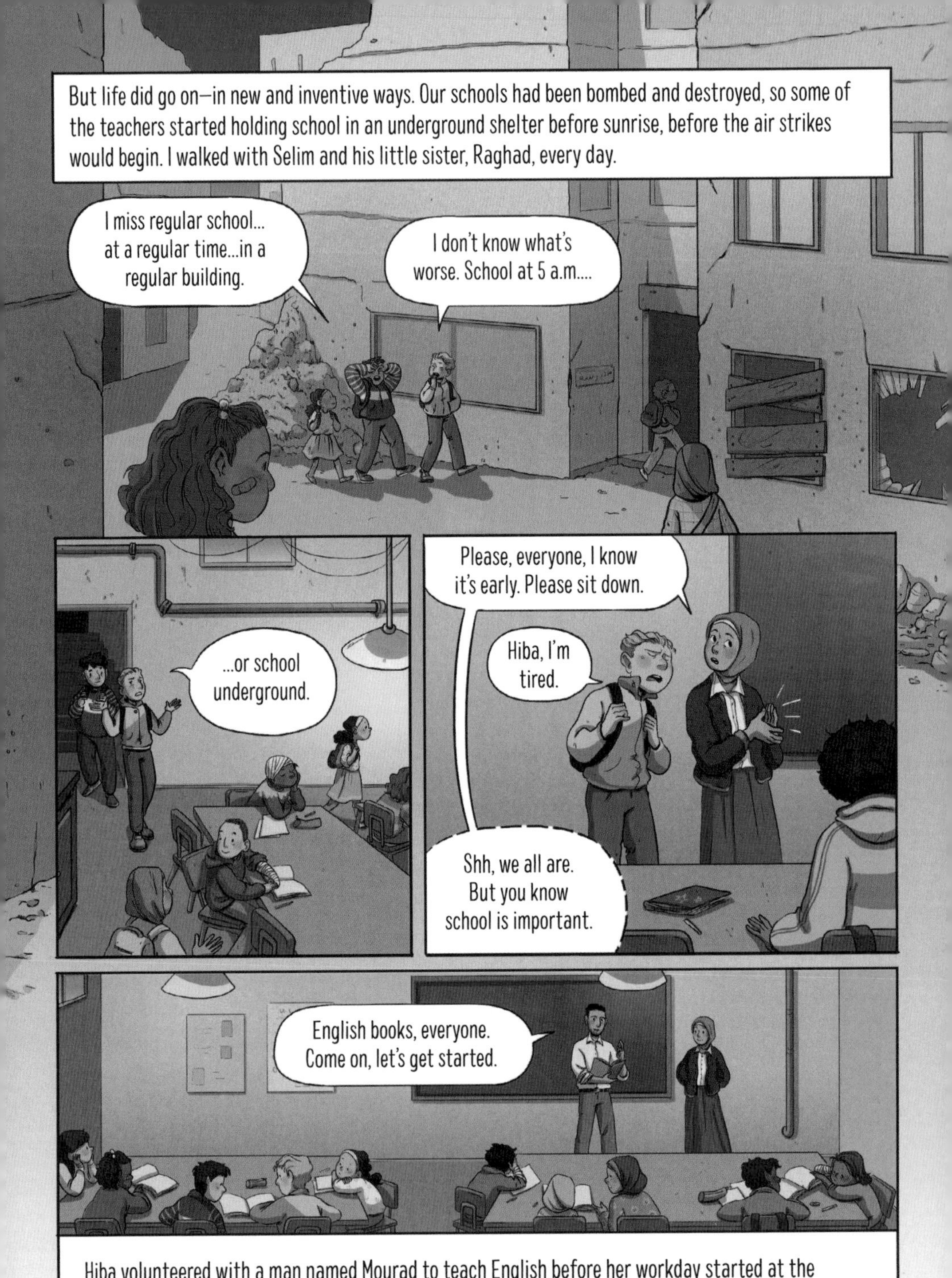
But life did go on—in new and inventive ways. Our schools had been bombed and destroyed, so some of the teachers started holding school in an underground shelter before sunrise, before the air strikes would begin. I walked with Selim and his little sister, Raghad, every day.
I miss regular school... at a regular time...in a regular building.
I don't know what's worse. School at 5 a.m....
...or school underground.
Please, everyone, I know it's early. Please sit down.
Hiba, I'm tired.
Shh, we all are. But you know school is important.
English books, everyone. Come on, let's get started.
Hiba volunteered with a man named Mourad to teach English before her workday started at the medical clinic. I was glad she had Mourad to help her, because I didn't know when Hiba slept anymore.

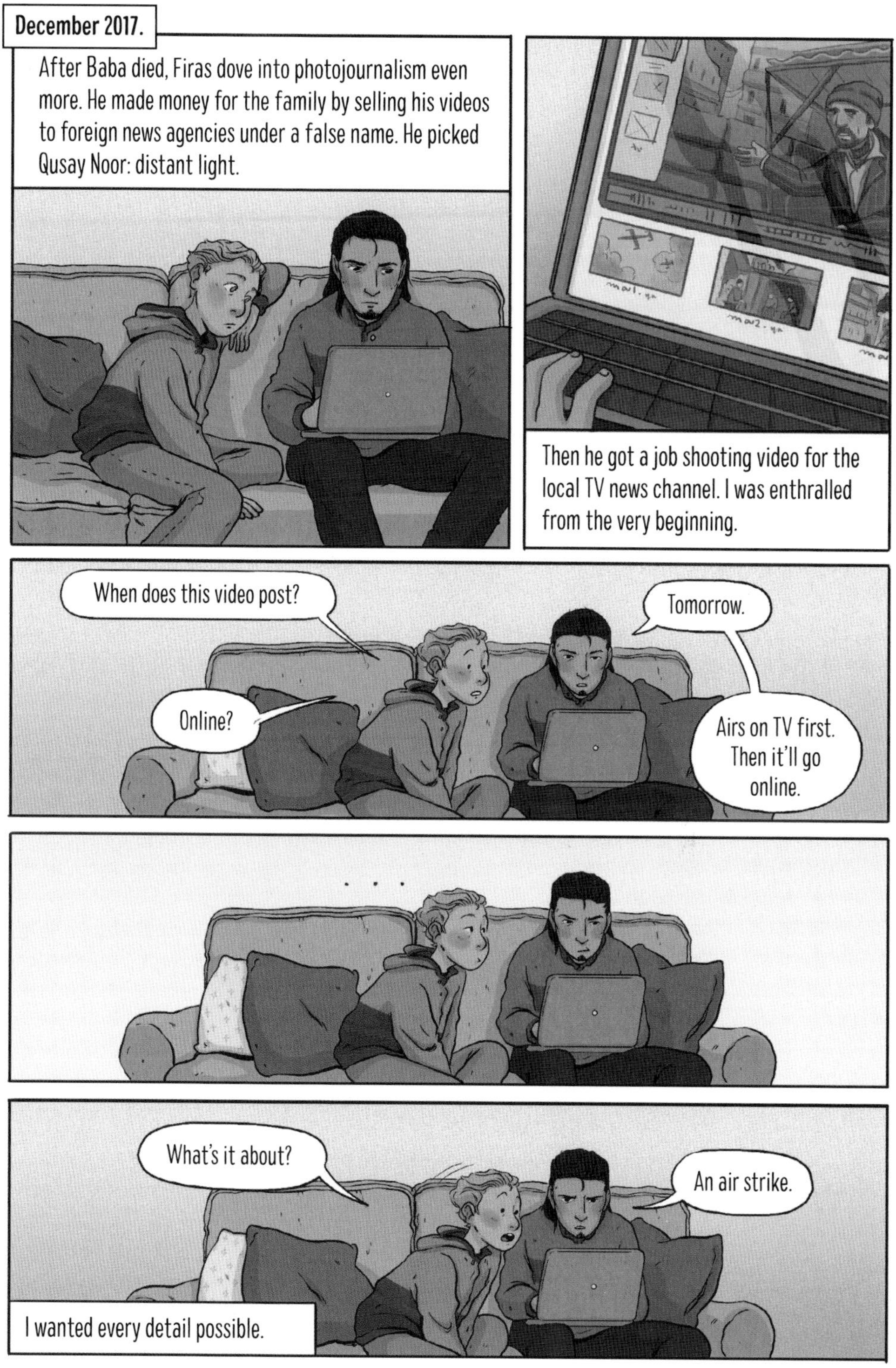
December 2017.
After Baba died, Firas dove into photojournalism even more. He made money for the family by selling his videos to foreign news agencies under a false name. He picked Qusay Noor: distant light.
Then he got a job shooting video for the local TV news channel. I was enthralled from the very beginning.
When does this video post?
Tomorrow.
Online?
Airs on TV first. Then it'll go online.
. . .
What's it about?
An air strike.
I wanted every detail possible.

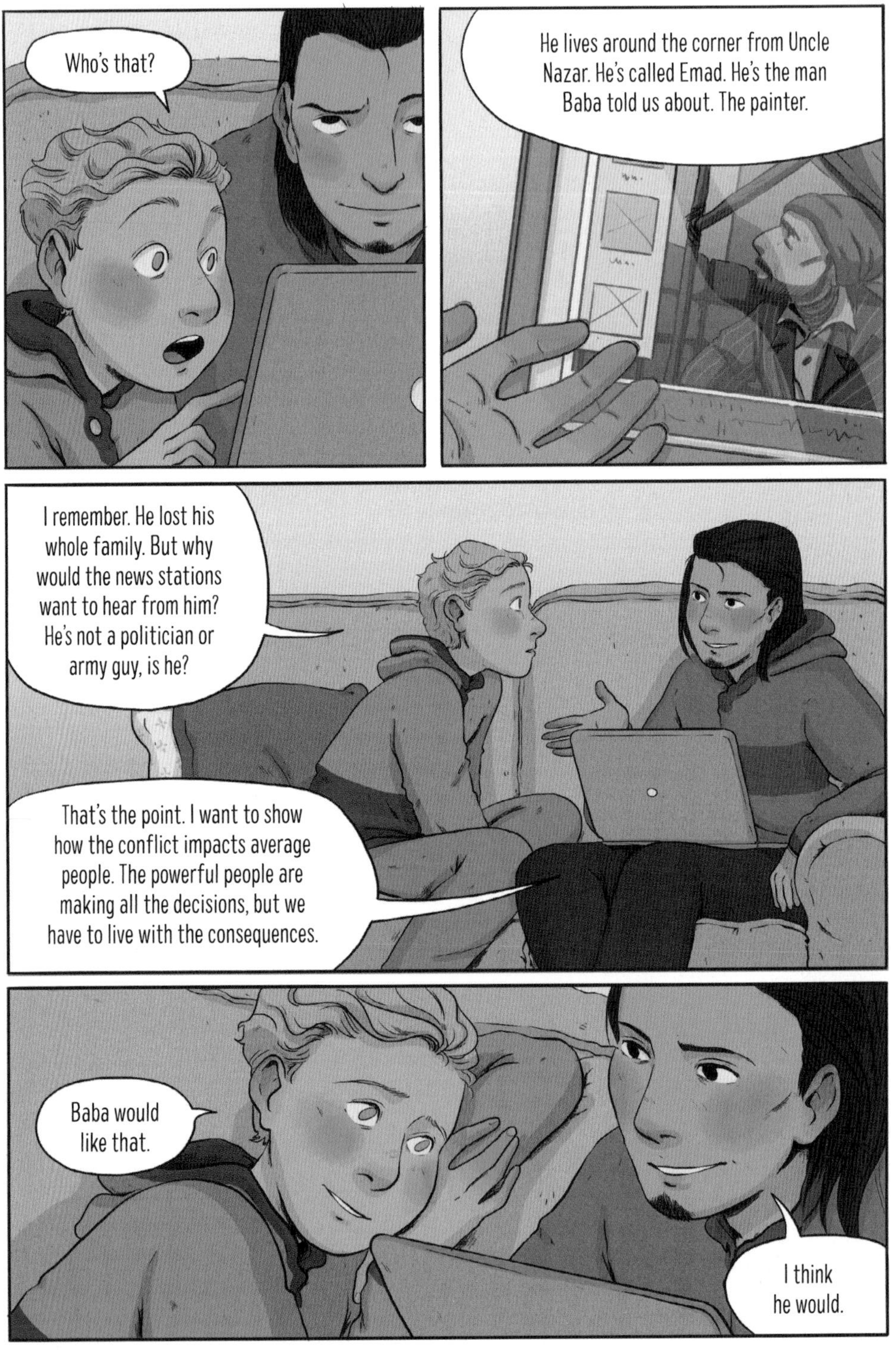
Who's that?
He lives around the corner from Uncle Nazar. He's called Emad. He's the man Baba told us about. The painter.
I remember. He lost his whole family. But why would the news stations want to hear from him? He's not a politician or army guy, is he?
That's the point. I want to show how the conflict impacts average people. The powerful people are making all the decisions, but we have to live with the consequences.
Baba would like that.
I think he would.

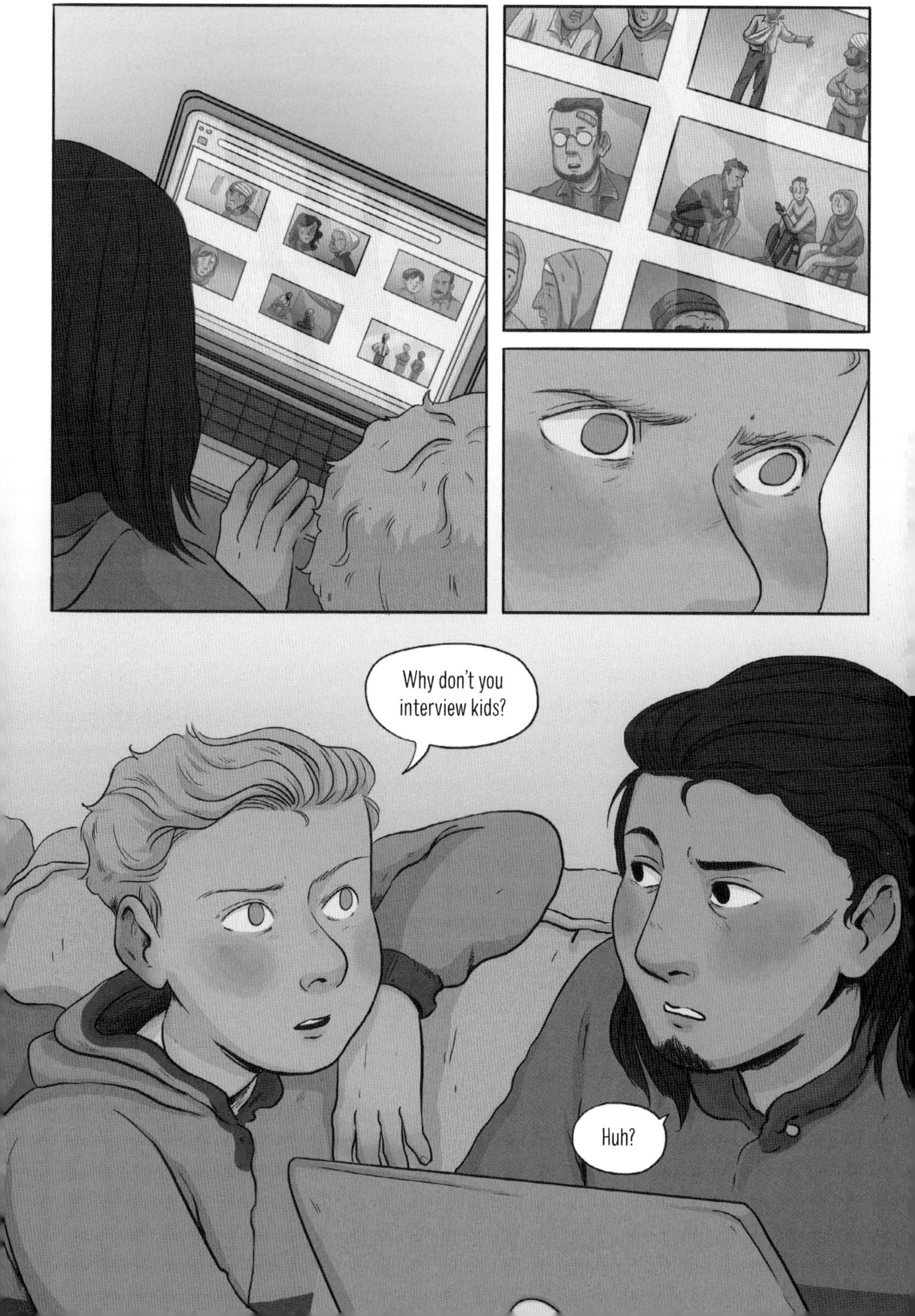
Why don't you
interview kids?
Huh?

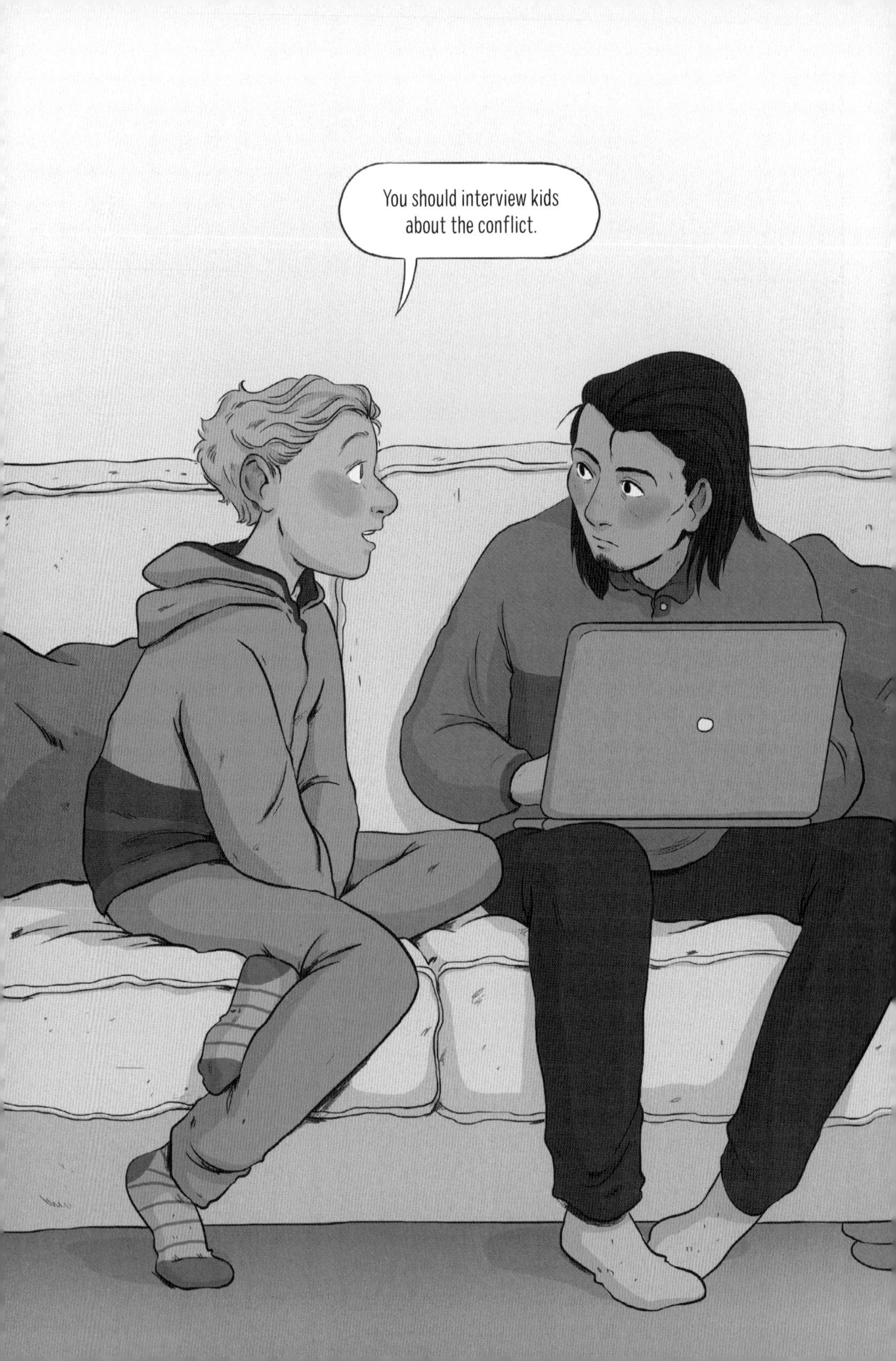
You should interview kids about the conflict.

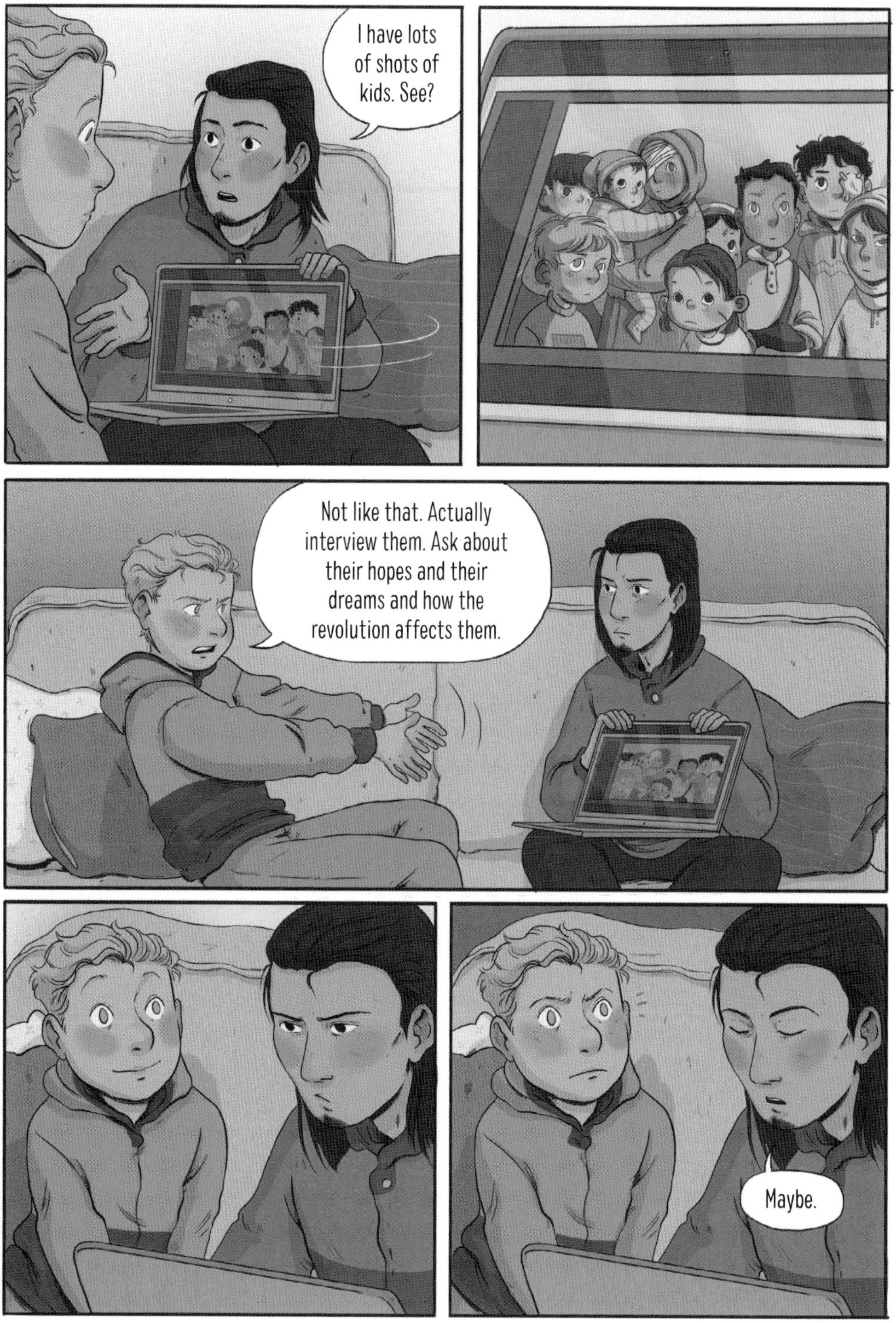
I have lots of shots of kids. See?
Not like that. Actually interview them. Ask about their hopes and their dreams and how the revolution affects them.
Maybe.

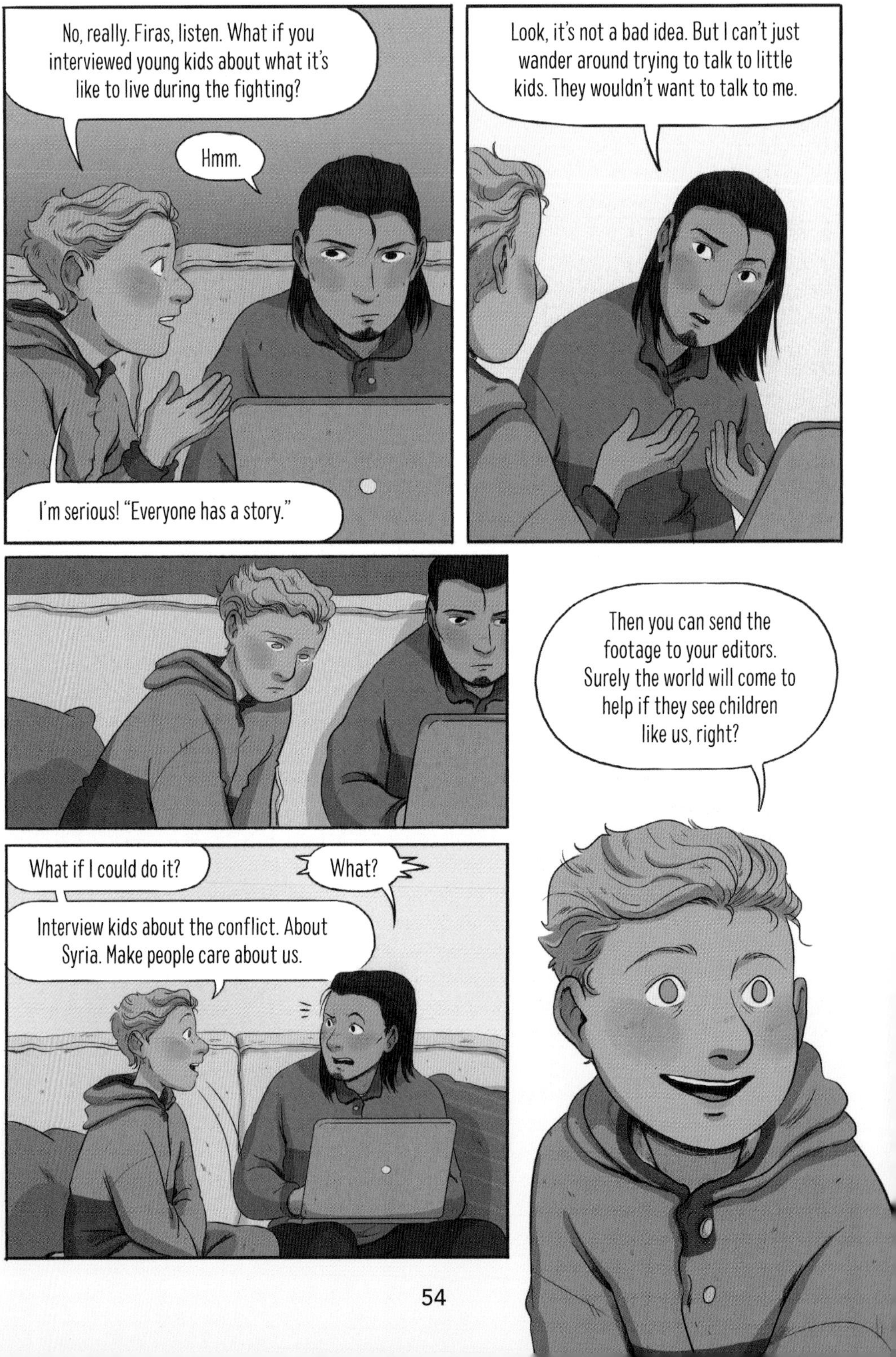
No, really. Firas, listen. What if you interviewed young kids about what it's like to live during the fighting?
Hmm.
I'm serious! "Everyone has a story."
Look, it's not a bad idea. But I can't just wander around trying to talk to little kids. They wouldn't want to talk to me.
Then you can send the footage to your editors. Surely the world will come to help if they see children like us, right?
What if I could do it?
What?
Interview kids about the conflict. About Syria. Make people care about us.

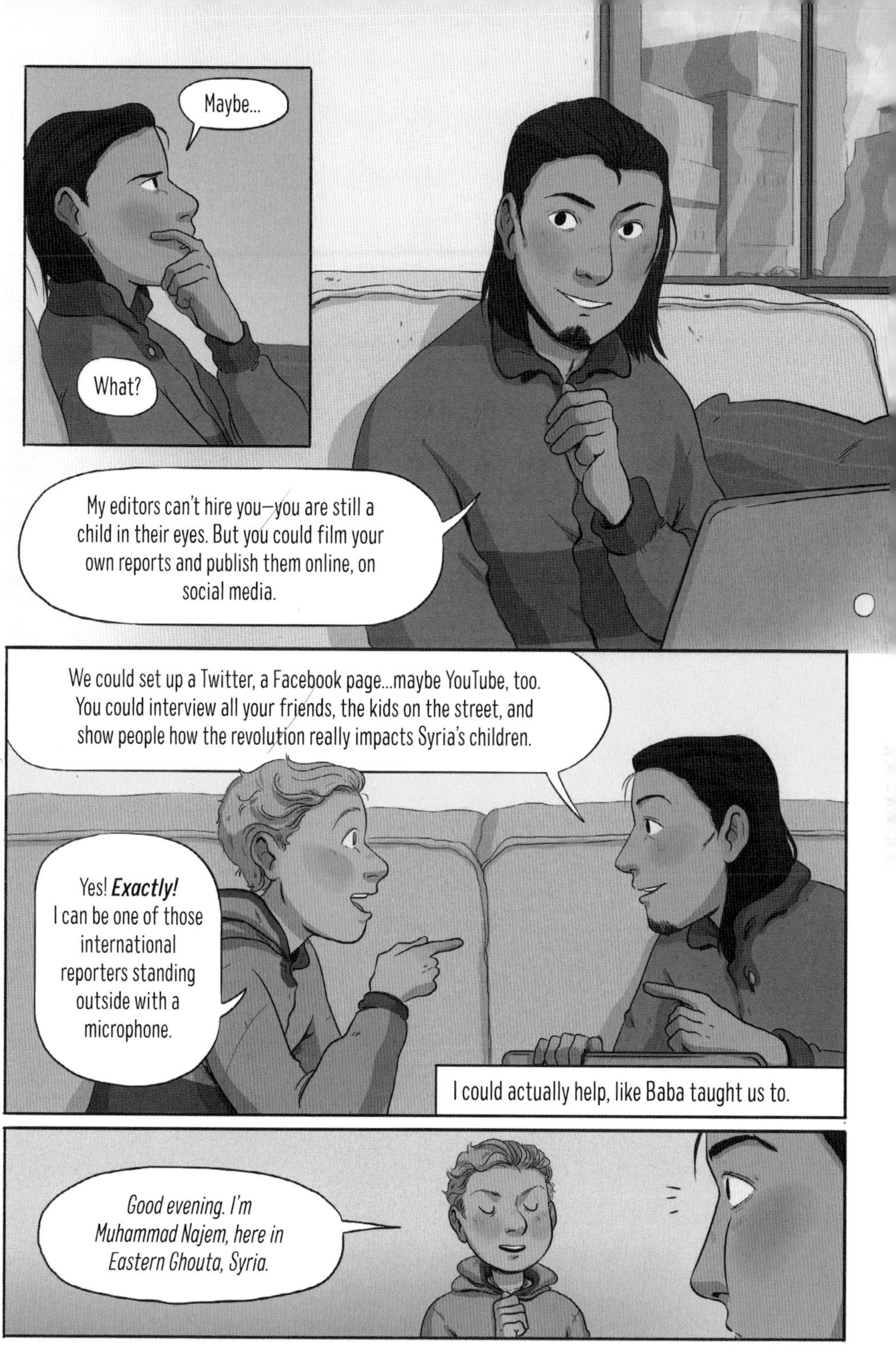

Maybe...
What?
My editors can't hire you—you are still a child in their eyes. But you could film your own reports and publish them online, on social media.
We could set up a Twitter, a Facebook page...maybe YouTube, too. You could interview all your friends, the kids on the street, and show people how the revolution really impacts Syria's children.
Yes! ***Exactly!*** I can be one of those international reporters standing outside with a microphone.
I could actually help, like Baba taught us to.
Good evening. I'm Muhammad Najem, here in Eastern Ghouta, Syria.

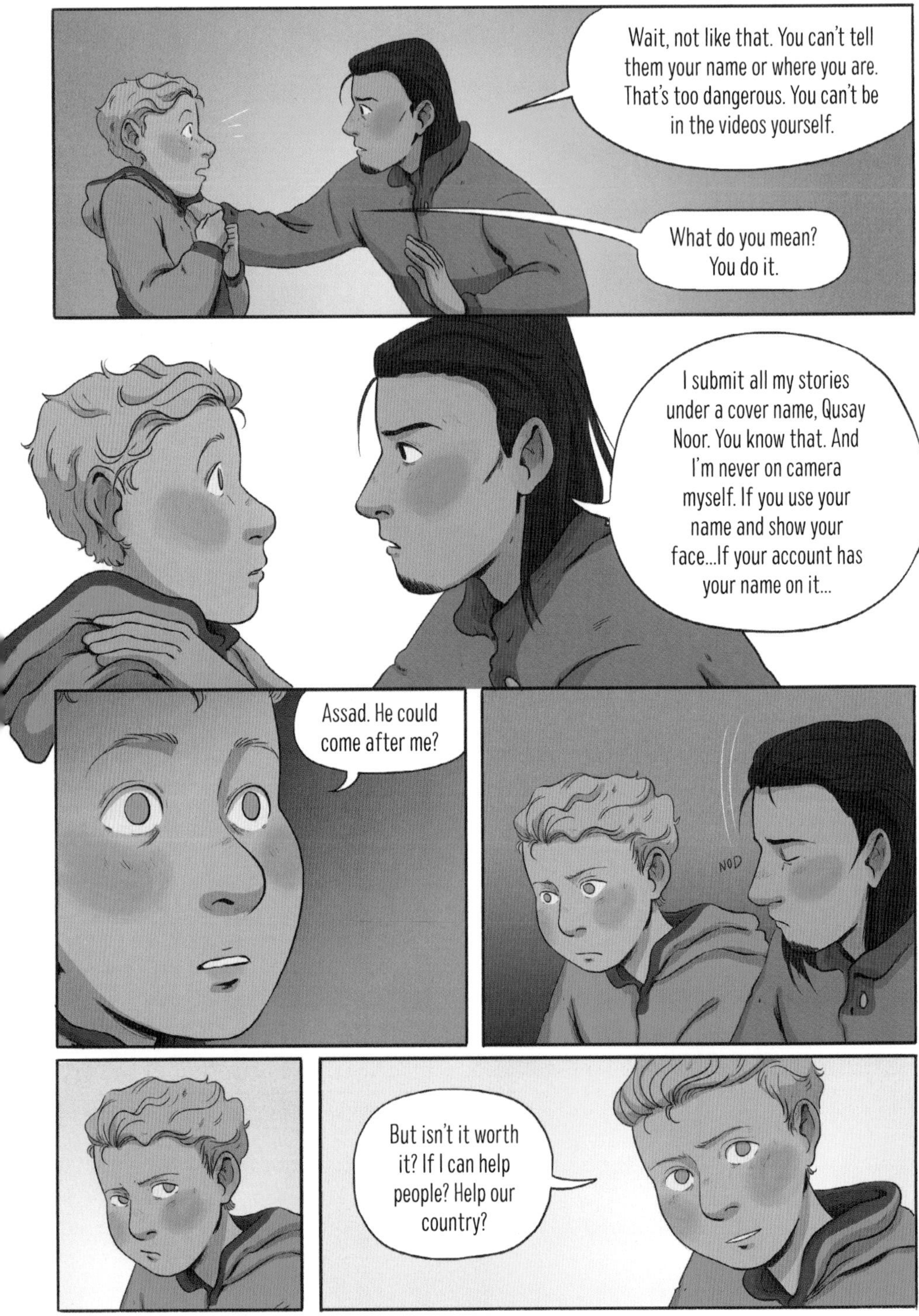
Wait, not like that. You can't tell them your name or where you are. That's too dangerous. You can't be in the videos yourself.
What do you mean? You do it.
I submit all my stories under a cover name, Qusay Noor. You know that. And I'm never on camera myself. If you use your name and show your face...If your account has your name on it...
Assad. He could come after me?
NOD
But isn't it worth it? If I can help people? Help our country?

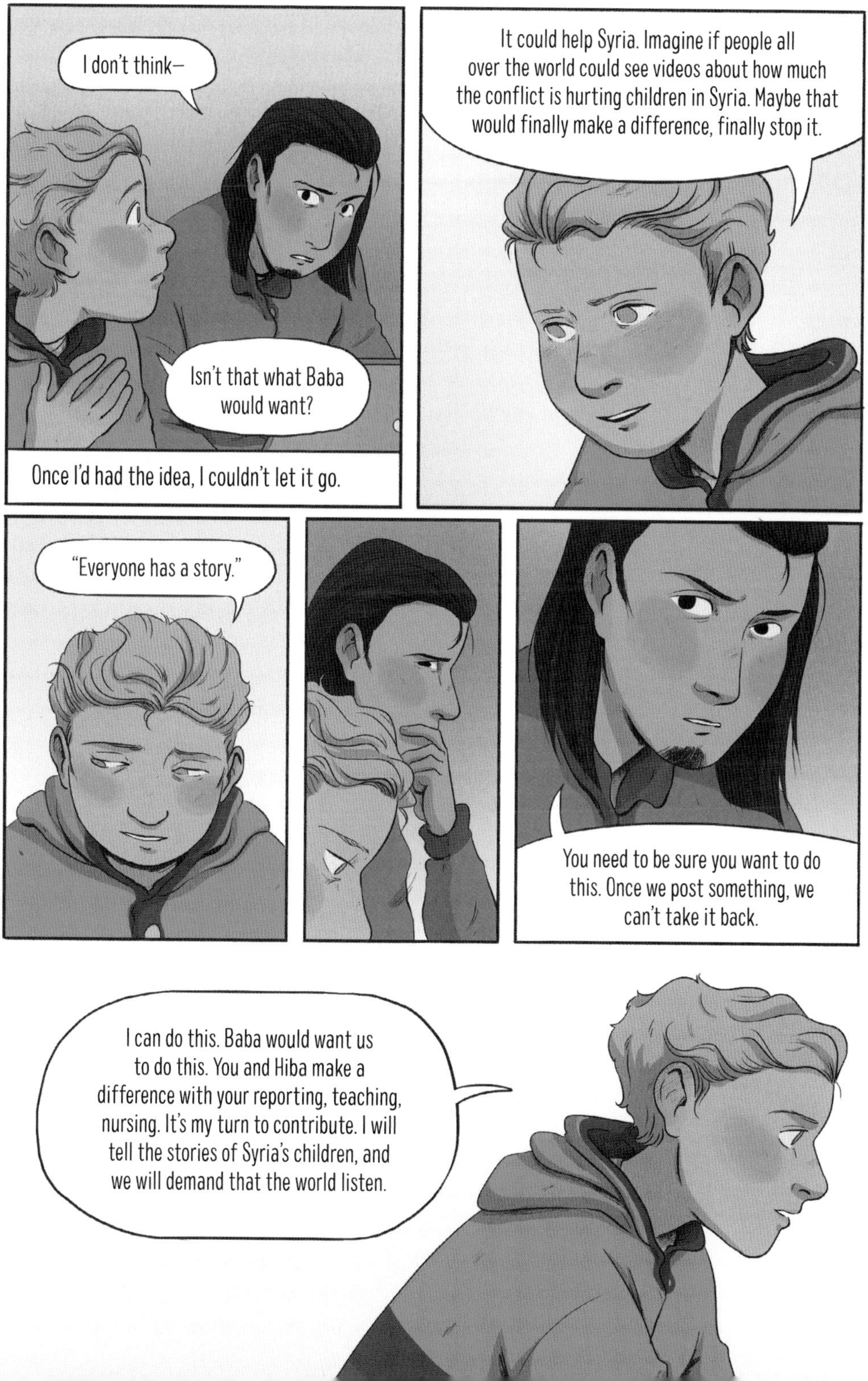
I don't think–
Isn't that what Baba would want?
Once I'd had the idea, I couldn't let it go.
It could help Syria. Imagine if people all over the world could see videos about how much the conflict is hurting children in Syria. Maybe that would finally make a difference, finally stop it.
"Everyone has a story."
You need to be sure you want to do this. Once we post something, we can't take it back.
I can do this. Baba would want us to do this. You and Hiba make a difference with your reporting, teaching, nursing. It's my turn to contribute. I will tell the stories of Syria's children, and we will demand that the world listen.

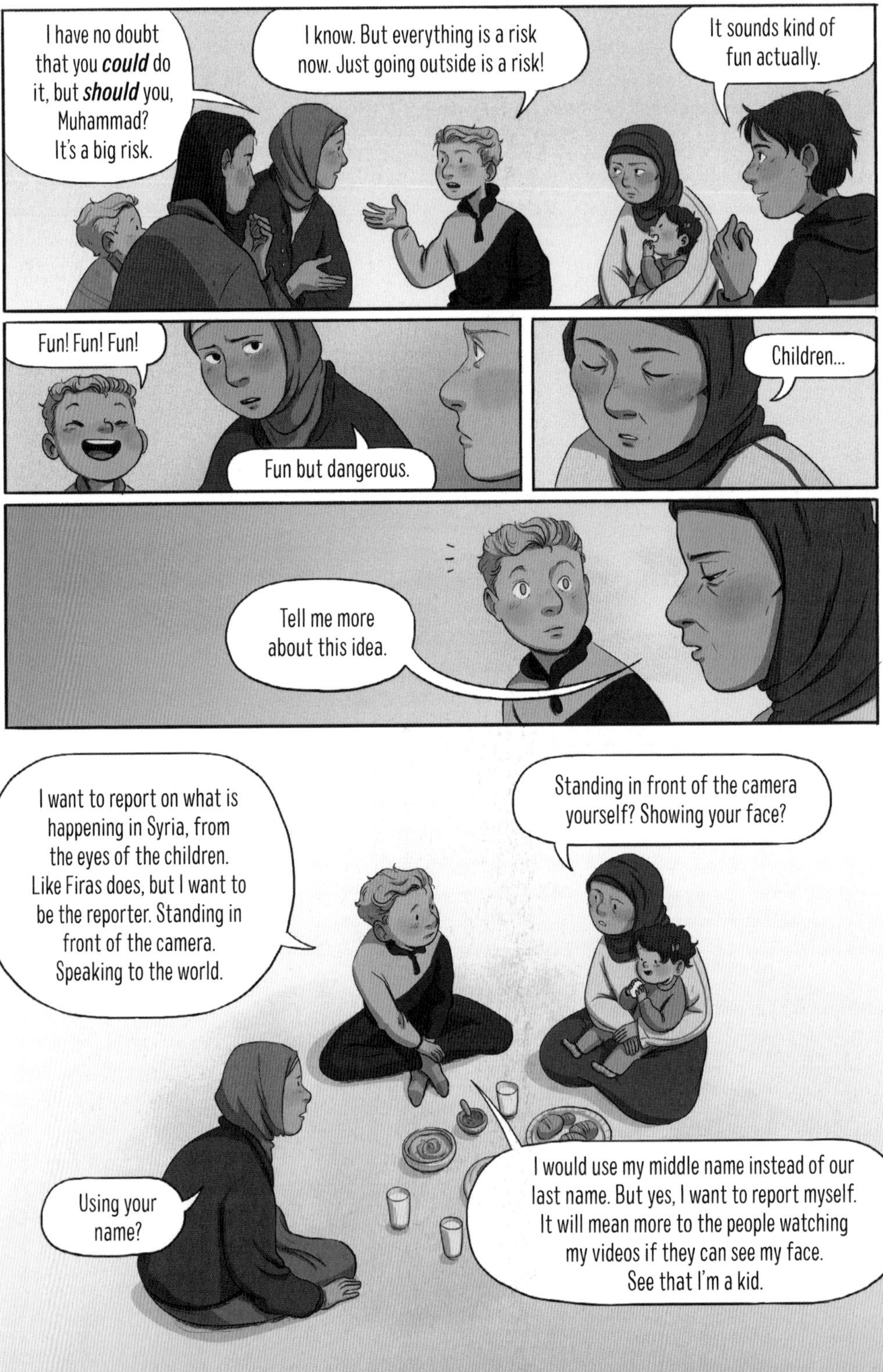
I have no doubt that you ***could*** do it, but ***should*** you, Muhammad? It's a big risk.
I know. But everything is a risk now. Just going outside is a risk!
It sounds kind of fun actually.
Fun! Fun! Fun!
Fun but dangerous.
Children...
Tell me more about this idea.
I want to report on what is happening in Syria, from the eyes of the children. Like Firas does, but I want to be the reporter. Standing in front of the camera. Speaking to the world.
Standing in front of the camera yourself? Showing your face?
Using your name?
I would use my middle name instead of our last name. But yes, I want to report myself. It will mean more to the people watching my videos if they can see my face. See that I'm a kid.

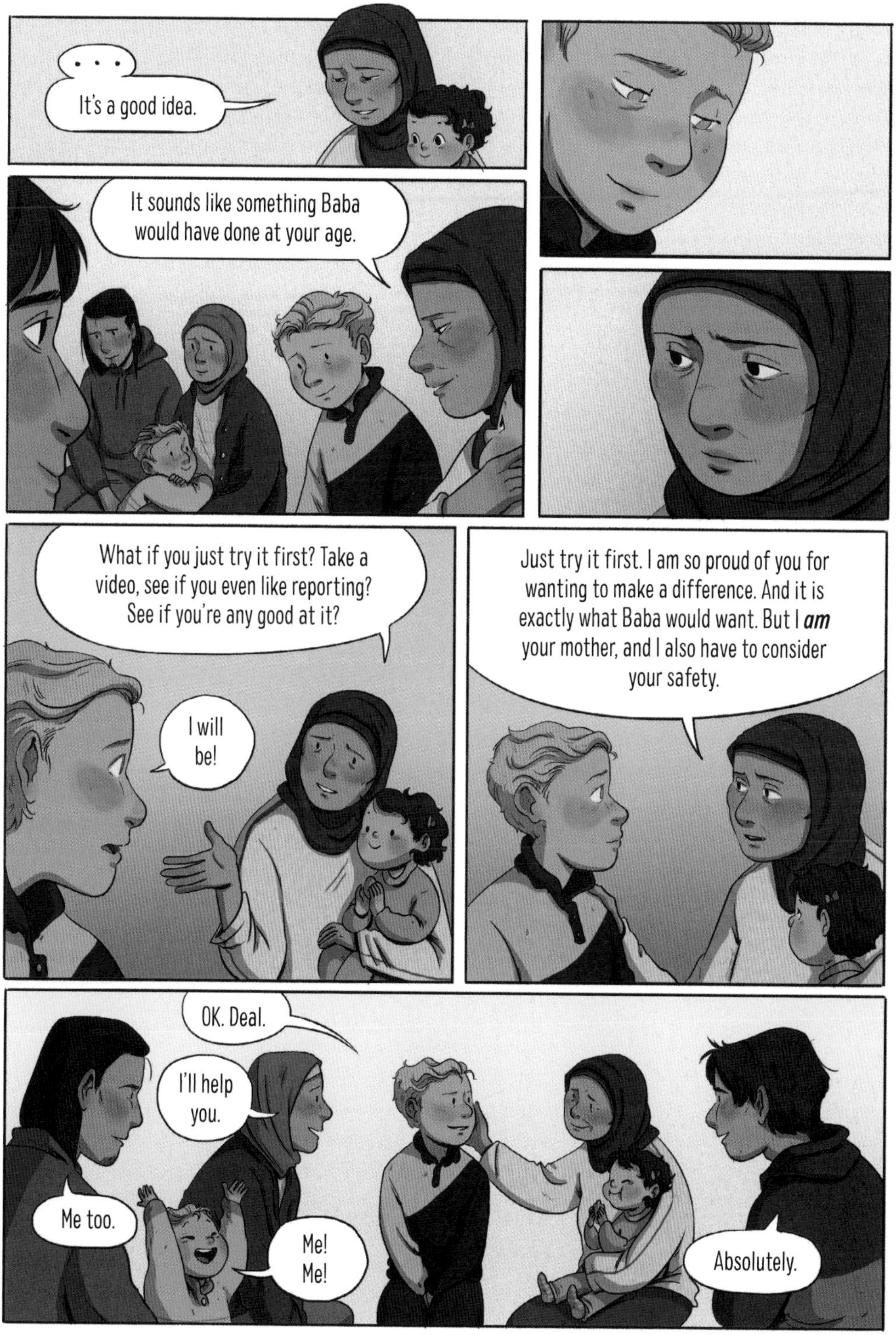
. . .
It's a good idea.
It sounds like something Baba would have done at your age.
What if you just try it first? Take a video, see if you even like reporting? See if you're any good at it?
I will be!
Just try it first. I am so proud of you for wanting to make a difference. And it is exactly what Baba would want. But I ***am*** your mother, and I also have to consider your safety.
OK. Deal.
I'll help you.
Me too.
Me! Me!
Absolutely.

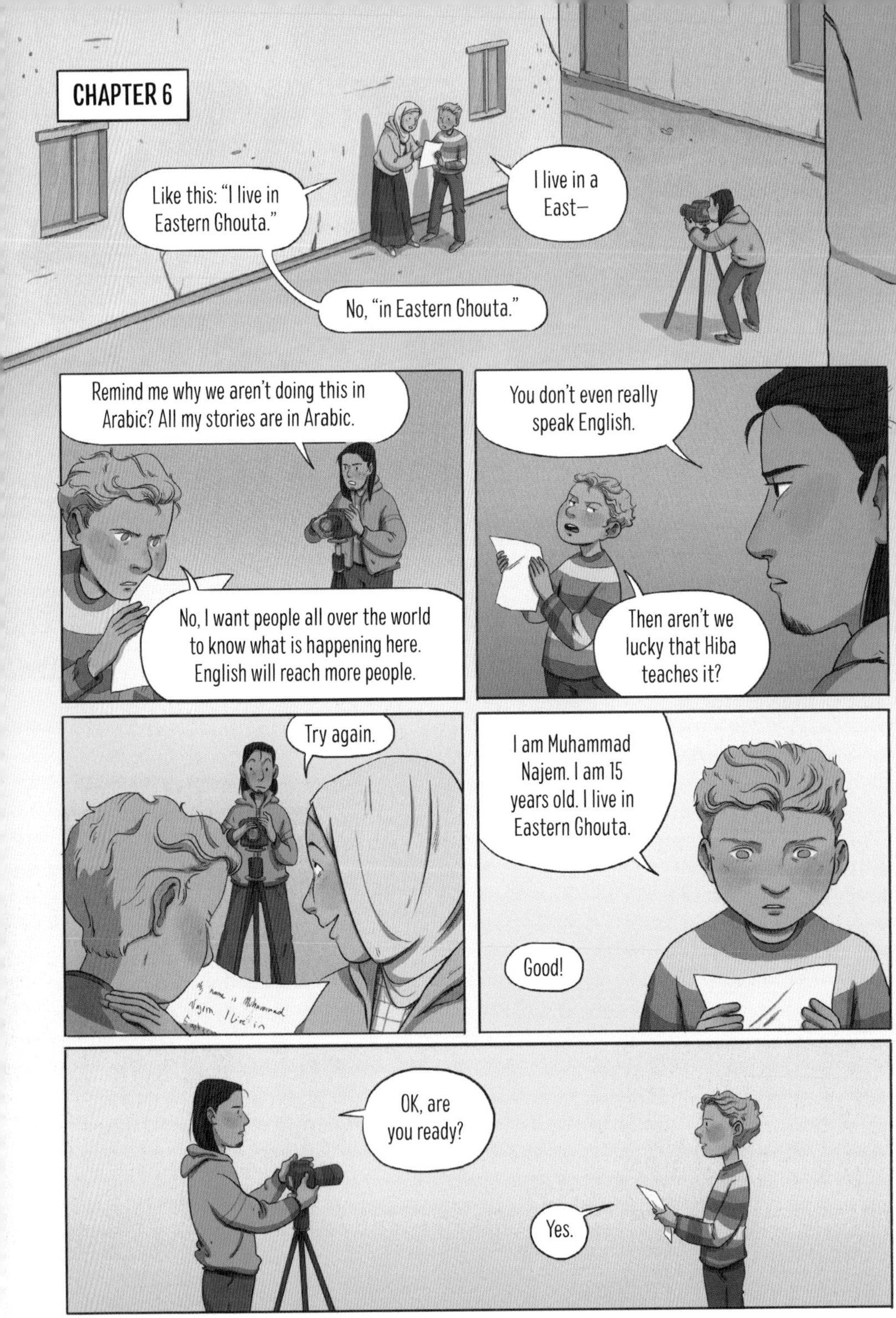
CHAPTER 6
Like this: "I live in Eastern Ghouta."
I live in a East—
No, "in Eastern Ghouta."
Remind me why we aren't doing this in Arabic? All my stories are in Arabic.
No, I want people all over the world to know what is happening here. English will reach more people.
You don't even really speak English.
Then aren't we lucky that Hiba teaches it?
Try again.
I am Muhammad Najem. I am 15 years old. I live in Eastern Ghouta.
Good!
OK, are you ready?
Yes.

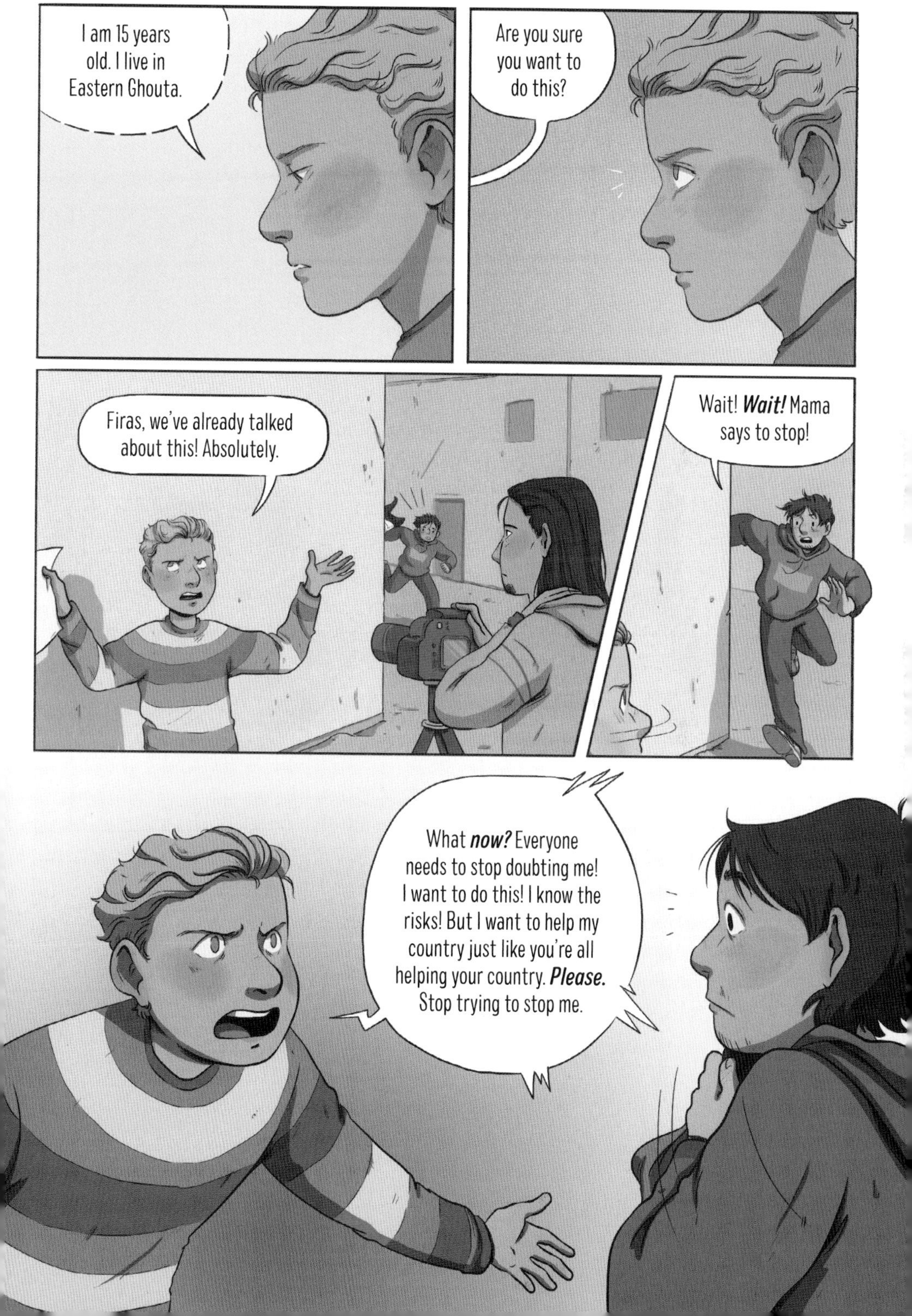
I am 15 years old. I live in Eastern Ghouta.
Are you sure you want to do this?
Firas, we've already talked about this! Absolutely.
Wait! ***Wait!*** Mama says to stop!
What ***now?*** Everyone needs to stop doubting me! I want to do this! I know the risks! But I want to help my country just like you're all helping your country. ***Please.*** Stop trying to stop me.

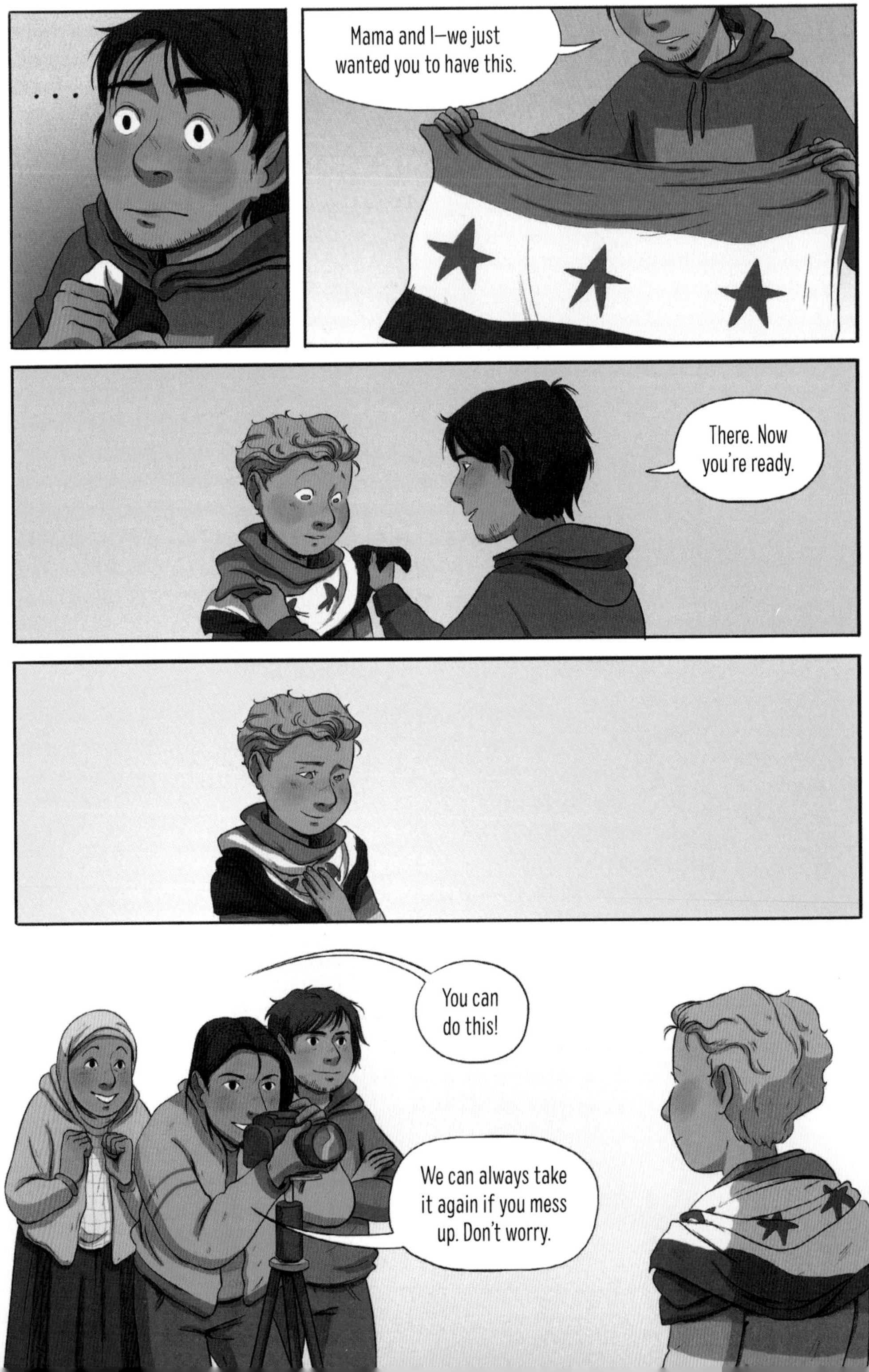
. . .
Mama and I—we just wanted you to have this.
There. Now you're ready.
You can do this!
We can always take it again if you mess up. Don't worry.

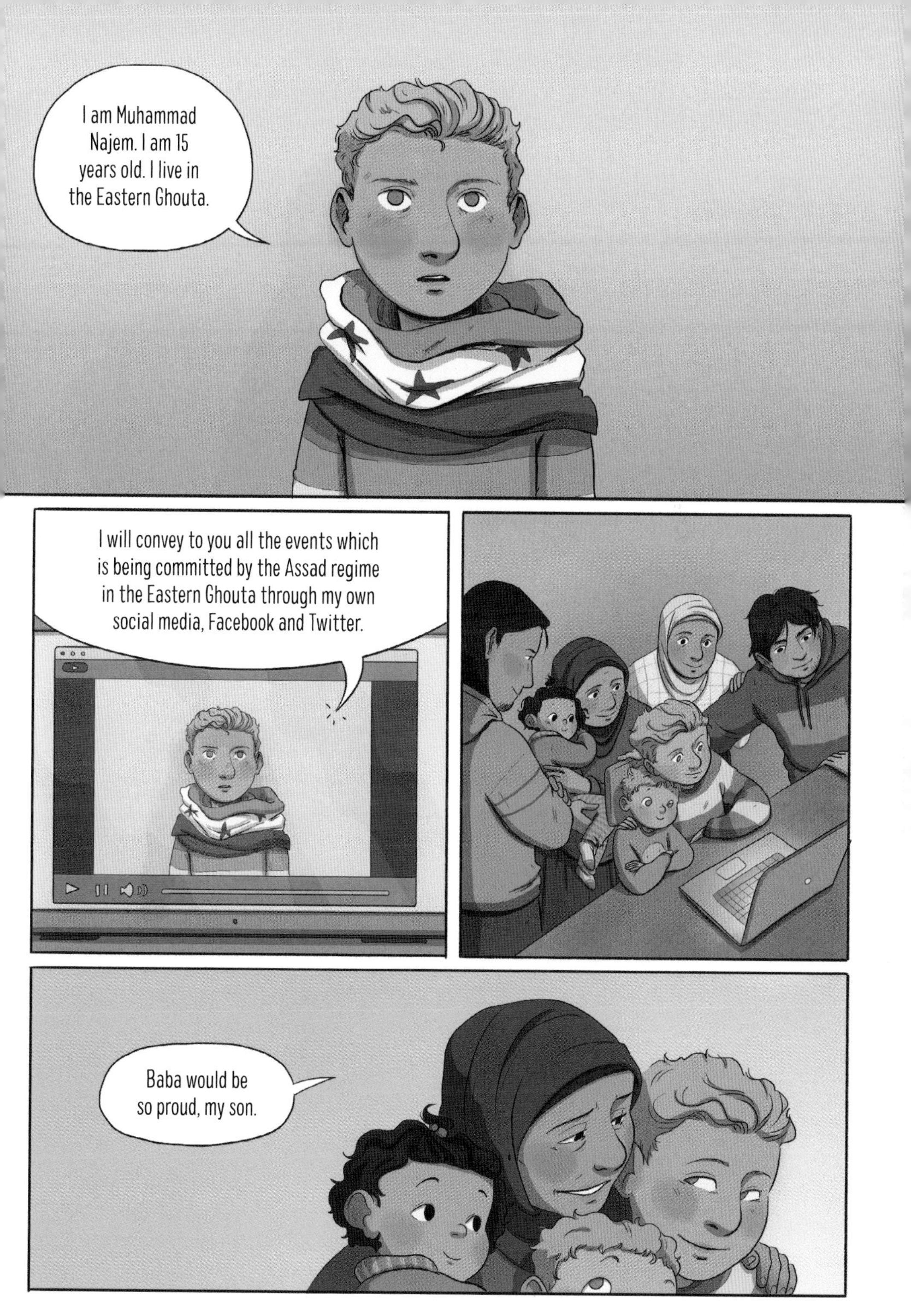
I am Muhammad Najem. I am 15 years old. I live in the Eastern Ghouta.
I will convey to you all the events which is being committed by the Assad regime in the Eastern Ghouta through my own social media, Facebook and Twitter.
Baba would be so proud, my son.

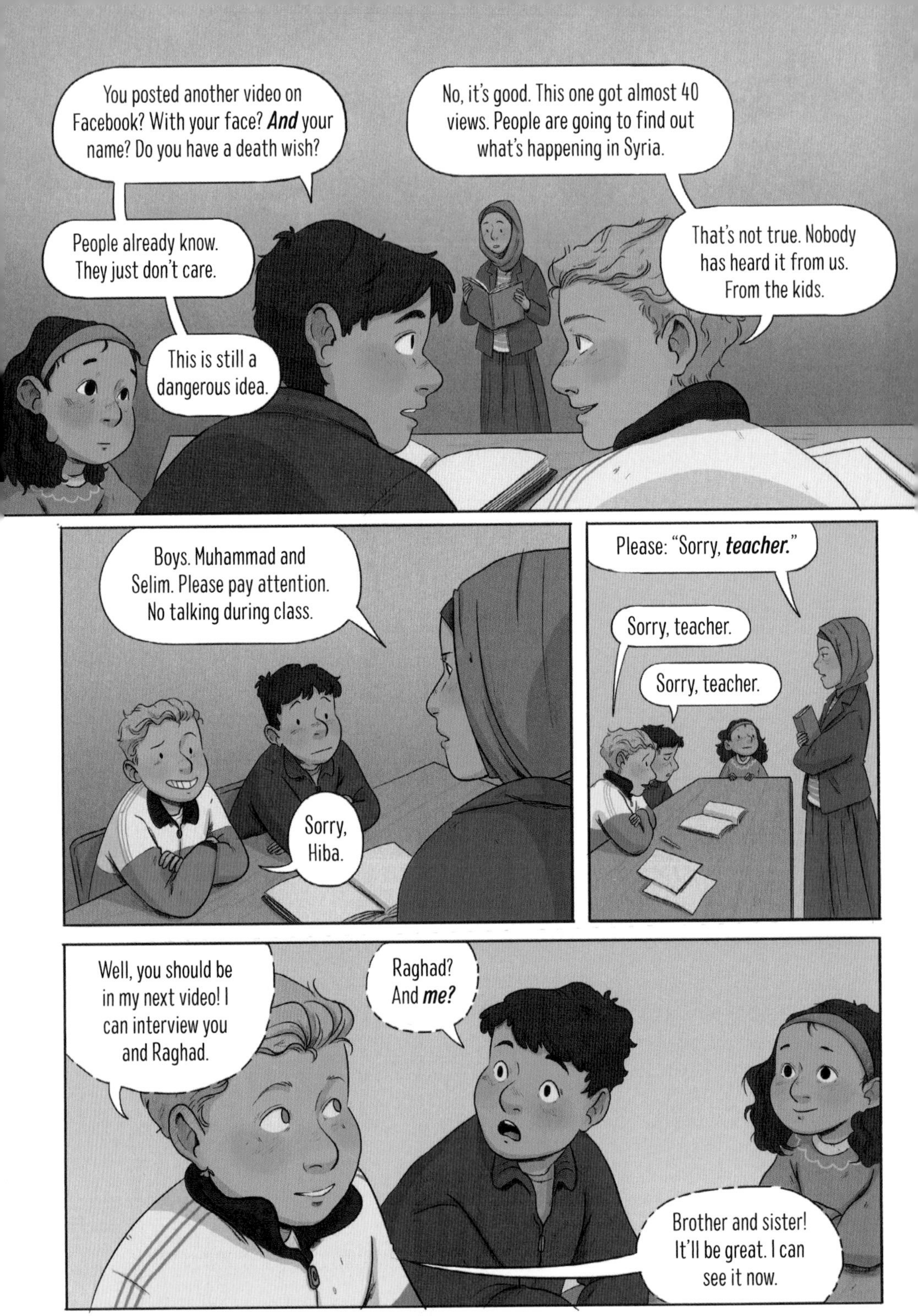
You posted another video on Facebook? With your face? ***And*** your name? Do you have a death wish?
No, it's good. This one got almost 40 views. People are going to find out what's happening in Syria.
People already know. They just don't care.
That's not true. Nobody has heard it from us. From the kids.
This is still a dangerous idea.
Boys. Muhammad and Selim. Please pay attention. No talking during class.
Sorry, Hiba.
Please: "Sorry, ***teacher.***"
Sorry, teacher.
Sorry, teacher.
Well, you should be in my next video! I can interview you and Raghad.
Raghad? And ***me?***
Brother and sister! It'll be great. I can see it now.

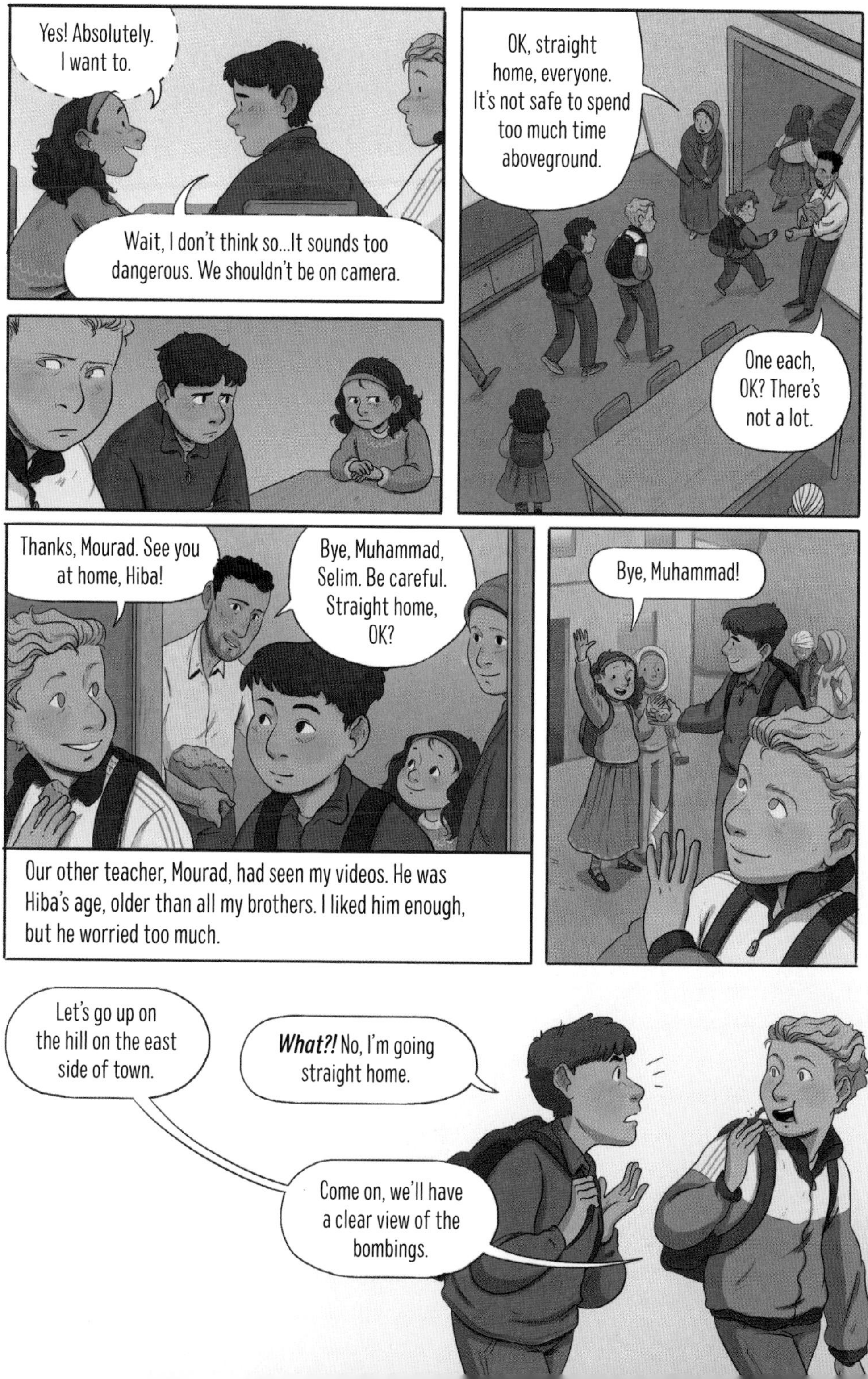

Yes! Absolutely. I want to.
Wait, I don't think so...It sounds too dangerous. We shouldn't be on camera.
OK, straight home, everyone. It's not safe to spend too much time aboveground.
One each, OK? There's not a lot.
Thanks, Mourad. See you at home, Hiba!
Bye, Muhammad, Selim. Be careful. Straight home, OK?
Our other teacher, Mourad, had seen my videos. He was Hiba's age, older than all my brothers. I liked him enough, but he worried too much.
Bye, Muhammad!
Let's go up on the hill on the east side of town.
What?! No, I'm going straight home.
Come on, we'll have a clear view of the bombings.

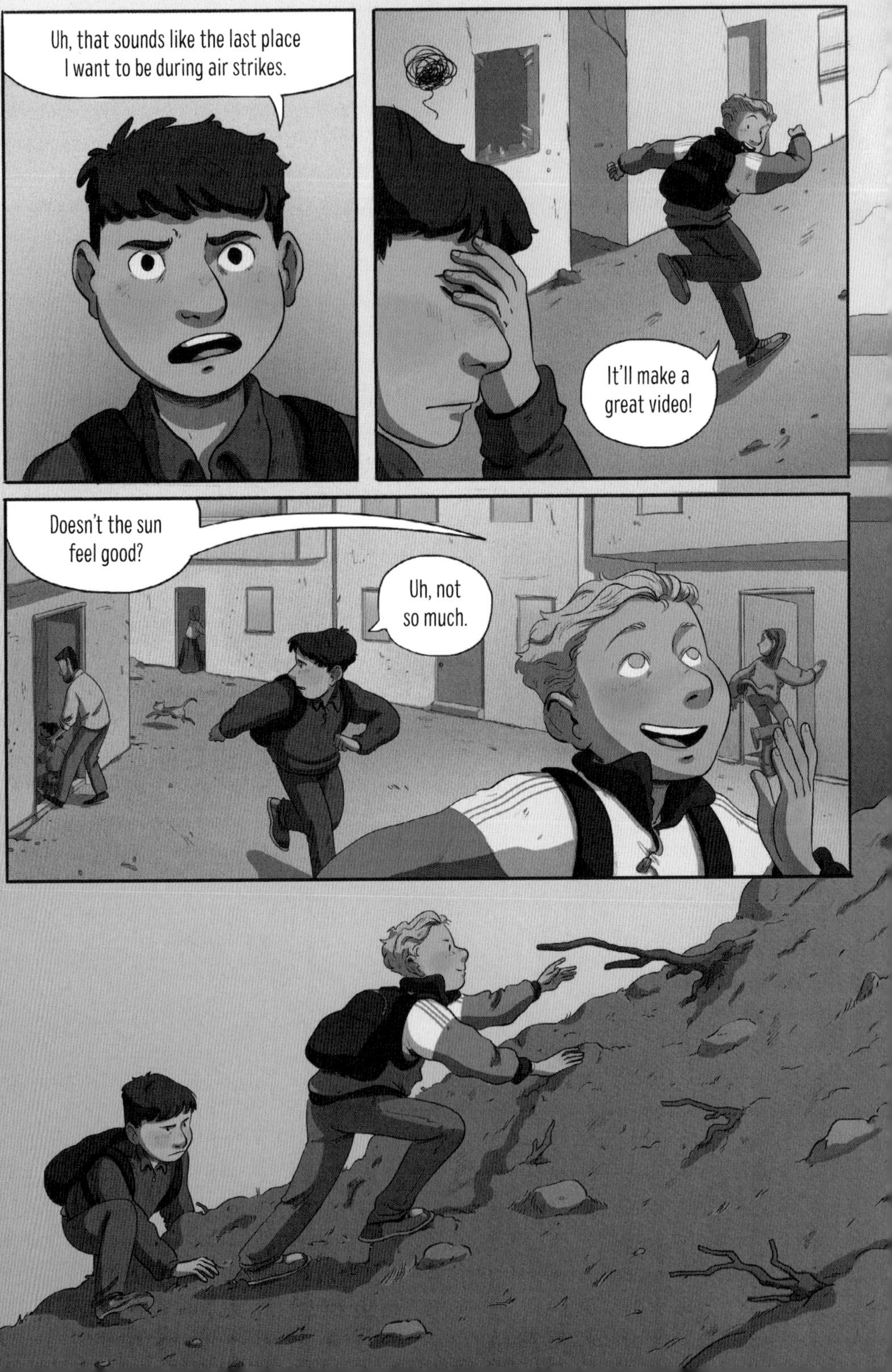
Uh, that sounds like the last place I want to be during air strikes.
It'll make a great video!
Doesn't the sun feel good?
Uh, not so much.

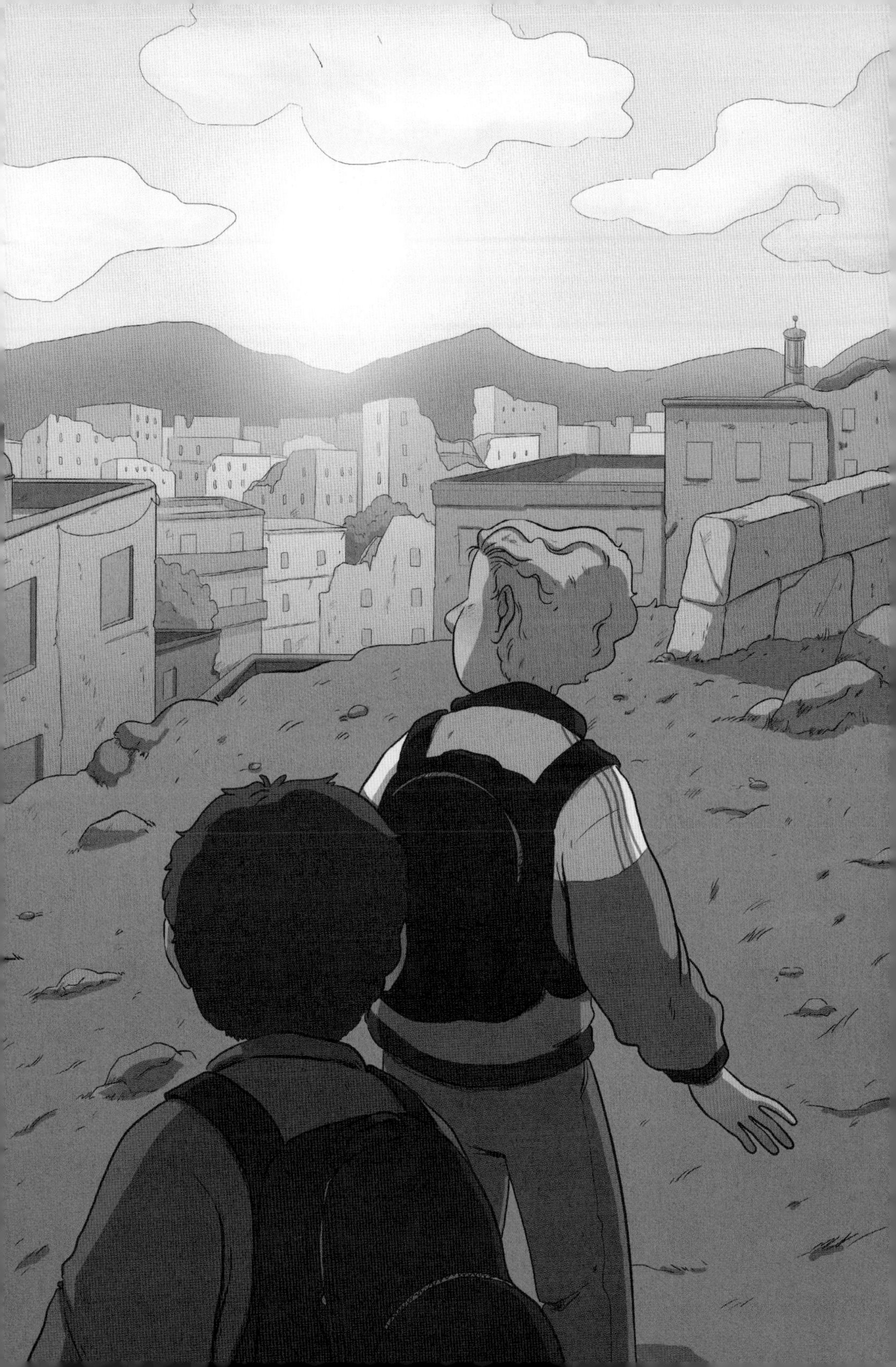

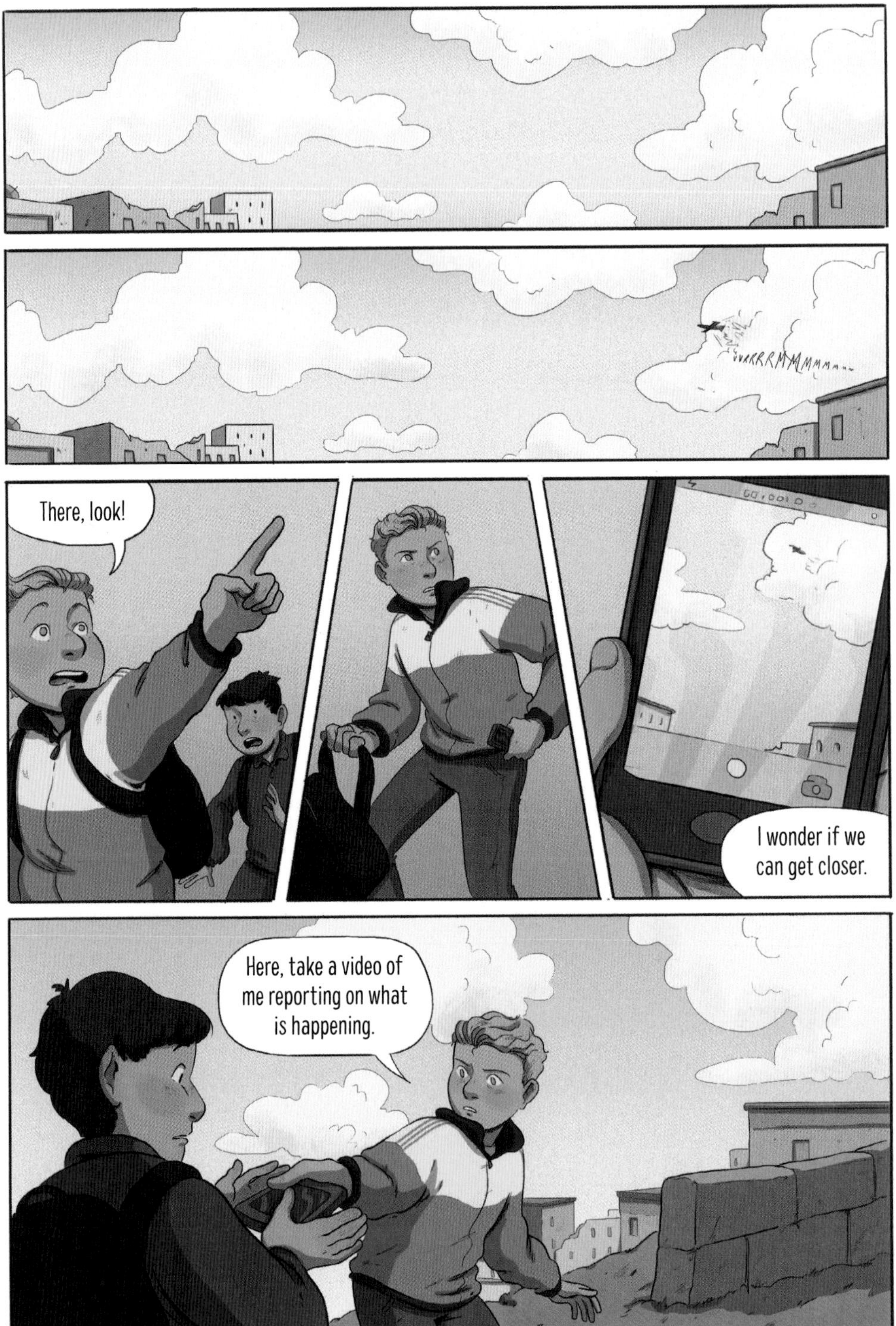

VRRRRRMMMMMM...
There, look!
I wonder if we can get closer.
Here, take a video of me reporting on what is happening.

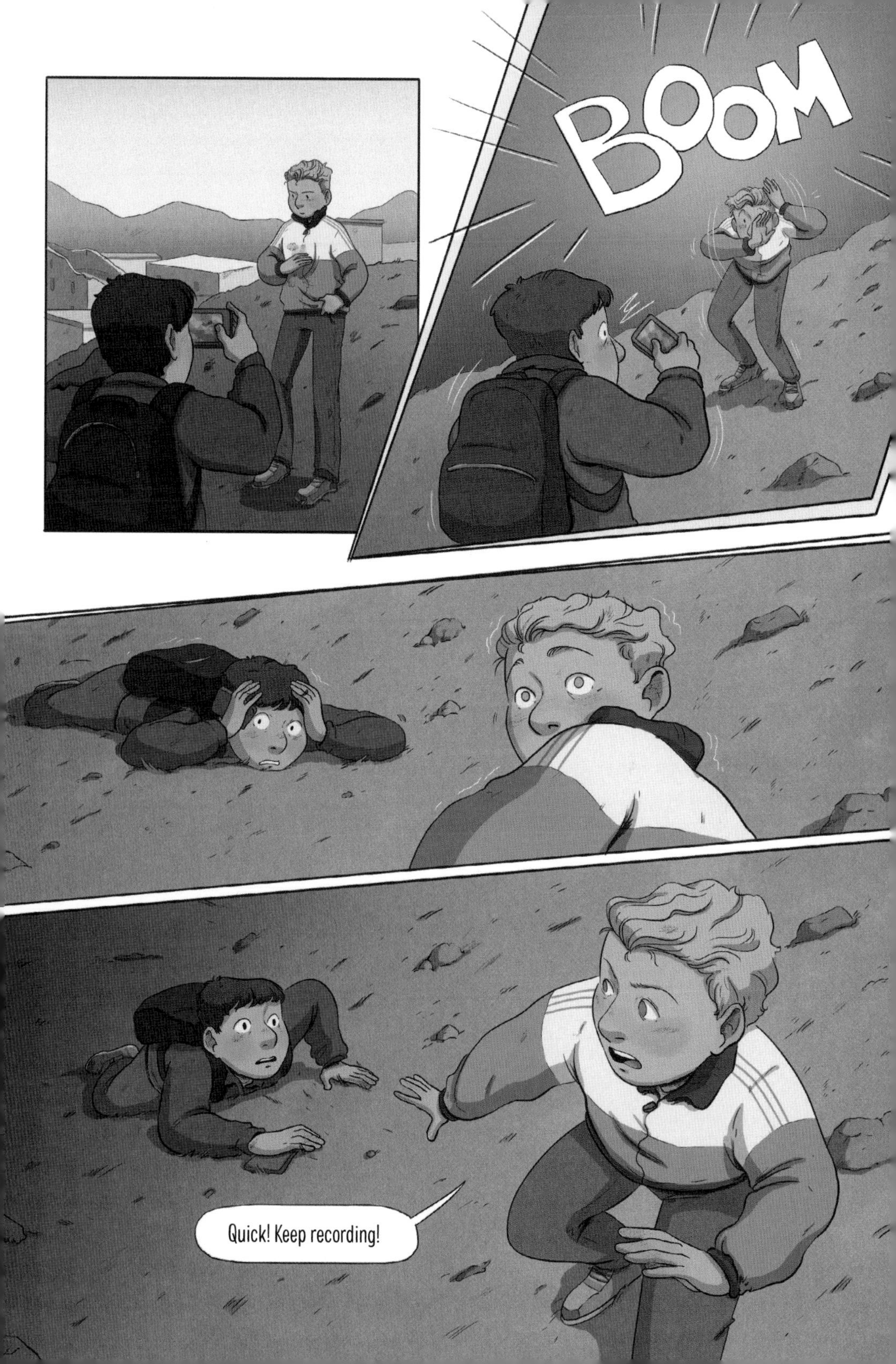
BOOM
Quick! Keep recording!

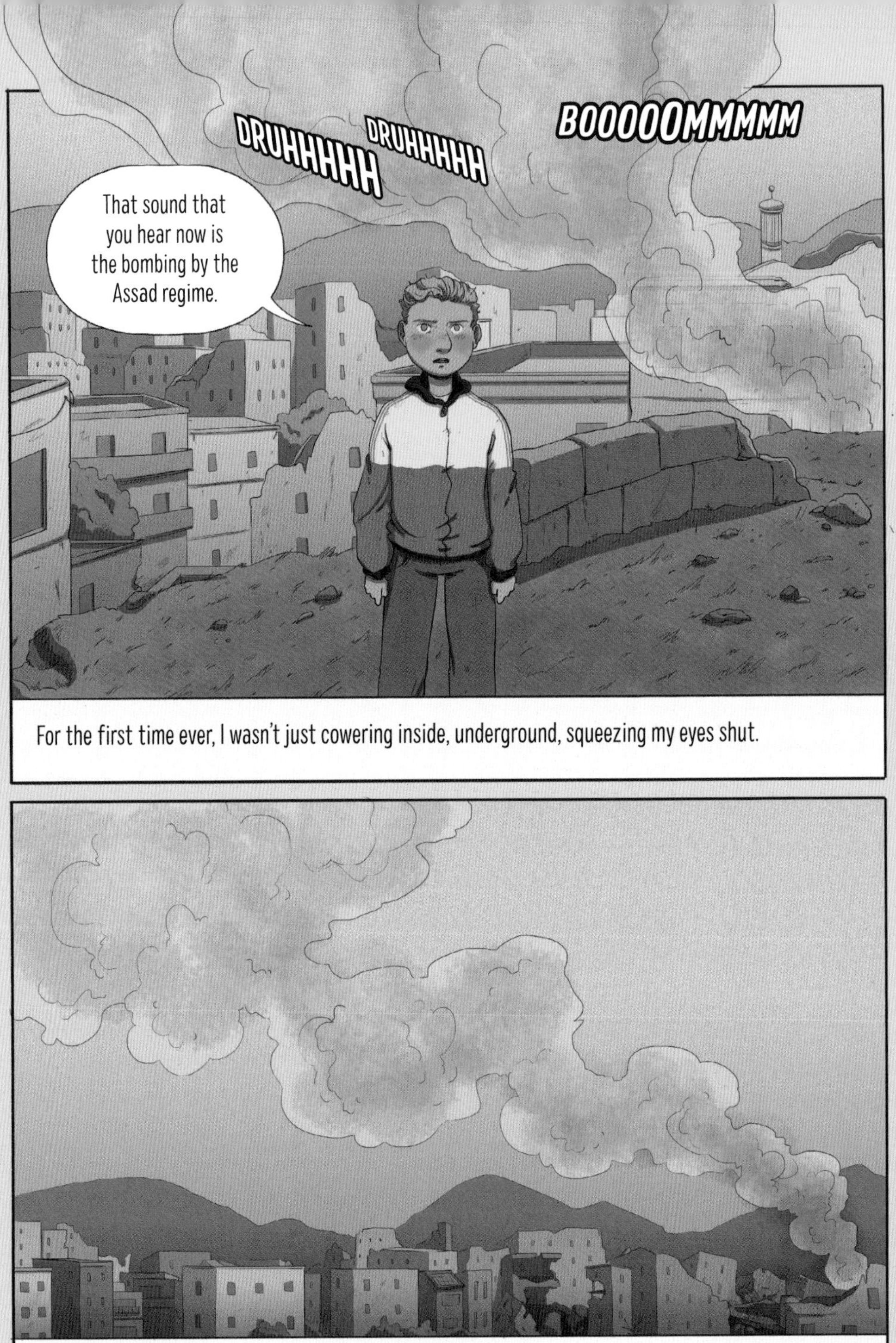
DRUHHHHH
DRUHHHHH
BOOOOOMMMMM
That sound that you hear now is the bombing by the Assad regime.
For the first time ever, I wasn't just cowering inside, underground, squeezing my eyes shut.
My eyes were wide open.

The rest of the world would see everything I saw.
The pain and the destruction.

I was going to show everyone what was happening in Syria.

I was going to help my country.

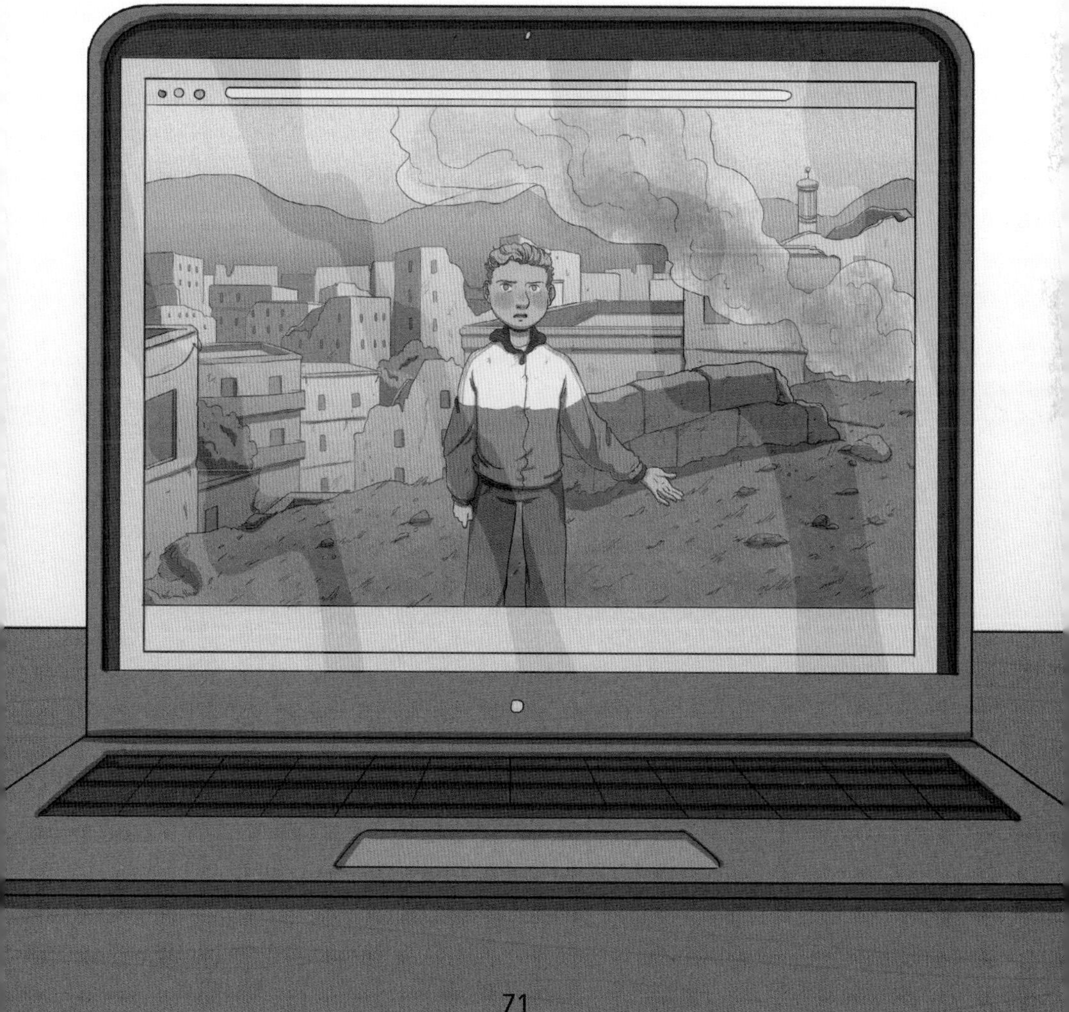

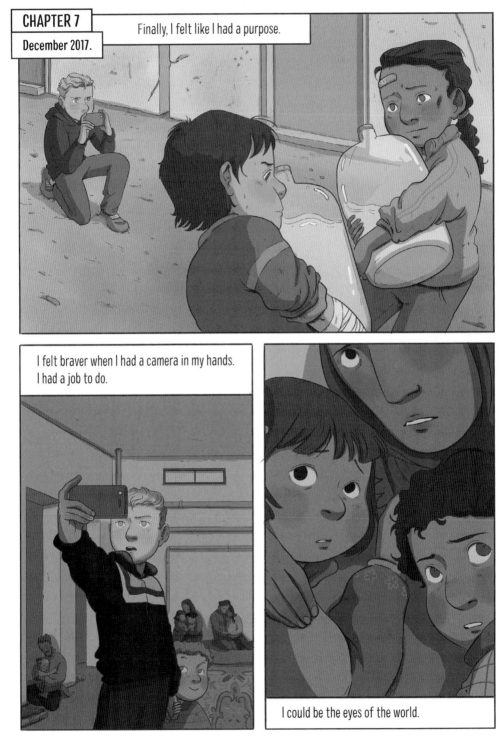

CHAPTER 7

December 2017.

Finally, I felt like I had a purpose.

I felt braver when I had a camera in my hands. I had a job to do.

I could be the eyes of the world.

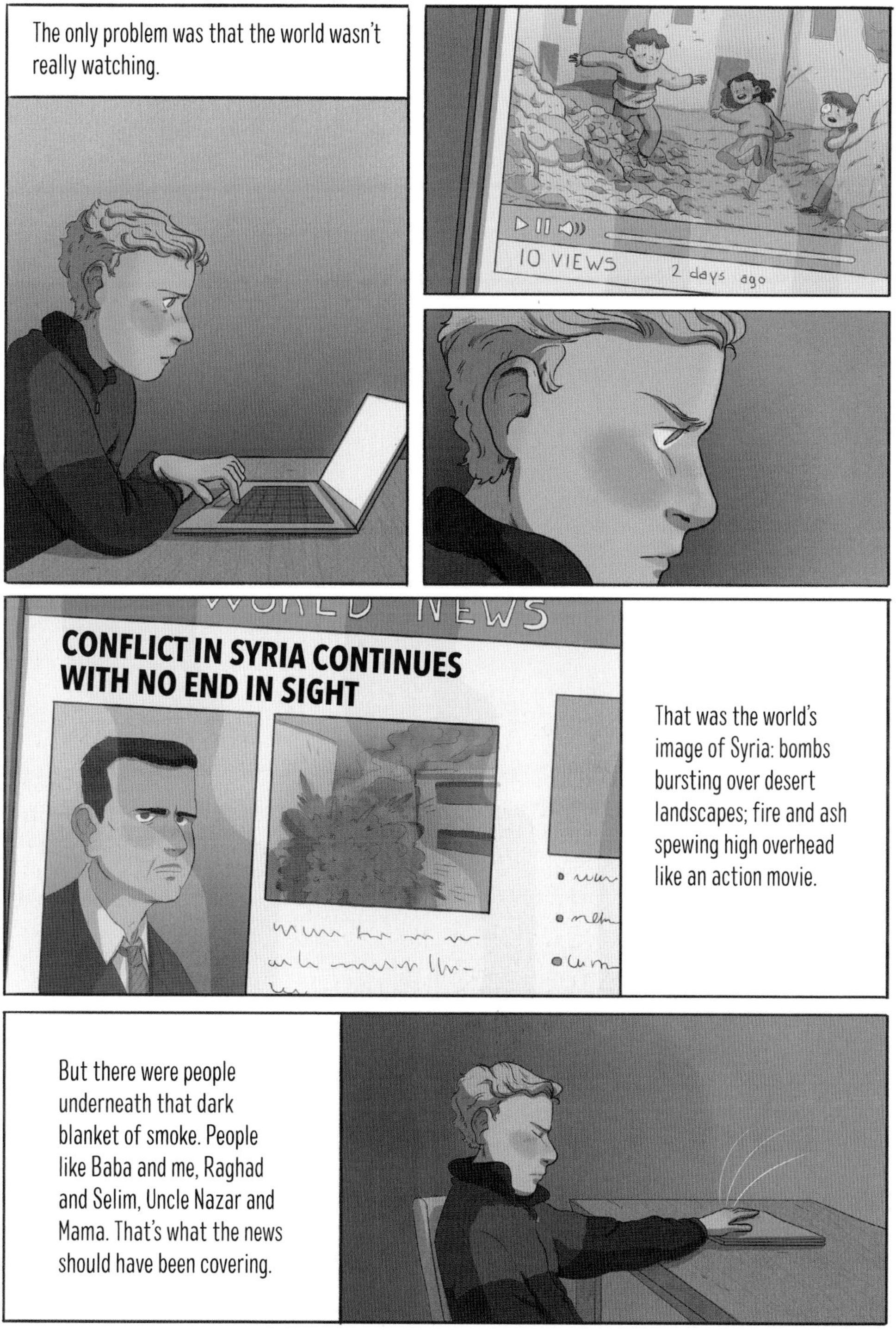
The only problem was that the world wasn't really watching.
10 VIEWS
2 days ago
WORLD NEWS
CONFLICT IN SYRIA CONTINUES WITH NO END IN SIGHT
That was the world's image of Syria: bombs bursting over desert landscapes; fire and ash spewing high overhead like an action movie.
But there were people underneath that dark blanket of smoke. People like Baba and me, Raghad and Selim, Uncle Nazar and Mama. That's what the news should have been covering.

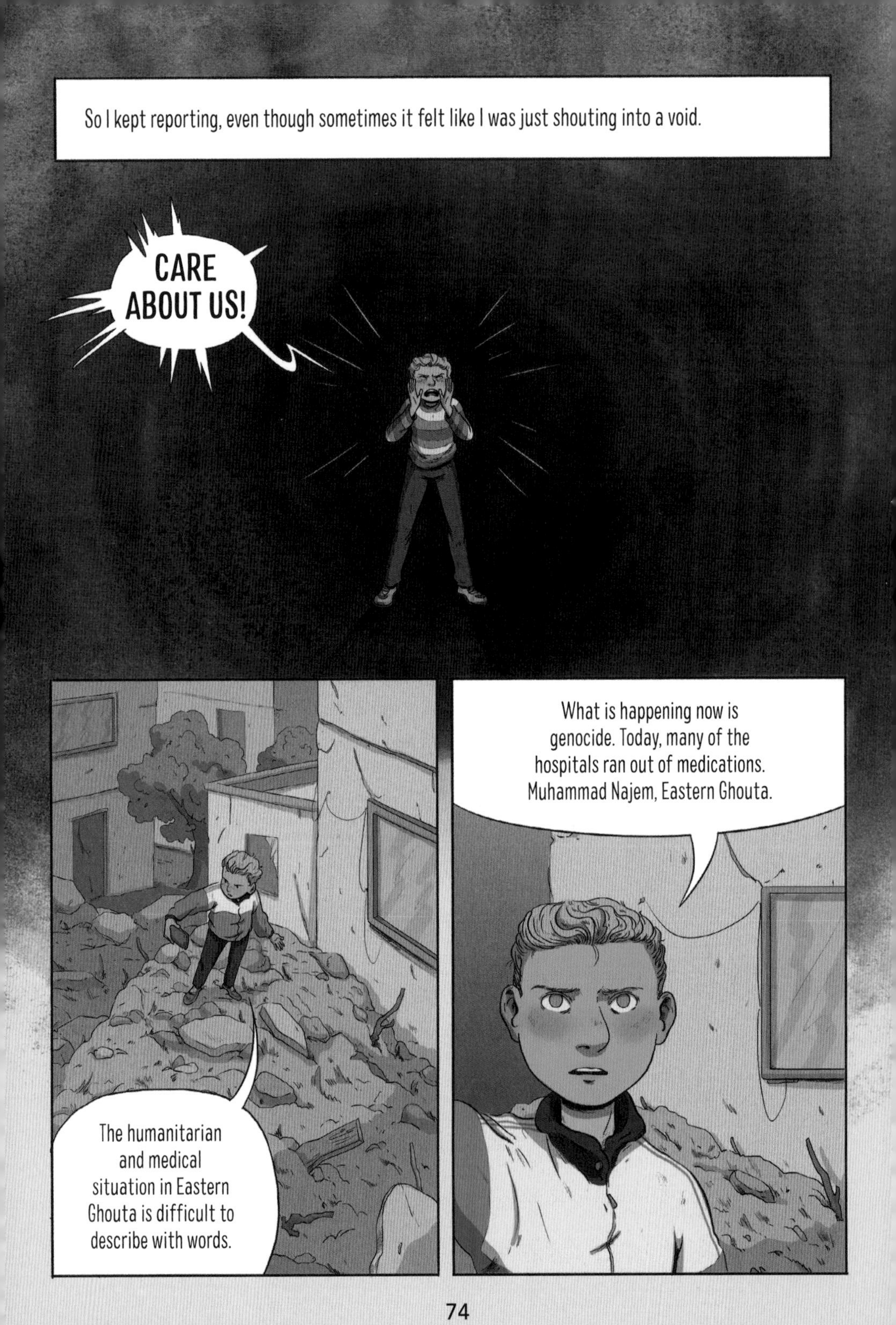
So I kept reporting, even though sometimes it felt like I was just shouting into a void.
CARE ABOUT US!
The humanitarian and medical situation in Eastern Ghouta is difficult to describe with words.
What is happening now is genocide. Today, many of the hospitals ran out of medications. Muhammad Najem, Eastern Ghouta.

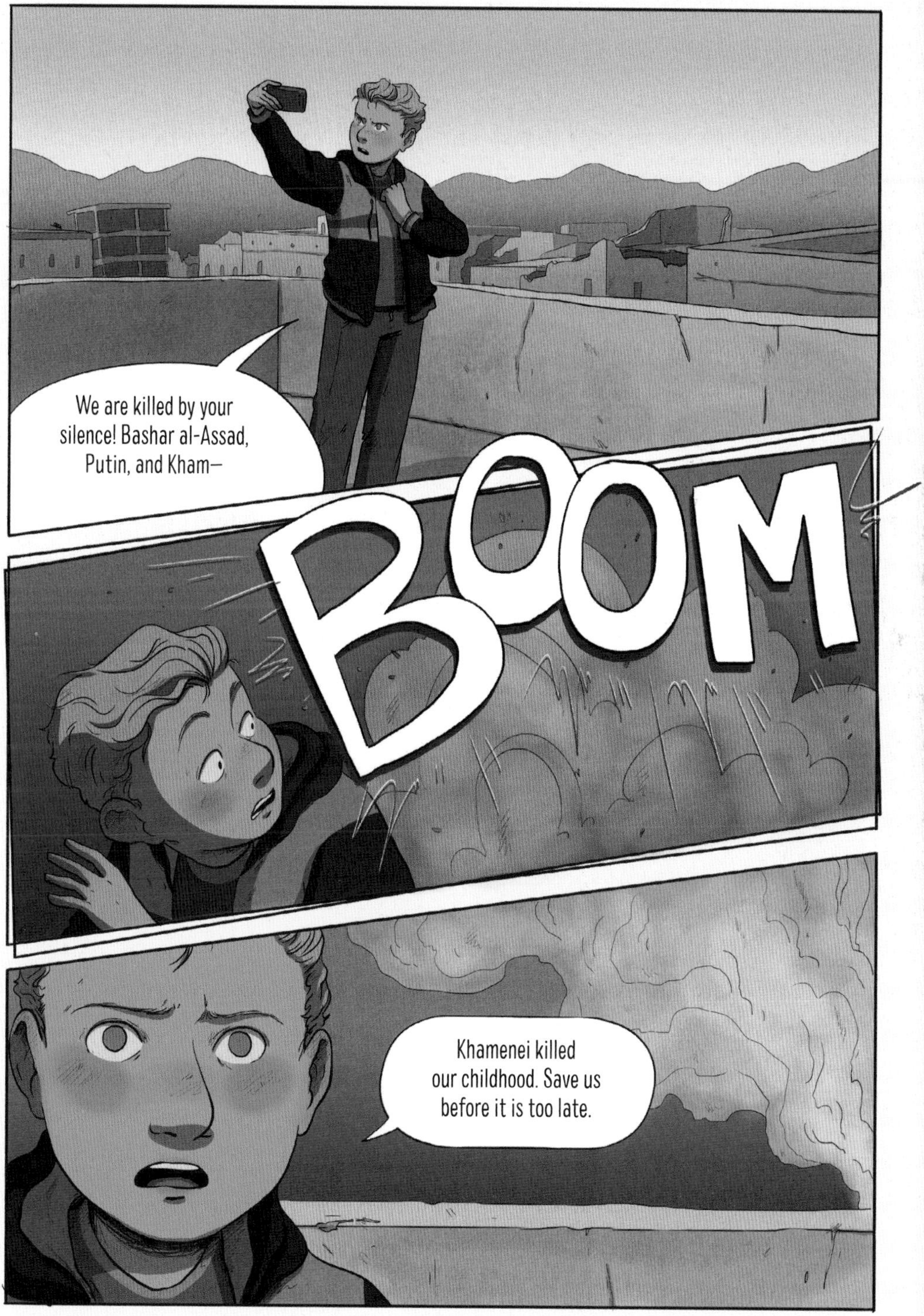
We are killed by your silence! Bashar al-Assad, Putin, and Kham—
BOOM
Khamenei killed our childhood. Save us before it is too late.

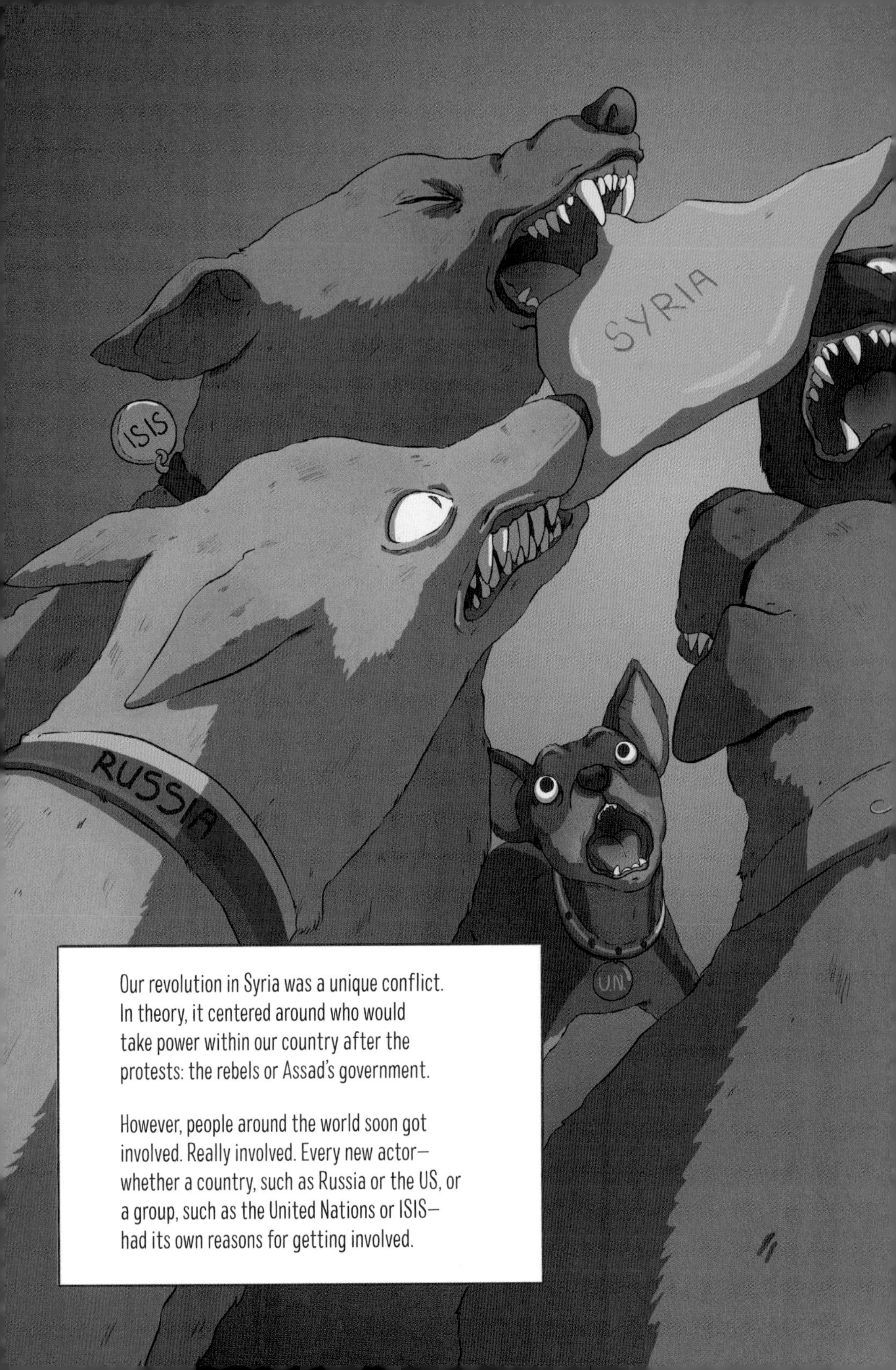
SYRIA
ISIS
RUSSIA
U.N.
Our revolution in Syria was a unique conflict. In theory, it centered around who would take power within our country after the protests: the rebels or Assad's government.
However, people around the world soon got involved. Really involved. Every new actor—whether a country, such as Russia or the US, or a group, such as the United Nations or ISIS—had its own reasons for getting involved.

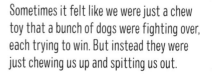

Sometimes it felt like we were just a chew toy that a bunch of dogs were fighting over, each trying to win. But instead they were just chewing us up and spitting us out.

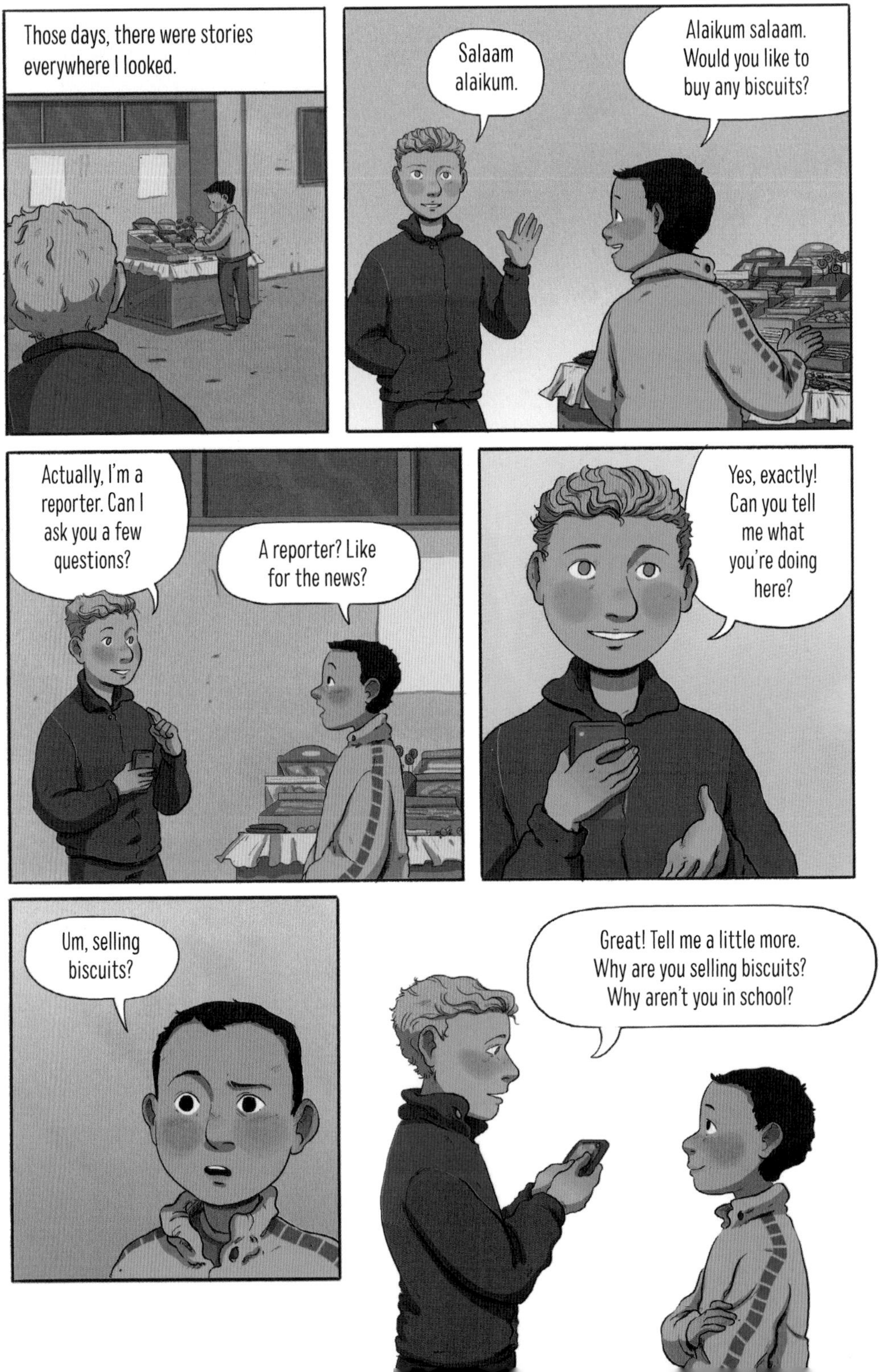
Those days, there were stories everywhere I looked.
Salaam alaikum.
Alaikum salaam. Would you like to buy any biscuits?
Actually, I'm a reporter. Can I ask you a few questions?
A reporter? Like for the news?
Yes, exactly! Can you tell me what you're doing here?
Um, selling biscuits?
Great! Tell me a little more. Why are you selling biscuits? Why aren't you in school?

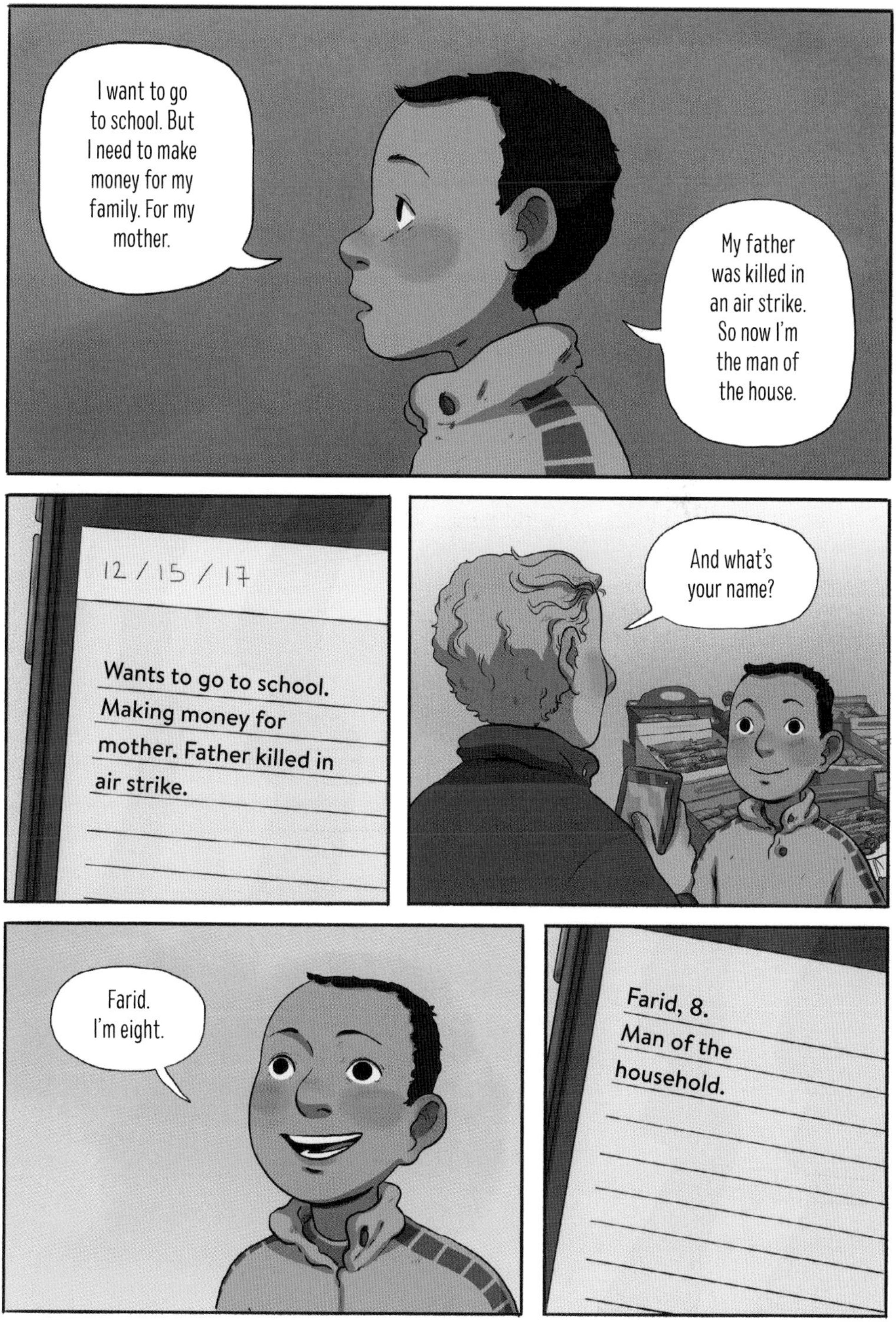
I want to go to school. But I need to make money for my family. For my mother.
My father was killed in an air strike. So now I'm the man of the house.
12 / 15 / 17
Wants to go to school. Making money for mother. Father killed in air strike.
And what's your name?
Farid. I'm eight.
Farid, 8. Man of the household.

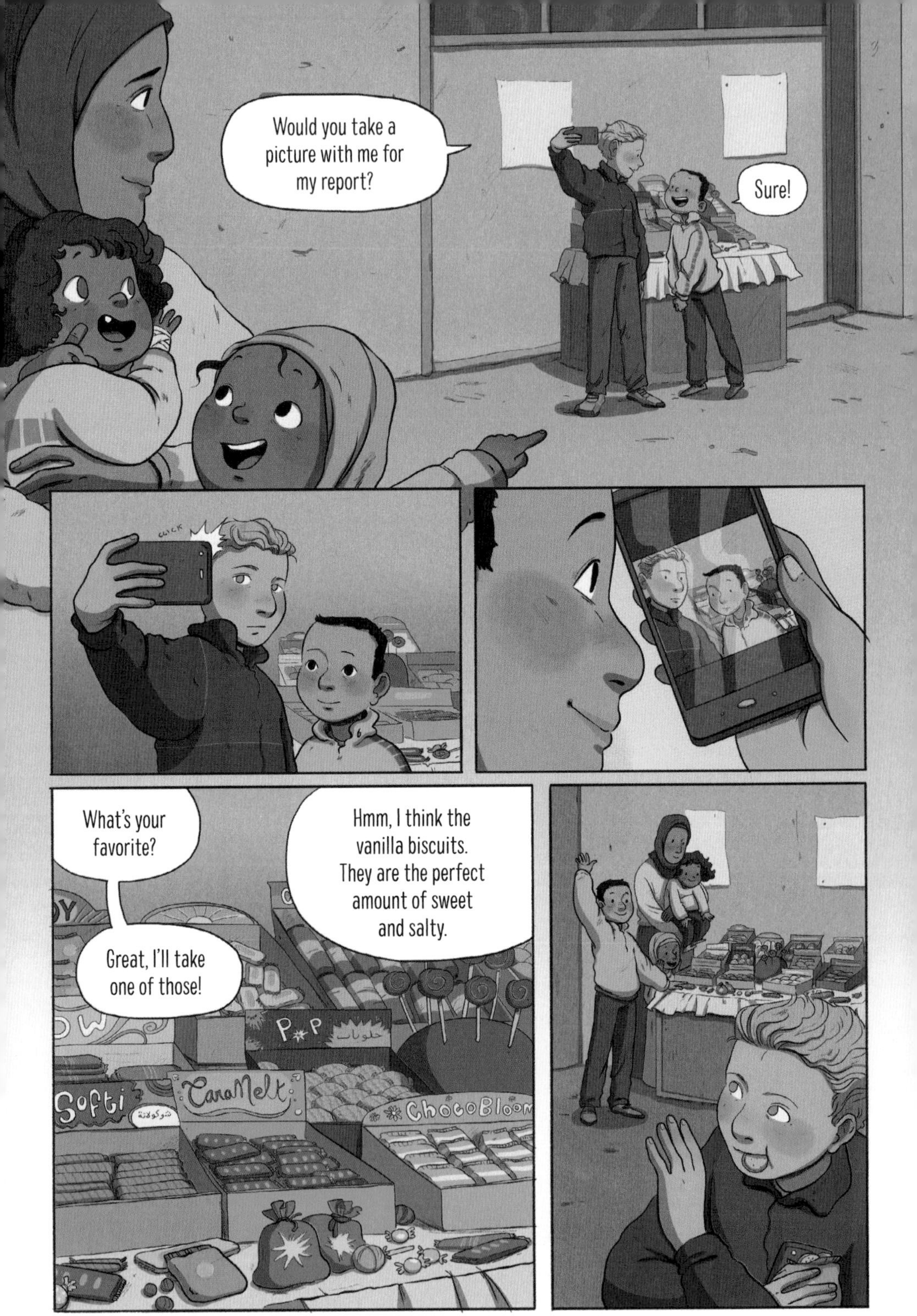
Would you take a picture with me for my report?
Sure!
What's your favorite?
Hmm, I think the vanilla biscuits. They are the perfect amount of sweet and salty.
Great, I'll take one of those!
Softi
CaraMelt

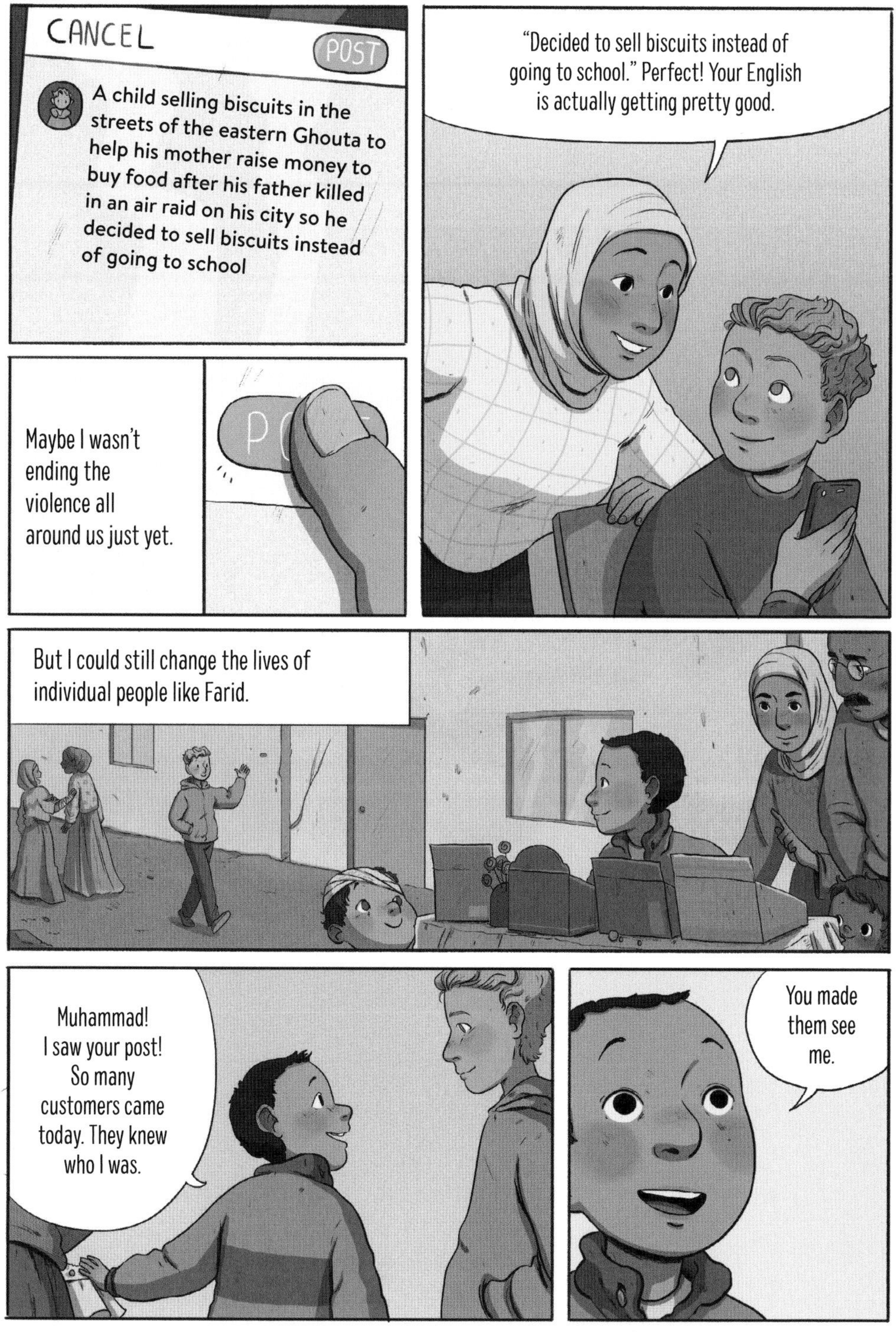

CANCEL POST

A child selling biscuits in the streets of the eastern Ghouta to help his mother raise money to buy food after his father killed in an air raid on his city so he decided to sell biscuits instead of going to school

"Decided to sell biscuits instead of going to school." Perfect! Your English is actually getting pretty good.

Maybe I wasn't ending the violence all around us just yet.

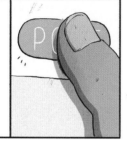

But I could still change the lives of individual people like Farid.

Muhammad! I saw your post! So many customers came today. They knew who I was.

You made them see me.

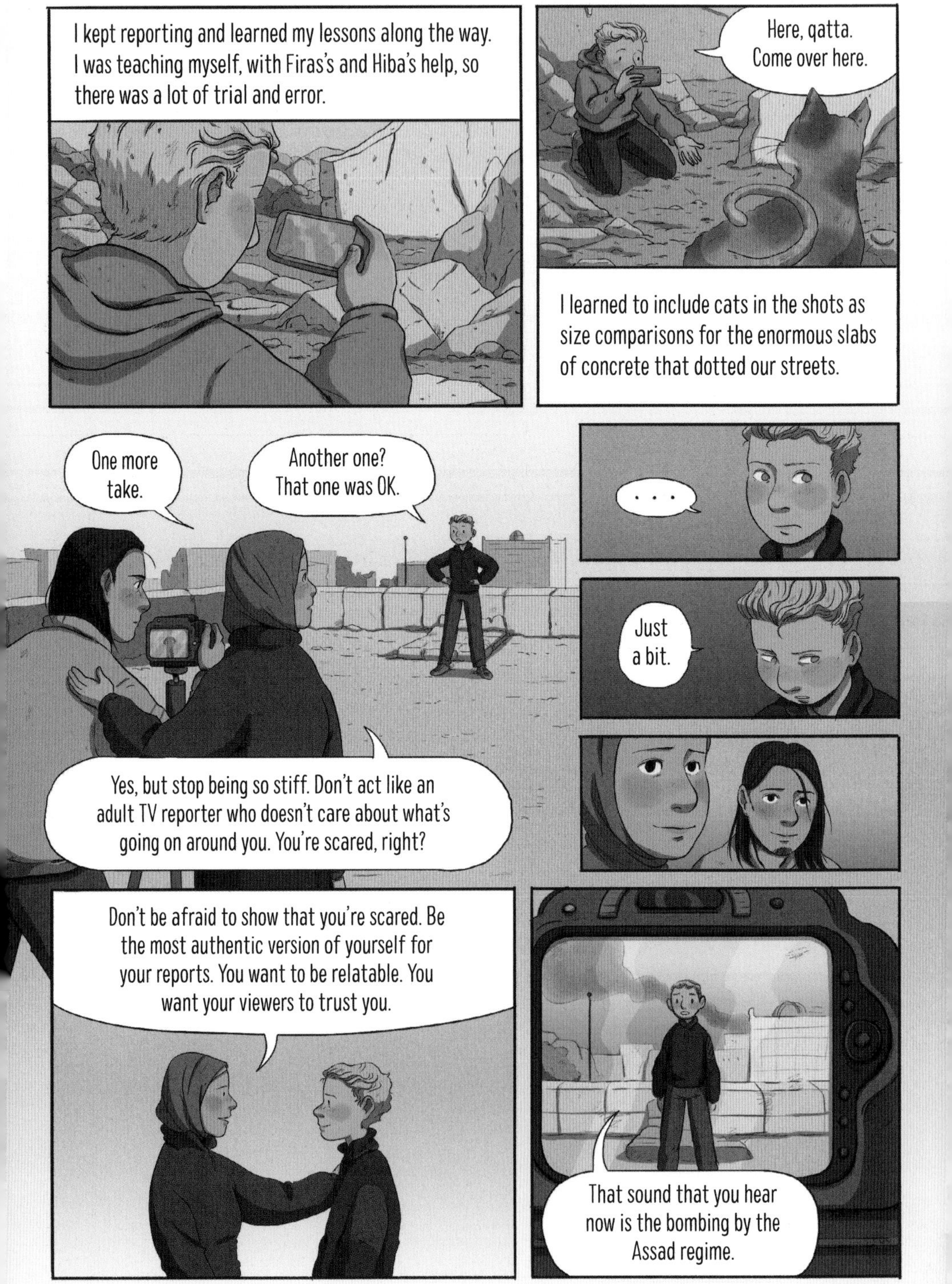
I kept reporting and learned my lessons along the way. I was teaching myself, with Firas's and Hiba's help, so there was a lot of trial and error.
Here, qatta. Come over here.
I learned to include cats in the shots as size comparisons for the enormous slabs of concrete that dotted our streets.
One more take.
Another one? That one was OK.
. . .
Just a bit.
Yes, but stop being so stiff. Don't act like an adult TV reporter who doesn't care about what's going on around you. You're scared, right?
Don't be afraid to show that you're scared. Be the most authentic version of yourself for your reports. You want to be relatable. You want your viewers to trust you.
That sound that you hear now is the bombing by the Assad regime.

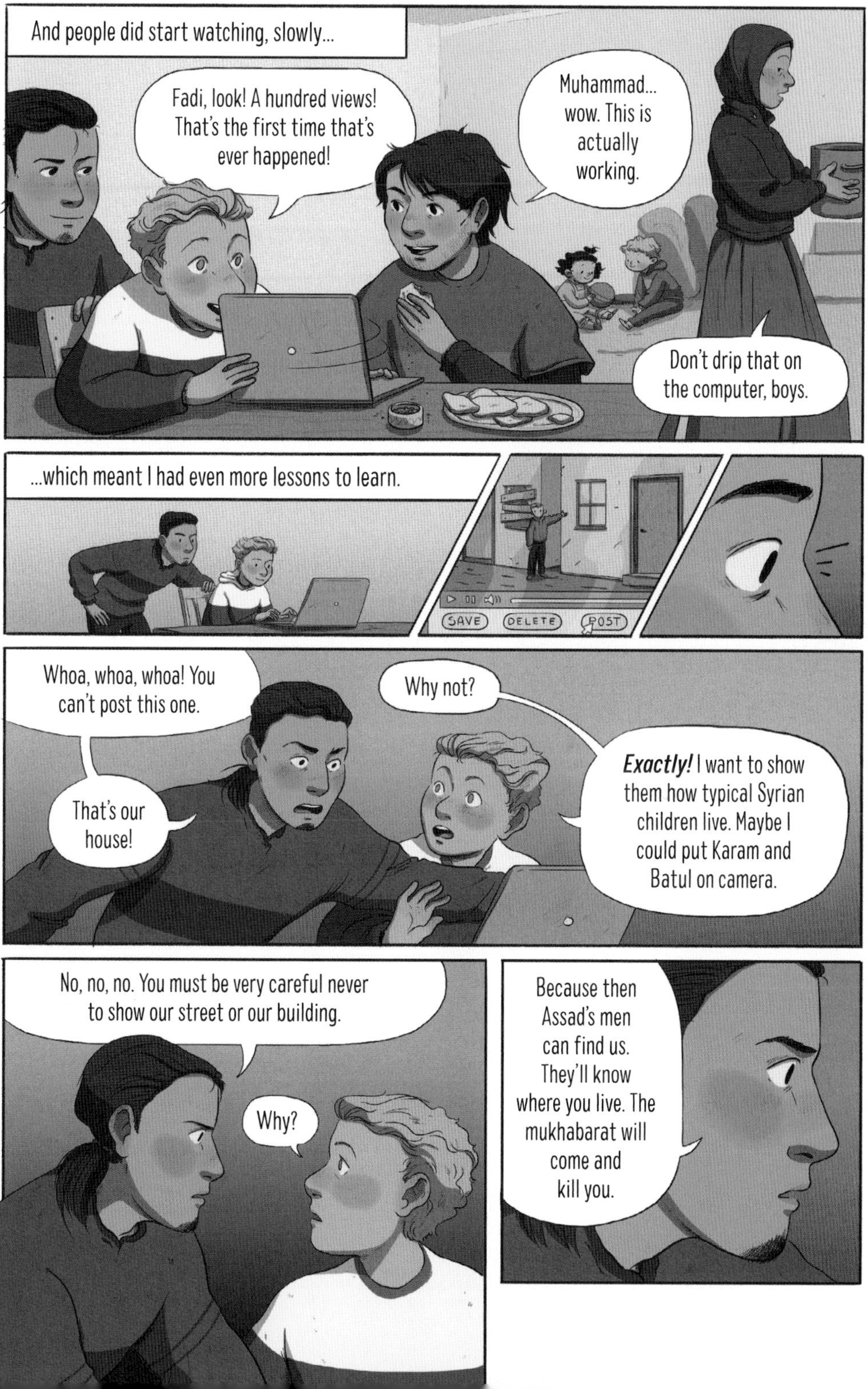

And people did start watching, slowly...
Fadi, look! A hundred views! That's the first time that's ever happened!
Muhammad... wow. This is actually working.
Don't drip that on the computer, boys.
...which meant I had even more lessons to learn.
SAVE
DELETE
POST
Whoa, whoa, whoa! You can't post this one.
That's our house!
Why not?
Exactly! I want to show them how typical Syrian children live. Maybe I could put Karam and Batul on camera.
No, no, no. You must be very careful never to show our street or our building.
Why?
Because then Assad's men can find us. They'll know where you live. The mukhabarat will come and kill you.

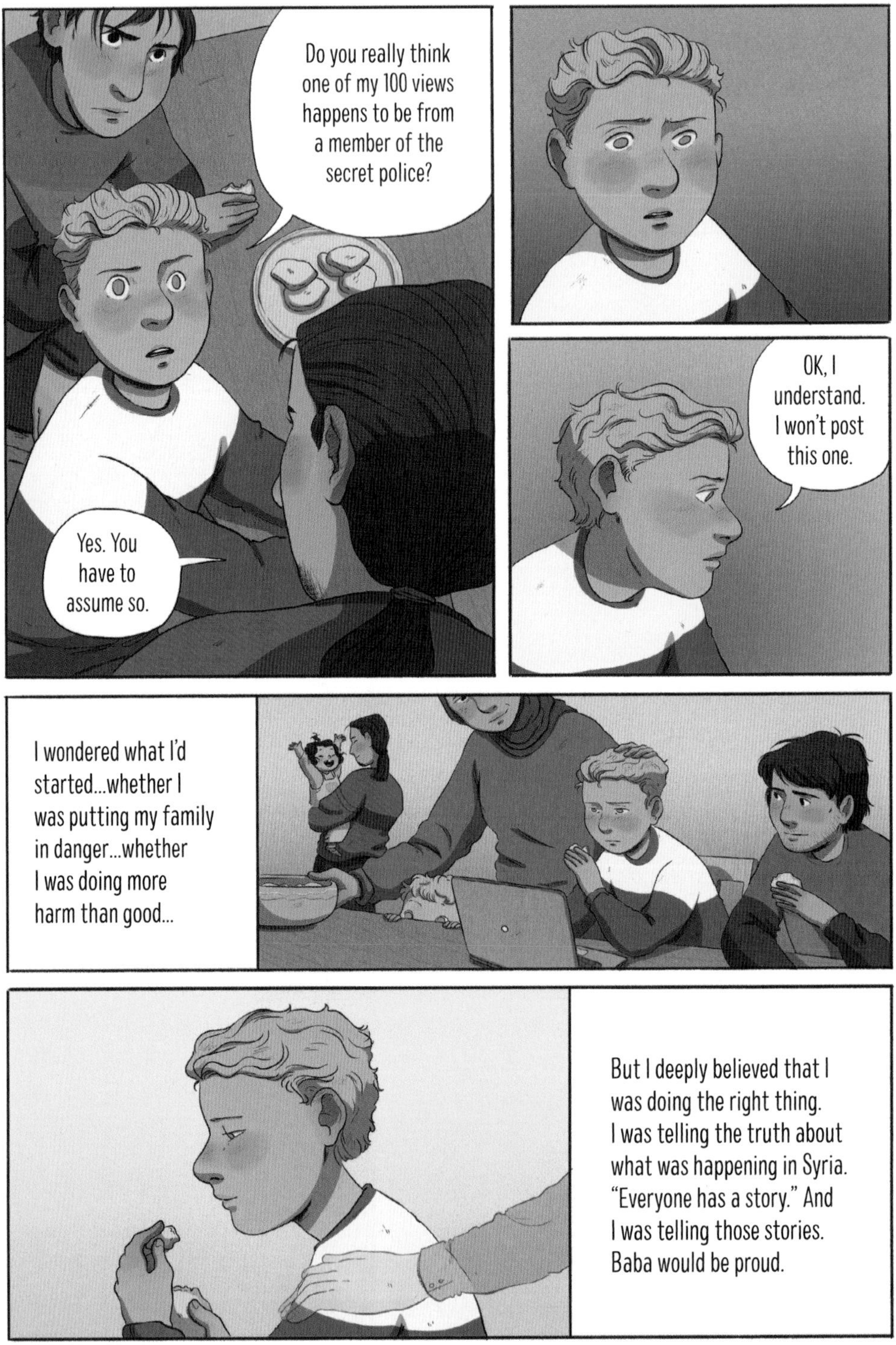
Do you really think one of my 100 views happens to be from a member of the secret police?
Yes. You have to assume so.
OK, I understand. I won't post this one.
I wondered what I'd started...whether I was putting my family in danger...whether I was doing more harm than good...
But I deeply believed that I was doing the right thing. I was telling the truth about what was happening in Syria. "Everyone has a story." And I was telling those stories. Baba would be proud.

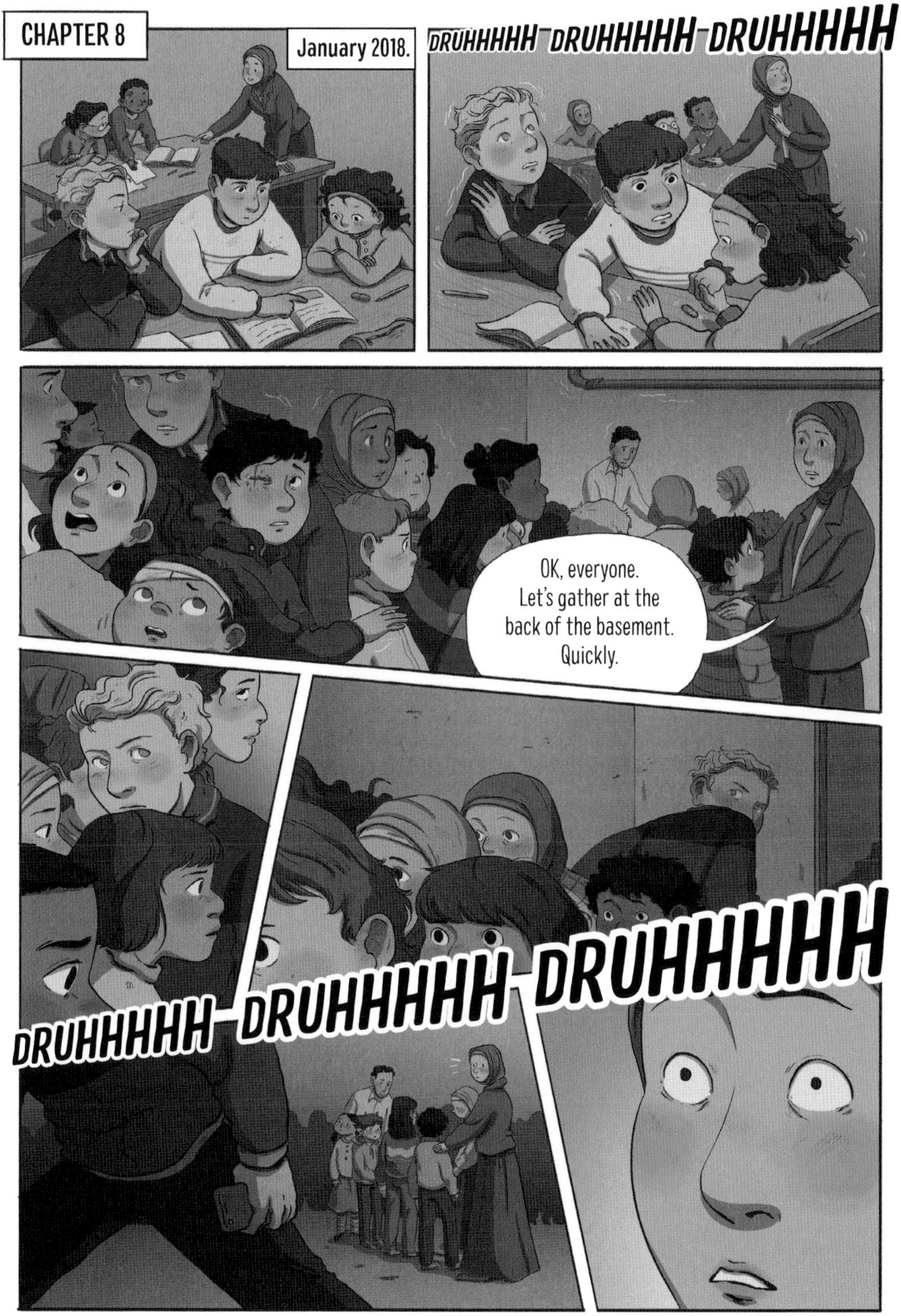
CHAPTER 8
January 2018.
DRUHHHHH DRUHHHHH DRUHHHHH
OK, everyone.
Let's gather at the back of the basement.
Quickly.
DRUHHHHH DRUHHHHH DRUHHHHH

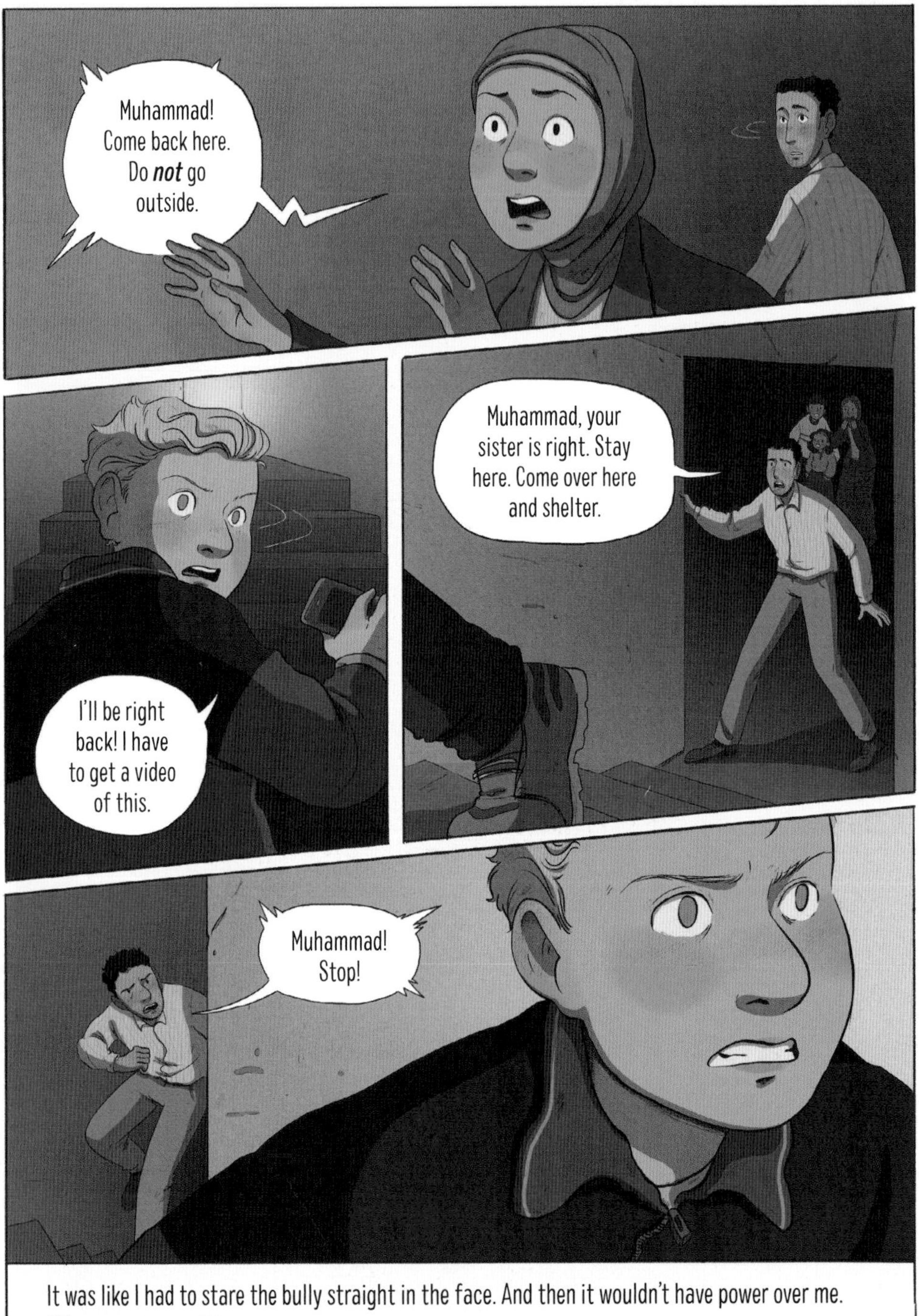
Muhammad! Come back here. Do ***not*** go outside.
I'll be right back! I have to get a video of this.
Muhammad, your sister is right. Stay here. Come over here and shelter.
Muhammad! Stop!

It was like I had to stare the bully straight in the face. And then it wouldn't have power over me. I'd have power over it.

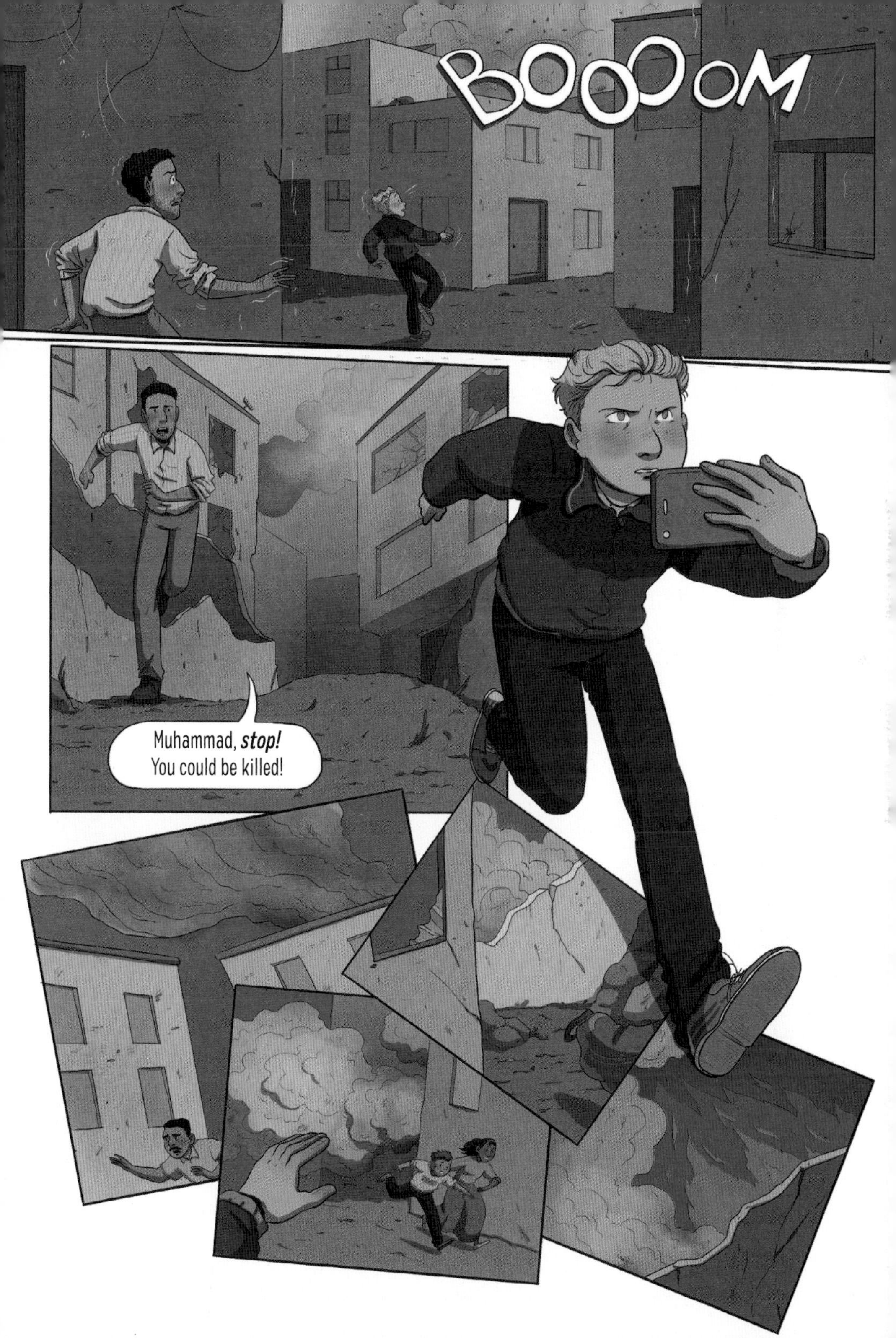
BOOOOM
Muhammad, *stop!*
You could be killed!

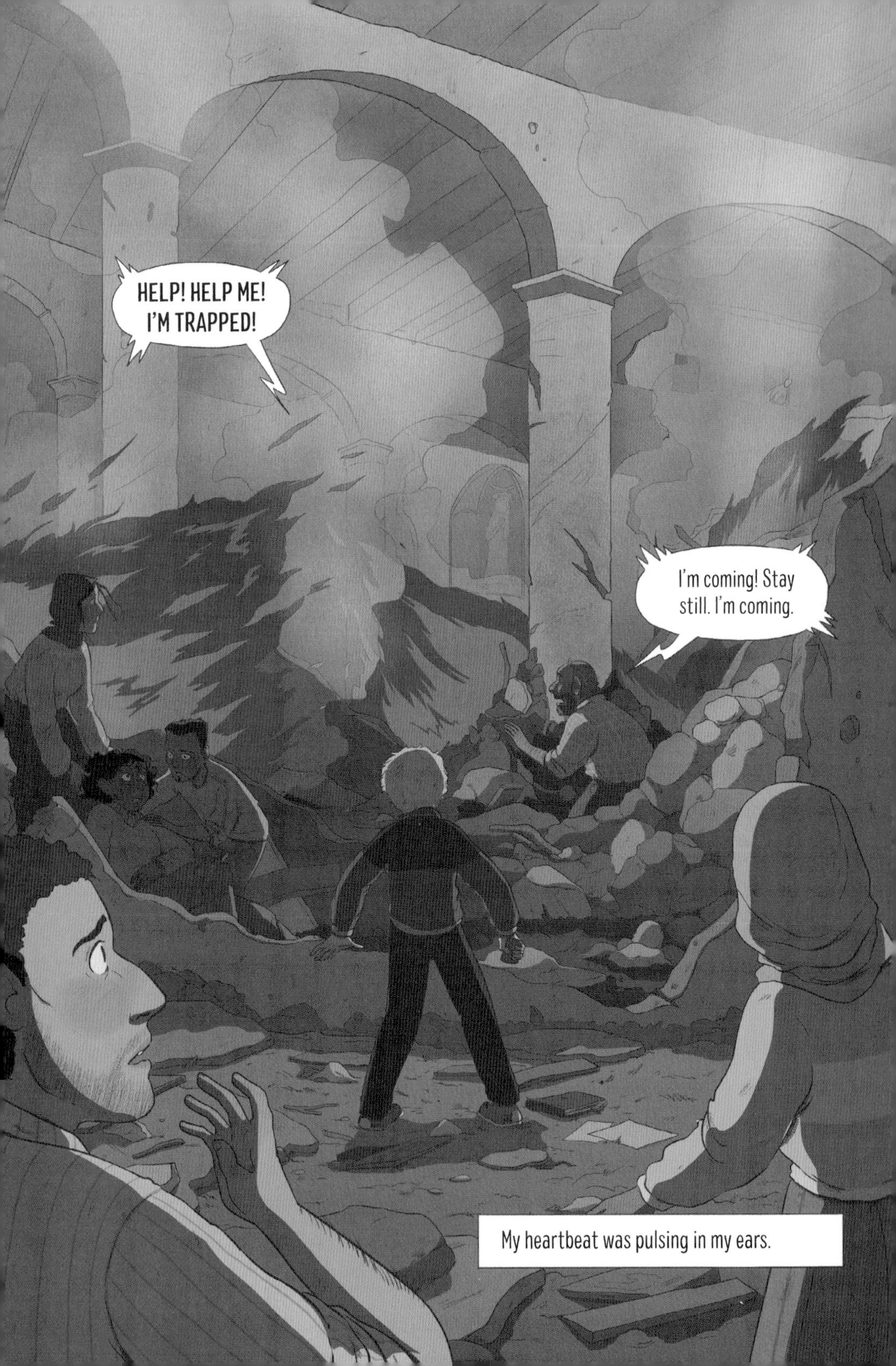
HELP! HELP ME!
I'M TRAPPED!
I'm coming! Stay
still. I'm coming.
My heartbeat was pulsing in my ears.

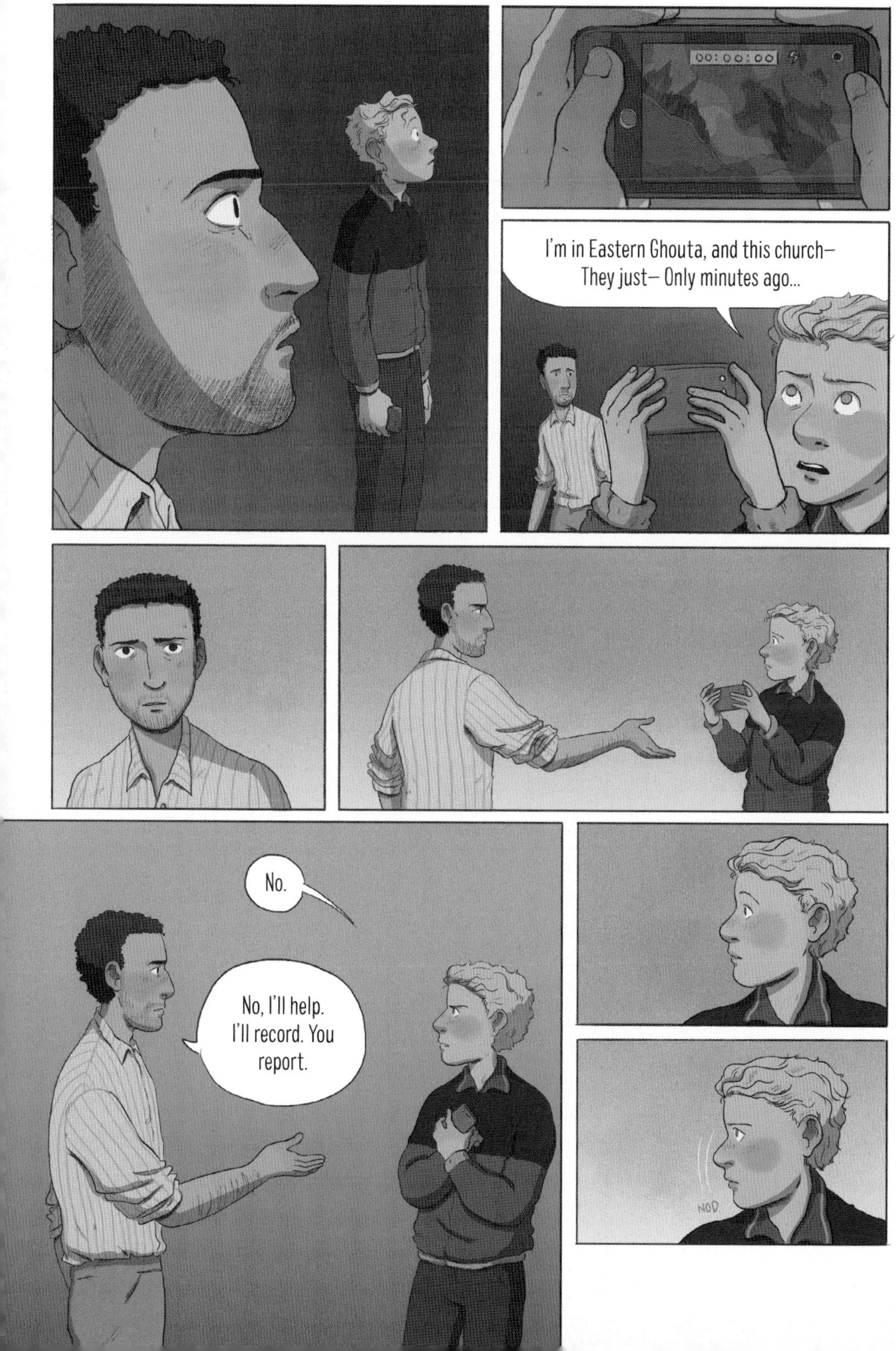
00:00:00
I'm in Eastern Ghouta, and this church— They just— Only minutes ago...
No.
No, I'll help. I'll record. You report.
NOD

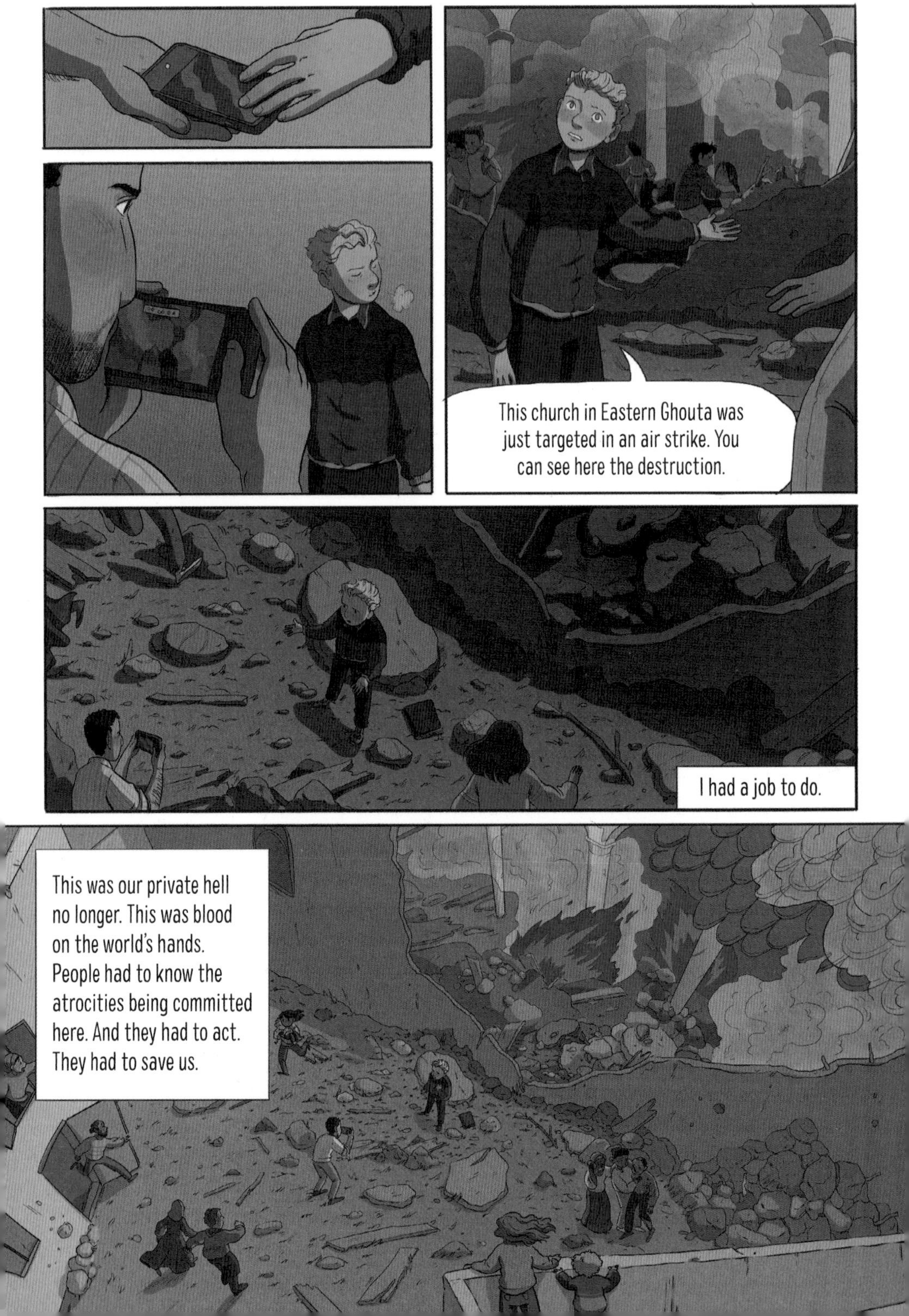
This church in Eastern Ghouta was just targeted in an air strike. You can see here the destruction.
I had a job to do.
This was our private hell no longer. This was blood on the world's hands. People had to know the atrocities being committed here. And they had to act. They had to save us.

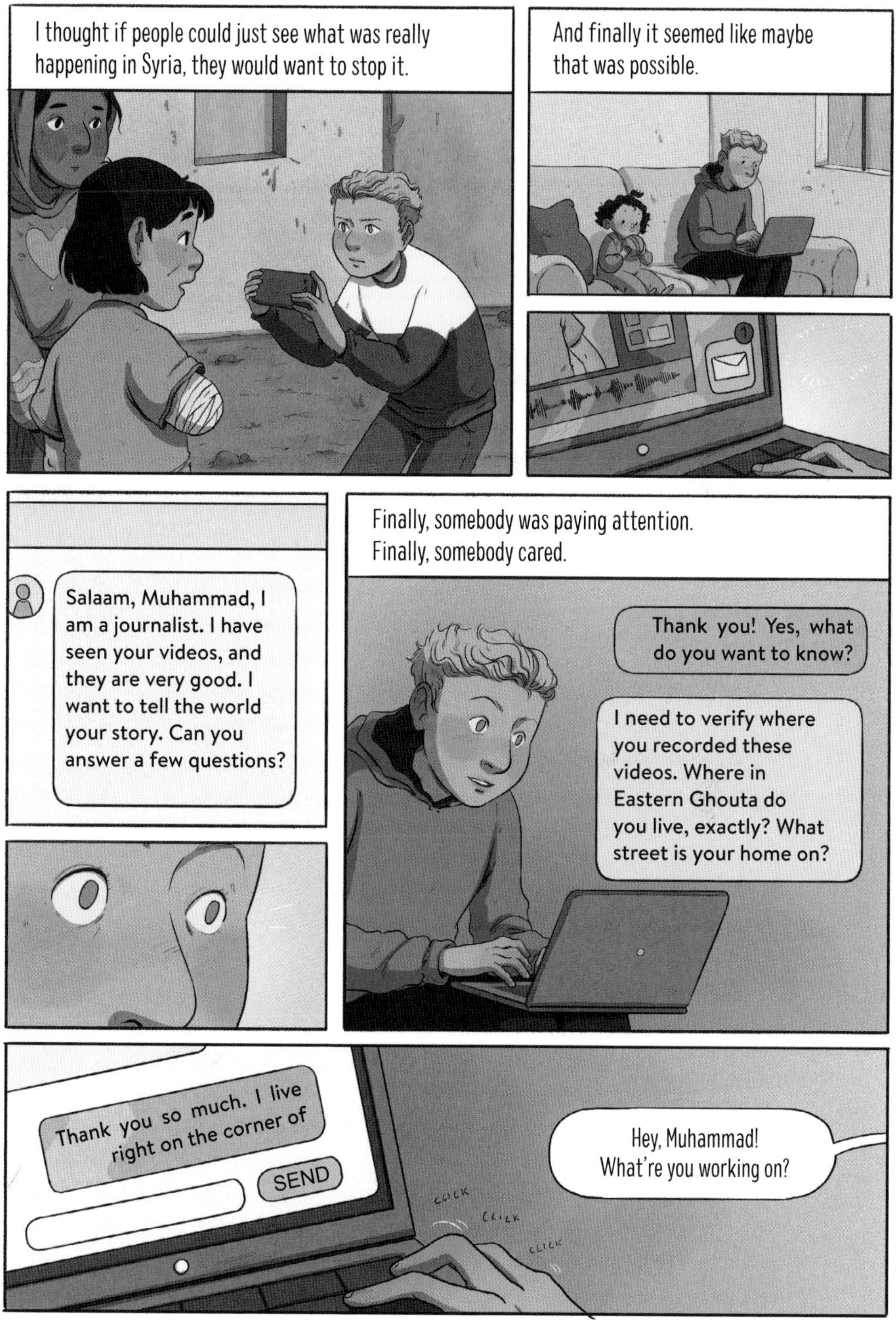
I thought if people could just see what was really happening in Syria, they would want to stop it.
And finally it seemed like maybe that was possible.
Salaam, Muhammad, I am a journalist. I have seen your videos, and they are very good. I want to tell the world your story. Can you answer a few questions?
Finally, somebody was paying attention. Finally, somebody cared.
Thank you! Yes, what do you want to know?
I need to verify where you recorded these videos. Where in Eastern Ghouta do you live, exactly? What street is your home on?
Thank you so much. I live right on the corner of
SEND
CLICK
CLICK
CLICK
Hey, Muhammad! What're you working on?

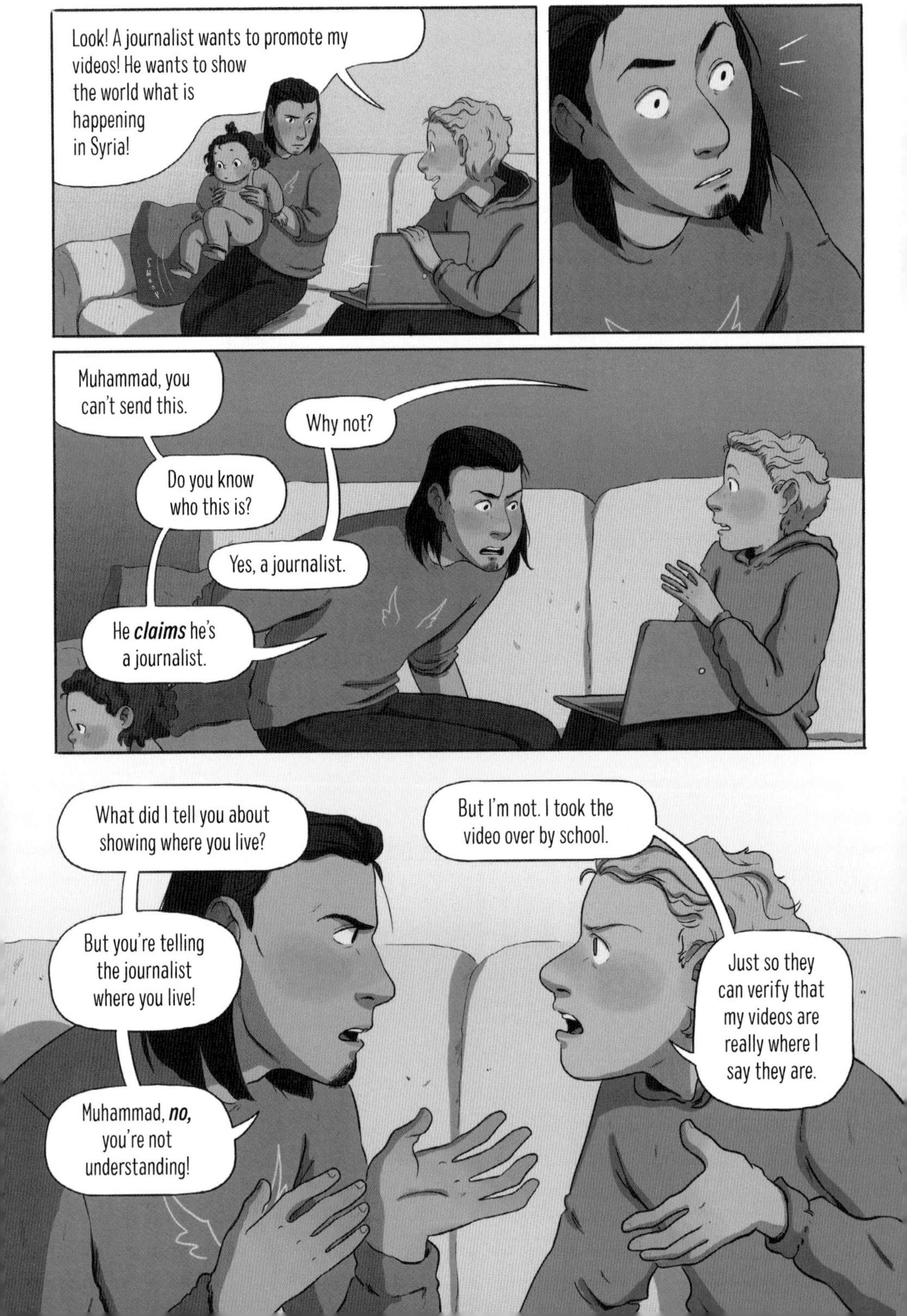
Look! A journalist wants to promote my videos! He wants to show the world what is happening in Syria!
Muhammad, you can't send this.
Why not?
Do you know who this is?
Yes, a journalist.
He *claims* he's a journalist.
What did I tell you about showing where you live?
But I'm not. I took the video over by school.
But you're telling the journalist where you live!
Just so they can verify that my videos are really where I say they are.
Muhammad, *no,* you're not understanding!

Look—remember the candy seller? On the street when we were kids?

Yes?

It's like that. You can't trust that anybody is who they say they are. This person claims they're a journalist, but what if they're mukhabarat?

What if you led Assad's men directly to our apartment...told them where to find you...and me and Fadi...and Mama and Hiba and Karam and Batul?

I know!

Muhammad, if you had sent that message, you could have gotten us all killed!

I know. I'll be more careful. I promise.

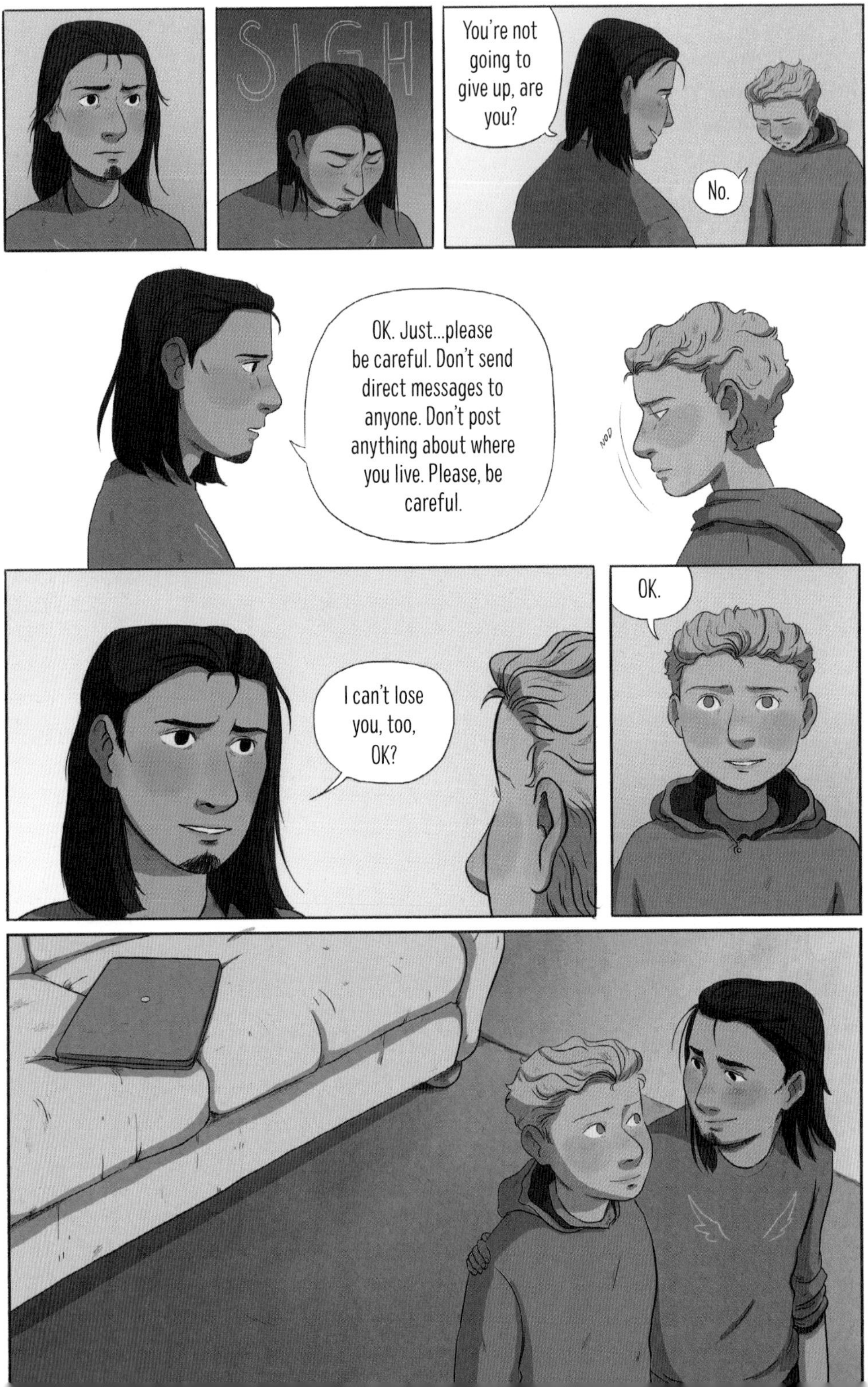
SIGH
You're not going to give up, are you?
No.
OK. Just...please be careful. Don't send direct messages to anyone. Don't post anything about where you live. Please, be careful.
NOD
I can't lose you, too, OK?
OK.

CHAPTER 9

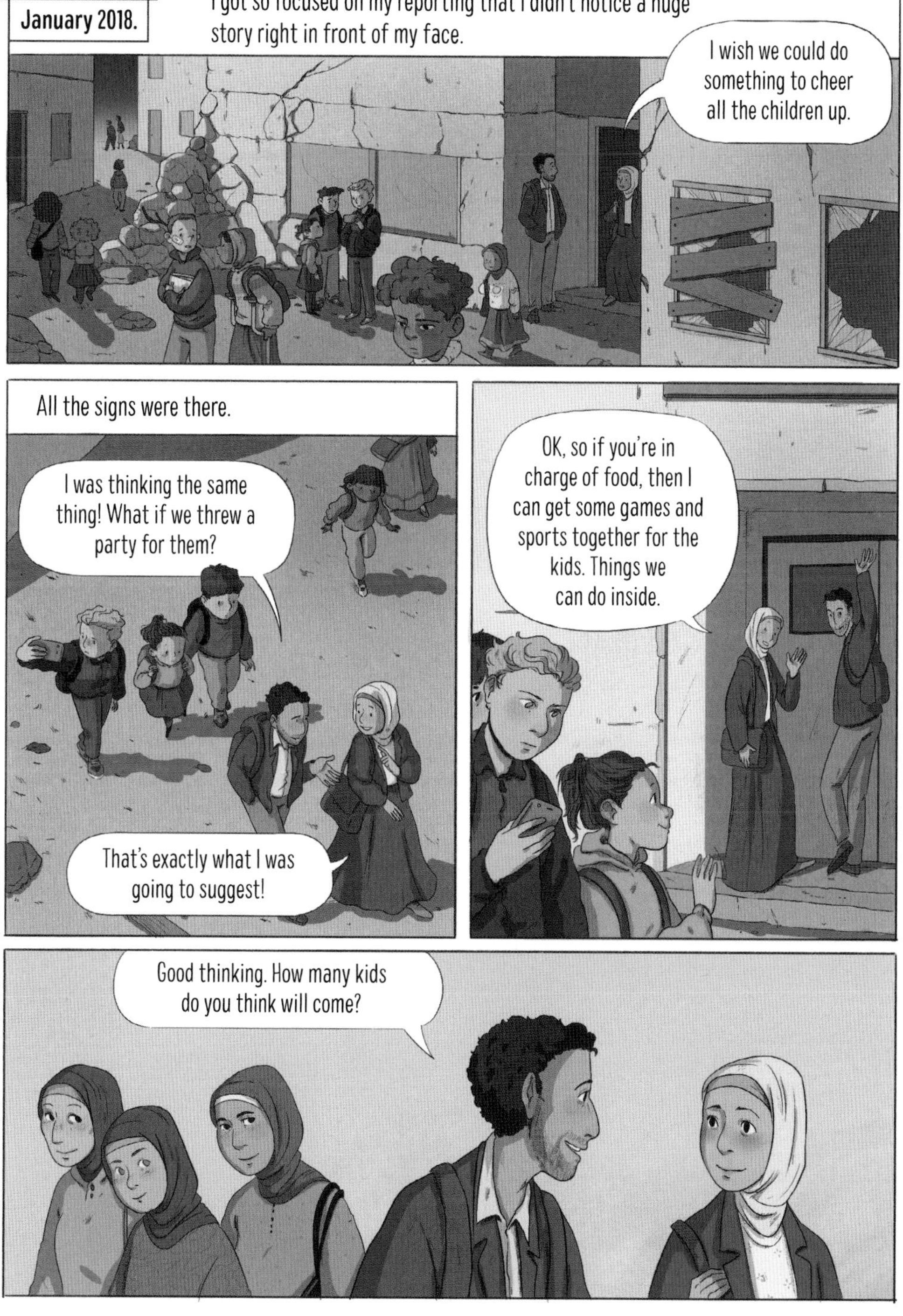
January 2018.
I got so focused on my reporting that I didn't notice a huge story right in front of my face.
I wish we could do something to cheer all the children up.
All the signs were there.
I was thinking the same thing! What if we threw a party for them?
That's exactly what I was going to suggest!
OK, so if you're in charge of food, then I can get some games and sports together for the kids. Things we can do inside.
Good thinking. How many kids do you think will come?

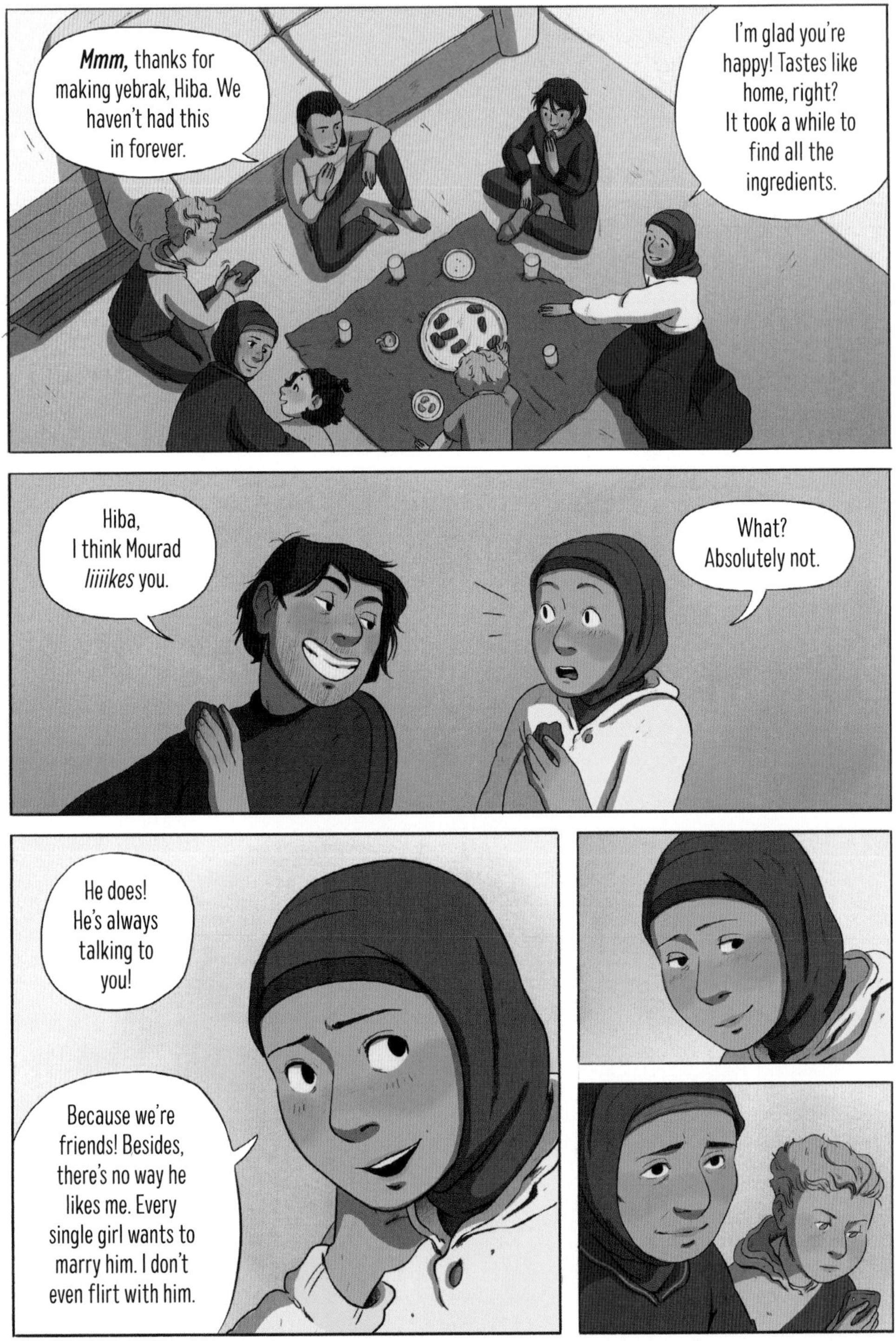
Mmm, thanks for making yebrak, Hiba. We haven't had this in forever.
I'm glad you're happy! Tastes like home, right? It took a while to find all the ingredients.
Hiba, I think Mourad *liiiikes* you.
What? Absolutely not.
He does! He's always talking to you!
Because we're friends! Besides, there's no way he likes me. Every single girl wants to marry him. I don't even flirt with him.

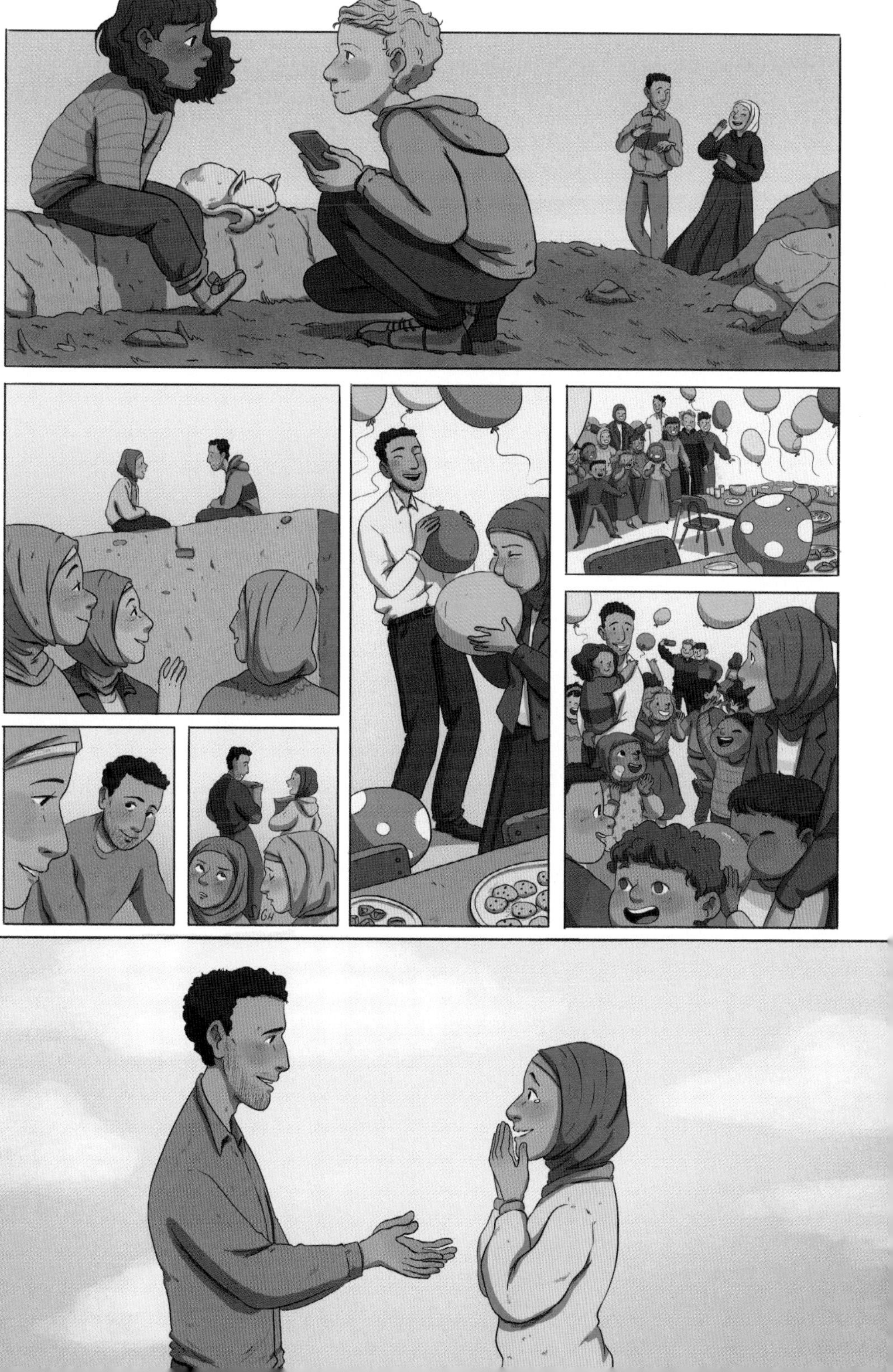
SIGH

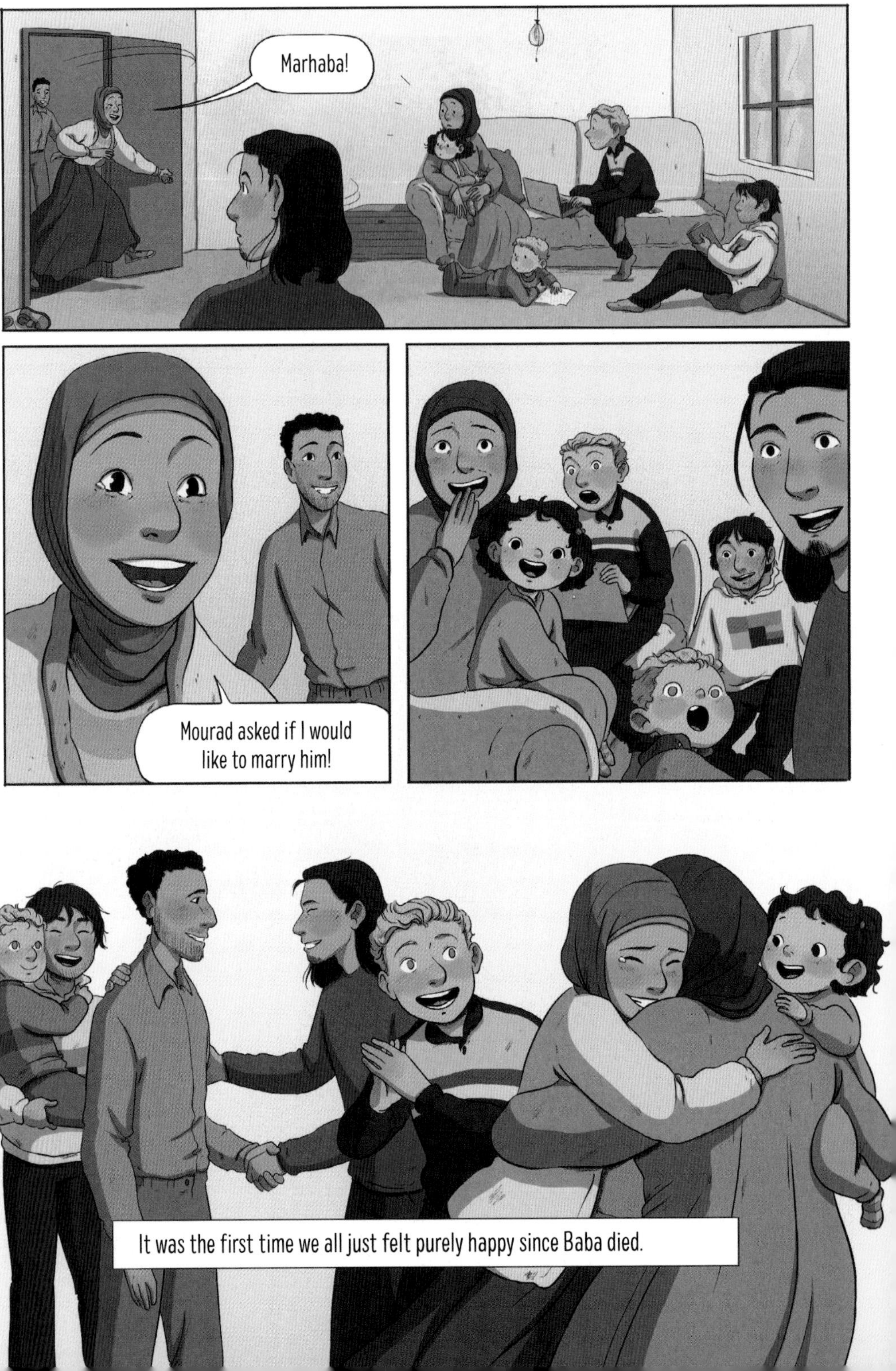
Marhaba!
Mourad asked if I would like to marry him!
It was the first time we all just felt purely happy since Baba died.

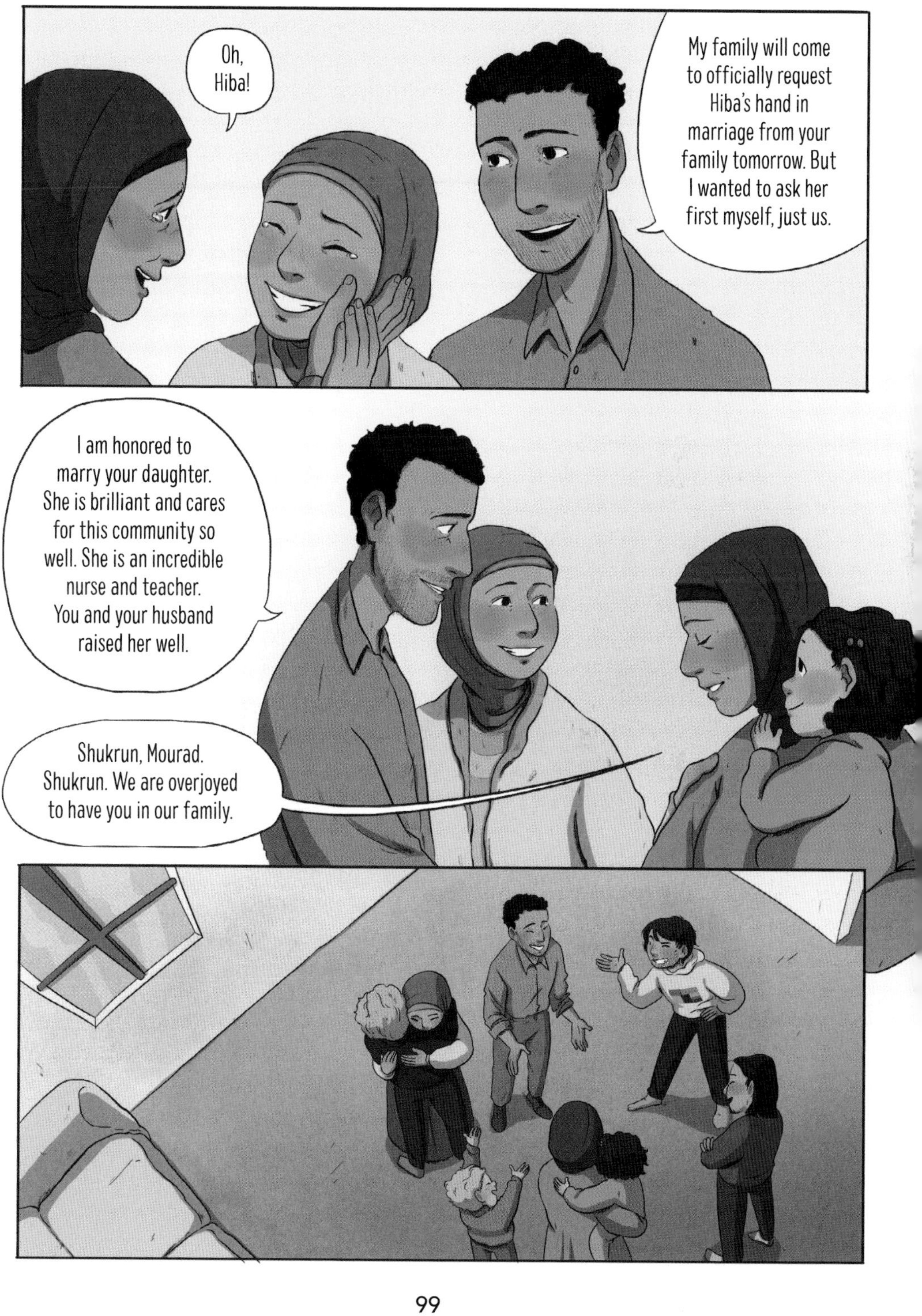
Oh, Hiba!
My family will come to officially request Hiba's hand in marriage from your family tomorrow. But I wanted to ask her first myself, just us.
I am honored to marry your daughter. She is brilliant and cares for this community so well. She is an incredible nurse and teacher. You and your husband raised her well.
Shukrun, Mourad. Shukrun. We are overjoyed to have you in our family.

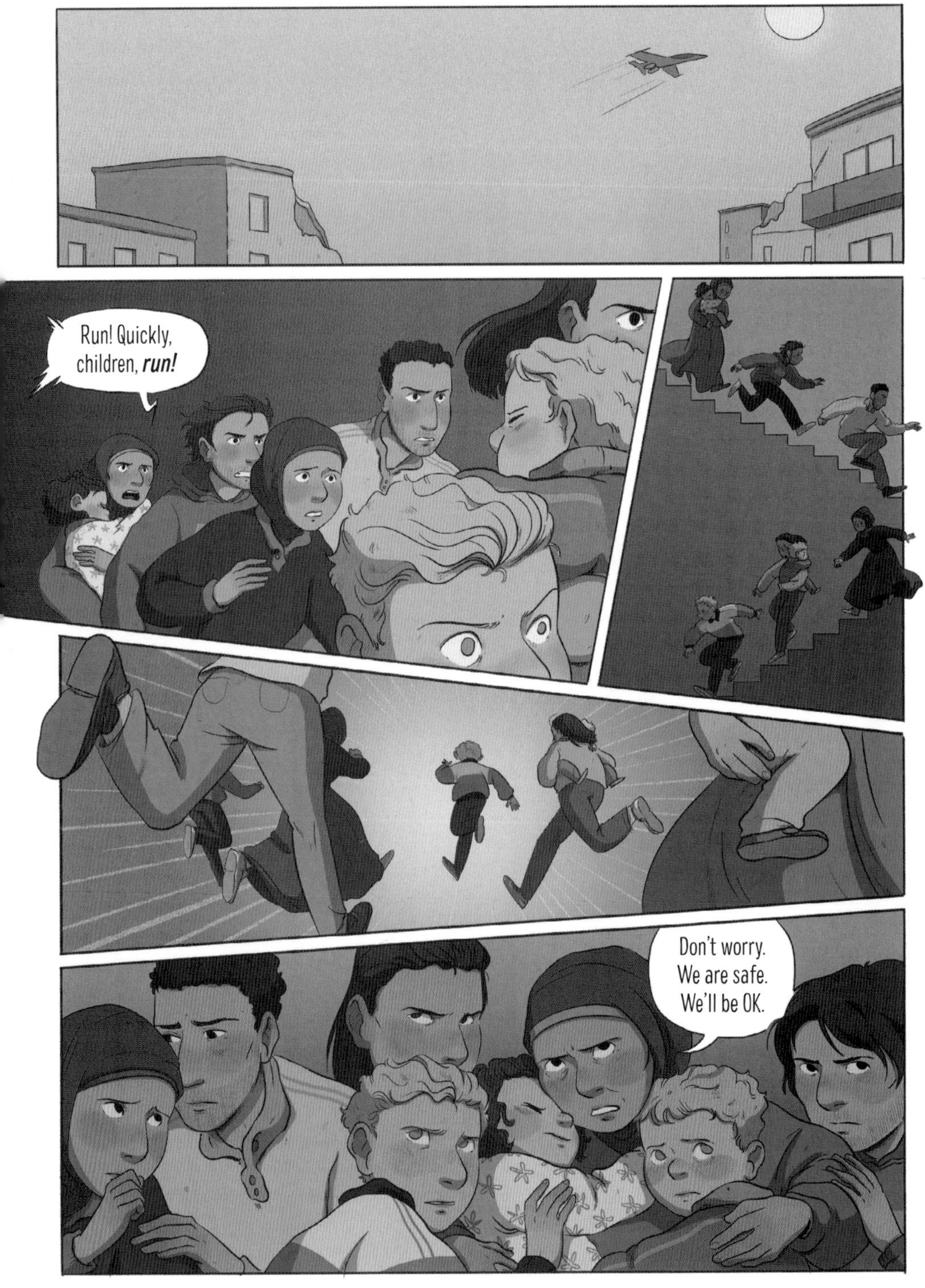
Run! Quickly, children, *run!*
Don't worry. We are safe. We'll be OK.

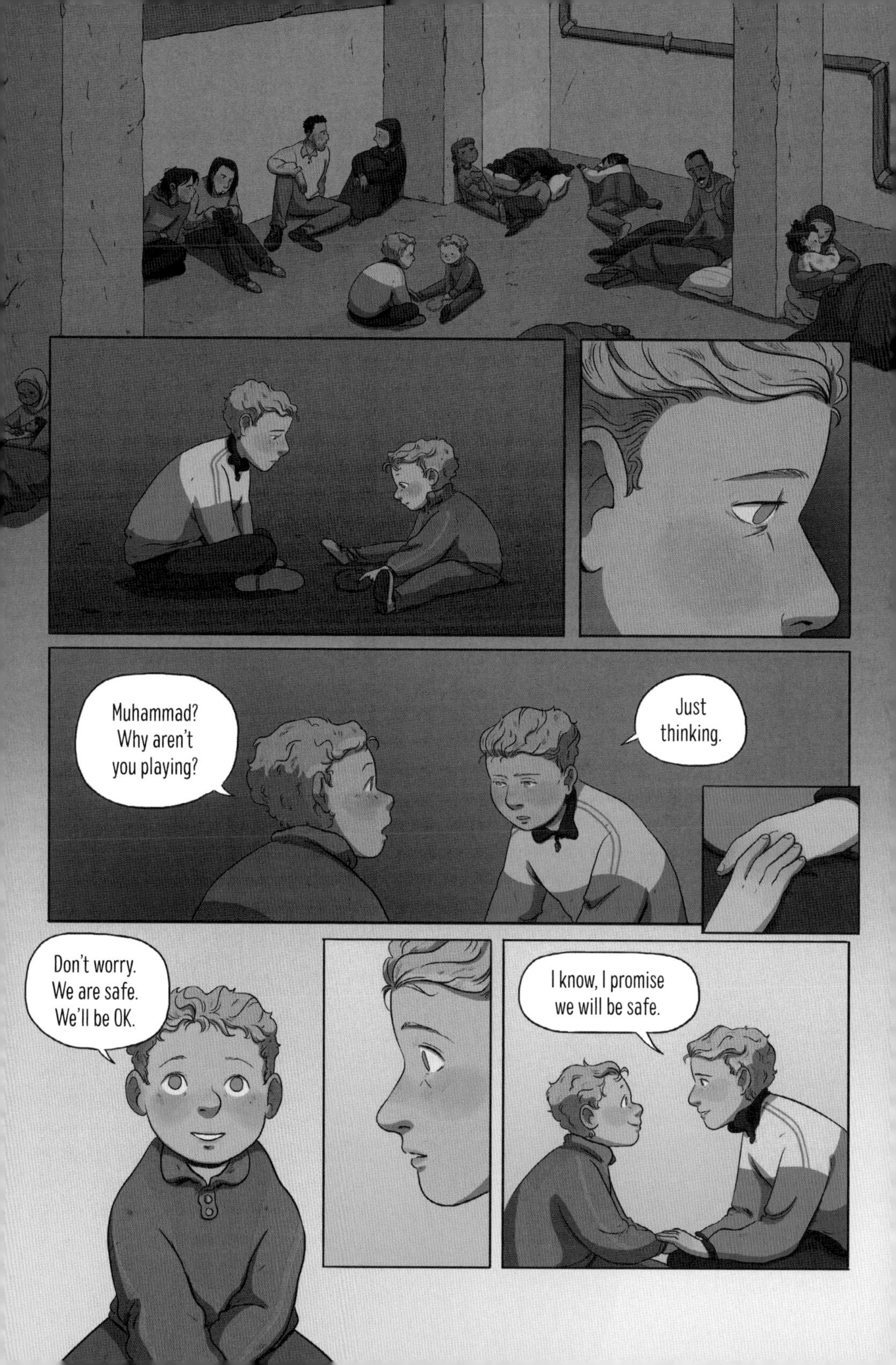
Muhammad? Why aren't you playing?
Just thinking.
Don't worry. We are safe. We'll be OK.
I know, I promise we will be safe.

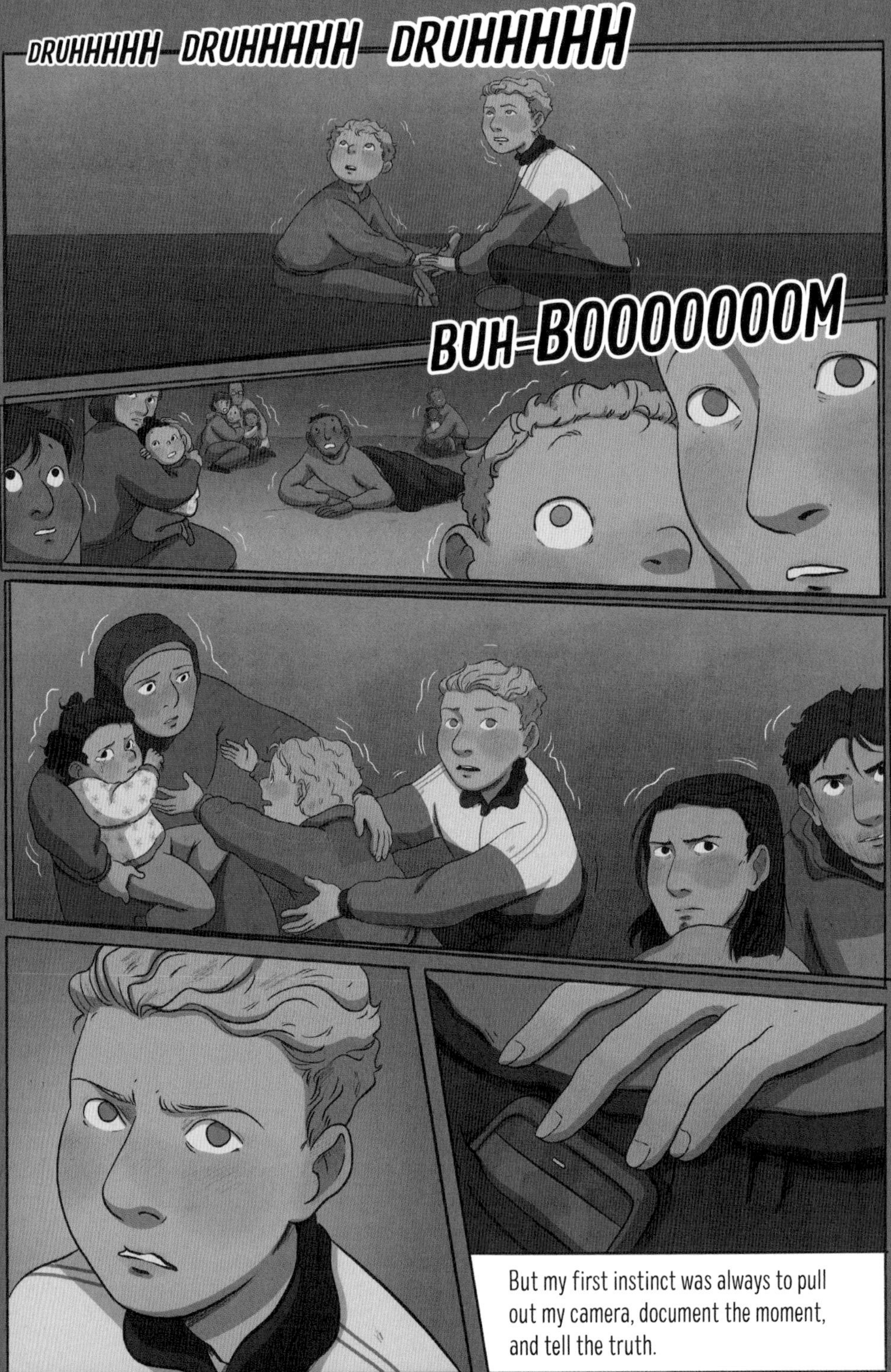
DRUHHHHH DRUHHHHH DRUHHHHH
BUH-BOOOOOOOM
But my first instinct was always to pull out my camera, document the moment, and tell the truth.

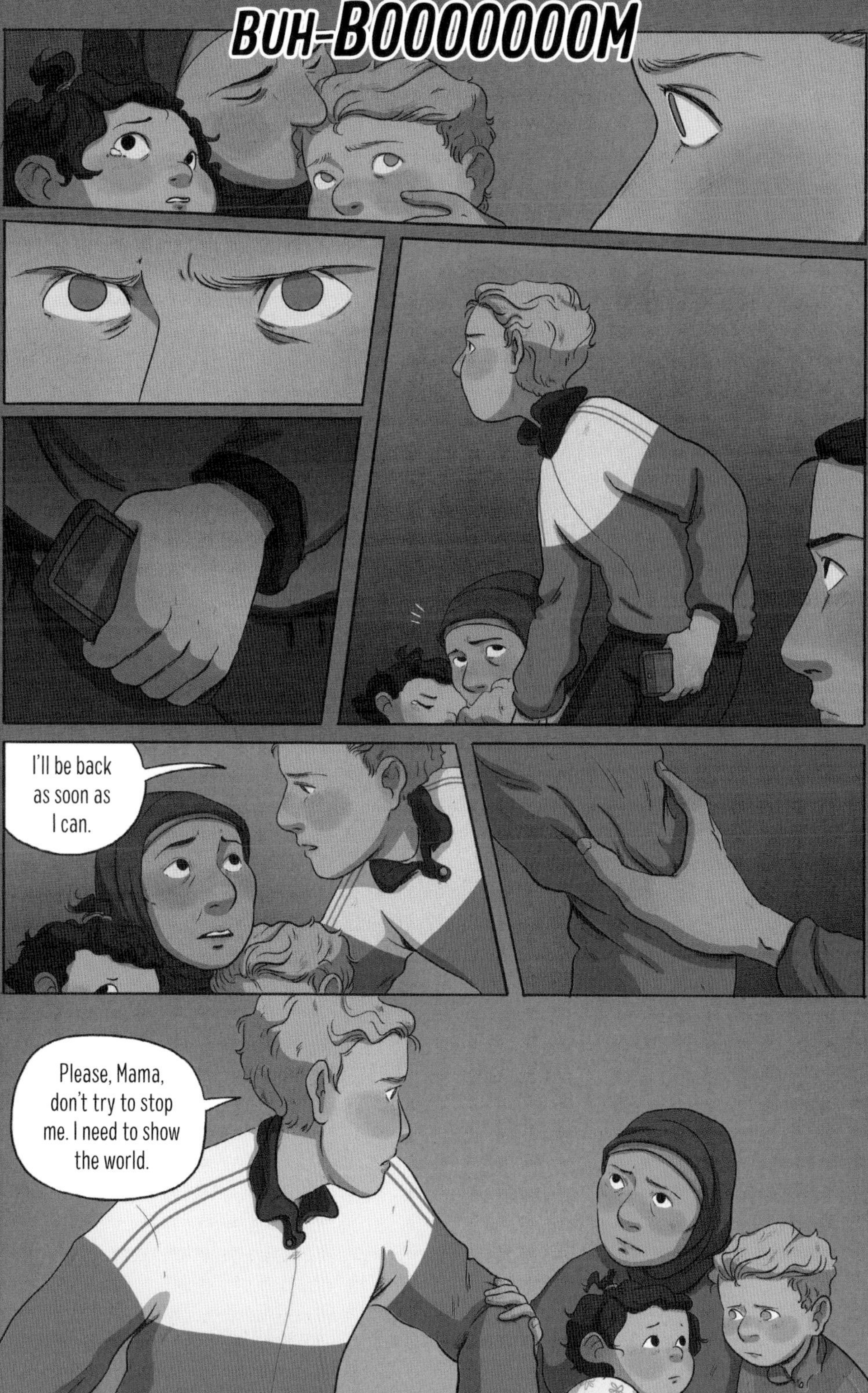
BUH-BOOOOOOOM
I'll be back as soon as I can.
Please, Mama, don't try to stop me. I need to show the world.

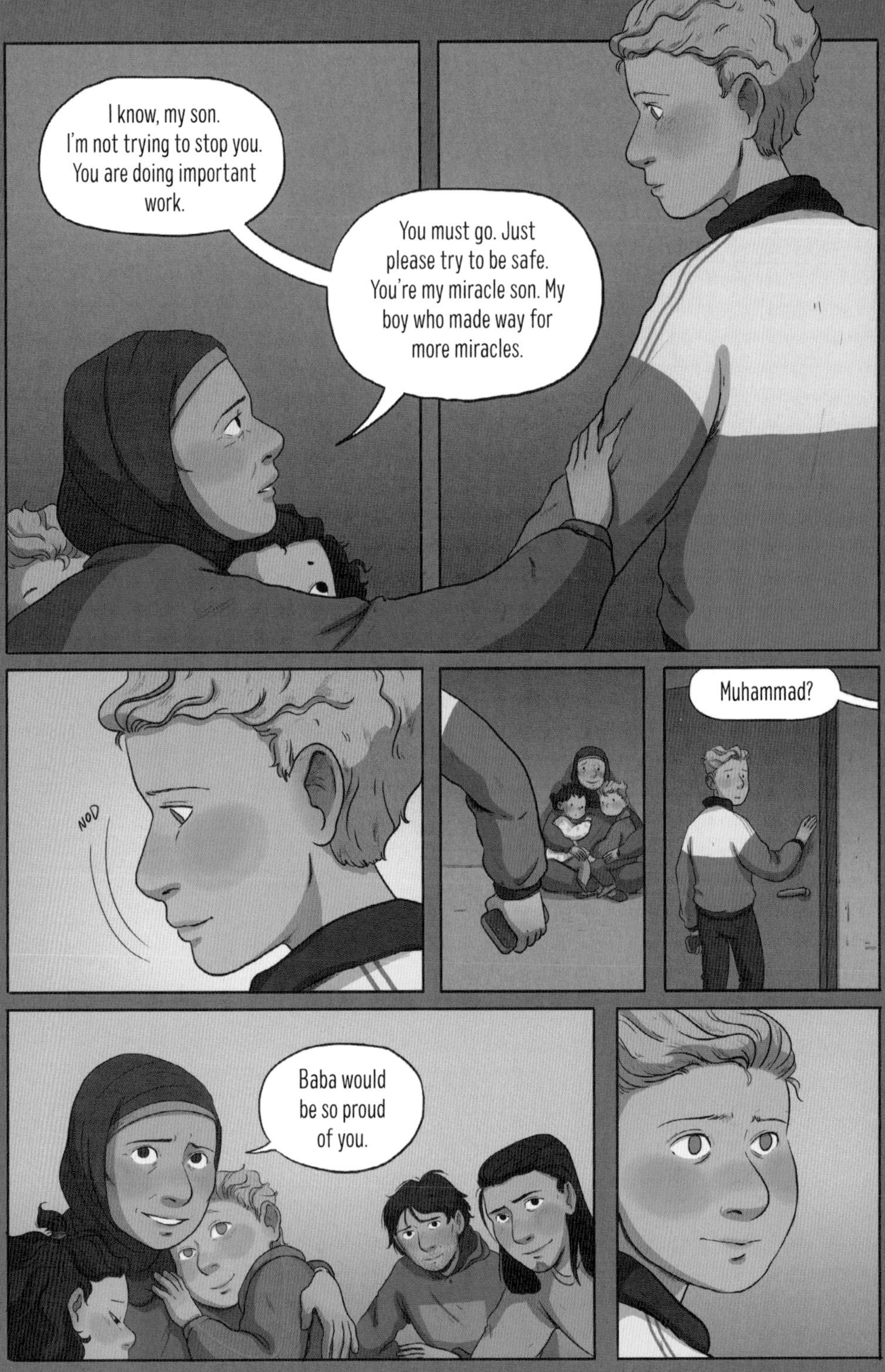
I know, my son. I'm not trying to stop you. You are doing important work.
You must go. Just please try to be safe. You're my miracle son. My boy who made way for more miracles.
NOD
Muhammad?
Baba would be so proud of you.

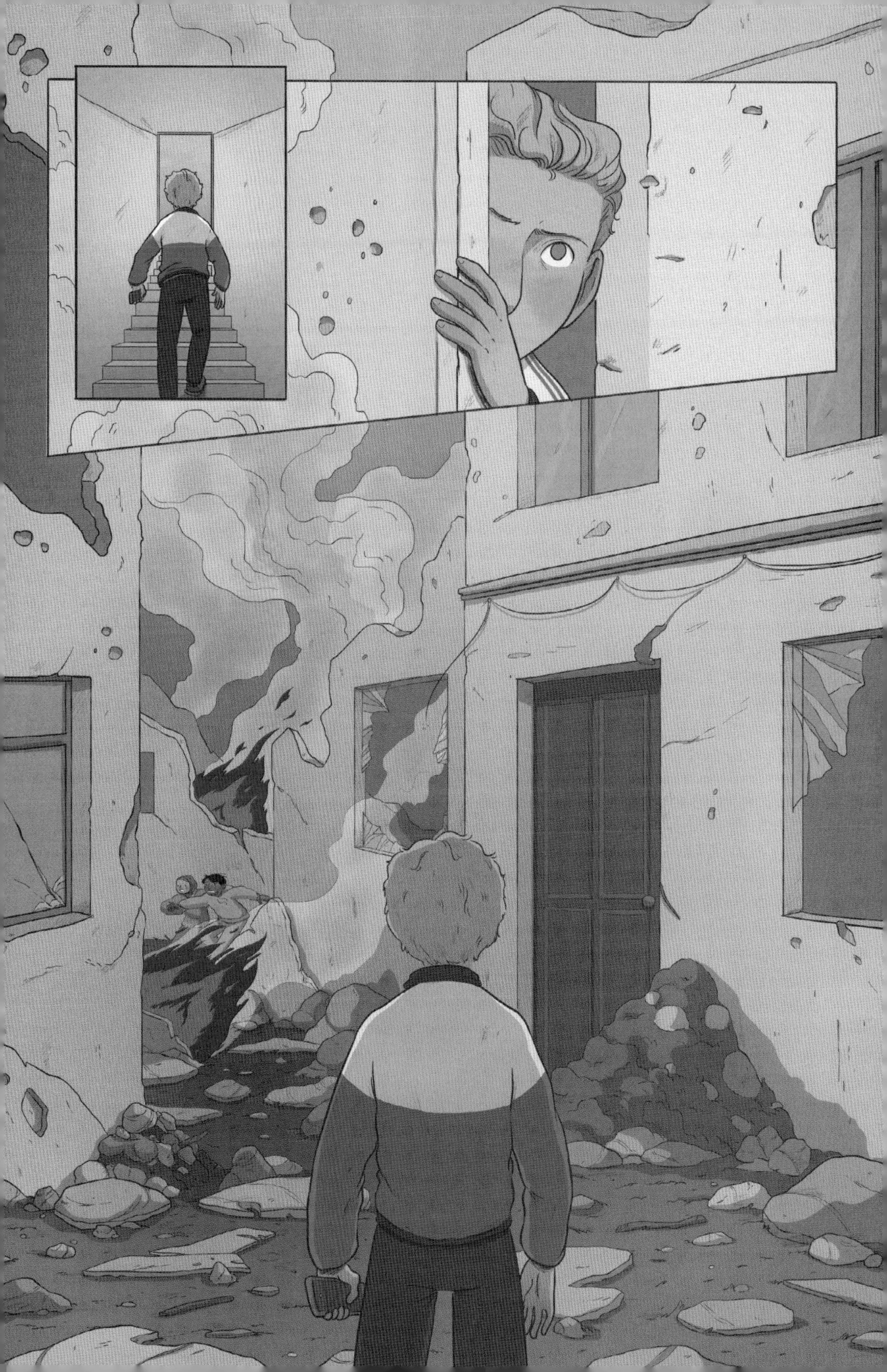

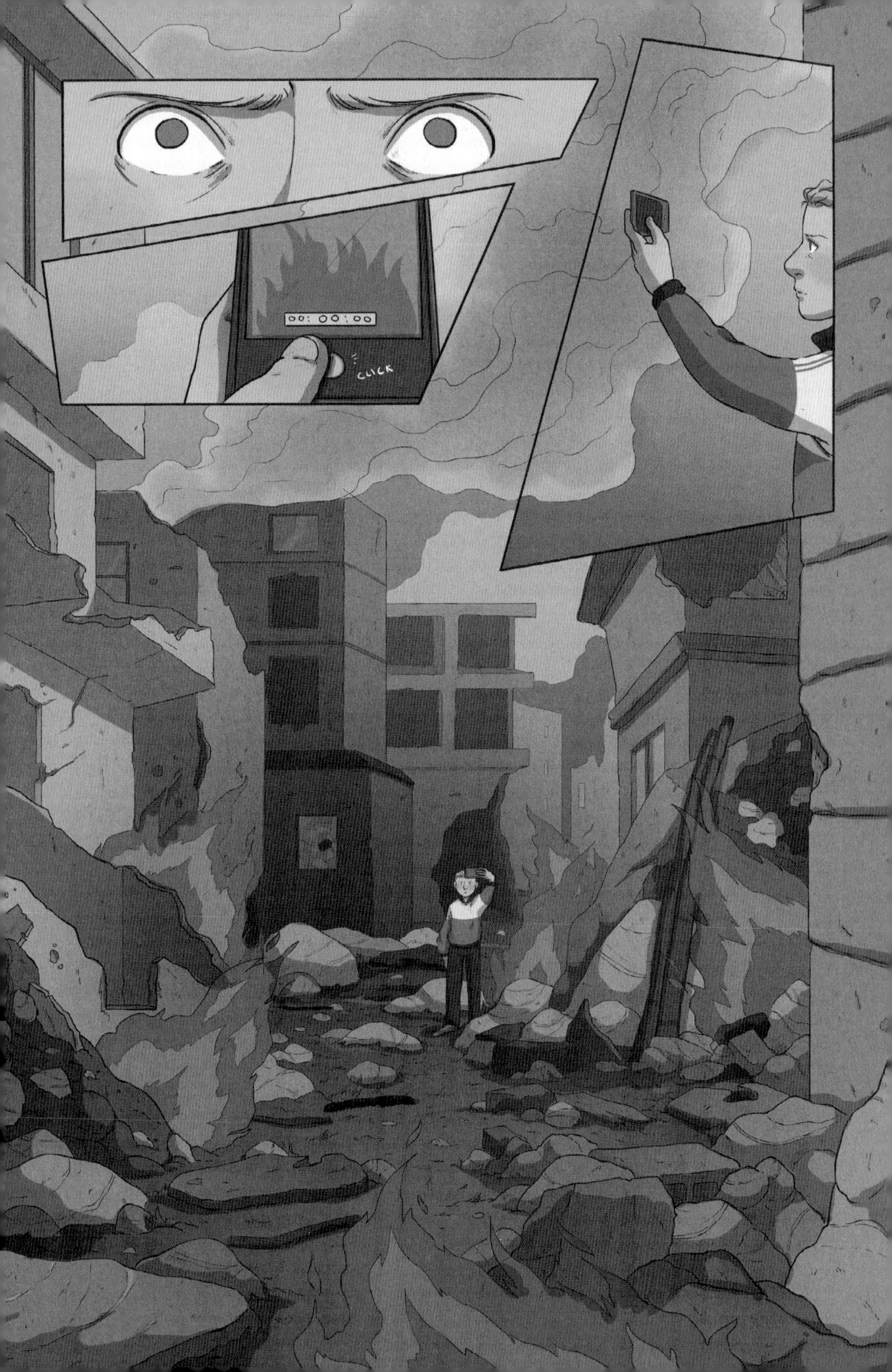
00:00:00
CLICK

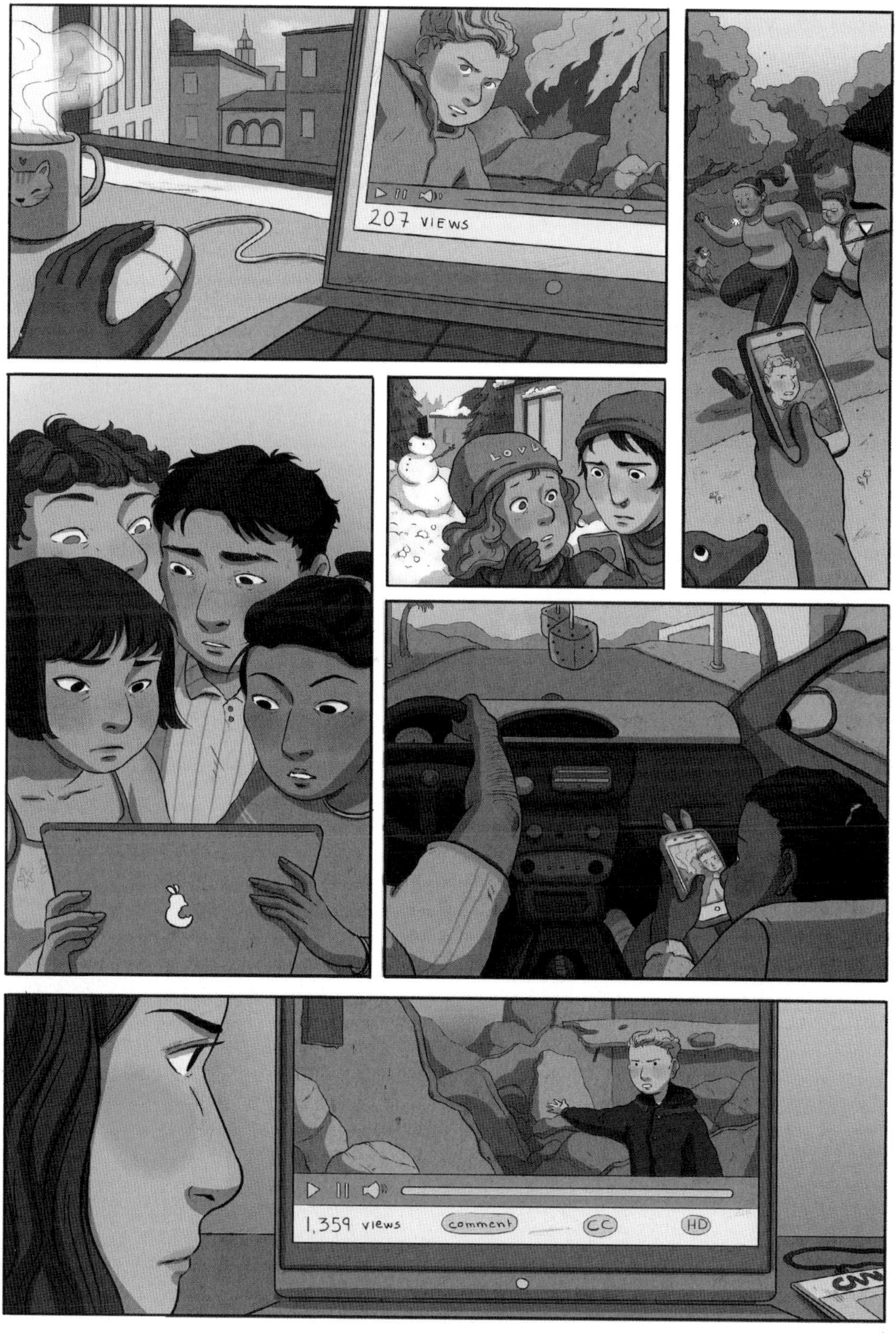

207 VIEWS
LOVE
1,359 views
comment
CC
HD

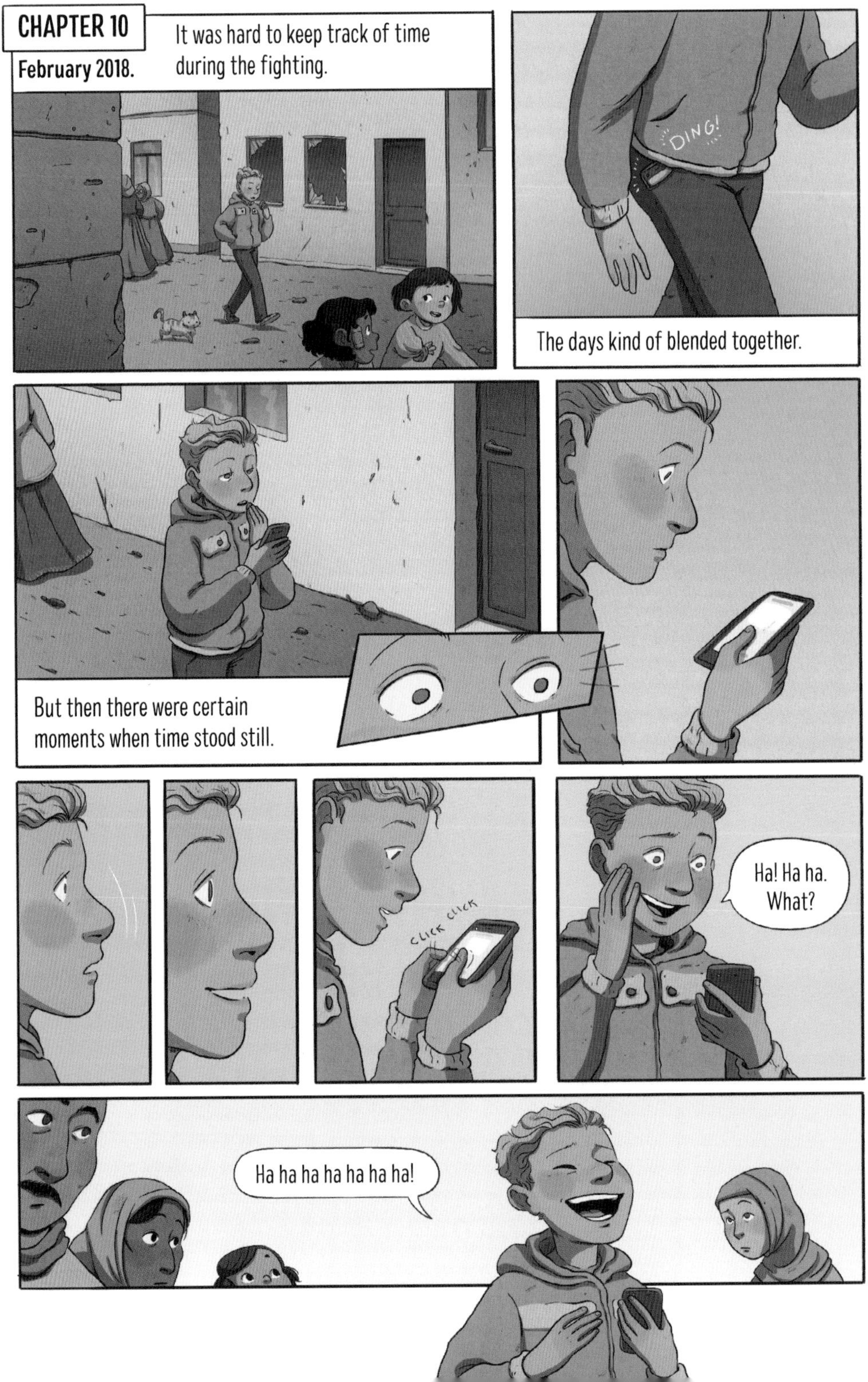
CHAPTER 10
February 2018.
It was hard to keep track of time during the fighting.
DING!
The days kind of blended together.
But then there were certain moments when time stood still.
CLICK CLICK
Ha! Ha ha. What?
Ha ha ha ha ha ha ha!

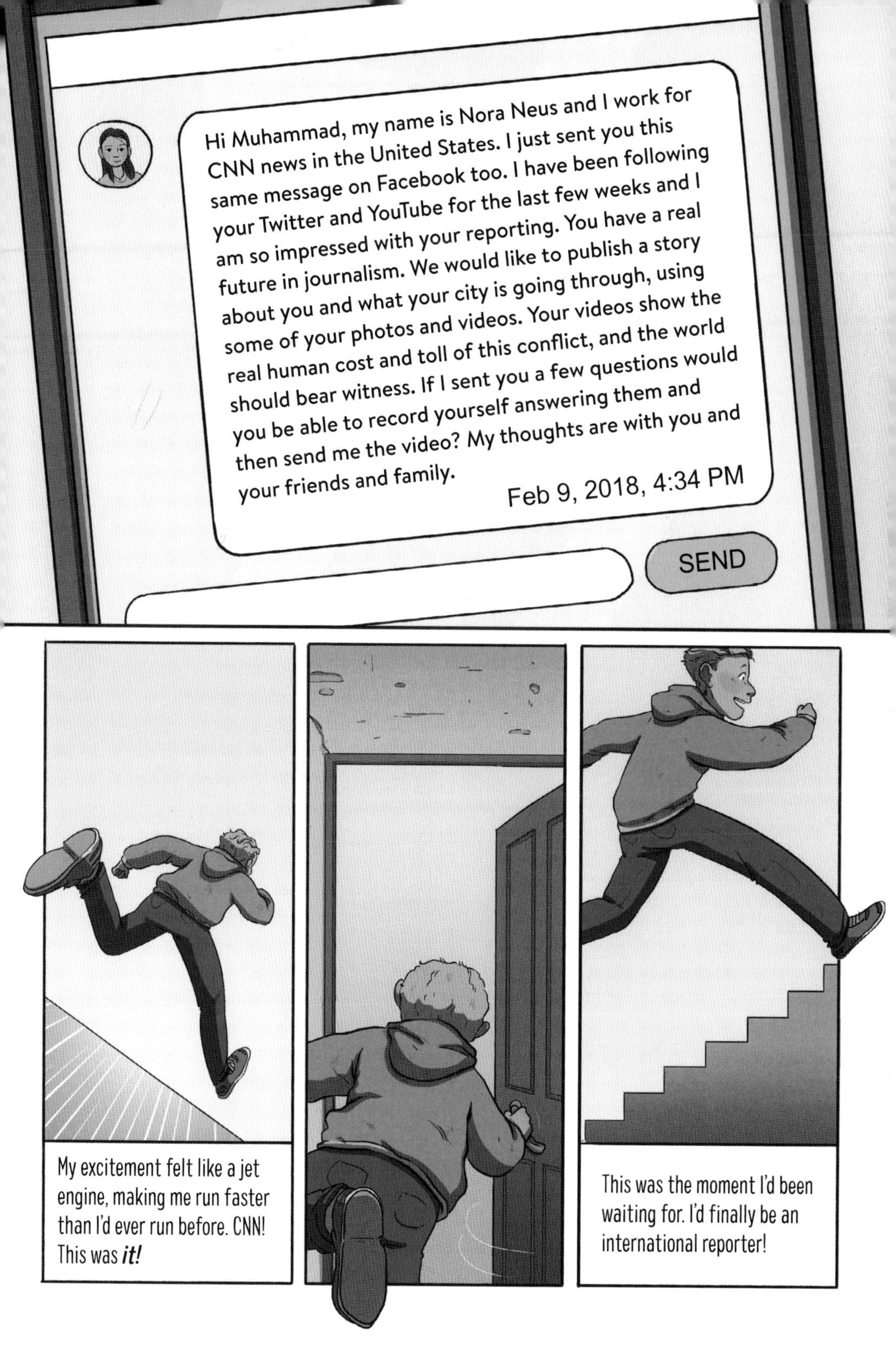
Hi Muhammad, my name is Nora Neus and I work for CNN news in the United States. I just sent you this same message on Facebook too. I have been following your Twitter and YouTube for the last few weeks and I am so impressed with your reporting. You have a real future in journalism. We would like to publish a story about you and what your city is going through, using some of your photos and videos. Your videos show the real human cost and toll of this conflict, and the world should bear witness. If I sent you a few questions would you be able to record yourself answering them and then send me the video? My thoughts are with you and your friends and family.
Feb 9, 2018, 4:34 PM
SEND
My excitement felt like a jet engine, making me run faster than I'd ever run before. CNN! This was *it!*
This was the moment I'd been waiting for. I'd finally be an international reporter!

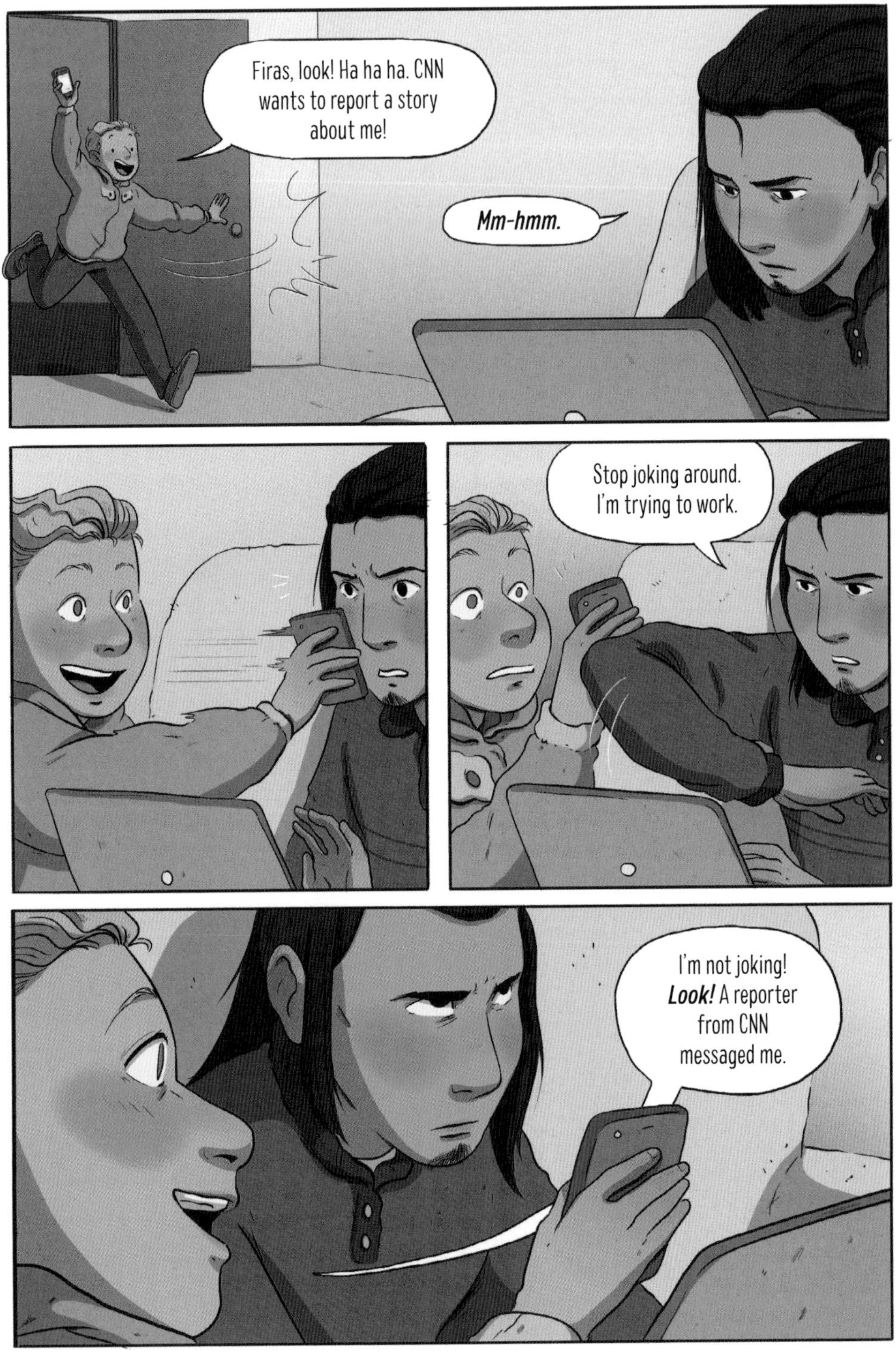
Firas, look! Ha ha ha. CNN wants to report a story about me!
Mm-hmm.
Stop joking around. I'm trying to work.
I'm not joking! **Look!** A reporter from CNN messaged me.

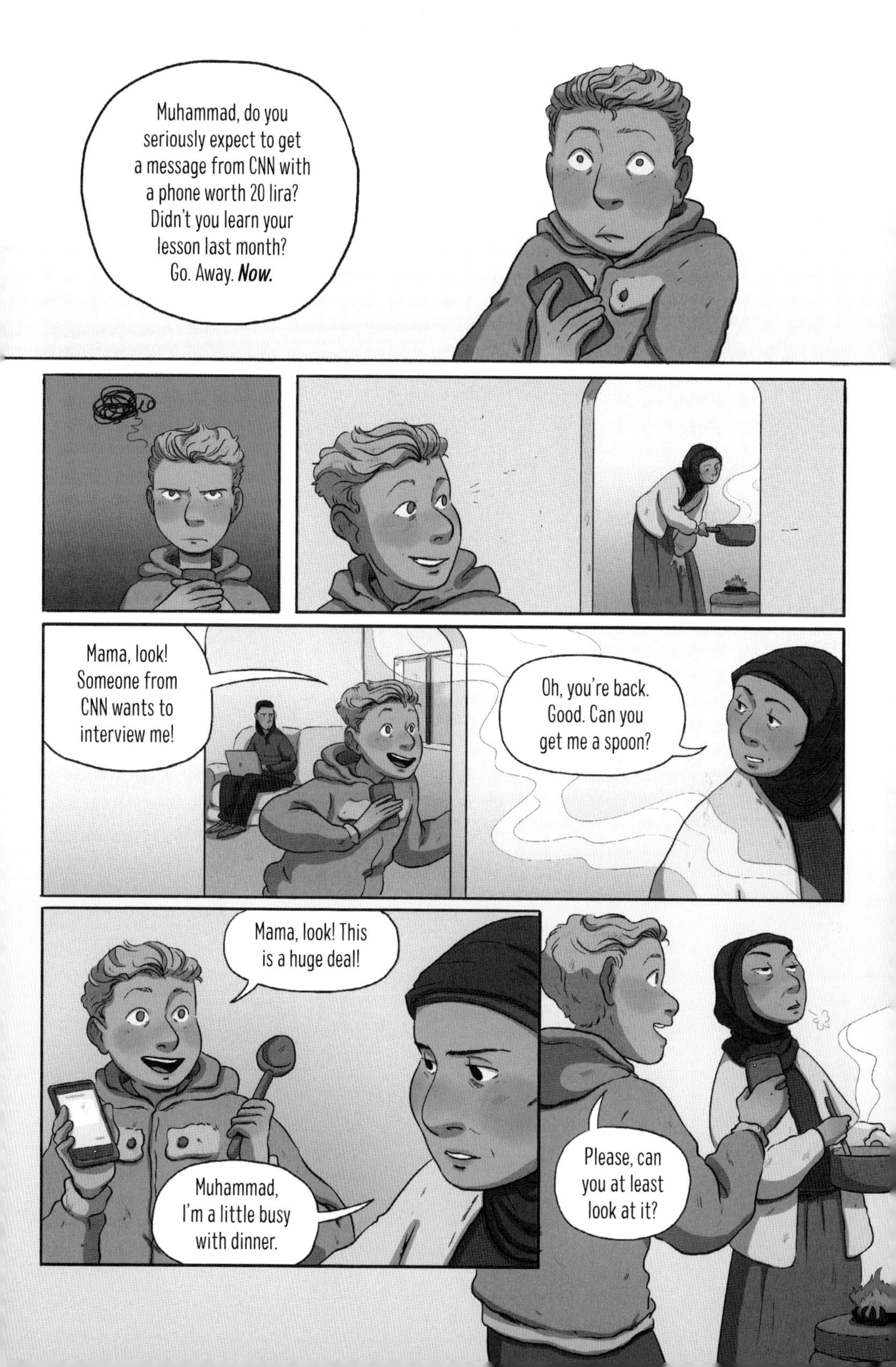
Muhammad, do you seriously expect to get a message from CNN with a phone worth 20 lira? Didn't you learn your lesson last month? Go. Away. ***Now.***
Mama, look! Someone from CNN wants to interview me!
Oh, you're back. Good. Can you get me a spoon?
Mama, look! This is a huge deal!
Muhammad, I'm a little busy with dinner.
Please, can you at least look at it?

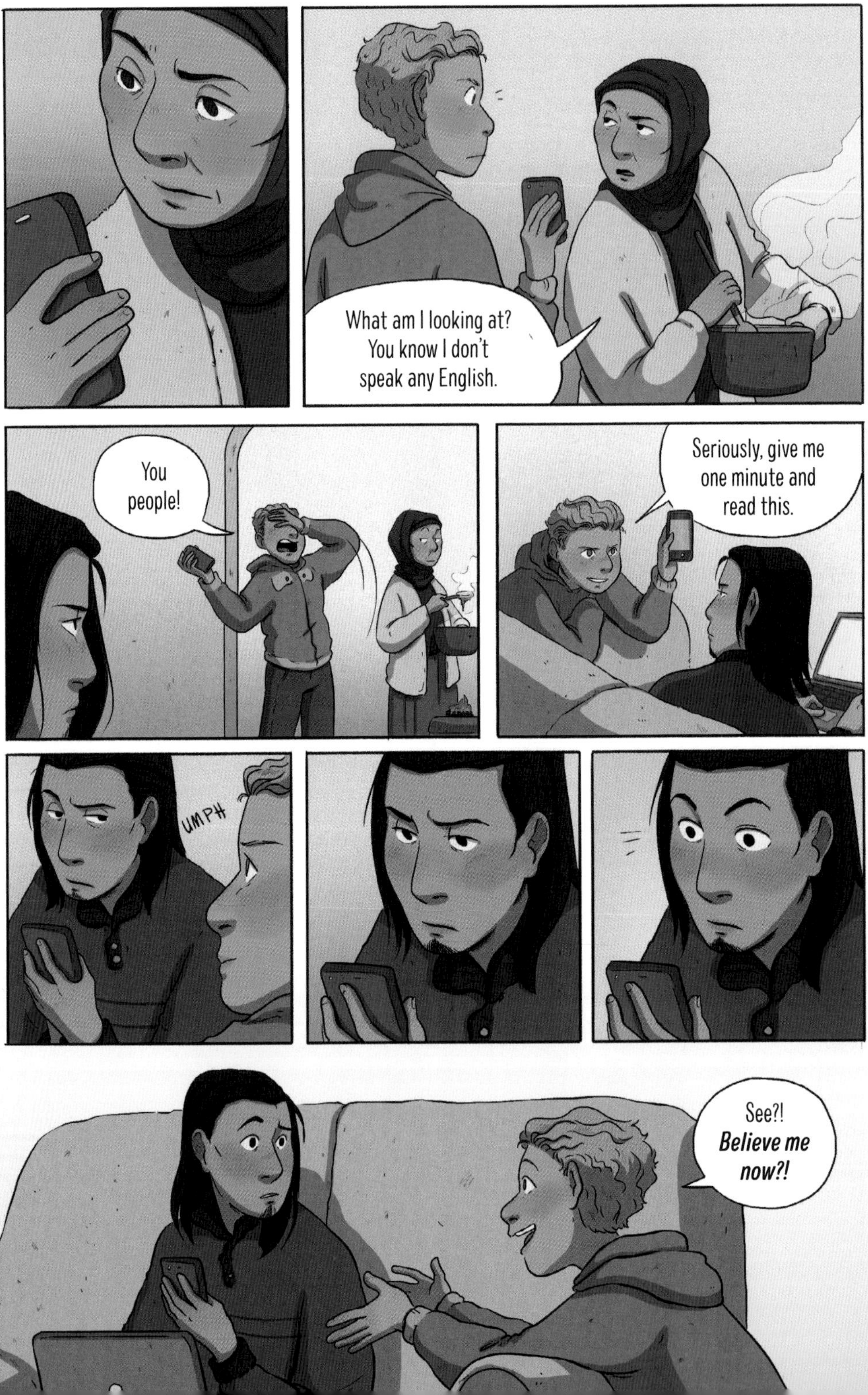
What am I looking at? You know I don't speak any English.
You people!
Seriously, give me one minute and read this.
UMPH
See?! **Believe me now?!**

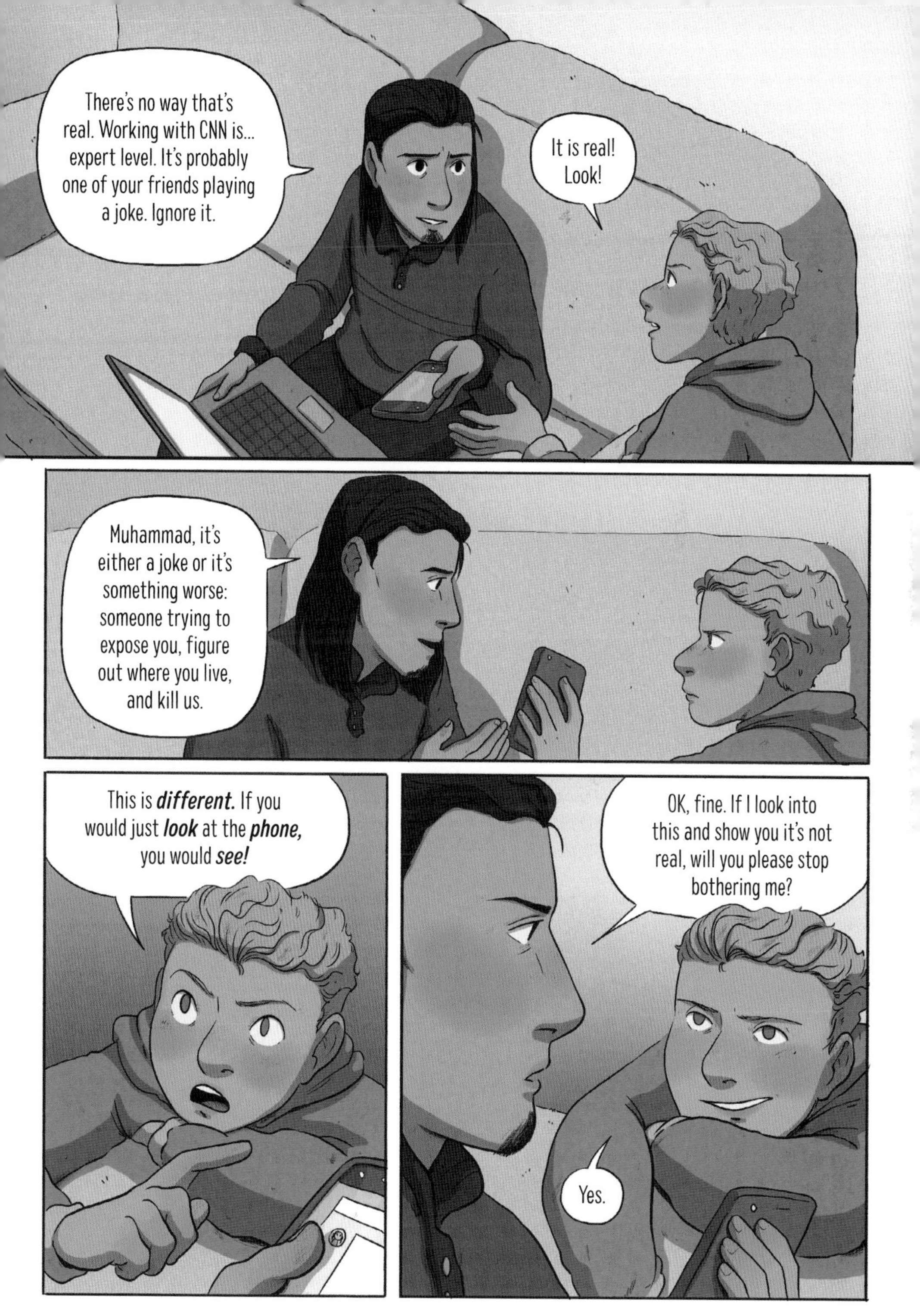
There's no way that's real. Working with CNN is... expert level. It's probably one of your friends playing a joke. Ignore it.
It is real! Look!
Muhammad, it's either a joke or it's something worse: someone trying to expose you, figure out where you live, and kill us.
This is ***different.*** If you would just ***look*** at the ***phone,*** you would ***see!***
OK, fine. If I look into this and show you it's not real, will you please stop bothering me?
Yes.

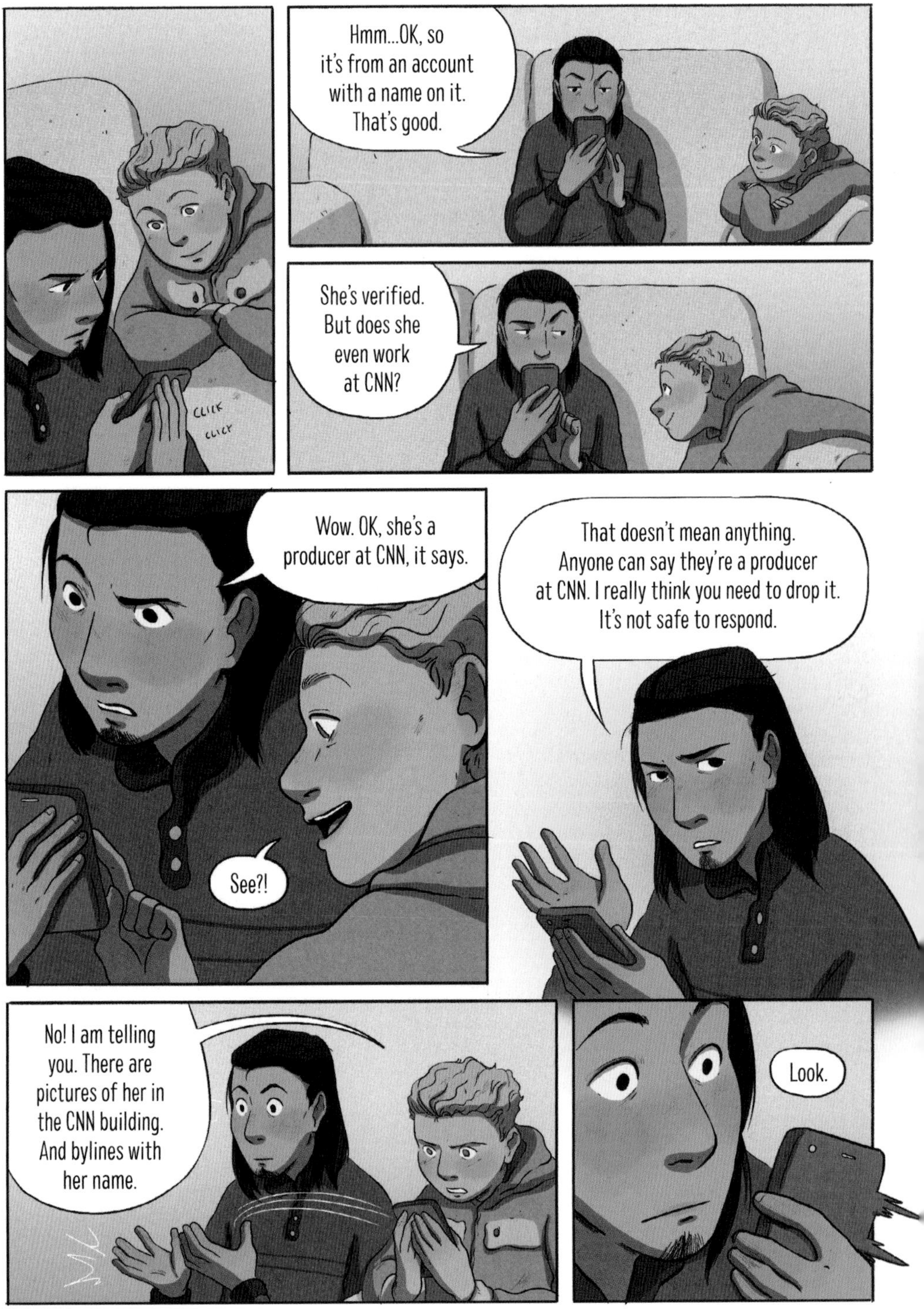

CLICK
CLICK
Hmm...OK, so it's from an account with a name on it. That's good.
She's verified. But does she even work at CNN?
Wow. OK, she's a producer at CNN, it says.
See?!
That doesn't mean anything. Anyone can say they're a producer at CNN. I really think you need to drop it. It's not safe to respond.
No! I am telling you. There are pictures of her in the CNN building. And bylines with her name.
Look.

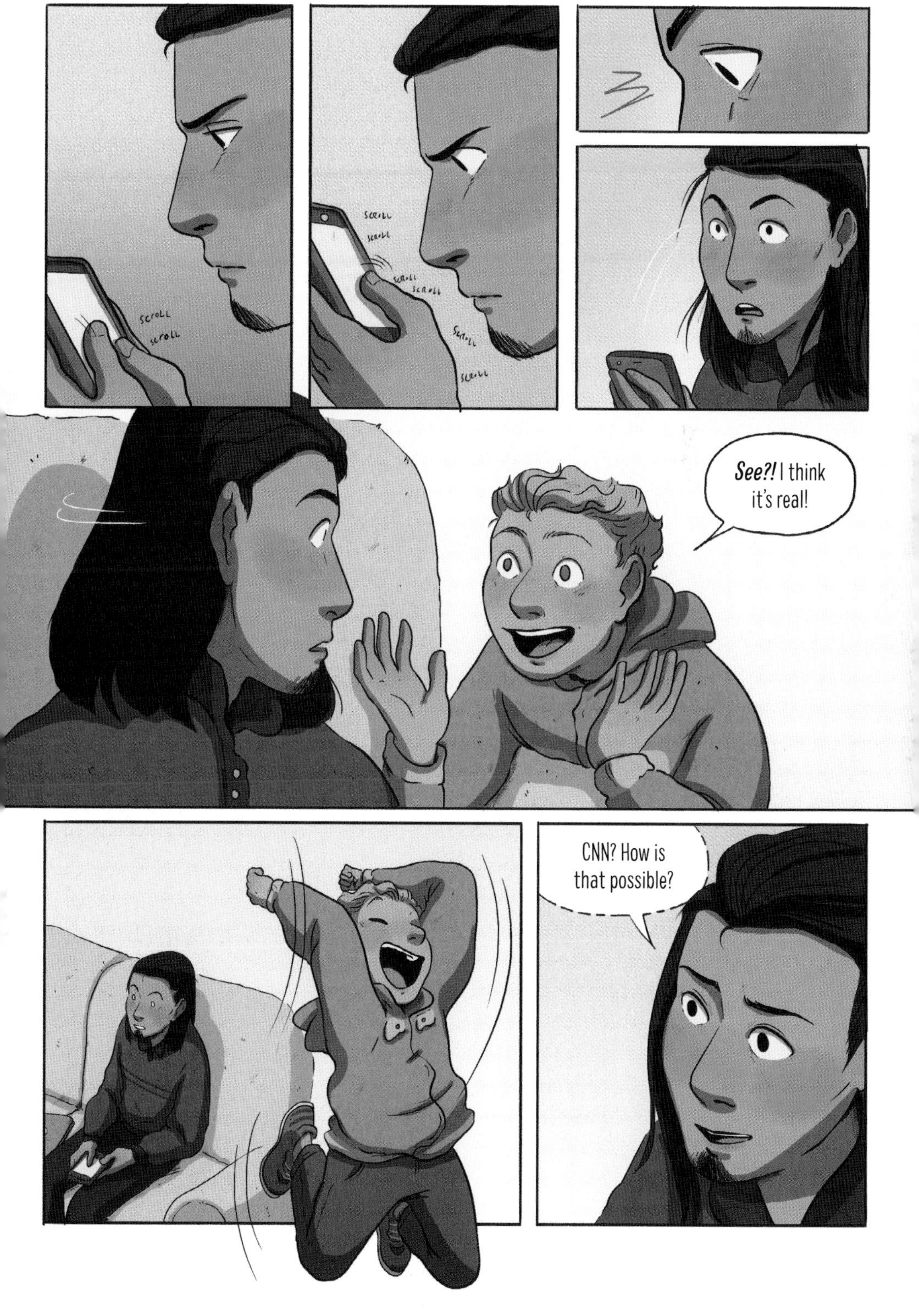
SCROLL
SCROLL
SCROLL
SCROLL
SCROLL
SCROLL
SCROLL
SCROLL
See?! I think it's real!
CNN? How is that possible?

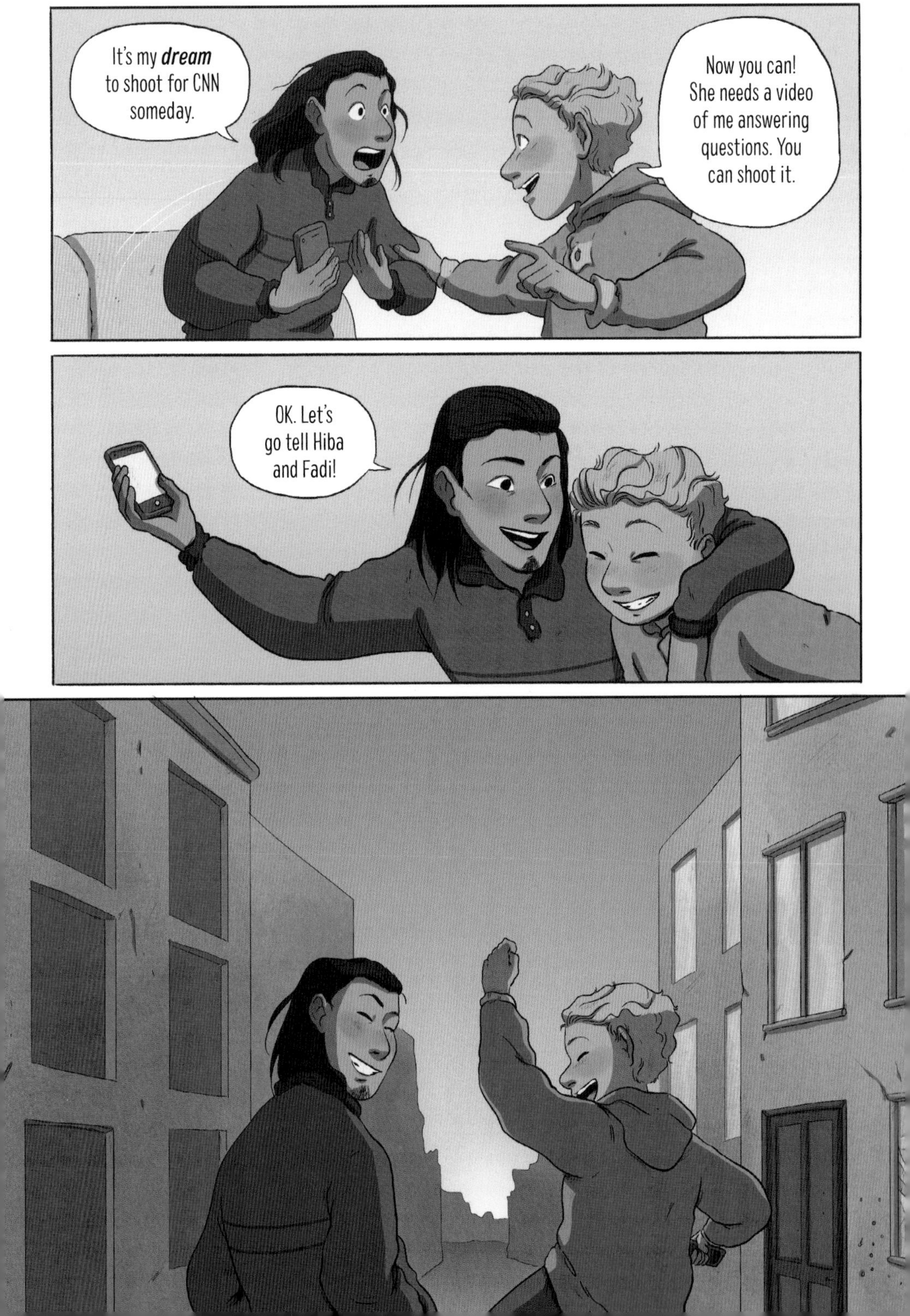
It's my ***dream*** to shoot for CNN someday.
Now you can! She needs a video of me answering questions. You can shoot it.
OK. Let's go tell Hiba and Fadi!

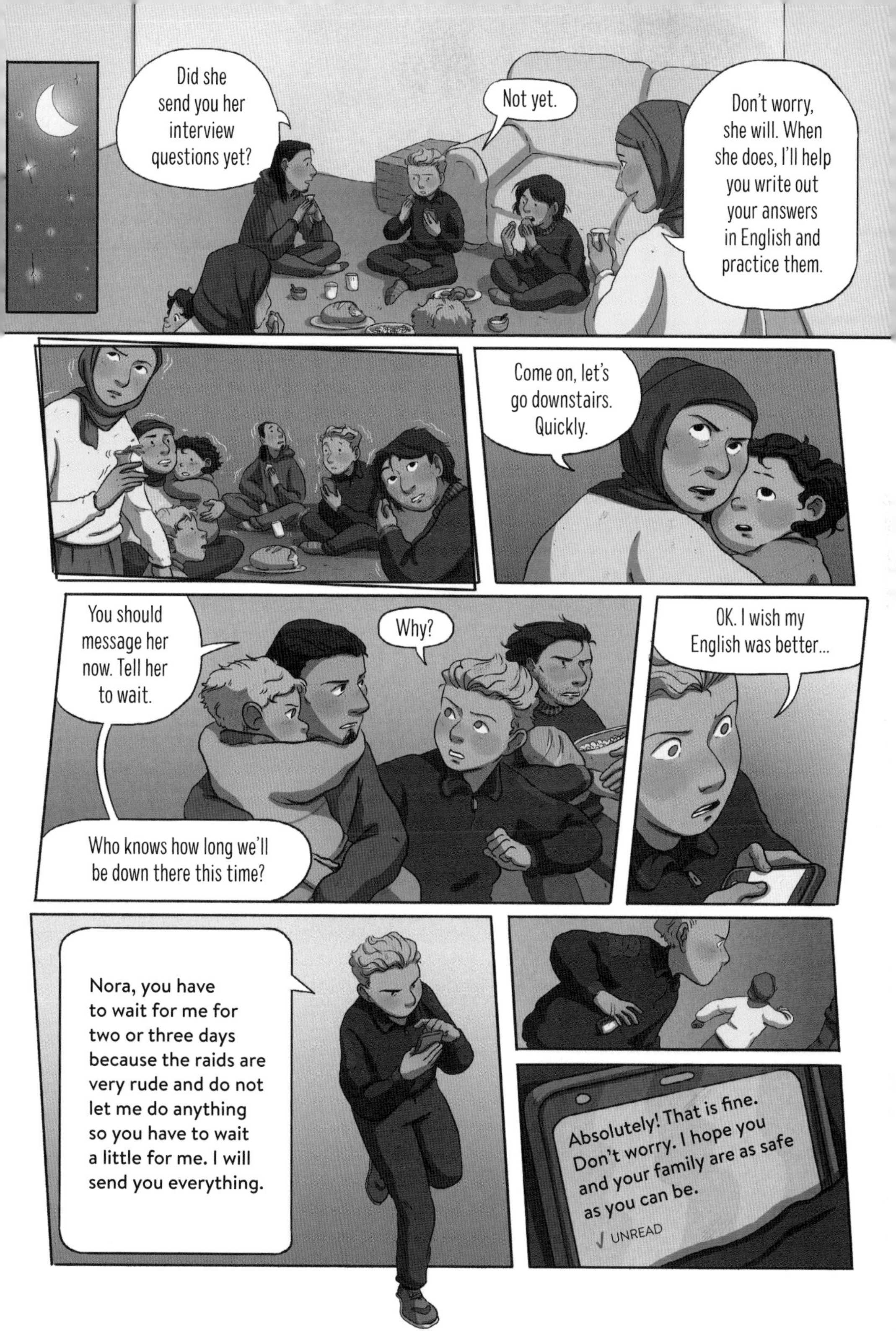
Did she send you her interview questions yet?
Not yet.
Don't worry, she will. When she does, I'll help you write out your answers in English and practice them.
Come on, let's go downstairs. Quickly.
You should message her now. Tell her to wait.
Why?
Who knows how long we'll be down there this time?
OK. I wish my English was better...
Nora, you have to wait for me for two or three days because the raids are very rude and do not let me do anything so you have to wait a little for me. I will send you everything.
Absolutely! That is fine. Don't worry. I hope you and your family are as safe as you can be.
UNREAD

By the start of that month, we knew how to live during the revolution. We knew to drop everything at the first sound of a plane overhead. We knew to go to school in the basement early in the morning before the air strikes began. We knew to never leave an argument cross with someone, because you didn't know if that would be the last time you saw them. We knew how to live during the revolution. But then everything changed once again.

The siege of Eastern Ghouta began.

It started on February 4. Eastern Ghouta was controlled by the rebels at that point. There were already frequent bombings; we would go about our days until we heard the *druhhh druhh druuuhhhh* of the planes and dive for shelter. But then Assad's men launched a targeted campaign to take over Eastern Ghouta entirely.

At the time, we didn't know exactly what was happening, but we did know that Assad's men had tried something similar in other parts of Syria, such as Aleppo and Daraya: launching a bombing campaign against civilians and homes to try to force the rebels to surrender.

Assad claimed he was just trying to hit radicals. He claimed there weren't many civilians left in Eastern Ghouta.

But what about us?

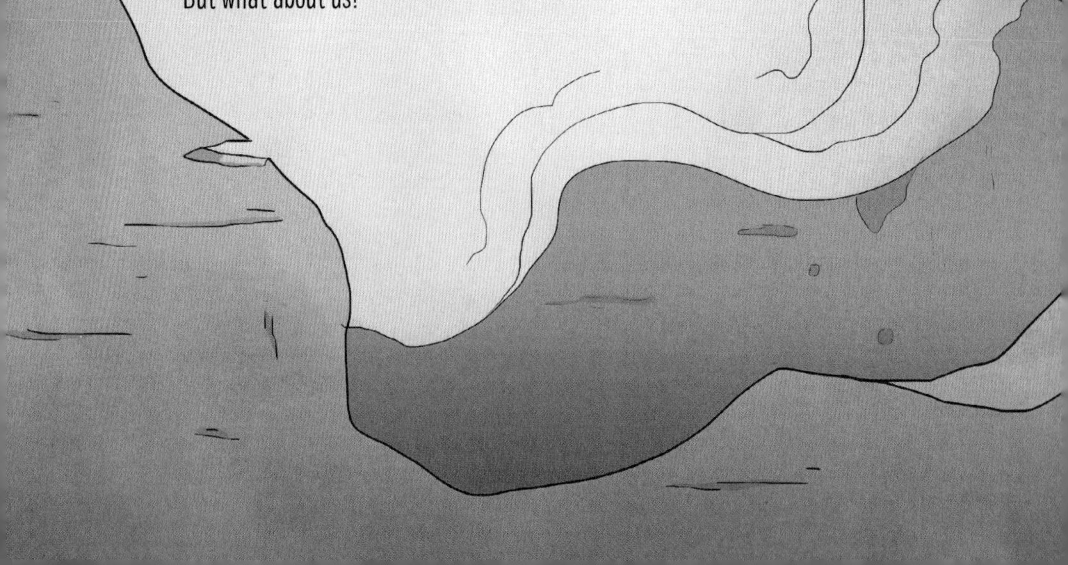

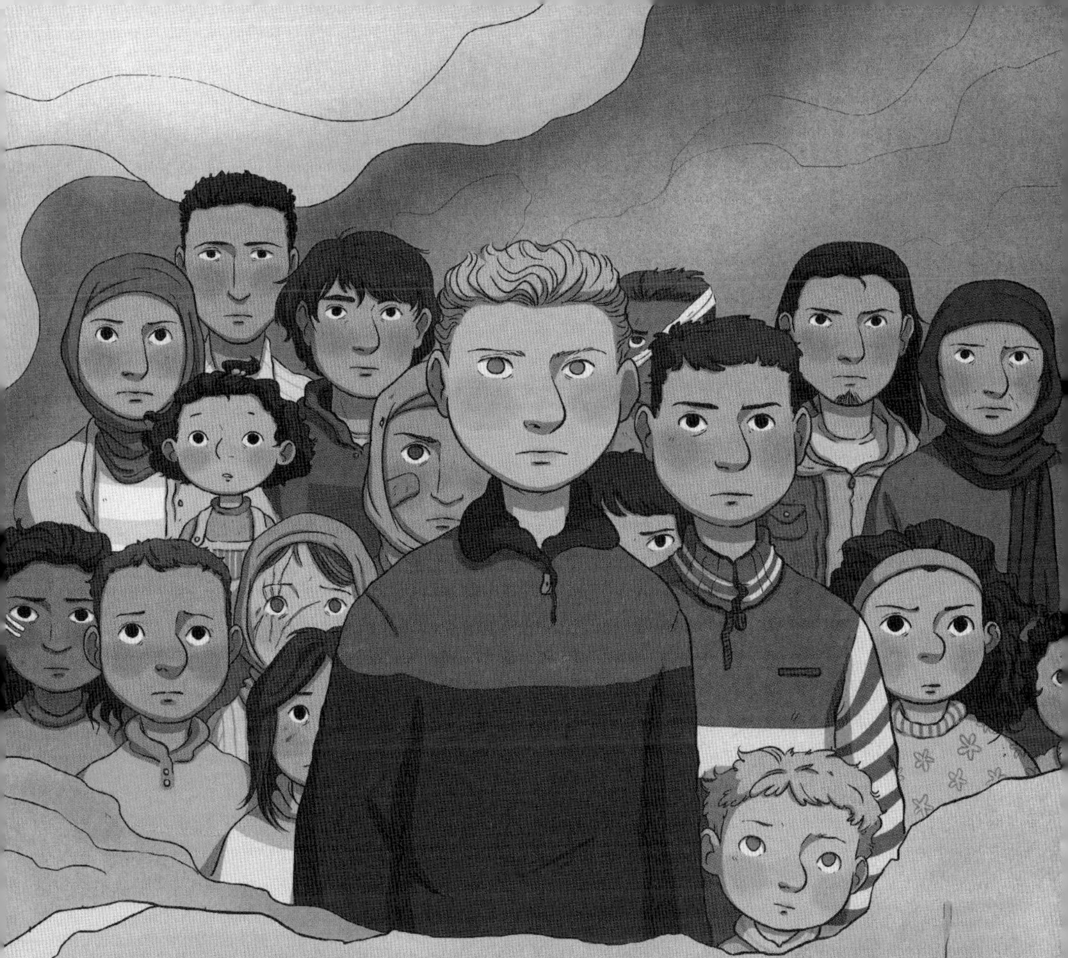

In reality, there were almost 350,000 civilians caught in the siege. We were pawns in their war.

But this time, we couldn't leave. Government forces blocked the roads. Instead, we were driven underground.

The men in our community dug out even more shelters and built tunnels connecting them so we could move from house to house without going aboveground and risking our lives.

Hundreds of people died almost every day.

The secretary-general of the United Nations called it "hell on Earth."

He was right.

CHAPTER 11

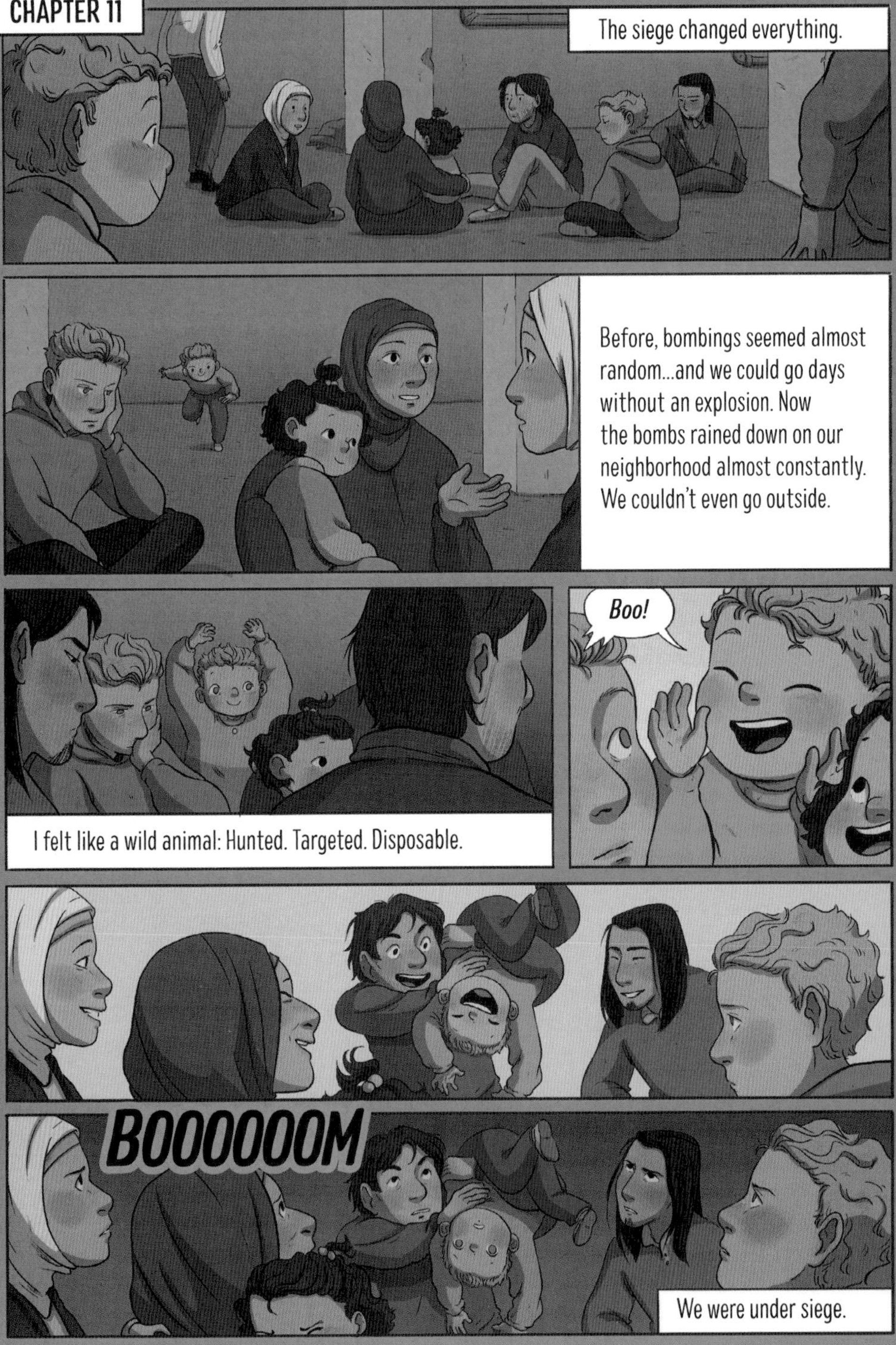
The siege changed everything.
Before, bombings seemed almost random...and we could go days without an explosion. Now the bombs rained down on our neighborhood almost constantly. We couldn't even go outside.
I felt like a wild animal: Hunted. Targeted. Disposable.
Boo!
BOOOOOOM
We were under siege.

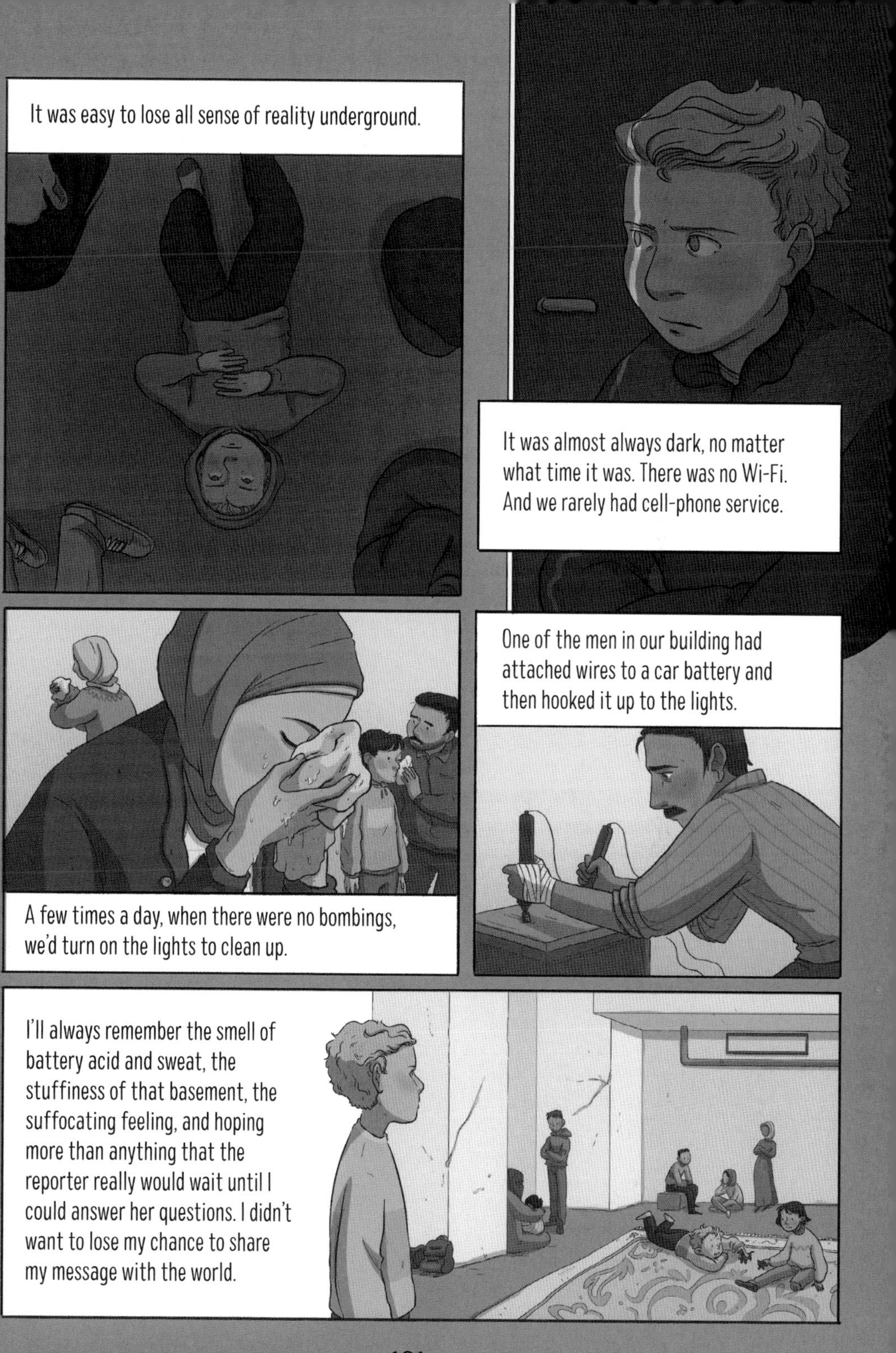
It was easy to lose all sense of reality underground.
It was almost always dark, no matter what time it was. There was no Wi-Fi. And we rarely had cell-phone service.
A few times a day, when there were no bombings, we'd turn on the lights to clean up.
One of the men in our building had attached wires to a car battery and then hooked it up to the lights.
I'll always remember the smell of battery acid and sweat, the stuffiness of that basement, the suffocating feeling, and hoping more than anything that the reporter really would wait until I could answer her questions. I didn't want to lose my chance to share my message with the world.

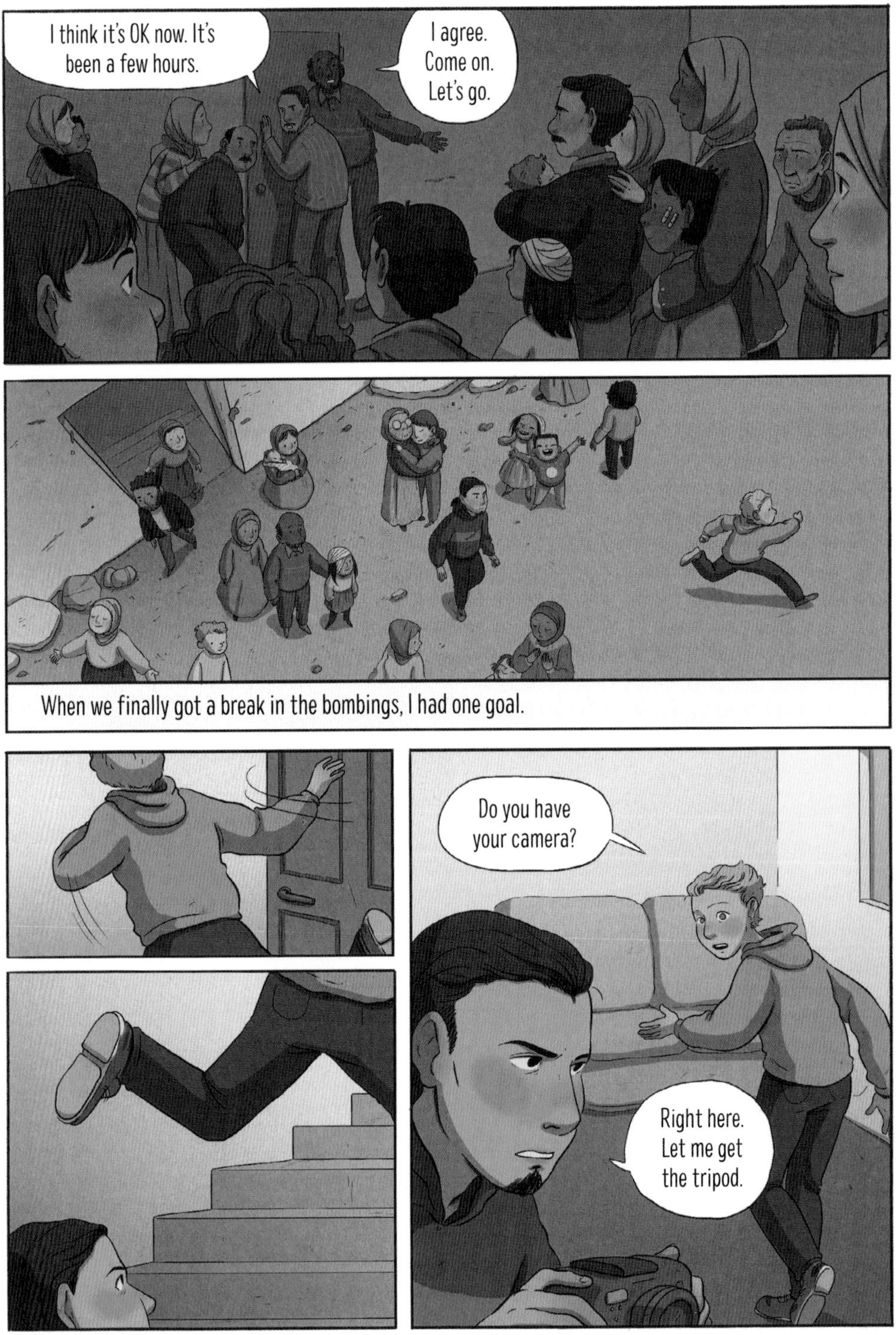
I think it's OK now. It's been a few hours.
I agree. Come on. Let's go.
When we finally got a break in the bombings, I had one goal.
Do you have your camera?
Right here. Let me get the tripod.

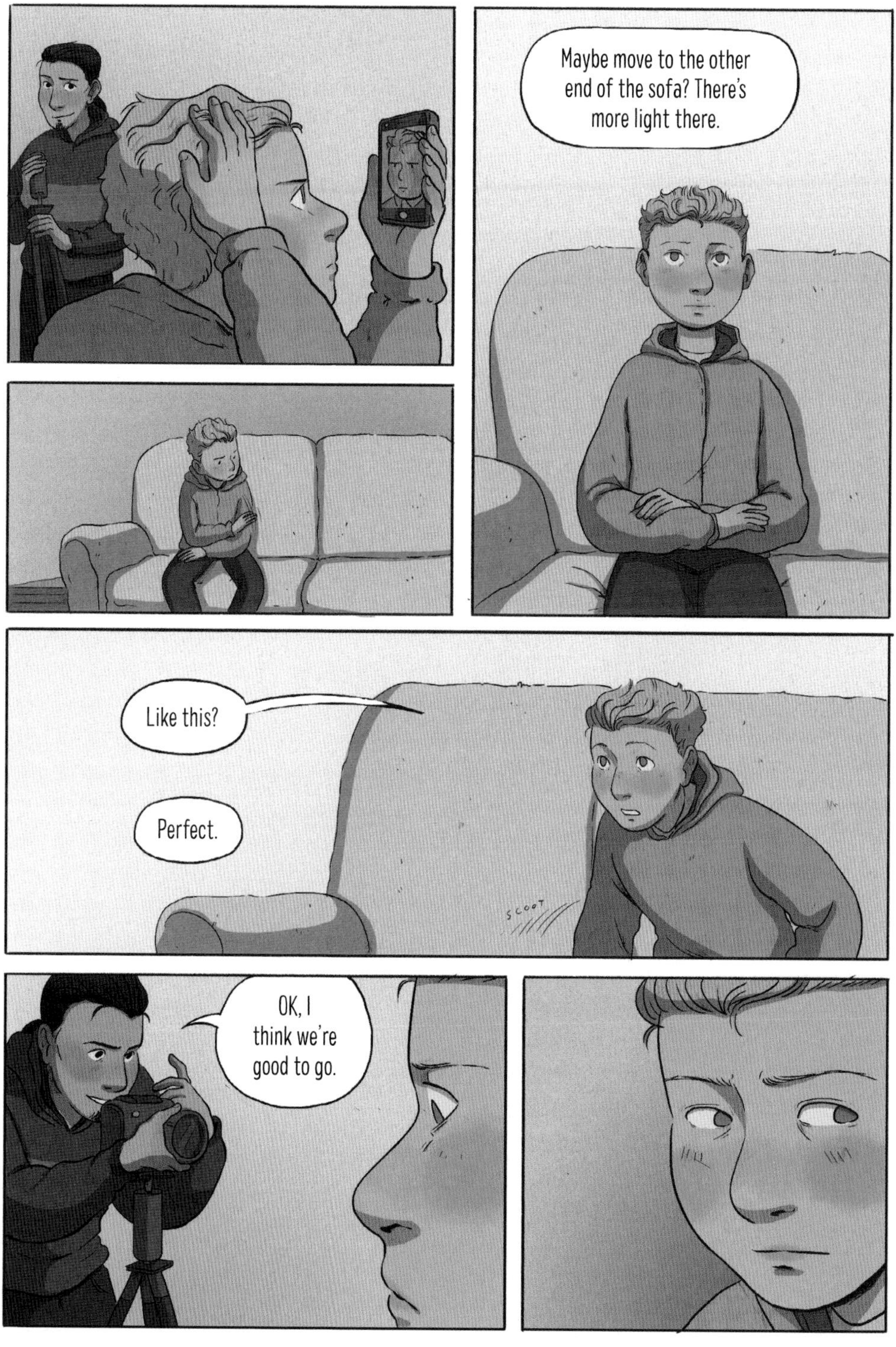
Maybe move to the other end of the sofa? There's more light there.
Like this?
Perfect.
SCOOT
OK, I think we're good to go.

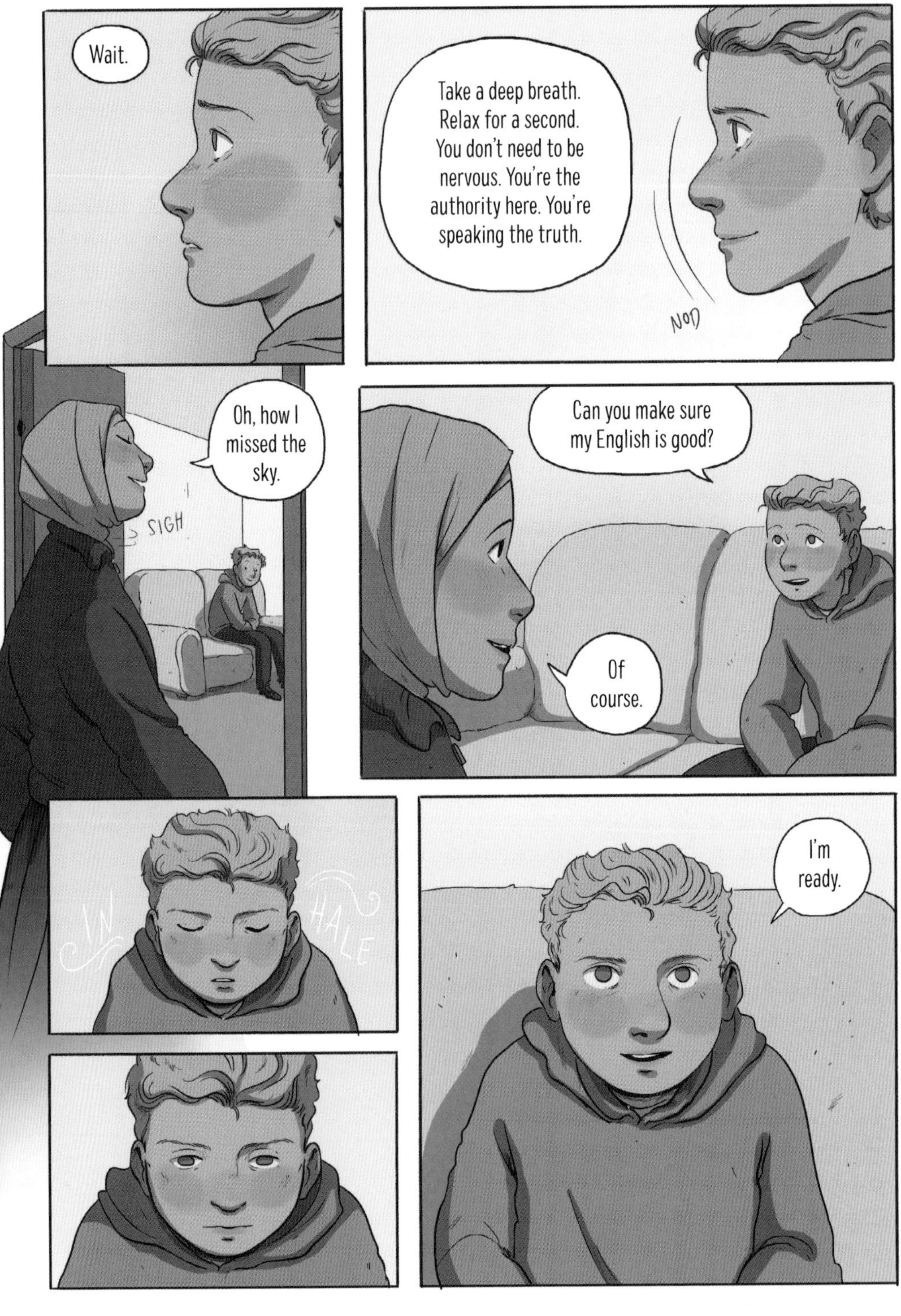
Wait.
Take a deep breath. Relax for a second. You don't need to be nervous. You're the authority here. You're speaking the truth.
NOD
Oh, how I missed the sky.
SIGH
Can you make sure my English is good?
Of course.
IN HALE
I'm ready.

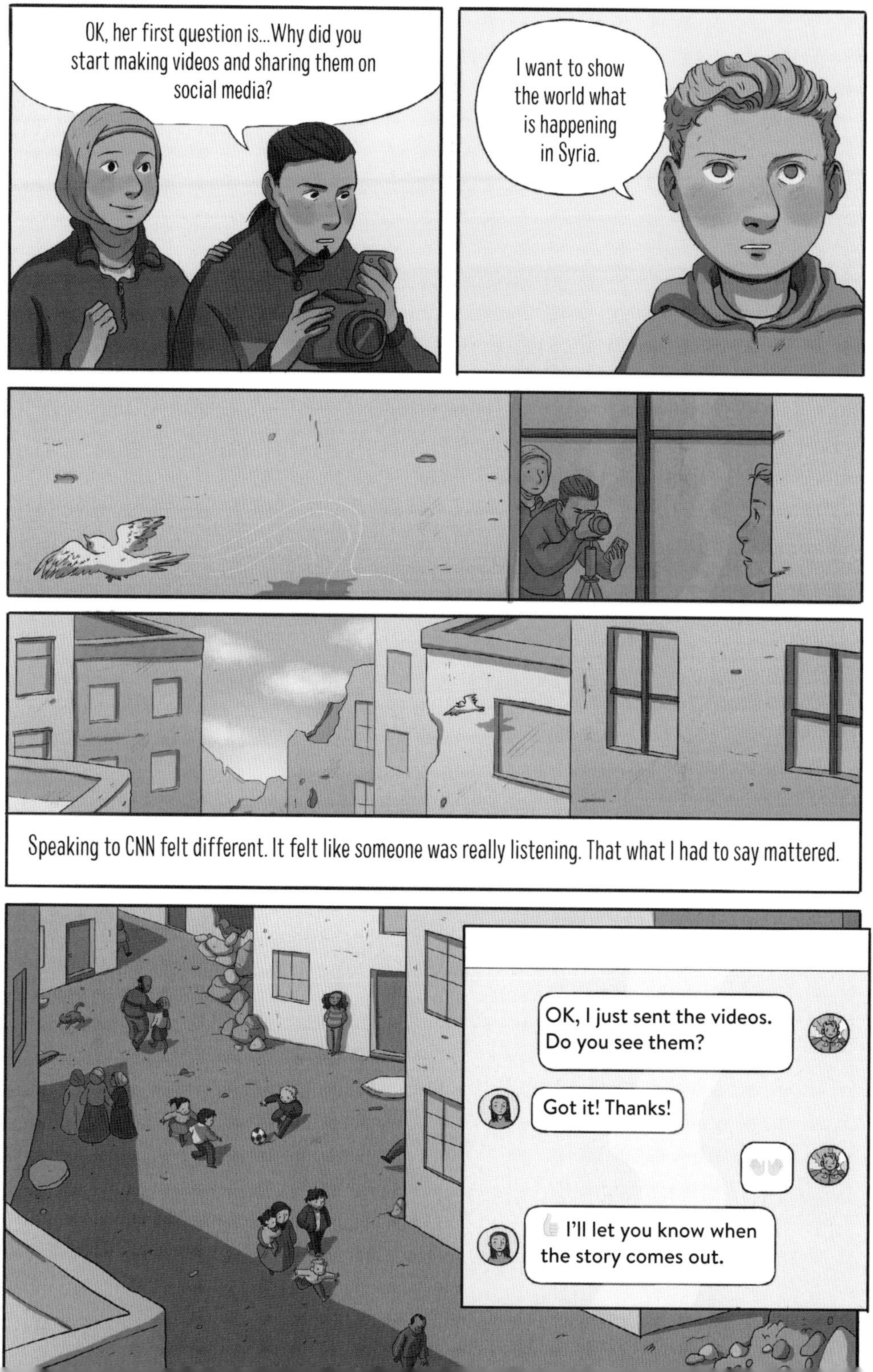
OK, her first question is...Why did you start making videos and sharing them on social media?
I want to show the world what is happening in Syria.
Speaking to CNN felt different. It felt like someone was really listening. That what I had to say mattered.
OK, I just sent the videos. Do you see them?
Got it! Thanks!
I'll let you know when the story comes out.

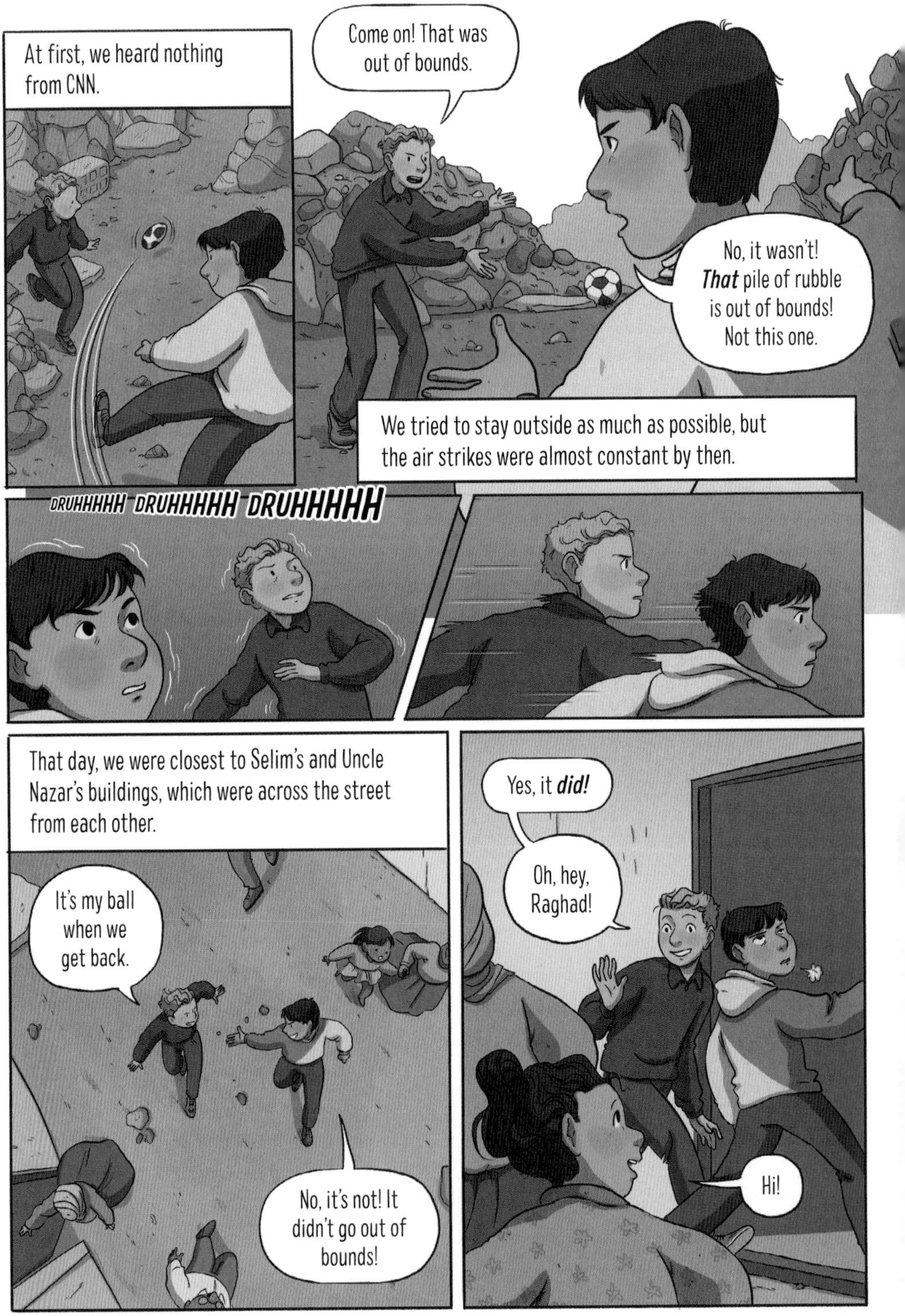
At first, we heard nothing from CNN.
Come on! That was out of bounds.
No, it wasn't! *That* pile of rubble is out of bounds! Not this one.
We tried to stay outside as much as possible, but the air strikes were almost constant by then.
DRUHHHHH DRUHHHHH DRUHHHHH
That day, we were closest to Selim's and Uncle Nazar's buildings, which were across the street from each other.
It's my ball when we get back.
No, it's not! It didn't go out of bounds!
Yes, it *did!*
Oh, hey, Raghad!
Hi!

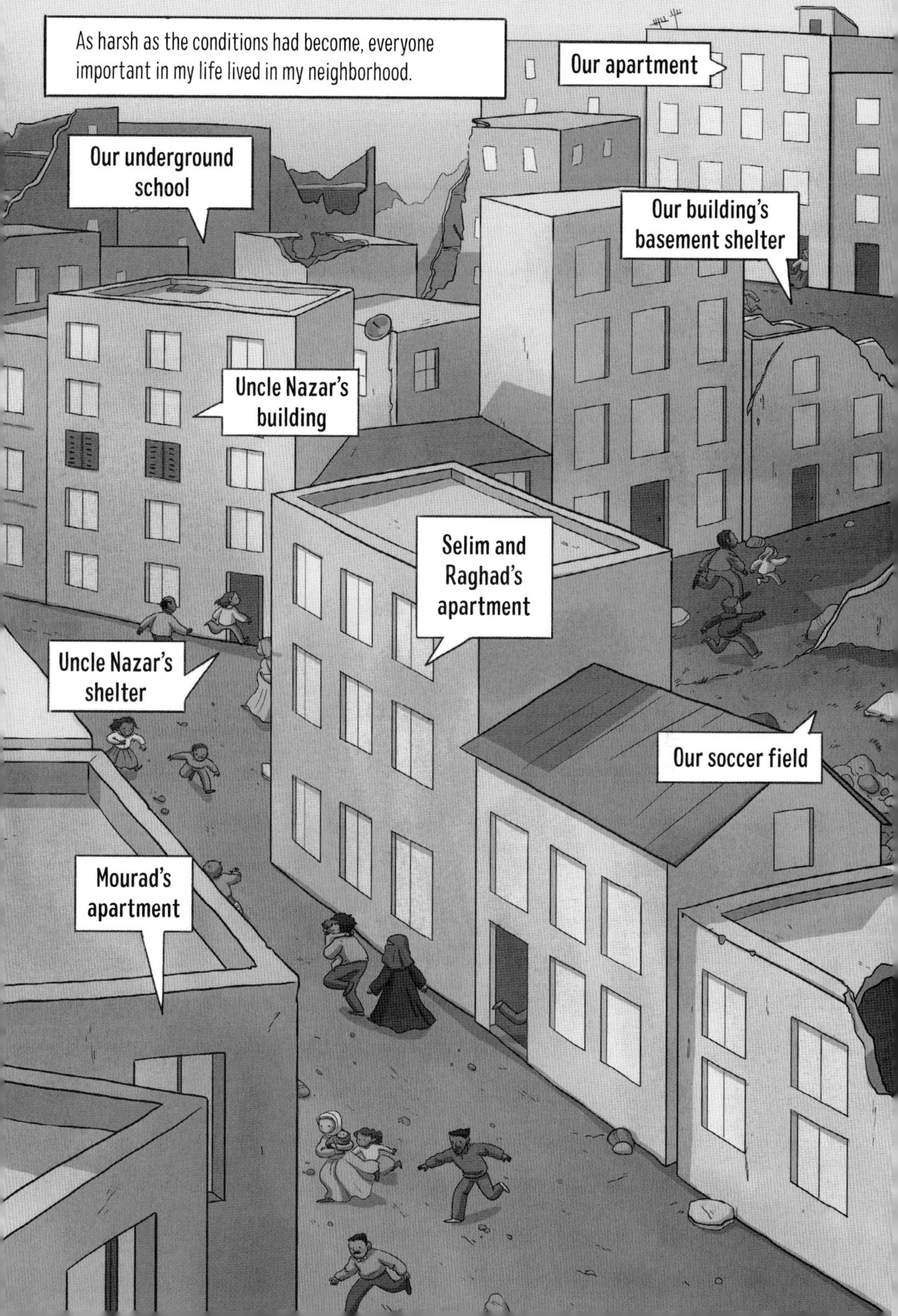

As harsh as the conditions had become, everyone important in my life lived in my neighborhood.
Our apartment
Our underground school
Our building's basement shelter
Uncle Nazar's building
Selim and Raghad's apartment
Uncle Nazar's shelter
Our soccer field
Mourad's apartment

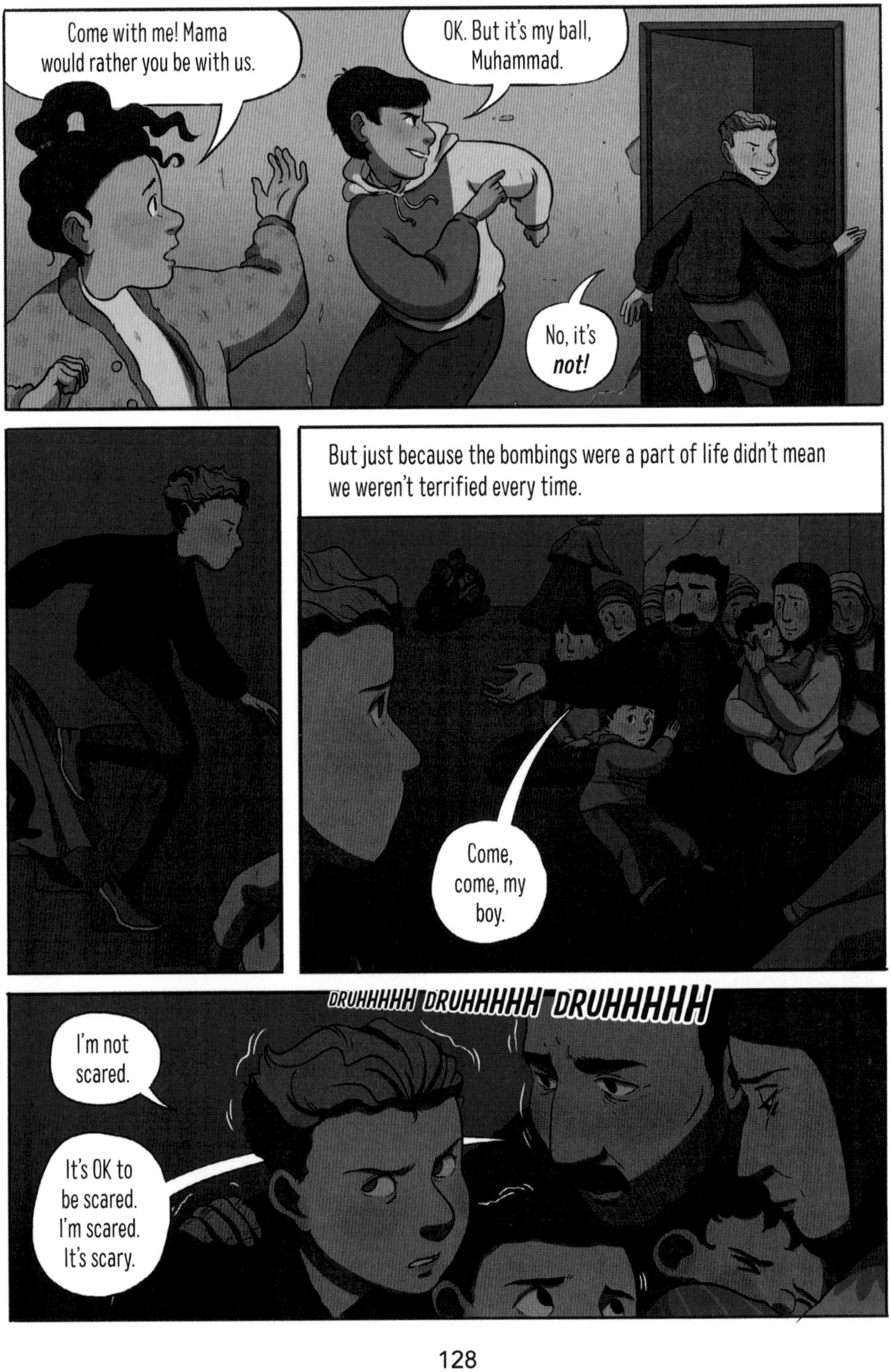
Come with me! Mama would rather you be with us.
OK. But it's my ball, Muhammad.
No, it's *not!*
But just because the bombings were a part of life didn't mean we weren't terrified every time.
Come, come, my boy.
DRUHHHHH DRUHHHHH DRUHHHHH
I'm not scared.
It's OK to be scared. I'm scared. It's scary.

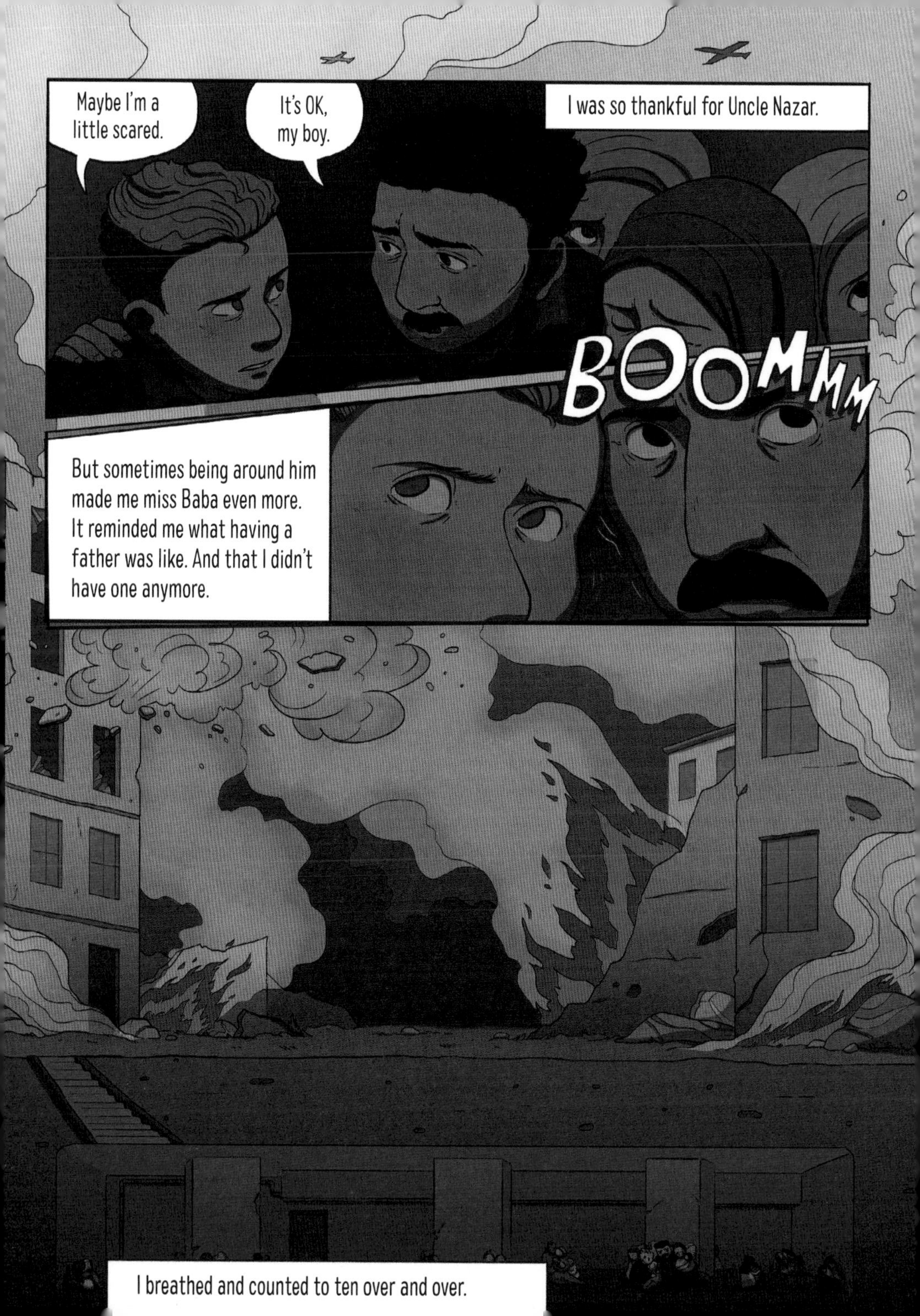
Maybe I'm a little scared.
It's OK, my boy.
I was so thankful for Uncle Nazar.
BOOMMM
But sometimes being around him made me miss Baba even more. It reminded me what having a father was like. And that I didn't have one anymore.
I breathed and counted to ten over and over.

CHAPTER 12

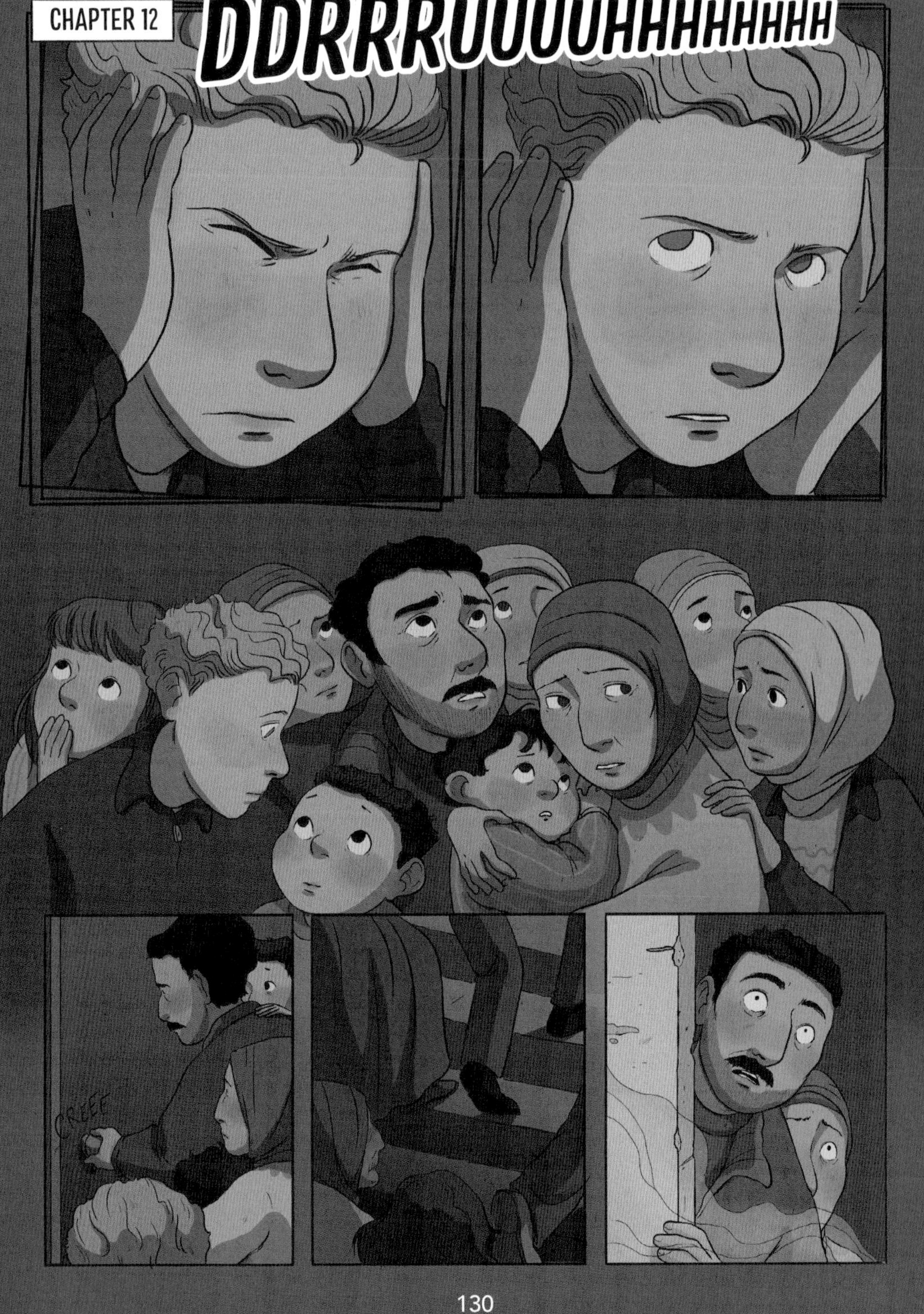
DDRRRUUUUHHHHHHHH
CREEE

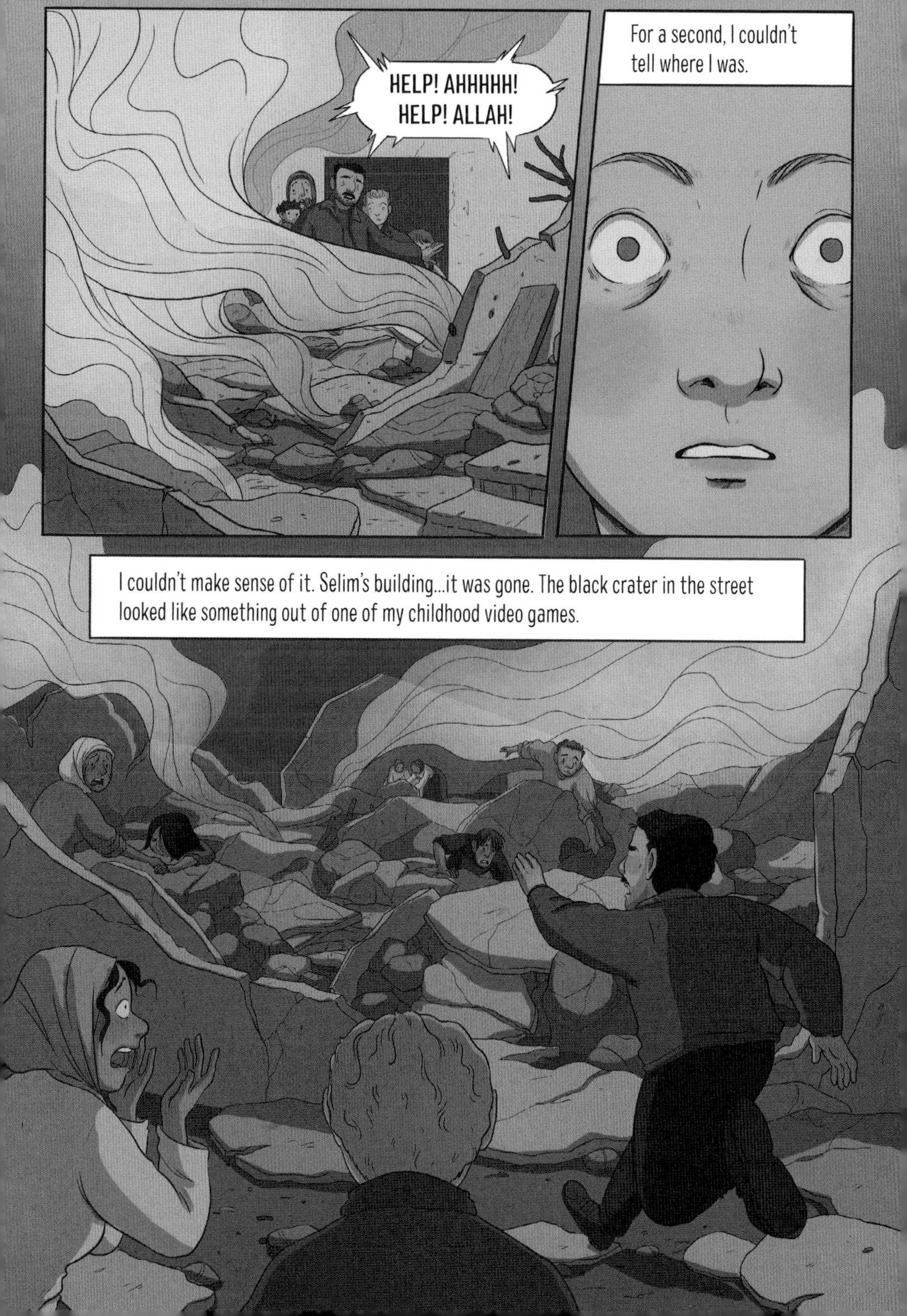
HELP! AHHHHH! HELP! ALLAH!
For a second, I couldn't tell where I was.
I couldn't make sense of it. Selim's building...it was gone. The black crater in the street looked like something out of one of my childhood video games.

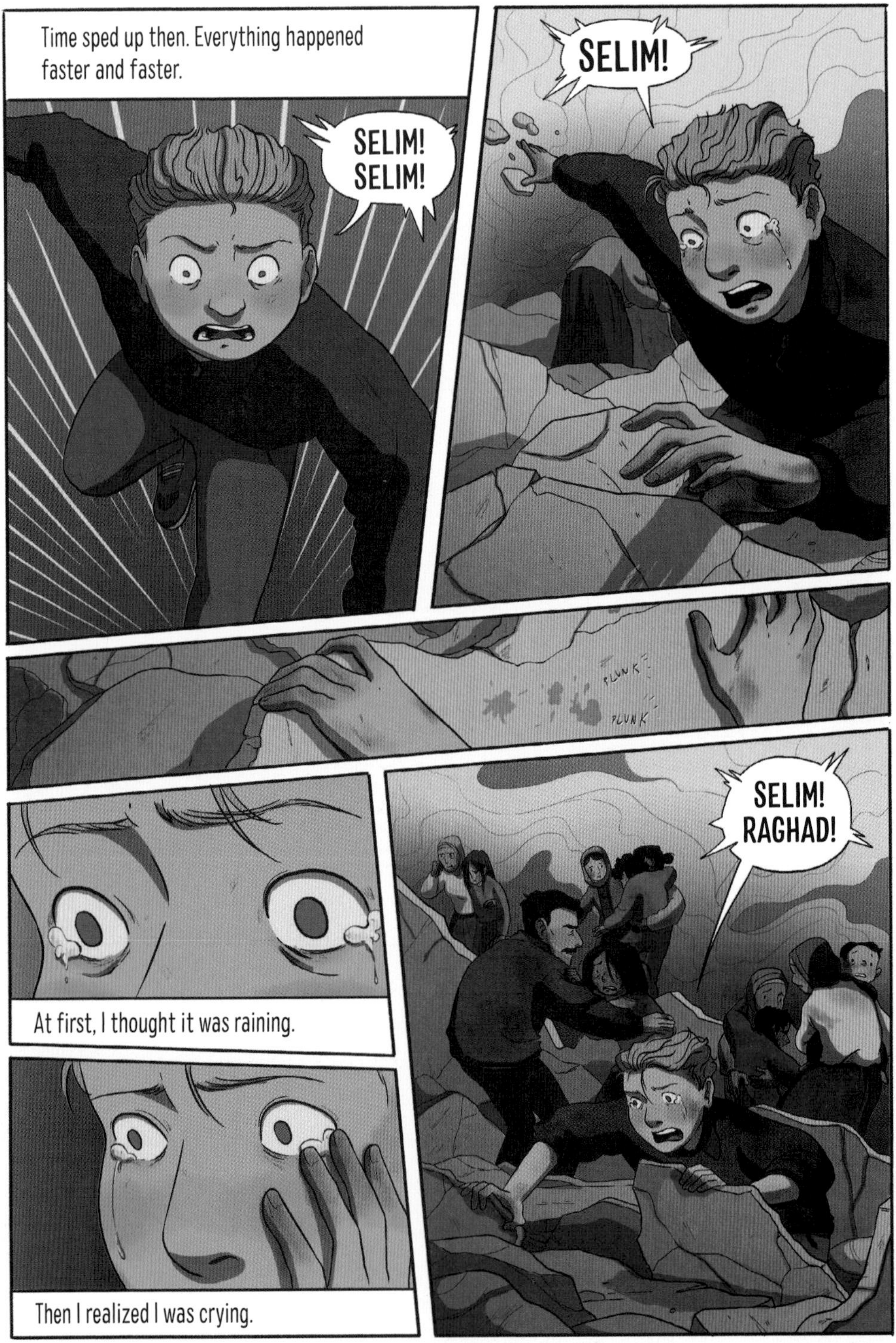
Time sped up then. Everything happened faster and faster.
SELIM! SELIM!
SELIM!
PLUNK
PLUNK
At first, I thought it was raining.
Then I realized I was crying.
SELIM! RAGHAD!

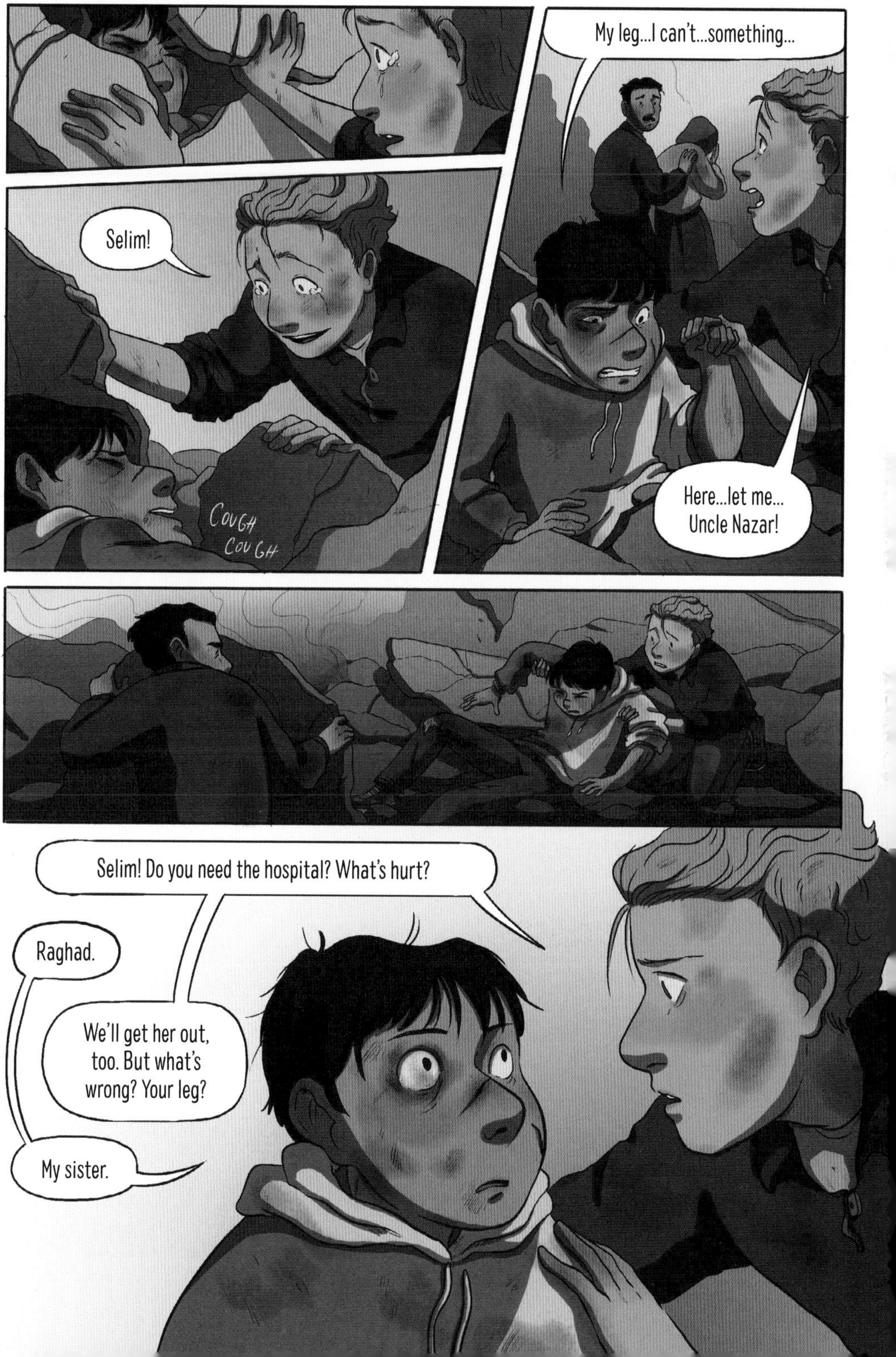
My leg...I can't...something...
Selim!
COUGH
COUGH
Here...let me...
Uncle Nazar!
Selim! Do you need the hospital? What's hurt?
Raghad.
We'll get her out, too. But what's wrong? Your leg?
My sister.

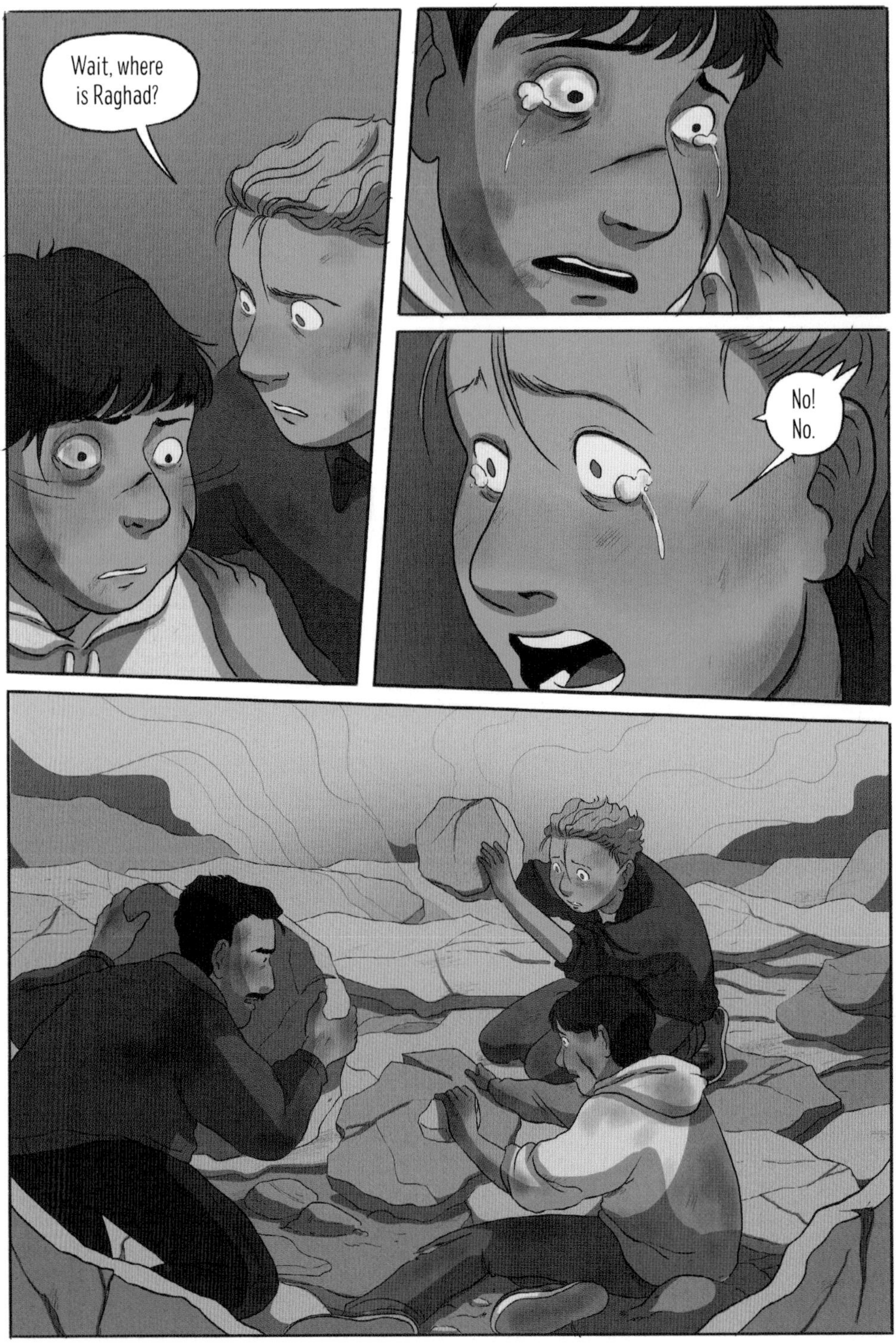
Wait, where is Raghad?
No! No.

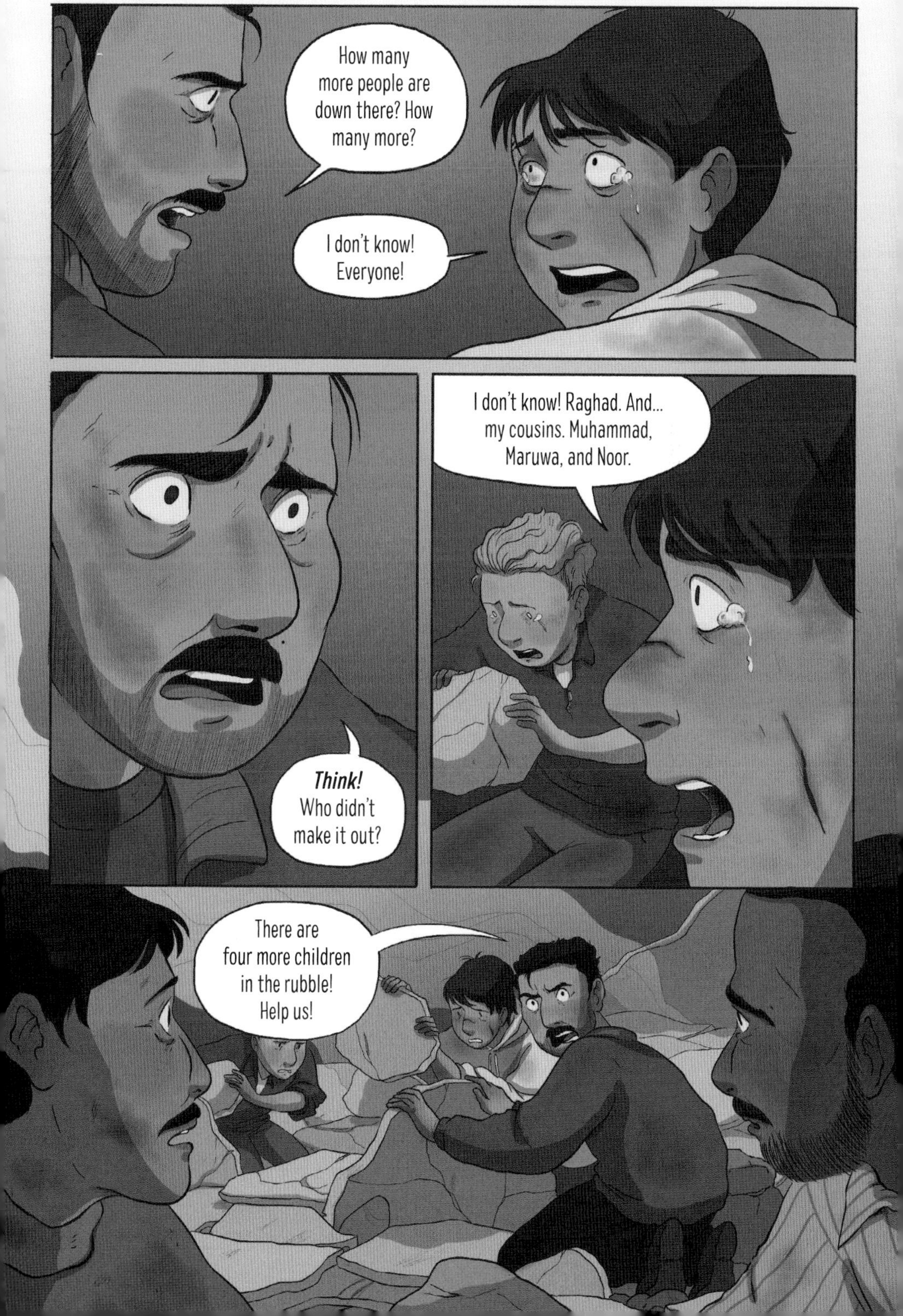
How many more people are down there? How many more?
I don't know! Everyone!
Think! Who didn't make it out?
I don't know! Raghad. And... my cousins. Muhammad, Maruwa, and Noor.
There are four more children in the rubble! Help us!

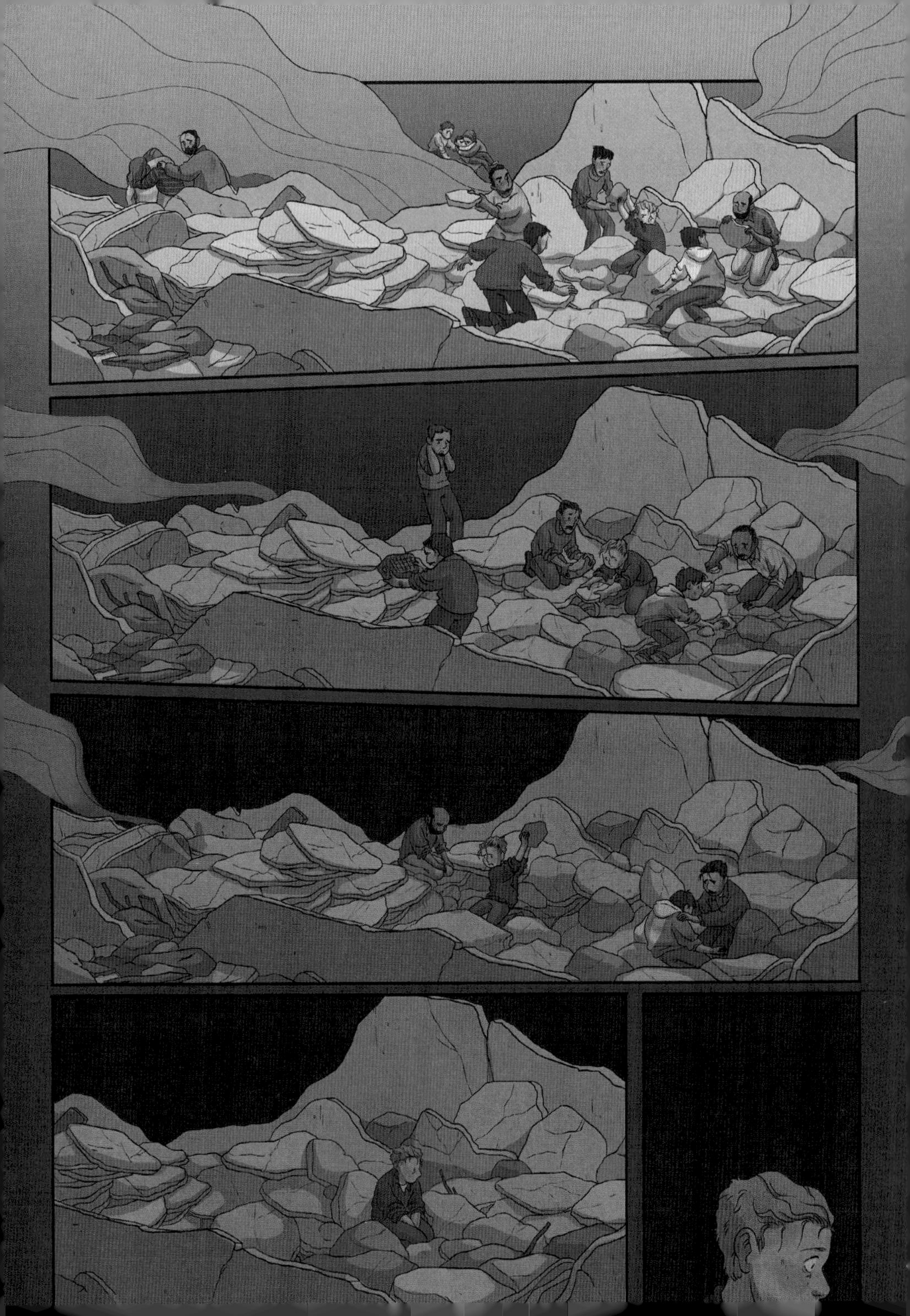

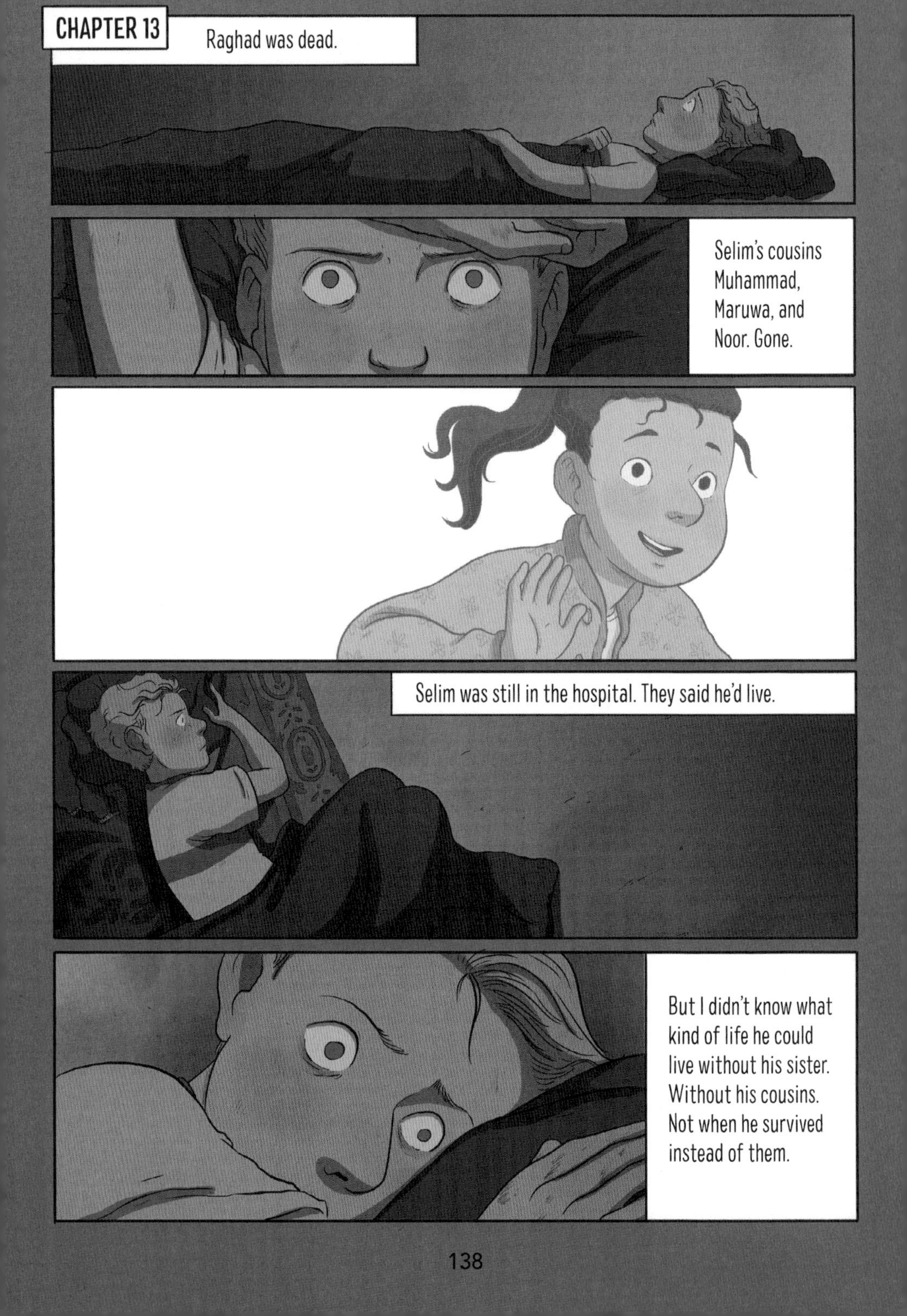
CHAPTER 13
Raghad was dead.
Selim's cousins Muhammad, Maruwa, and Noor. Gone.
Selim was still in the hospital. They said he'd live.
But I didn't know what kind of life he could live without his sister. Without his cousins. Not when he survived instead of them.

The next few days felt a little like after Baba died.

It felt a little like sleepwalking.

But also I felt like I didn't deserve to be this upset.

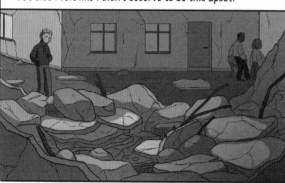

It wasn't *my* sister.

But it felt like it. Selim felt like family. If only I'd told them to come with me...to come shelter in Uncle Nazar's building...

Thoughts of "what if" are never helpful, my boy.

He knew just what I was thinking.

Did you know I was next to your father when he was killed?

You were?

We were praying. Like every Friday. We placed our mats next to each other, right in front—near the only window—so we could pray in the light.

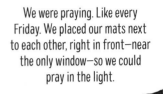

The missile came straight through the window. It was a small one. Somehow it hit your father and nobody else. I could feel the heat. I fell backward. But I was OK. And your father...

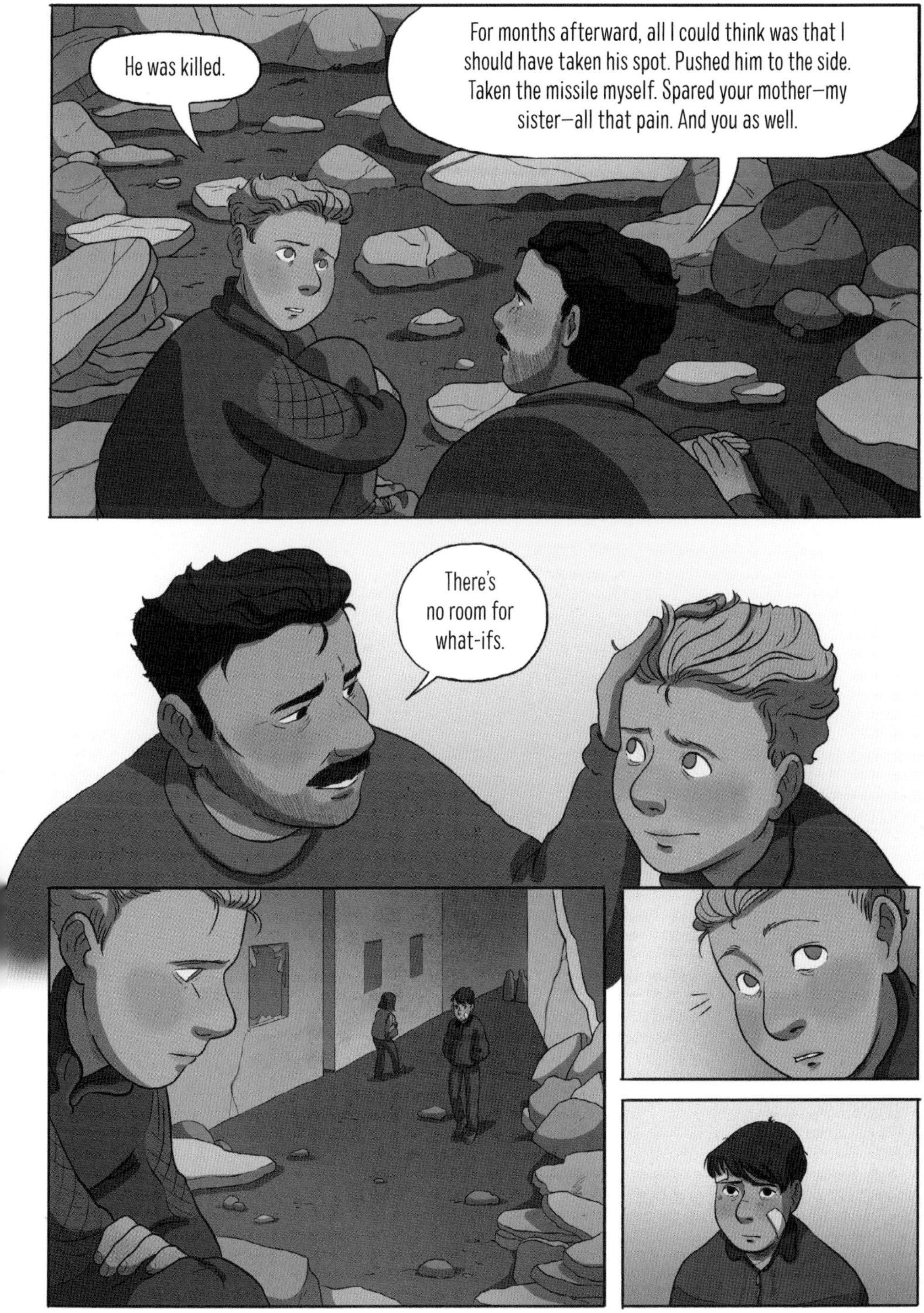
He was killed.
For months afterward, all I could think was that I should have taken his spot. Pushed him to the side. Taken the missile myself. Spared your mother—my sister—all that pain. And you as well.
There's no room for what-ifs.

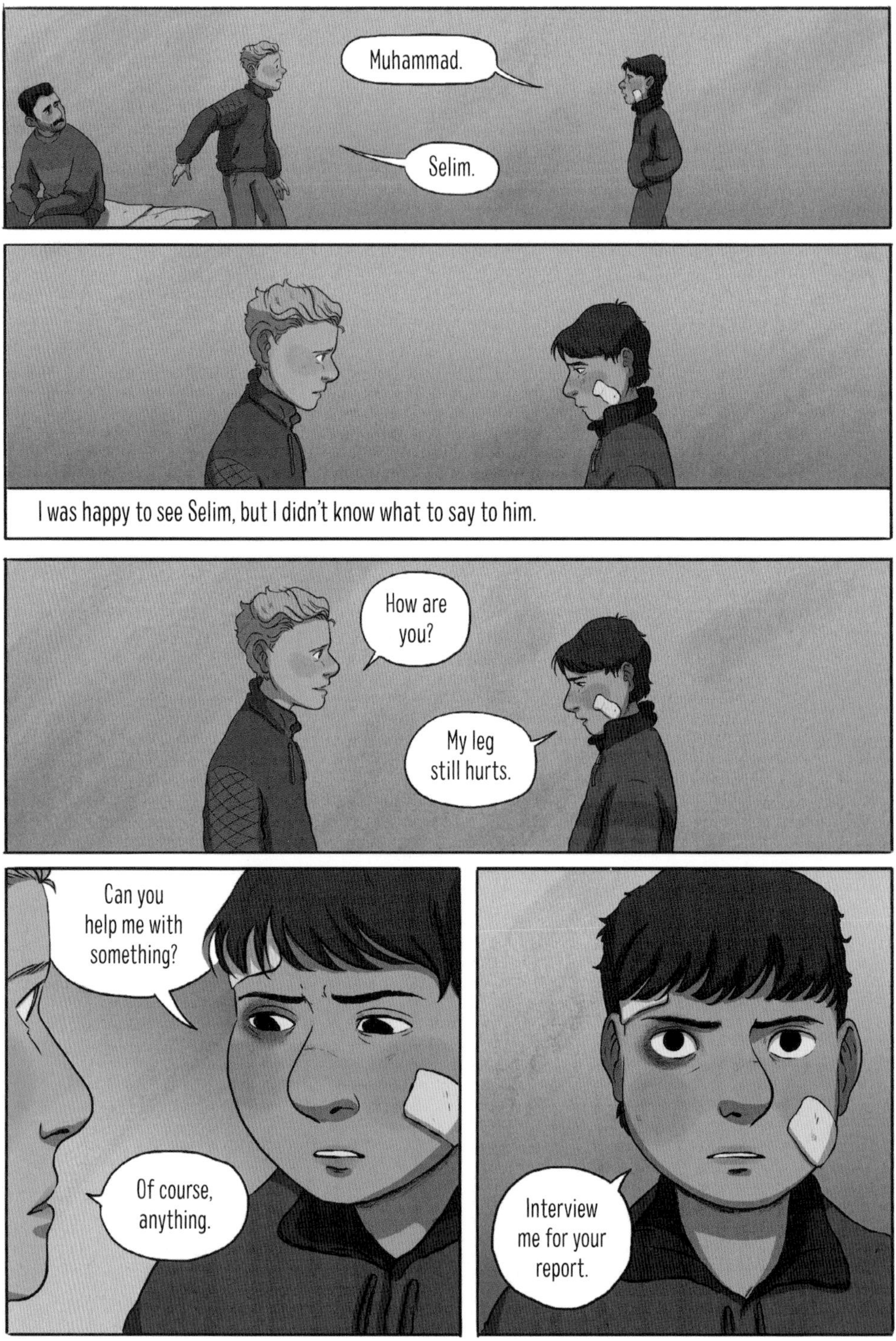
Muhammad.
Selim.
I was happy to see Selim, but I didn't know what to say to him.
How are you?
My leg still hurts.
Can you help me with something?
Of course, anything.
Interview me for your report.

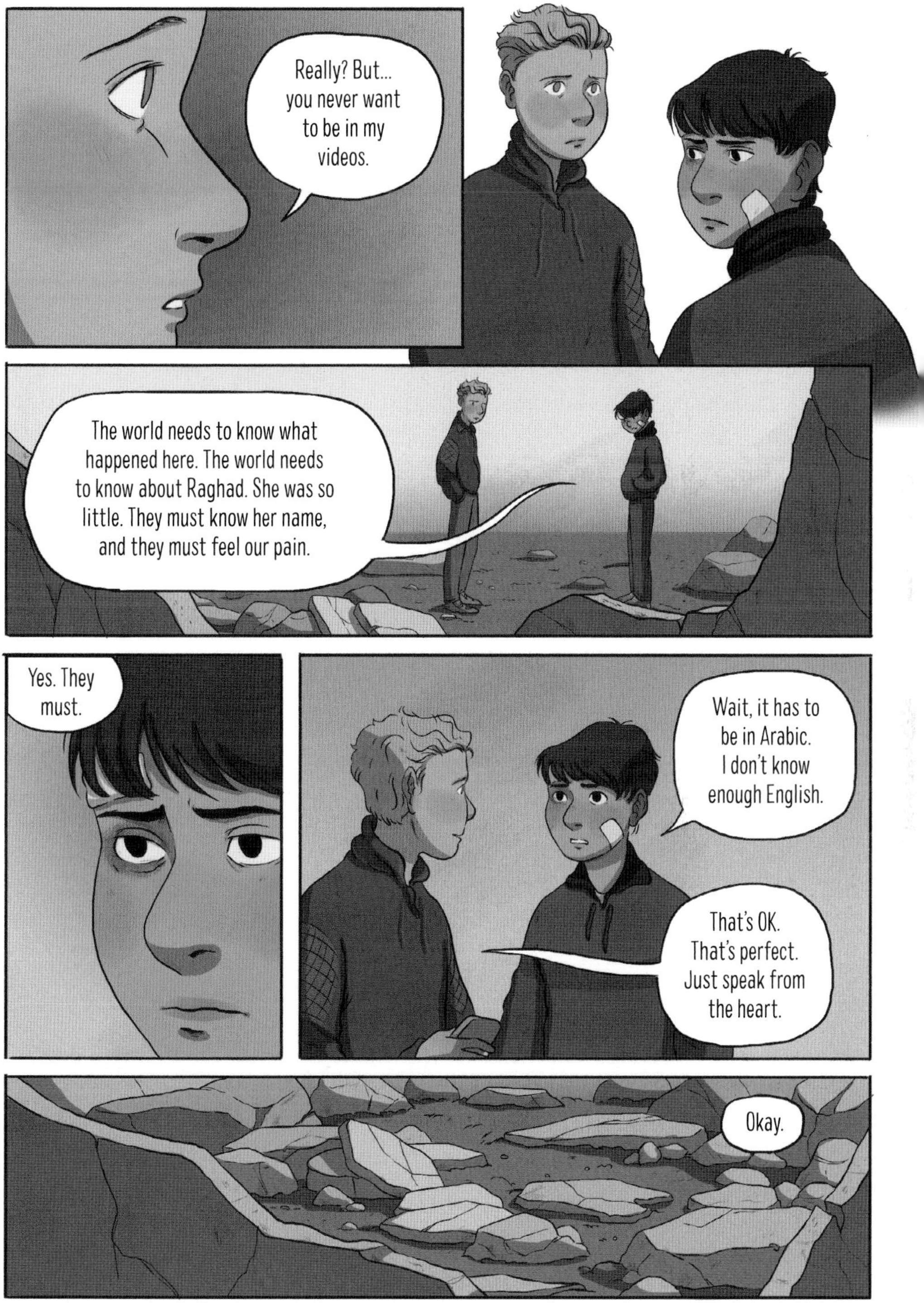

Really? But... you never want to be in my videos.
The world needs to know what happened here. The world needs to know about Raghad. She was so little. They must know her name, and they must feel our pain.
Yes. They must.
Wait, it has to be in Arabic. I don't know enough English.
That's OK. That's perfect. Just speak from the heart.
Okay.

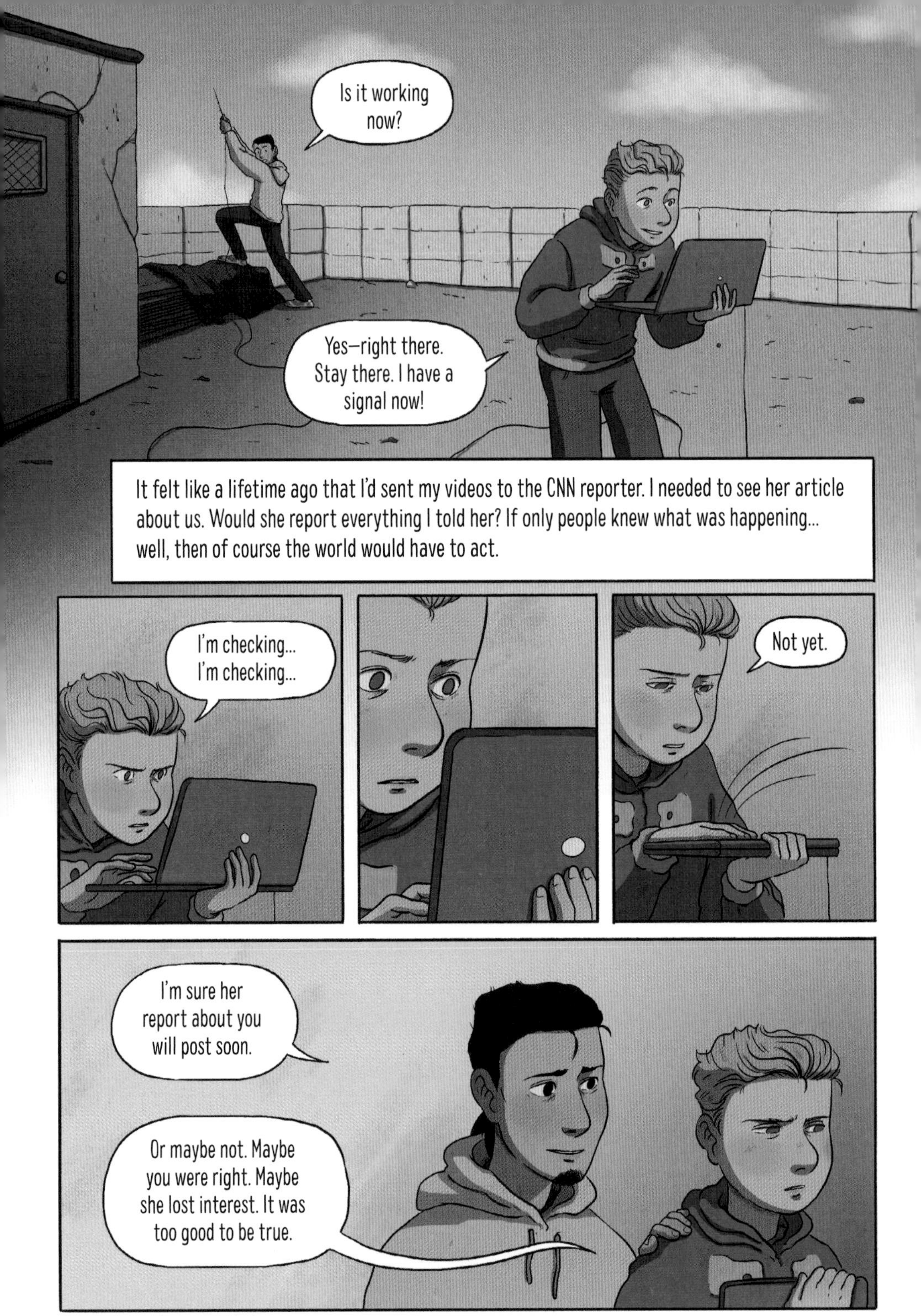
Is it working now?
Yes—right there. Stay there. I have a signal now!
It felt like a lifetime ago that I'd sent my videos to the CNN reporter. I needed to see her article about us. Would she report everything I told her? If only people knew what was happening... well, then of course the world would have to act.
I'm checking... I'm checking...
Not yet.
I'm sure her report about you will post soon.
Or maybe not. Maybe you were right. Maybe she lost interest. It was too good to be true.

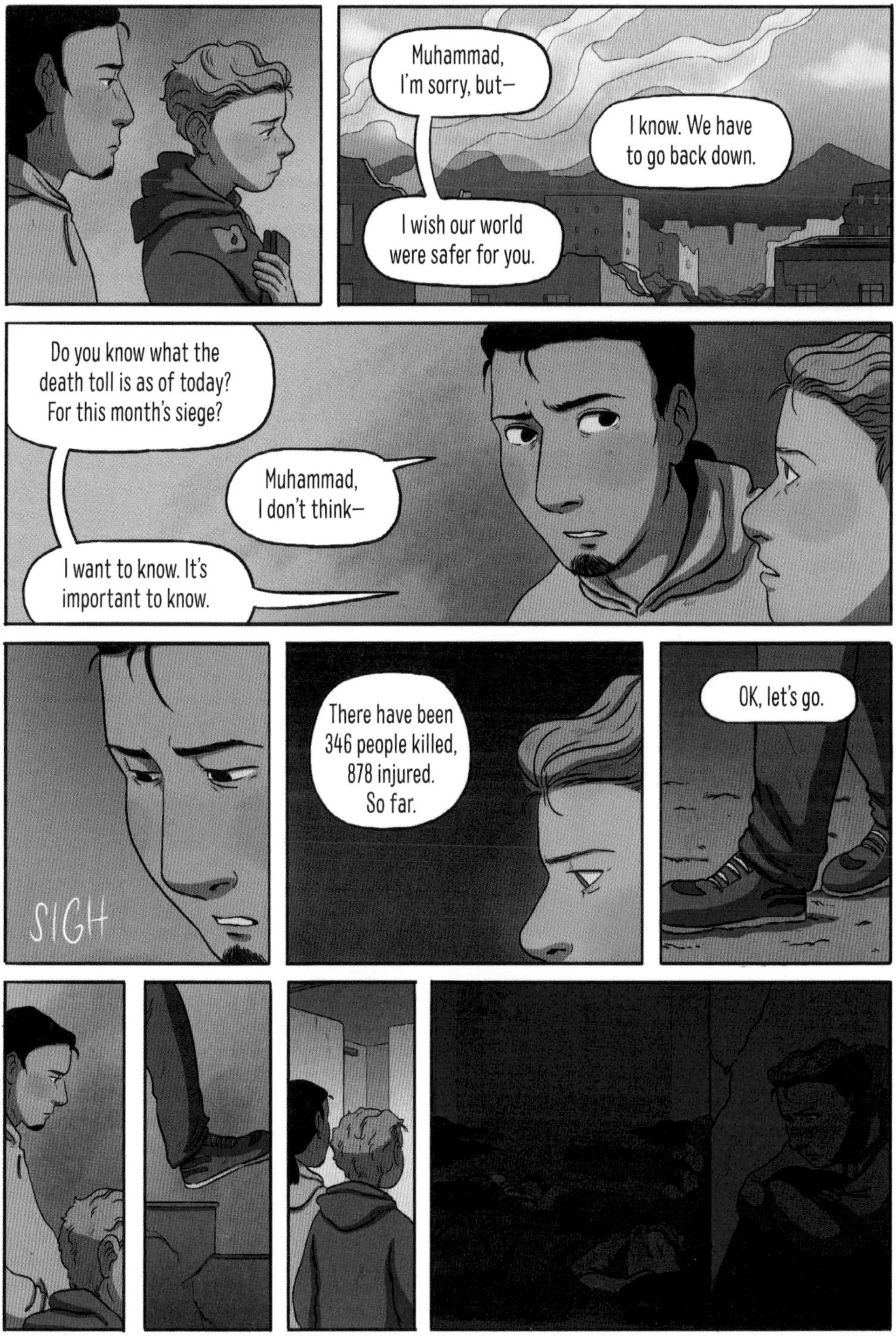
Muhammad, I'm sorry, but–
I wish our world were safer for you.
I know. We have to go back down.
Do you know what the death toll is as of today? For this month's siege?
Muhammad, I don't think–
I want to know. It's important to know.
SIGH
There have been 346 people killed, 878 injured. So far.
OK, let's go.

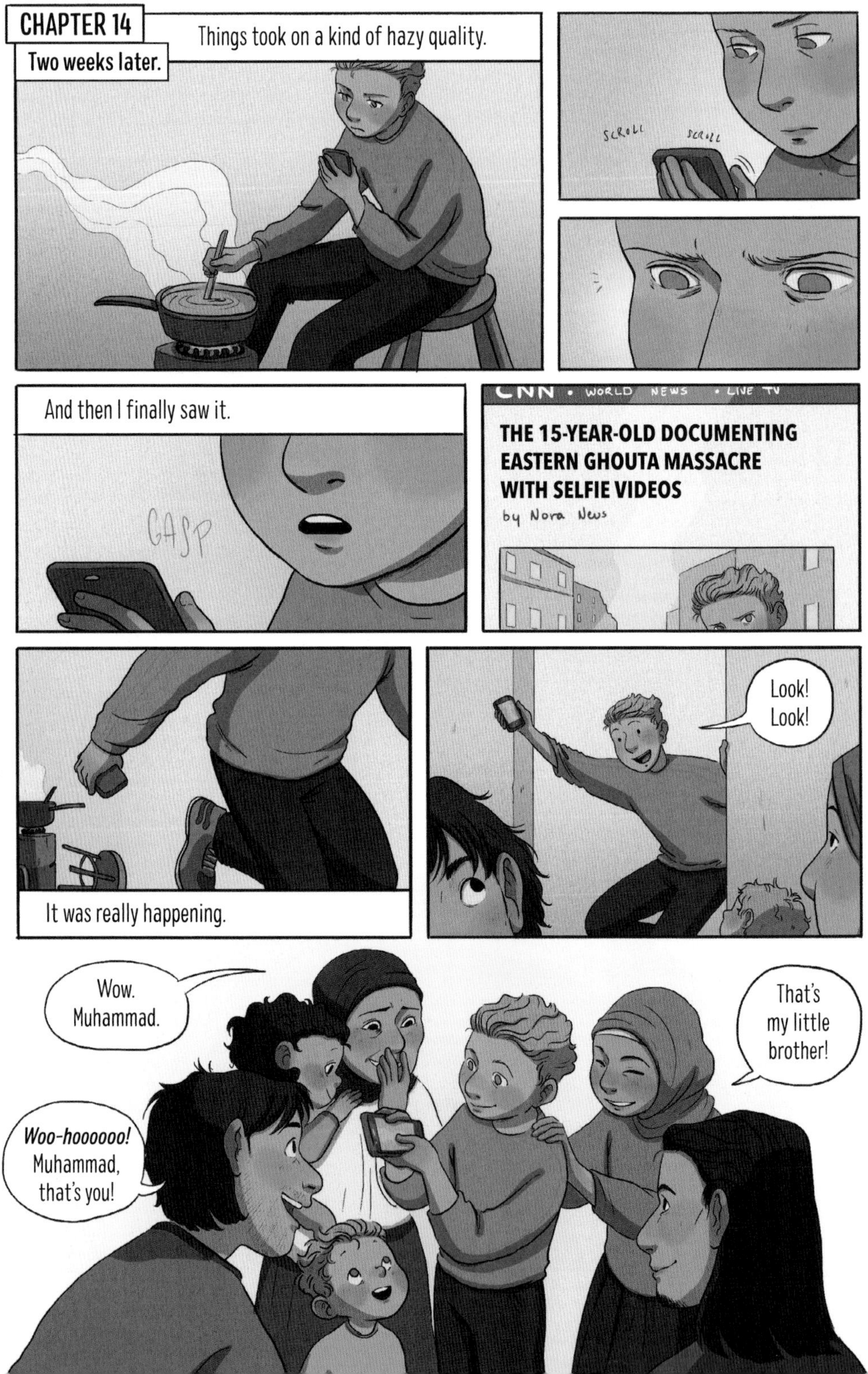
CHAPTER 14
Two weeks later.
Things took on a kind of hazy quality.
SCROLL
SCROLL
And then I finally saw it.
GASP
CNN • WORLD NEWS • LIVE TV
THE 15-YEAR-OLD DOCUMENTING EASTERN GHOUTA MASSACRE WITH SELFIE VIDEOS
by Nora News
It was really happening.
Look! Look!
Wow. Muhammad.
That's my little brother!
Woo-hoooooo! Muhammad, that's you!

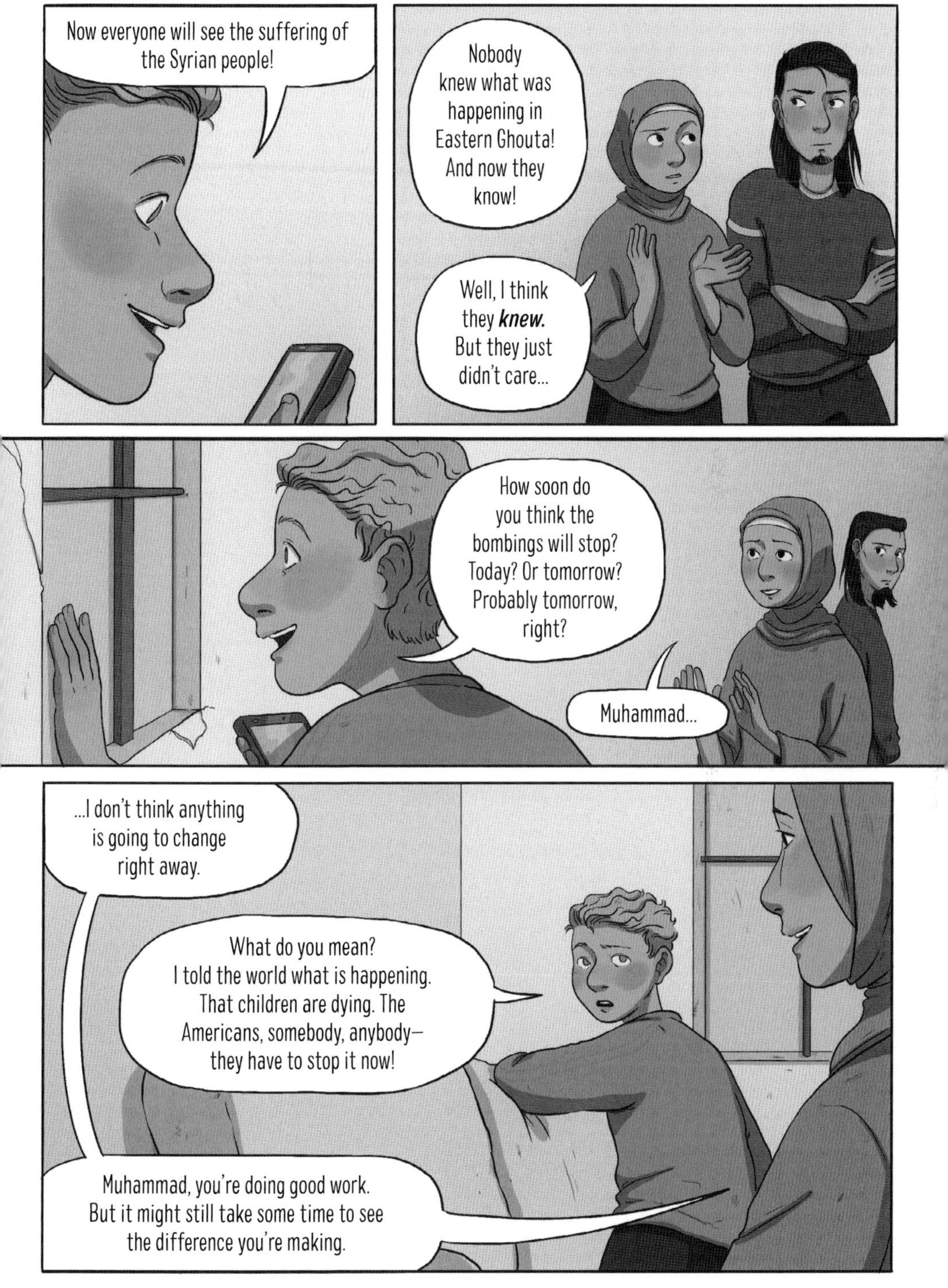
Now everyone will see the suffering of the Syrian people!
Nobody knew what was happening in Eastern Ghouta! And now they know!
Well, I think they ***knew.*** But they just didn't care...
How soon do you think the bombings will stop? Today? Or tomorrow? Probably tomorrow, right?
Muhammad...
...I don't think anything is going to change right away.
What do you mean? I told the world what is happening. That children are dying. The Americans, somebody, anybody—they have to stop it now!
Muhammad, you're doing good work. But it might still take some time to see the difference you're making.

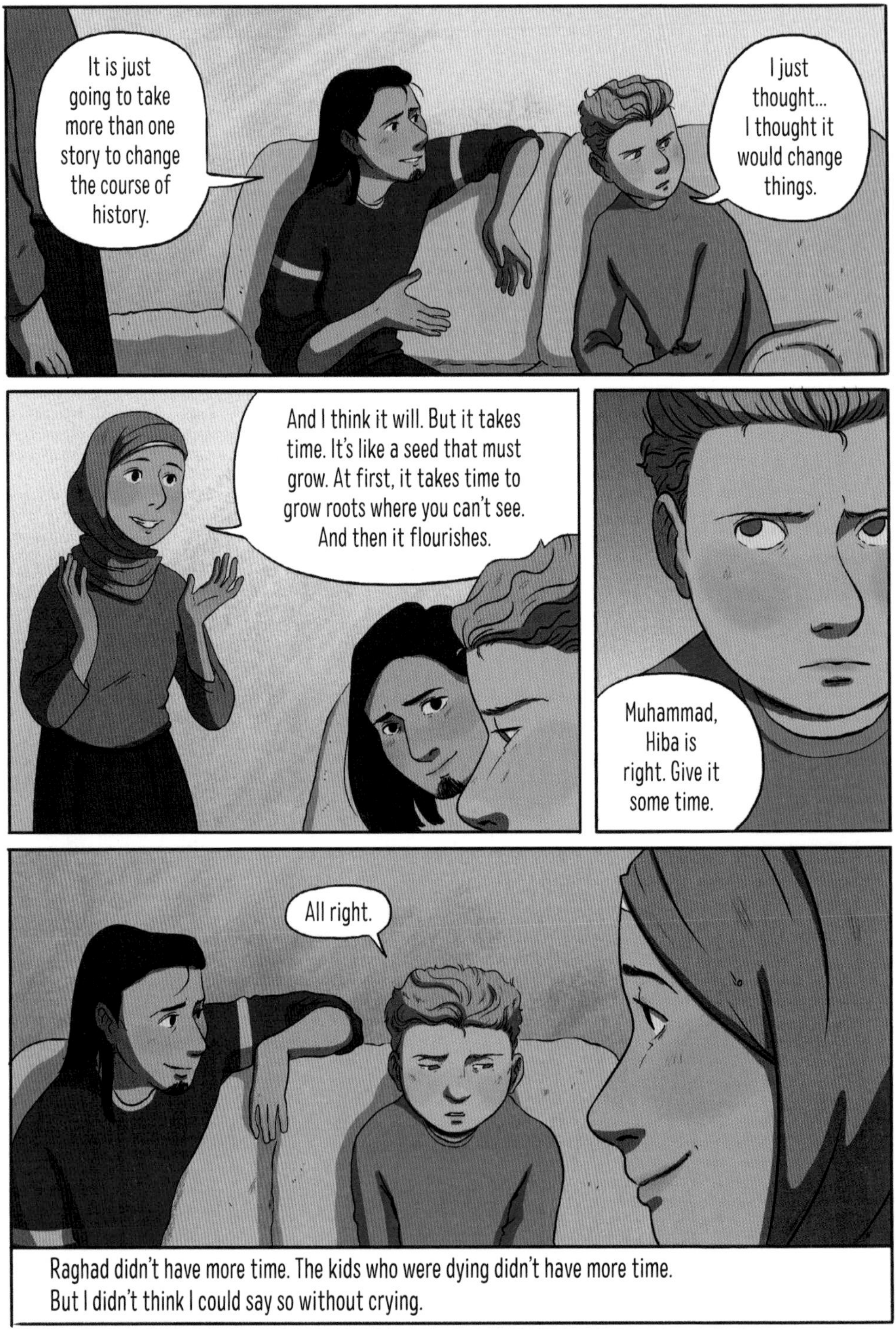
It is just going to take more than one story to change the course of history.
I just thought... I thought it would change things.
And I think it will. But it takes time. It's like a seed that must grow. At first, it takes time to grow roots where you can't see. And then it flourishes.
Muhammad, Hiba is right. Give it some time.
All right.
Raghad didn't have more time. The kids who were dying didn't have more time.
But I didn't think I could say so without crying.

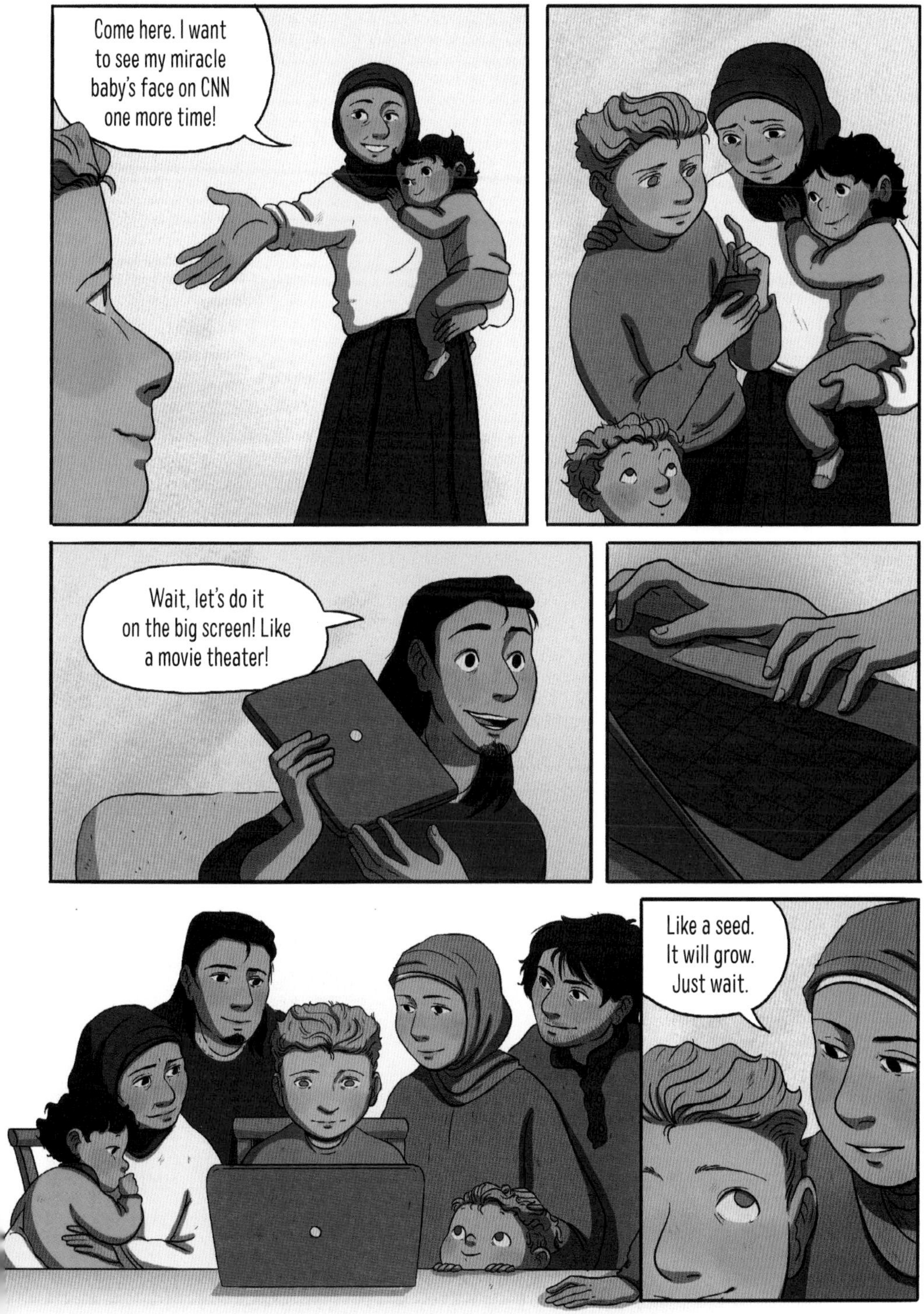
Come here. I want to see my miracle baby's face on CNN one more time!
Wait, let's do it on the big screen! Like a movie theater!
Like a seed. It will grow. Just wait.

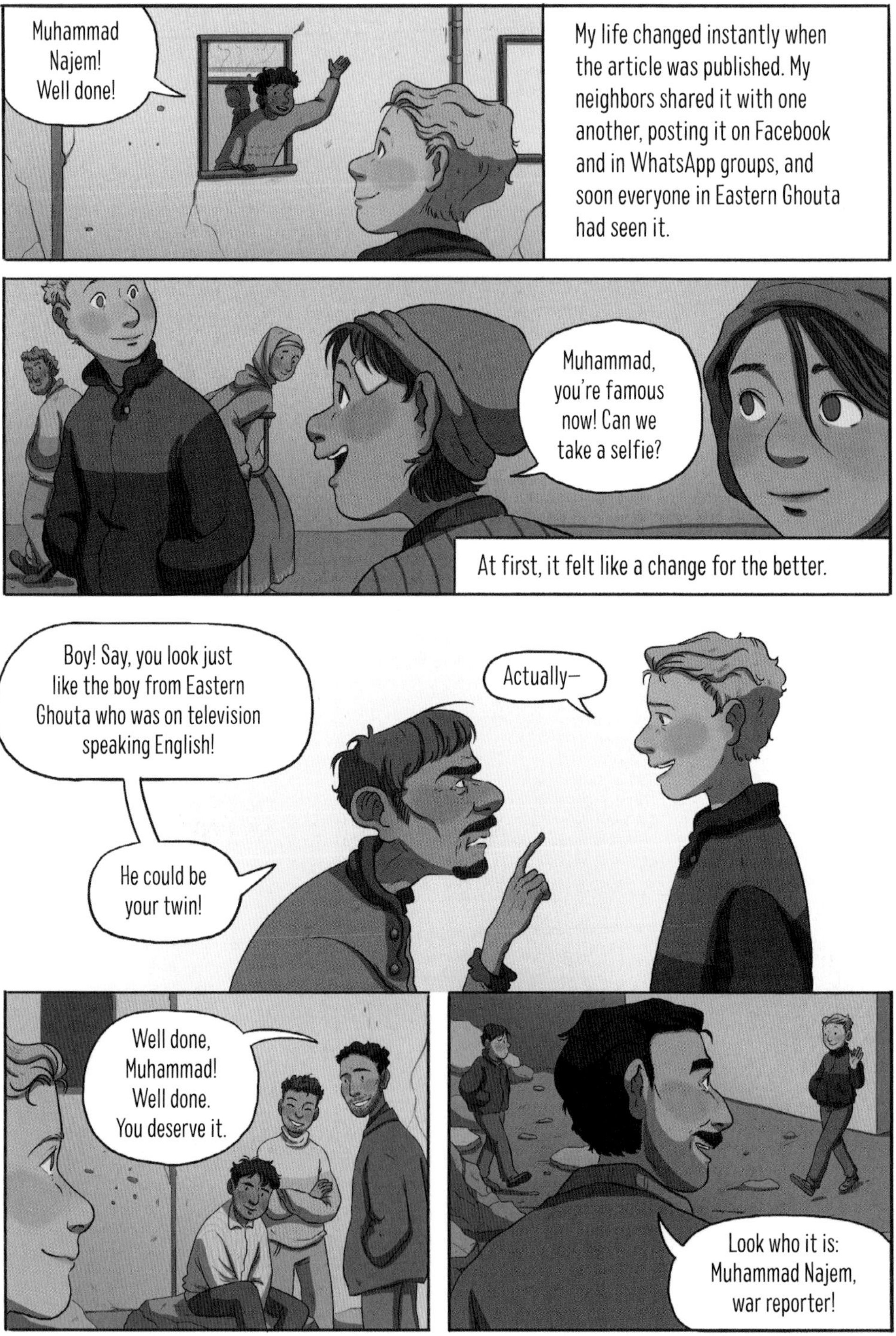

Muhammad Najem! Well done!
My life changed instantly when the article was published. My neighbors shared it with one another, posting it on Facebook and in WhatsApp groups, and soon everyone in Eastern Ghouta had seen it.
Muhammad, you're famous now! Can we take a selfie?
At first, it felt like a change for the better.
Boy! Say, you look just like the boy from Eastern Ghouta who was on television speaking English!
He could be your twin!
Actually—
Well done, Muhammad! Well done. You deserve it.
Look who it is: Muhammad Najem, war reporter!

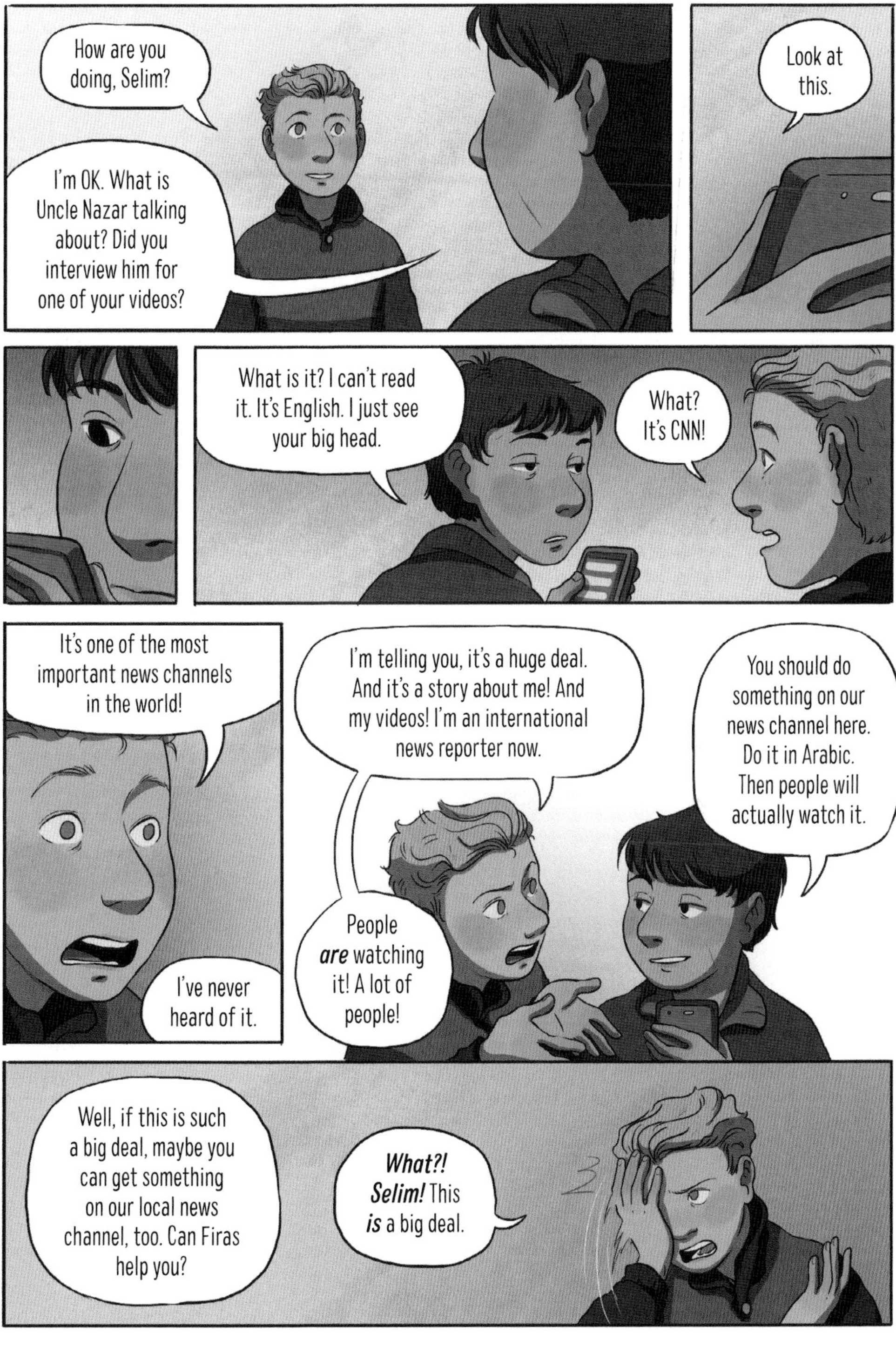
How are you doing, Selim?
I'm OK. What is Uncle Nazar talking about? Did you interview him for one of your videos?
Look at this.
What is it? I can't read it. It's English. I just see your big head.
What? It's CNN!
It's one of the most important news channels in the world!
I've never heard of it.
I'm telling you, it's a huge deal. And it's a story about me! And my videos! I'm an international news reporter now.
You should do something on our news channel here. Do it in Arabic. Then people will actually watch it.
People *are* watching it! A lot of people!
Well, if this is such a big deal, maybe you can get something on our local news channel, too. Can Firas help you?
What?! Selim! This ***is*** a big deal.

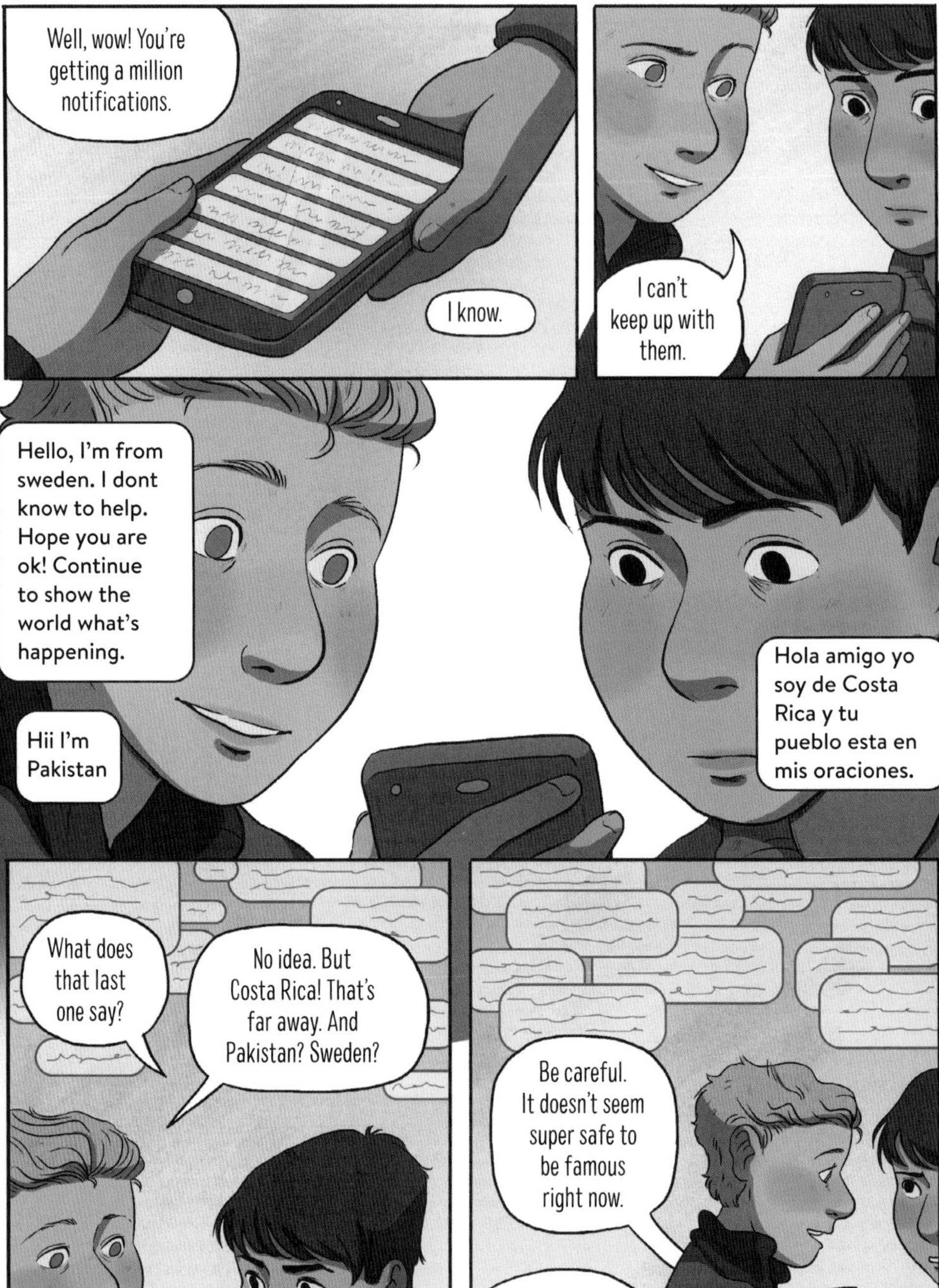
Well, wow! You're getting a million notifications.
I know.
I can't keep up with them.
Hello, I'm from sweden. I dont know to help. Hope you are ok! Continue to show the world what's happening.
Hii I'm Pakistan
Hola amigo yo soy de Costa Rica y tu pueblo esta en mis oraciones.
What does that last one say?
No idea. But Costa Rica! That's far away. And Pakistan? Sweden?
Be careful. It doesn't seem super safe to be famous right now.
You sound just like Firas. It'll be fine!

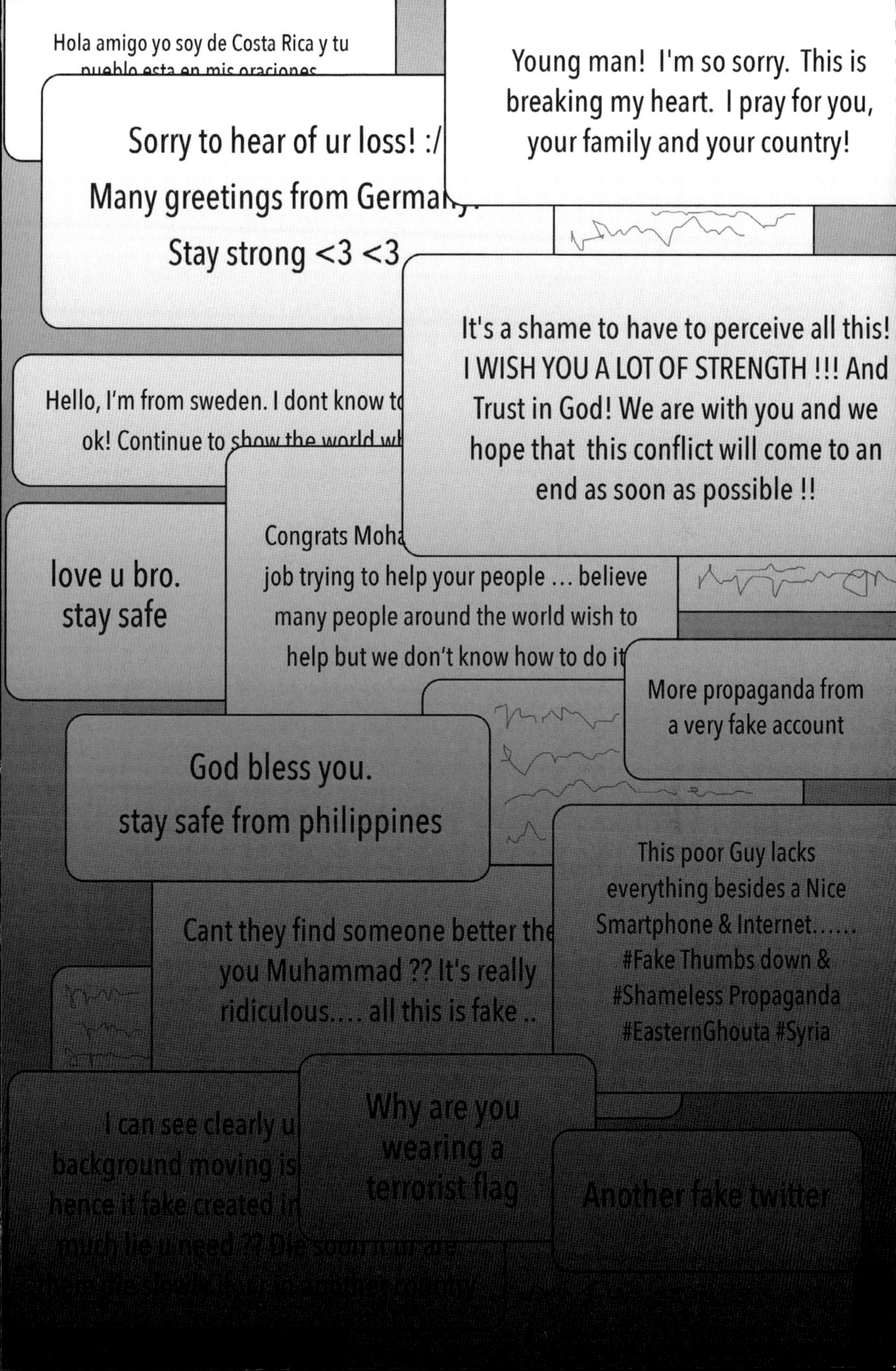
Hola amigo yo soy de Costa Rica y tu
Young man! I'm so sorry. This is breaking my heart. I pray for you, your family and your country!
Sorry to hear of ur loss! :/
Many greetings from Germa
Stay strong <3 <3
It's a shame to have to perceive all this! I WISH YOU A LOT OF STRENGTH !!! And Trust in God! We are with you and we hope that this conflict will come to an end as soon as possible !!
Hello, I'm from sweden. I dont know t
ok! Continue to
Congrats Moh
job trying to help your people … believe many people around the world wish to help but we don't know how to do it
love u bro. stay safe
More propaganda from a very fake account
God bless you. stay safe from philippines
This poor Guy lacks everything besides a Nice Smartphone & Internet…… #Fake Thumbs down & #Shameless Propaganda #EasternGhouta #Syria
Cant they find someone better th
you Muhammad ?? It's really ridiculous…. all this is fake ..
I can see clearly u
background moving is
hence it fake created in
much lie u need ?? Die soon
Why are you wearing a terrorist flag
Another fake twitter

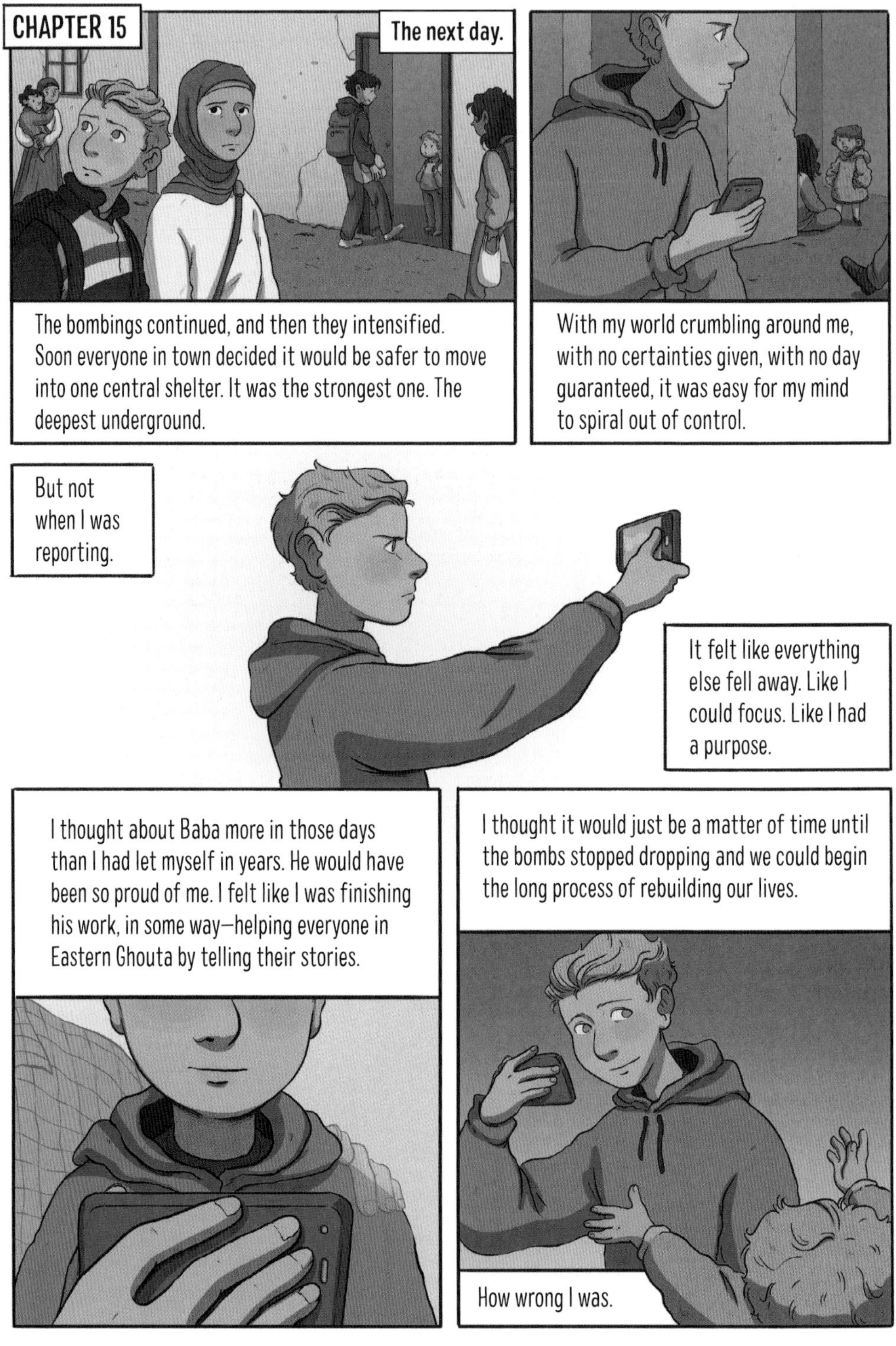
CHAPTER 15
The next day.
The bombings continued, and then they intensified. Soon everyone in town decided it would be safer to move into one central shelter. It was the strongest one. The deepest underground.
With my world crumbling around me, with no certainties given, with no day guaranteed, it was easy for my mind to spiral out of control.
But not when I was reporting.
It felt like everything else fell away. Like I could focus. Like I had a purpose.
I thought about Baba more in those days than I had let myself in years. He would have been so proud of me. I felt like I was finishing his work, in some way—helping everyone in Eastern Ghouta by telling their stories.
I thought it would just be a matter of time until the bombs stopped dropping and we could begin the long process of rebuilding our lives.
How wrong I was.

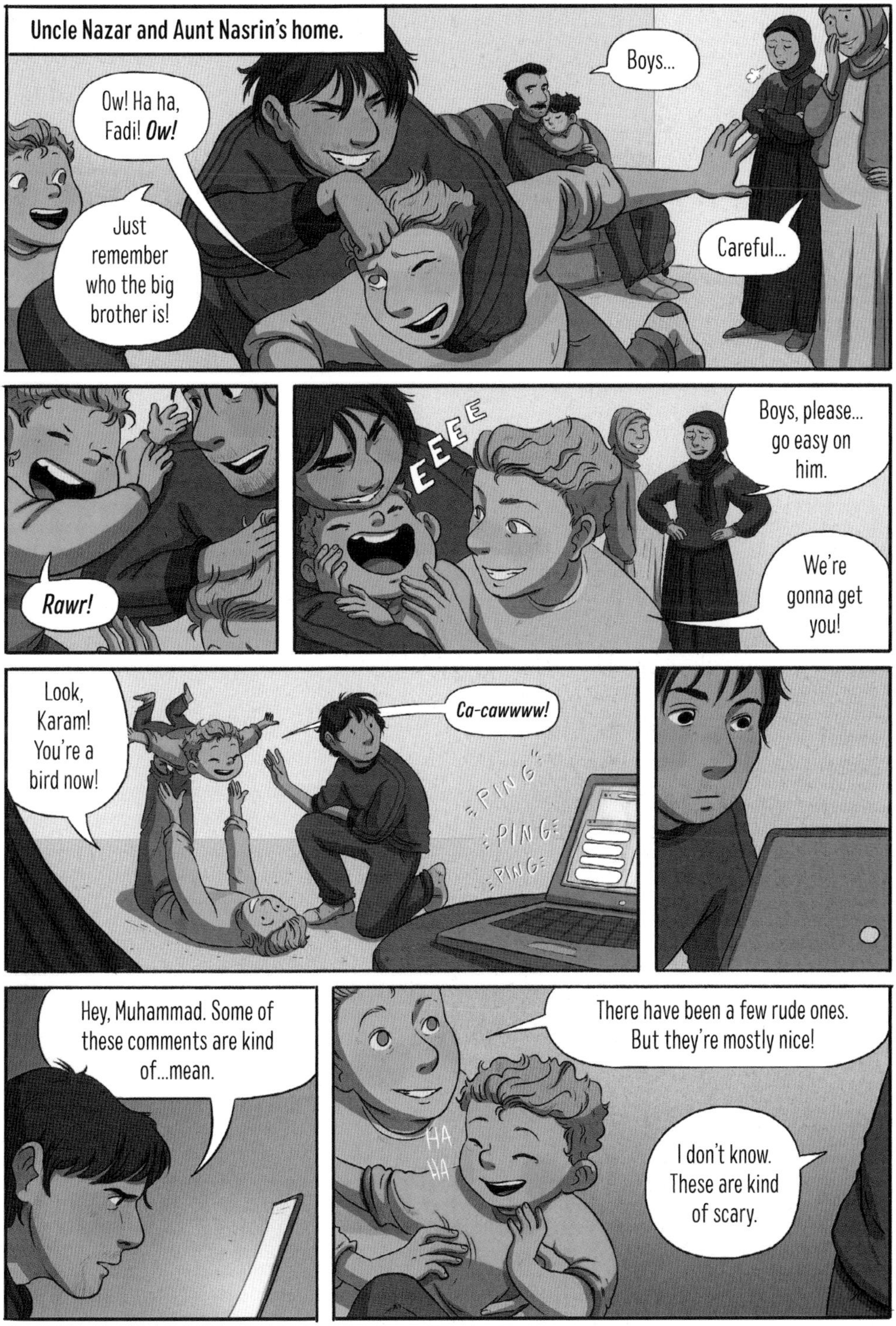
Uncle Nazar and Aunt Nasrin's home.
Ow! Ha ha, Fadi! **Ow!**
Just remember who the big brother is!
Boys...
Careful...
Rawr!
EEEE
Boys, please... go easy on him.
We're gonna get you!
Look, Karam! You're a bird now!
Ca-cawwww!
PING
PING
PING
Hey, Muhammad. Some of these comments are kind of...mean.
There have been a few rude ones. But they're mostly nice!
HA HA
I don't know. These are kind of scary.

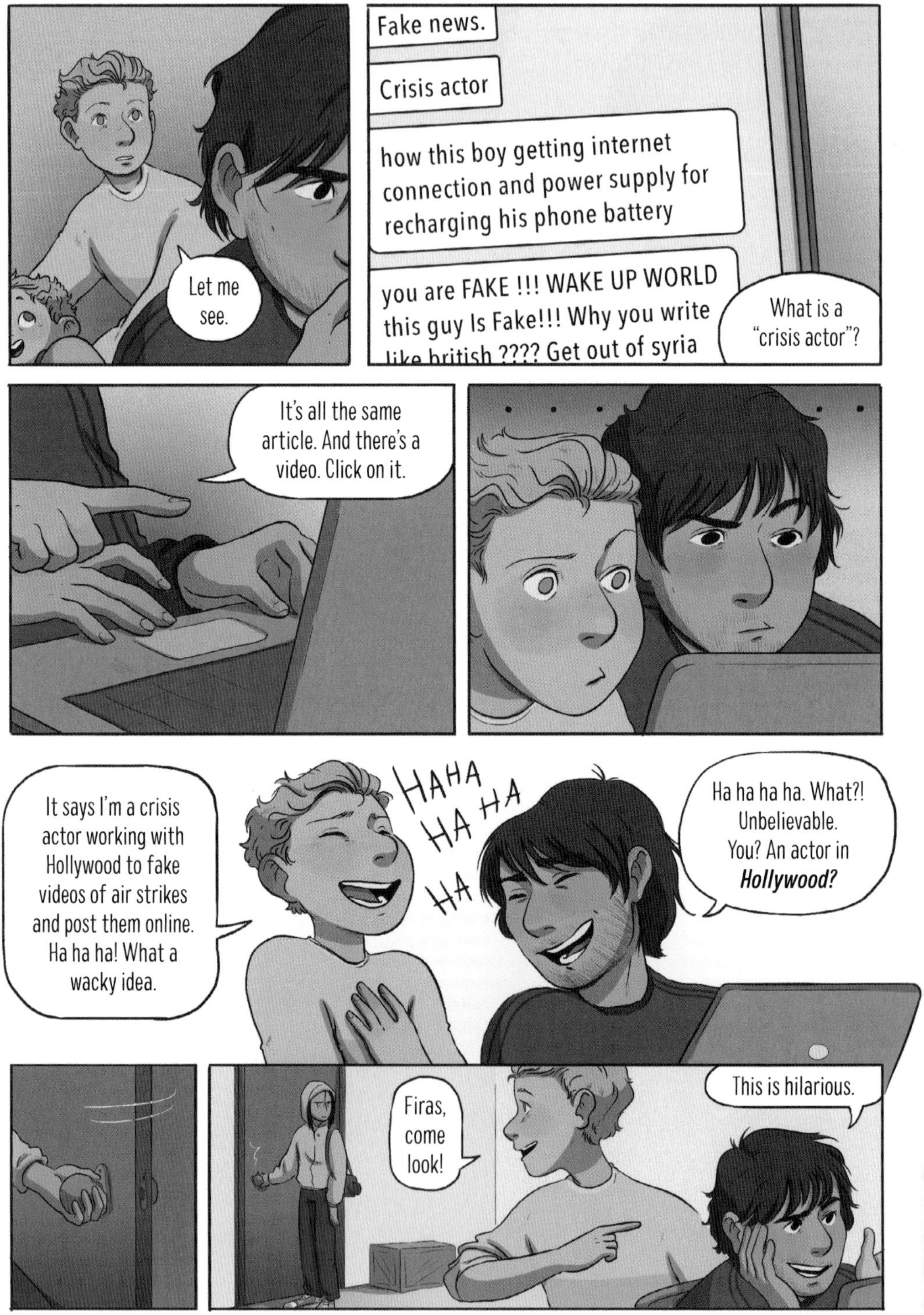

Let me see.
Fake news.
Crisis actor
how this boy getting internet connection and power supply for recharging his phone battery
you are FAKE !!! WAKE UP WORLD this guy Is Fake!!! Why you write like british ???? Get out of syria
What is a "crisis actor"?
It's all the same article. And there's a video. Click on it.
It says I'm a crisis actor working with Hollywood to fake videos of air strikes and post them online. Ha ha ha! What a wacky idea.
HAHA HA HA HA
Ha ha ha ha. What?! Unbelievable. You? An actor in ***Hollywood?***
Firas, come look!
This is hilarious.

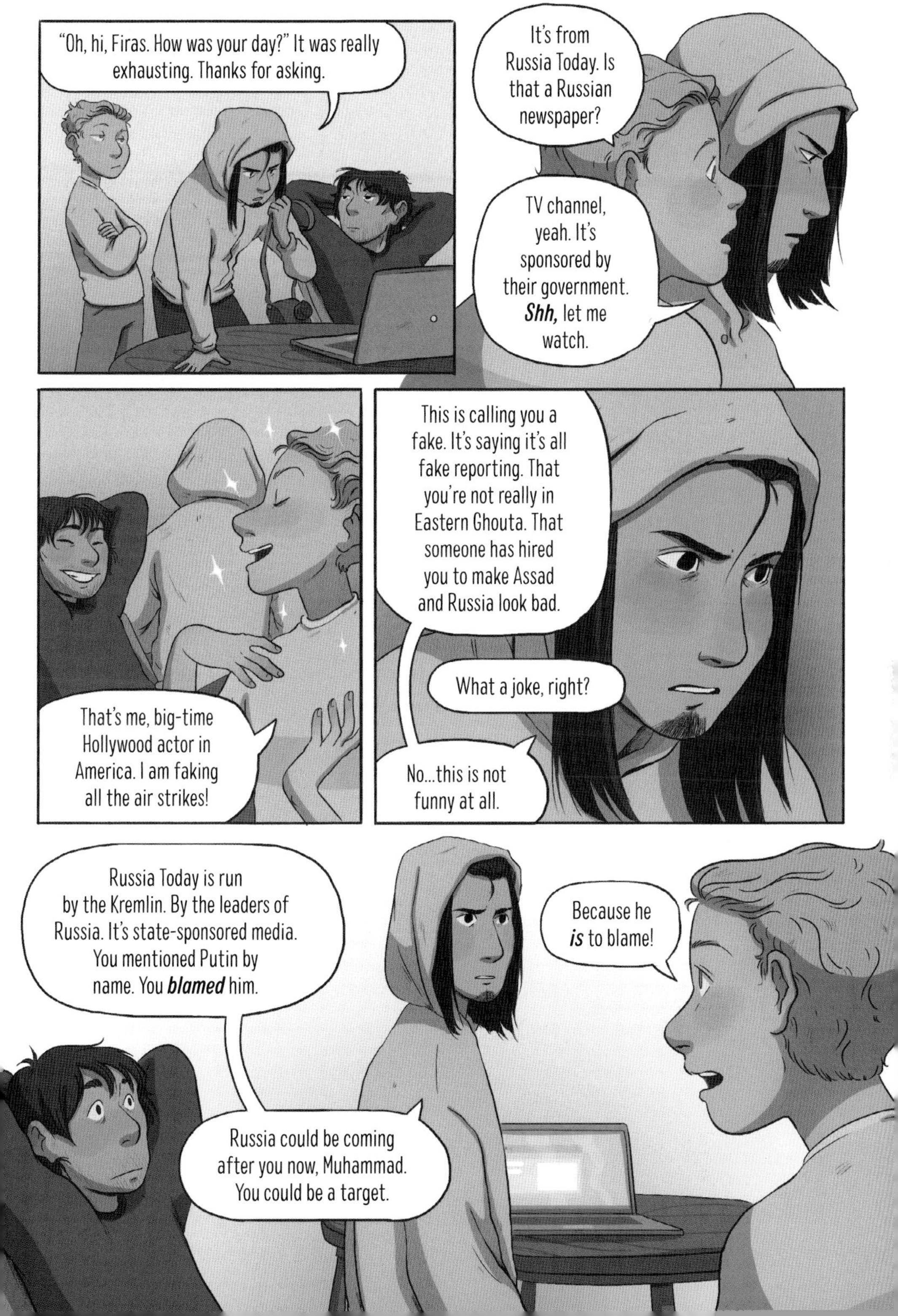
"Oh, hi, Firas. How was your day?" It was really exhausting. Thanks for asking.
It's from Russia Today. Is that a Russian newspaper?
TV channel, yeah. It's sponsored by their government. ***Shh,*** let me watch.
That's me, big-time Hollywood actor in America. I am faking all the air strikes!
This is calling you a fake. It's saying it's all fake reporting. That you're not really in Eastern Ghouta. That someone has hired you to make Assad and Russia look bad.
What a joke, right?
No...this is not funny at all.
Russia Today is run by the Kremlin. By the leaders of Russia. It's state-sponsored media. You mentioned Putin by name. You ***blamed*** him.
Because he ***is*** to blame!
Russia could be coming after you now, Muhammad. You could be a target.

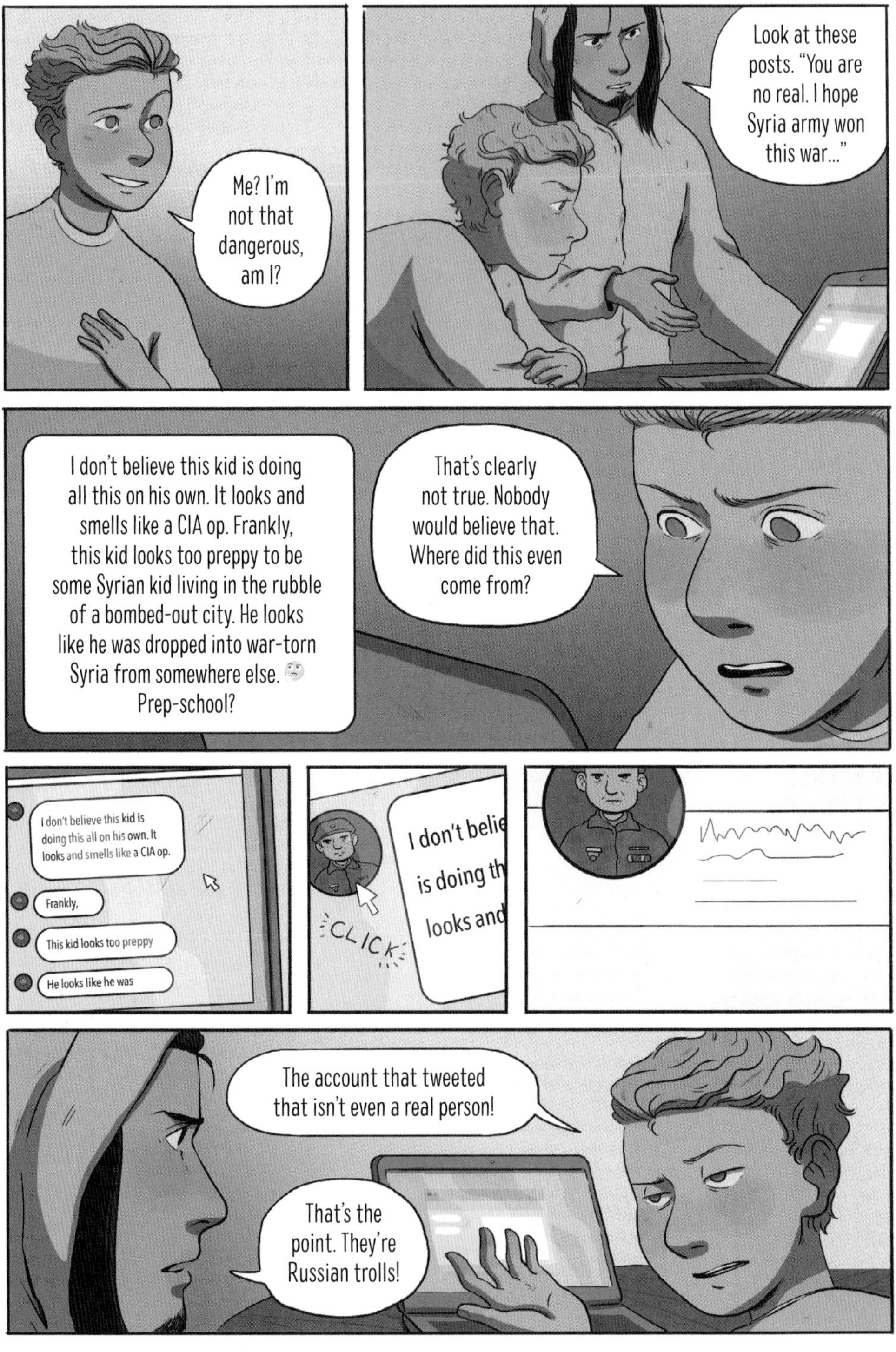

Me? I'm not that dangerous, am I?
Look at these posts. "You are no real. I hope Syria army won this war..."
I don't believe this kid is doing all this on his own. It looks and smells like a CIA op. Frankly, this kid looks too preppy to be some Syrian kid living in the rubble of a bombed-out city. He looks like he was dropped into war-torn Syria from somewhere else. Prep-school?
That's clearly not true. Nobody would believe that. Where did this even come from?
I don't believe this kid is doing this all on his own. It looks and smells like a CIA op.
Frankly,
This kid looks too preppy
He looks like he was
CLICK
The account that tweeted that isn't even a real person!
That's the point. They're Russian trolls!

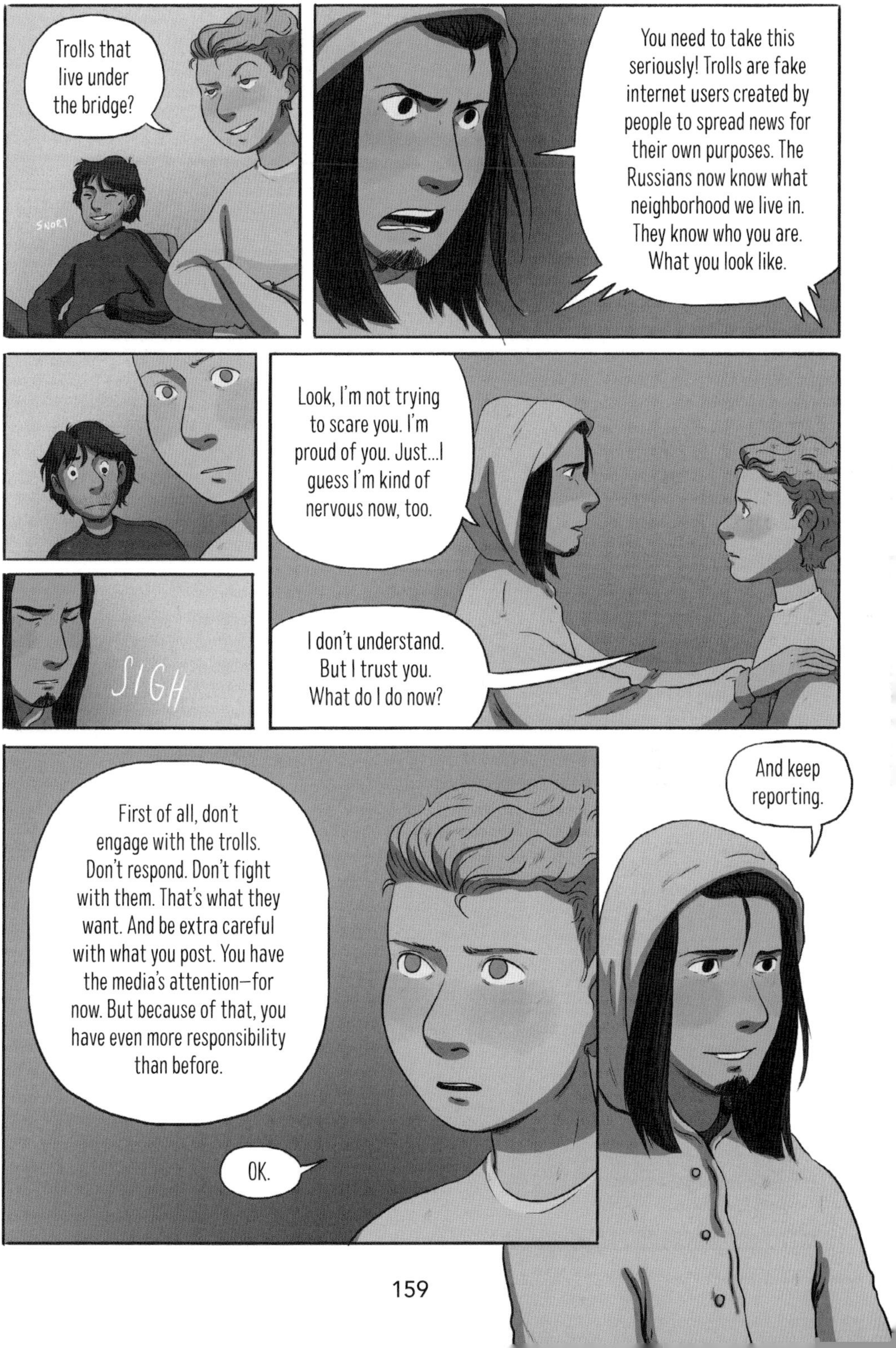
Trolls that live under the bridge?
SNORT
You need to take this seriously! Trolls are fake internet users created by people to spread news for their own purposes. The Russians now know what neighborhood we live in. They know who you are. What you look like.
SIGH
Look, I'm not trying to scare you. I'm proud of you. Just...I guess I'm kind of nervous now, too.
I don't understand. But I trust you. What do I do now?
First of all, don't engage with the trolls. Don't respond. Don't fight with them. That's what they want. And be extra careful with what you post. You have the media's attention—for now. But because of that, you have even more responsibility than before.
OK.
And keep reporting.

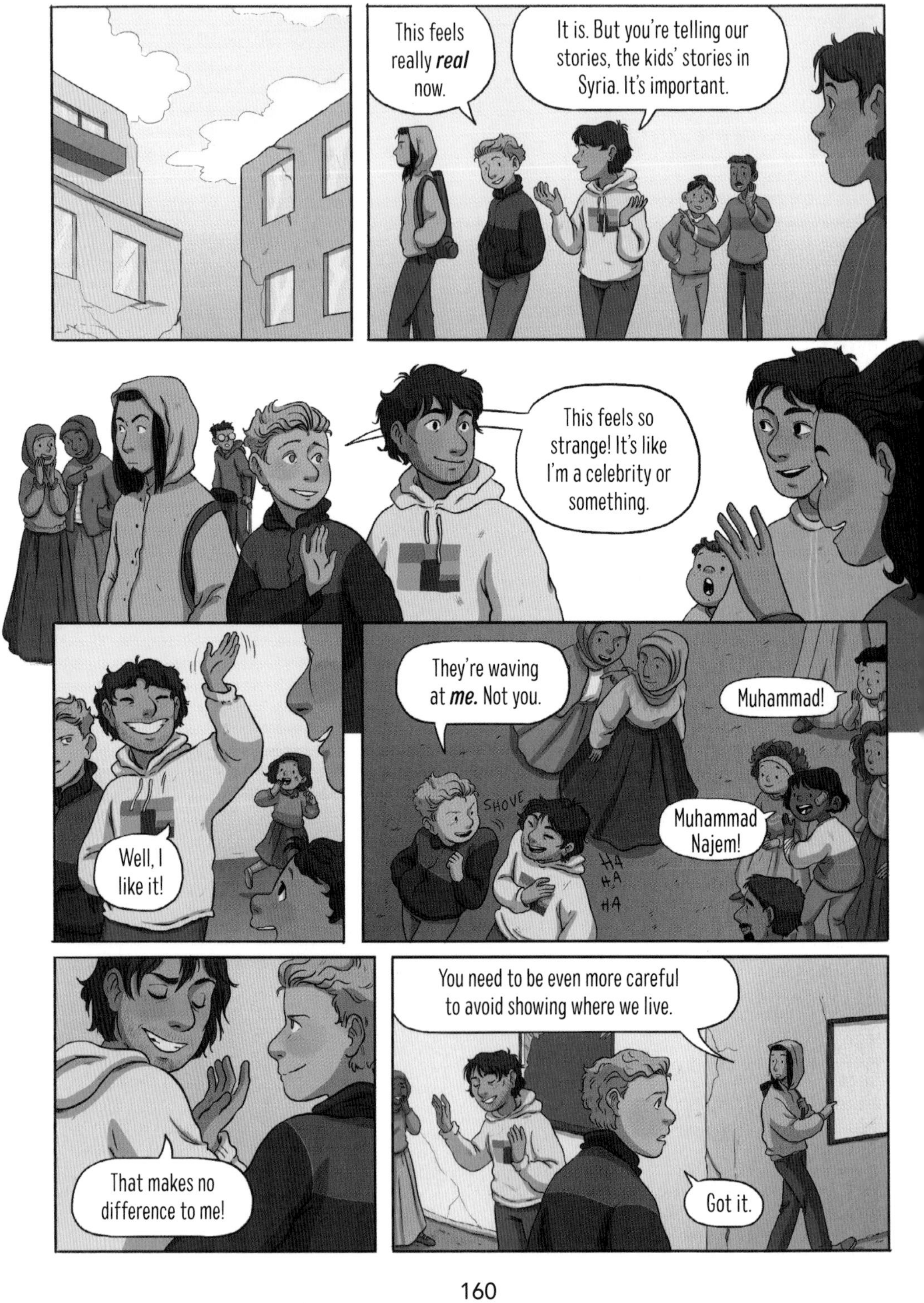
This feels really *real* now.
It is. But you're telling our stories, the kids' stories in Syria. It's important.
This feels so strange! It's like I'm a celebrity or something.
Well, I like it!
They're waving at *me.* Not you.
SHOVE
Muhammad!
Muhammad Najem!
HA HA HA
That makes no difference to me!
You need to be even more careful to avoid showing where we live.
Got it.

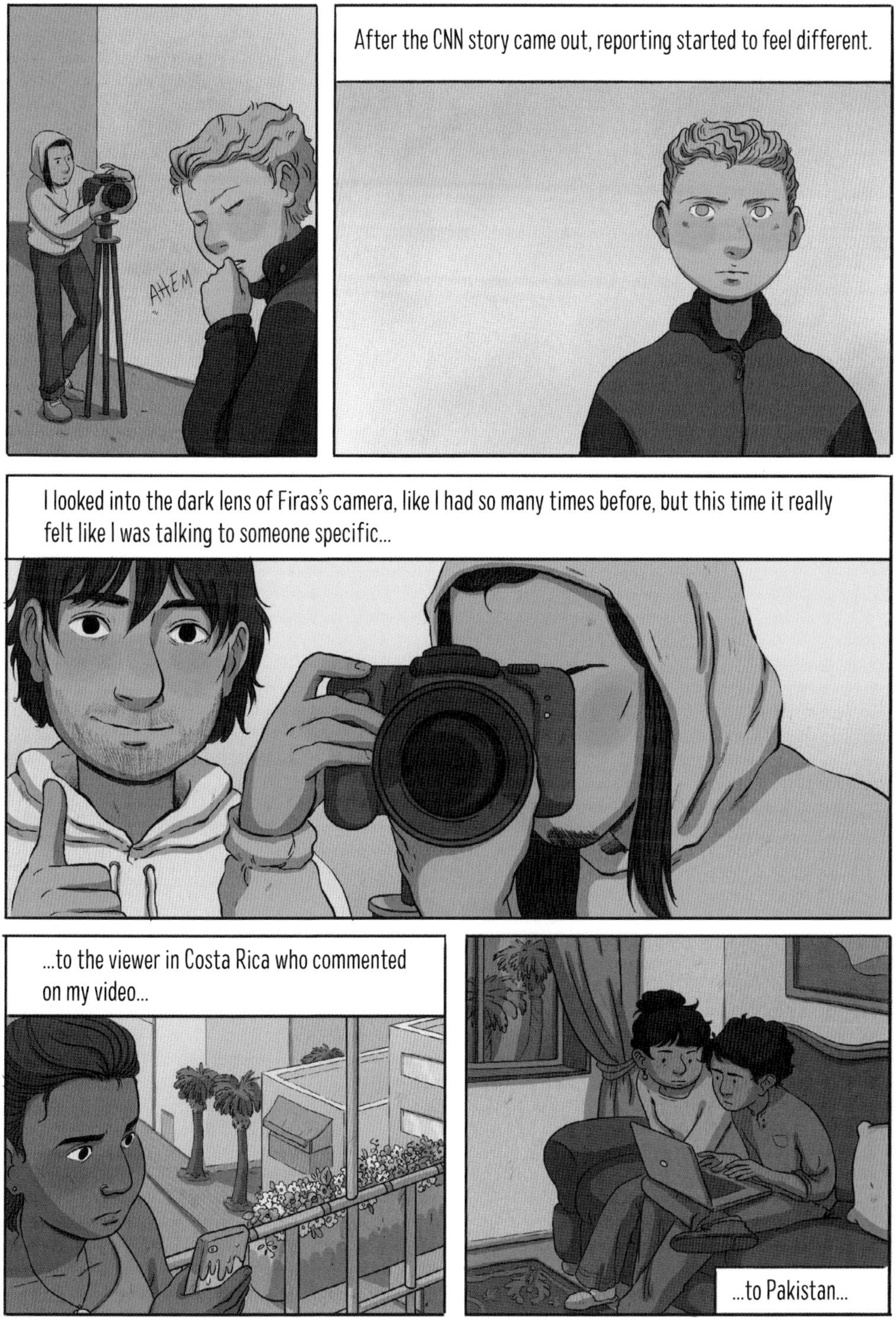
AHEM
After the CNN story came out, reporting started to feel different.
I looked into the dark lens of Firas's camera, like I had so many times before, but this time it really felt like I was talking to someone specific...
...to the viewer in Costa Rica who commented on my video...
...to Pakistan...

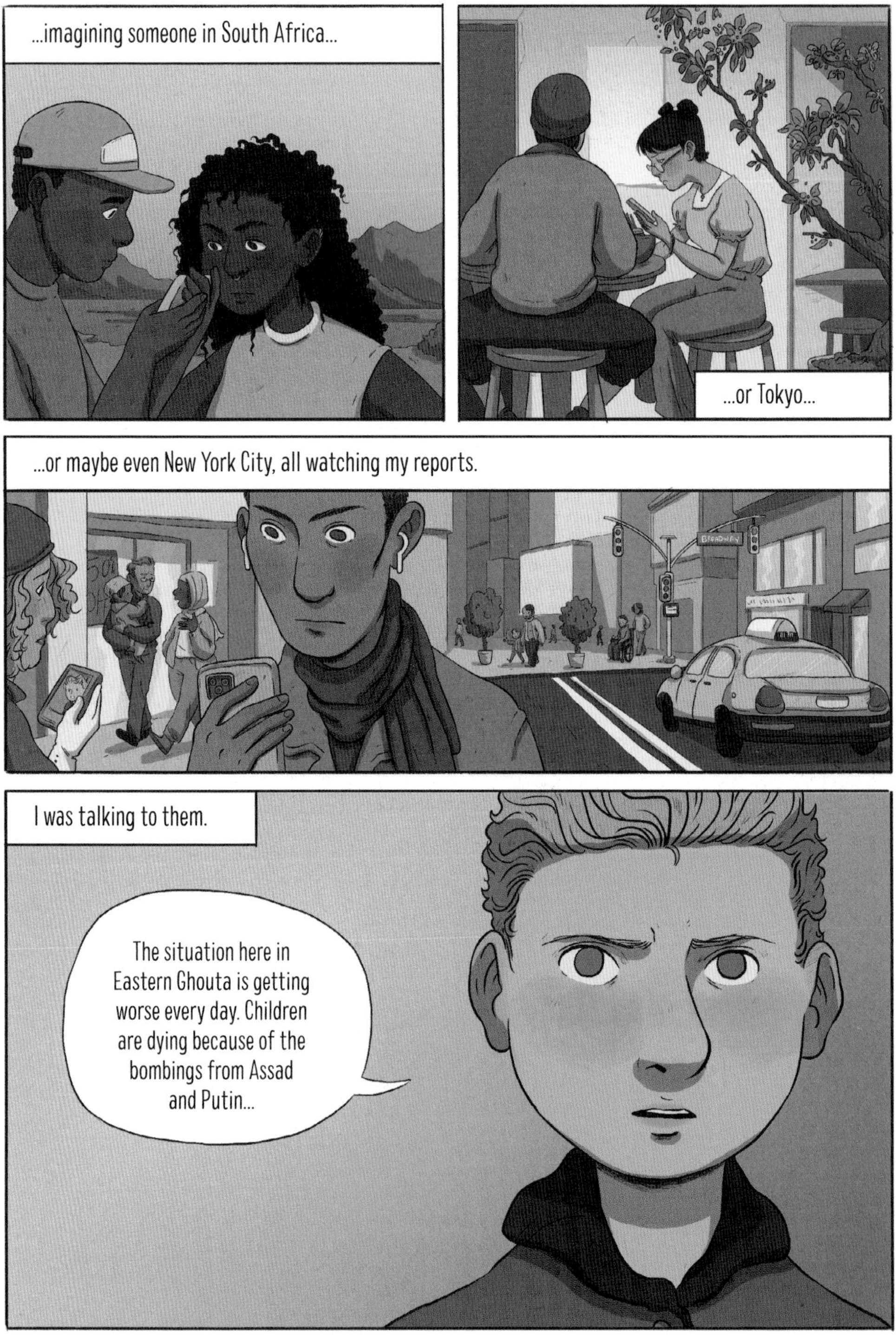
...imagining someone in South Africa...
...or Tokyo...
...or maybe even New York City, all watching my reports.
BROADWAY
I was talking to them.
The situation here in Eastern Ghouta is getting worse every day. Children are dying because of the bombings from Assad and Putin...

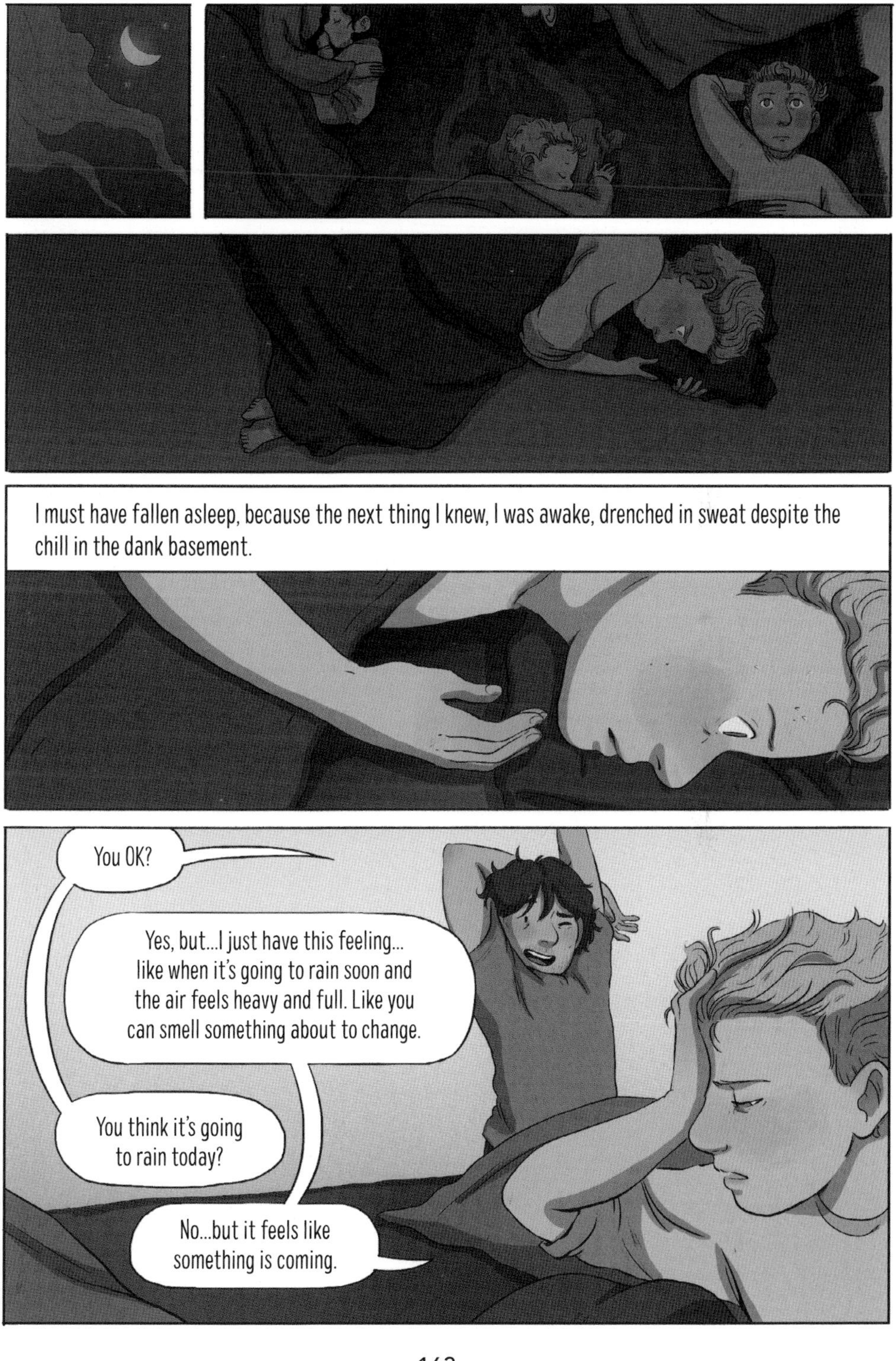
I must have fallen asleep, because the next thing I knew, I was awake, drenched in sweat despite the chill in the dank basement.
You OK?
Yes, but...I just have this feeling... like when it's going to rain soon and the air feels heavy and full. Like you can smell something about to change.
You think it's going to rain today?
No...but it feels like something is coming.

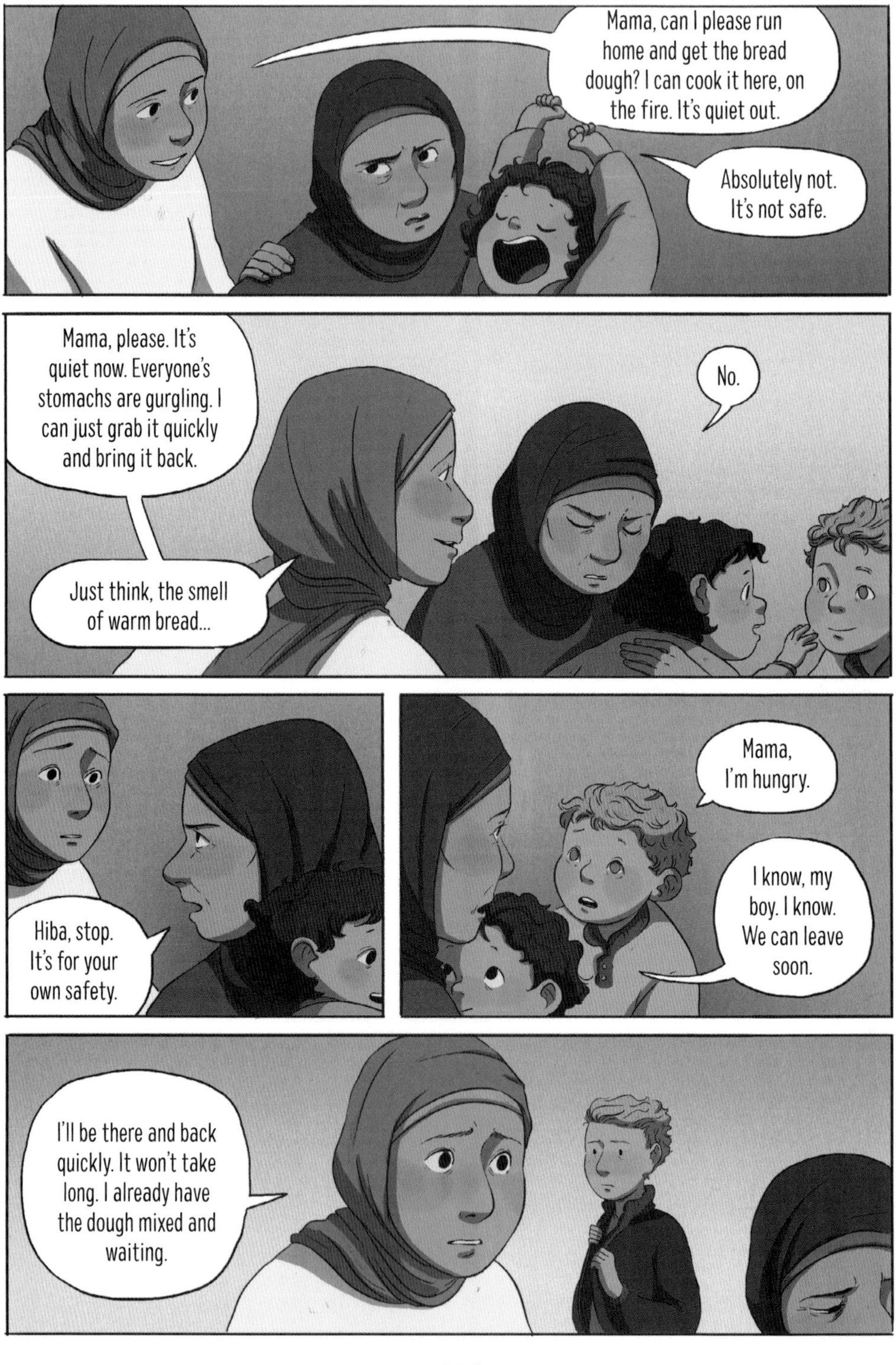

Mama, can I please run home and get the bread dough? I can cook it here, on the fire. It's quiet out.
Absolutely not. It's not safe.
Mama, please. It's quiet now. Everyone's stomachs are gurgling. I can just grab it quickly and bring it back.
Just think, the smell of warm bread...
No.
Hiba, stop. It's for your own safety.
Mama, I'm hungry.
I know, my boy. I know. We can leave soon.
I'll be there and back quickly. It won't take long. I already have the dough mixed and waiting.

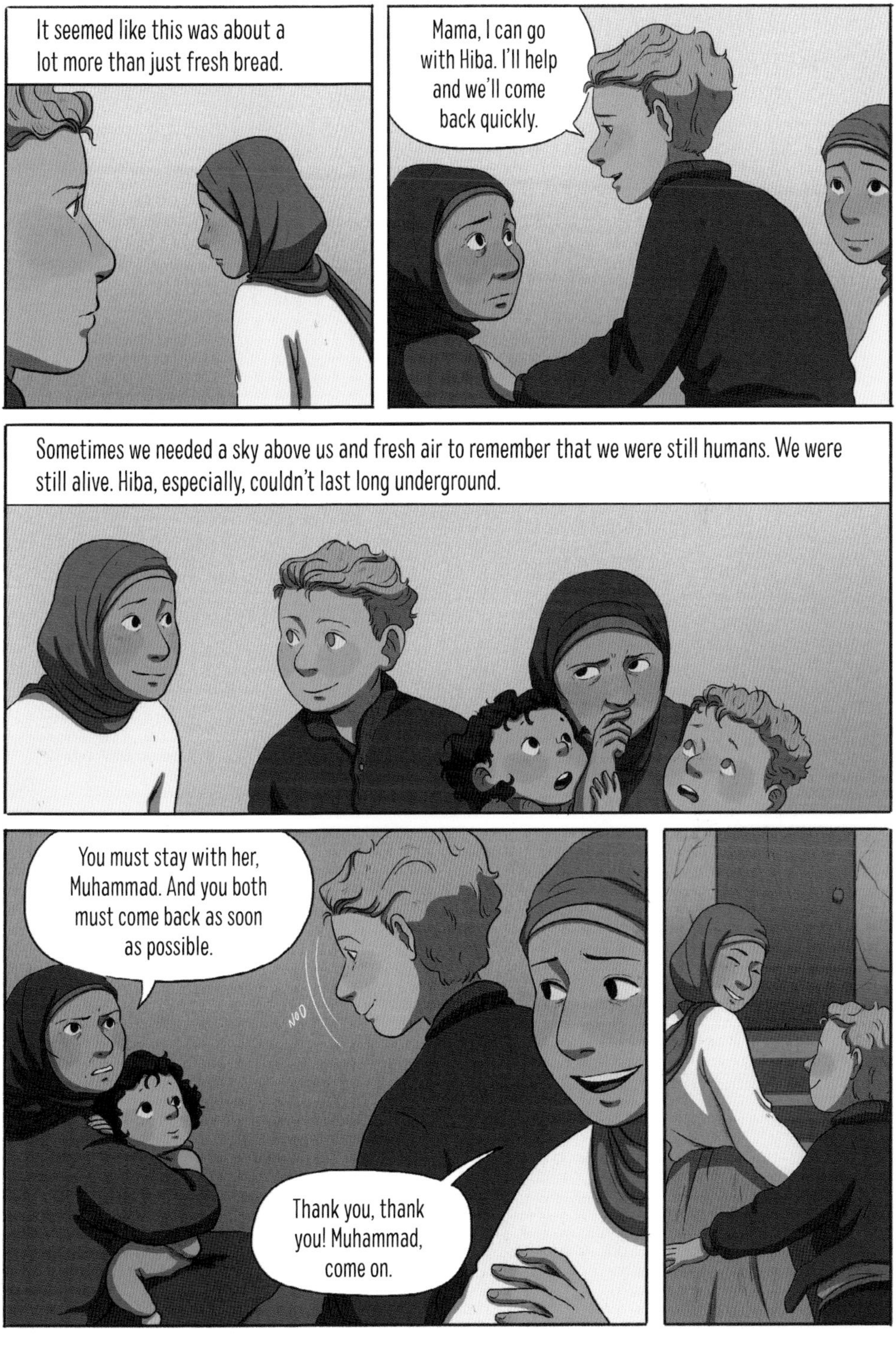
It seemed like this was about a lot more than just fresh bread.
Mama, I can go with Hiba. I'll help and we'll come back quickly.
Sometimes we needed a sky above us and fresh air to remember that we were still humans. We were still alive. Hiba, especially, couldn't last long underground.
You must stay with her, Muhammad. And you both must come back as soon as possible.
NOD
Thank you, thank you! Muhammad, come on.

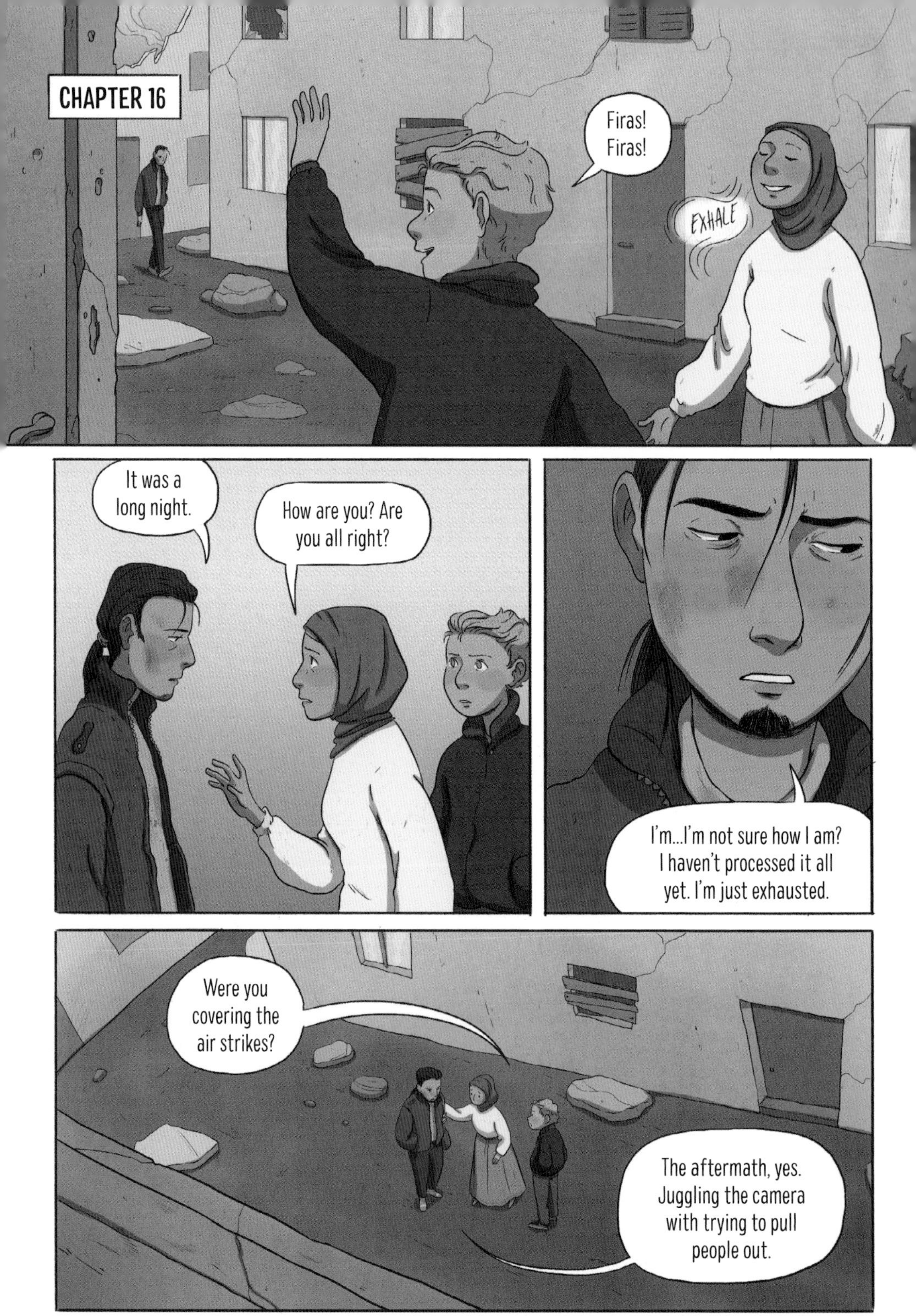
CHAPTER 16
Firas!
Firas!
EXHALE
It was a long night.
How are you? Are you all right?
I'm...I'm not sure how I am? I haven't processed it all yet. I'm just exhausted.
Were you covering the air strikes?
The aftermath, yes. Juggling the camera with trying to pull people out.

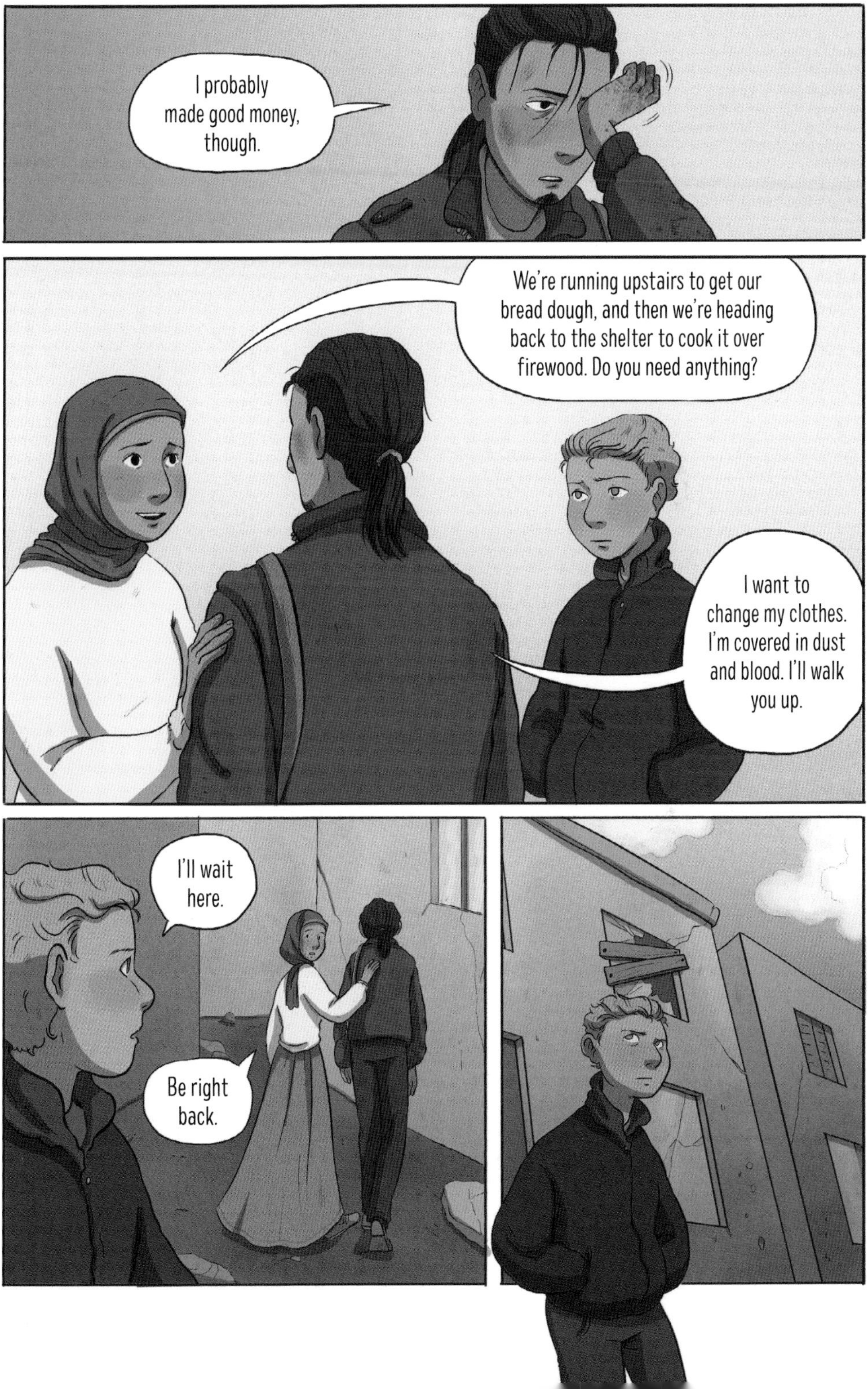
I probably made good money, though.
We're running upstairs to get our bread dough, and then we're heading back to the shelter to cook it over firewood. Do you need anything?
I want to change my clothes. I'm covered in dust and blood. I'll walk you up.
I'll wait here.
Be right back.

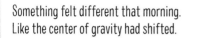
Something felt different that morning.
Like the center of gravity had shifted.

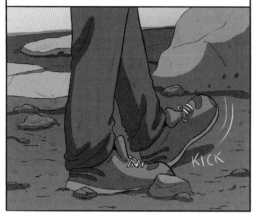
KICK

Like we were being watched.

And then suddenly, there it came.

DRUHHHHH DRUHHHHH DRRUUUHHHH

FIRAS! HIBA!
COME BACK!

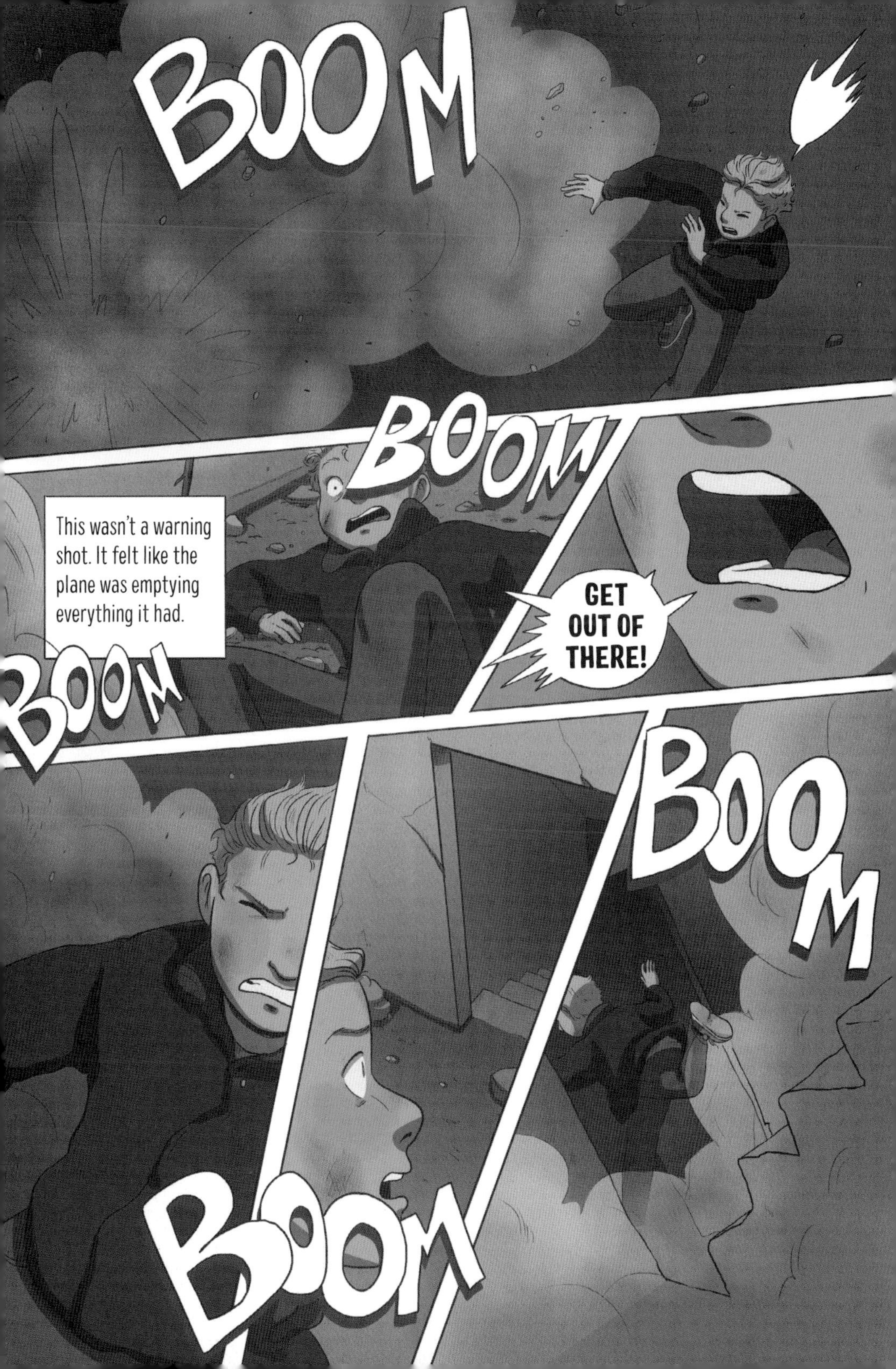
BOOM
BOOM
This wasn't a warning shot. It felt like the plane was emptying everything it had.
BOOM
GET OUT OF THERE!
BOOM
BOOM

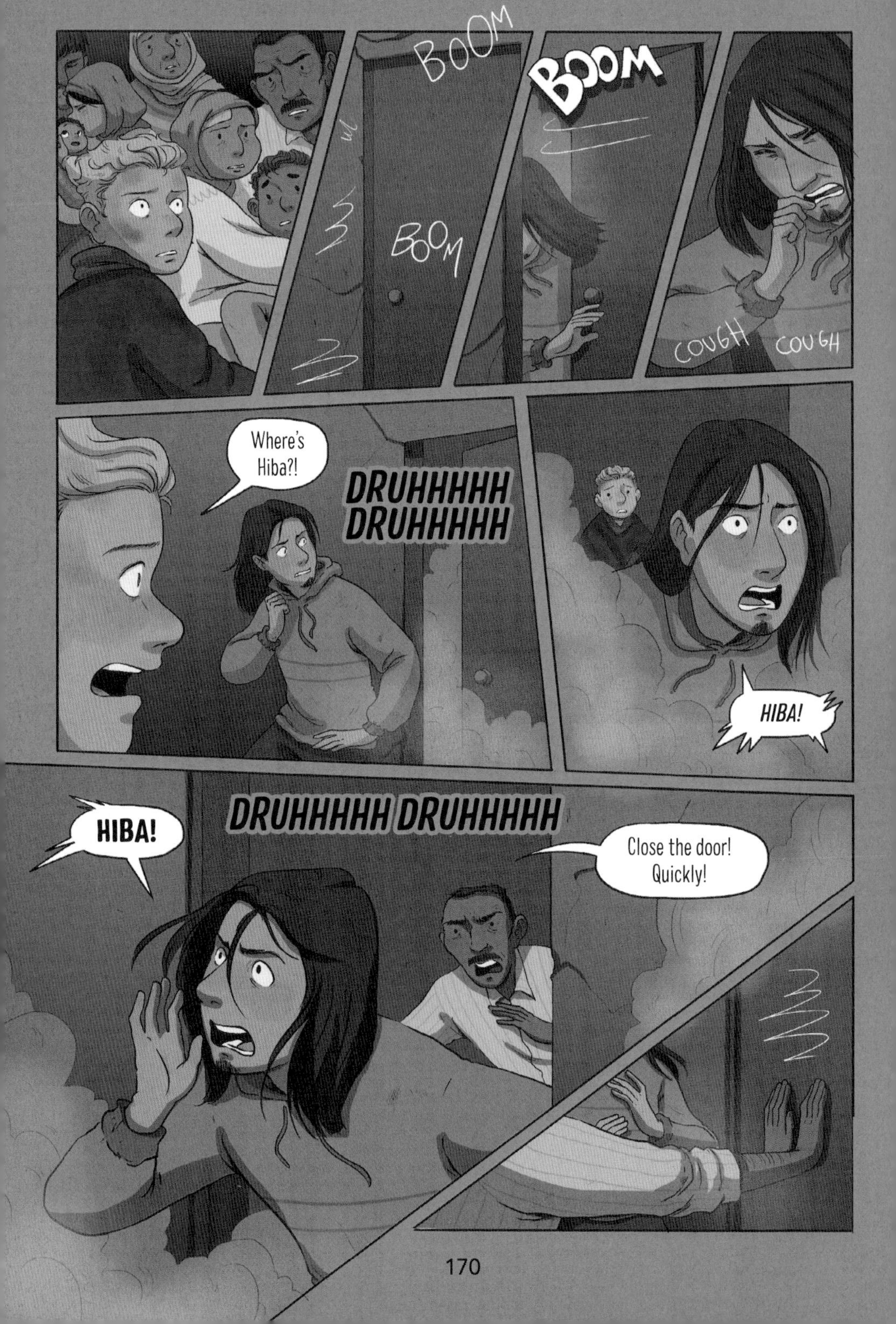
BOOM
BOOM
BOOM
COUGH
COUGH
Where's Hiba?!
DRUHHHHH DRUHHHHH
HIBA!
HIBA!
DRUHHHHH DRUHHHHH
Close the door! Quickly!

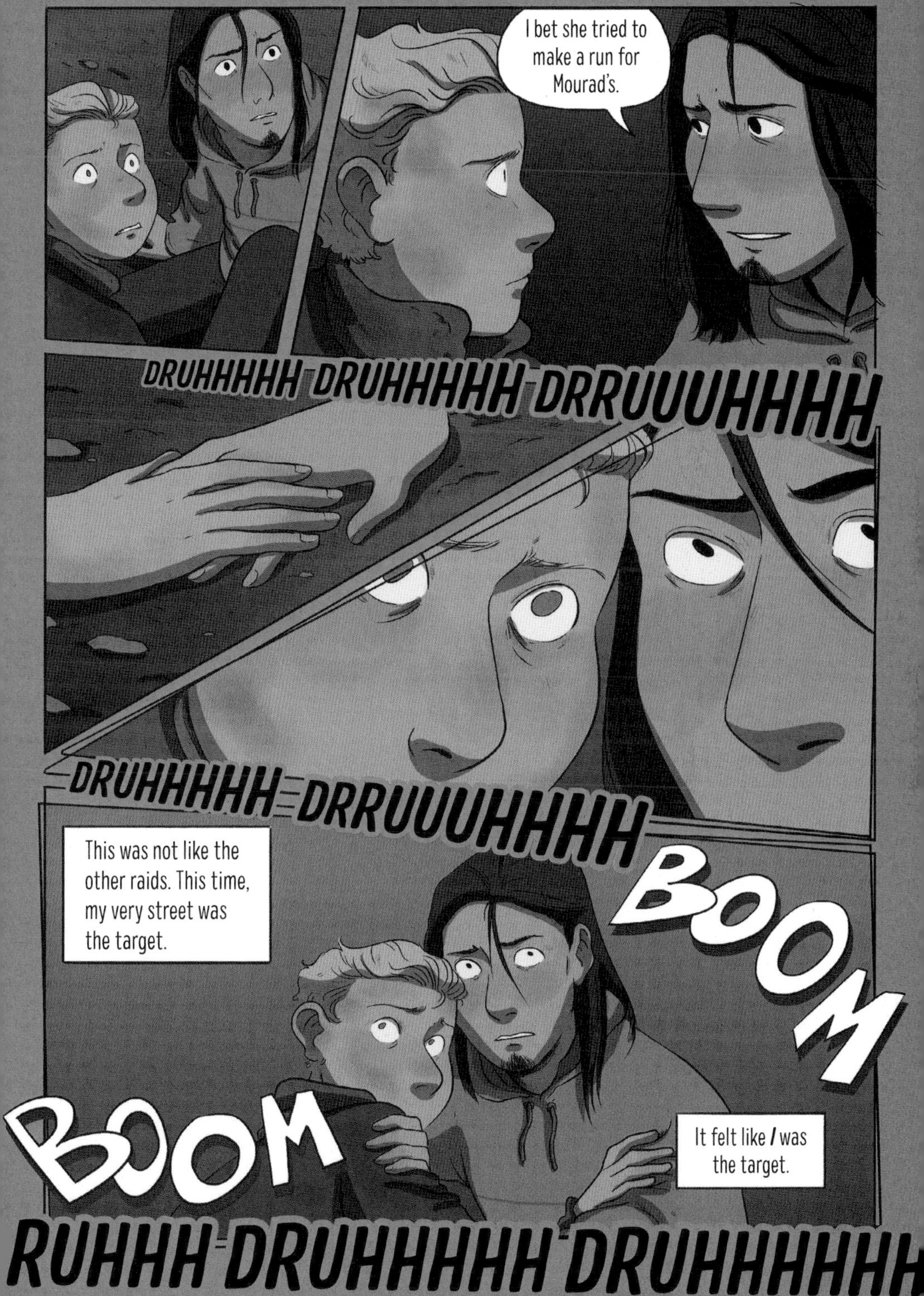

I bet she tried to make a run for Mourad's.
DRUHHHHH DRUHHHHH DRRUUUUHHHH
DRUHHHHH DRRUUUUHHHH
This was not like the other raids. This time, my very street was the target.
BOOM
BOOM
It felt like **I** was the target.
RUHHH DRUHHHHHH DRUHHHHHH

The ceiling rained cement and ash and darkness. The bomb directly overhead was the loudest noise I had ever heard in my life.

But just as I noticed the noise, it was replaced with ringing in my ears.

I couldn't hear anything except my own blood pulsing against my eardrums, faster and faster and faster.

It was as if it were happening in slow motion.

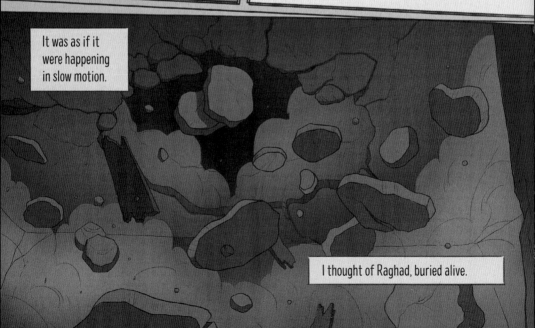

I thought of Raghad, buried alive.

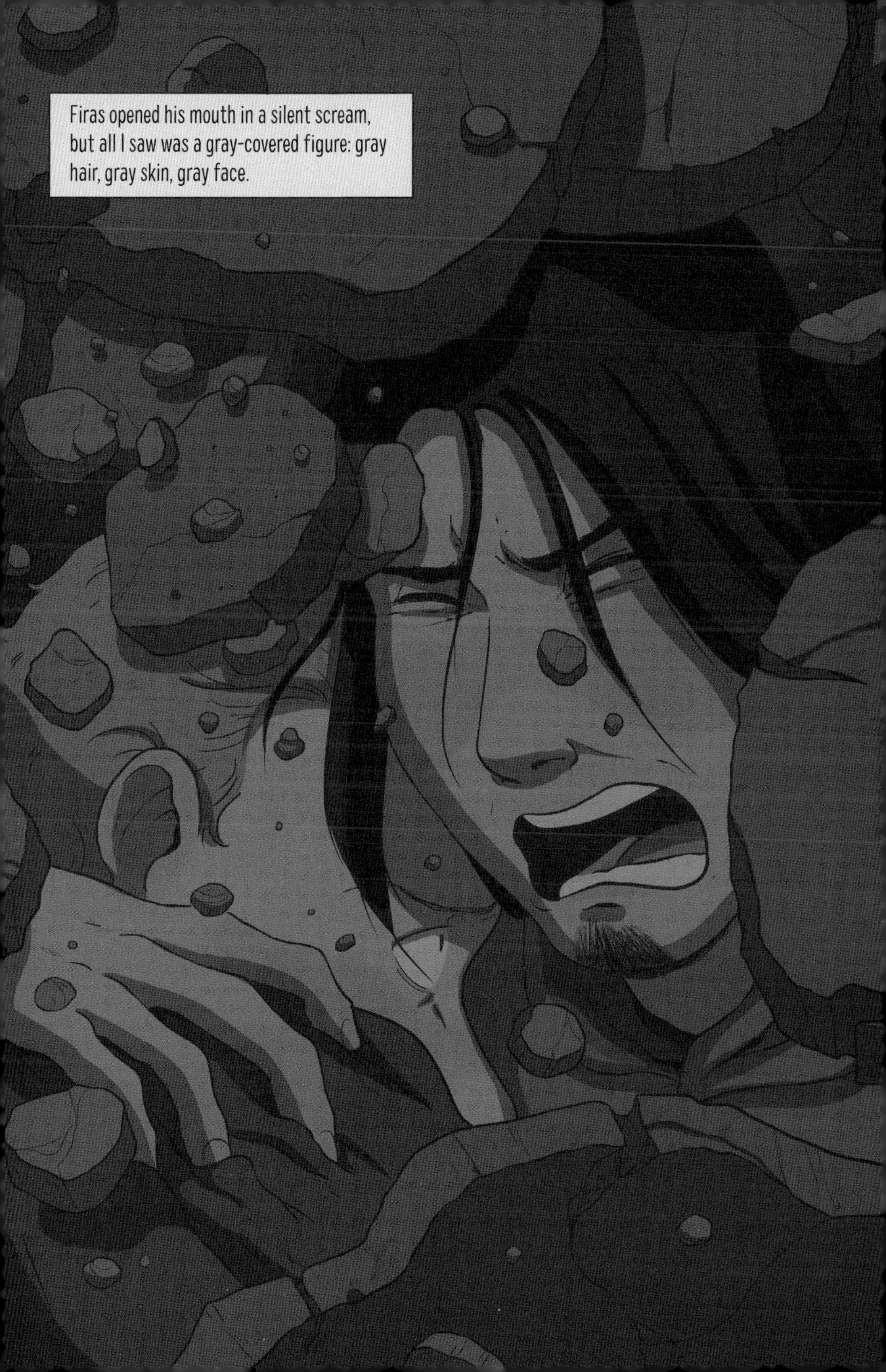
Firas opened his mouth in a silent scream, but all I saw was a gray-covered figure: gray hair, gray skin, gray face.

And then I couldn't
see anything at all.

I prayed frantically for my mother, for my brothers and sisters.
That they were alive. I apologized to them for letting Hiba get
bread. We should've stayed with them. And now it was too late.

But...

...I didn't feel dead.

I was still alive.

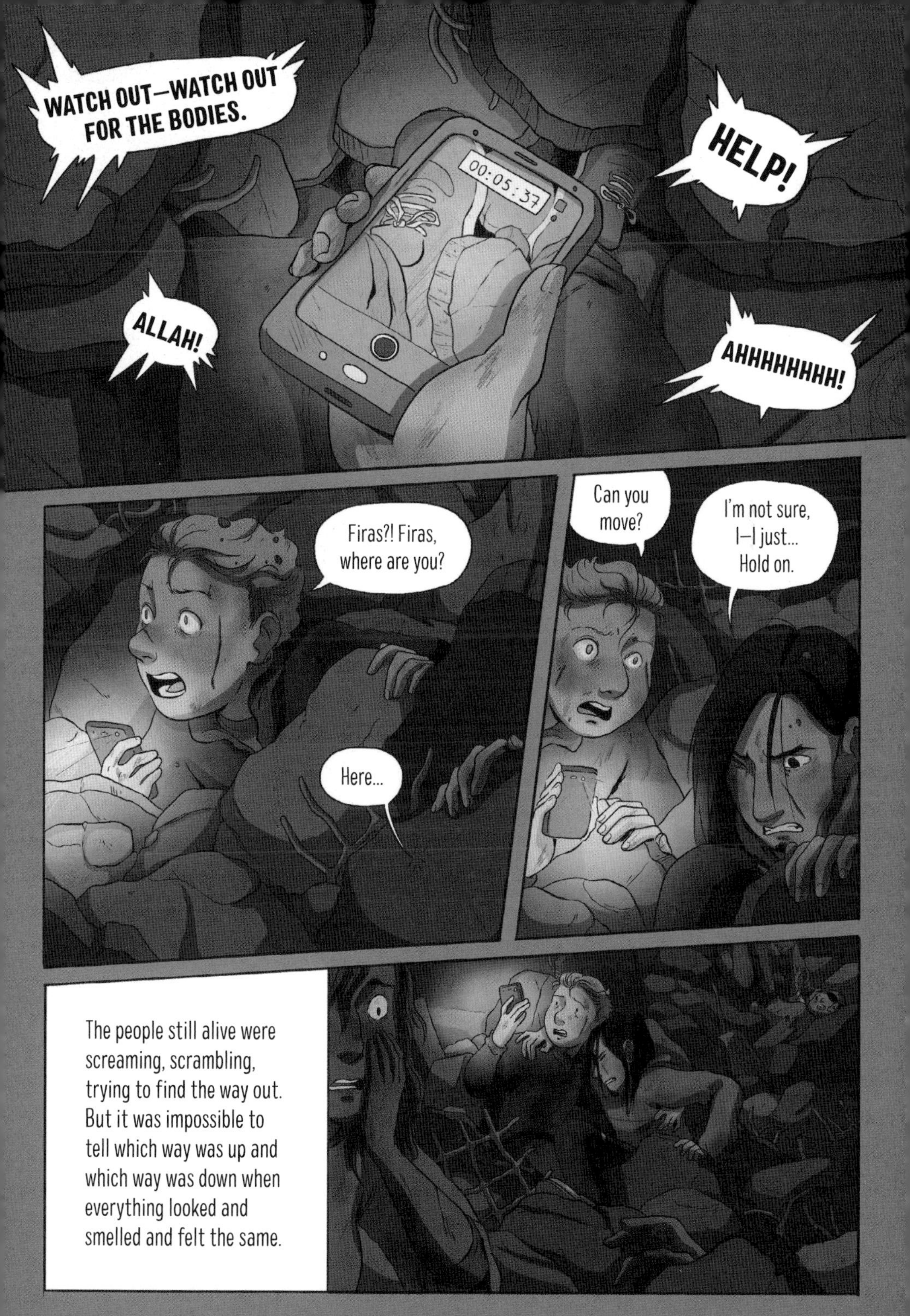
WATCH OUT—WATCH OUT FOR THE BODIES.
HELP!
00:05:37
ALLAH!
AHHHHHHHH!
Firas?! Firas, where are you?
Here...
Can you move?
I'm not sure, I—I just... Hold on.
The people still alive were screaming, scrambling, trying to find the way out. But it was impossible to tell which way was up and which way was down when everything looked and smelled and felt the same.

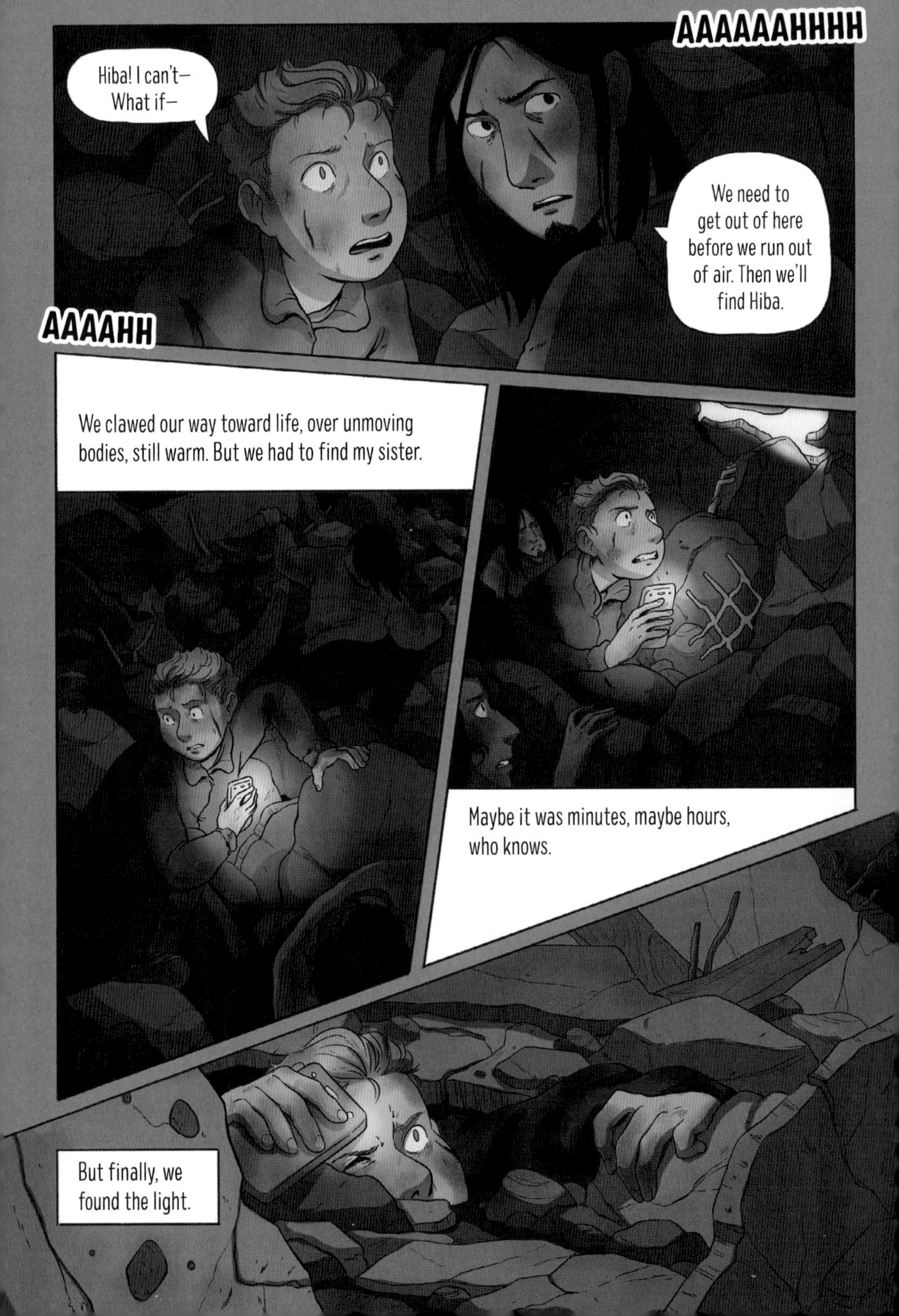
AAAAAAHHHH
Hiba! I can't— What if—
We need to get out of here before we run out of air. Then we'll find Hiba.
AAAAHH
We clawed our way toward life, over unmoving bodies, still warm. But we had to find my sister.
Maybe it was minutes, maybe hours, who knows.
But finally, we found the light.

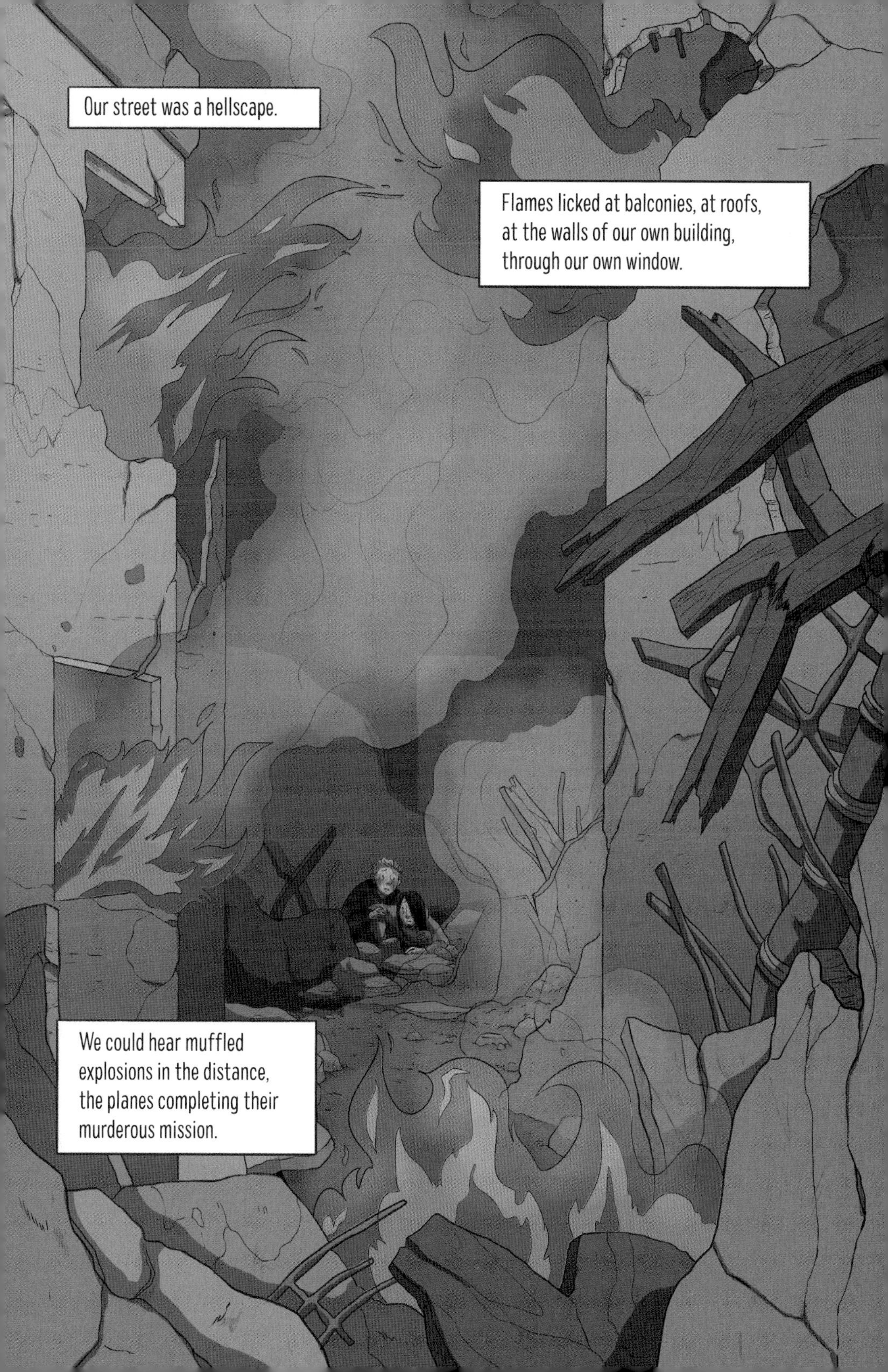
Our street was a hellscape.
Flames licked at balconies, at roofs, at the walls of our own building, through our own window.
We could hear muffled explosions in the distance, the planes completing their murderous mission.

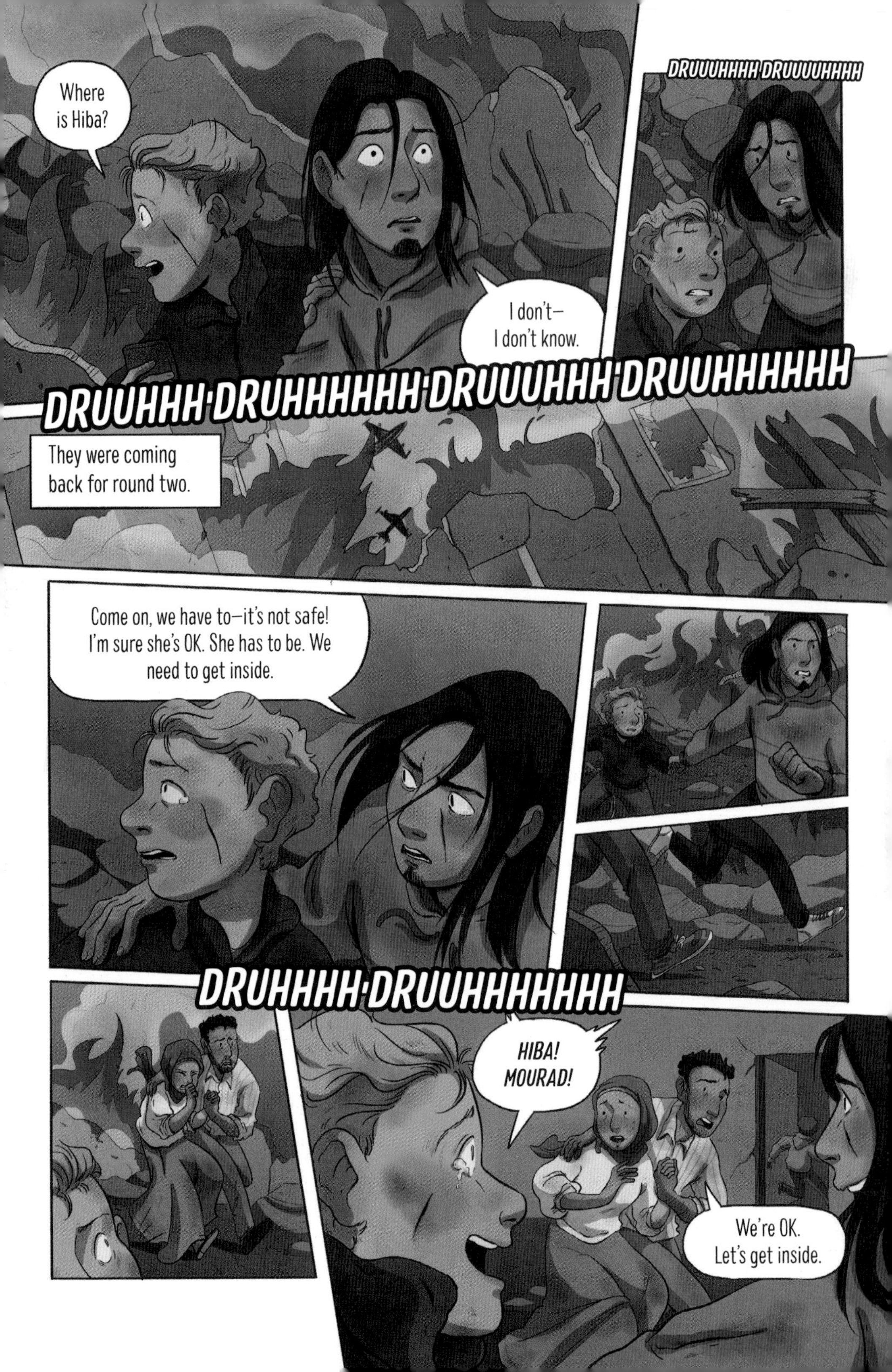
Where is Hiba?
I don't—
I don't know.
DRUUUHHHH DRUUUUHHHH
DRUUHHH DRUHHHHHH DRUUUHHH DRUUHHHHHH
They were coming back for round two.
Come on, we have to—it's not safe! I'm sure she's OK. She has to be. We need to get inside.
DRUHHHH DRUUHHHHHHH
HIBA! MOURAD!
We're OK. Let's get inside.

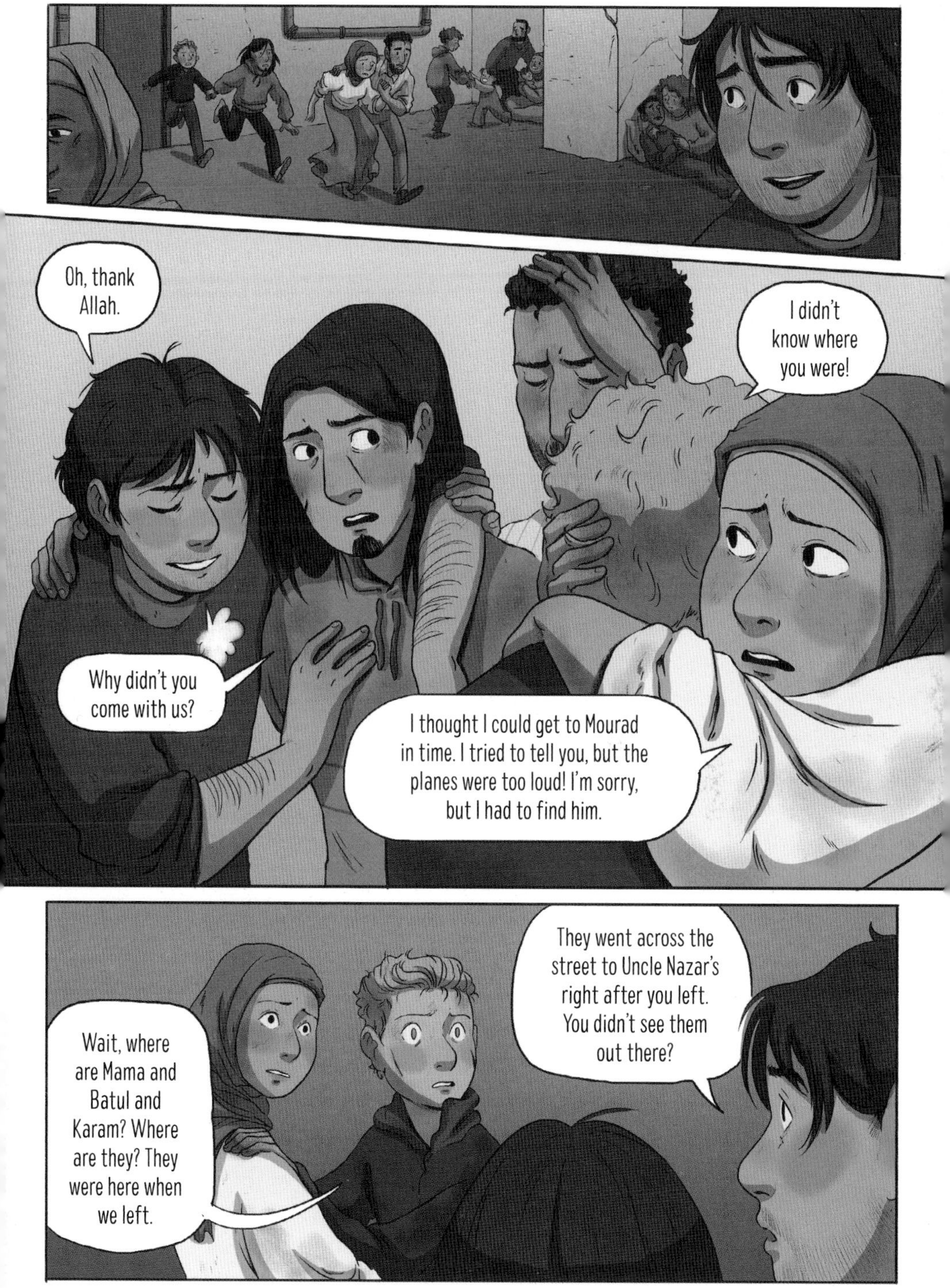
Oh, thank Allah.
I didn't know where you were!
Why didn't you come with us?
I thought I could get to Mourad in time. I tried to tell you, but the planes were too loud! I'm sorry, but I had to find him.
Wait, where are Mama and Batul and Karam? Where are they? They were here when we left.
They went across the street to Uncle Nazar's right after you left. You didn't see them out there?

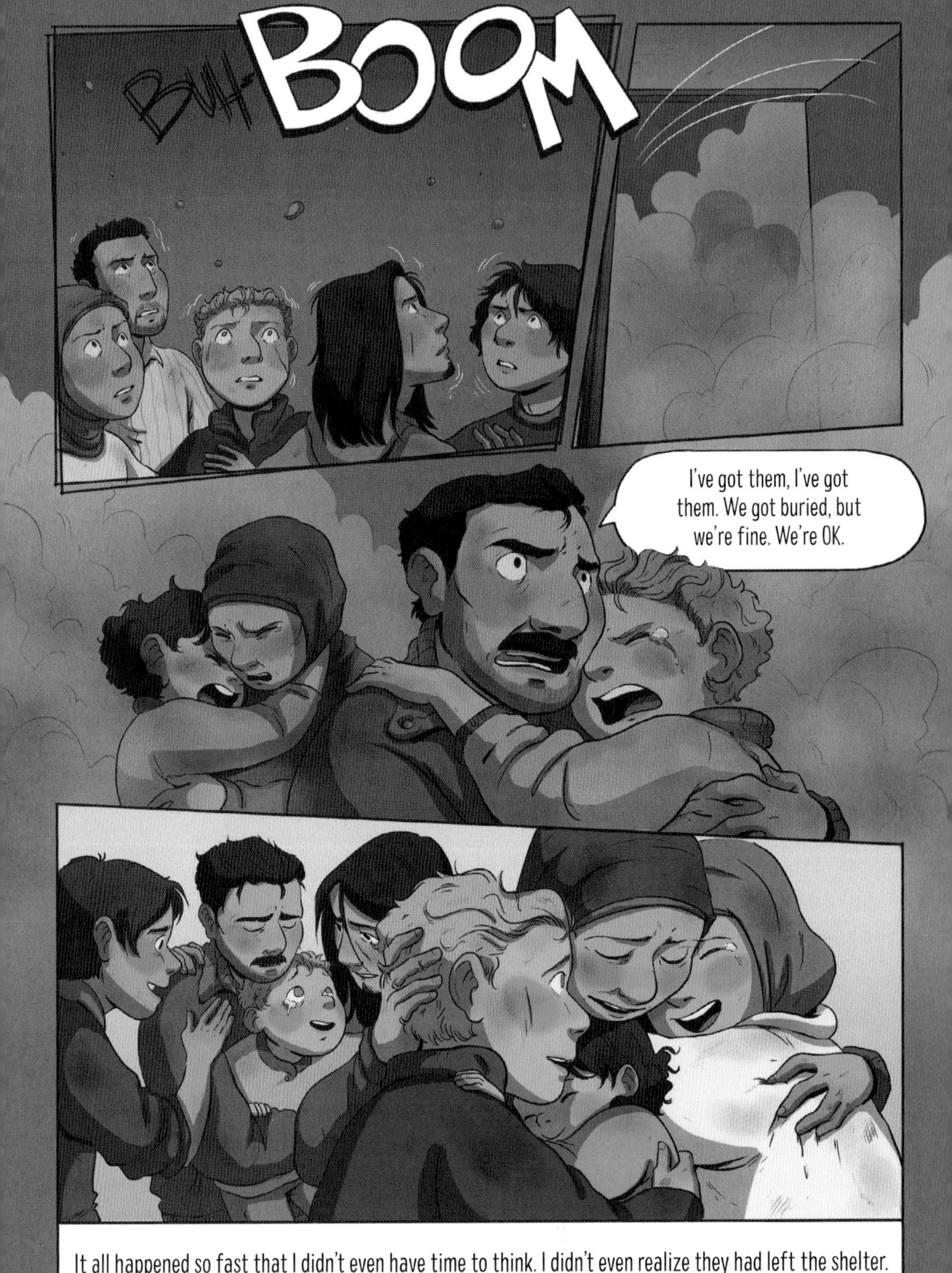
BUH-BOOM
I've got them, I've got them. We got buried, but we're fine. We're OK.
It all happened so fast that I didn't even have time to think. I didn't even realize they had left the shelter.

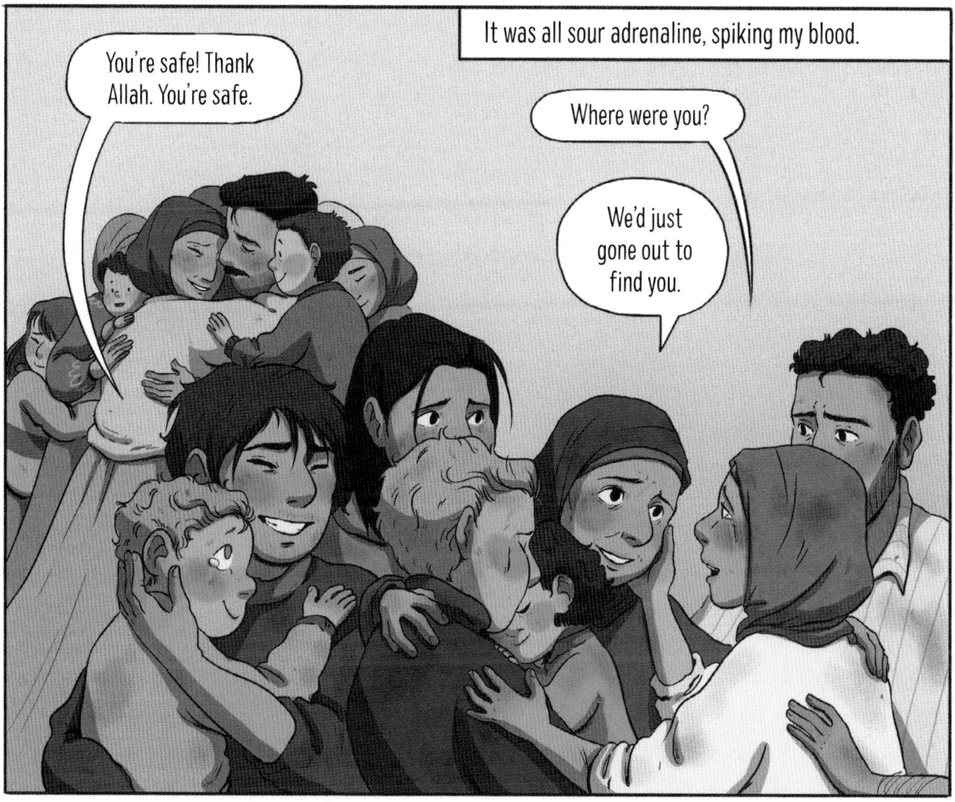
It was all sour adrenaline, spiking my blood.
You're safe! Thank Allah. You're safe.
Where were you?
We'd just gone out to find you.

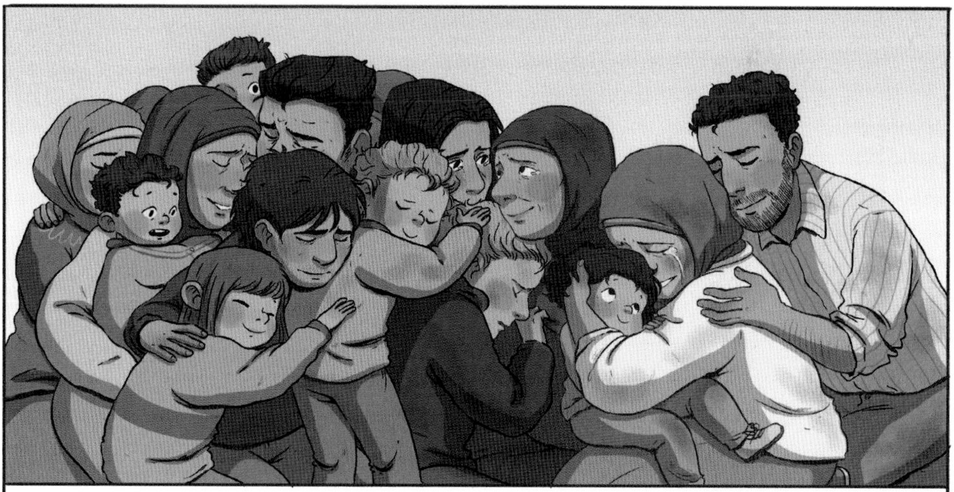
It wasn't until we were finally safe—until we were finally together—that the relief hit me like a physical thing, almost painful in its intensity, pushing the air out of my lungs and any coherent thoughts from my head.

Suddenly I couldn't breathe. I gasped for air. It was OK.
It was going to be OK. We were all alive.

We still had one another.

And I never wanted that to change.

CHAPTER 17

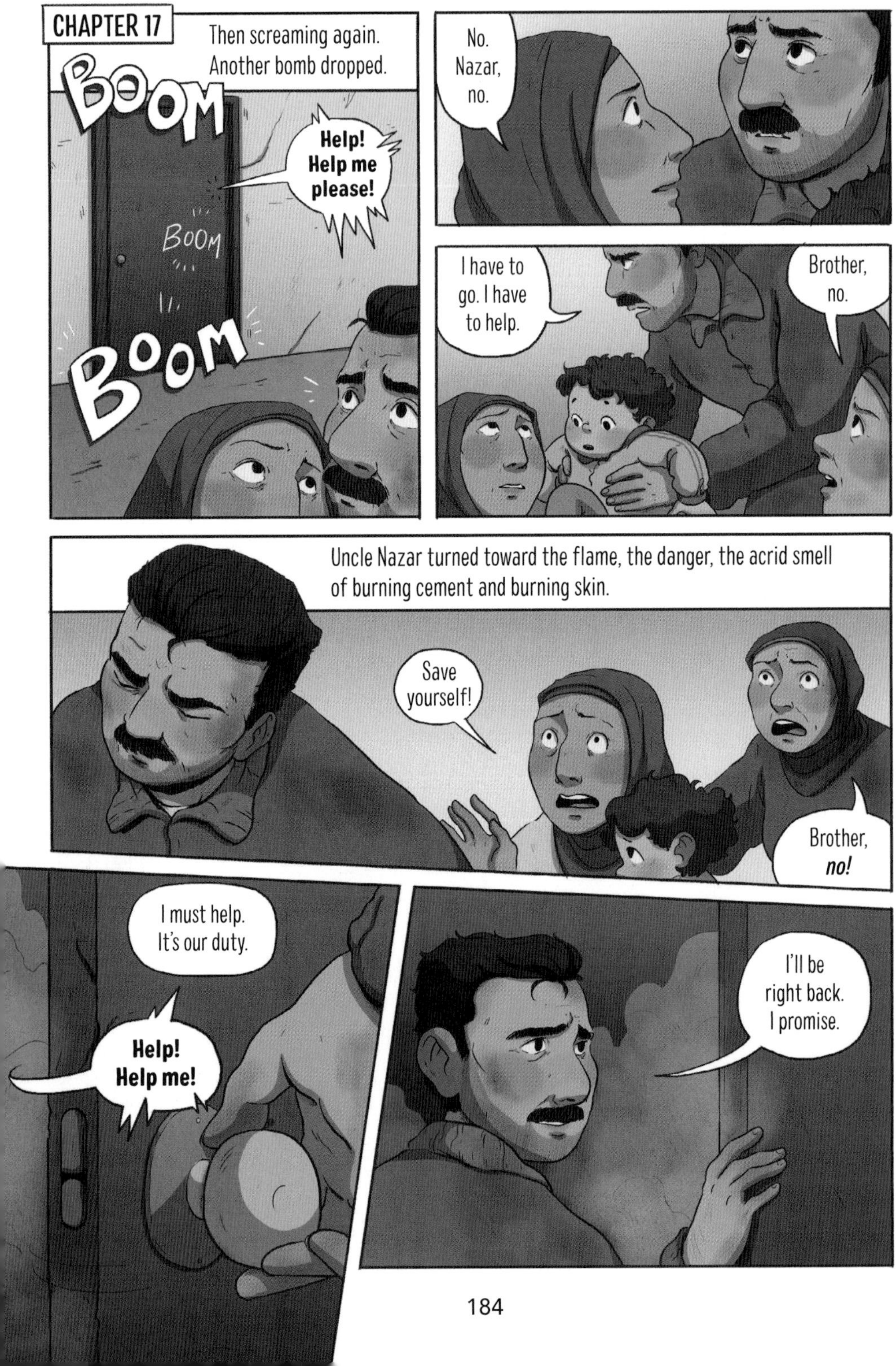
Then screaming again.
Another bomb dropped.
BOOM
Help! Help me please!
BOOM
BOOM
No. Nazar, no.
I have to go. I have to help.
Brother, no.
Uncle Nazar turned toward the flame, the danger, the acrid smell of burning cement and burning skin.
Save yourself!
Brother, *no!*
I must help. It's our duty.
Help! Help me!
I'll be right back. I promise.

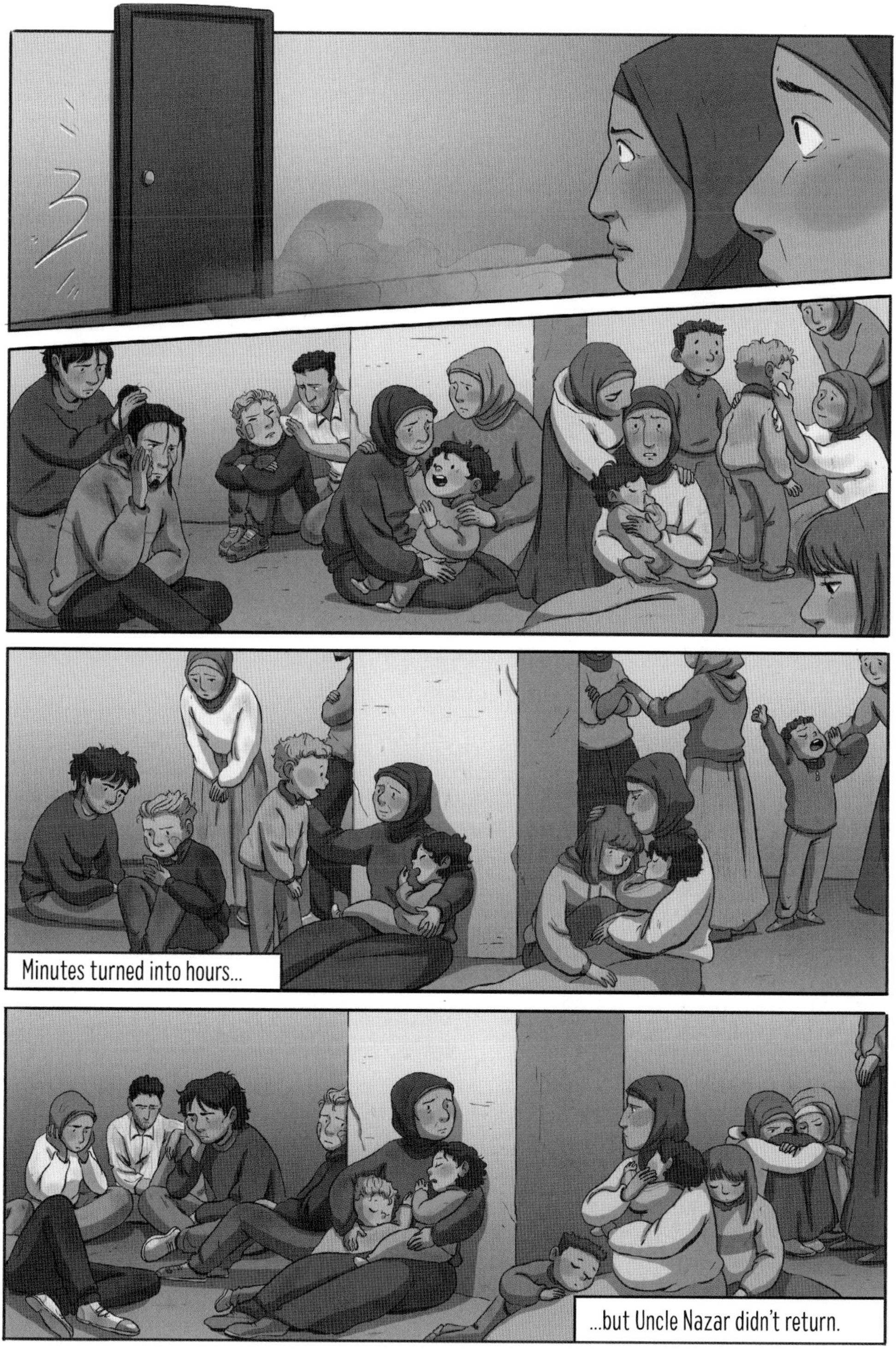
Minutes turned into hours...
...but Uncle Nazar didn't return.

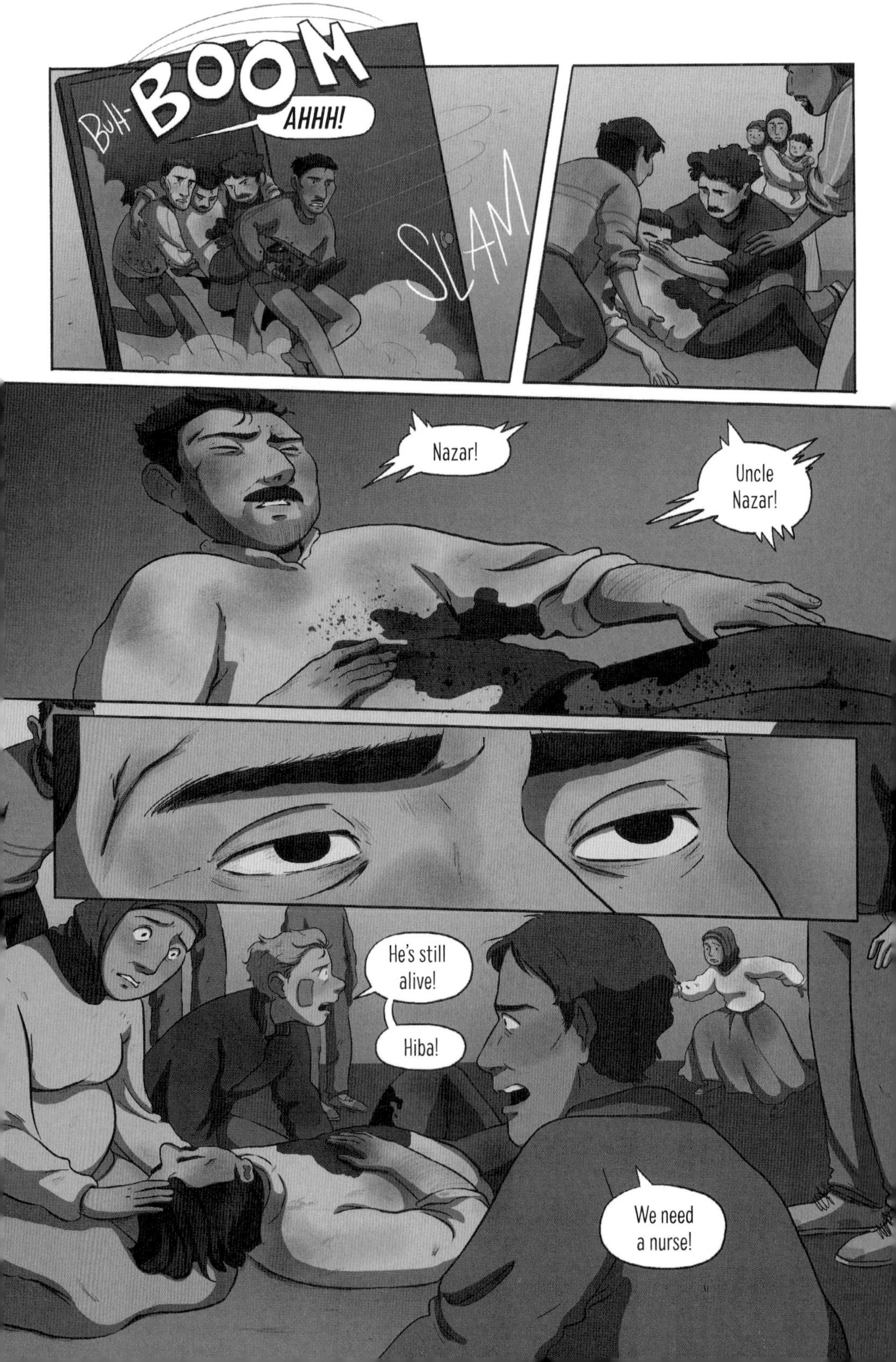
BUH-BOOM
AHHH!
SLAM
Nazar!
Uncle Nazar!
He's still alive!
Hiba!
We need a nurse!

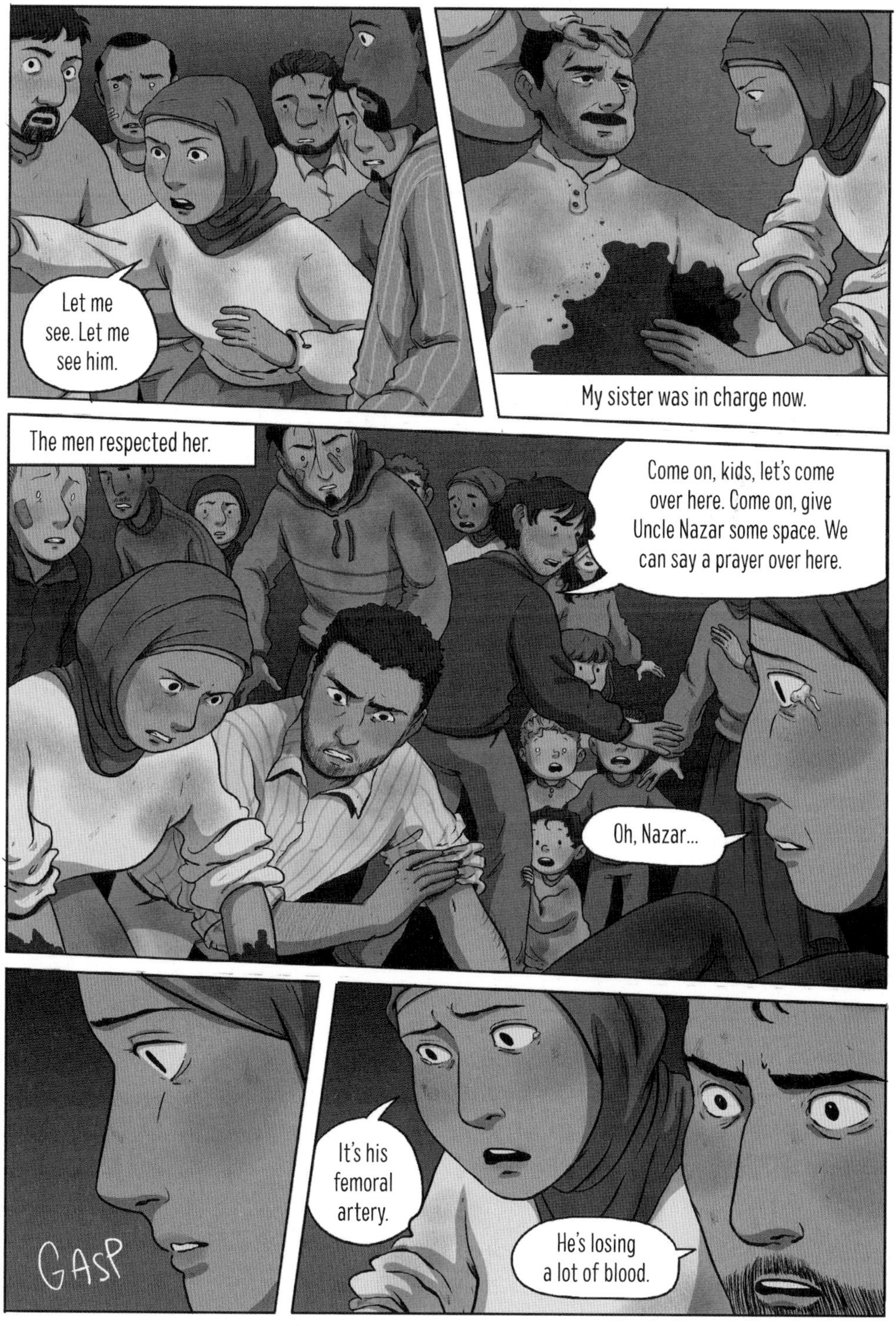
Let me see. Let me see him.
My sister was in charge now.
The men respected her.
Come on, kids, let's come over here. Come on, give Uncle Nazar some space. We can say a prayer over here.
Oh, Nazar...
GASP
It's his femoral artery.
He's losing a lot of blood.

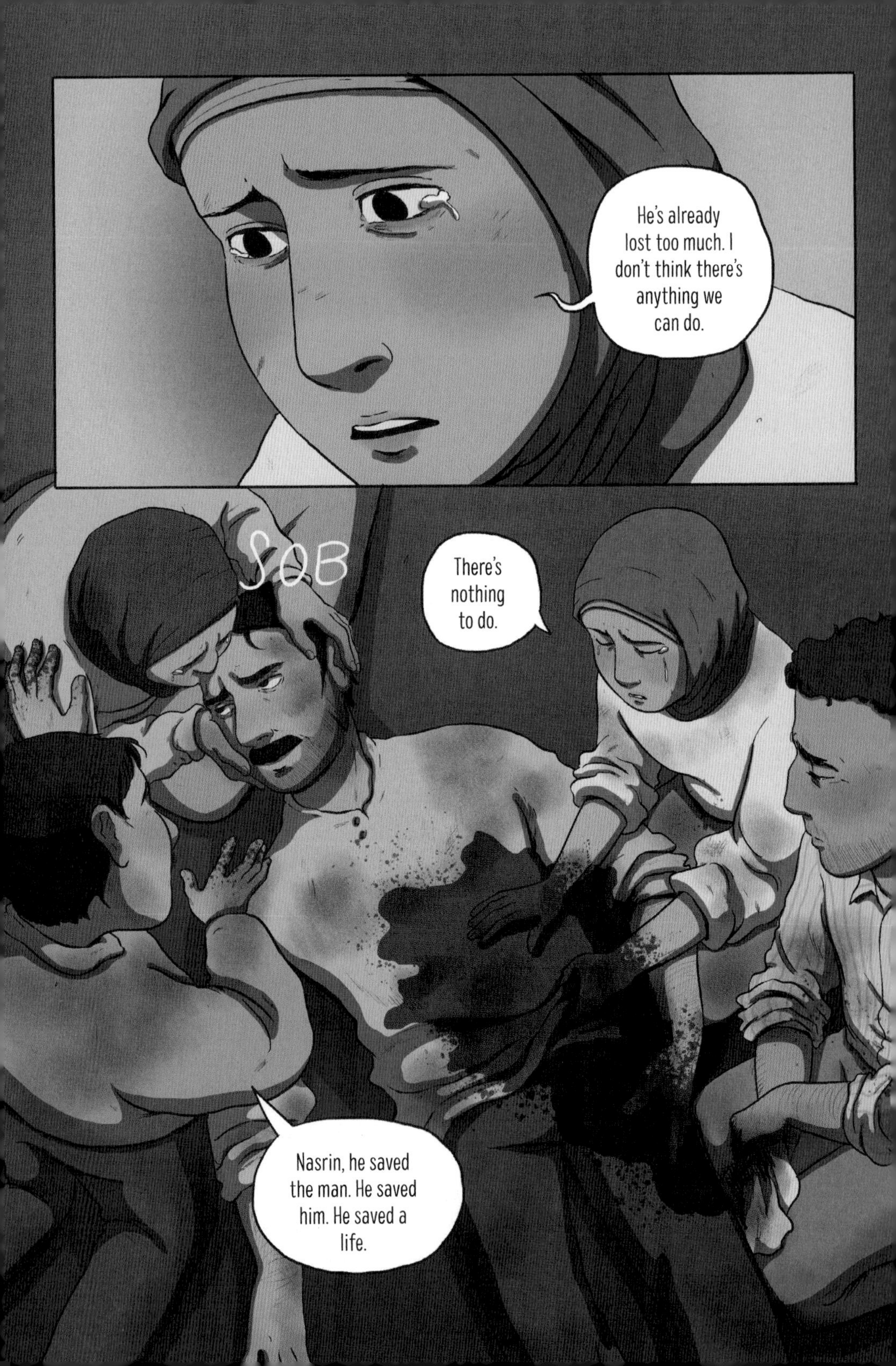
He's already lost too much. I don't think there's anything we can do.
SOB
There's nothing to do.
Nasrin, he saved the man. He saved him. He saved a life.

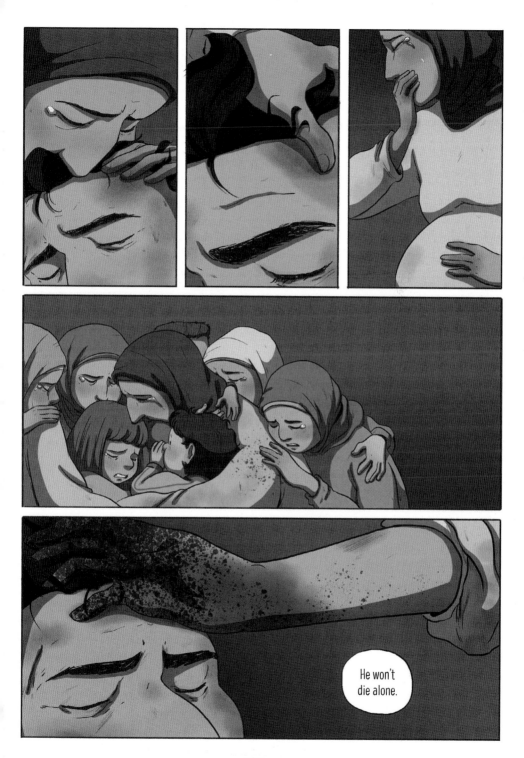

He won't
die alone.

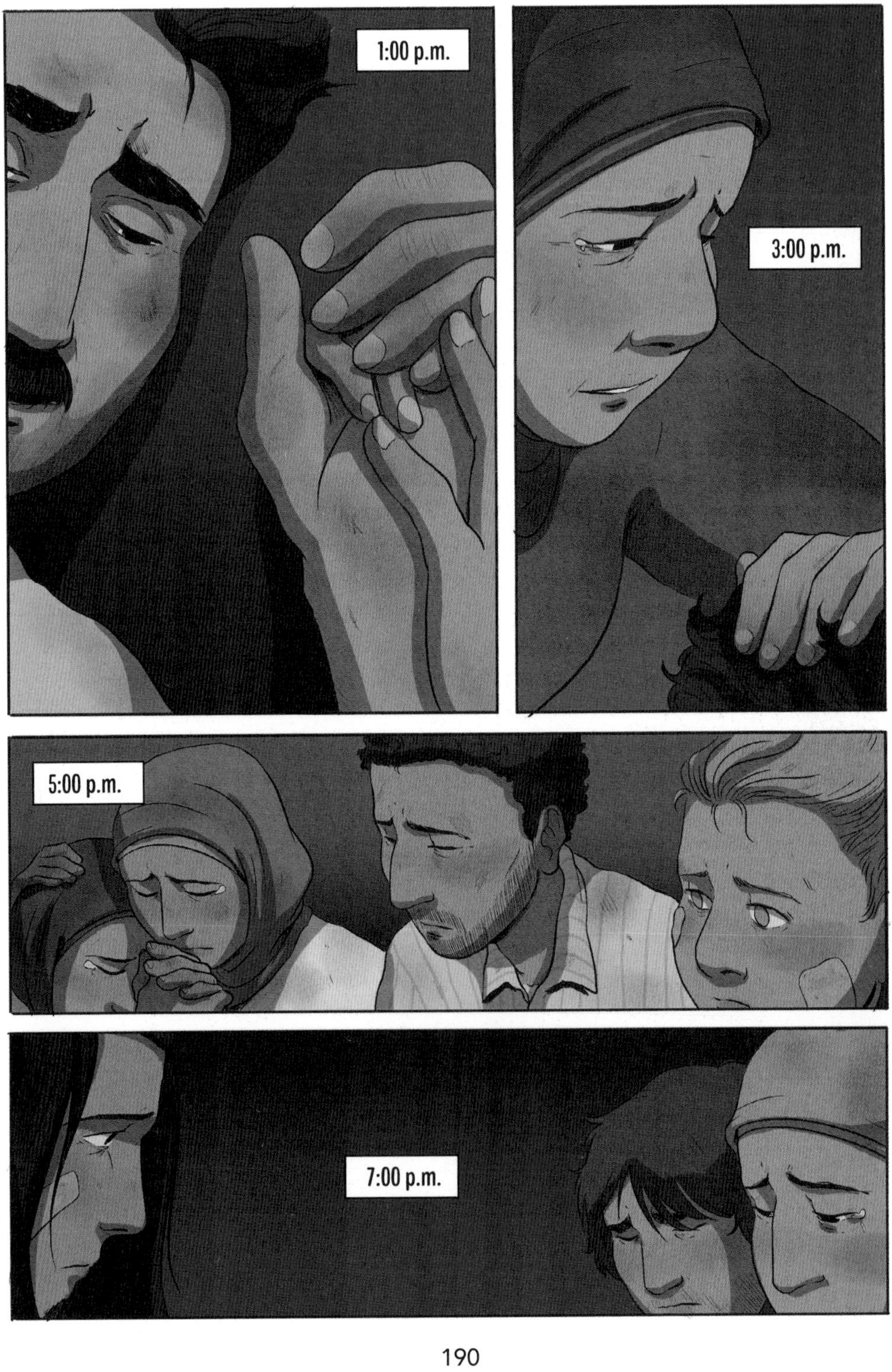
1:00 p.m.
3:00 p.m.
5:00 p.m.
7:00 p.m.

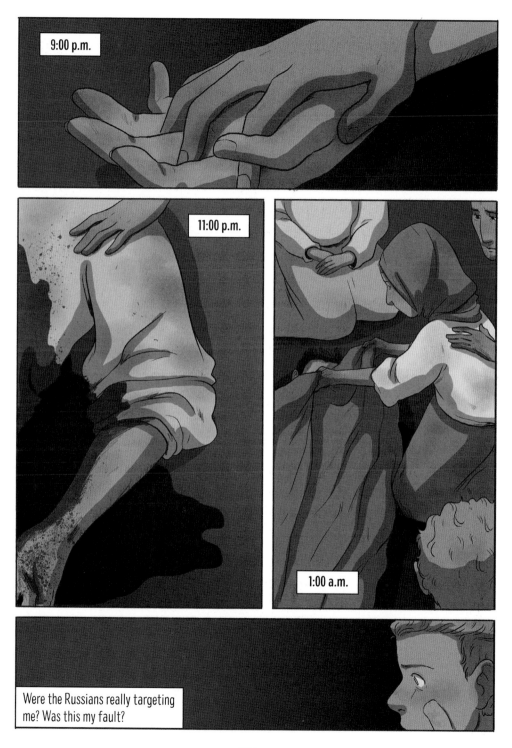

9:00 p.m.

11:00 p.m.

1:00 a.m.

Were the Russians really targeting me? Was this my fault?

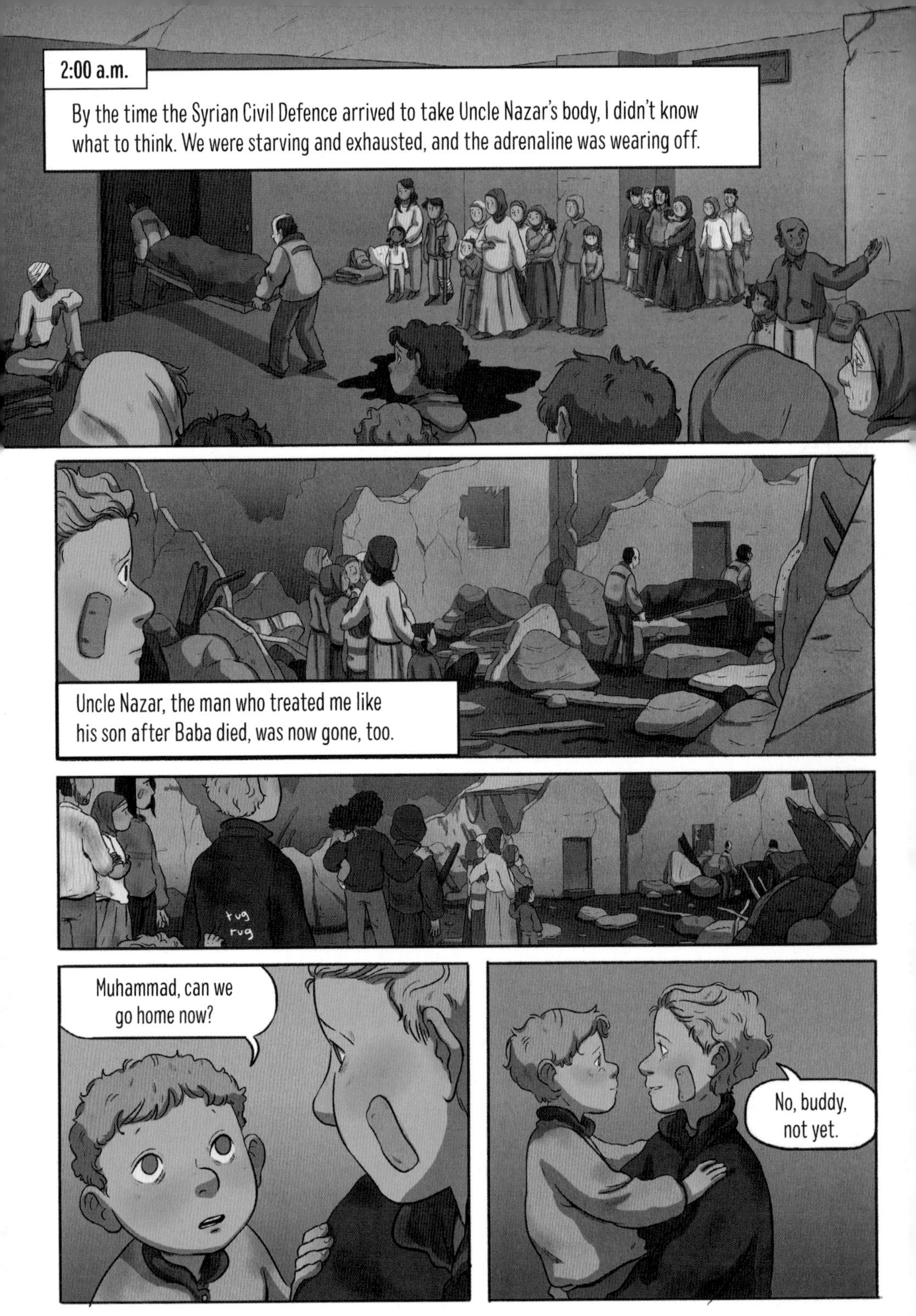
2:00 a.m.
By the time the Syrian Civil Defence arrived to take Uncle Nazar's body, I didn't know what to think. We were starving and exhausted, and the adrenaline was wearing off.
Uncle Nazar, the man who treated me like his son after Baba died, was now gone, too.
tug tug
Muhammad, can we go home now?
No, buddy, not yet.

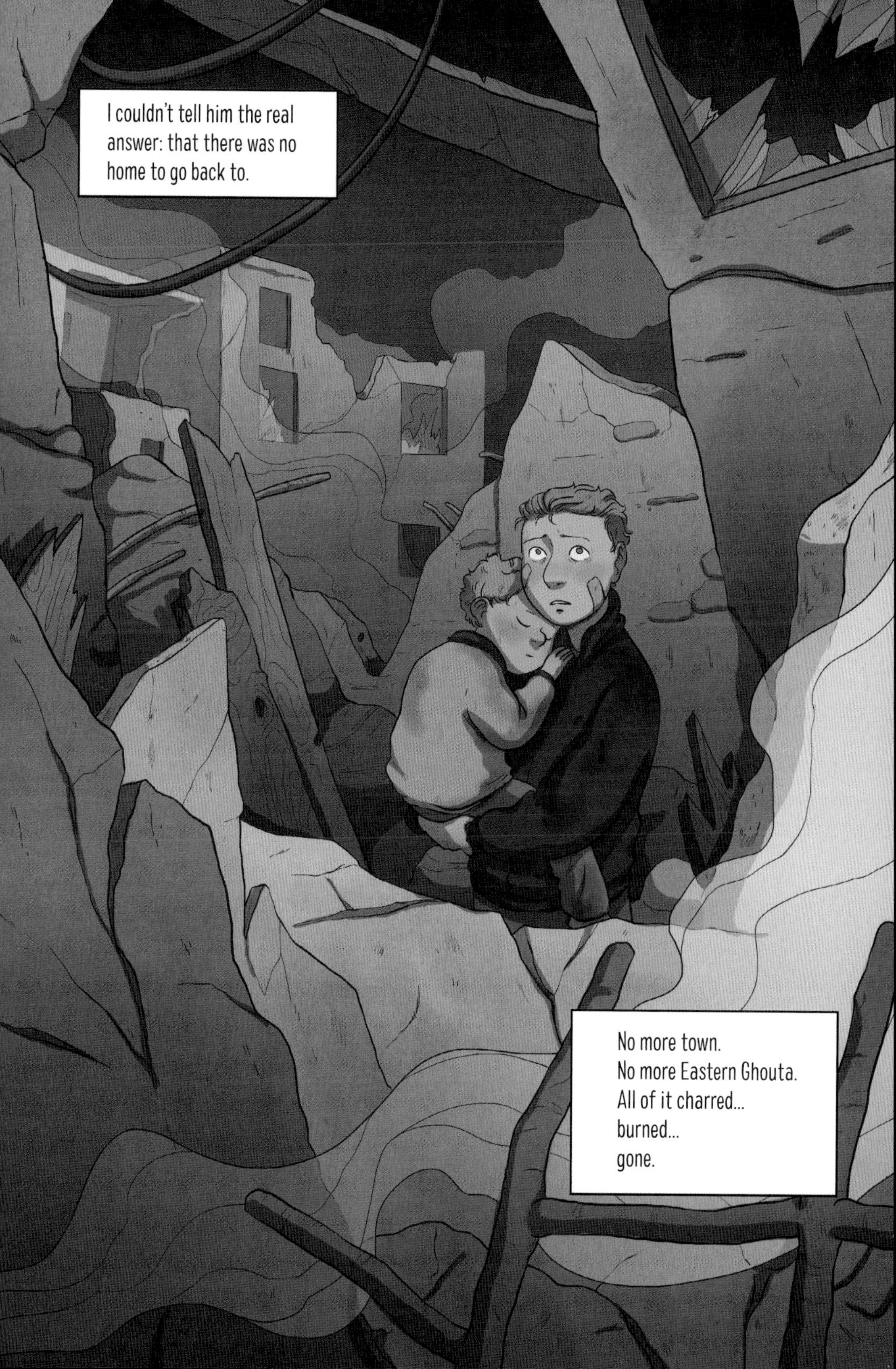
I couldn't tell him the real answer: that there was no home to go back to.
No more town.
No more Eastern Ghouta.
All of it charred...
burned...
gone.

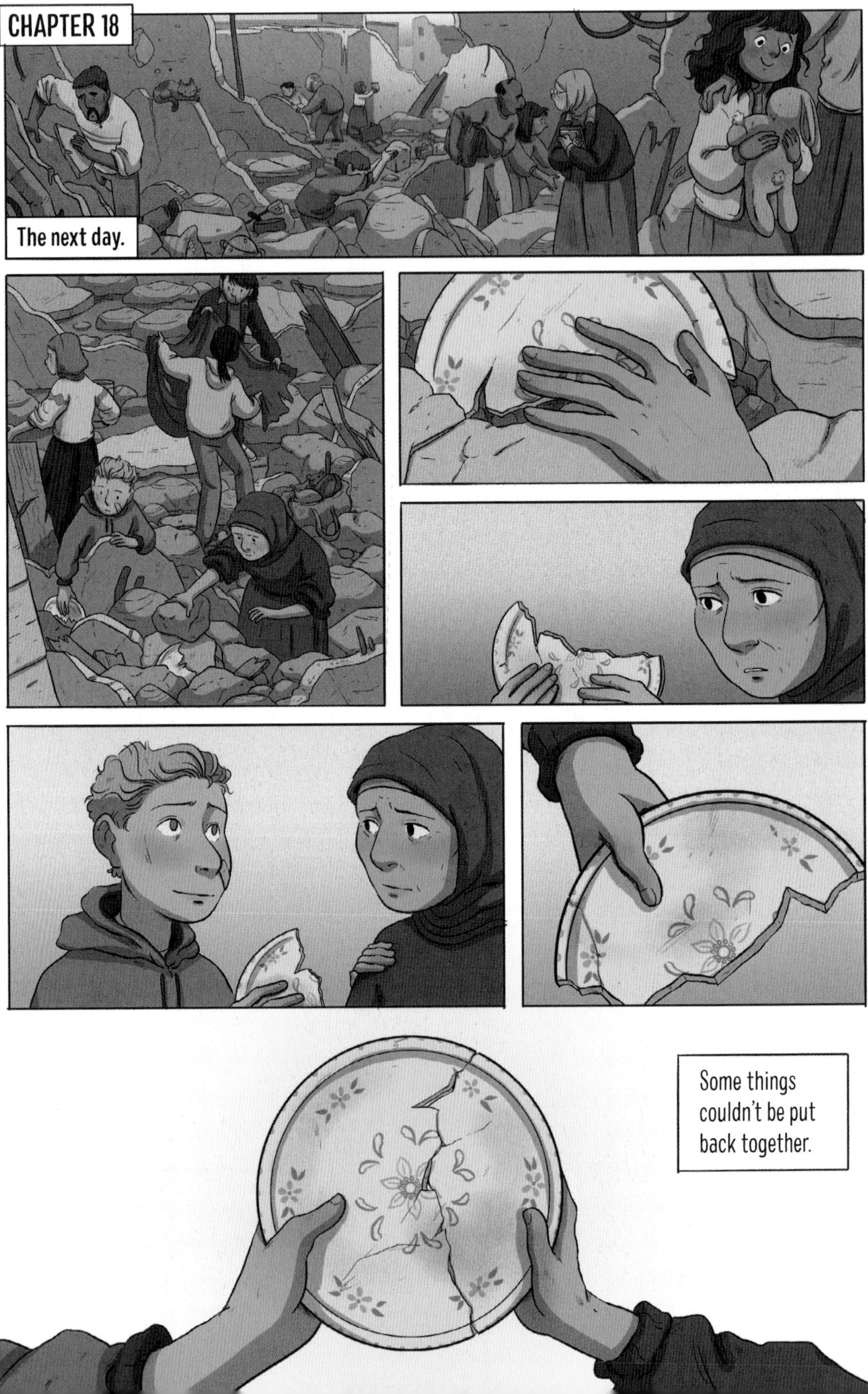
CHAPTER 18
The next day.
Some things couldn't be put back together.

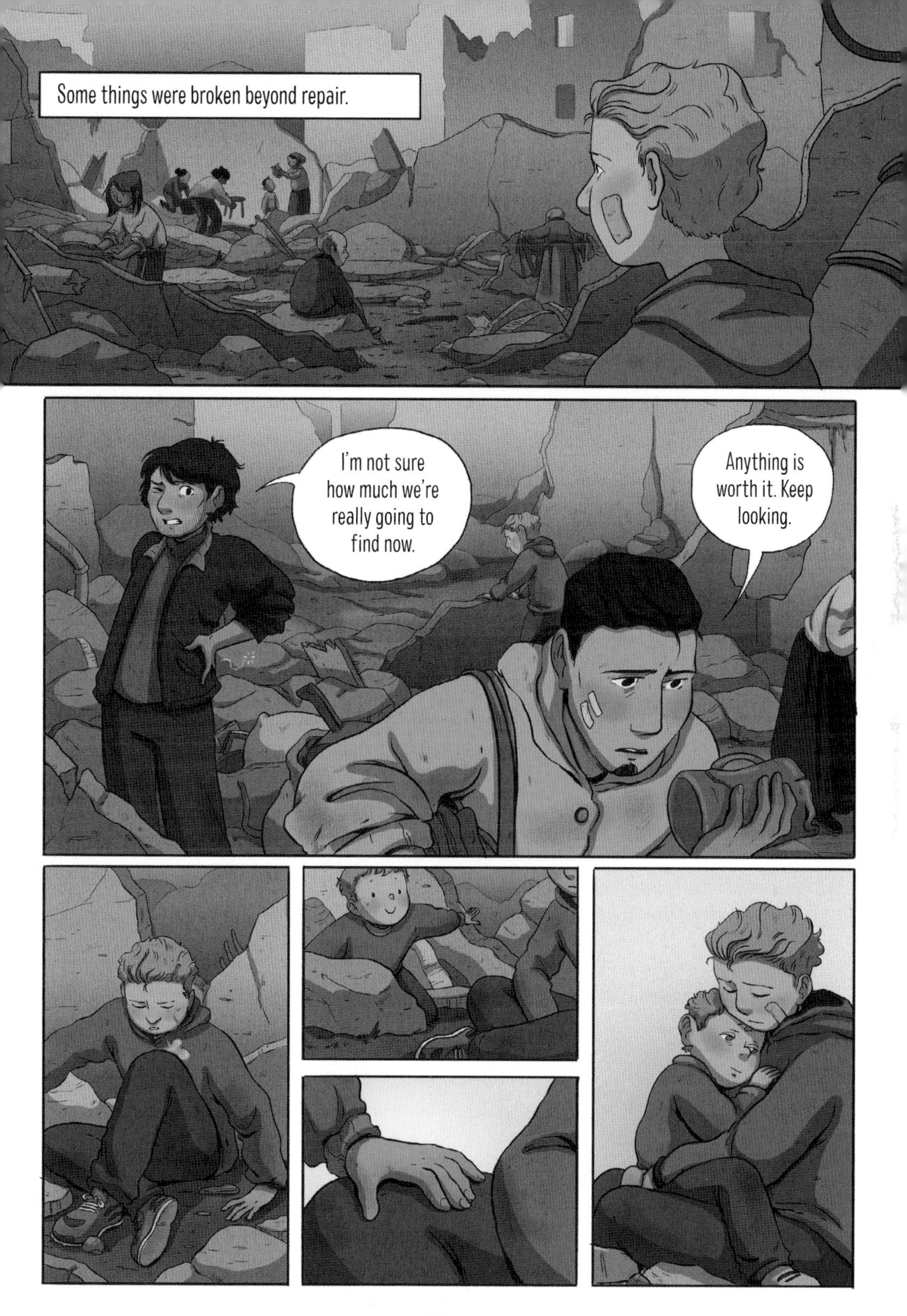
Some things were broken beyond repair.
I'm not sure how much we're really going to find now.
Anything is worth it. Keep looking.

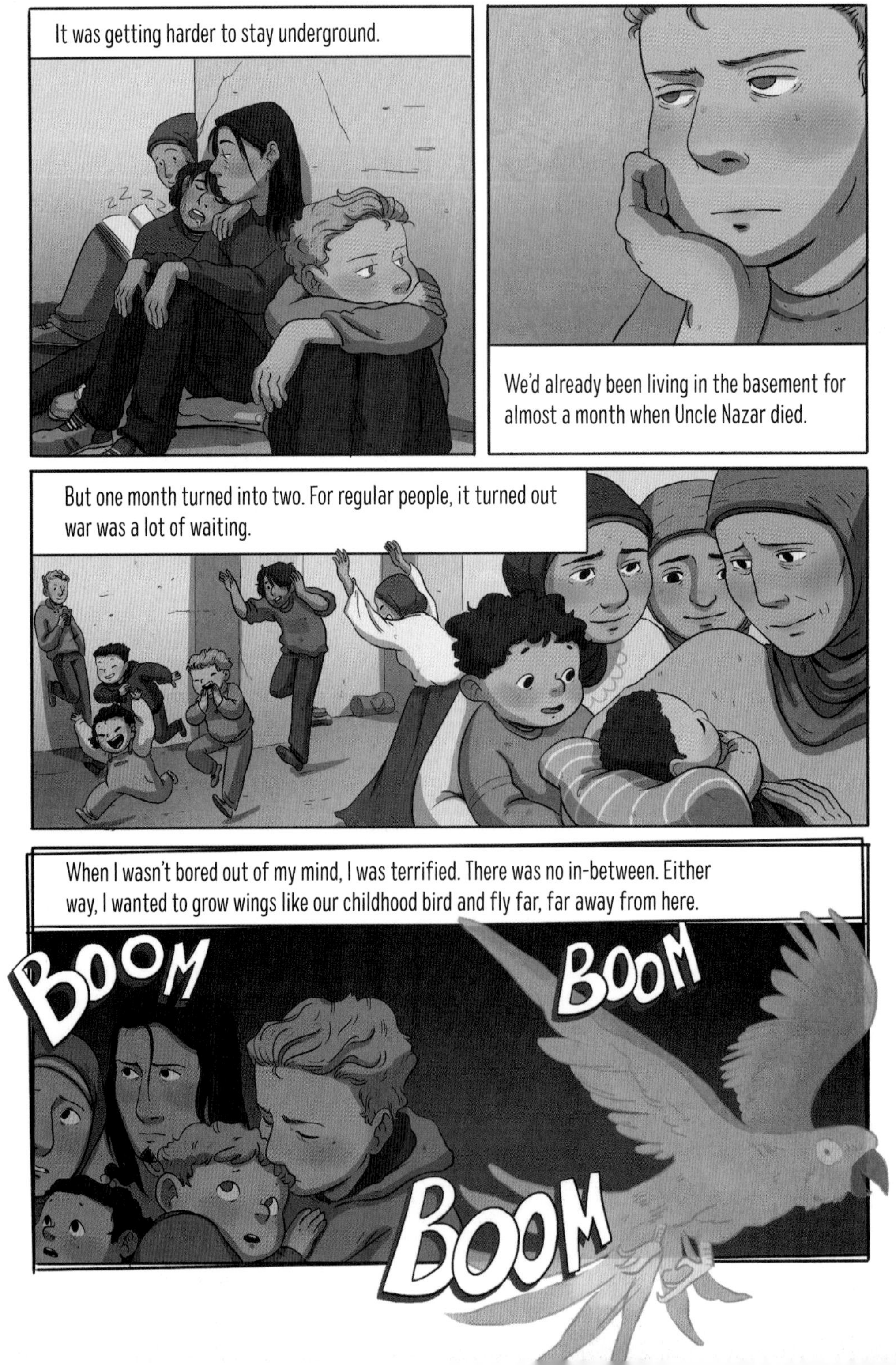
It was getting harder to stay underground.
We'd already been living in the basement for almost a month when Uncle Nazar died.
But one month turned into two. For regular people, it turned out war was a lot of waiting.
When I wasn't bored out of my mind, I was terrified. There was no in-between. Either way, I wanted to grow wings like our childhood bird and fly far, far away from here.
BOOM
BOOM
BOOM

We didn't have much after the siege.

But I still had my reporting.

`09:26:47`

I had the video I took during the strike.

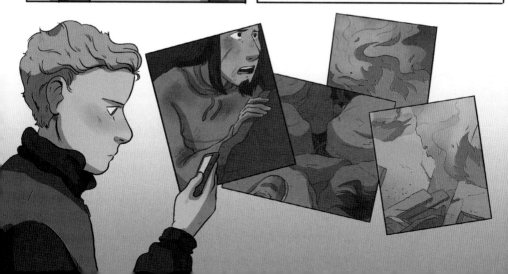

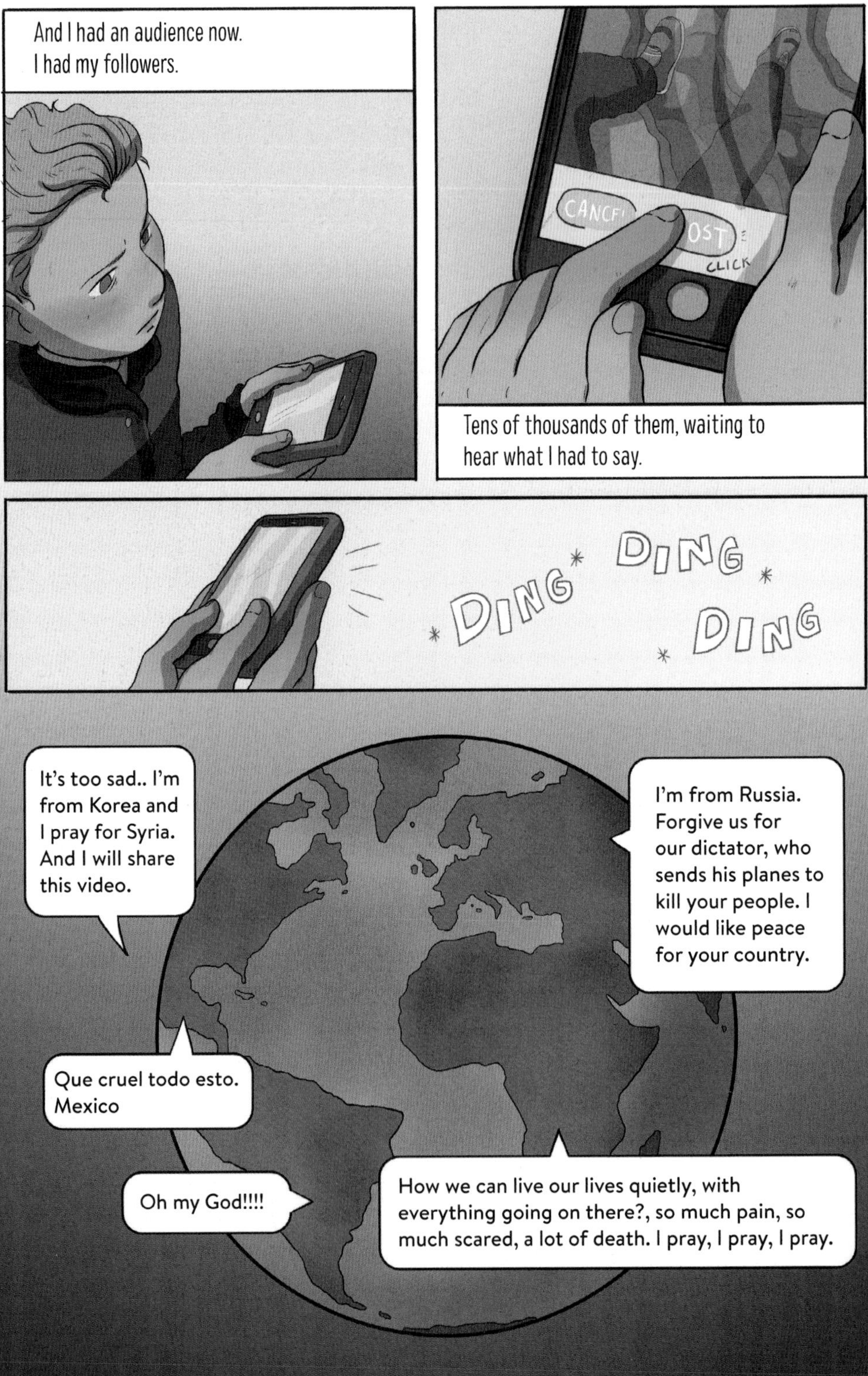
And I had an audience now.
I had my followers.
Tens of thousands of them, waiting to hear what I had to say.
DING DING DING
It's too sad.. I'm from Korea and I pray for Syria. And I will share this video.
I'm from Russia. Forgive us for our dictator, who sends his planes to kill your people. I would like peace for your country.
Que cruel todo esto. Mexico
Oh my God!!!!
How we can live our lives quietly, with everything going on there?, so much pain, so much scared, a lot of death. I pray, I pray, I pray.

Soon we began running out of food in the basement. We couldn't wash our hands. There was no bathroom. And people kept dying if they went outside.

But where would we even go?

I don't know.

They weren't talking to me directly, but I knew what they were considering.

How would we even leave? We'd be killed on the road before we got out of town.

I don't know, Hiba. I don't know.

But we can't stay here.

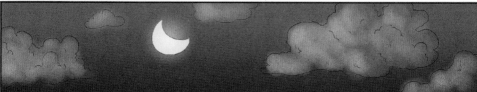

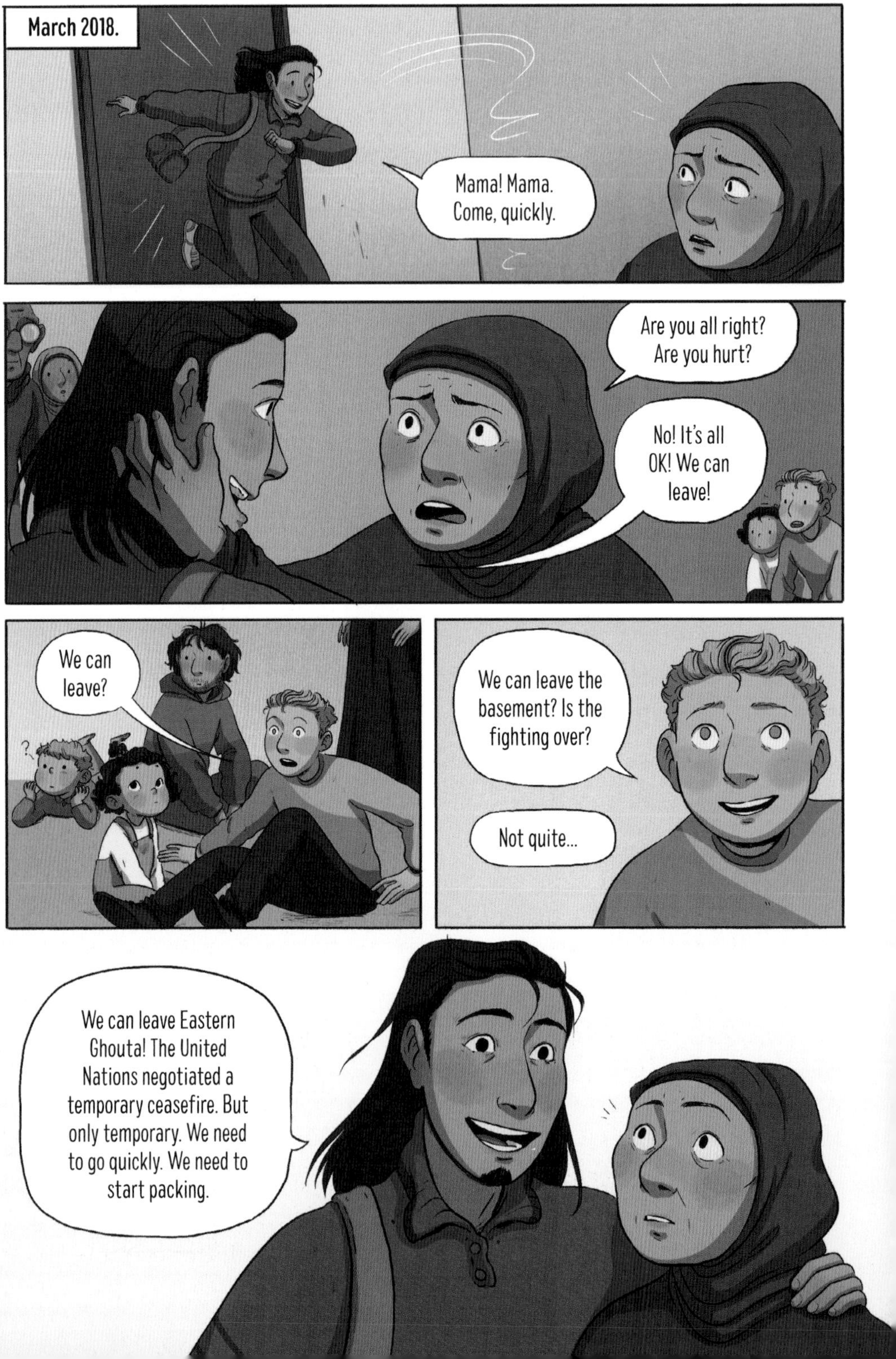
March 2018.
Mama! Mama. Come, quickly.
Are you all right? Are you hurt?
No! It's all OK! We can leave!
We can leave?
We can leave the basement? Is the fighting over?
Not quite...
We can leave Eastern Ghouta! The United Nations negotiated a temporary ceasefire. But only temporary. We need to go quickly. We need to start packing.

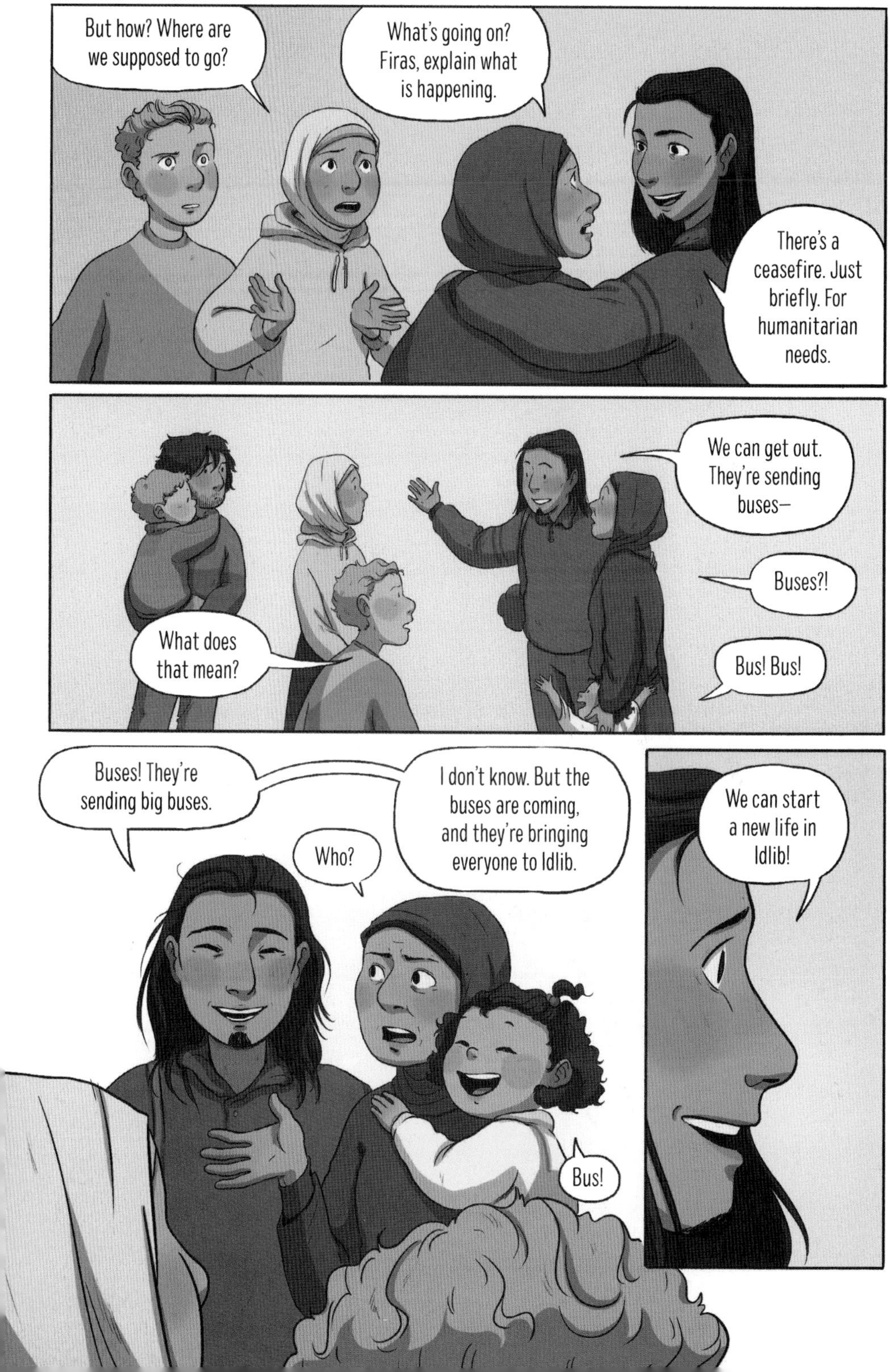
But how? Where are we supposed to go?
What's going on? Firas, explain what is happening.
There's a ceasefire. Just briefly. For humanitarian needs.
We can get out. They're sending buses—
Buses?!
What does that mean?
Bus! Bus!
Buses! They're sending big buses.
Who?
I don't know. But the buses are coming, and they're bringing everyone to Idlib.
Bus!
We can start a new life in Idlib!

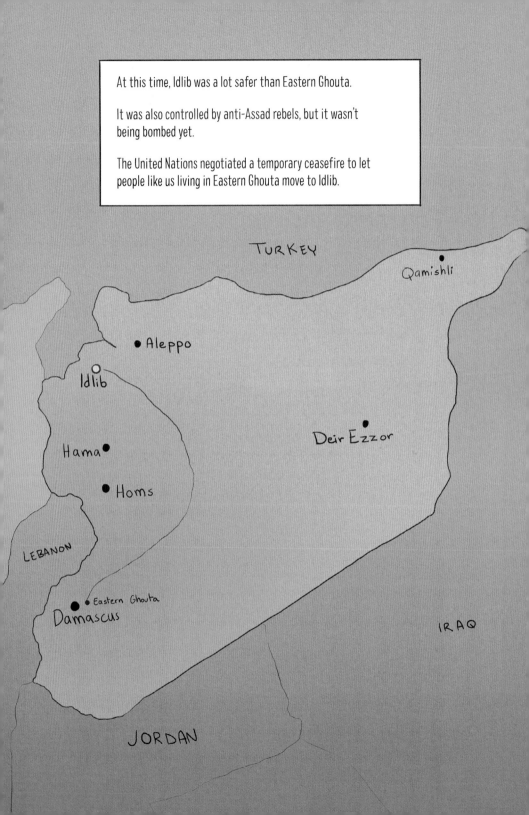

At this time, Idlib was a lot safer than Eastern Ghouta.

It was also controlled by anti-Assad rebels, but it wasn't being bombed yet.

The United Nations negotiated a temporary ceasefire to let people like us living in Eastern Ghouta move to Idlib.

TURKEY

Qamishli

Aleppo

Idlib

Deir Ezzor

Hama

Homs

LEBANON

Eastern Ghouta

Damascus

IRAQ

JORDAN

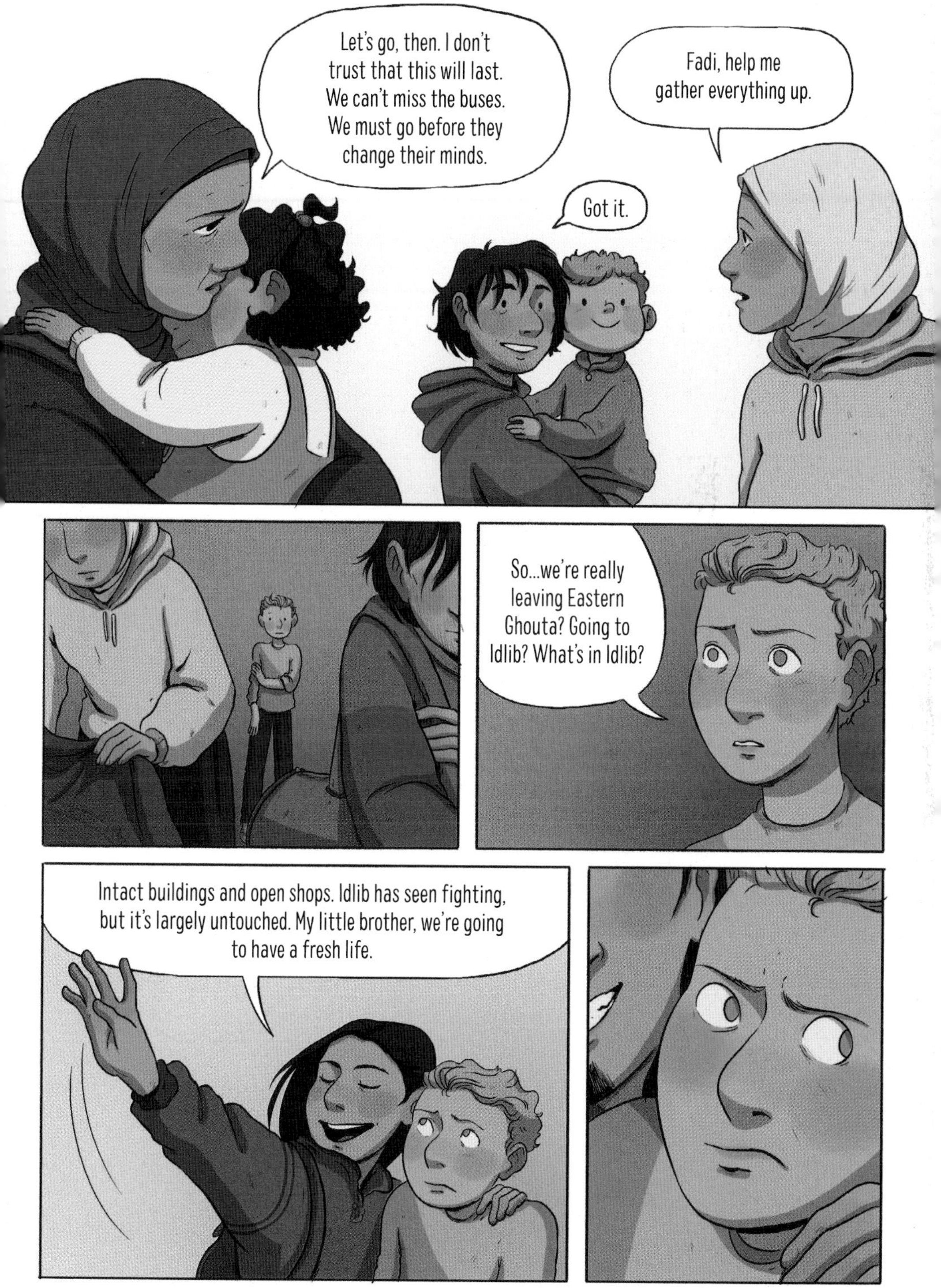
Let's go, then. I don't trust that this will last. We can't miss the buses. We must go before they change their minds.
Fadi, help me gather everything up.
Got it.
So...we're really leaving Eastern Ghouta? Going to Idlib? What's in Idlib?
Intact buildings and open shops. Idlib has seen fighting, but it's largely untouched. My little brother, we're going to have a fresh life.

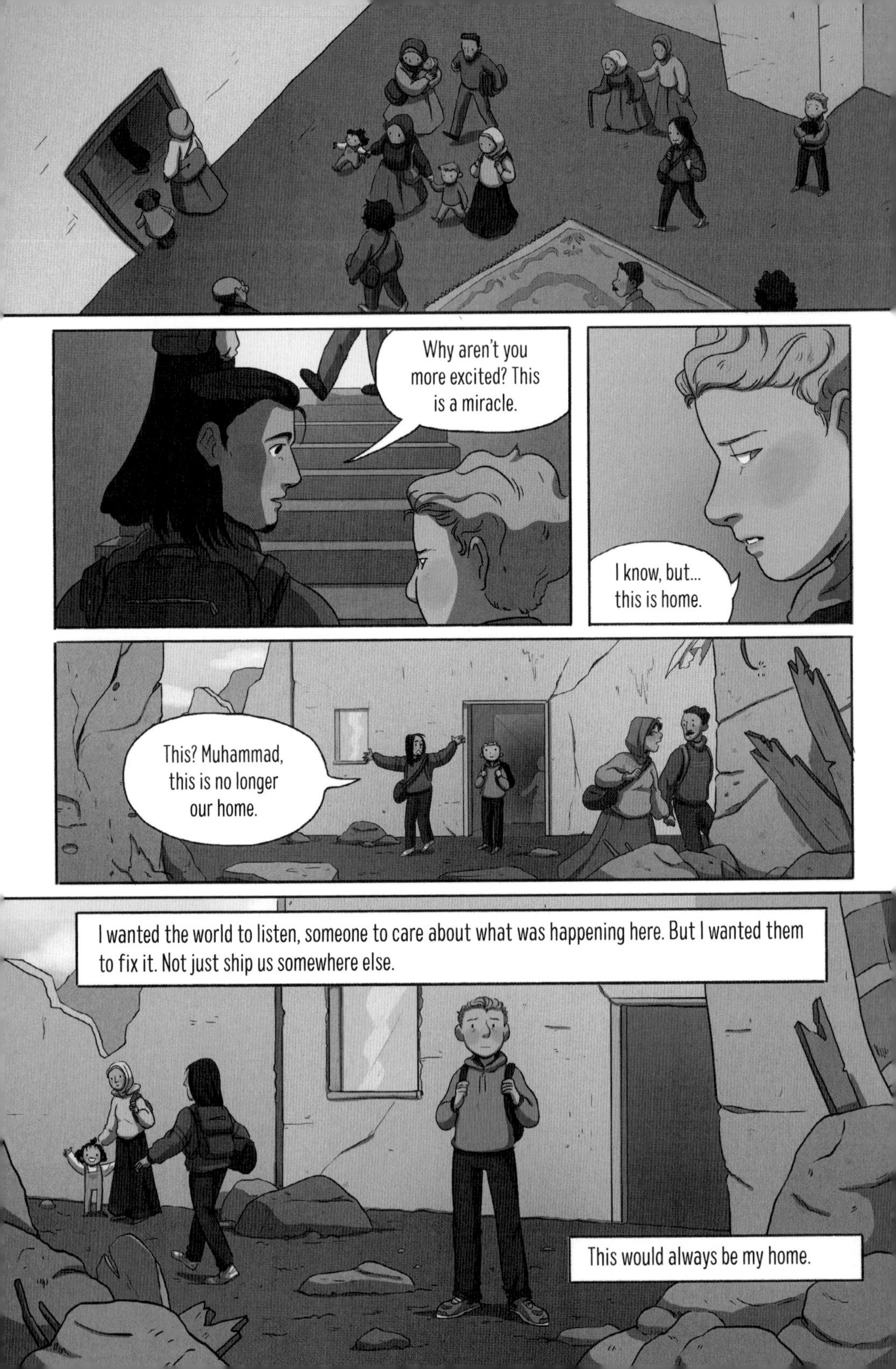
Why aren't you more excited? This is a miracle.
I know, but... this is home.
This? Muhammad, this is no longer our home.
I wanted the world to listen, someone to care about what was happening here. But I wanted them to fix it. Not just ship us somewhere else.
This would always be my home.

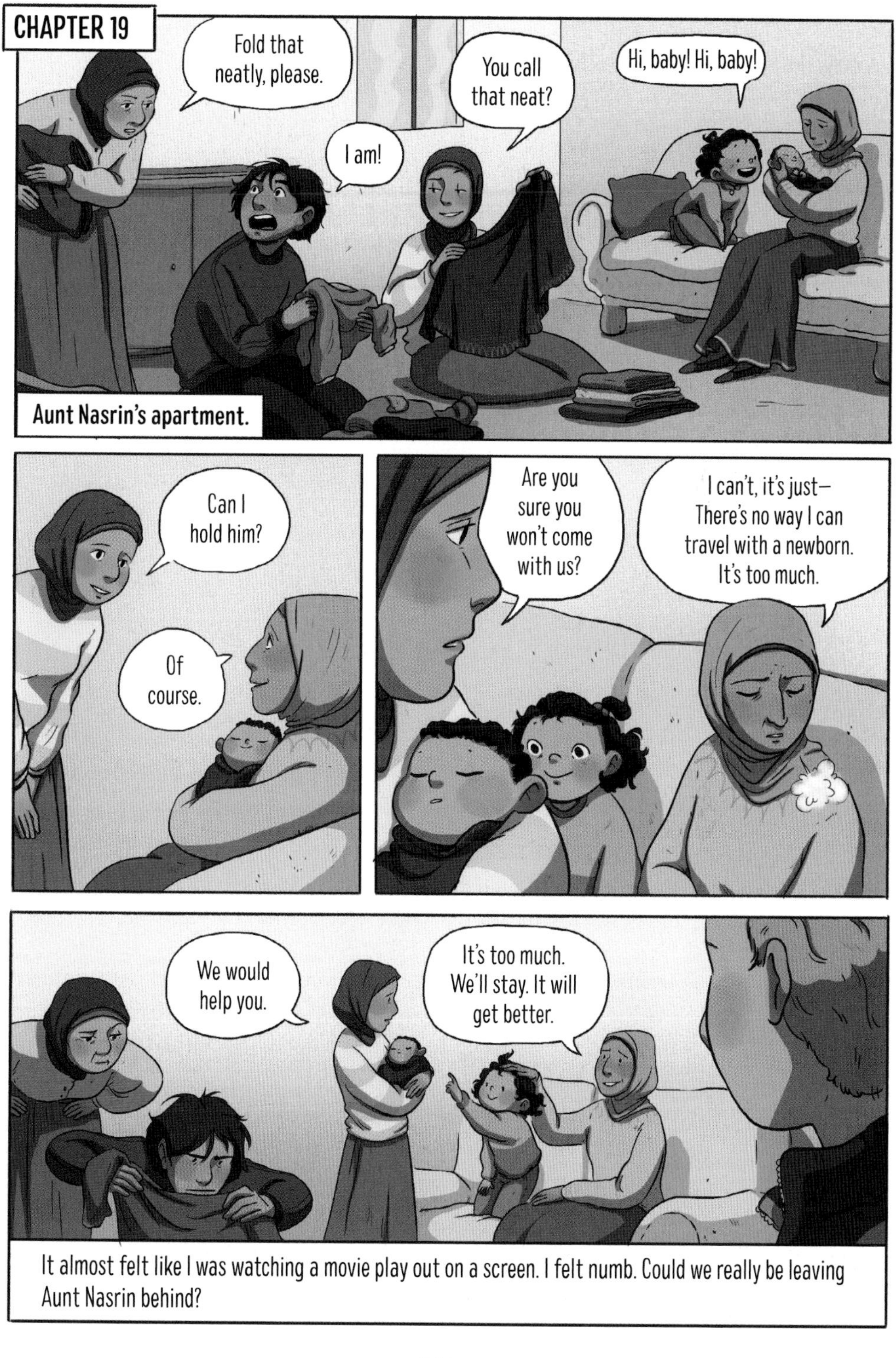
CHAPTER 19
Fold that neatly, please.
I am!
You call that neat?
Hi, baby! Hi, baby!
Aunt Nasrin's apartment.
Can I hold him?
Of course.
Are you sure you won't come with us?
I can't, it's just— There's no way I can travel with a newborn. It's too much.
We would help you.
It's too much. We'll stay. It will get better.
It almost felt like I was watching a movie play out on a screen. I felt numb. Could we really be leaving Aunt Nasrin behind?

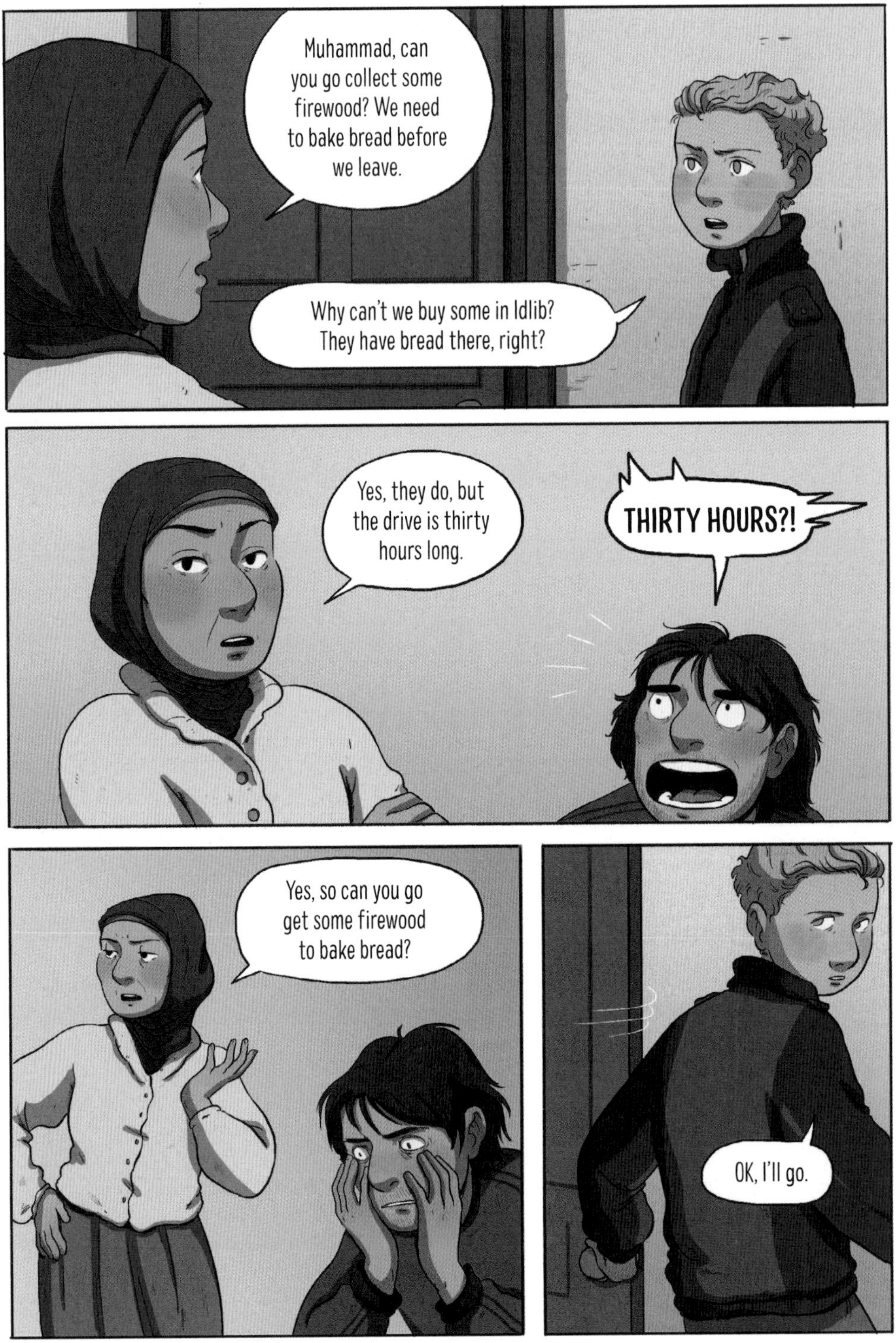
Muhammad, can you go collect some firewood? We need to bake bread before we leave.
Why can't we buy some in Idlib? They have bread there, right?
Yes, they do, but the drive is thirty hours long.
THIRTY HOURS?!
Yes, so can you go get some firewood to bake bread?
OK, I'll go.

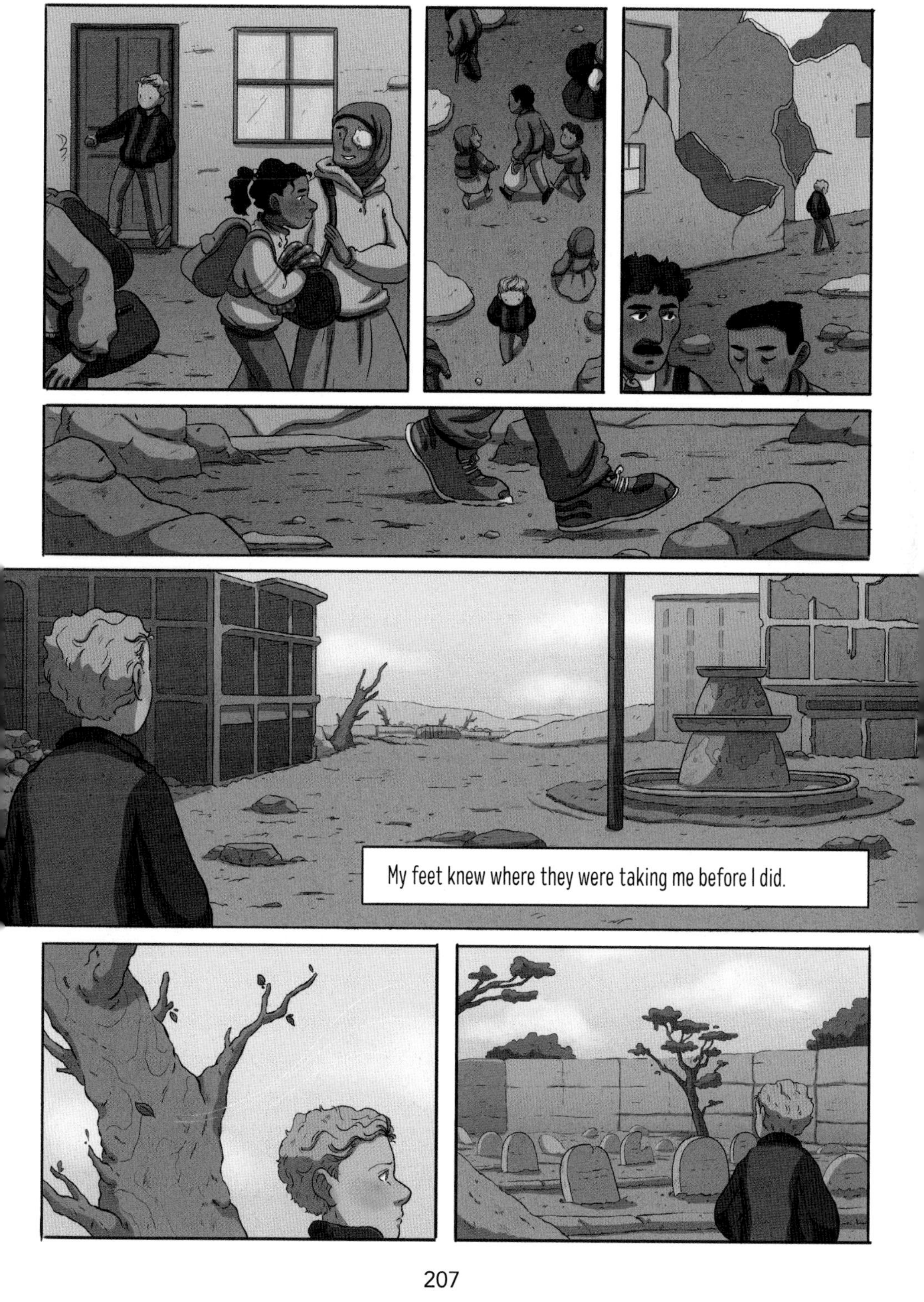
My feet knew where they were taking me before I did.

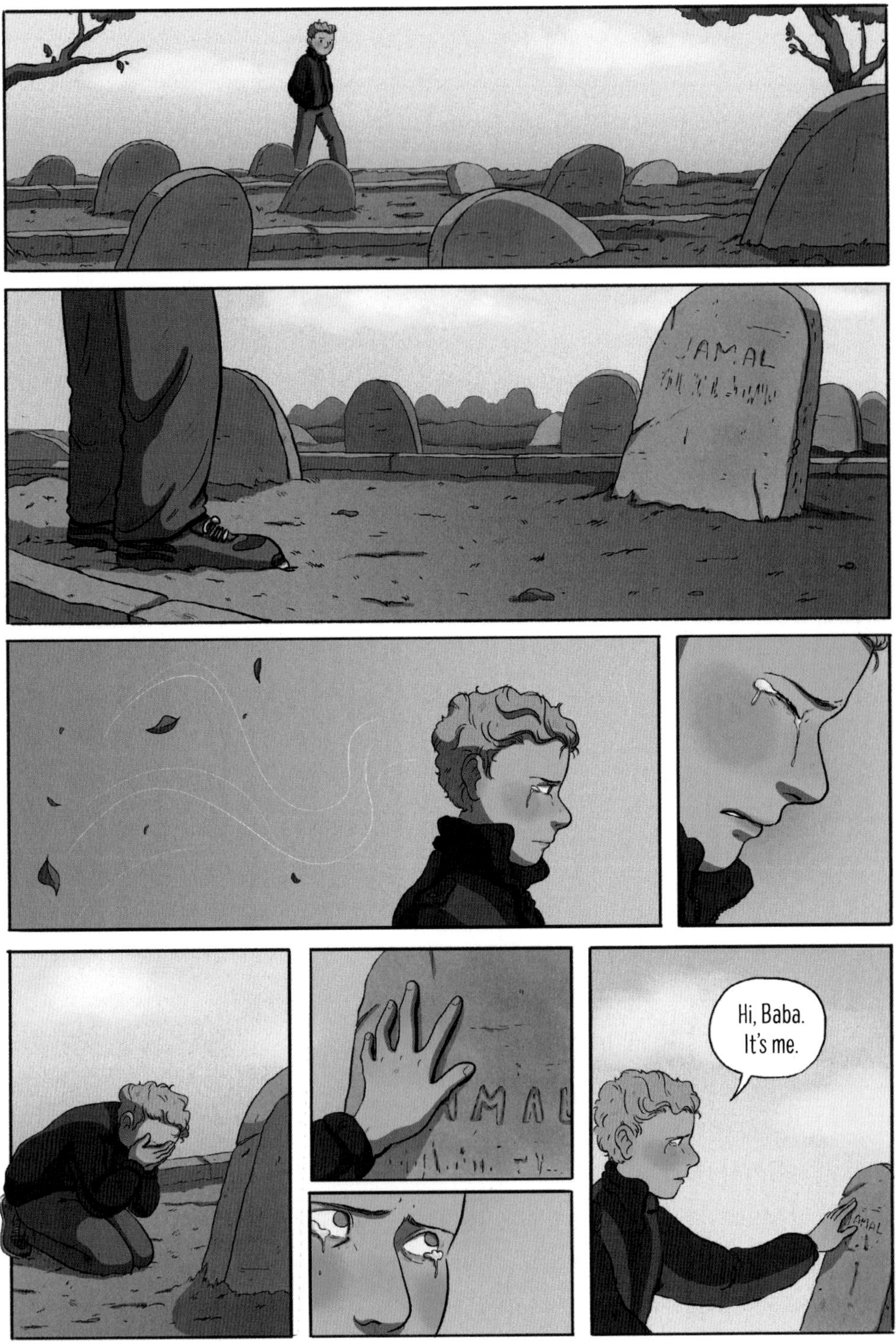
JAMAL
Hi, Baba. It's me.

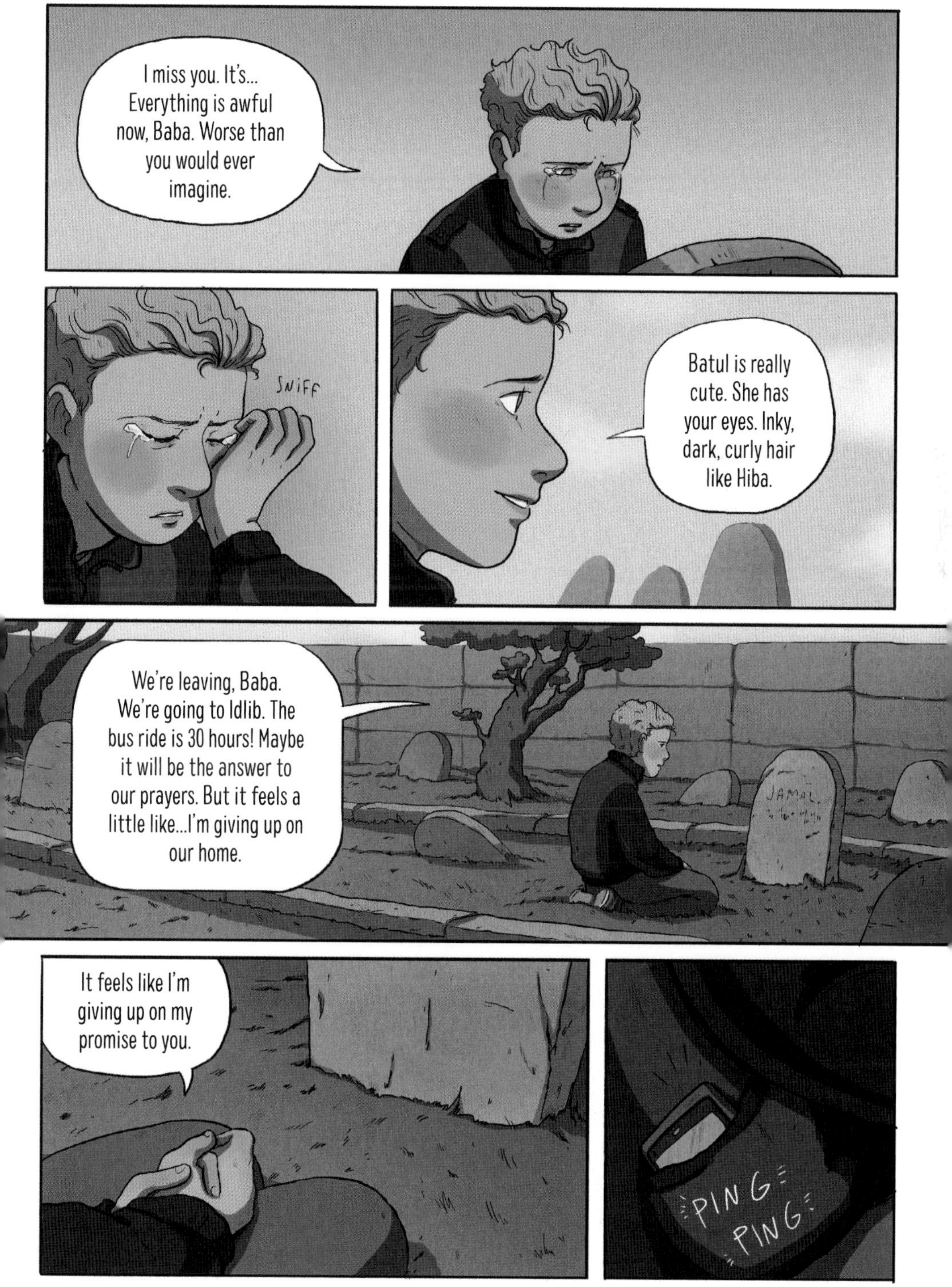
I miss you. It's... Everything is awful now, Baba. Worse than you would ever imagine.
SNIFF
Batul is really cute. She has your eyes. Inky, dark, curly hair like Hiba.
We're leaving, Baba. We're going to Idlib. The bus ride is 30 hours! Maybe it will be the answer to our prayers. But it feels a little like...I'm giving up on our home.
JAMAL
It feels like I'm giving up on my promise to you.
PING PING

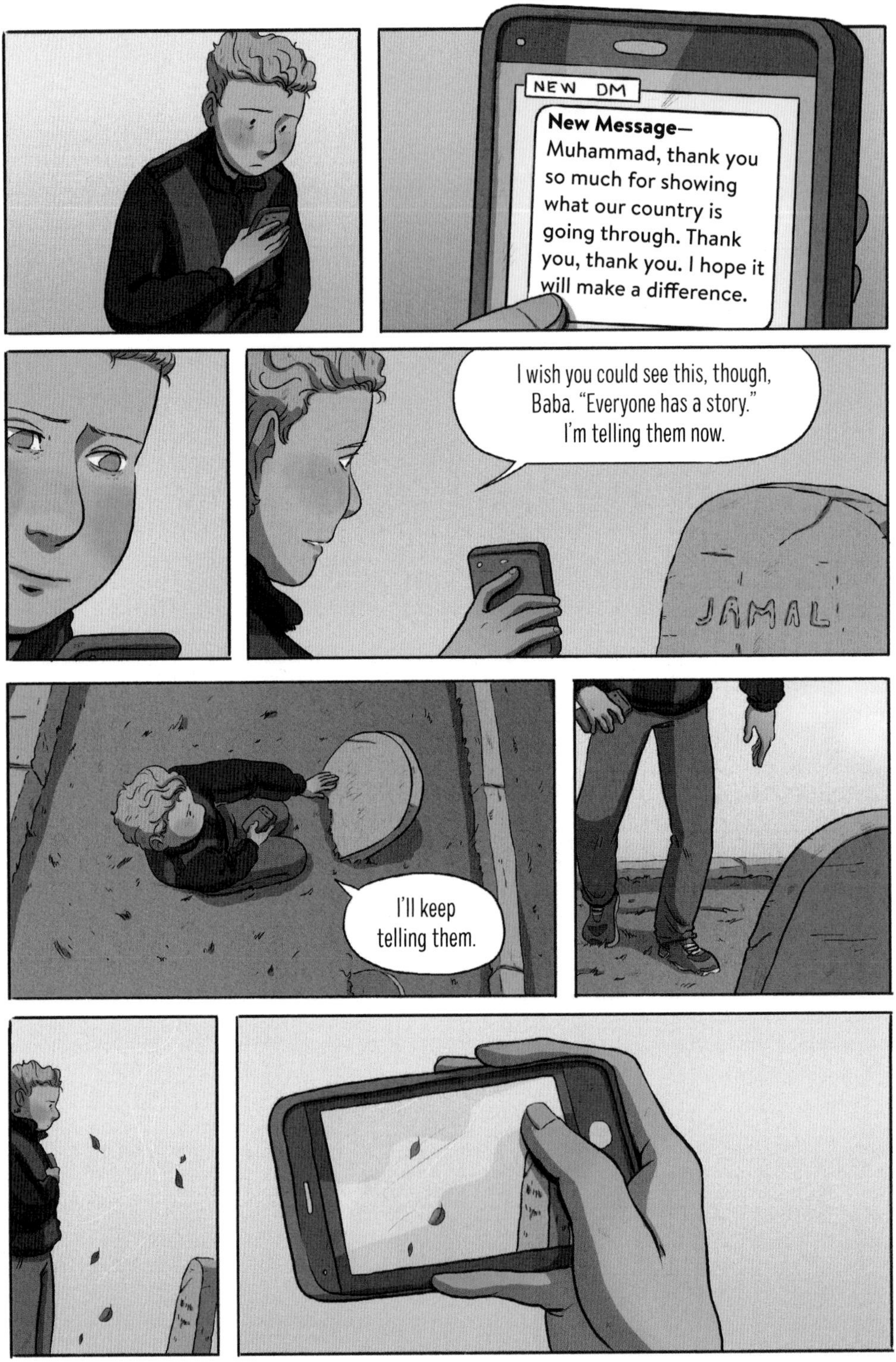
NEW DM
New Message—
Muhammad, thank you so much for showing what our country is going through. Thank you, thank you. I hope it will make a difference.
I wish you could see this, though, Baba. "Everyone has a story." I'm telling them now.
JAMAL
I'll keep telling them.

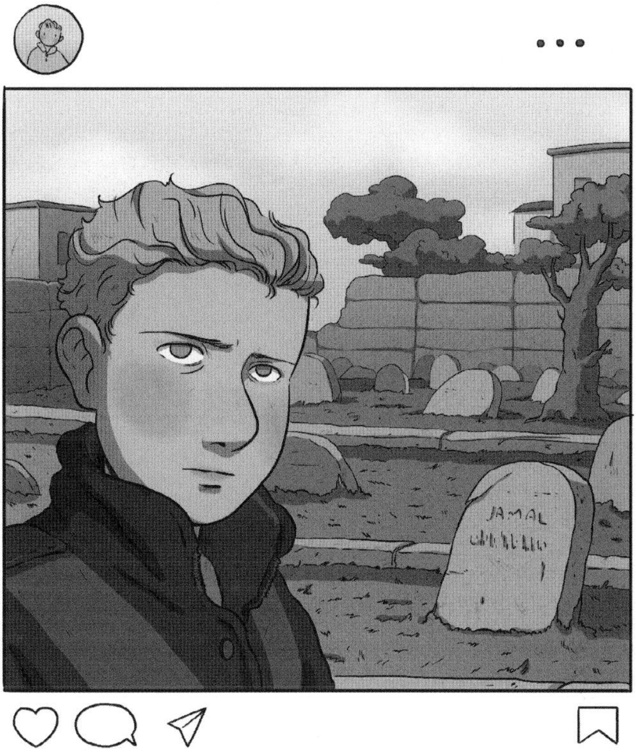
JAMAL

Despite the fact that my country is destroyed, it is still beautiful. I am leaving Eastern Ghouta for Idlib. Our bags are packed, but I am visiting my father's grave for the last time. I hope I can visit it again one day. I hope I can come home.

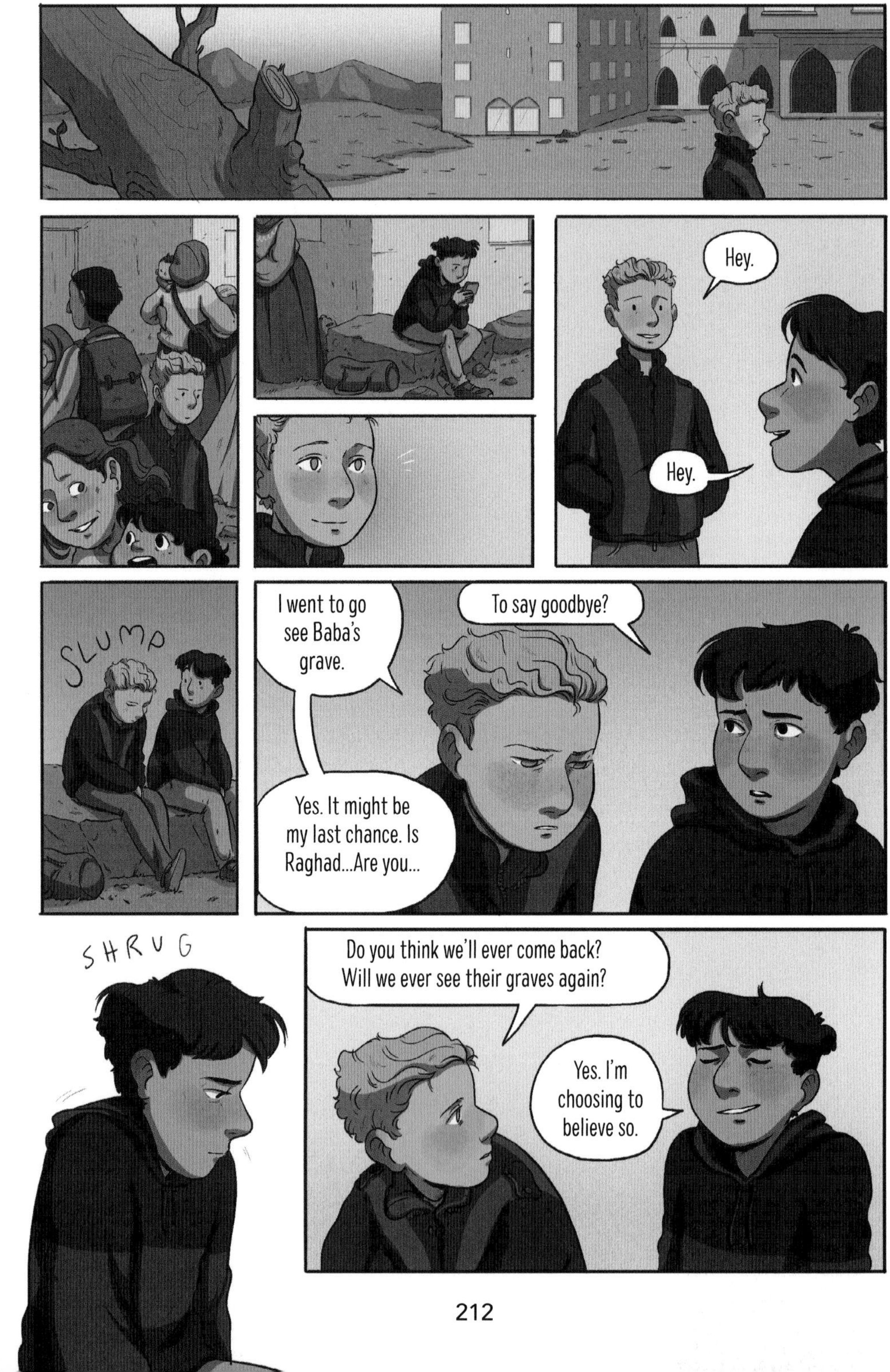
Hey.
Hey.
SLUMP
I went to go see Baba's grave.
To say goodbye?
Yes. It might be my last chance. Is Raghad...Are you...
SHRUG
Do you think we'll ever come back? Will we ever see their graves again?
Yes. I'm choosing to believe so.

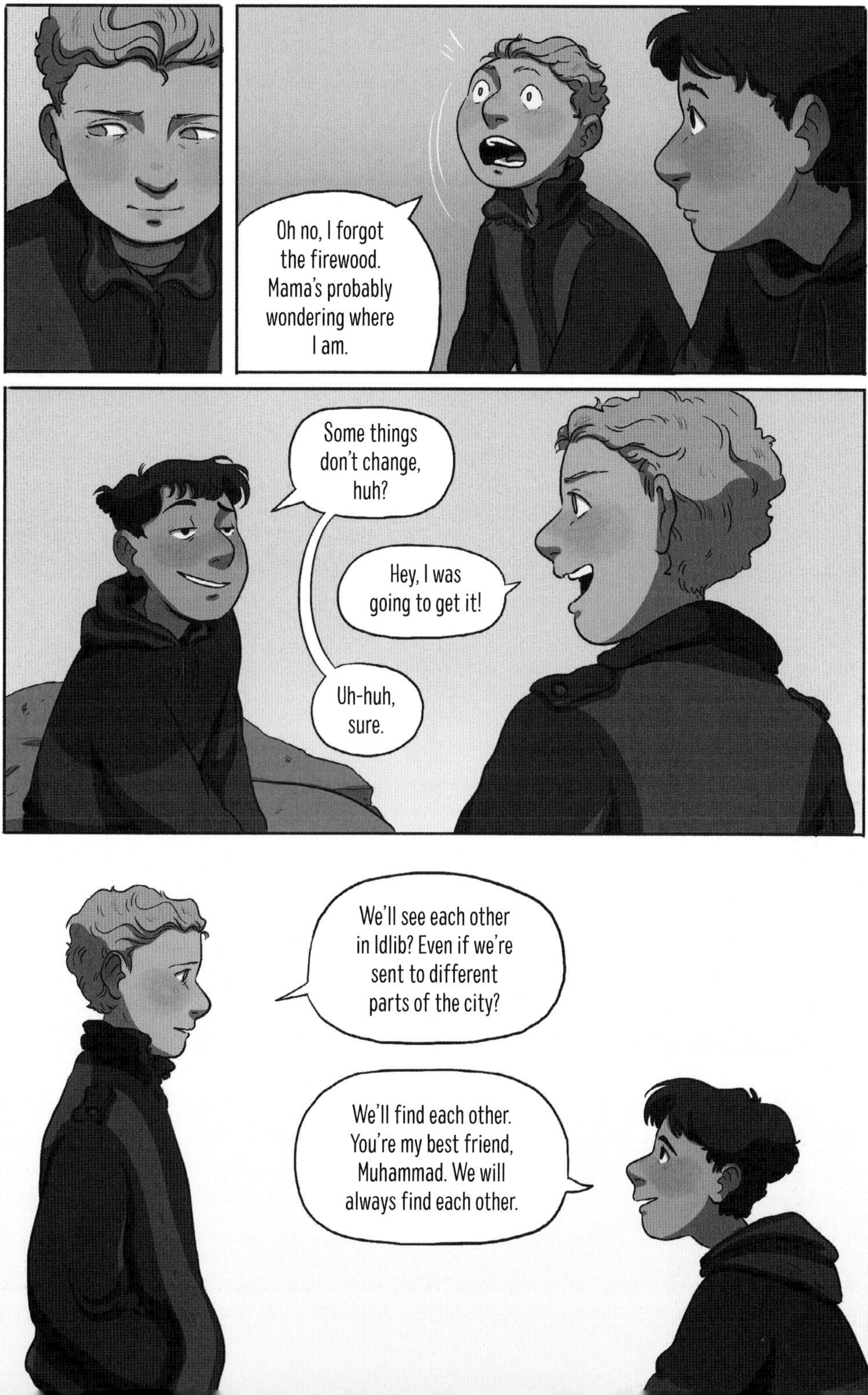
Oh no, I forgot the firewood. Mama's probably wondering where I am.
Some things don't change, huh?
Hey, I was going to get it!
Uh-huh, sure.
We'll see each other in Idlib? Even if we're sent to different parts of the city?
We'll find each other. You're my best friend, Muhammad. We will always find each other.

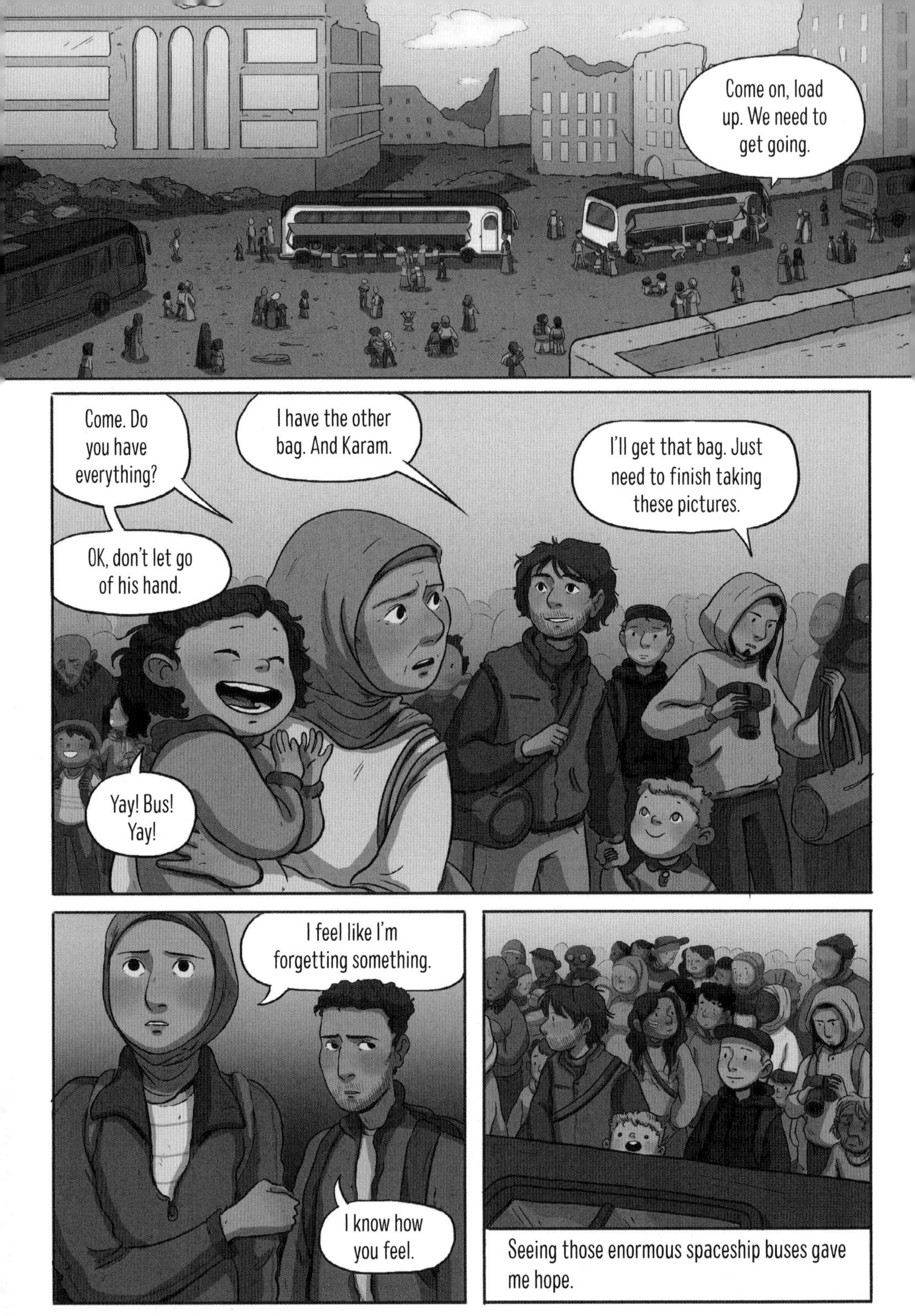
Come on, load up. We need to get going.
Come. Do you have everything?
I have the other bag. And Karam.
I'll get that bag. Just need to finish taking these pictures.
OK, don't let go of his hand.
Yay! Bus! Yay!
I feel like I'm forgetting something.
I know how you feel.
Seeing those enormous spaceship buses gave me hope.

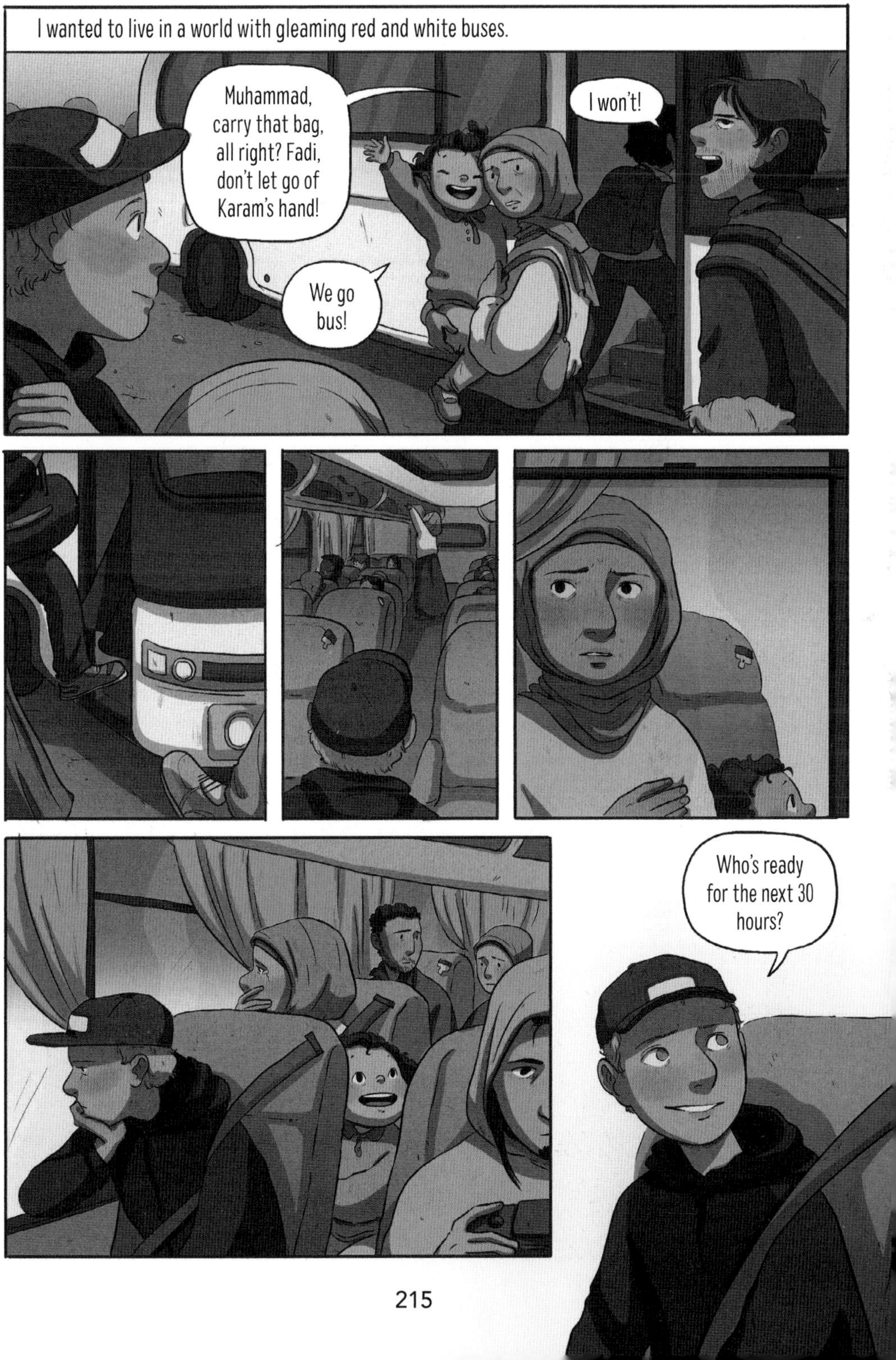
I wanted to live in a world with gleaming red and white buses.
Muhammad, carry that bag, all right? Fadi, don't let go of Karam's hand!
We go bus!
I won't!
Who's ready for the next 30 hours?

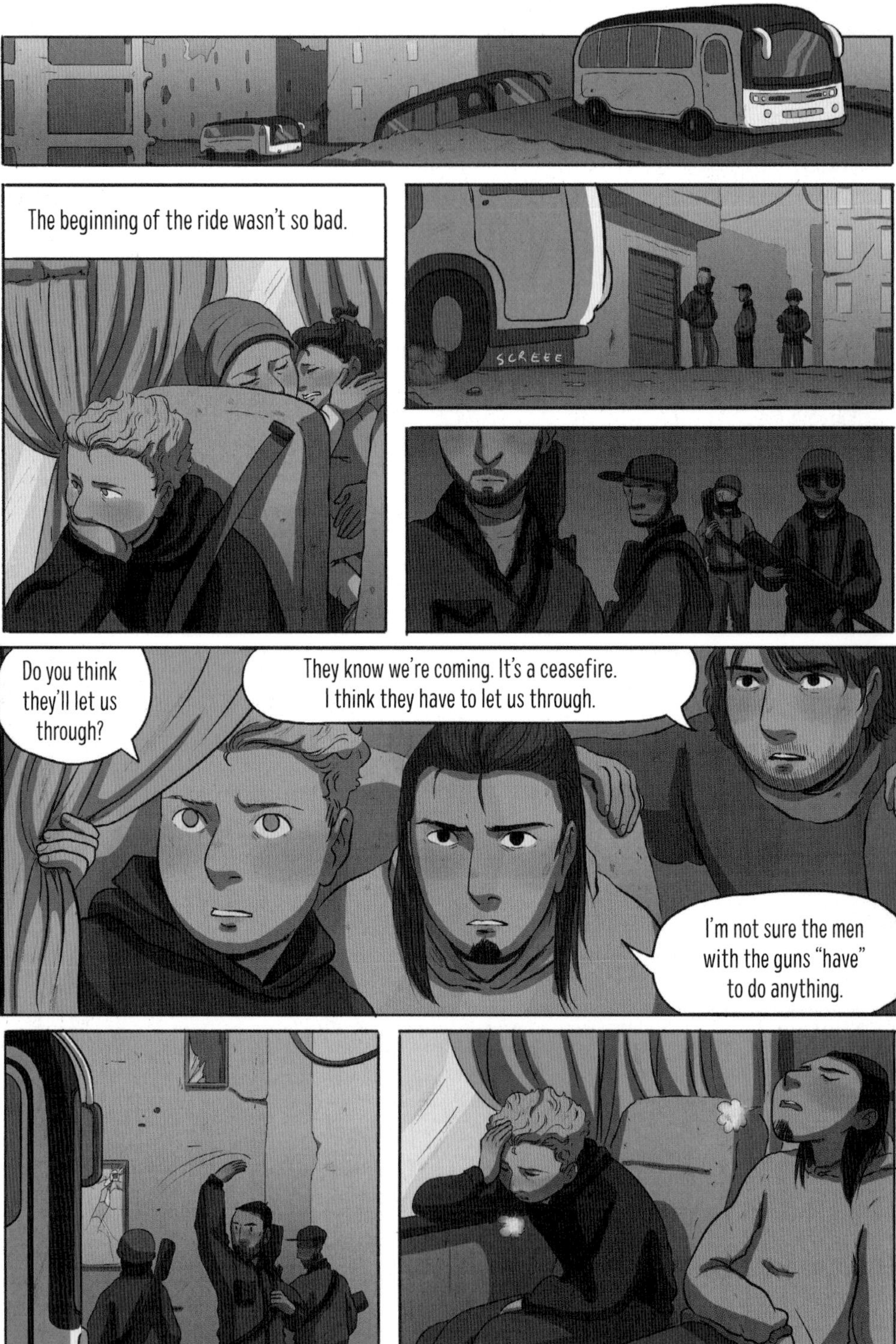

The beginning of the ride wasn't so bad.
SCREEE
Do you think they'll let us through?
They know we're coming. It's a ceasefire. I think they have to let us through.
I'm not sure the men with the guns "have" to do anything.

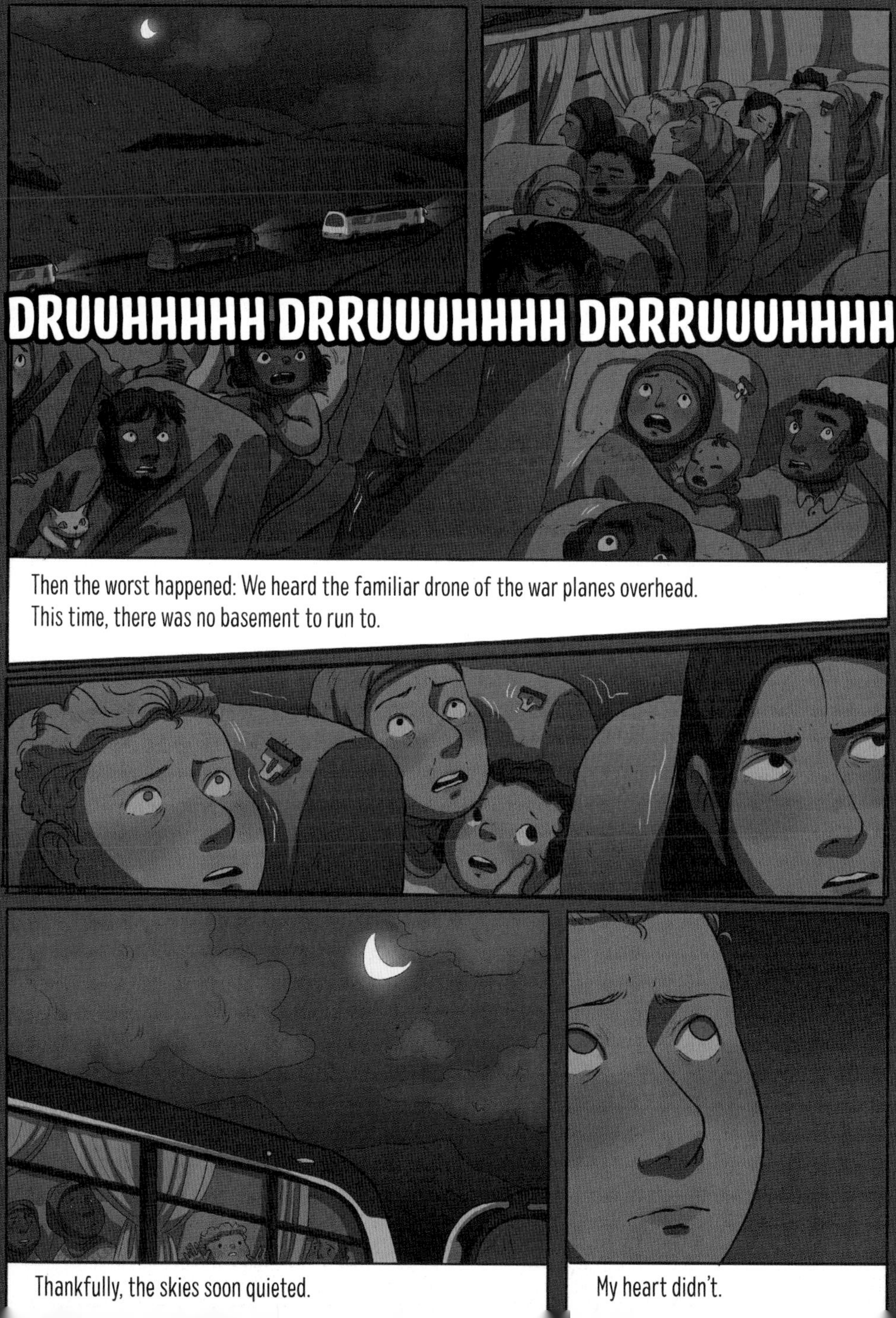
DRUUHHHHH DRRUUUHHHH DRRRUUUHHHH
Then the worst happened: We heard the familiar drone of the war planes overhead.
This time, there was no basement to run to.
Thankfully, the skies soon quieted.
My heart didn't.

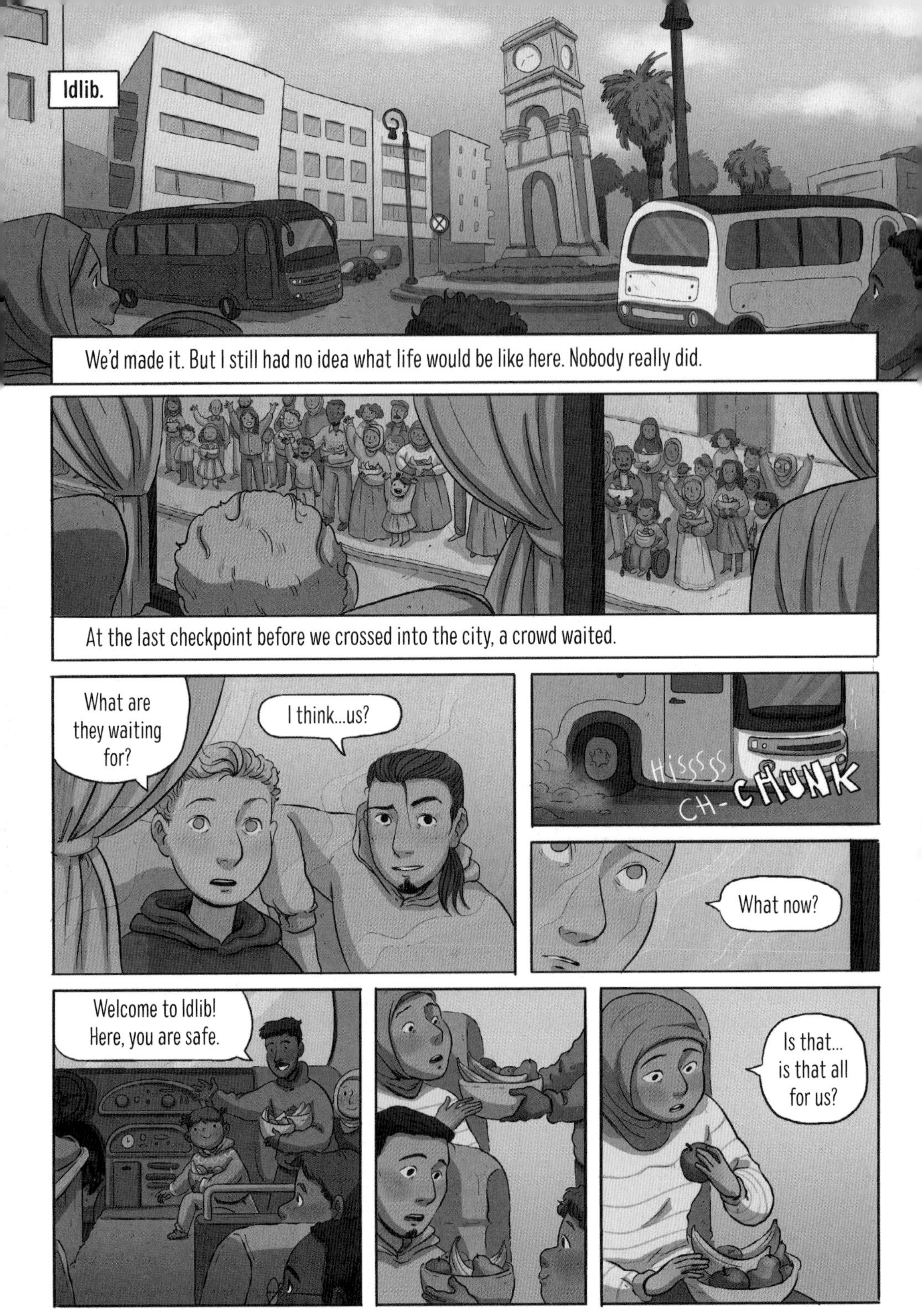

Idlib.
We'd made it. But I still had no idea what life would be like here. Nobody really did.
At the last checkpoint before we crossed into the city, a crowd waited.
What are they waiting for?
I think...us?
HISSSSS
CH-CHUNK
What now?
Welcome to Idlib! Here, you are safe.
Is that... is that all for us?

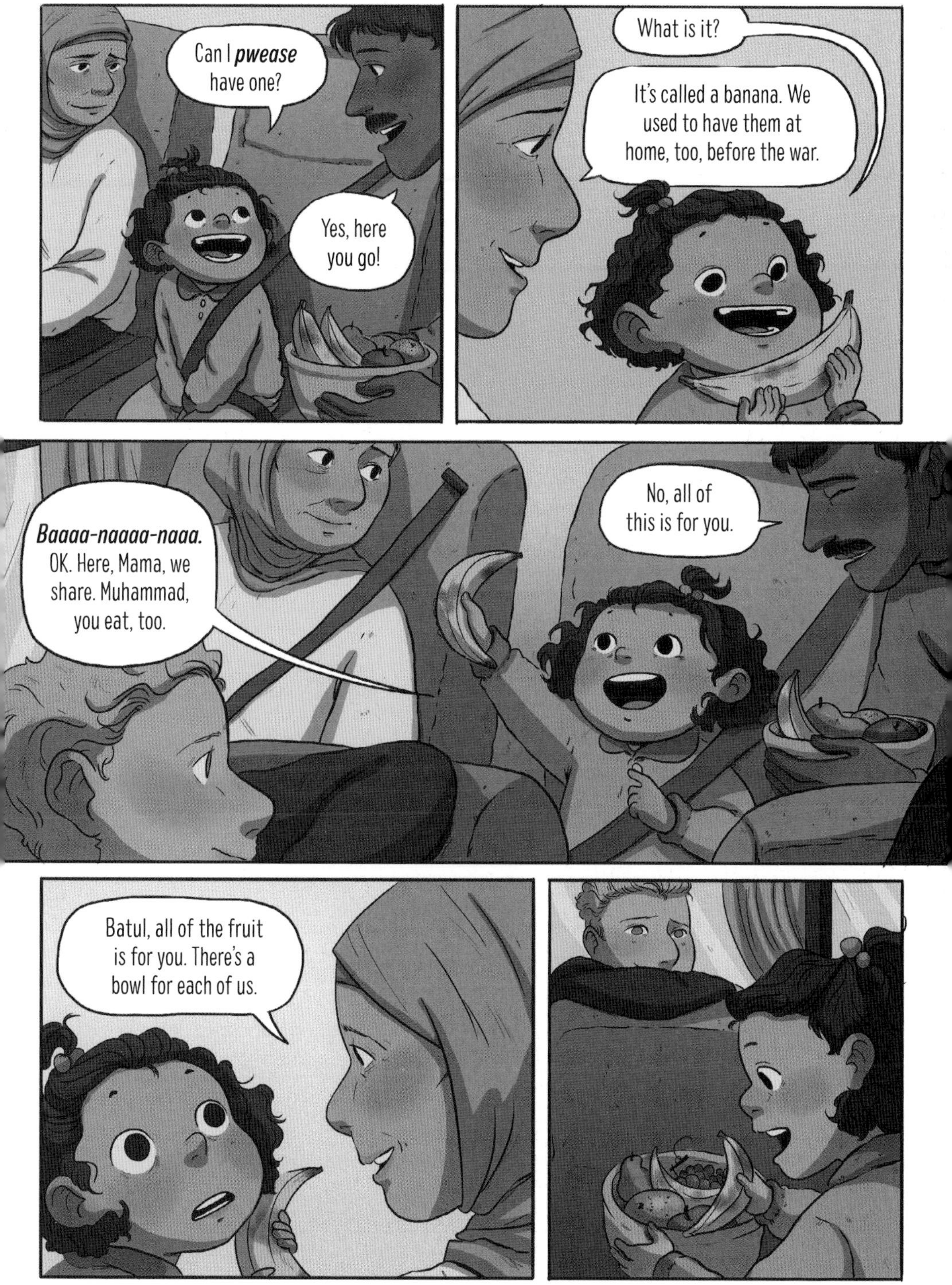
Can I ***pwease*** have one?
Yes, here you go!
What is it?
It's called a banana. We used to have them at home, too, before the war.
Baaaa-naaaa-naaa. OK. Here, Mama, we share. Muhammad, you eat, too.
No, all of this is for you.
Batul, all of the fruit is for you. There's a bowl for each of us.

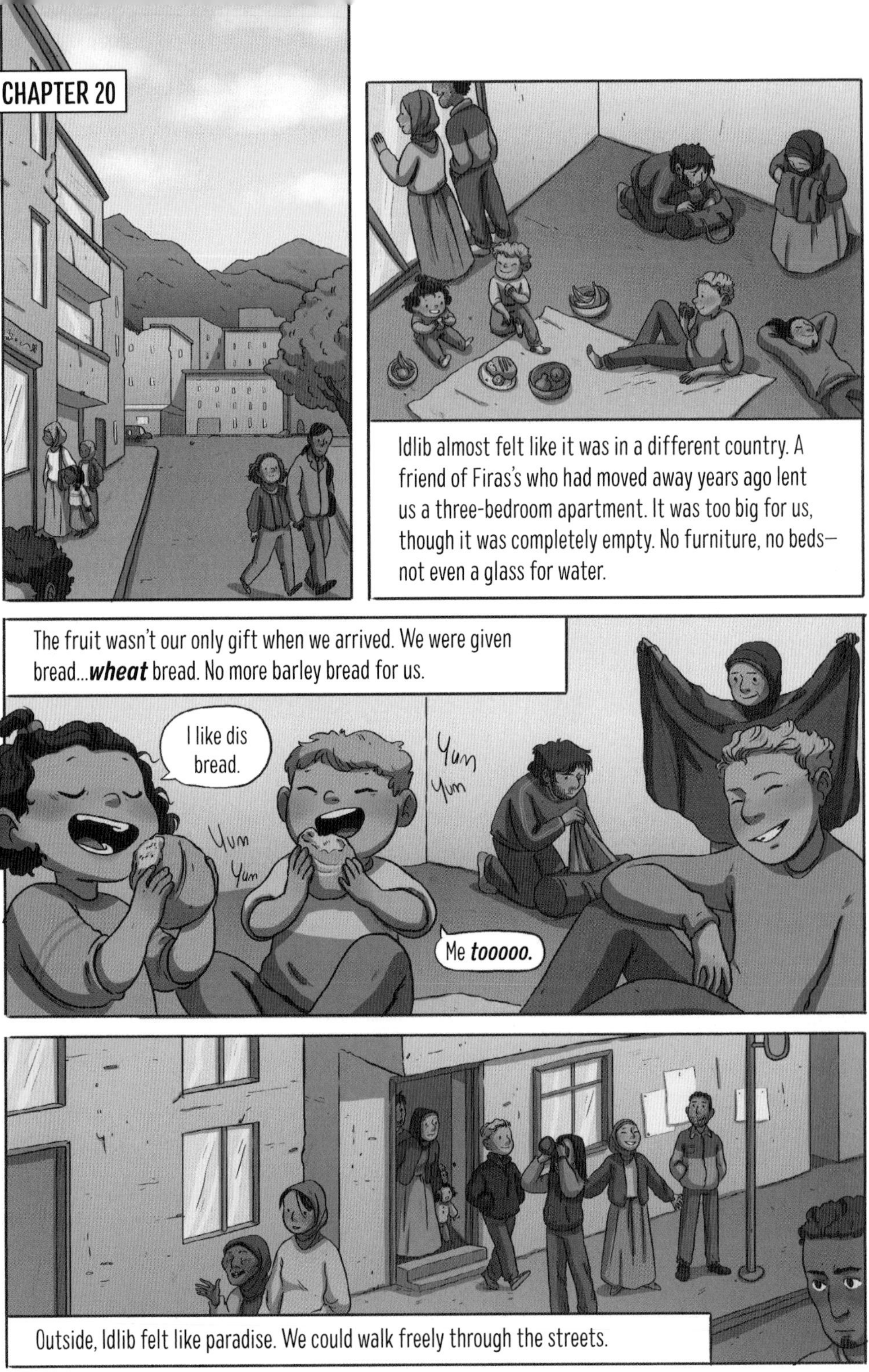
CHAPTER 20
Idlib almost felt like it was in a different country. A friend of Firas's who had moved away years ago lent us a three-bedroom apartment. It was too big for us, though it was completely empty. No furniture, no beds—not even a glass for water.
The fruit wasn't our only gift when we arrived. We were given bread...***wheat*** bread. No more barley bread for us.
I like dis bread.
Yum Yum
Yum Yum
Me ***tooooo.***
Outside, Idlib felt like paradise. We could walk freely through the streets.

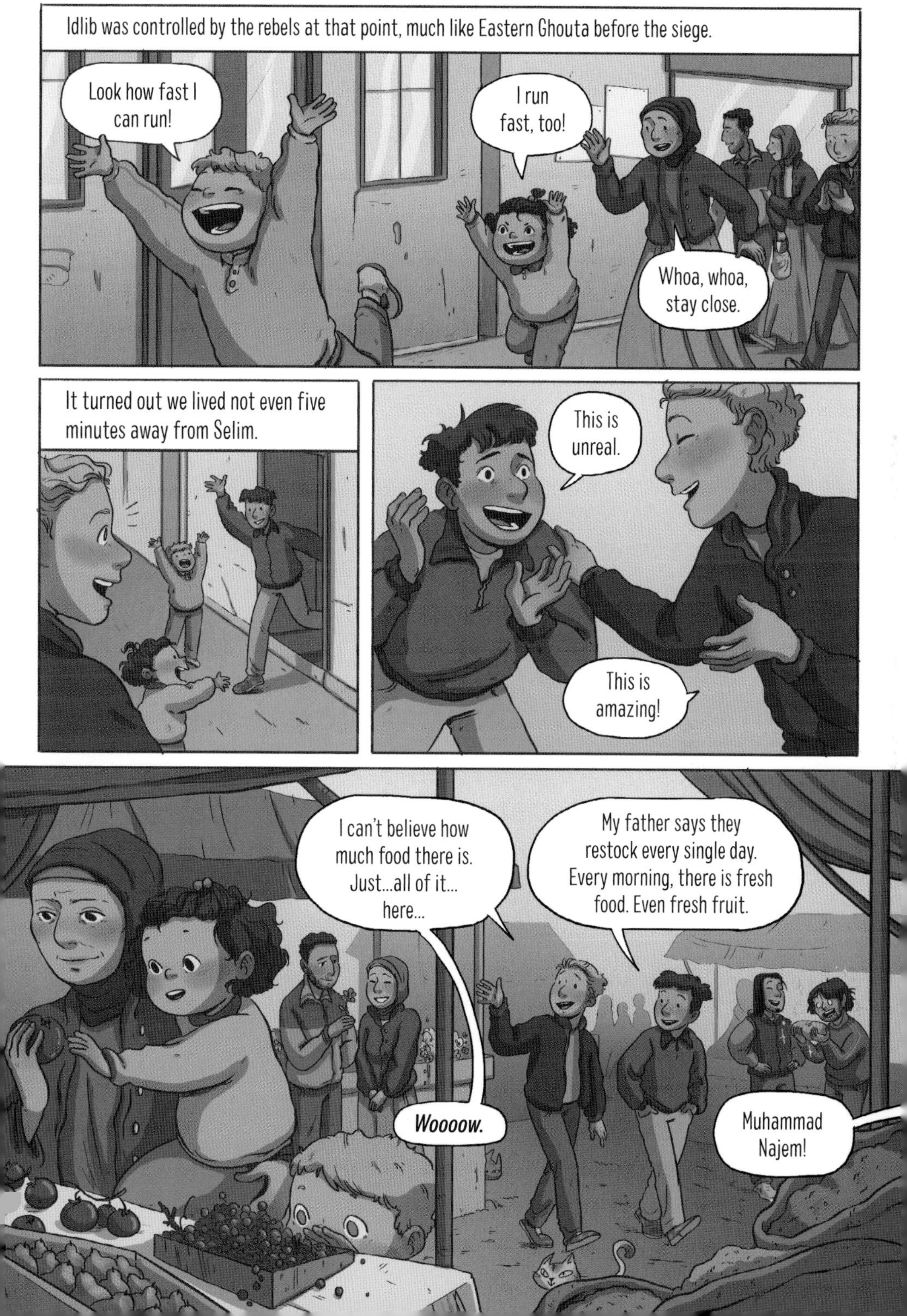

Idlib was controlled by the rebels at that point, much like Eastern Ghouta before the siege.
Look how fast I can run!
I run fast, too!
Whoa, whoa, stay close.
It turned out we lived not even five minutes away from Selim.
This is unreal.
This is amazing!
I can't believe how much food there is. Just...all of it... here...
Woooow.
My father says they restock every single day. Every morning, there is fresh food. Even fresh fruit.
Muhammad Najem!

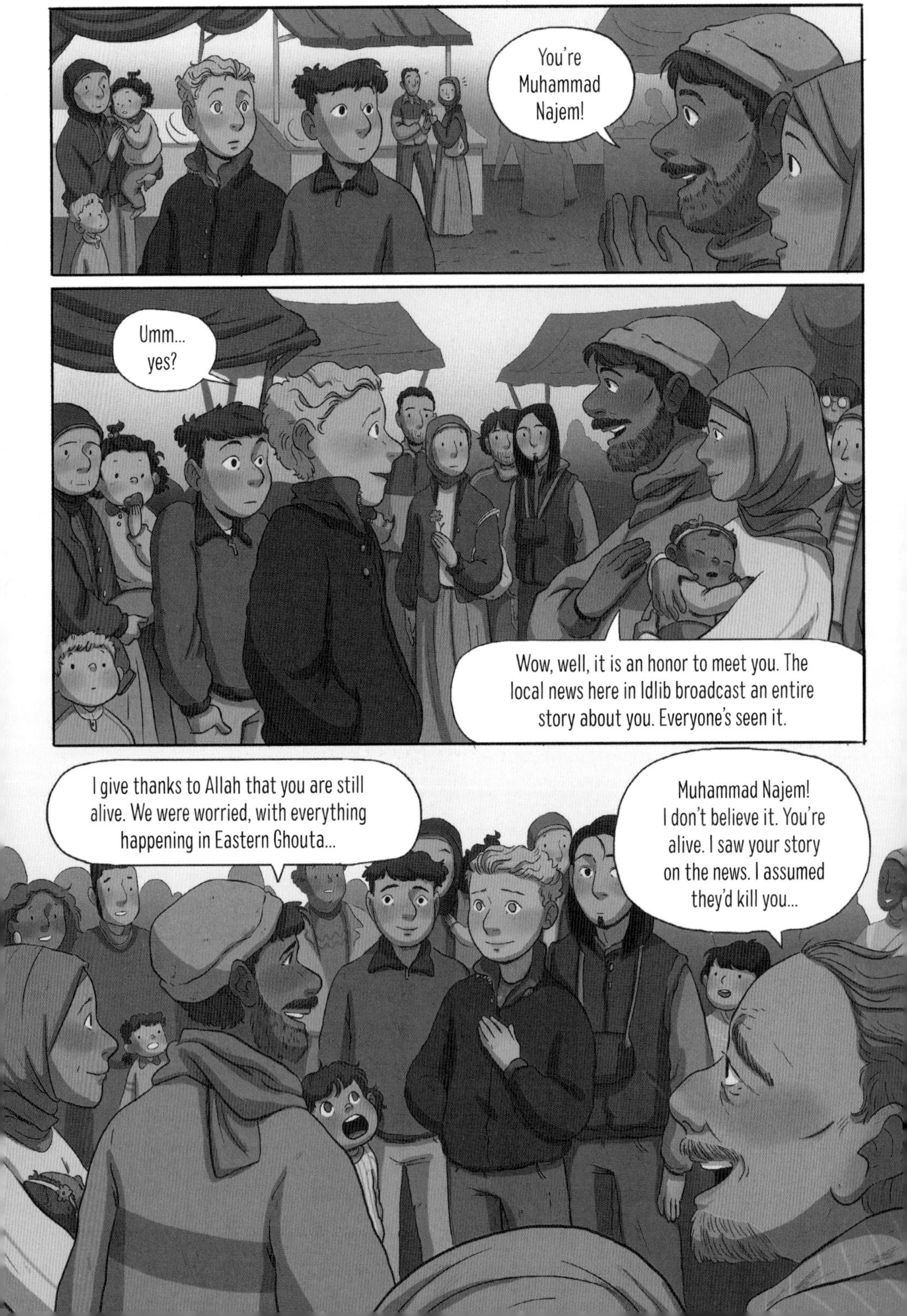
You're Muhammad Najem!
Umm... yes?
Wow, well, it is an honor to meet you. The local news here in Idlib broadcast an entire story about you. Everyone's seen it.
I give thanks to Allah that you are still alive. We were worried, with everything happening in Eastern Ghouta...
Muhammad Najem! I don't believe it. You're alive. I saw your story on the news. I assumed they'd kill you...

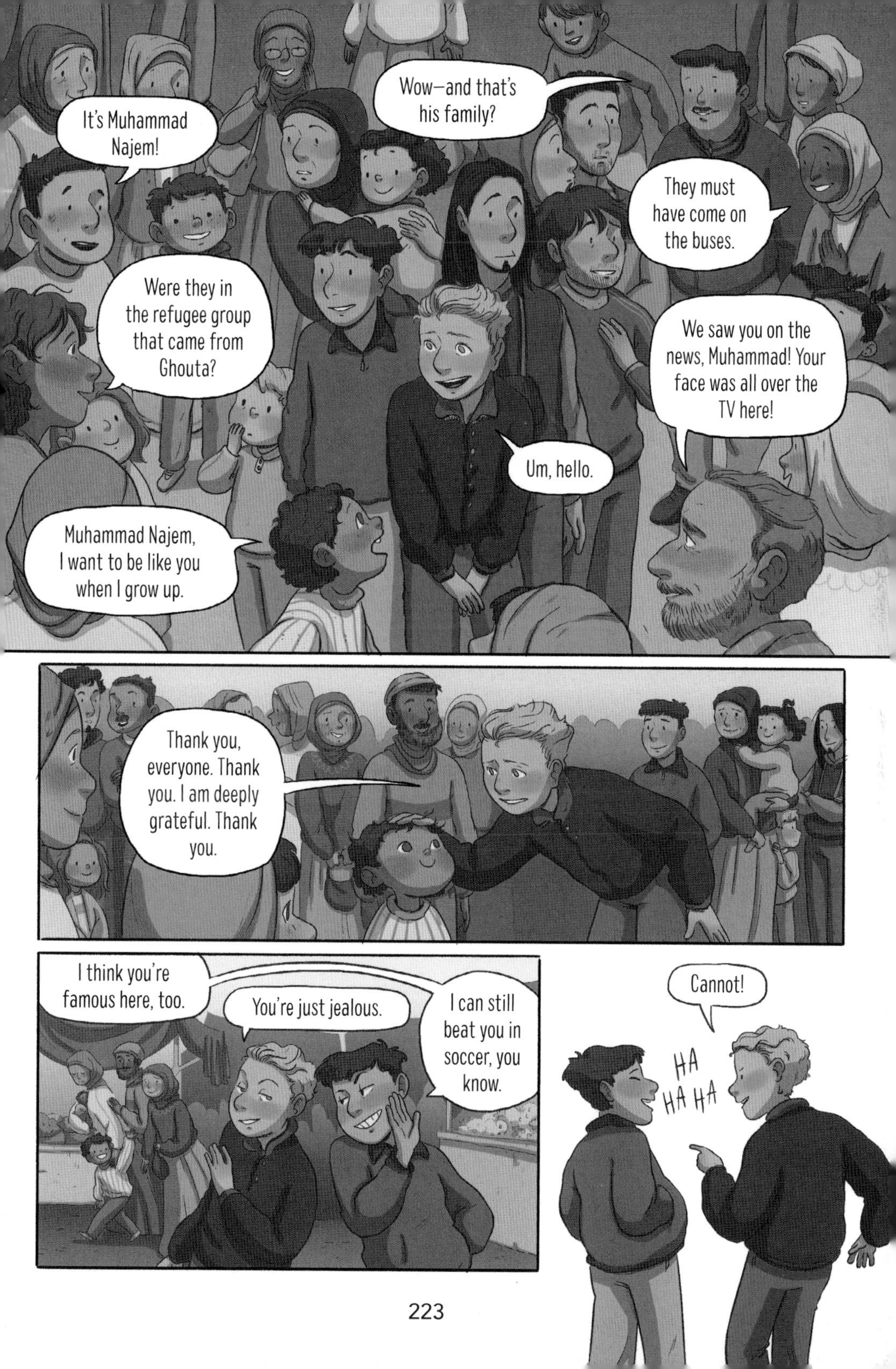
It's Muhammad Najem!
Wow—and that's his family?
They must have come on the buses.
Were they in the refugee group that came from Ghouta?
We saw you on the news, Muhammad! Your face was all over the TV here!
Um, hello.
Muhammad Najem, I want to be like you when I grow up.
Thank you, everyone. Thank you. I am deeply grateful. Thank you.
I think you're famous here, too.
You're just jealous.
I can still beat you in soccer, you know.
Cannot!
HA HA HA

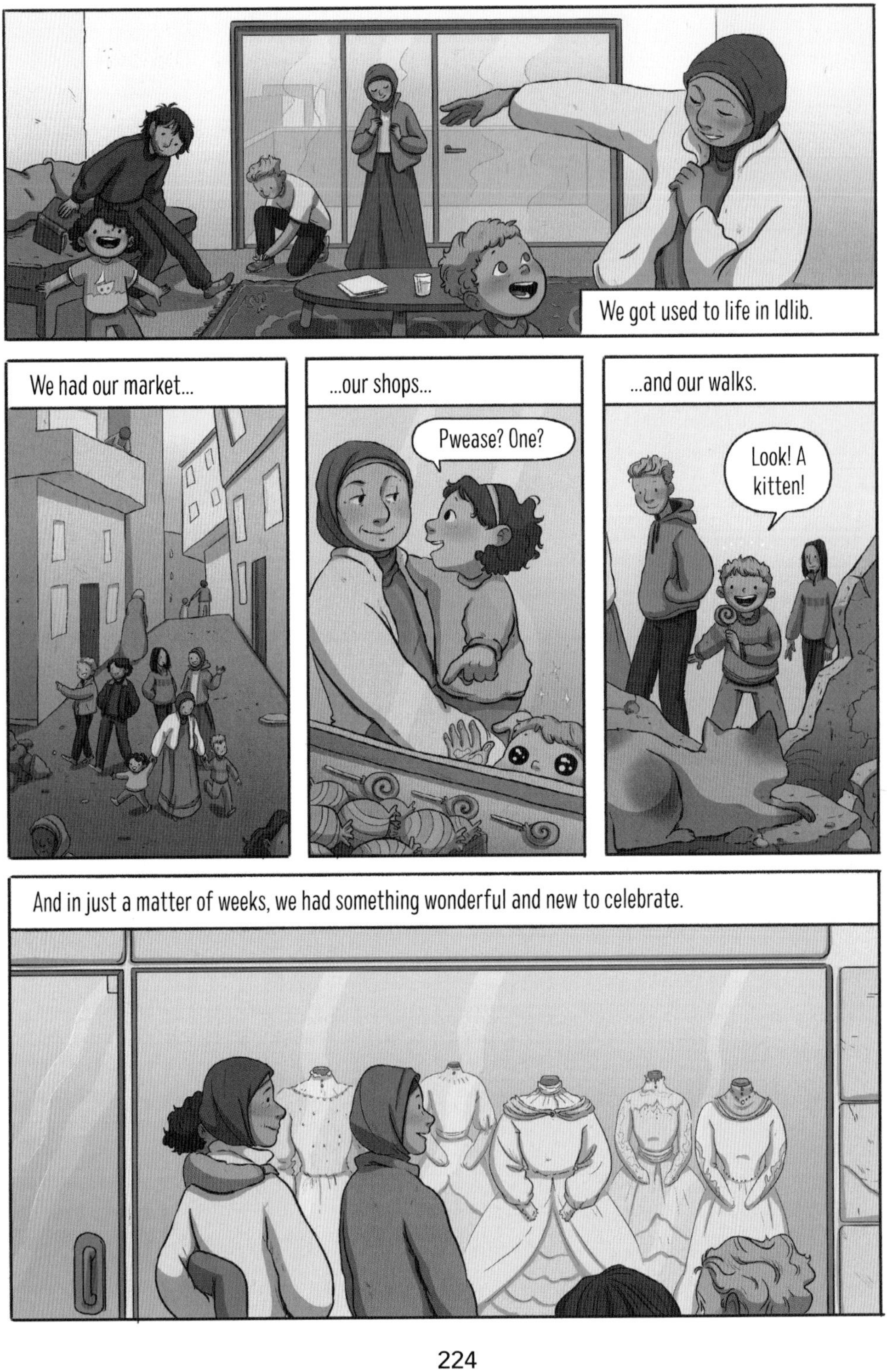
We got used to life in Idlib.
We had our market...
...our shops...
Pwease? One?
...and our walks.
Look! A kitten!
And in just a matter of weeks, we had something wonderful and new to celebrate.

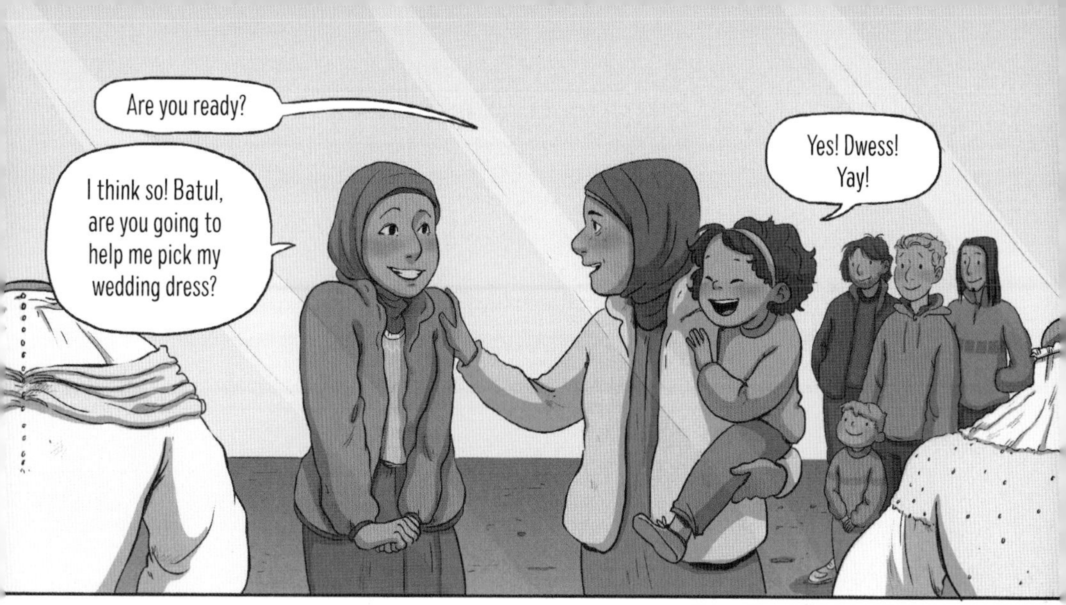
Are you ready?
I think so! Batul, are you going to help me pick my wedding dress?
Yes! Dwess! Yay!

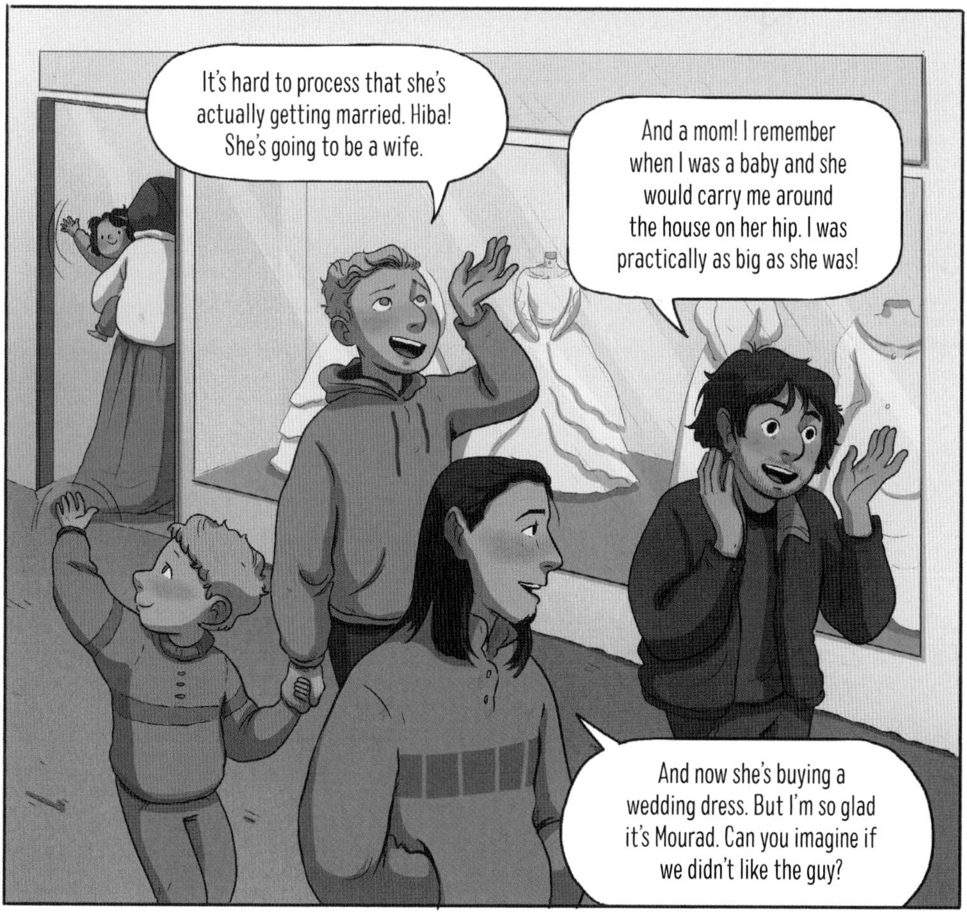
It's hard to process that she's actually getting married. Hiba! She's going to be a wife.
And a mom! I remember when I was a baby and she would carry me around the house on her hip. I was practically as big as she was!
And now she's buying a wedding dress. But I'm so glad it's Mourad. Can you imagine if we didn't like the guy?

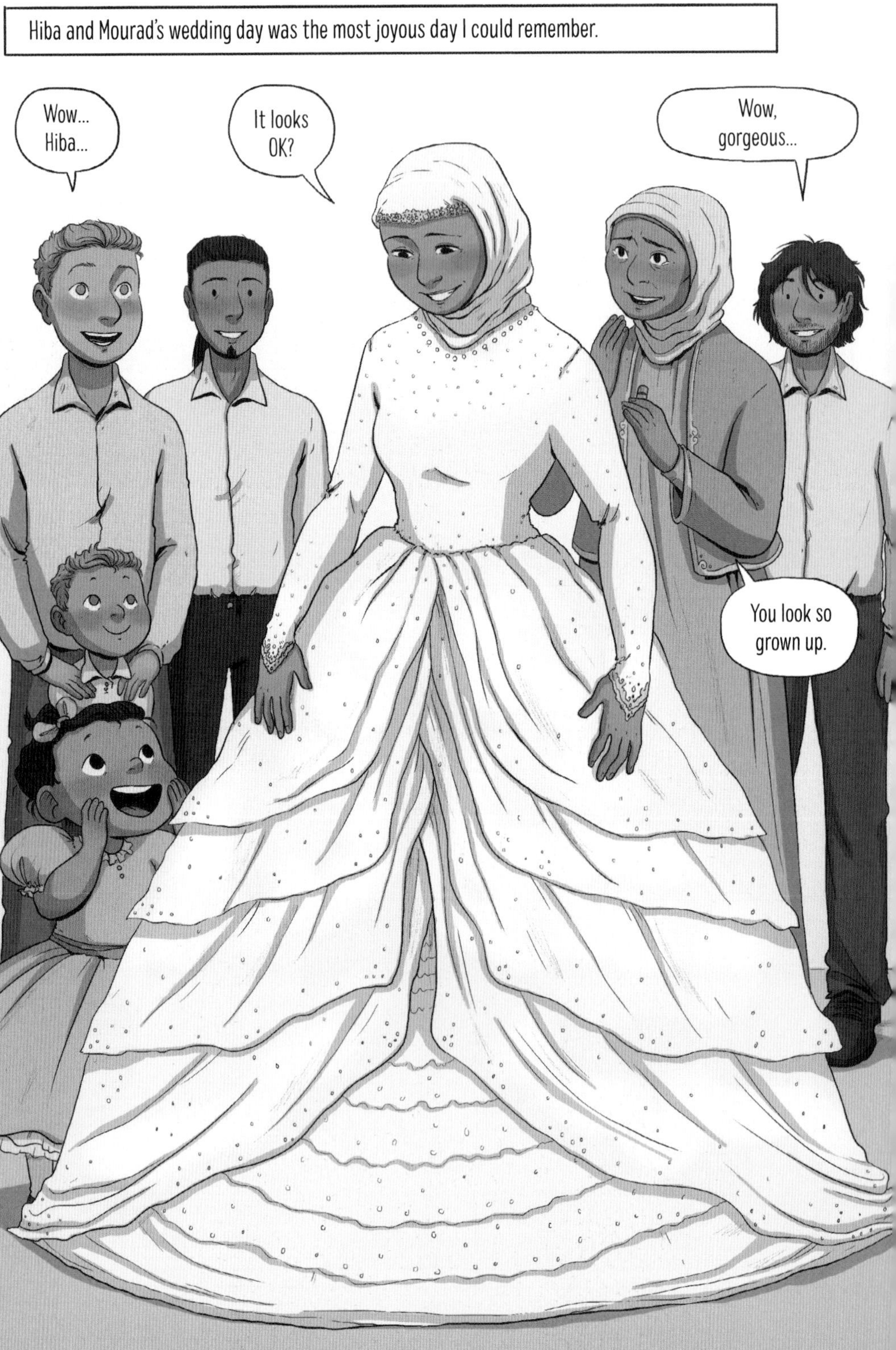
Hiba and Mourad's wedding day was the most joyous day I could remember.
Wow... Hiba...
It looks OK?
Wow, gorgeous...
You look so grown up.

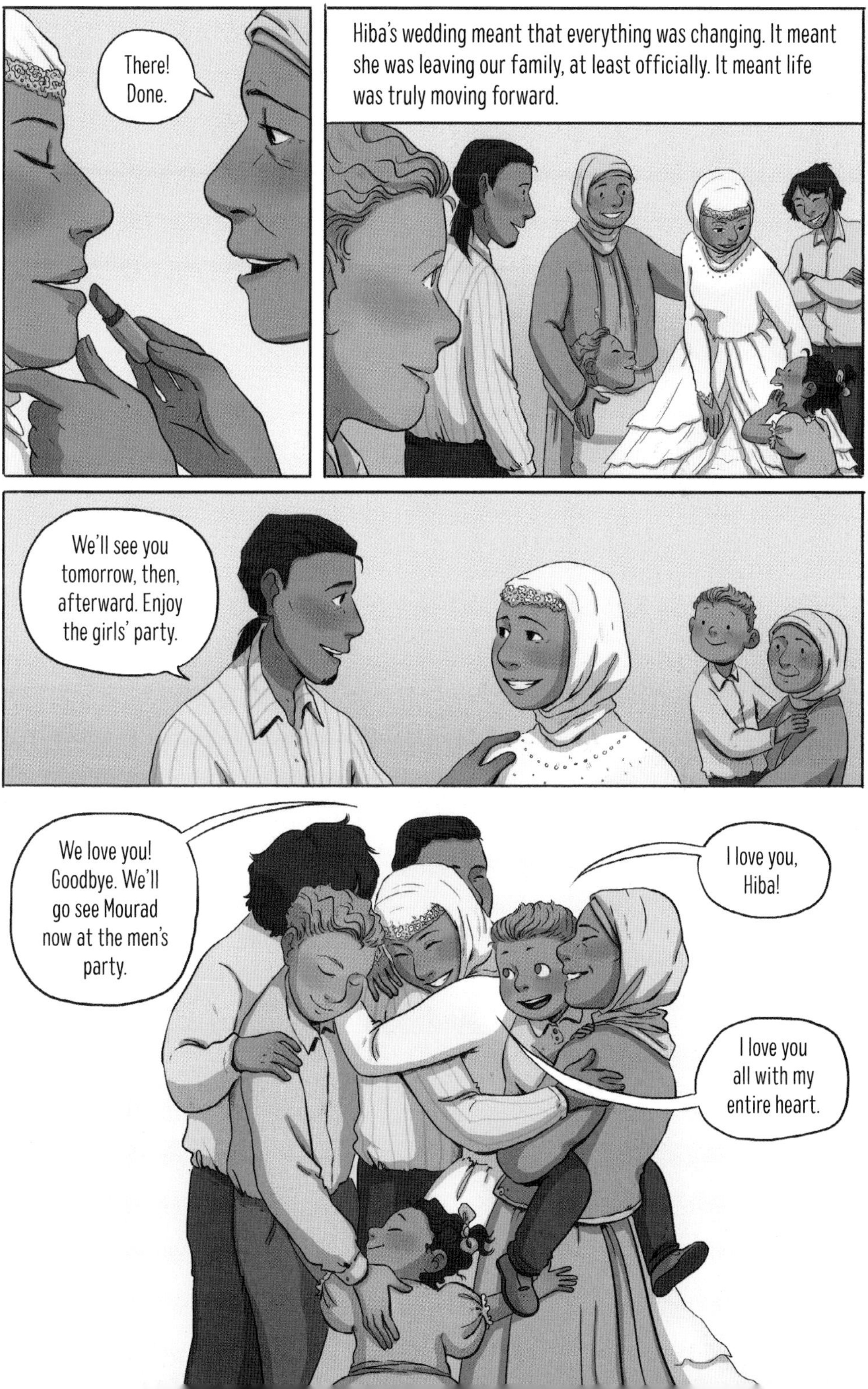
There! Done.
Hiba's wedding meant that everything was changing. It meant she was leaving our family, at least officially. It meant life was truly moving forward.
We'll see you tomorrow, then, afterward. Enjoy the girls' party.
We love you! Goodbye. We'll go see Mourad now at the men's party.
I love you, Hiba!
I love you all with my entire heart.

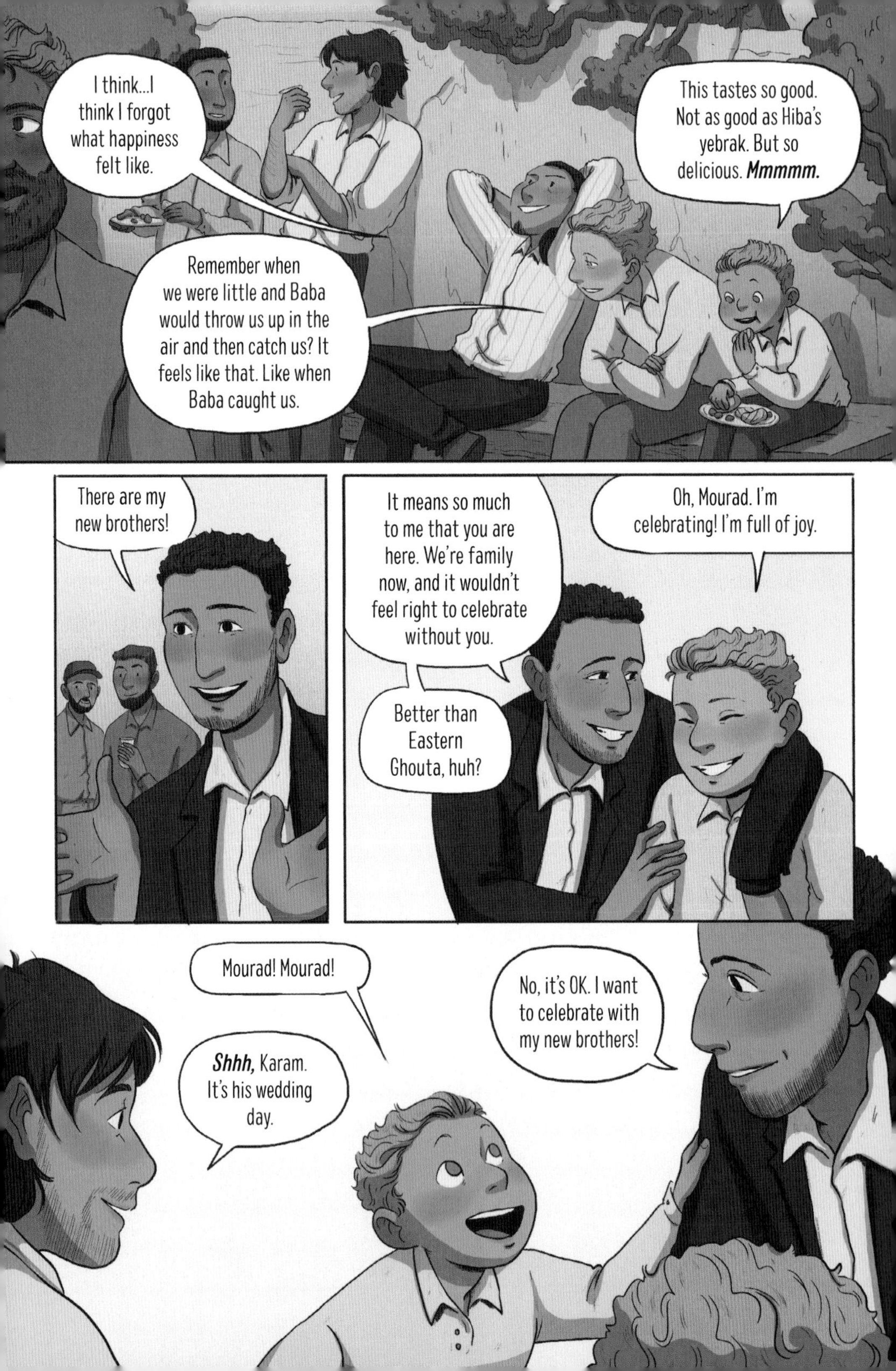
I think...I think I forgot what happiness felt like.
This tastes so good. Not as good as Hiba's yebrak. But so delicious. ***Mmmmm.***
Remember when we were little and Baba would throw us up in the air and then catch us? It feels like that. Like when Baba caught us.
There are my new brothers!
It means so much to me that you are here. We're family now, and it wouldn't feel right to celebrate without you.
Better than Eastern Ghouta, huh?
Oh, Mourad. I'm celebrating! I'm full of joy.
Mourad! Mourad!
Shhh, Karam. It's his wedding day.
No, it's OK. I want to celebrate with my new brothers!

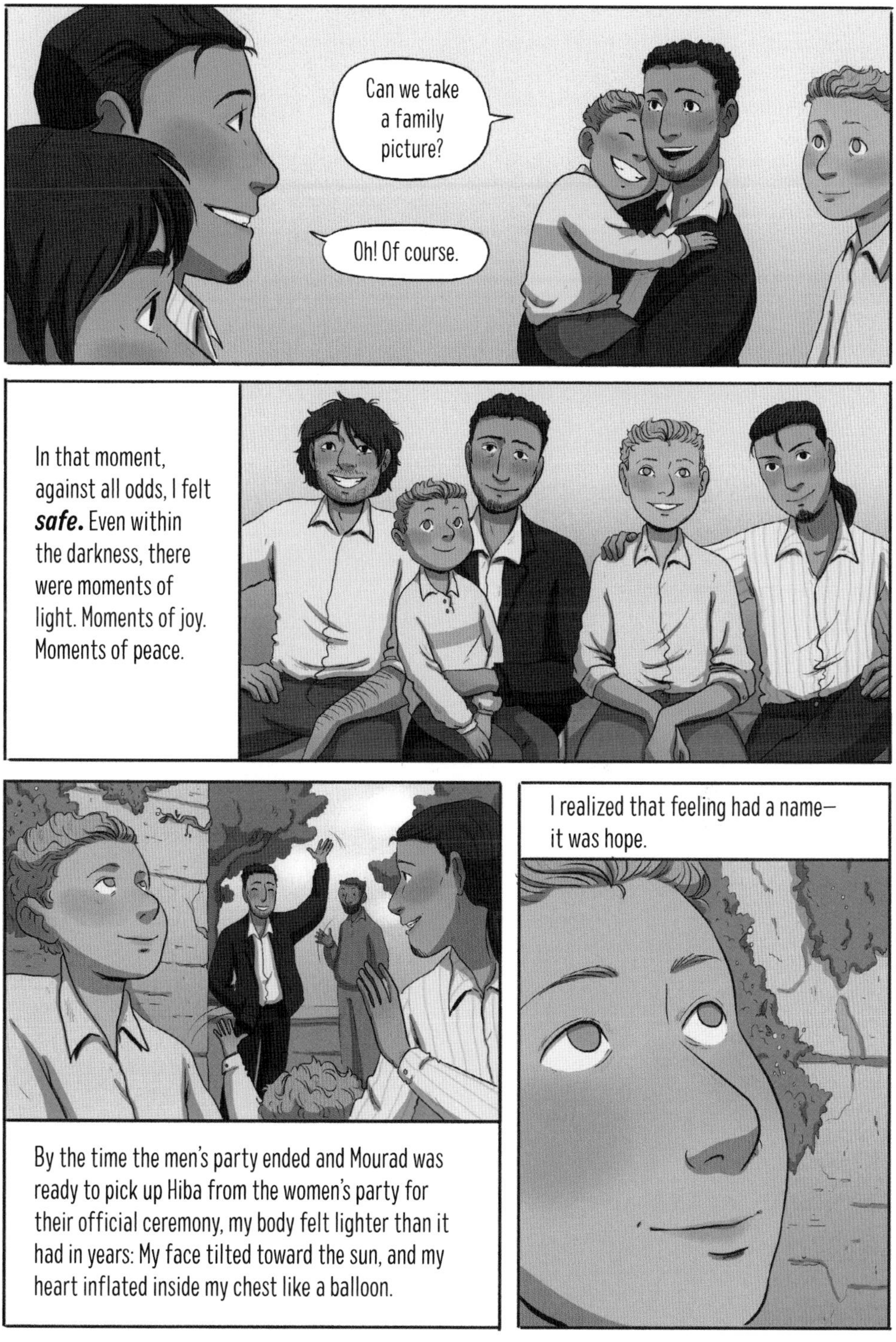

Can we take a family picture?
Oh! Of course.
In that moment, against all odds, I felt ***safe.*** Even within the darkness, there were moments of light. Moments of joy. Moments of peace.
By the time the men's party ended and Mourad was ready to pick up Hiba from the women's party for their official ceremony, my body felt lighter than it had in years: My face tilted toward the sun, and my heart inflated inside my chest like a balloon.
I realized that feeling had a name—it was hope.

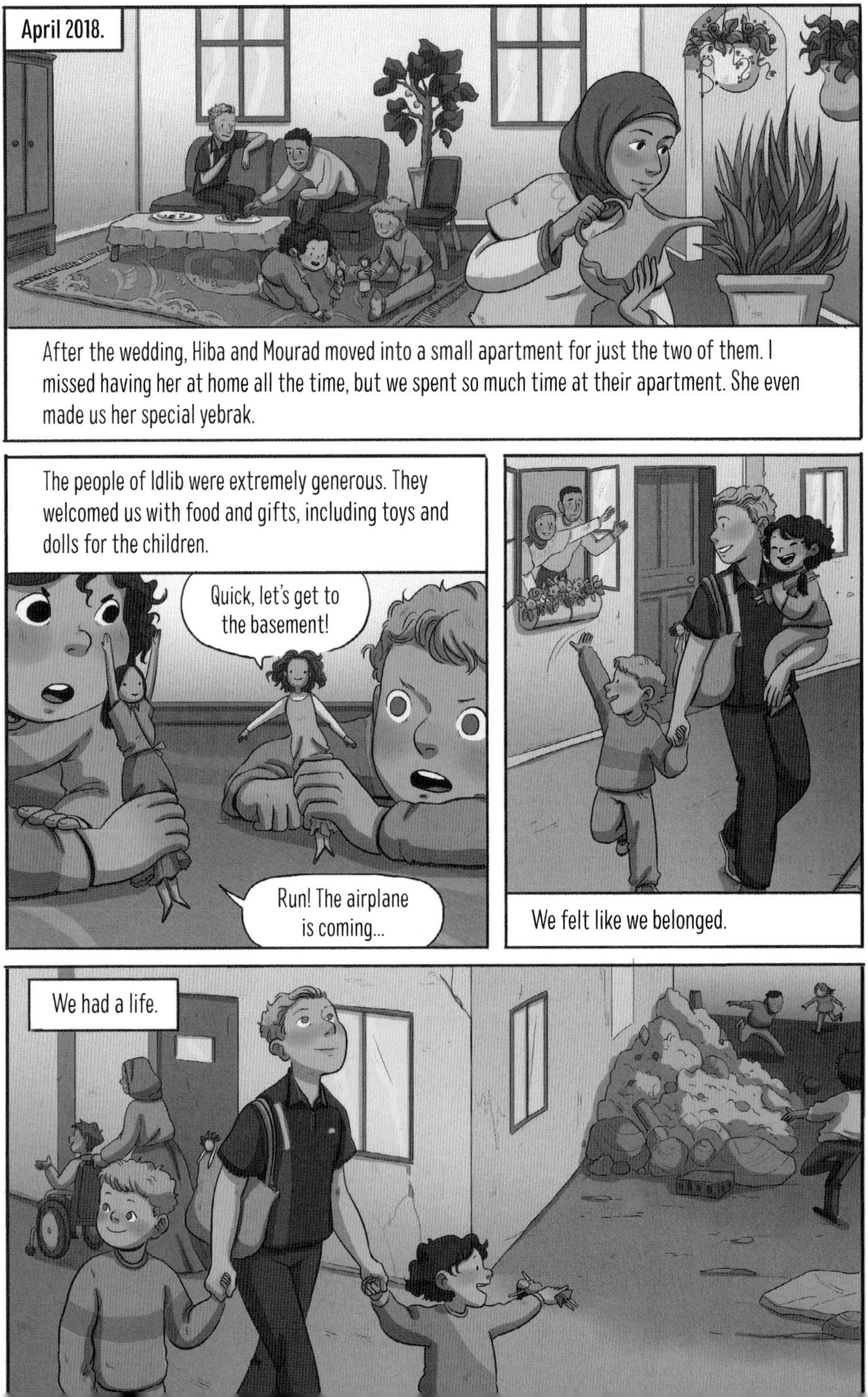
April 2018.
After the wedding, Hiba and Mourad moved into a small apartment for just the two of them. I missed having her at home all the time, but we spent so much time at their apartment. She even made us her special yebrak.
The people of Idlib were extremely generous. They welcomed us with food and gifts, including toys and dolls for the children.
Quick, let's get to the basement!
Run! The airplane is coming...
We felt like we belonged.
We had a life.

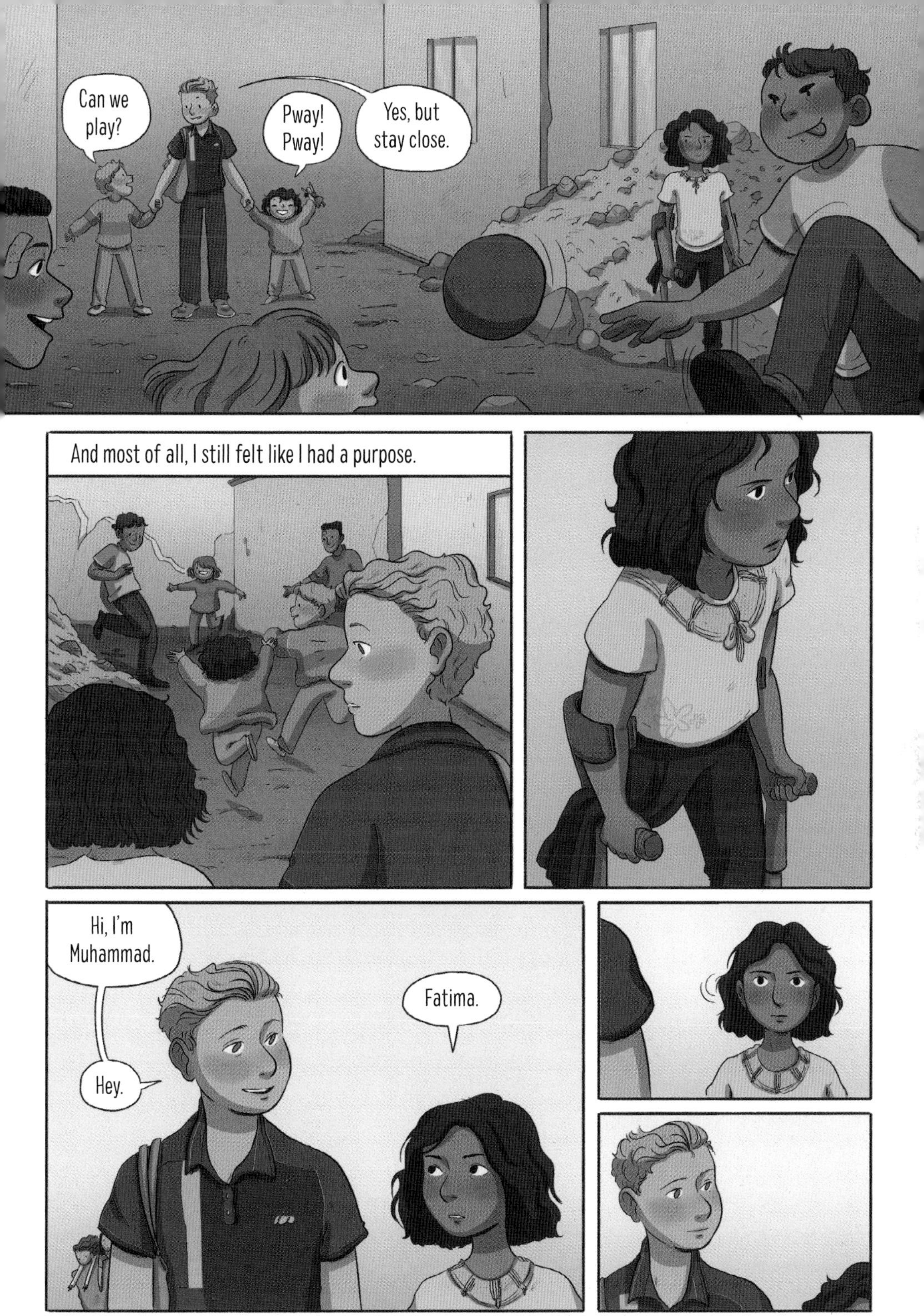

Can we play?
Pway! Pway!
Yes, but stay close.
And most of all, I still felt like I had a purpose.
Hi, I'm Muhammad.
Hey.
Fatima.

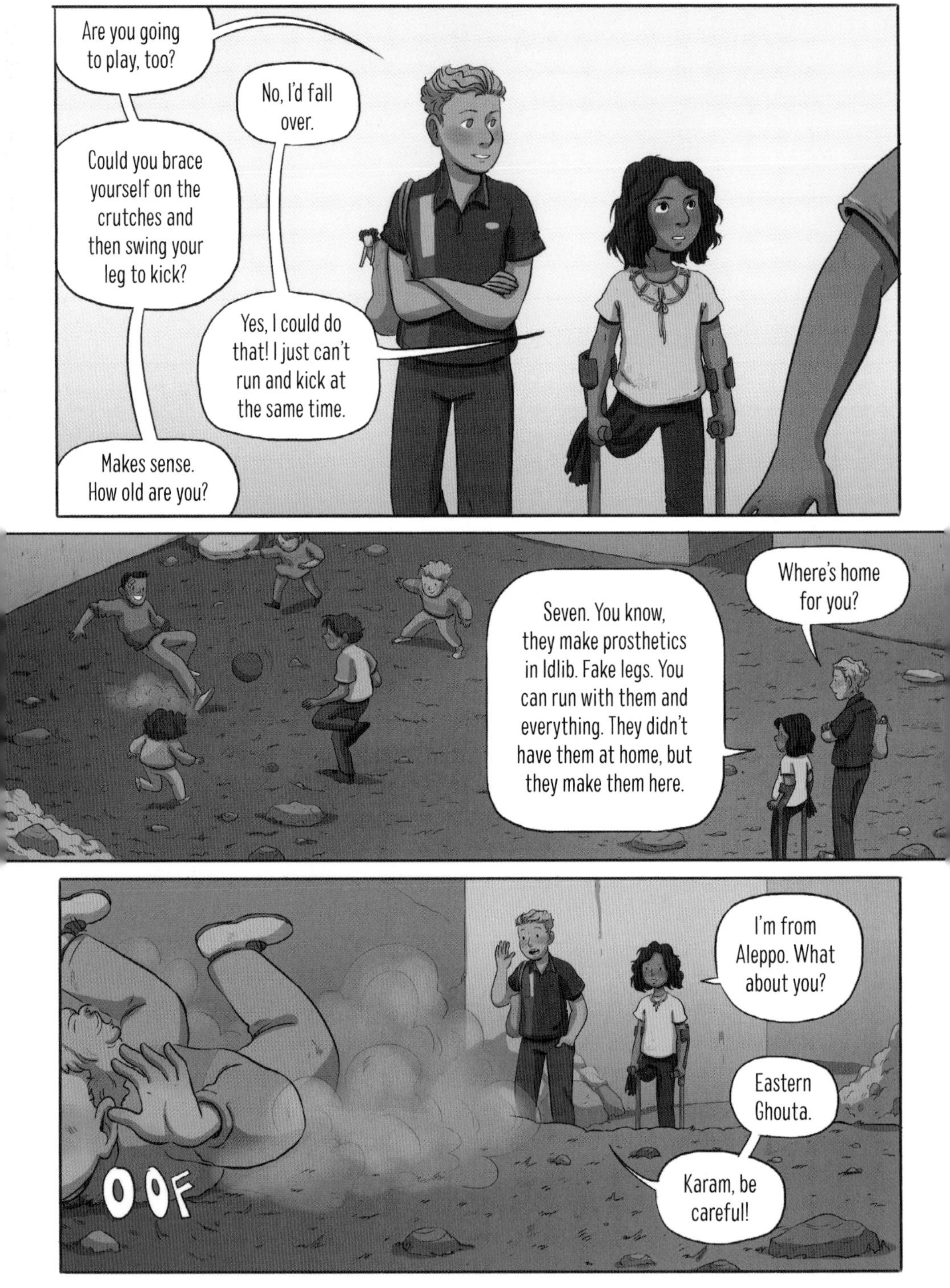
Are you going to play, too?
No, I'd fall over.
Could you brace yourself on the crutches and then swing your leg to kick?
Yes, I could do that! I just can't run and kick at the same time.
Makes sense. How old are you?
Seven. You know, they make prosthetics in Idlib. Fake legs. You can run with them and everything. They didn't have them at home, but they make them here.
Where's home for you?
OOF
I'm from Aleppo. What about you?
Eastern Ghouta.
Karam, be careful!

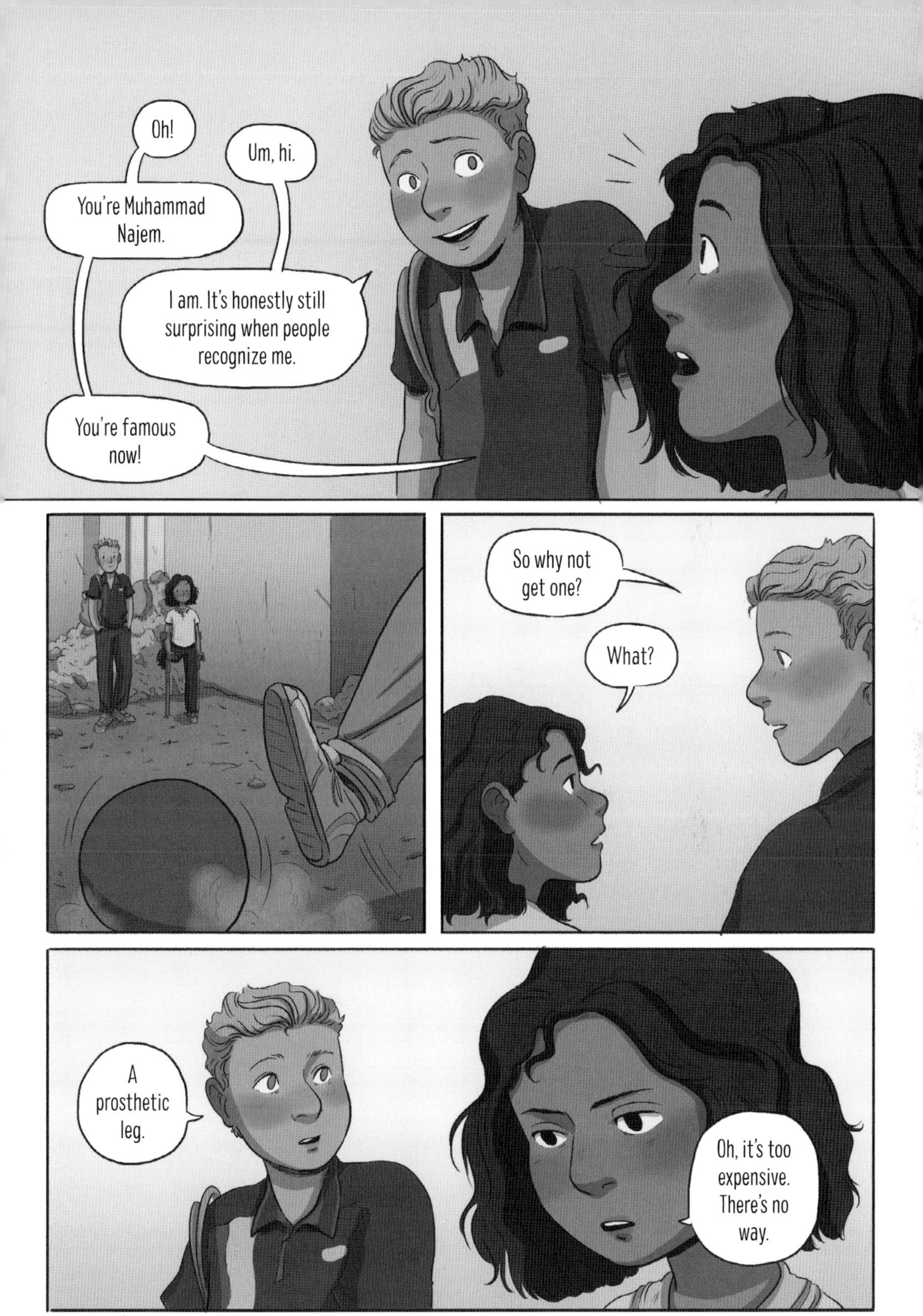
Oh!
Um, hi.
You're Muhammad Najem.
I am. It's honestly still surprising when people recognize me.
You're famous now!
So why not get one?
What?
A prosthetic leg.
Oh, it's too expensive. There's no way.

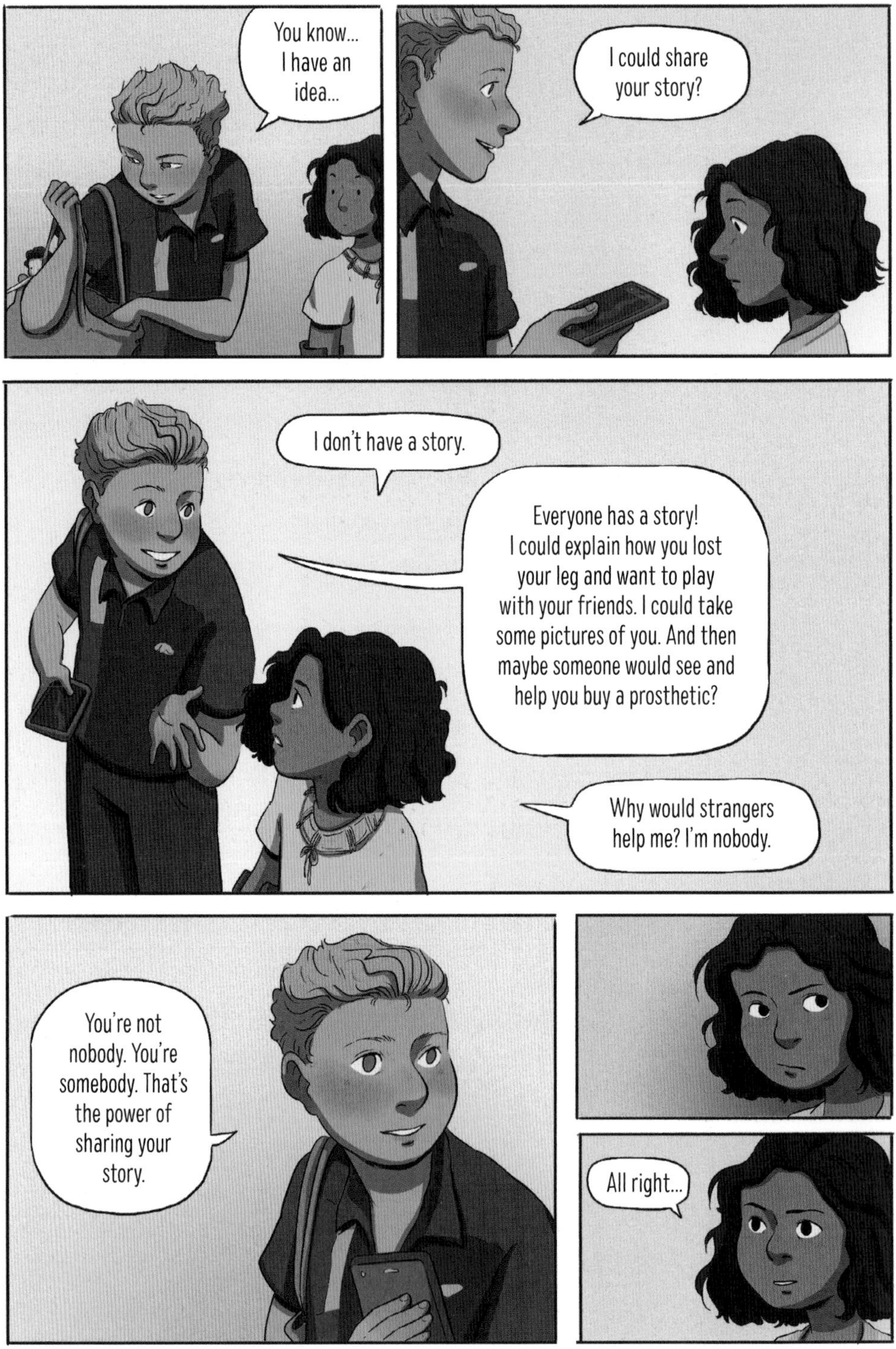

You know... I have an idea...
I could share your story?
I don't have a story.
Everyone has a story! I could explain how you lost your leg and want to play with your friends. I could take some pictures of you. And then maybe someone would see and help you buy a prosthetic?
Why would strangers help me? I'm nobody.
You're not nobody. You're somebody. That's the power of sharing your story.
All right...

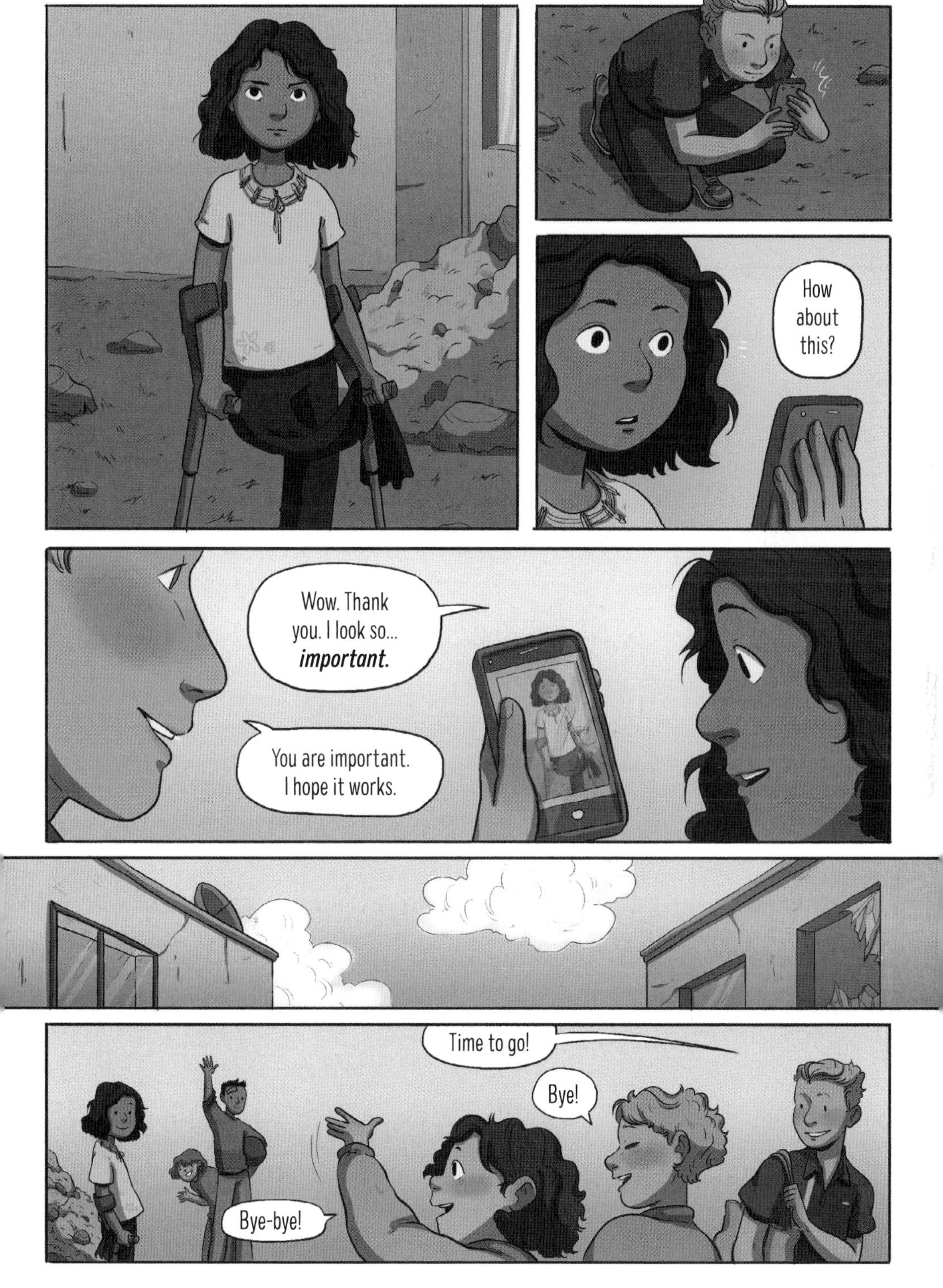
How about this?
Wow. Thank you. I look so... ***important.***
You are important. I hope it works.
Time to go!
Bye!
Bye-bye!

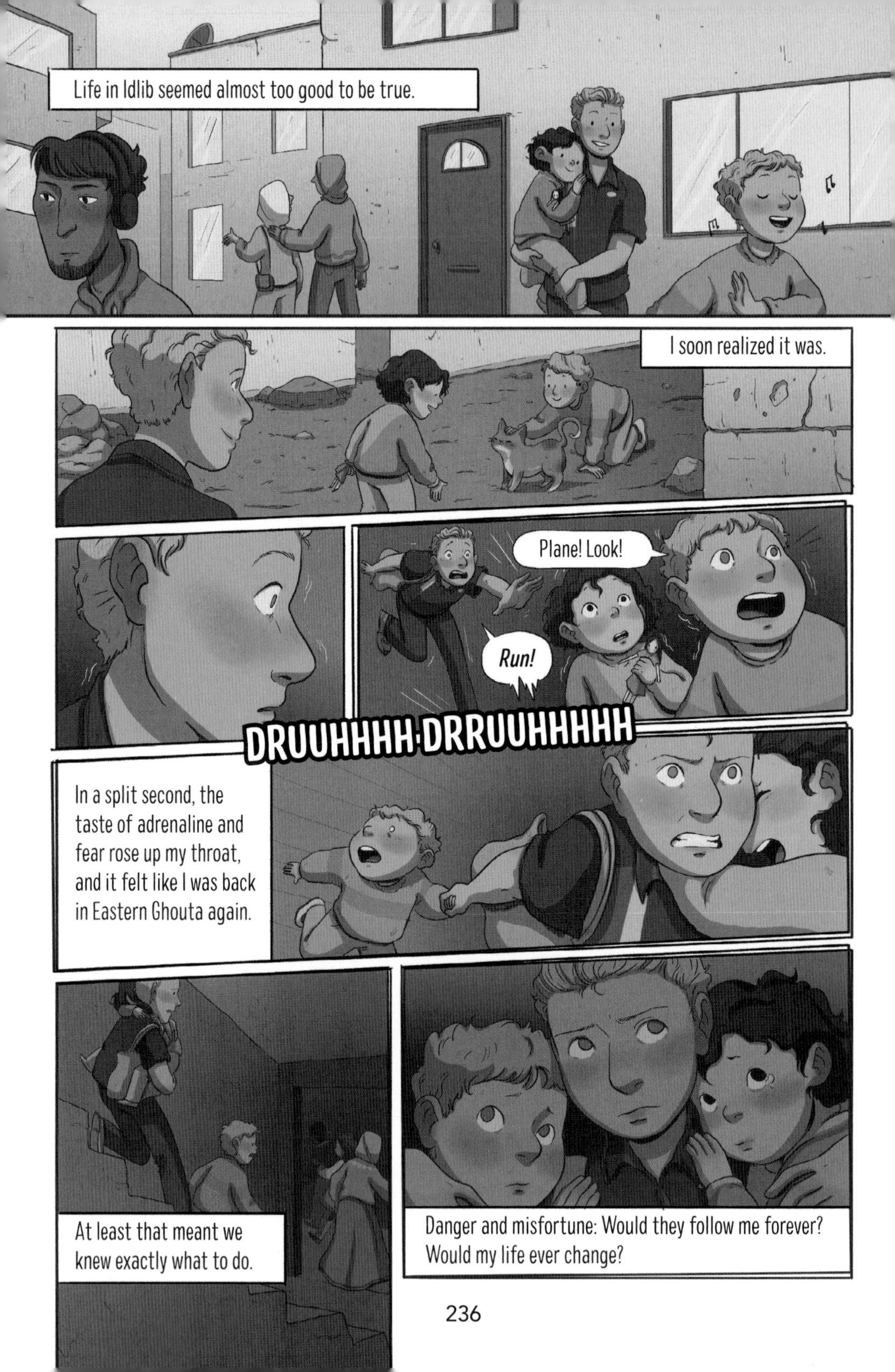

Life in Idlib seemed almost too good to be true.
I soon realized it was.
Plane! Look!
Run!
DRUUHHHH-DRRUUHHHHH
In a split second, the taste of adrenaline and fear rose up my throat, and it felt like I was back in Eastern Ghouta again.
At least that meant we knew exactly what to do.
Danger and misfortune: Would they follow me forever? Would my life ever change?

CHAPTER 21

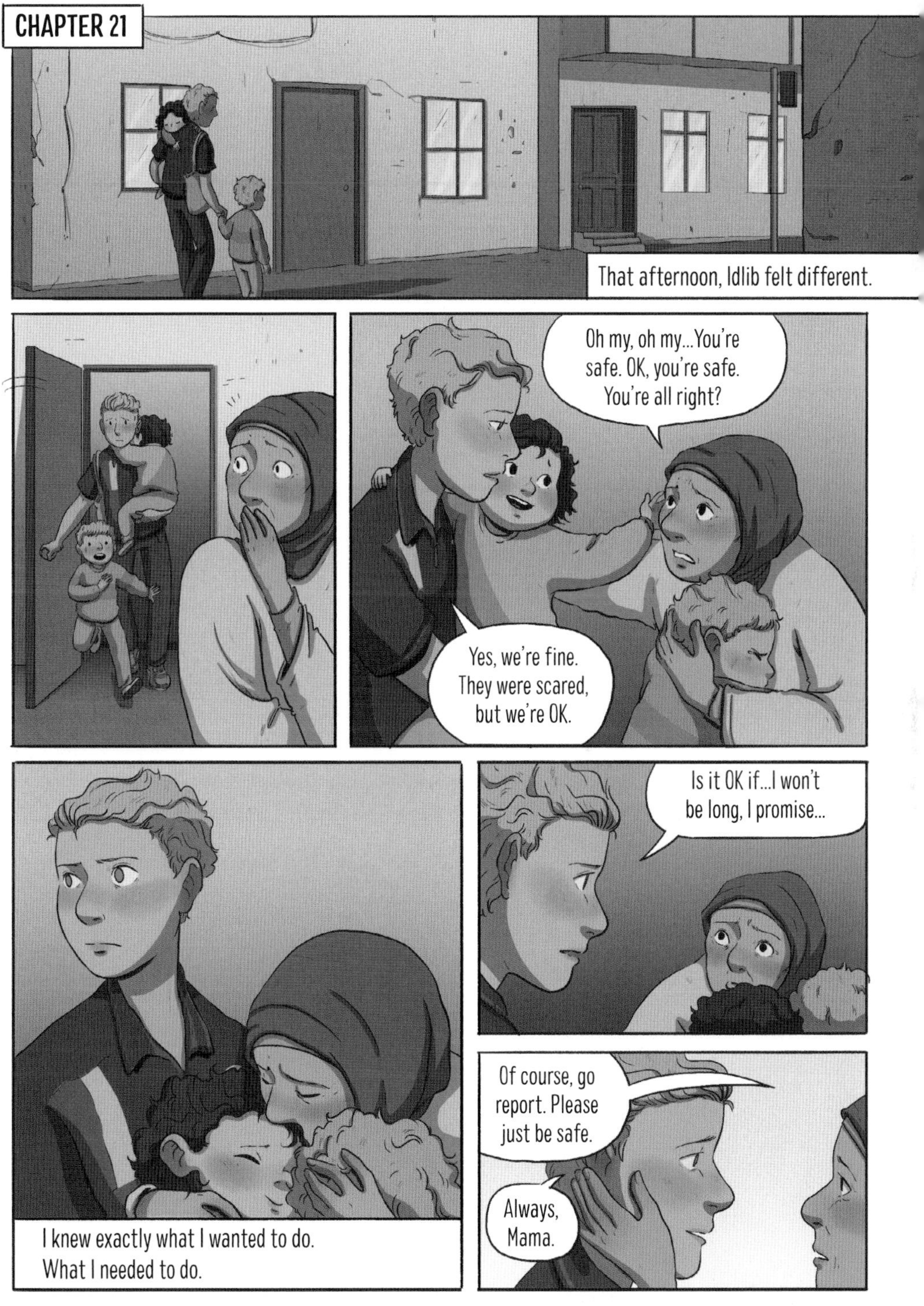

That afternoon, Idlib felt different.
Oh my, oh my...You're safe. OK, you're safe. You're all right?
Yes, we're fine. They were scared, but we're OK.
I knew exactly what I wanted to do. What I needed to do.
Is it OK if...I won't be long, I promise...
Of course, go report. Please just be safe.
Always, Mama.

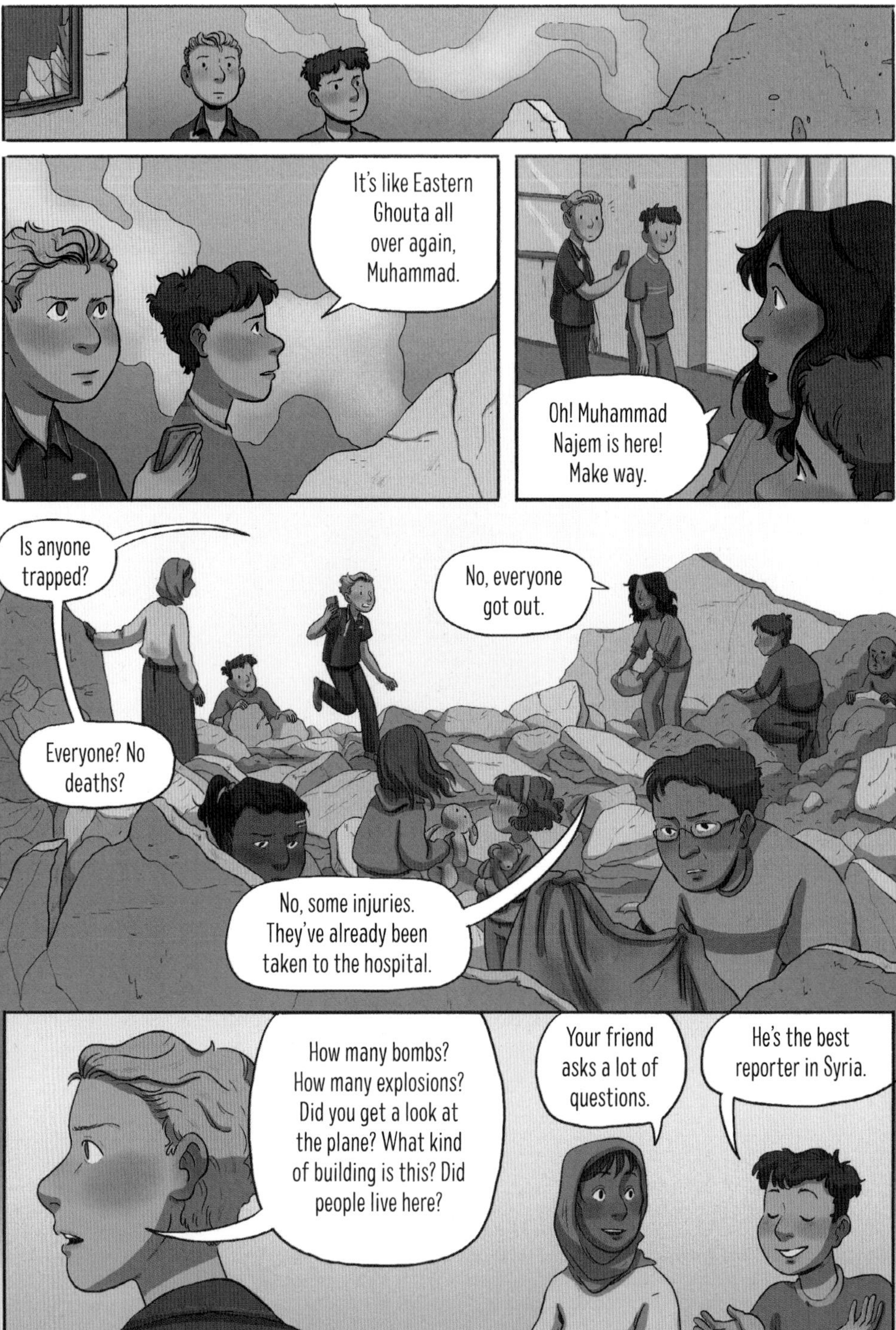
It's like Eastern Ghouta all over again, Muhammad.
Oh! Muhammad Najem is here! Make way.
Is anyone trapped?
No, everyone got out.
Everyone? No deaths?
No, some injuries. They've already been taken to the hospital.
How many bombs? How many explosions? Did you get a look at the plane? What kind of building is this? Did people live here?
Your friend asks a lot of questions.
He's the best reporter in Syria.

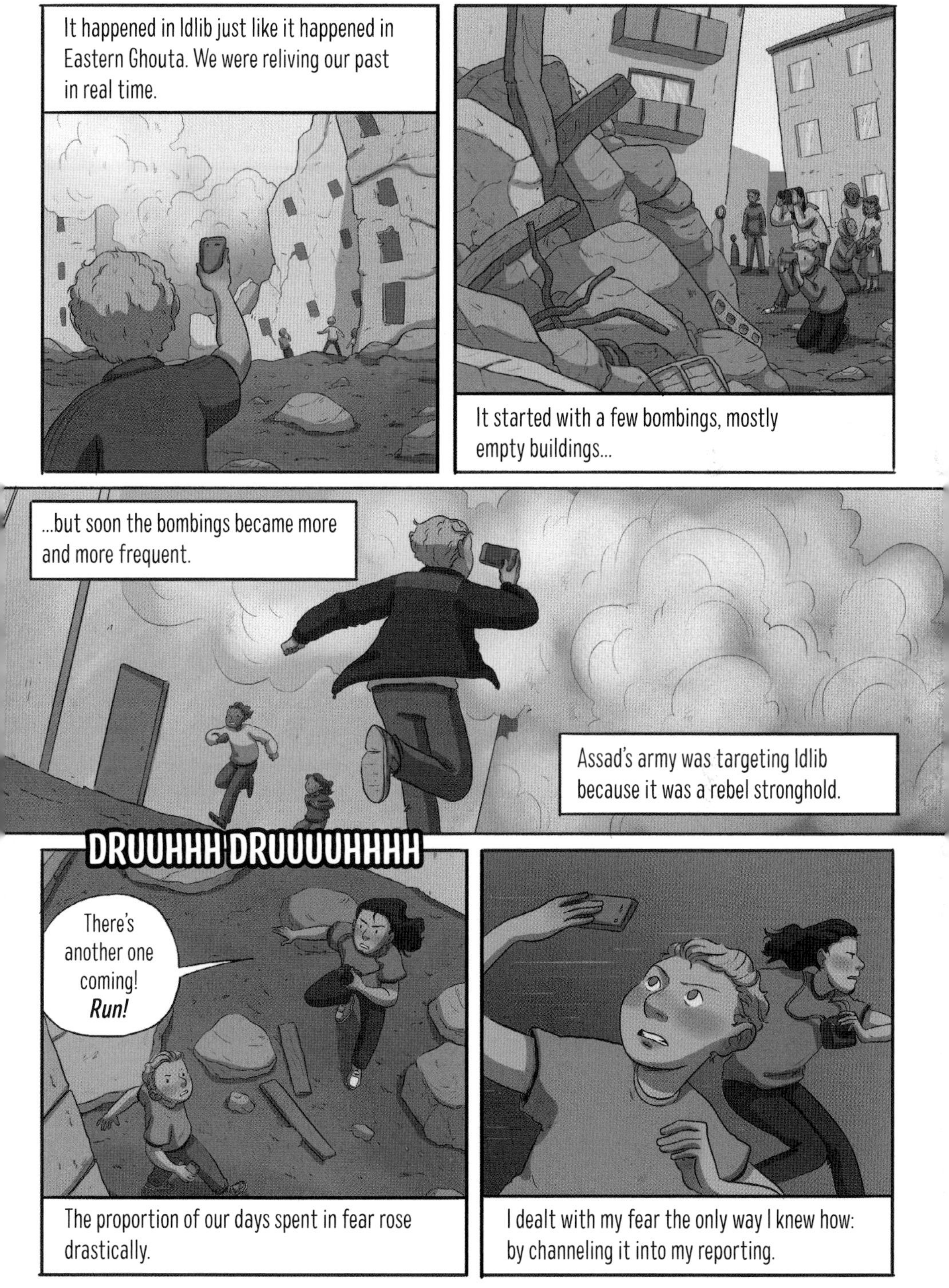
It happened in Idlib just like it happened in Eastern Ghouta. We were reliving our past in real time.
It started with a few bombings, mostly empty buildings...
...but soon the bombings became more and more frequent.
Assad's army was targeting Idlib because it was a rebel stronghold.
DRUUHHH DRUUUUHHHH
There's another one coming! *Run!*
The proportion of our days spent in fear rose drastically.
I dealt with my fear the only way I knew how: by channeling it into my reporting.

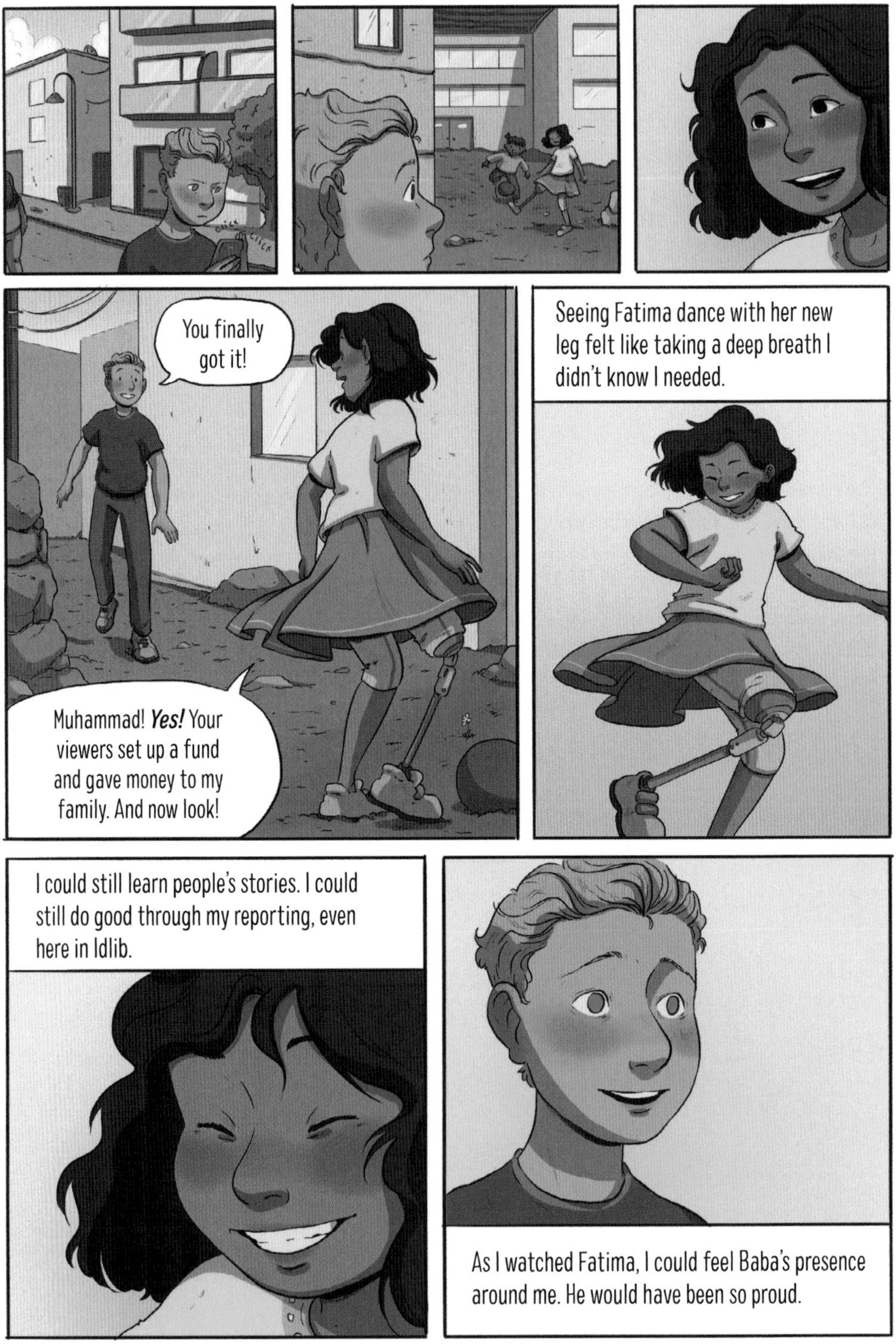
You finally got it!
Muhammad! ***Yes!*** Your viewers set up a fund and gave money to my family. And now look!
Seeing Fatima dance with her new leg felt like taking a deep breath I didn't know I needed.
I could still learn people's stories. I could still do good through my reporting, even here in Idlib.
As I watched Fatima, I could feel Baba's presence around me. He would have been so proud.

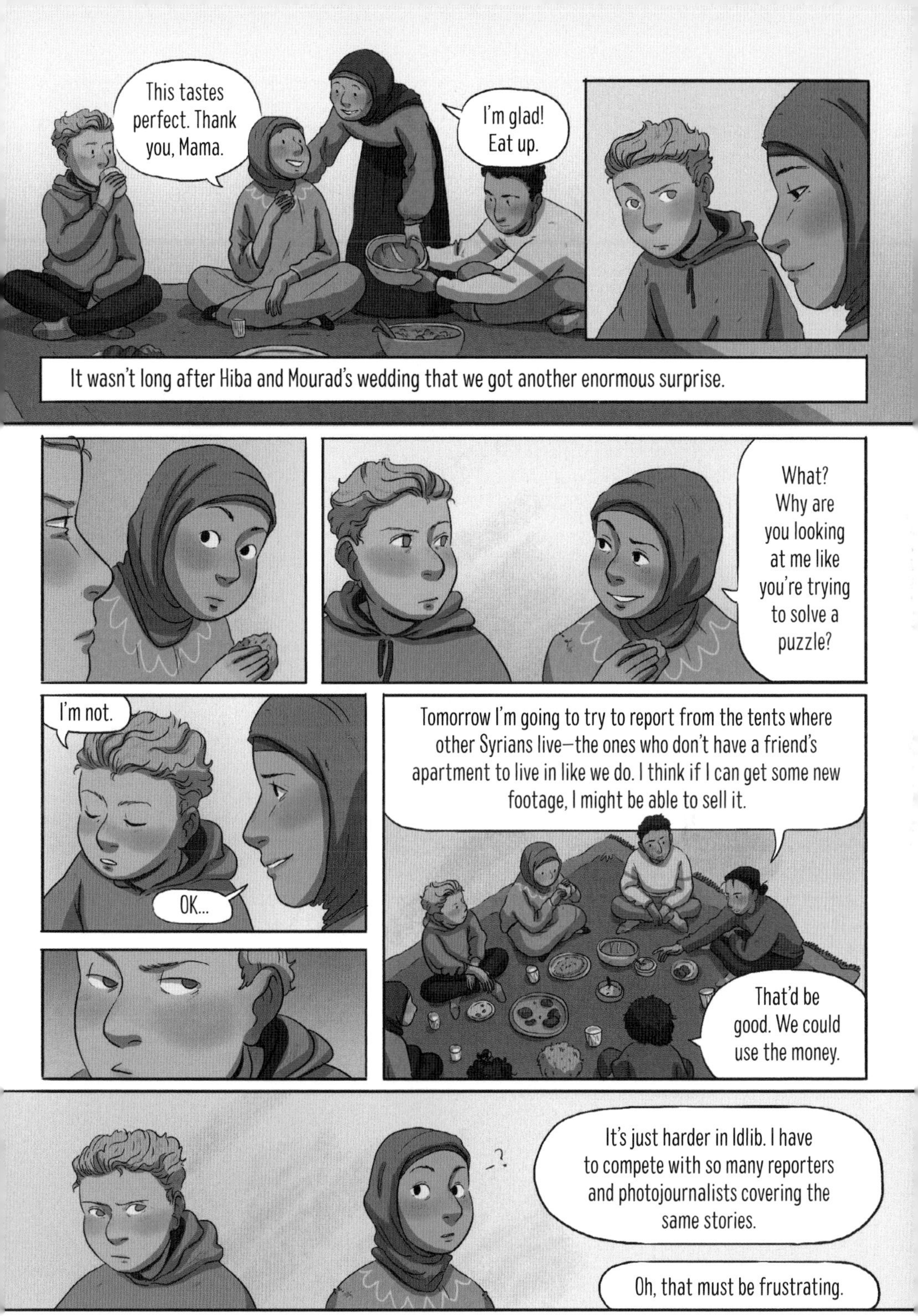

This tastes perfect. Thank you, Mama.
I'm glad! Eat up.
It wasn't long after Hiba and Mourad's wedding that we got another enormous surprise.
What? Why are you looking at me like you're trying to solve a puzzle?
I'm not.
OK...
Tomorrow I'm going to try to report from the tents where other Syrians live—the ones who don't have a friend's apartment to live in like we do. I think if I can get some new footage, I might be able to sell it.
That'd be good. We could use the money.
?
It's just harder in Idlib. I have to compete with so many reporters and photojournalists covering the same stories.
Oh, that must be frustrating.

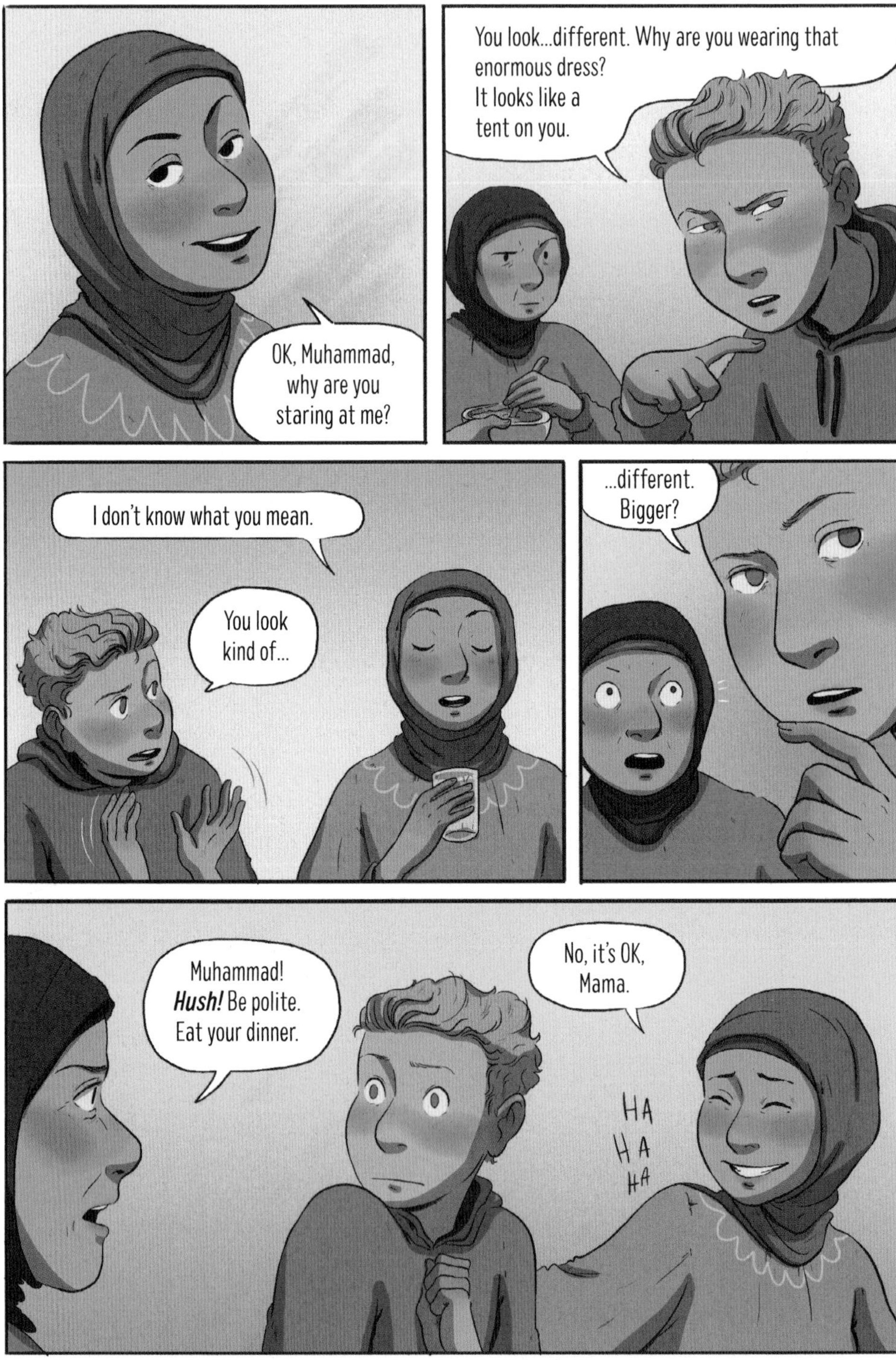
OK, Muhammad, why are you staring at me?
You look...different. Why are you wearing that enormous dress? It looks like a tent on you.
I don't know what you mean.
You look kind of...
...different. Bigger?
Muhammad! *Hush!* Be polite. Eat your dinner.
No, it's OK, Mama.
HA HA HA

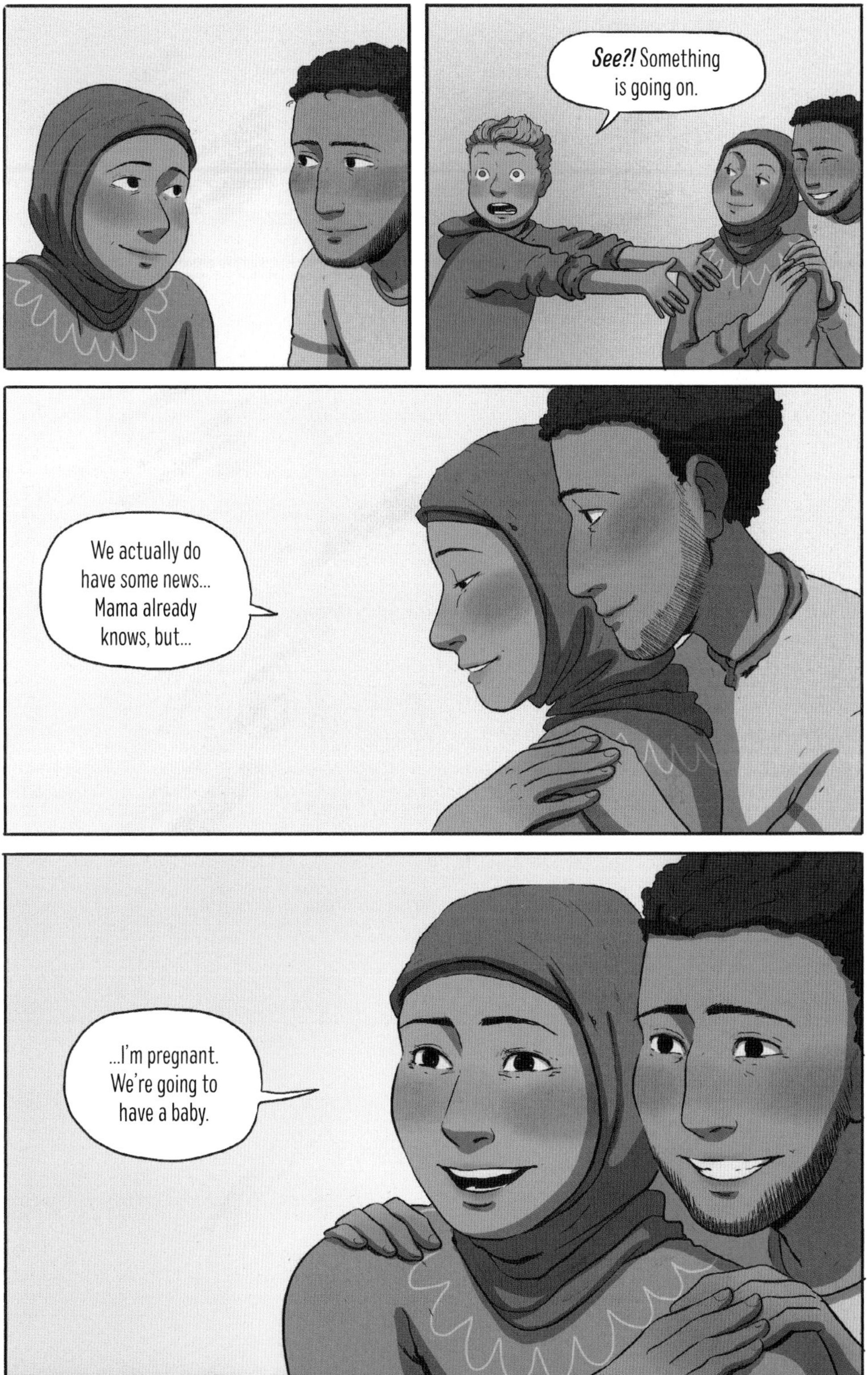
See?! Something is going on.
We actually do have some news... Mama already knows, but...
...I'm pregnant. We're going to have a baby.

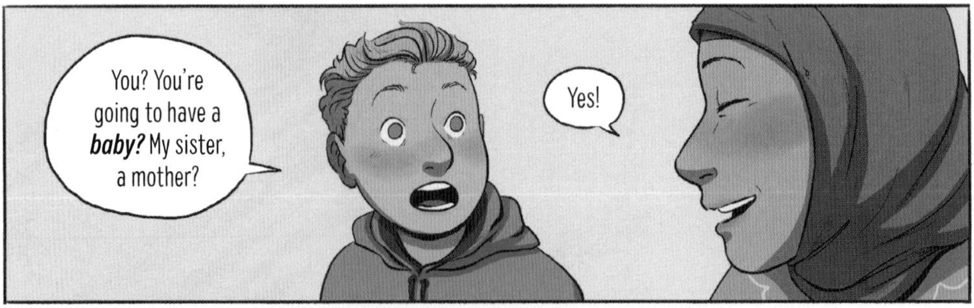
You? You're going to have a ***baby?*** My sister, a mother?
Yes!

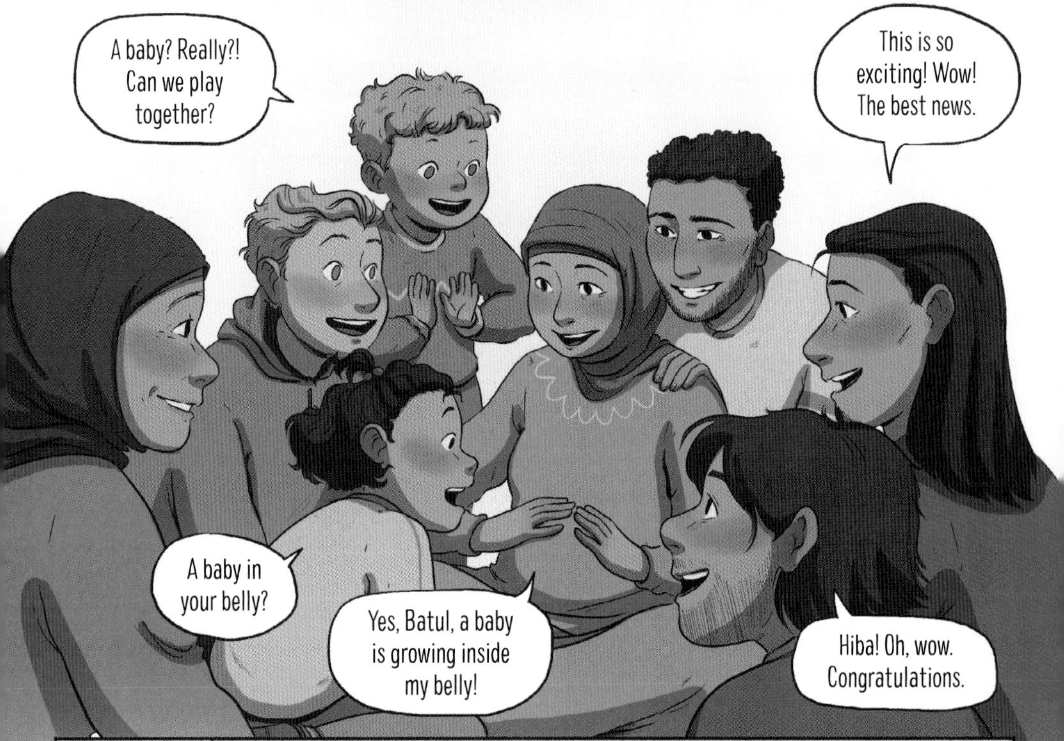
A baby? Really?! Can we play together?
This is so exciting! Wow! The best news.
A baby in your belly?
Yes, Batul, a baby is growing inside my belly!
Hiba! Oh, wow. Congratulations.

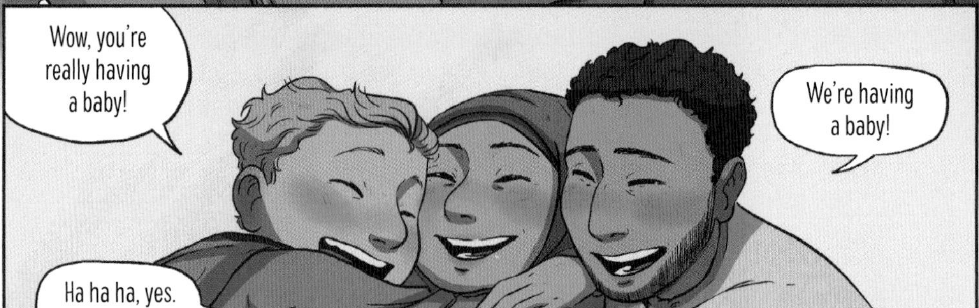
Wow, you're really having a baby!
We're having a baby!
Ha ha ha, yes. We are.

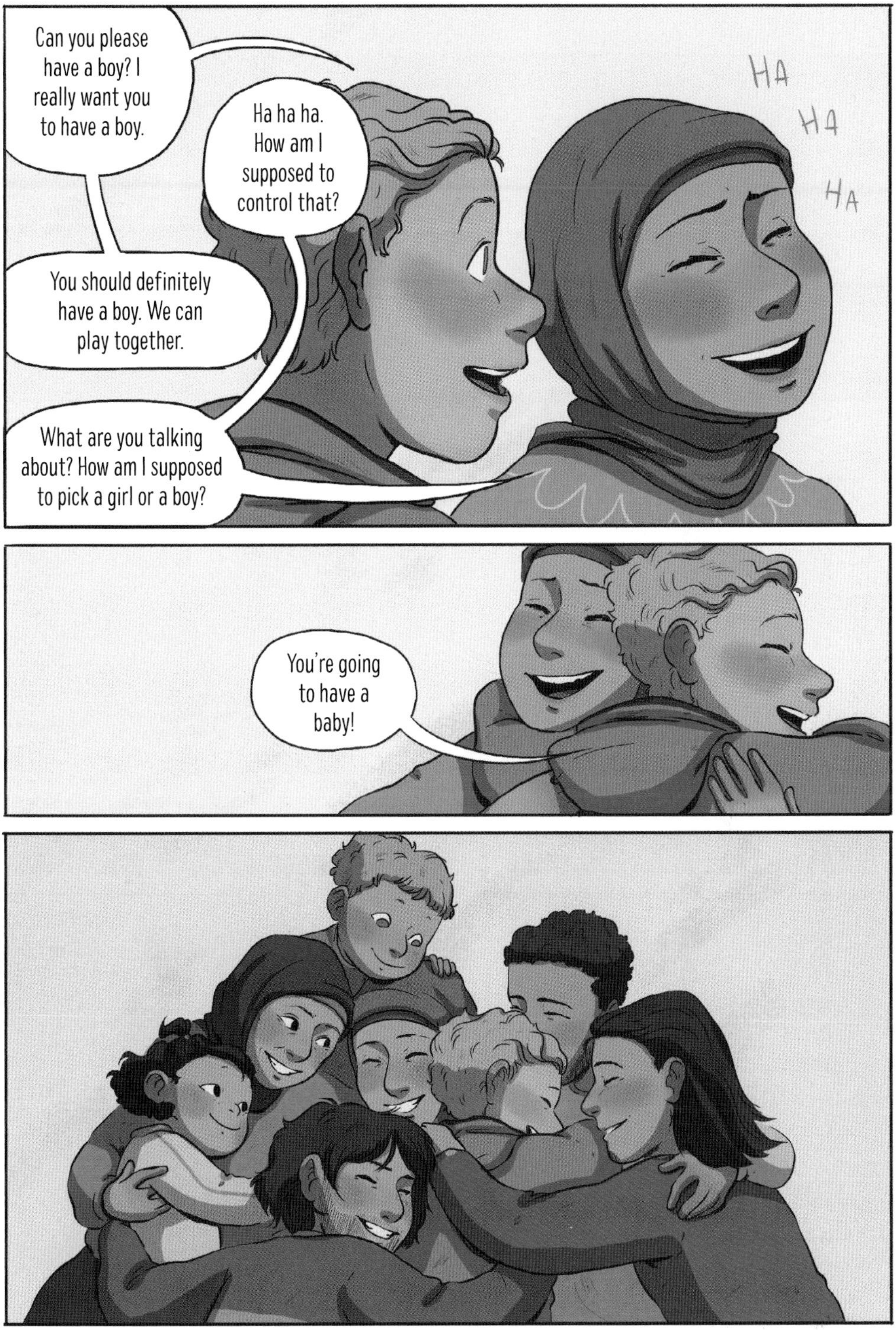
Can you please have a boy? I really want you to have a boy.
Ha ha ha. How am I supposed to control that?
HA HA HA
You should definitely have a boy. We can play together.
What are you talking about? How am I supposed to pick a girl or a boy?
You're going to have a baby!

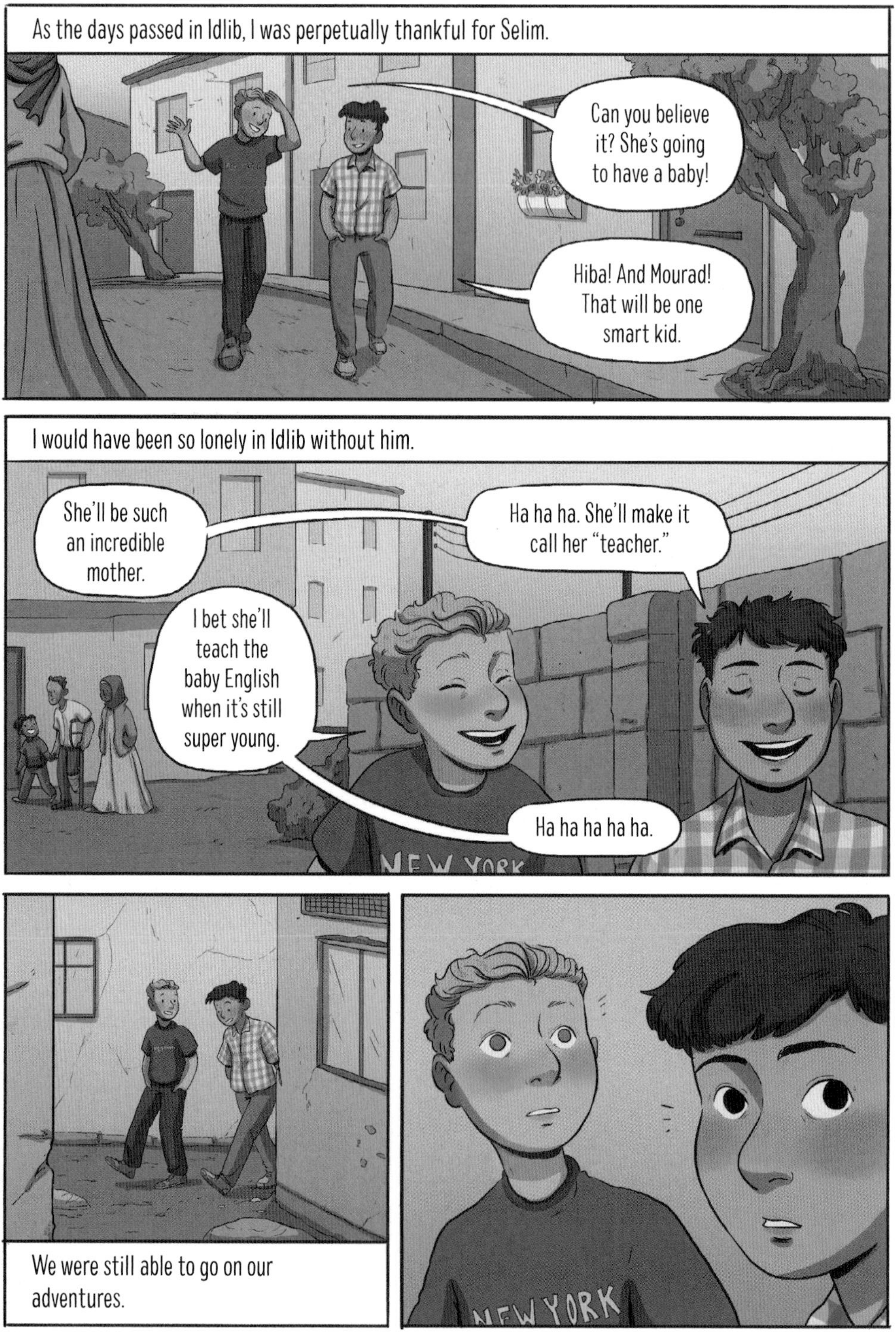
As the days passed in Idlib, I was perpetually thankful for Selim.
Can you believe it? She's going to have a baby!
Hiba! And Mourad! That will be one smart kid.
I would have been so lonely in Idlib without him.
She'll be such an incredible mother.
Ha ha ha. She'll make it call her "teacher."
I bet she'll teach the baby English when it's still super young.
Ha ha ha ha ha.
NEW YORK
We were still able to go on our adventures.
NEW YORK

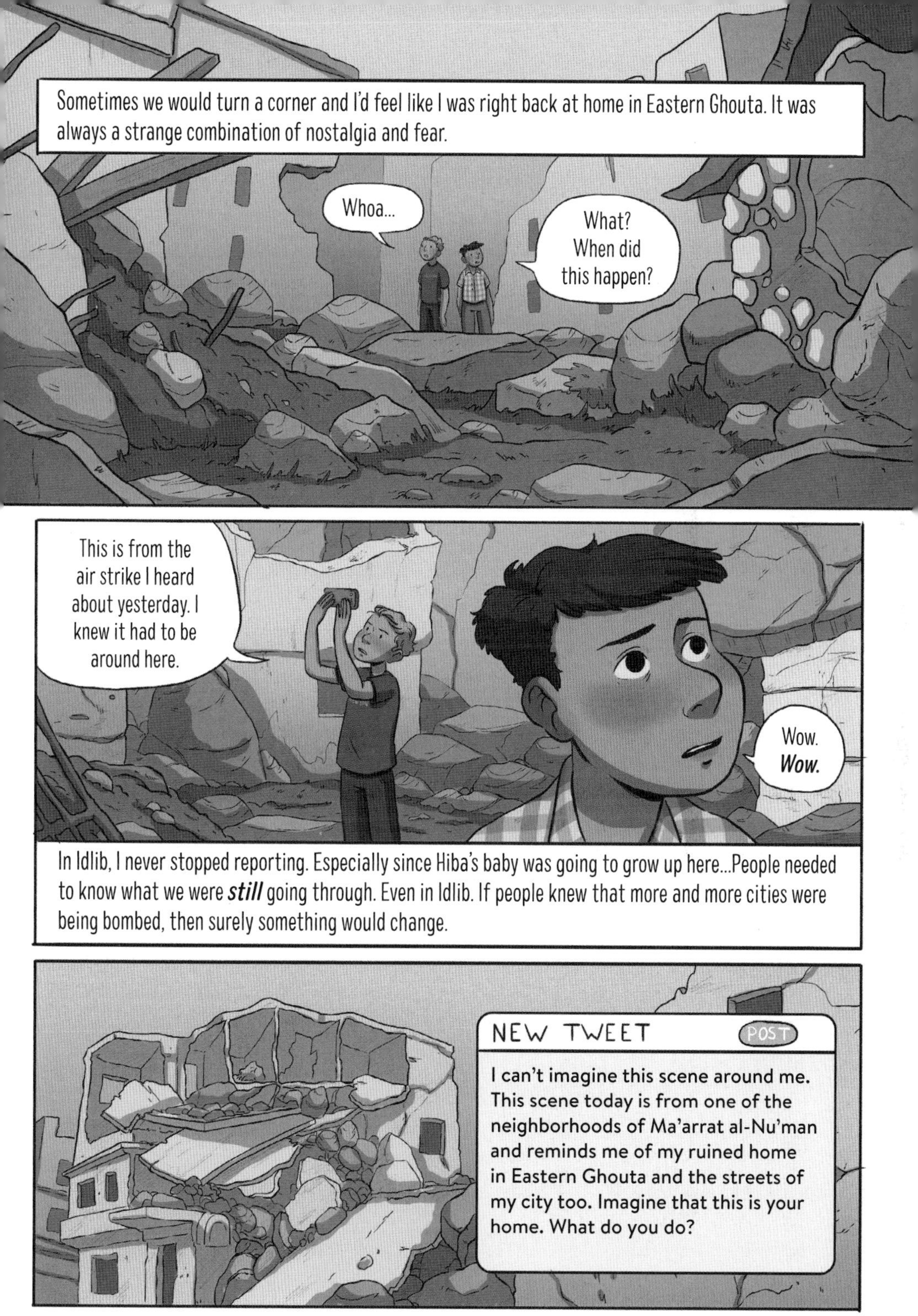
Sometimes we would turn a corner and I'd feel like I was right back at home in Eastern Ghouta. It was always a strange combination of nostalgia and fear.
Whoa...
What? When did this happen?
This is from the air strike I heard about yesterday. I knew it had to be around here.
Wow. *Wow.*
In Idlib, I never stopped reporting. Especially since Hiba's baby was going to grow up here...People needed to know what we were ***still*** going through. Even in Idlib. If people knew that more and more cities were being bombed, then surely something would change.
NEW TWEET
POST
I can't imagine this scene around me. This scene today is from one of the neighborhoods of Ma'arrat al-Nu'man and reminds me of my ruined home in Eastern Ghouta and the streets of my city too. Imagine that this is your home. What do you do?

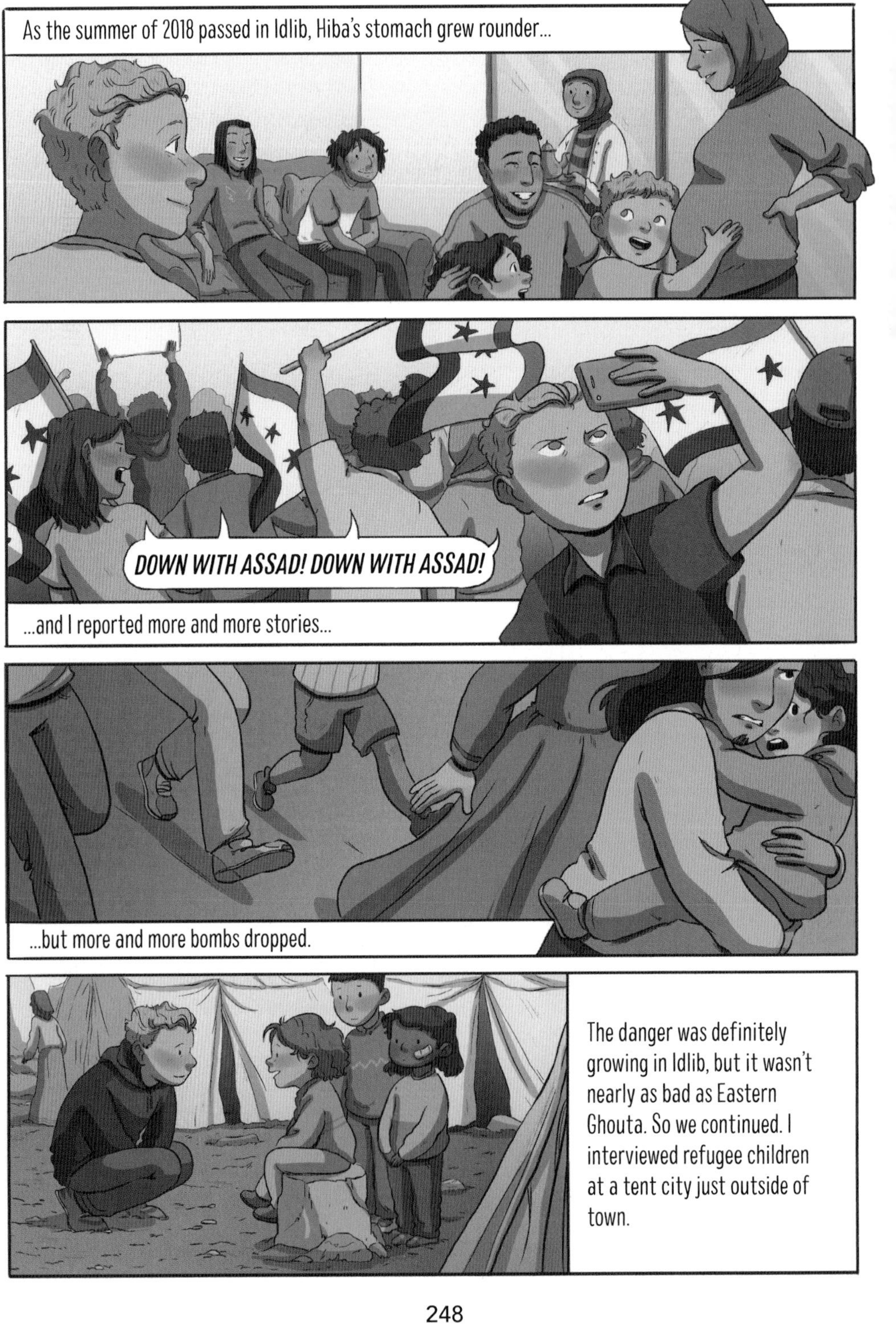
As the summer of 2018 passed in Idlib, Hiba's stomach grew rounder...
DOWN WITH ASSAD! DOWN WITH ASSAD!
...and I reported more and more stories...
...but more and more bombs dropped.
The danger was definitely growing in Idlib, but it wasn't nearly as bad as Eastern Ghouta. So we continued. I interviewed refugee children at a tent city just outside of town.

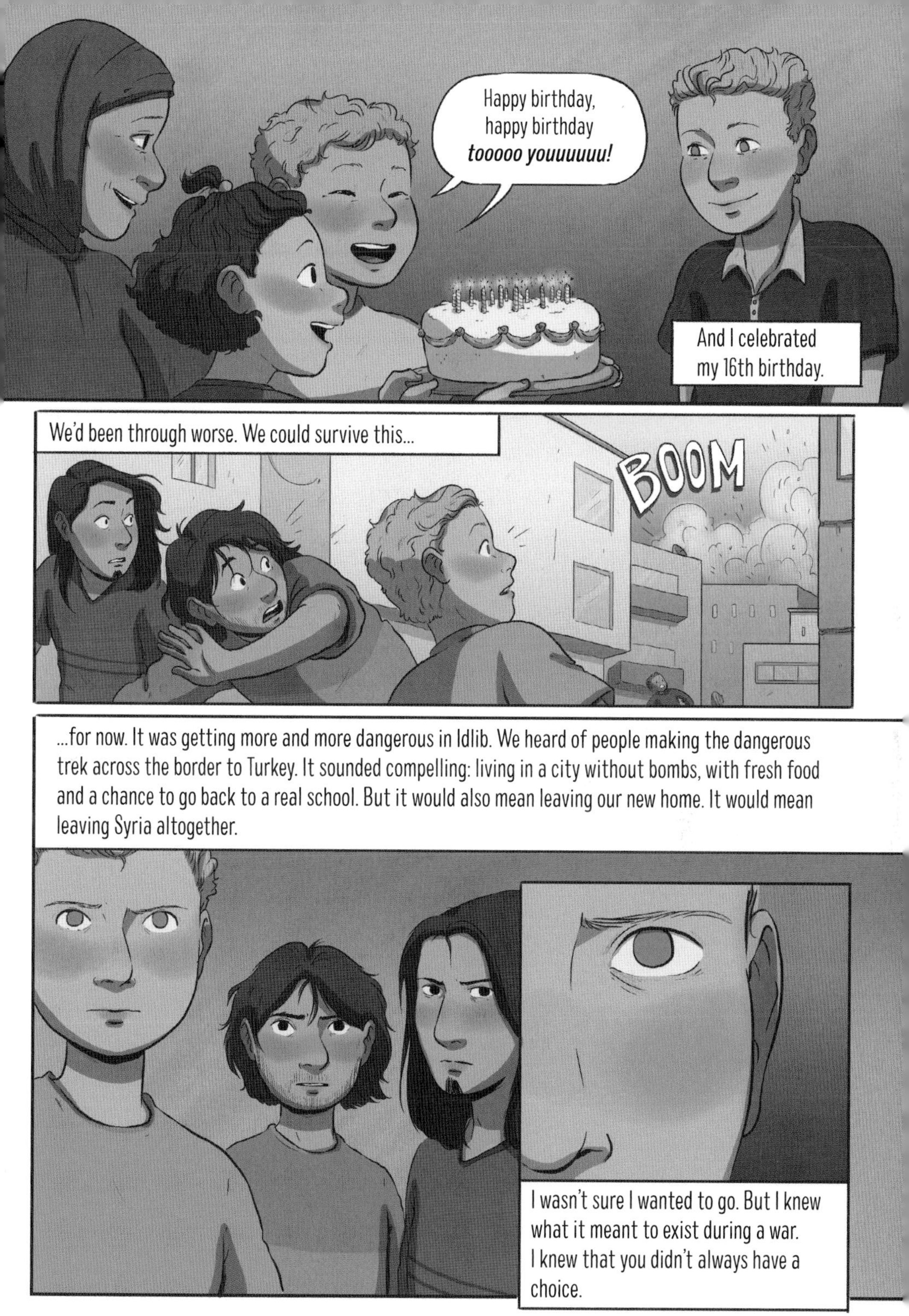
Happy birthday,
happy birthday
tooooo youuuuuu!
And I celebrated
my 16th birthday.
We'd been through worse. We could survive this...
BOOM
...for now. It was getting more and more dangerous in Idlib. We heard of people making the dangerous trek across the border to Turkey. It sounded compelling: living in a city without bombs, with fresh food and a chance to go back to a real school. But it would also mean leaving our new home. It would mean leaving Syria altogether.
I wasn't sure I wanted to go. But I knew what it meant to exist during a war. I knew that you didn't always have a choice.

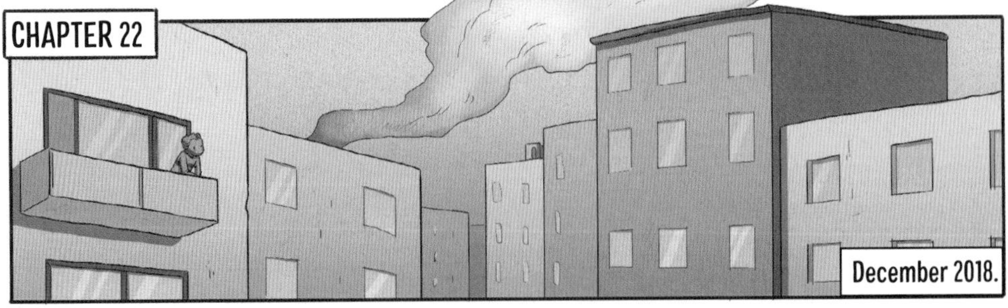
CHAPTER 22
December 2018.

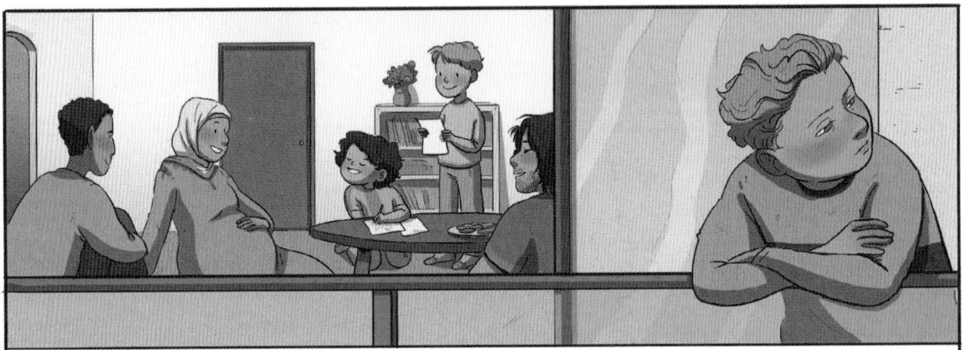

In Idlib, most days were fine, safe...even fun. But as the months went on, the danger grew. Soon there were more terrifying days than easy days.

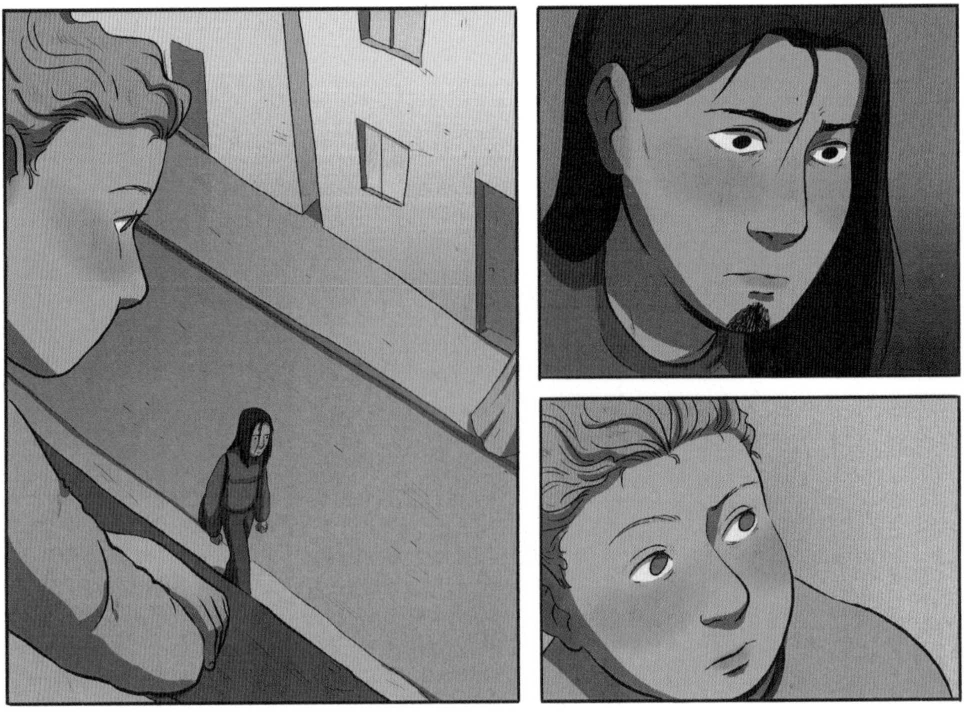

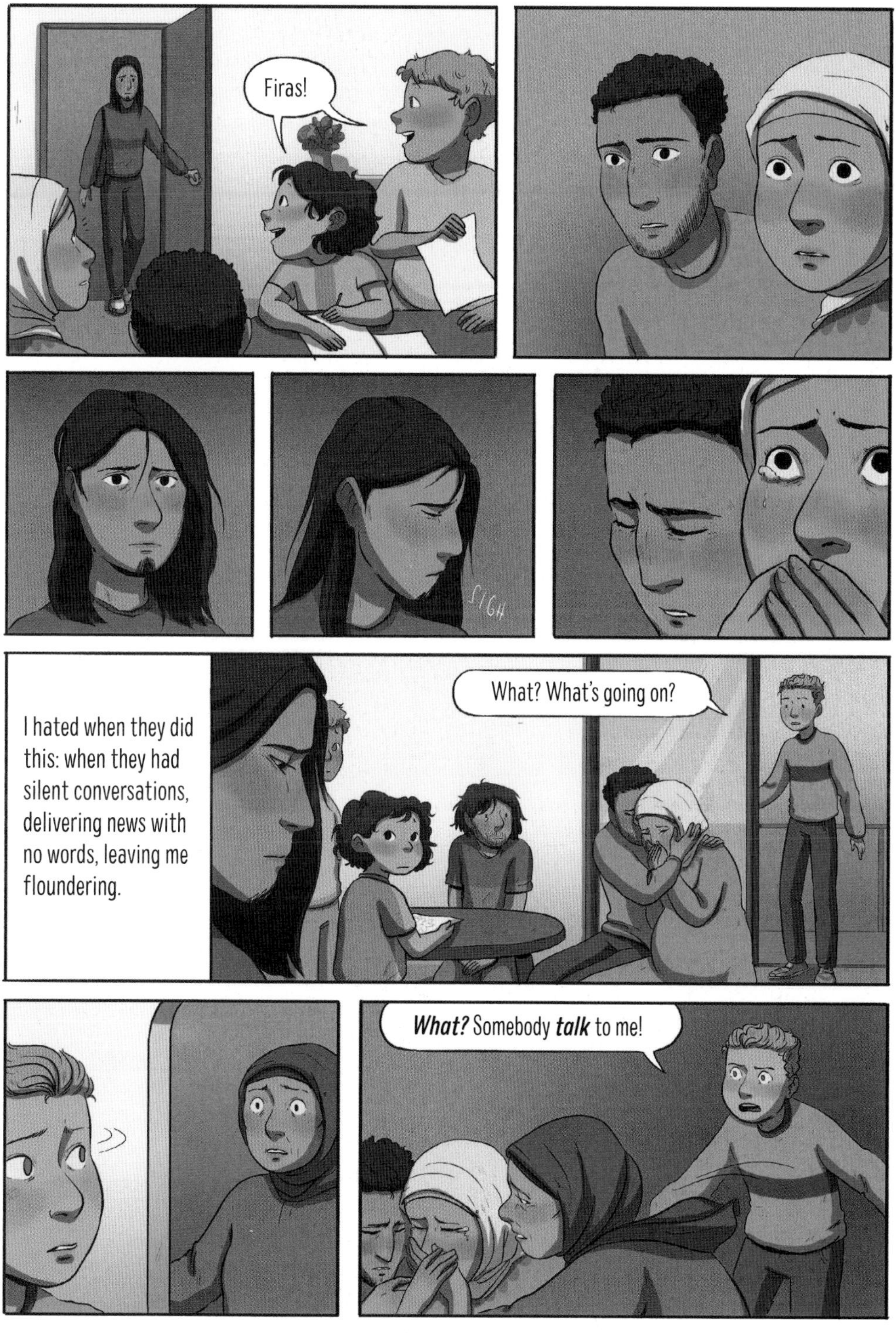
Firas!
SIGH
I hated when they did this: when they had silent conversations, delivering news with no words, leaving me floundering.
What? What's going on?
What? Somebody **talk** to me!

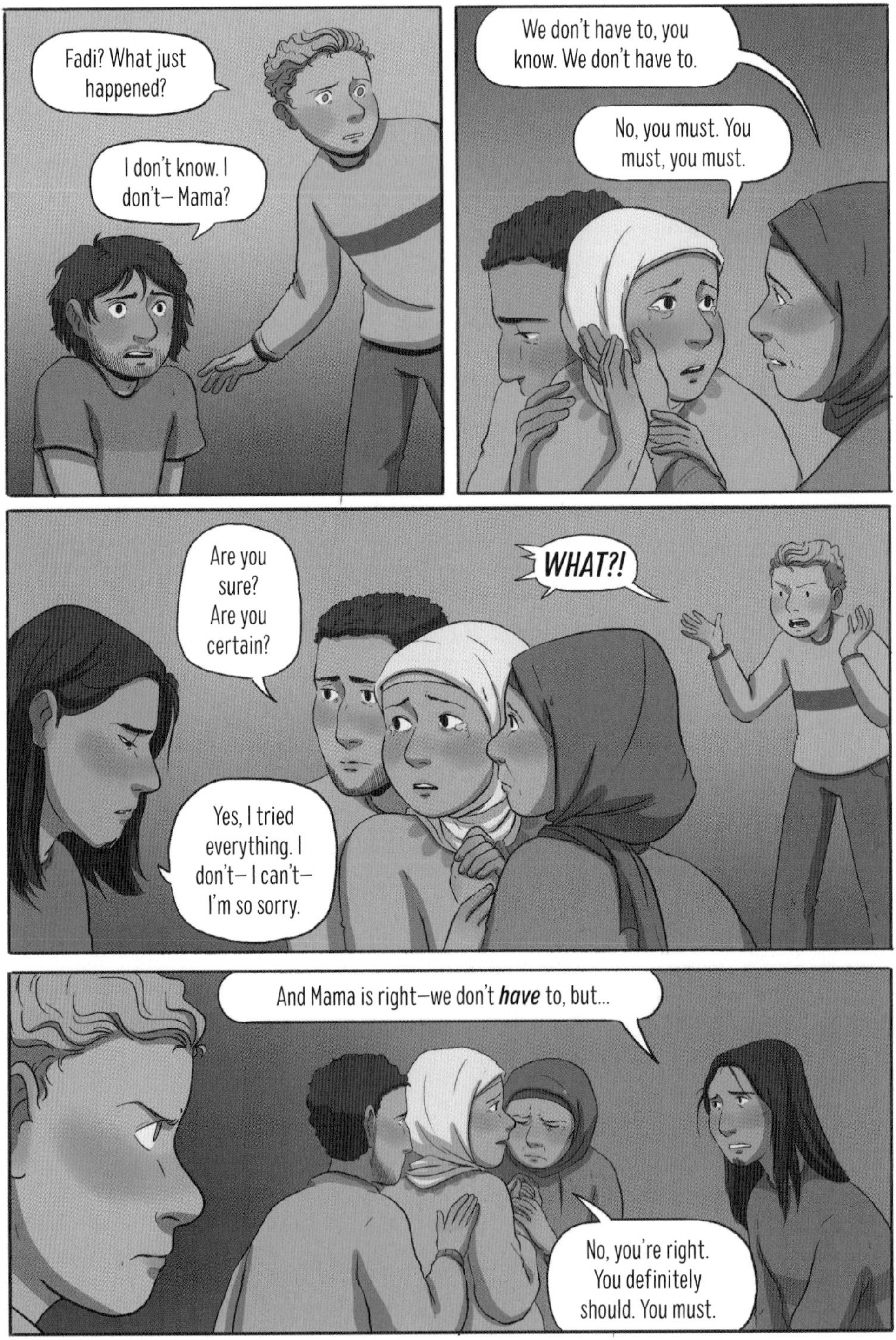

Fadi? What just happened?
I don't know. I don't– Mama?
We don't have to, you know. We don't have to.
No, you must. You must, you must.
Are you sure? Are you certain?
WHAT?!
Yes, I tried everything. I don't– I can't– I'm so sorry.
And Mama is right–we don't ***have*** to, but...
No, you're right. You definitely should. You must.

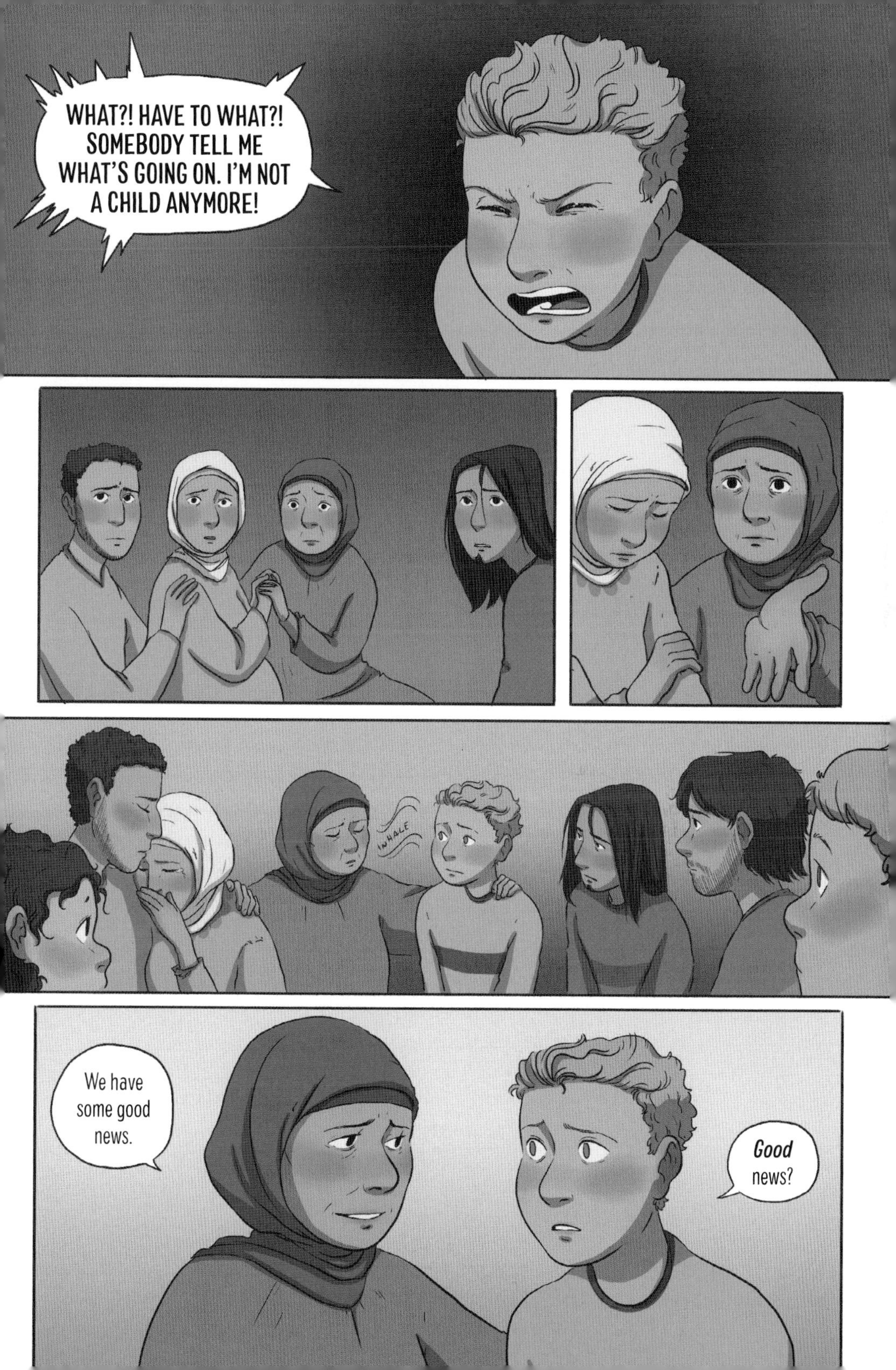
WHAT?! HAVE TO WHAT?! SOMEBODY TELL ME WHAT'S GOING ON. I'M NOT A CHILD ANYMORE!
INHALE
We have some good news.
Good news?

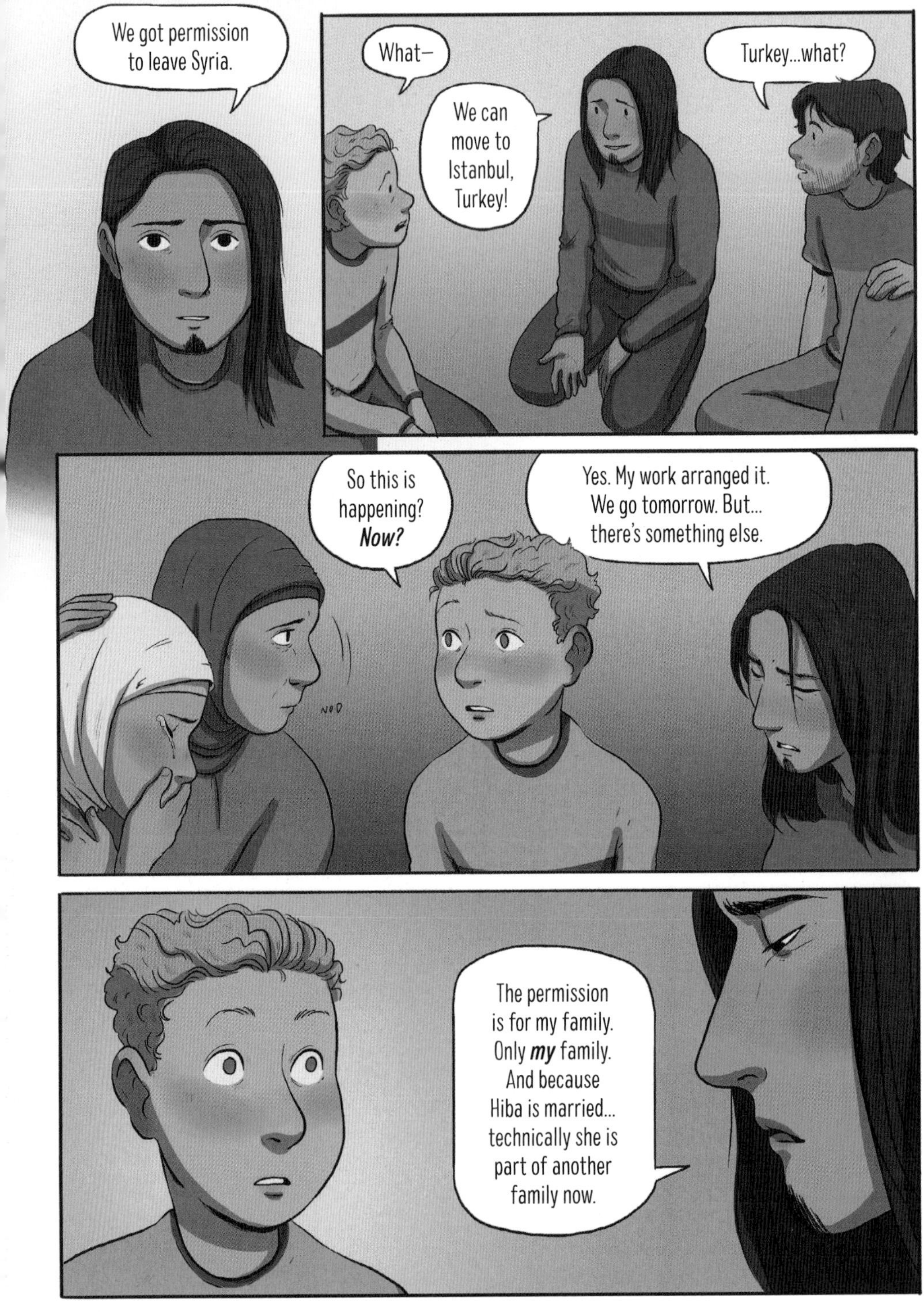
We got permission to leave Syria.
What–
We can move to Istanbul, Turkey!
Turkey...what?
So this is happening? *Now?*
NOD
Yes. My work arranged it. We go tomorrow. But... there's something else.
The permission is for my family. Only *my* family. And because Hiba is married... technically she is part of another family now.

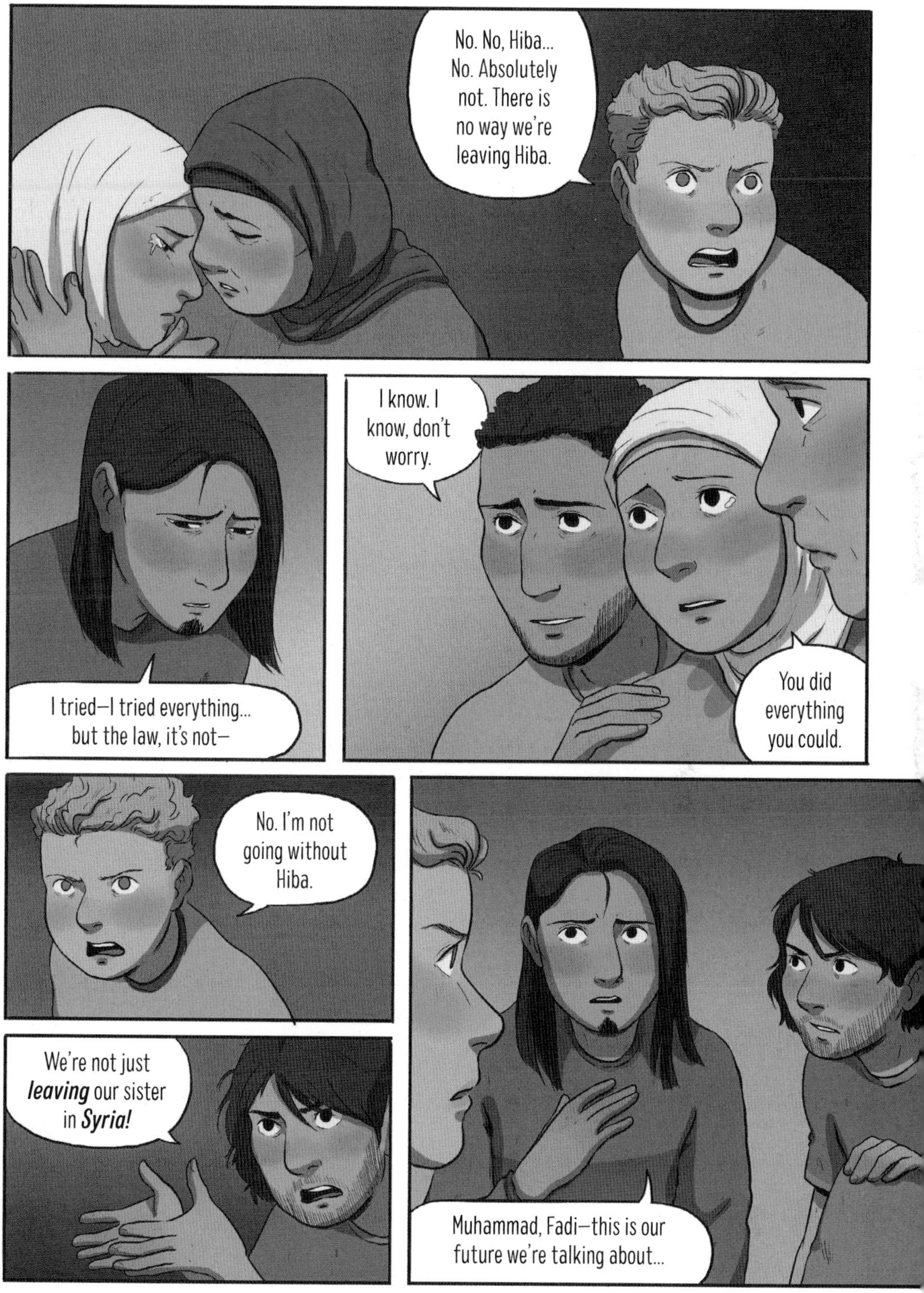
No. No, Hiba... No. Absolutely not. There is no way we're leaving Hiba.
I tried—I tried everything... but the law, it's not—
I know. I know, don't worry.
You did everything you could.
No. I'm not going without Hiba.
We're not just ***leaving*** our sister in ***Syria!***
Muhammad, Fadi—this is our future we're talking about...

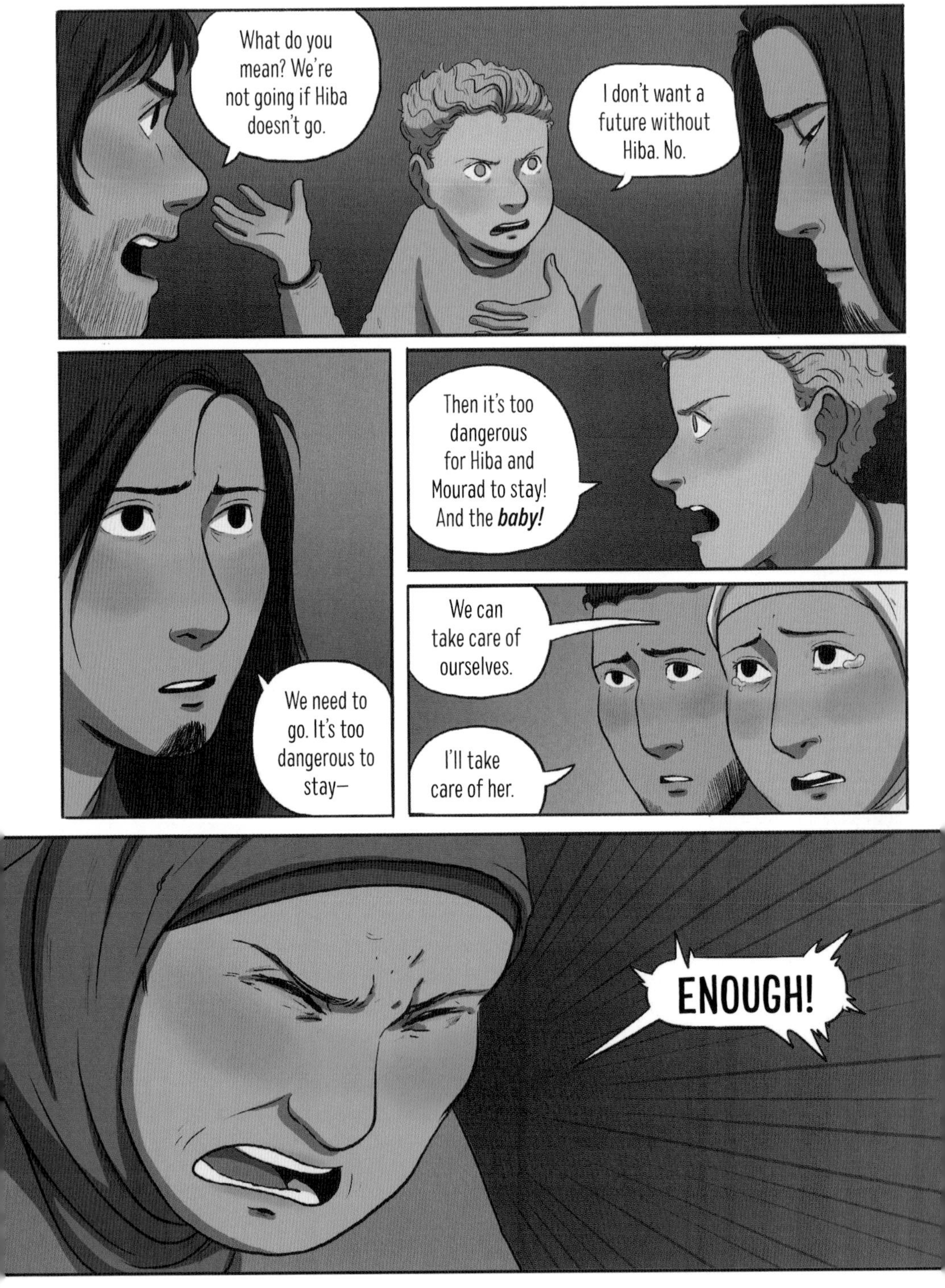

What do you mean? We're not going if Hiba doesn't go.
I don't want a future without Hiba. No.
We need to go. It's too dangerous to stay—
Then it's too dangerous for Hiba and Mourad to stay! And the *baby!*
We can take care of ourselves.
I'll take care of her.
ENOUGH!

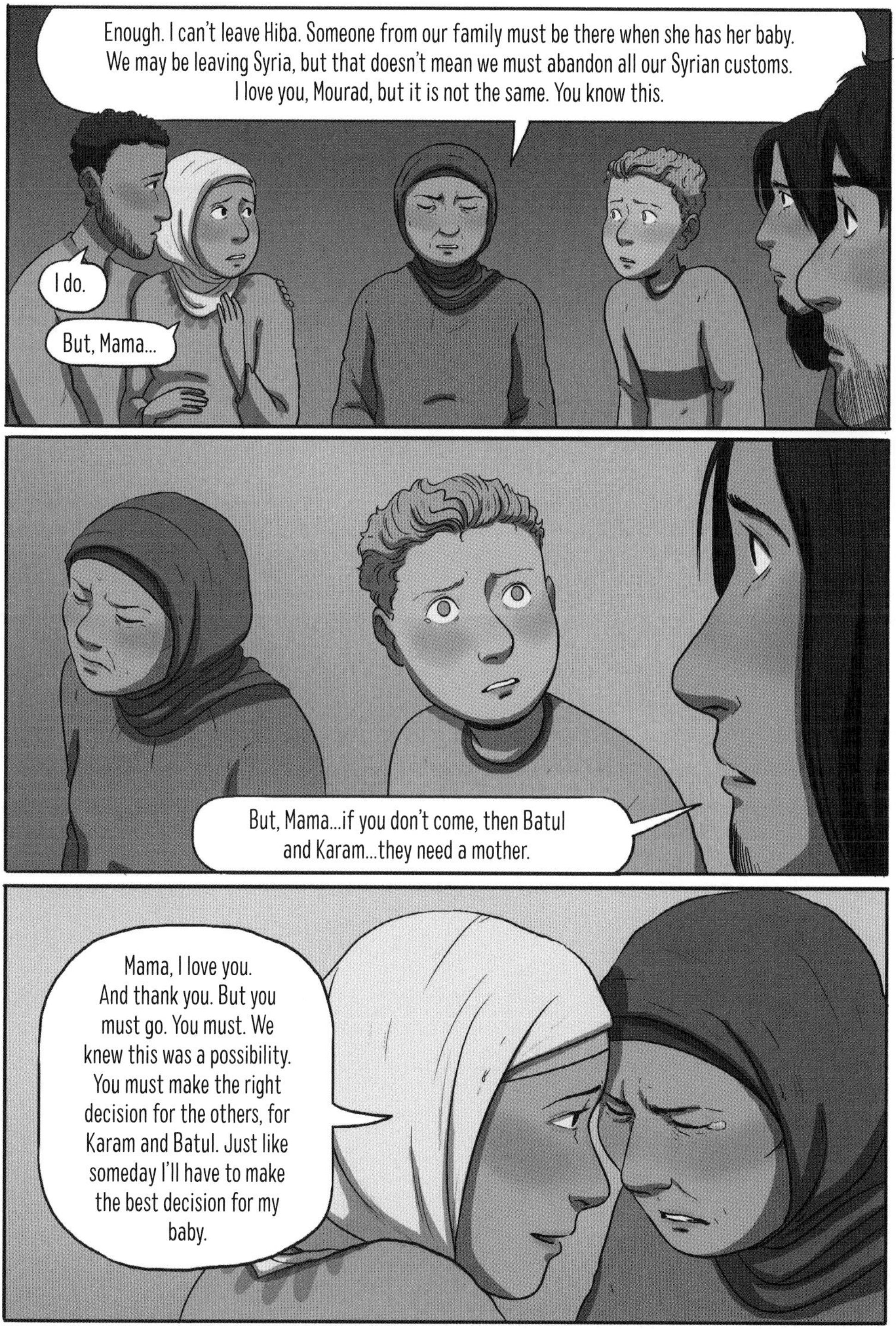
Enough. I can't leave Hiba. Someone from our family must be there when she has her baby. We may be leaving Syria, but that doesn't mean we must abandon all our Syrian customs. I love you, Mourad, but it is not the same. You know this.
I do.
But, Mama...
But, Mama...if you don't come, then Batul and Karam...they need a mother.
Mama, I love you. And thank you. But you must go. You must. We knew this was a possibility. You must make the right decision for the others, for Karam and Batul. Just like someday I'll have to make the best decision for my baby.

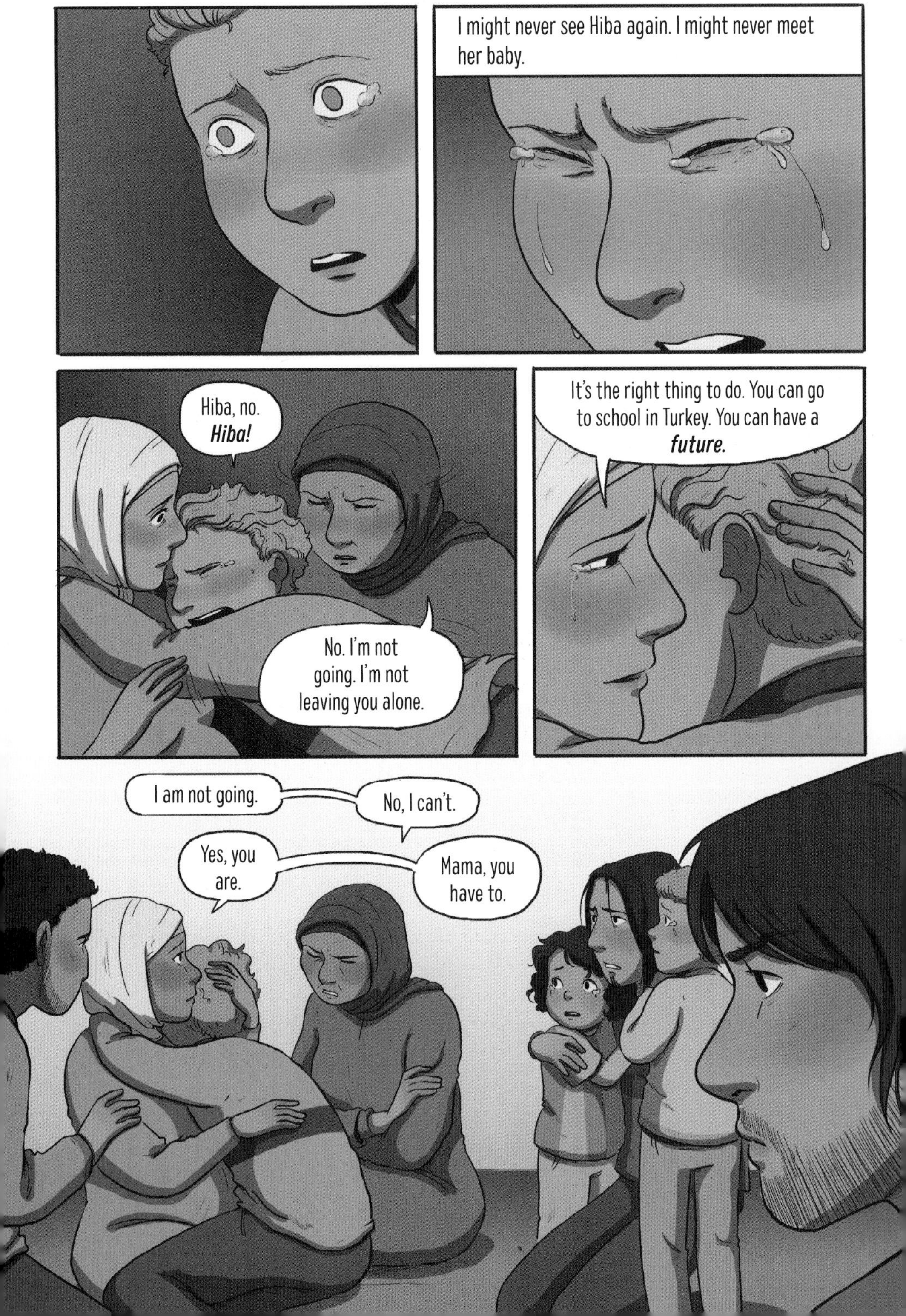

I might never see Hiba again. I might never meet her baby.
Hiba, no. *Hiba!*
No. I'm not going. I'm not leaving you alone.
It's the right thing to do. You can go to school in Turkey. You can have a *future.*
I am not going.
No, I can't.
Yes, you are.
Mama, you have to.

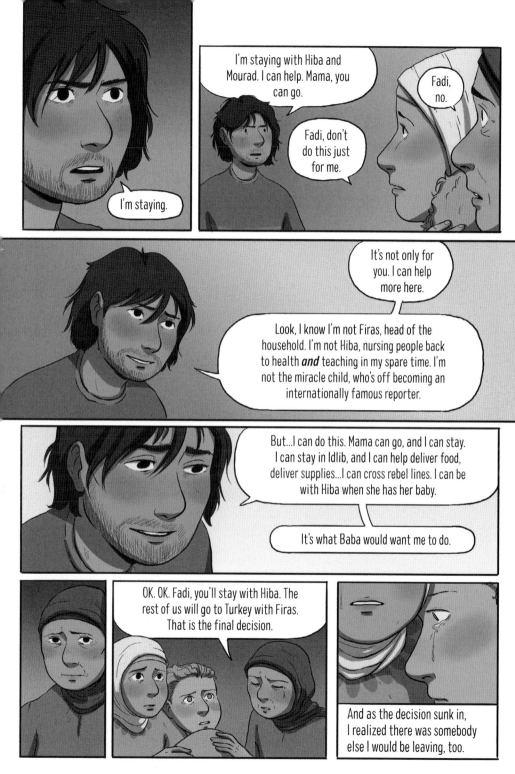

I'm staying with Hiba and Mourad. I can help. Mama, you can go.

Fadi, no.

Fadi, don't do this just for me.

I'm staying.

It's not only for you. I can help more here.

Look, I know I'm not Firas, head of the household. I'm not Hiba, nursing people back to health *and* teaching in my spare time. I'm not the miracle child, who's off becoming an internationally famous reporter.

But...I can do this. Mama can go, and I can stay. I can stay in Idlib, and I can help deliver food, deliver supplies...I can cross rebel lines. I can be with Hiba when she has her baby.

It's what Baba would want me to do.

OK. OK. Fadi, you'll stay with Hiba. The rest of us will go to Turkey with Firas. That is the final decision.

And as the decision sunk in, I realized there was somebody else I would be leaving, too.

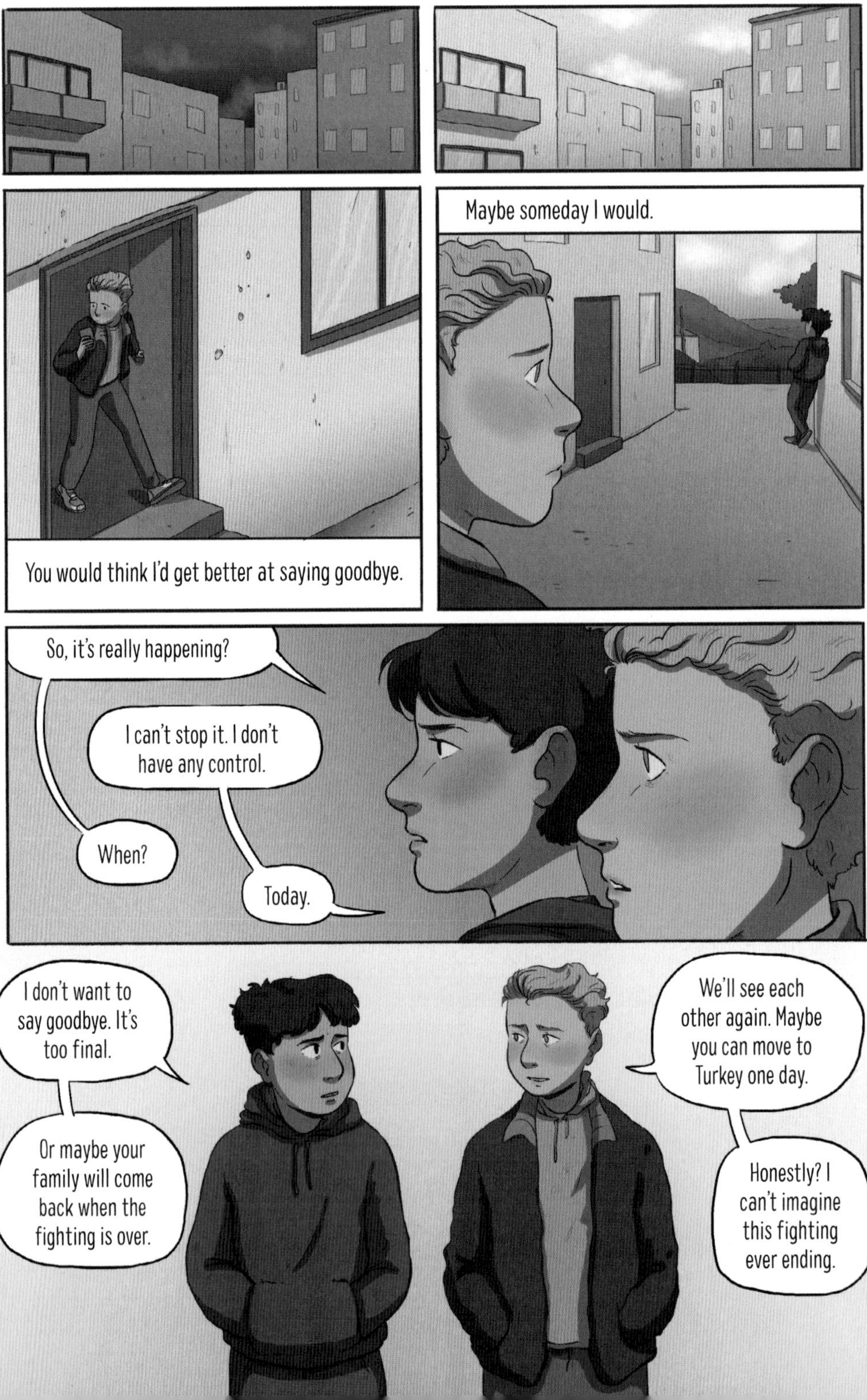

You would think I'd get better at saying goodbye.
Maybe someday I would.
So, it's really happening?
I can't stop it. I don't have any control.
When?
Today.
I don't want to say goodbye. It's too final.
We'll see each other again. Maybe you can move to Turkey one day.
Or maybe your family will come back when the fighting is over.
Honestly? I can't imagine this fighting ever ending.

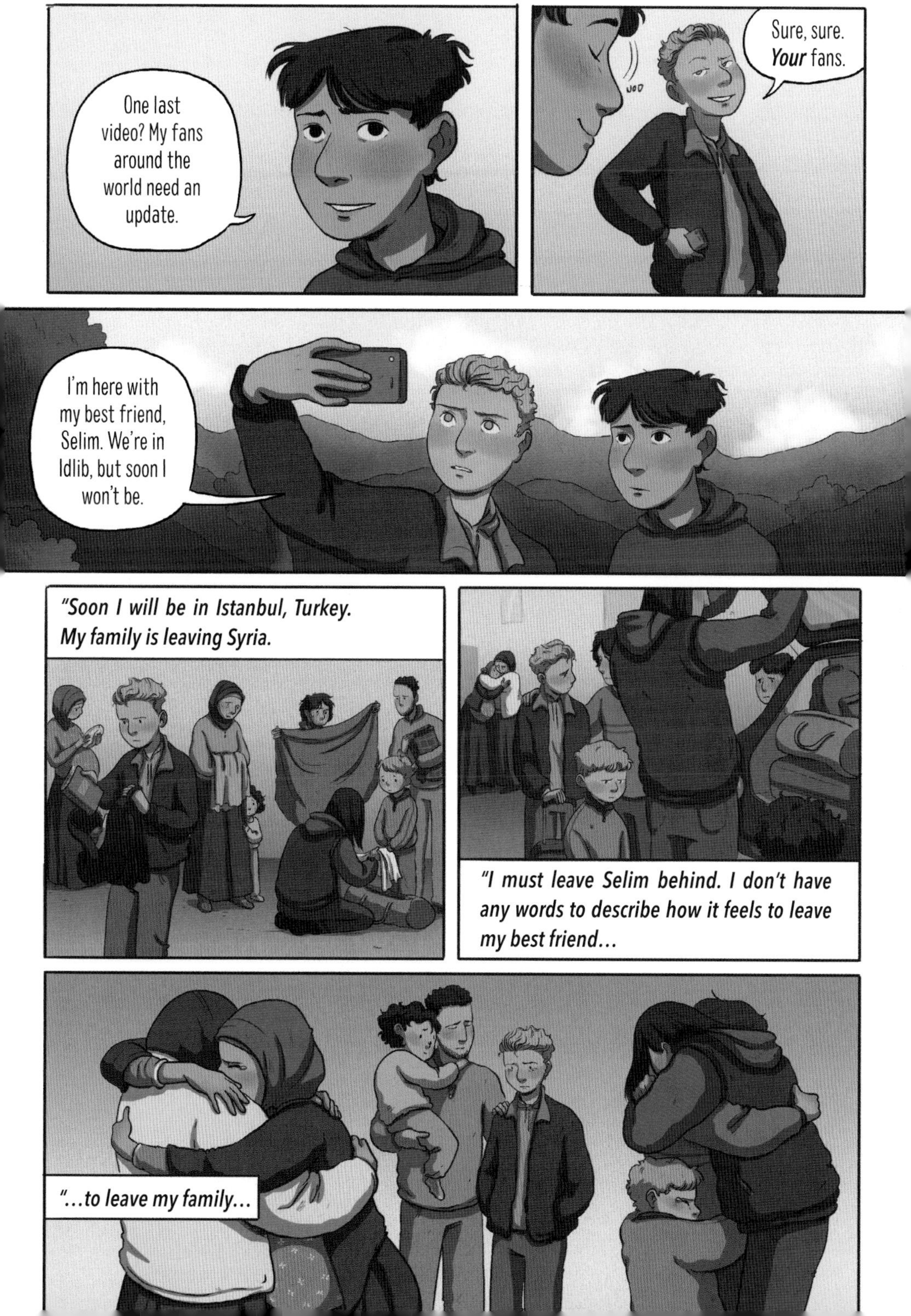

One last video? My fans around the world need an update.
NOD
Sure, sure. *Your* fans.
I'm here with my best friend, Selim. We're in Idlib, but soon I won't be.
"Soon I will be in Istanbul, Turkey. My family is leaving Syria.
"I must leave Selim behind. I don't have any words to describe how it feels to leave my best friend...
"...to leave my family...

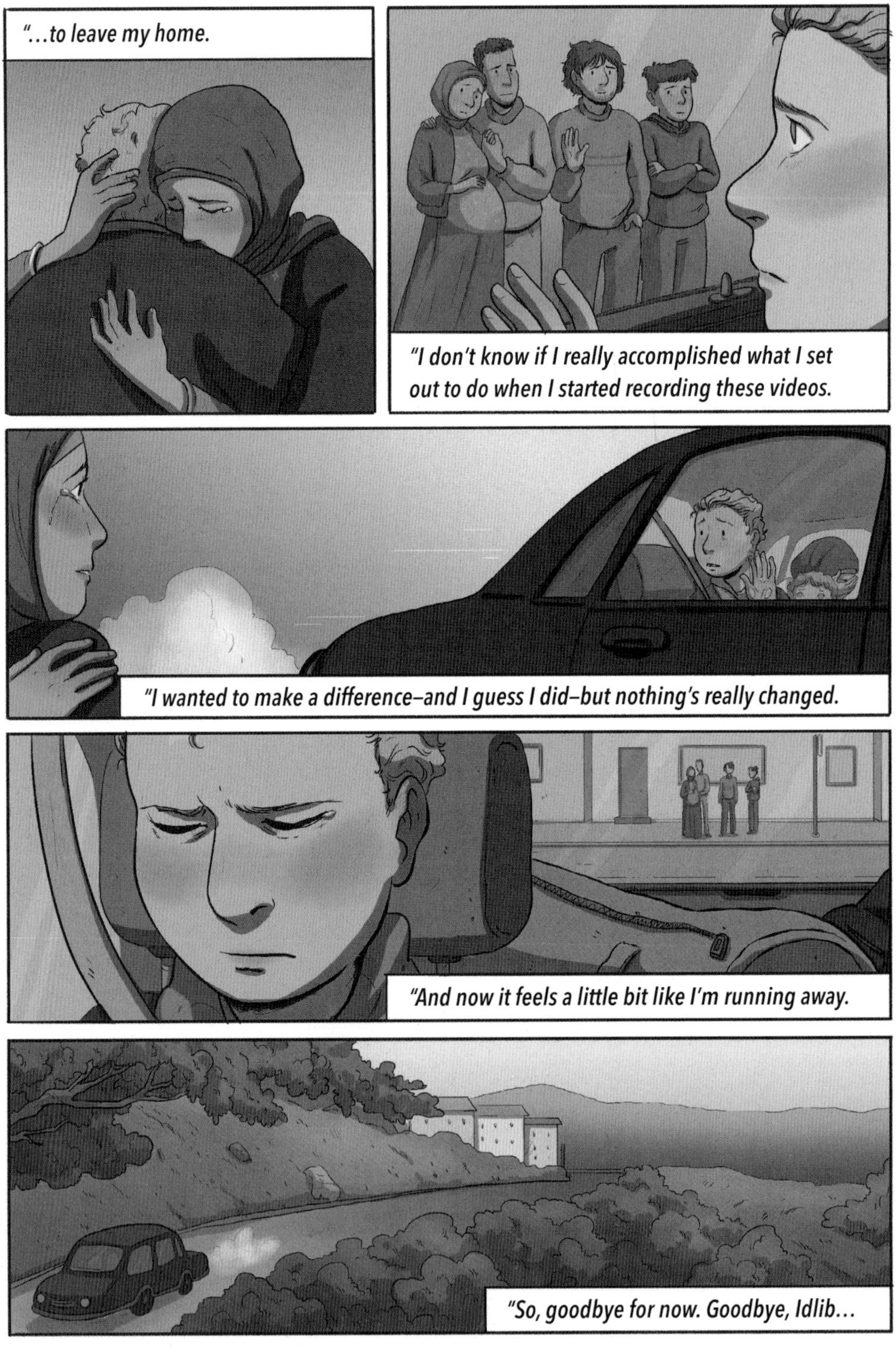
"...to leave my home.
"I don't know if I really accomplished what I set out to do when I started recording these videos.
"I wanted to make a difference–and I guess I did–but nothing's really changed.
"And now it feels a little bit like I'm running away.
"So, goodbye for now. Goodbye, Idlib...

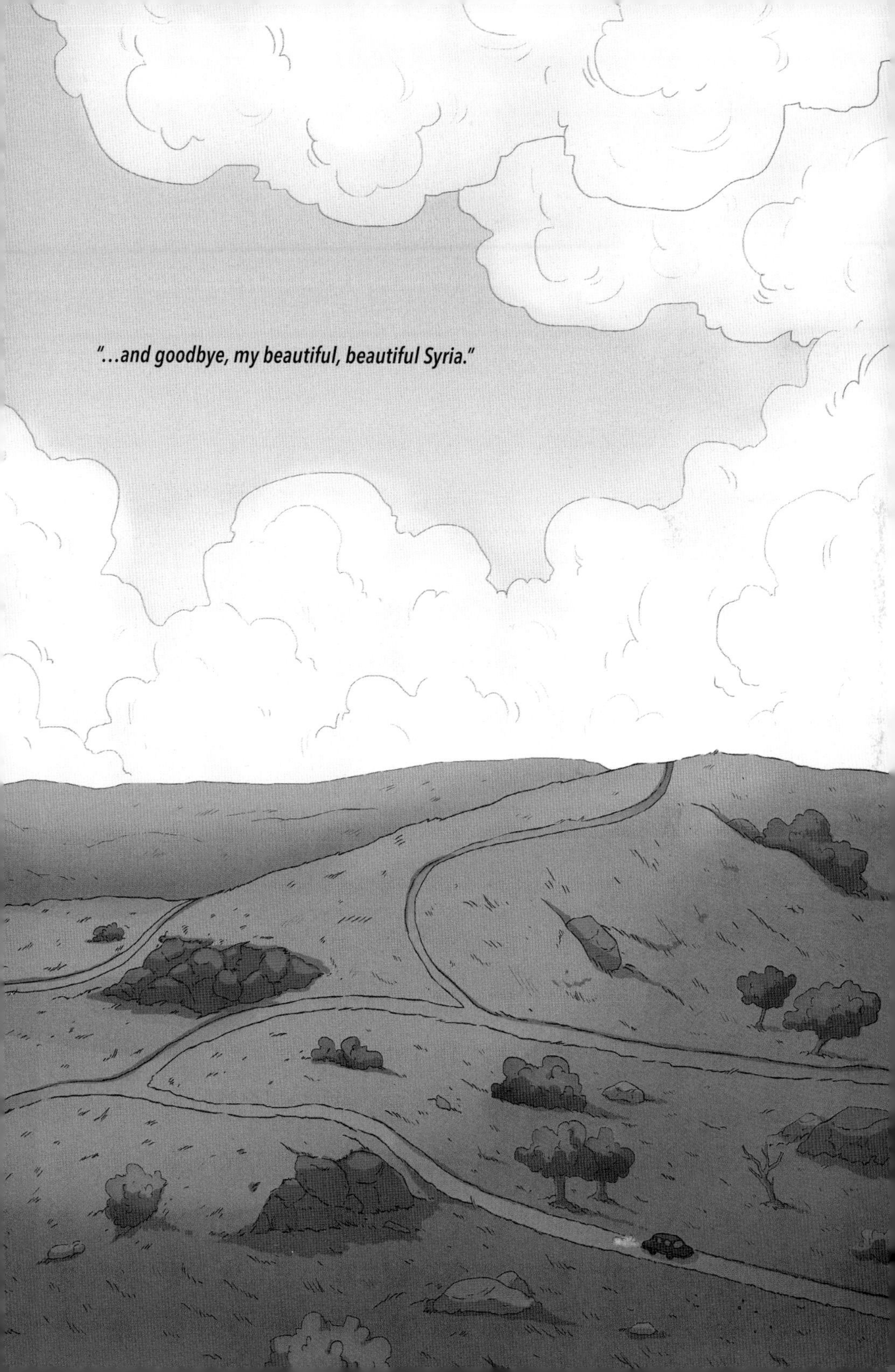
"...and goodbye, my beautiful, beautiful Syria."

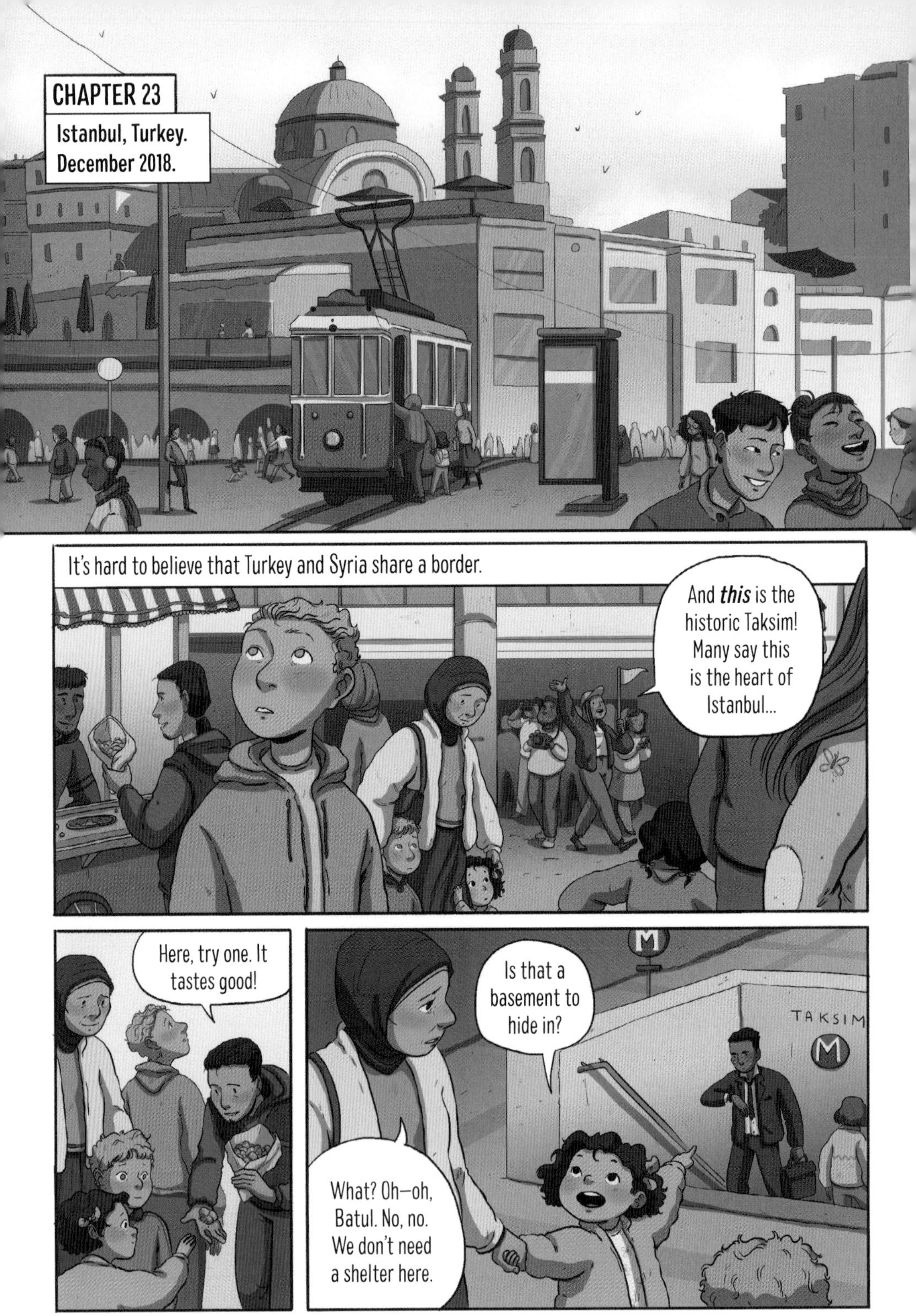
CHAPTER 23
Istanbul, Turkey. December 2018.
It's hard to believe that Turkey and Syria share a border.
And *this* is the historic Taksim! Many say this is the heart of Istanbul...
Here, try one. It tastes good!
Is that a basement to hide in?
TAKSIM
M
What? Oh—oh, Batul. No, no. We don't need a shelter here.

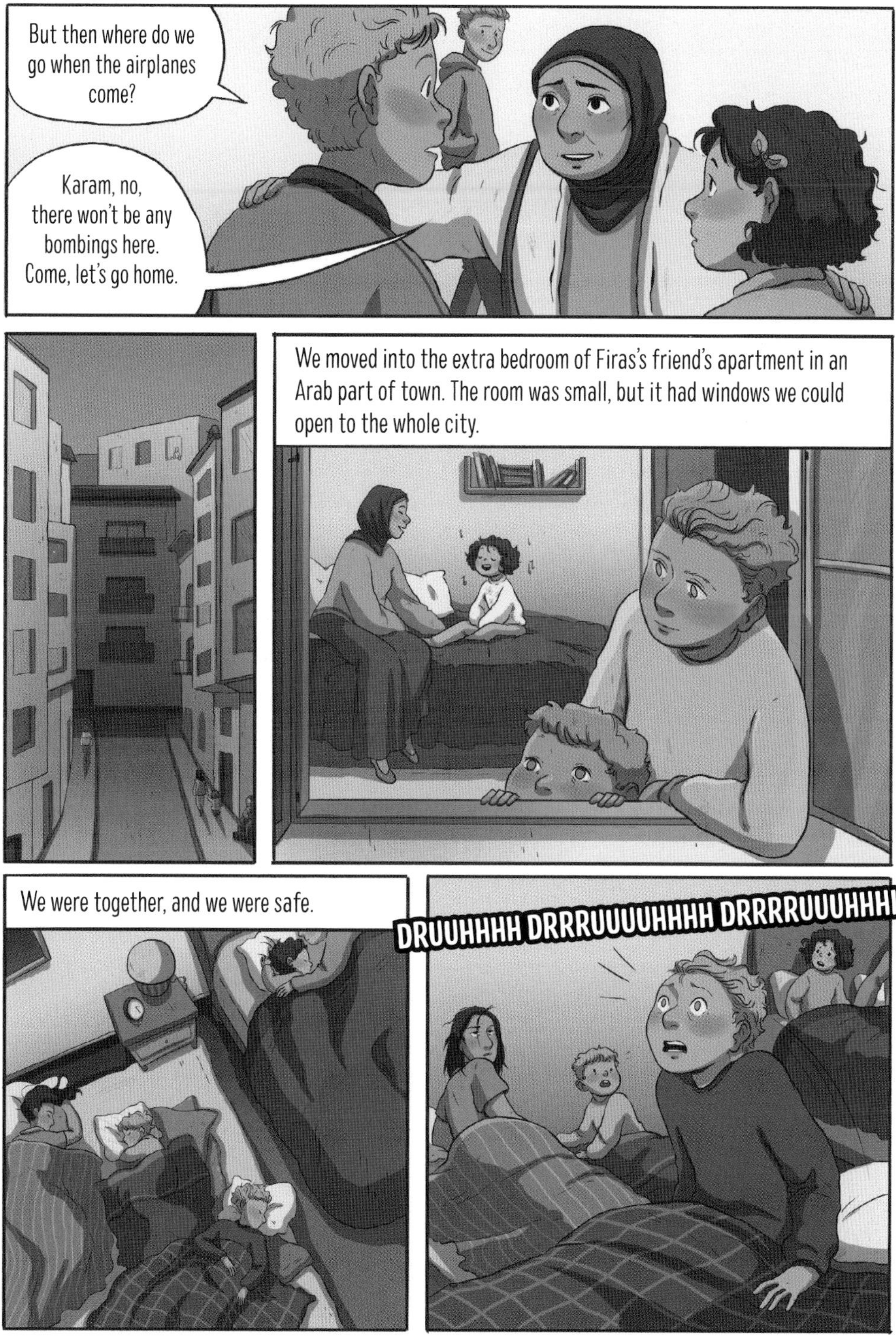

But then where do we go when the airplanes come?
Karam, no, there won't be any bombings here. Come, let's go home.
We moved into the extra bedroom of Firas's friend's apartment in an Arab part of town. The room was small, but it had windows we could open to the whole city.
We were together, and we were safe.
DRUUHHHH DRRRUUUUHHHH DRRRRUUUHHHHH

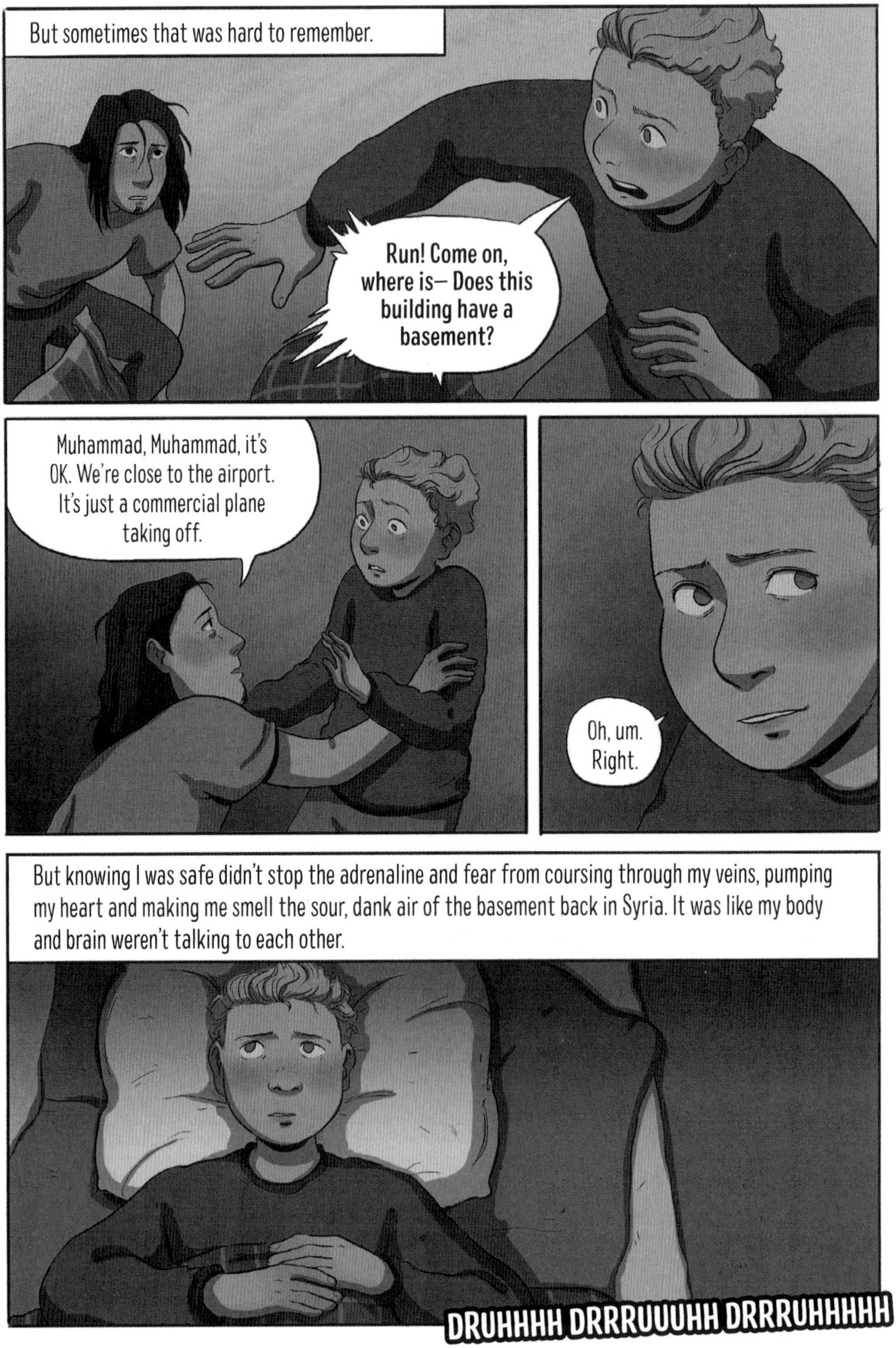
But sometimes that was hard to remember.
Run! Come on, where is— Does this building have a basement?
Muhammad, Muhammad, it's OK. We're close to the airport. It's just a commercial plane taking off.
Oh, um. Right.
But knowing I was safe didn't stop the adrenaline and fear from coursing through my veins, pumping my heart and making me smell the sour, dank air of the basement back in Syria. It was like my body and brain weren't talking to each other.
DRUHHHH DRRRUUUHH DRRRUHHHHH

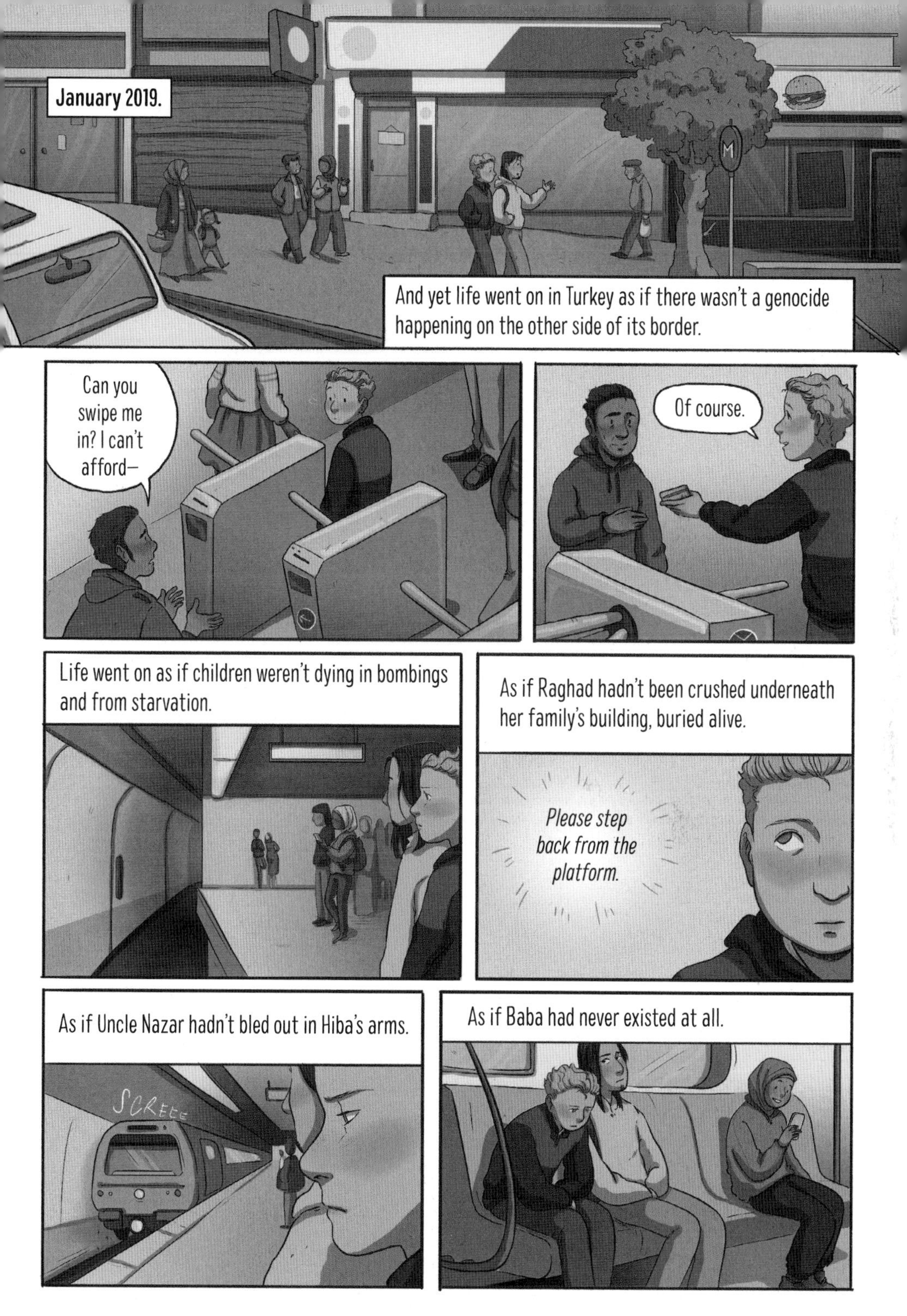
January 2019.
And yet life went on in Turkey as if there wasn't a genocide happening on the other side of its border.
Can you swipe me in? I can't afford—
Of course.
Life went on as if children weren't dying in bombings and from starvation.
As if Raghad hadn't been crushed underneath her family's building, buried alive.
Please step back from the platform.
As if Uncle Nazar hadn't bled out in Hiba's arms.
SCREEE
As if Baba had never existed at all.

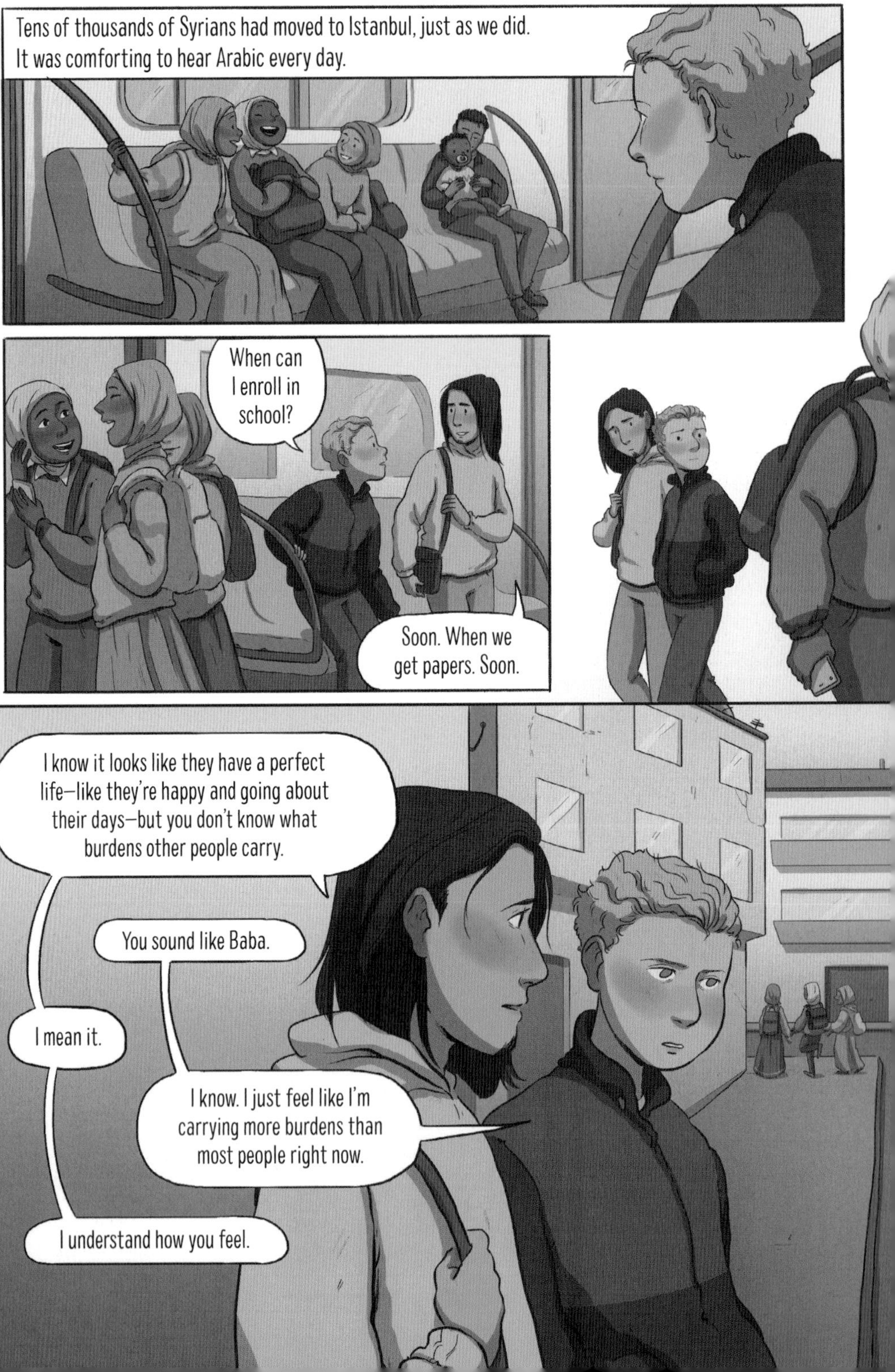
Tens of thousands of Syrians had moved to Istanbul, just as we did.
It was comforting to hear Arabic every day.
When can I enroll in school?
Soon. When we get papers. Soon.
I know it looks like they have a perfect life—like they're happy and going about their days—but you don't know what burdens other people carry.
You sound like Baba.
I mean it.
I know. I just feel like I'm carrying more burdens than most people right now.
I understand how you feel.

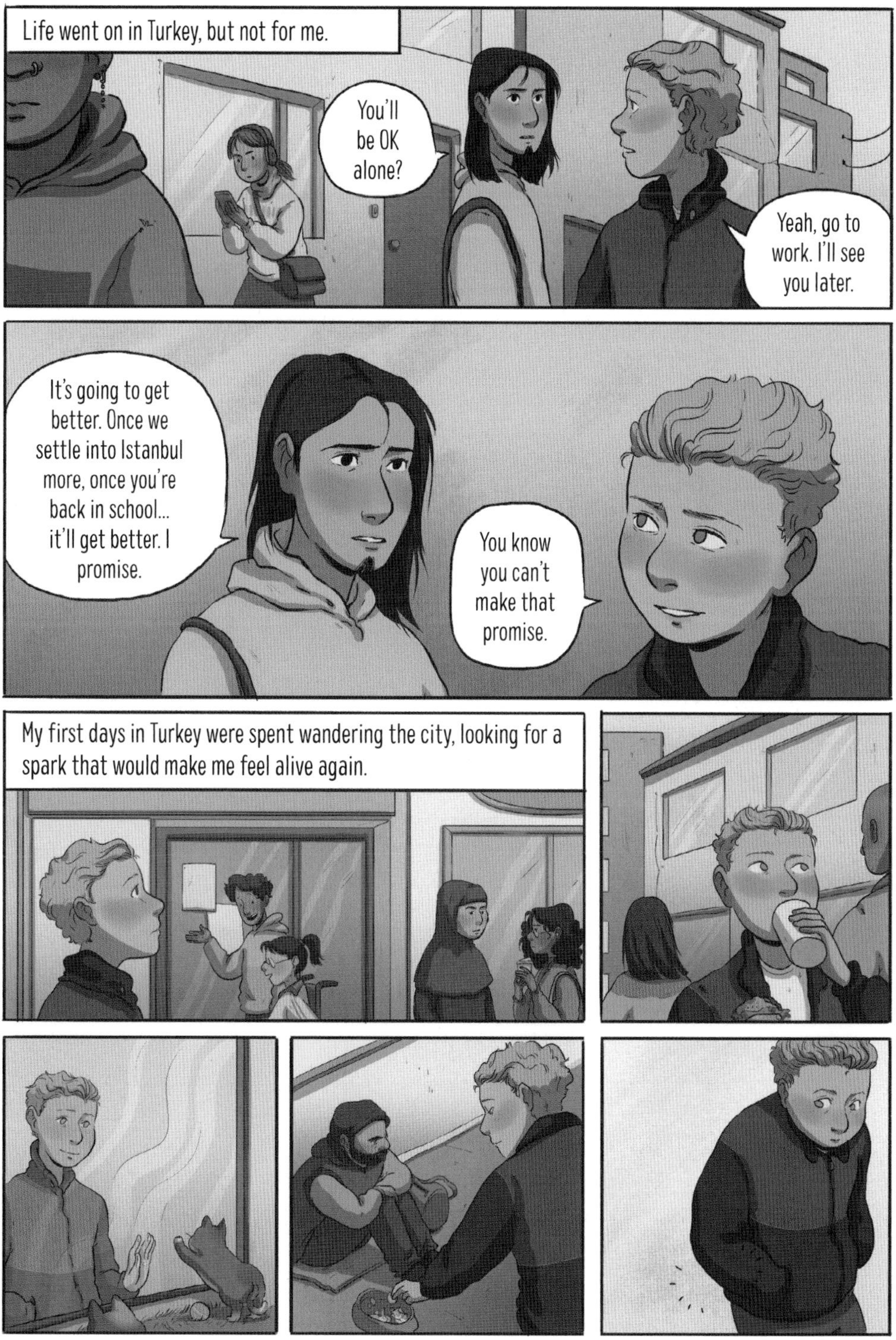
Life went on in Turkey, but not for me.
You'll be OK alone?
Yeah, go to work. I'll see you later.
It's going to get better. Once we settle into Istanbul more, once you're back in school... it'll get better. I promise.
You know you can't make that promise.
My first days in Turkey were spent wandering the city, looking for a spark that would make me feel alive again.

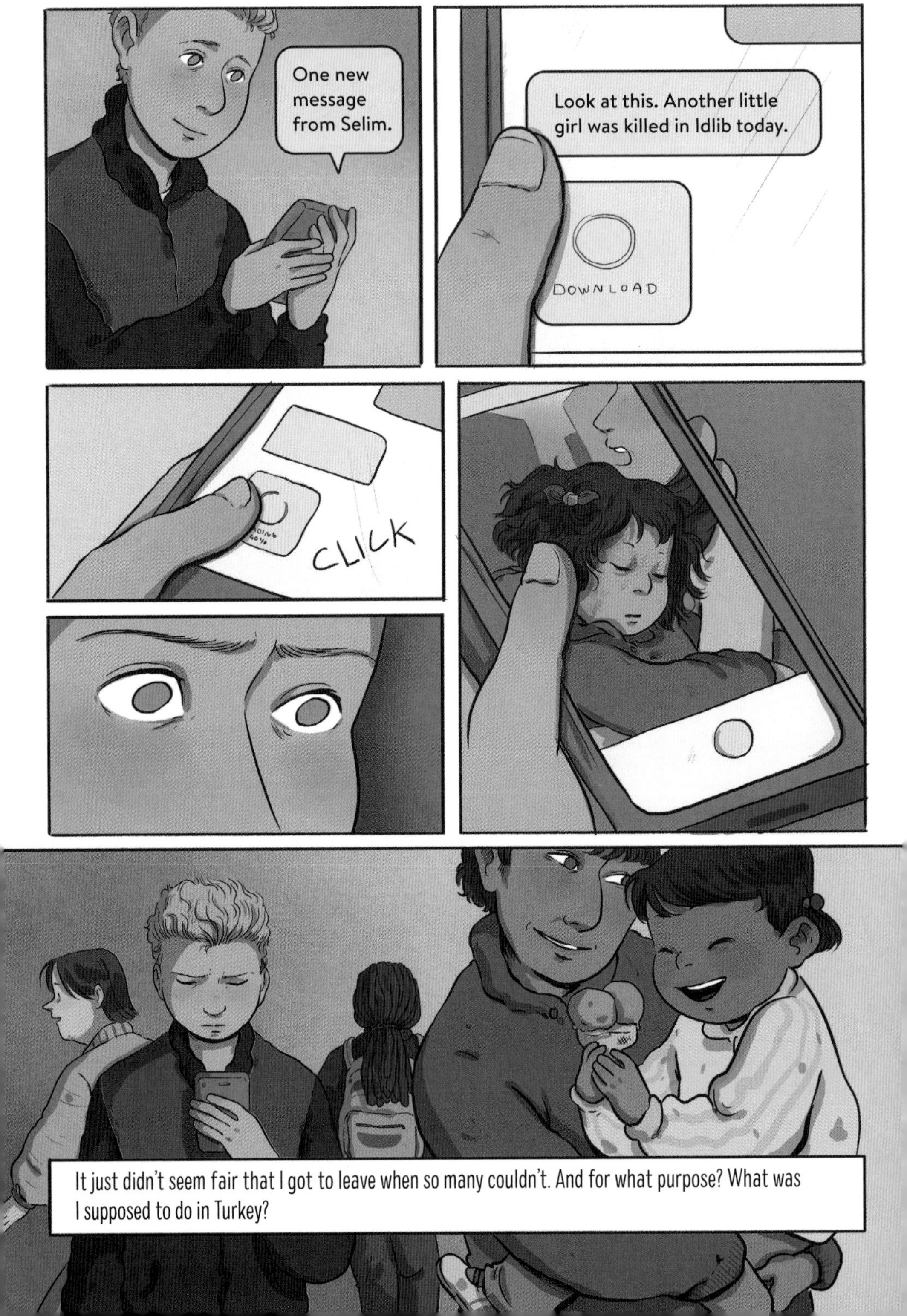
One new message from Selim.
Look at this. Another little girl was killed in Idlib today.
DOWNLOAD
CLICK
It just didn't seem fair that I got to leave when so many couldn't. And for what purpose? What was I supposed to do in Turkey?

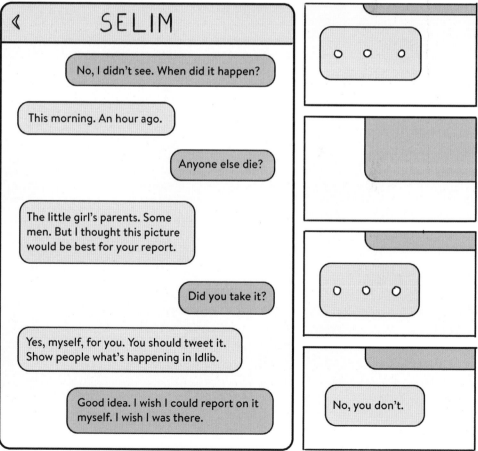

No, I didn't see. When did it happen?

This morning. An hour ago.

Anyone else die?

The little girl's parents. Some men. But I thought this picture would be best for your report.

Did you take it?

Yes, myself, for you. You should tweet it. Show people what's happening in Idlib.

Good idea. I wish I could report on it myself. I wish I was there.

No, you don't.

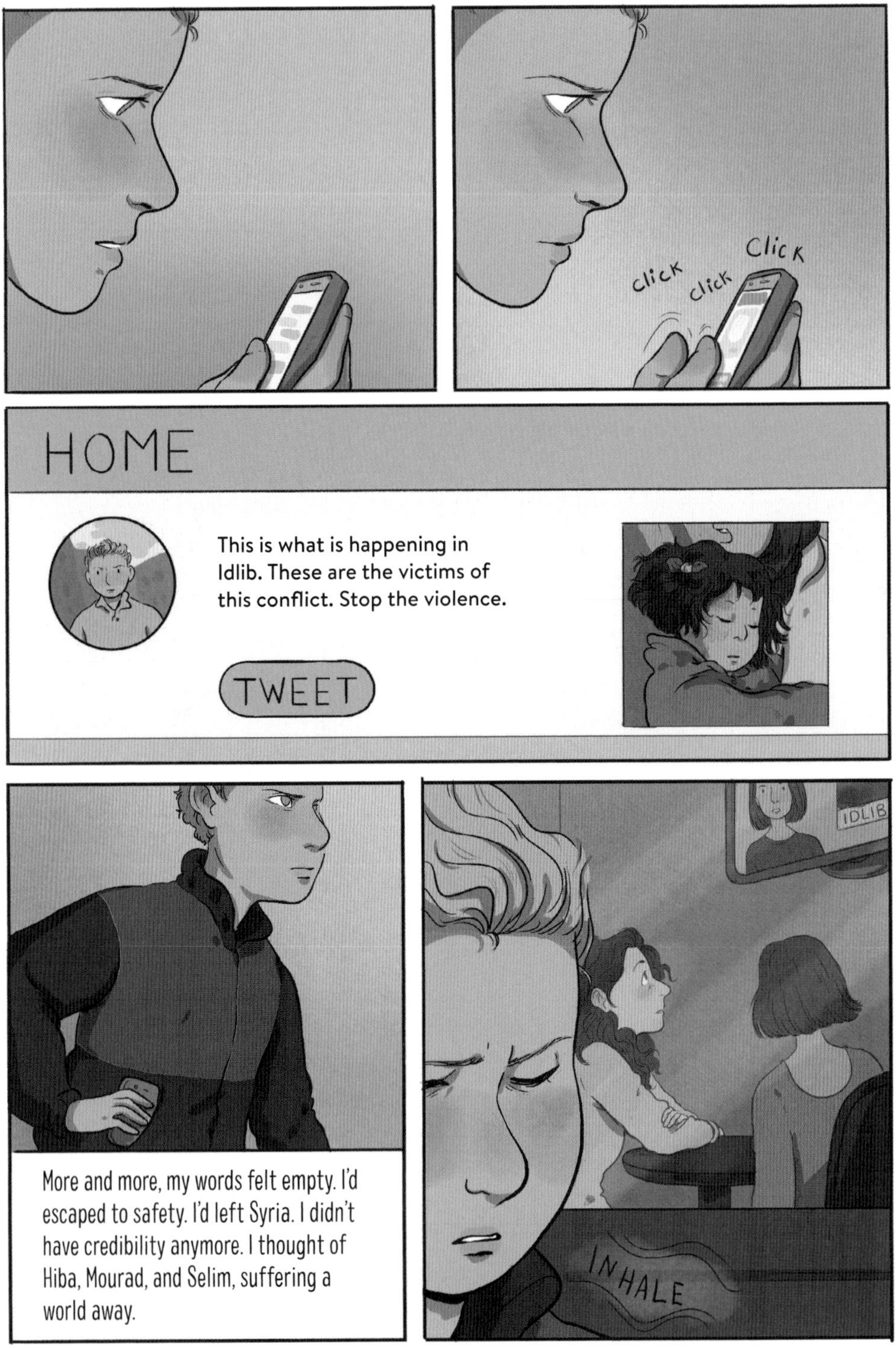
click
click
Click
HOME
This is what is happening in Idlib. These are the victims of this conflict. Stop the violence.
TWEET
More and more, my words felt empty. I'd escaped to safety. I'd left Syria. I didn't have credibility anymore. I thought of Hiba, Mourad, and Selim, suffering a world away.
IDLIB
INHALE

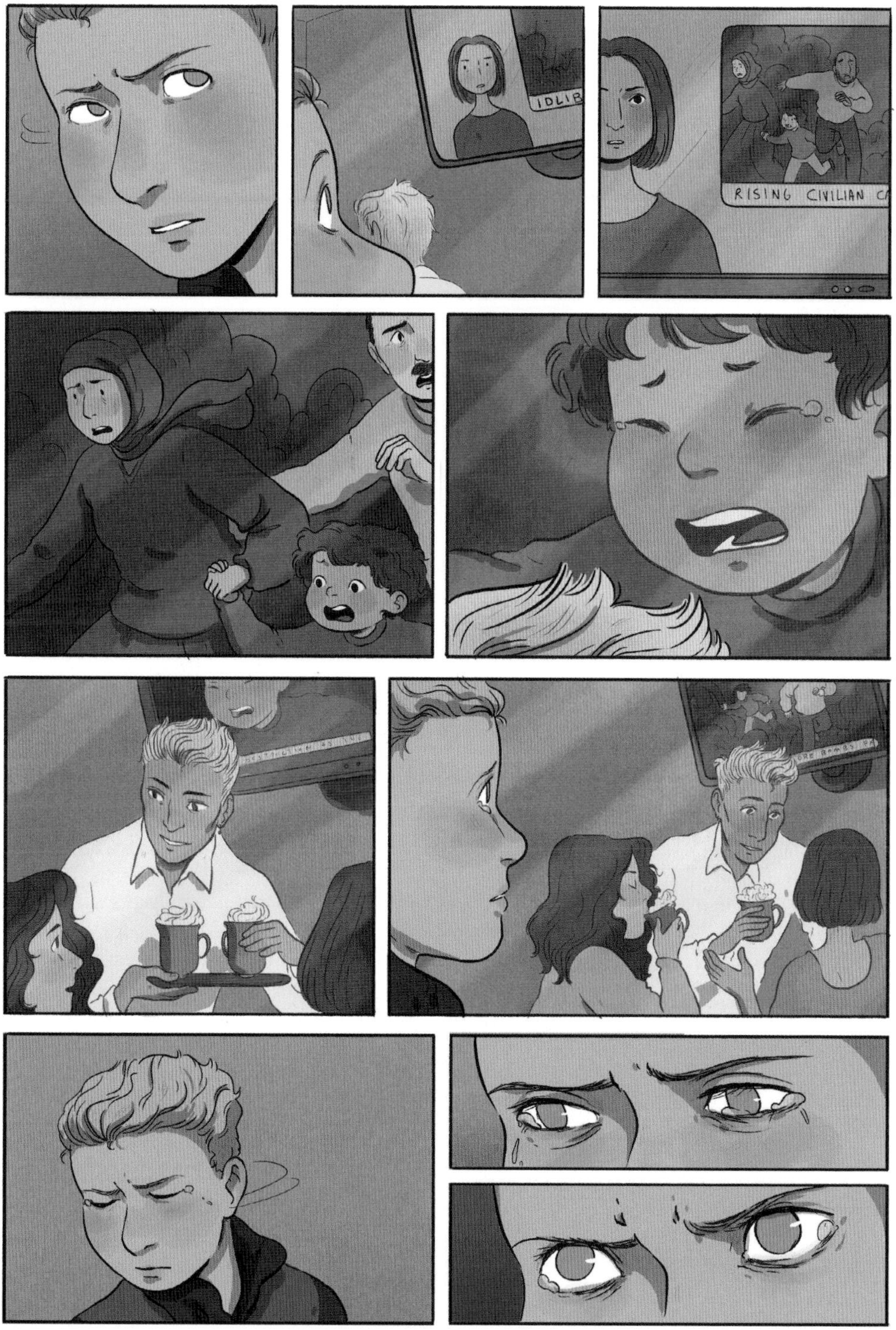
IDLIB
RISING CIVILIAN

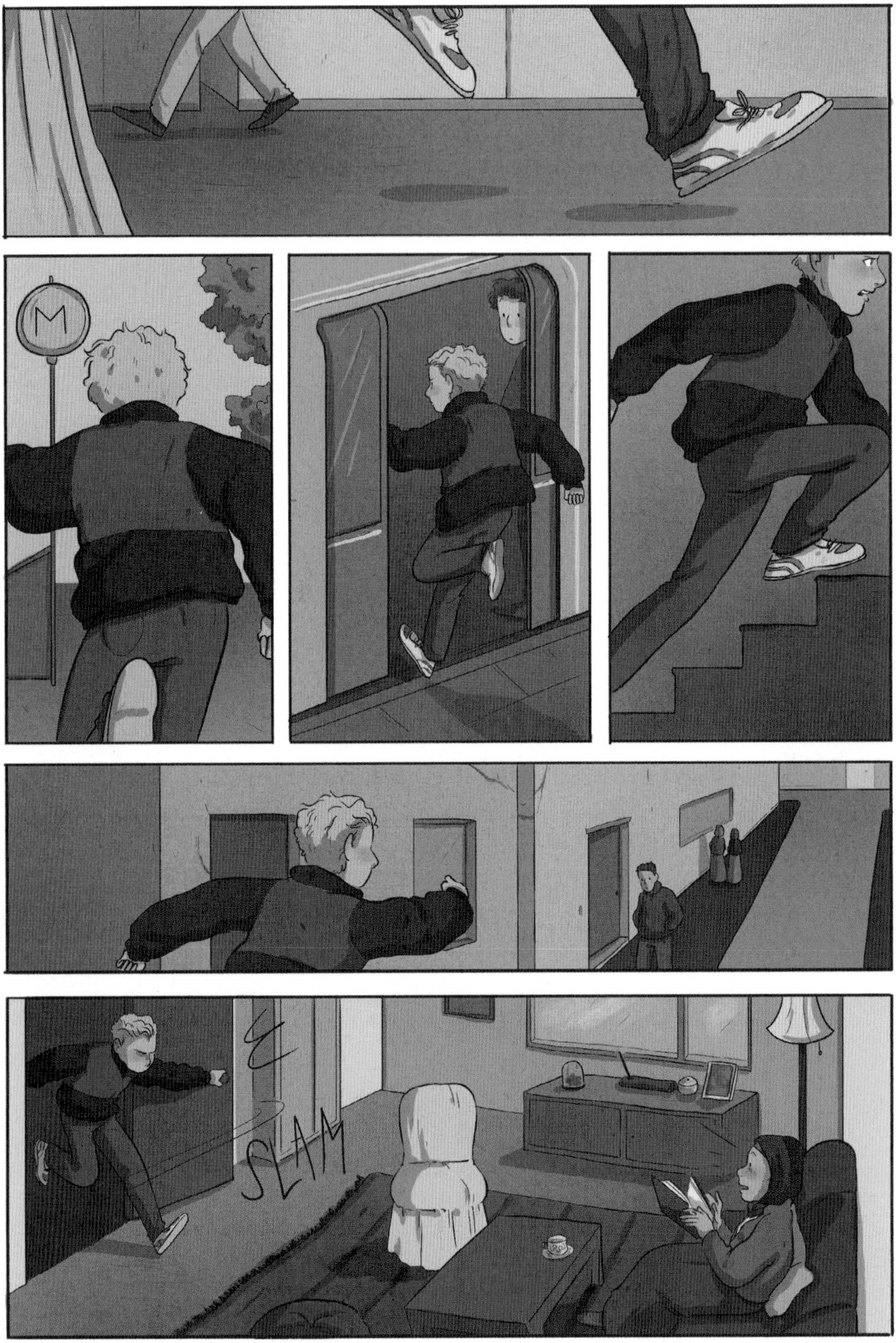
M
SLAM

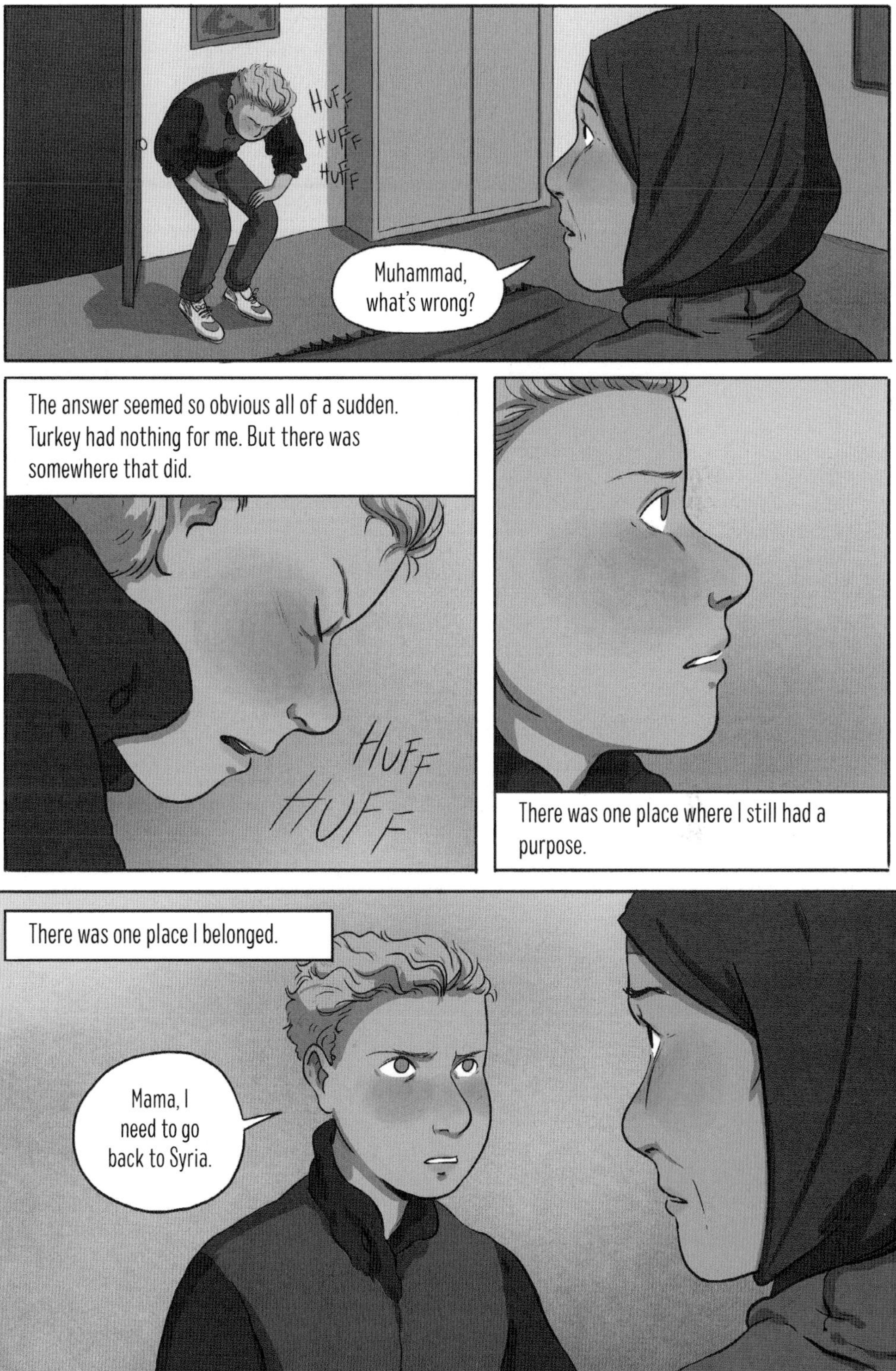
HUFF
HUFF
HUFF
Muhammad, what's wrong?
The answer seemed so obvious all of a sudden. Turkey had nothing for me. But there was somewhere that did.
HUFF
HUFF
There was one place where I still had a purpose.
There was one place I belonged.
Mama, I need to go back to Syria.

CHAPTER 24

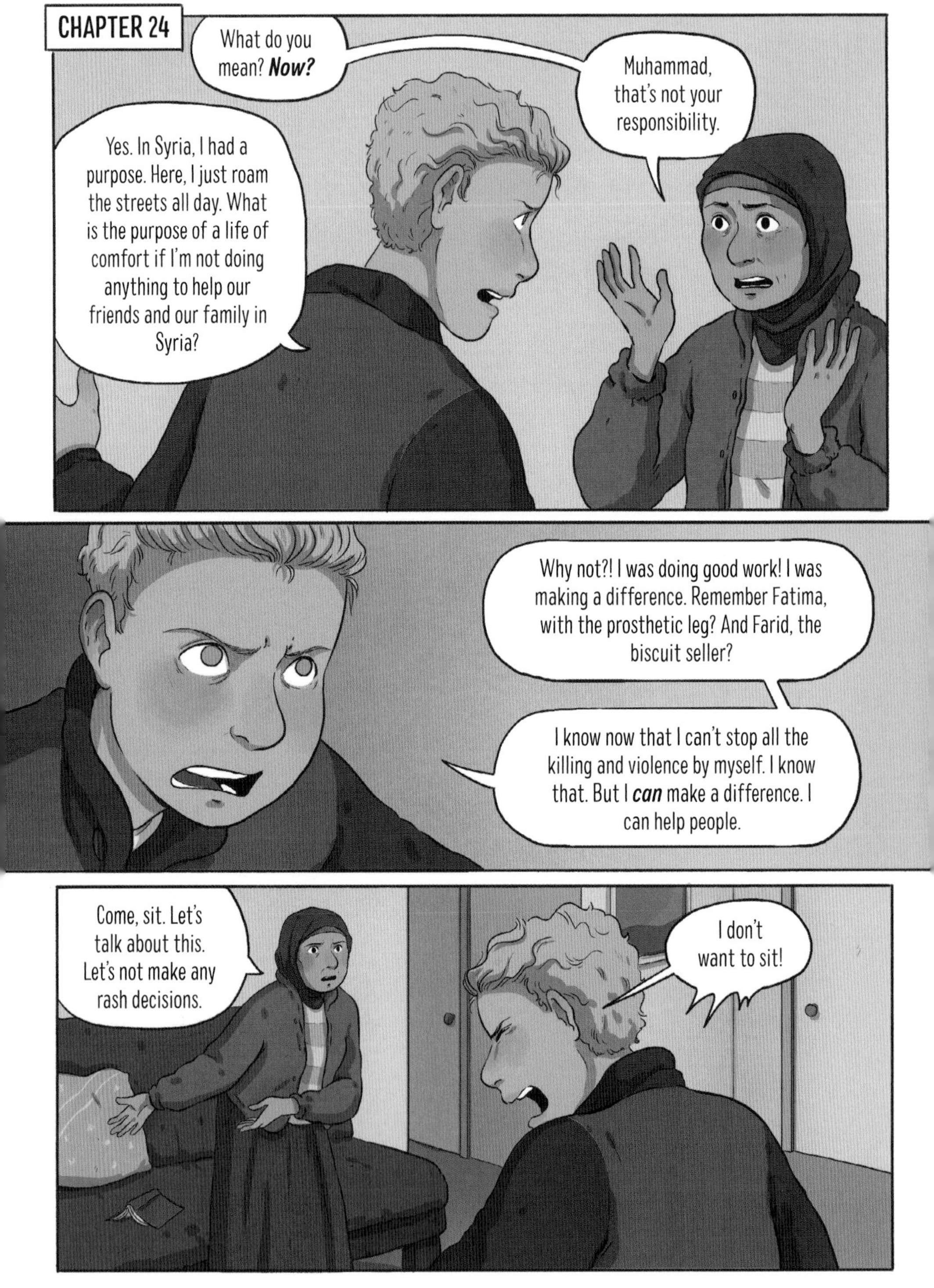
What do you mean? ***Now?***
Muhammad, that's not your responsibility.
Yes. In Syria, I had a purpose. Here, I just roam the streets all day. What is the purpose of a life of comfort if I'm not doing anything to help our friends and our family in Syria?
Why not?! I was doing good work! I was making a difference. Remember Fatima, with the prosthetic leg? And Farid, the biscuit seller?
I know now that I can't stop all the killing and violence by myself. I know that. But I ***can*** make a difference. I can help people.
Come, sit. Let's talk about this. Let's not make any rash decisions.
I don't want to sit!

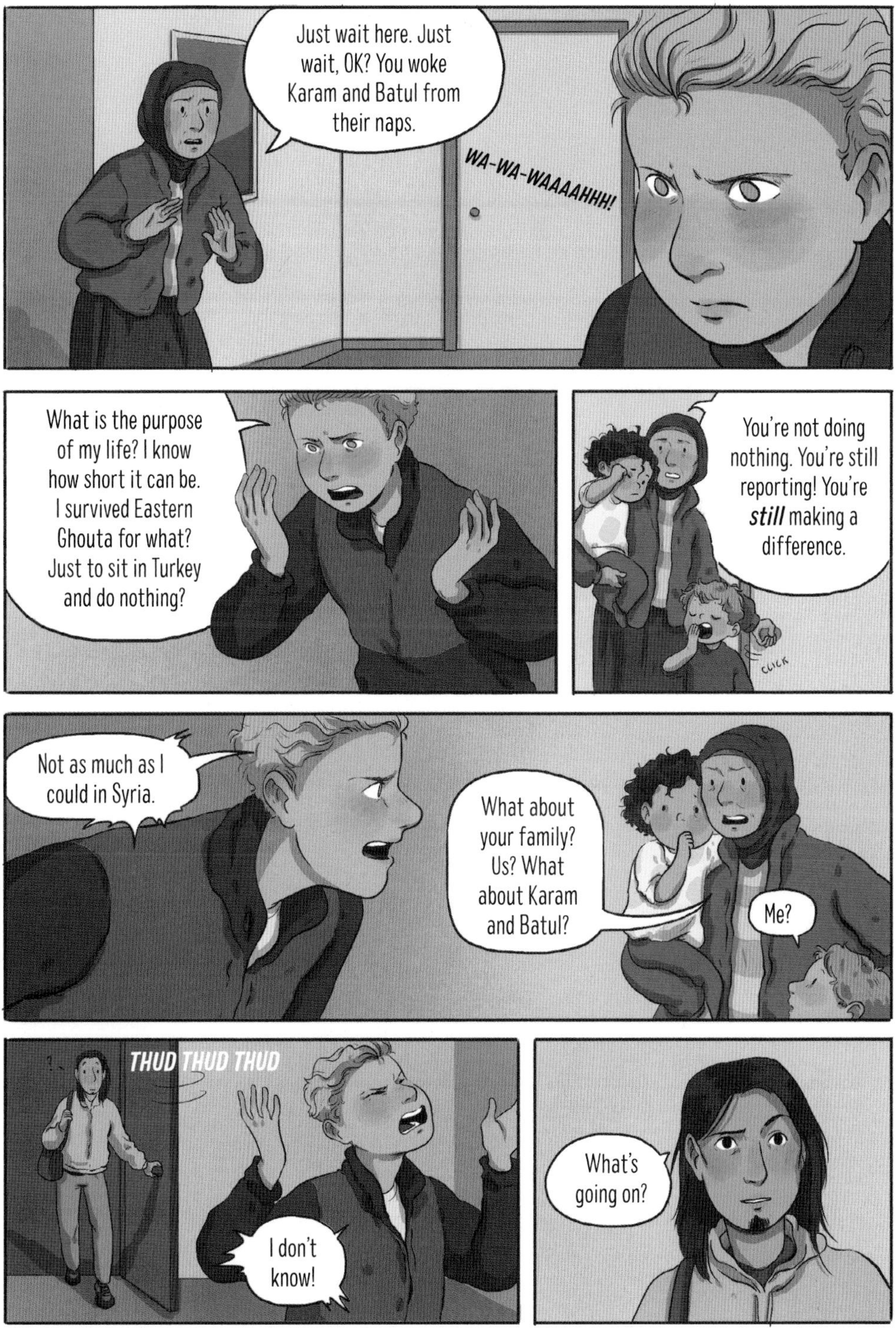
Just wait here. Just wait, OK? You woke Karam and Batul from their naps.
WA-WA-WAAAAHHH!
What is the purpose of my life? I know how short it can be. I survived Eastern Ghouta for what? Just to sit in Turkey and do nothing?
You're not doing nothing. You're still reporting! You're *still* making a difference.
CLICK
Not as much as I could in Syria.
What about your family? Us? What about Karam and Batul?
Me?
THUD THUD THUD
I don't know!
What's going on?

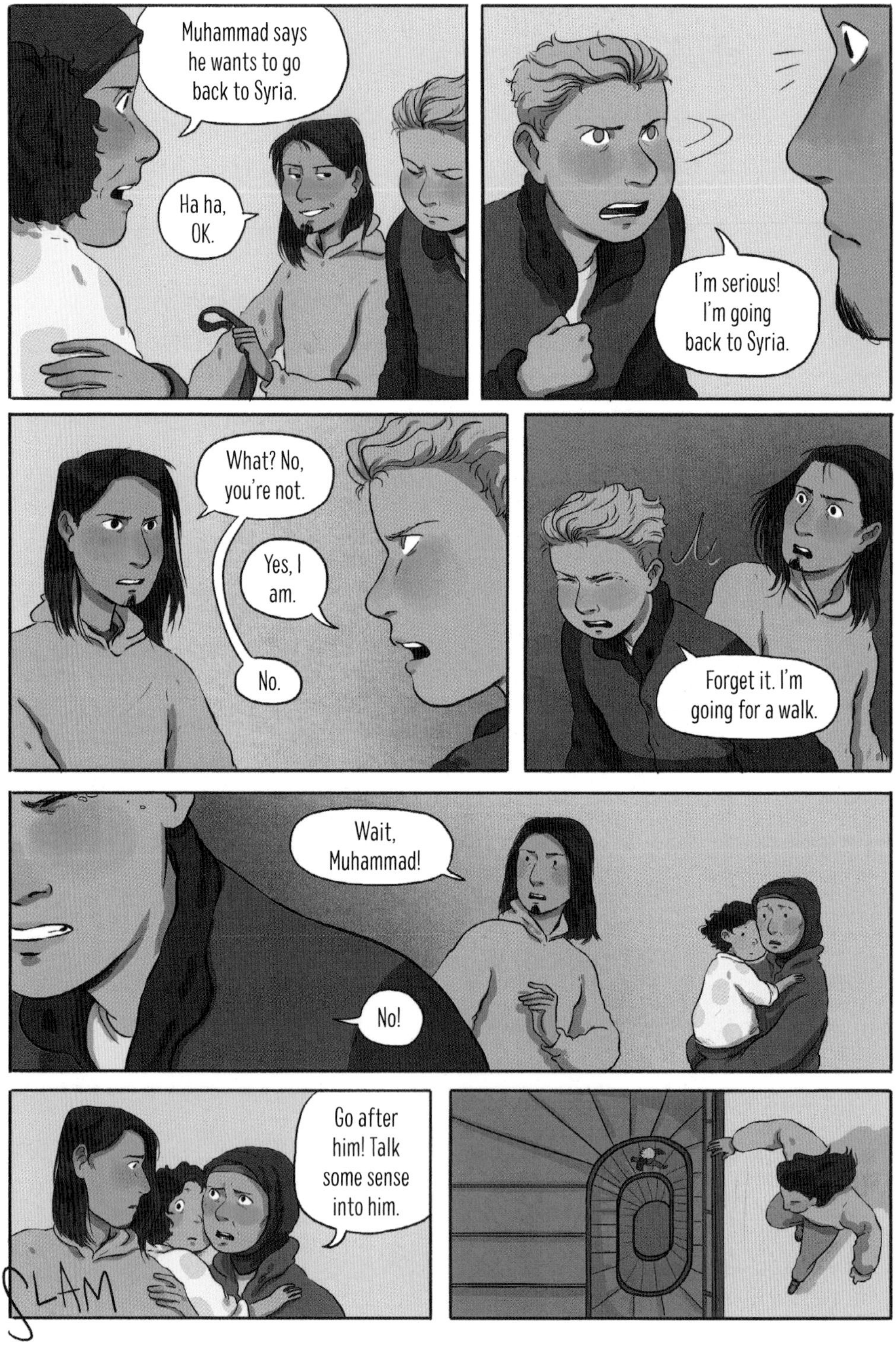
Muhammad says he wants to go back to Syria.
Ha ha, OK.
I'm serious! I'm going back to Syria.
What? No, you're not.
Yes, I am.
No.
Forget it. I'm going for a walk.
Wait, Muhammad!
No!
Go after him! Talk some sense into him.
SLAM

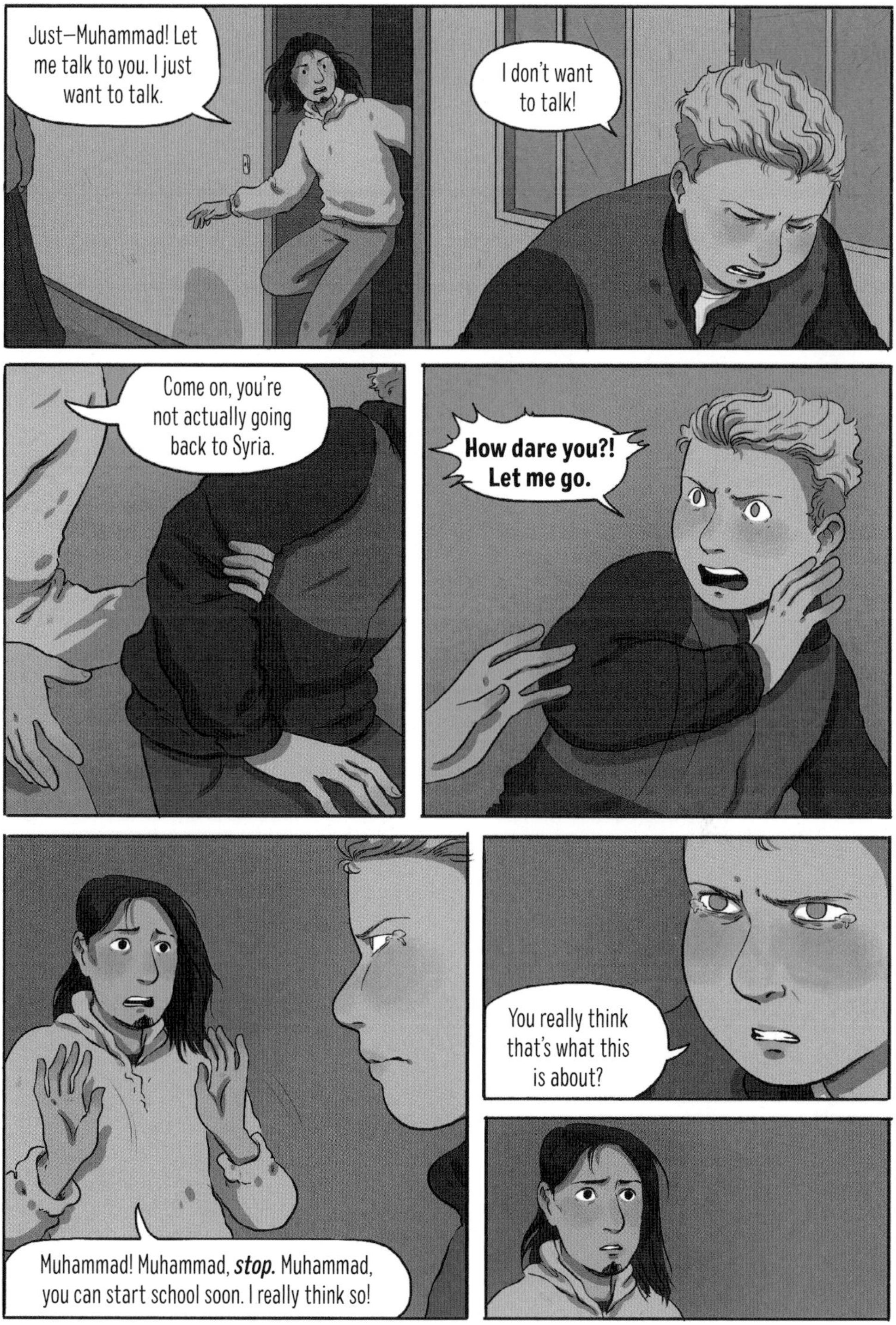
Just—Muhammad! Let me talk to you. I just want to talk.
I don't want to talk!
Come on, you're not actually going back to Syria.
How dare you?! Let me go.
Muhammad! Muhammad, stop. Muhammad, you can start school soon. I really think so!
You really think that's what this is about?

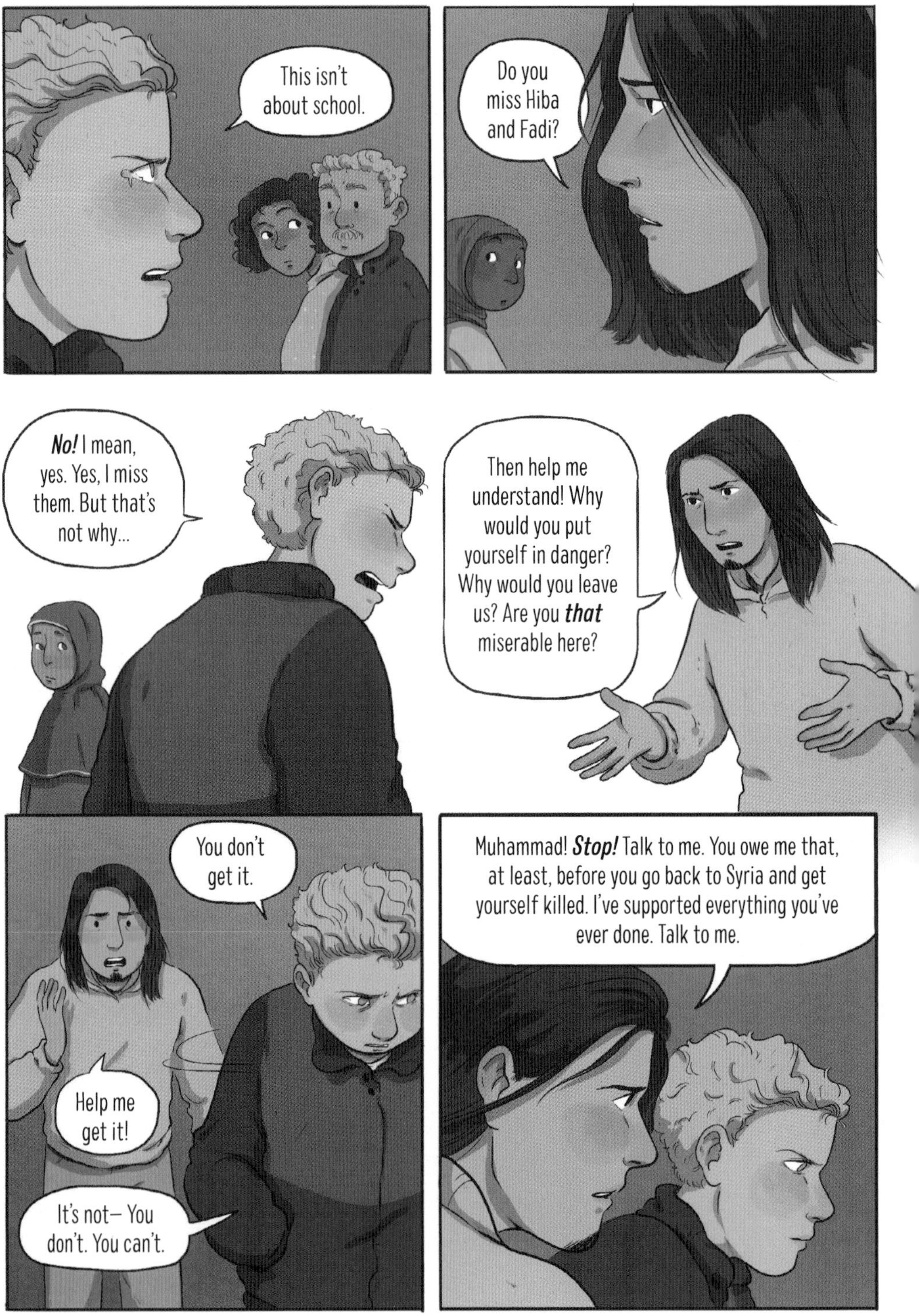
This isn't about school.
Do you miss Hiba and Fadi?
No! I mean, yes. Yes, I miss them. But that's not why...
Then help me understand! Why would you put yourself in danger? Why would you leave us? Are you ***that*** miserable here?
You don't get it.
Help me get it!
It's not— You don't. You can't.
Muhammad! ***Stop!*** Talk to me. You owe me that, at least, before you go back to Syria and get yourself killed. I've supported everything you've ever done. Talk to me.

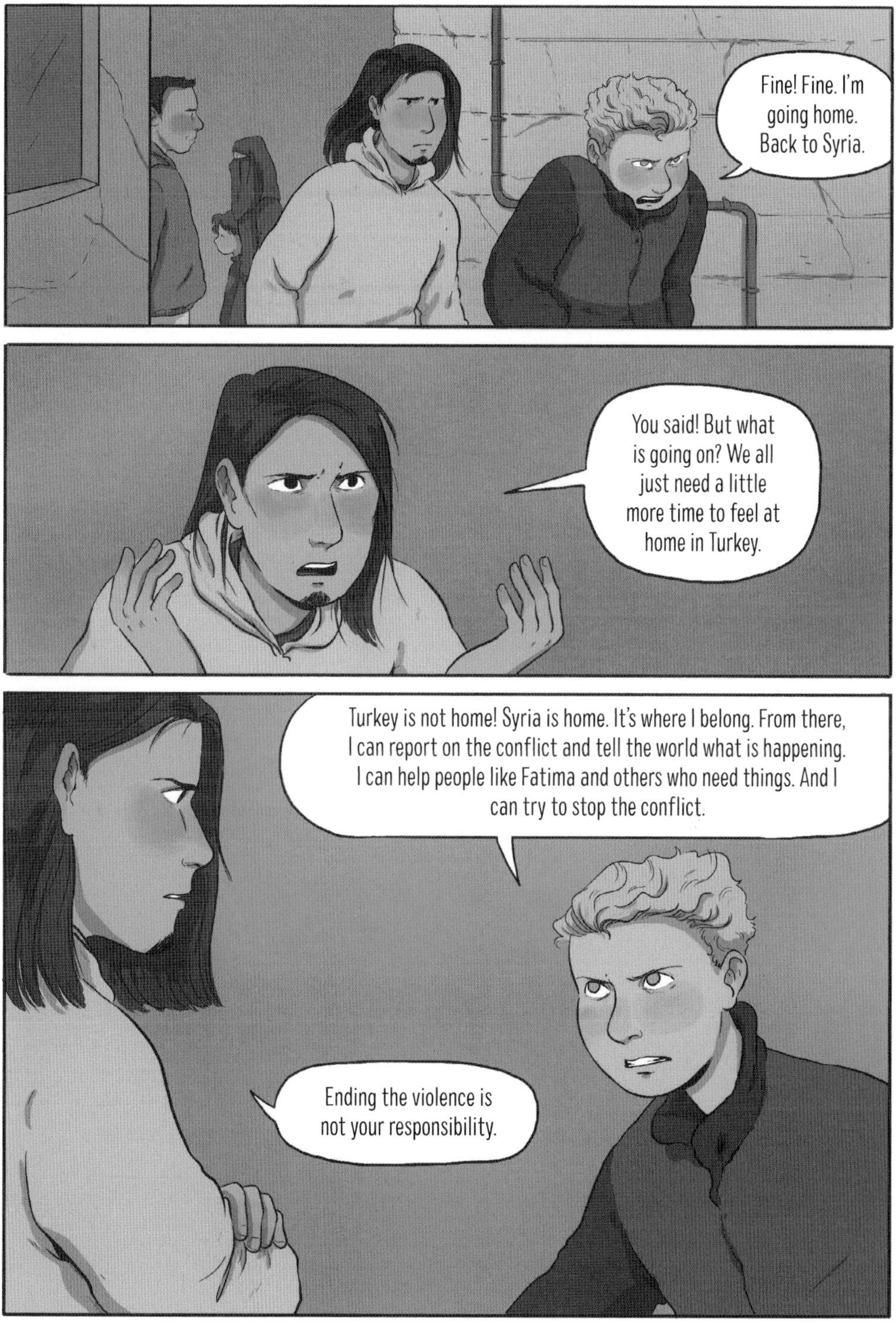
Fine! Fine. I'm going home. Back to Syria.
You said! But what is going on? We all just need a little more time to feel at home in Turkey.
Turkey is not home! Syria is home. It's where I belong. From there, I can report on the conflict and tell the world what is happening. I can help people like Fatima and others who need things. And I can try to stop the conflict.
Ending the violence is not your responsibility.

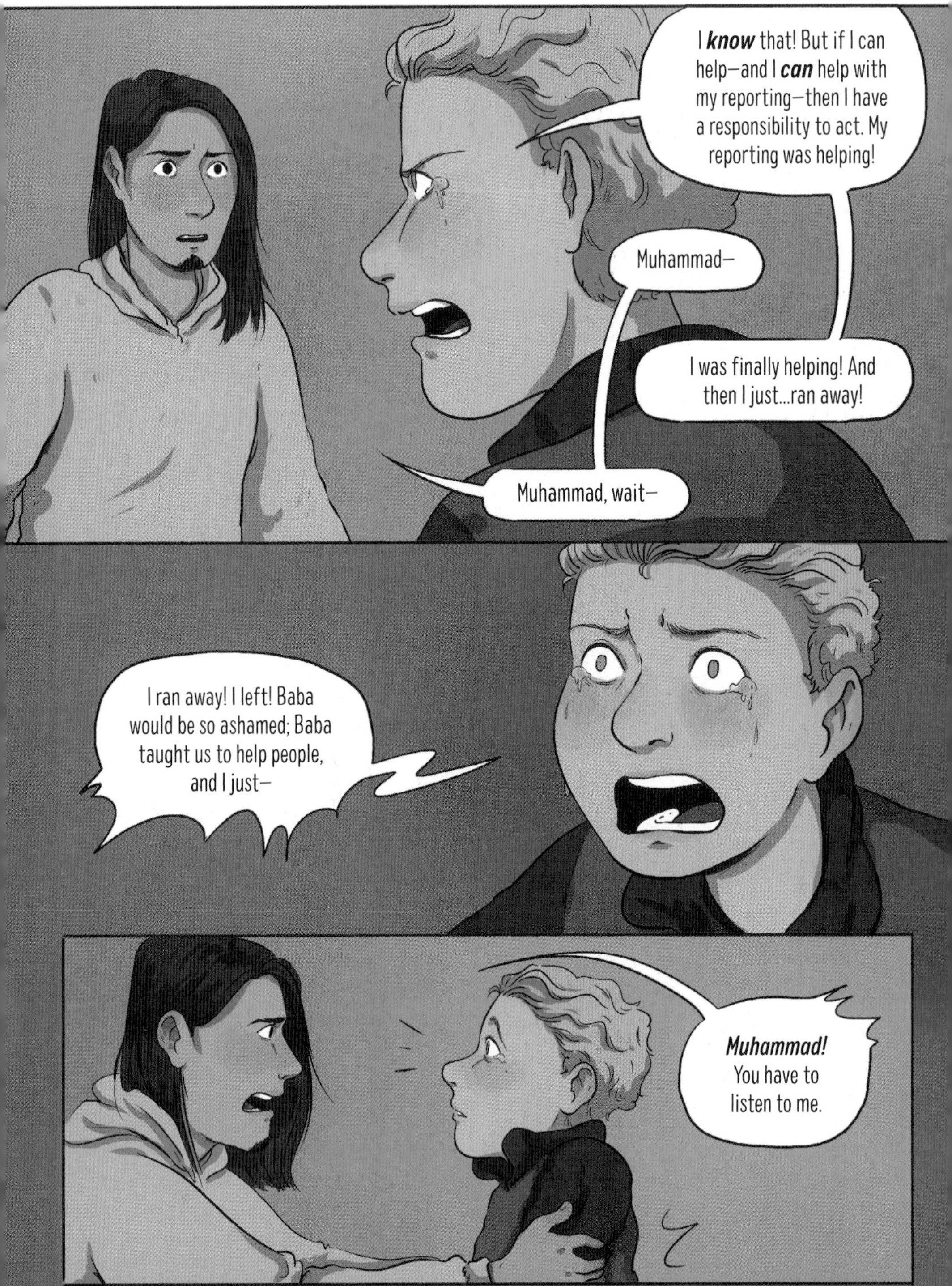
I **know** that! But if I can help—and I **can** help with my reporting—then I have a responsibility to act. My reporting was helping!
Muhammad—
I was finally helping! And then I just...ran away!
Muhammad, wait—
I ran away! I left! Baba would be so ashamed; Baba taught us to help people, and I just—
Muhammad! You have to listen to me.

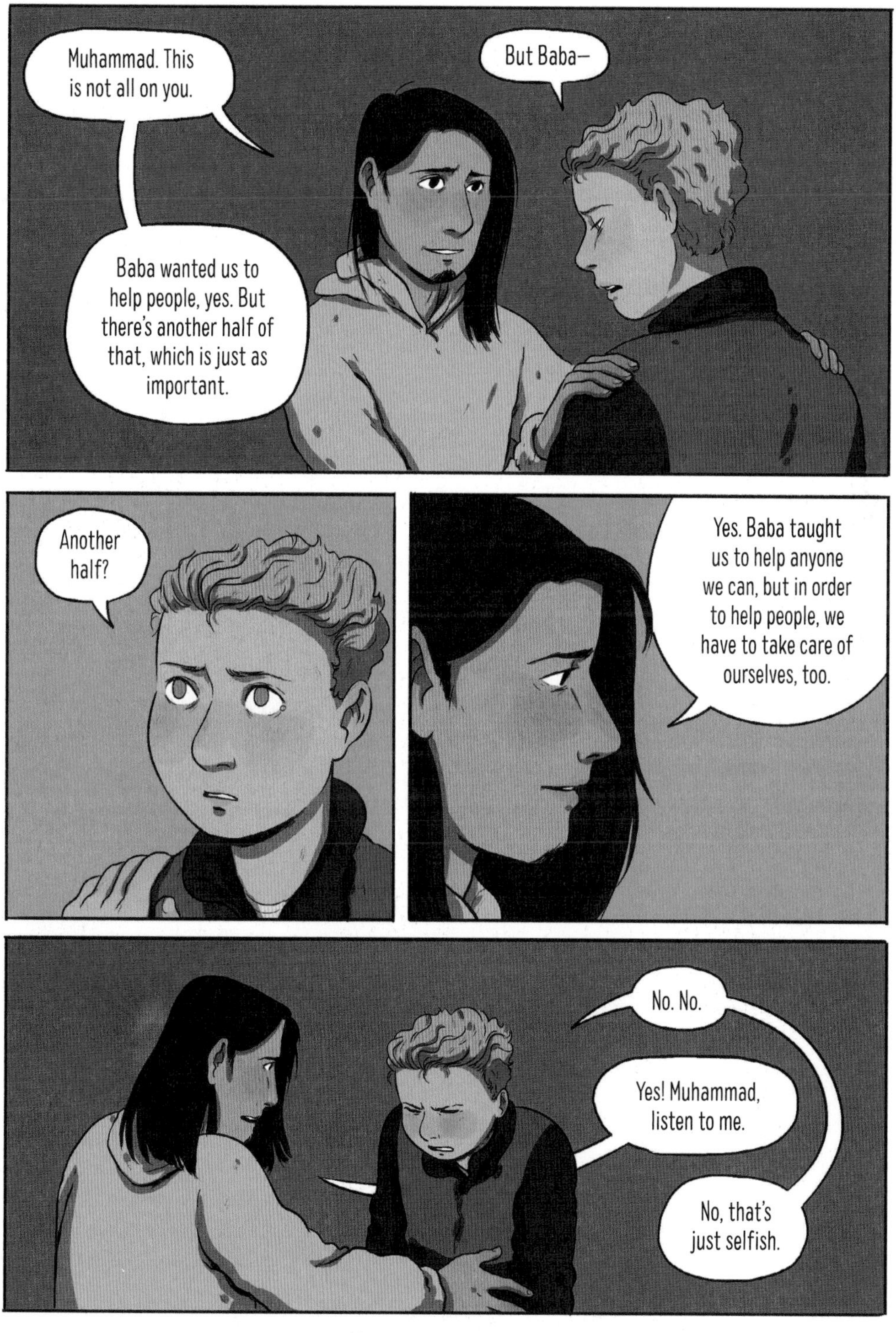

Muhammad. This is not all on you.
Baba wanted us to help people, yes. But there's another half of that, which is just as important.
But Baba—
Another half?
Yes. Baba taught us to help anyone we can, but in order to help people, we have to take care of ourselves, too.
No. No.
Yes! Muhammad, listen to me.
No, that's just selfish.

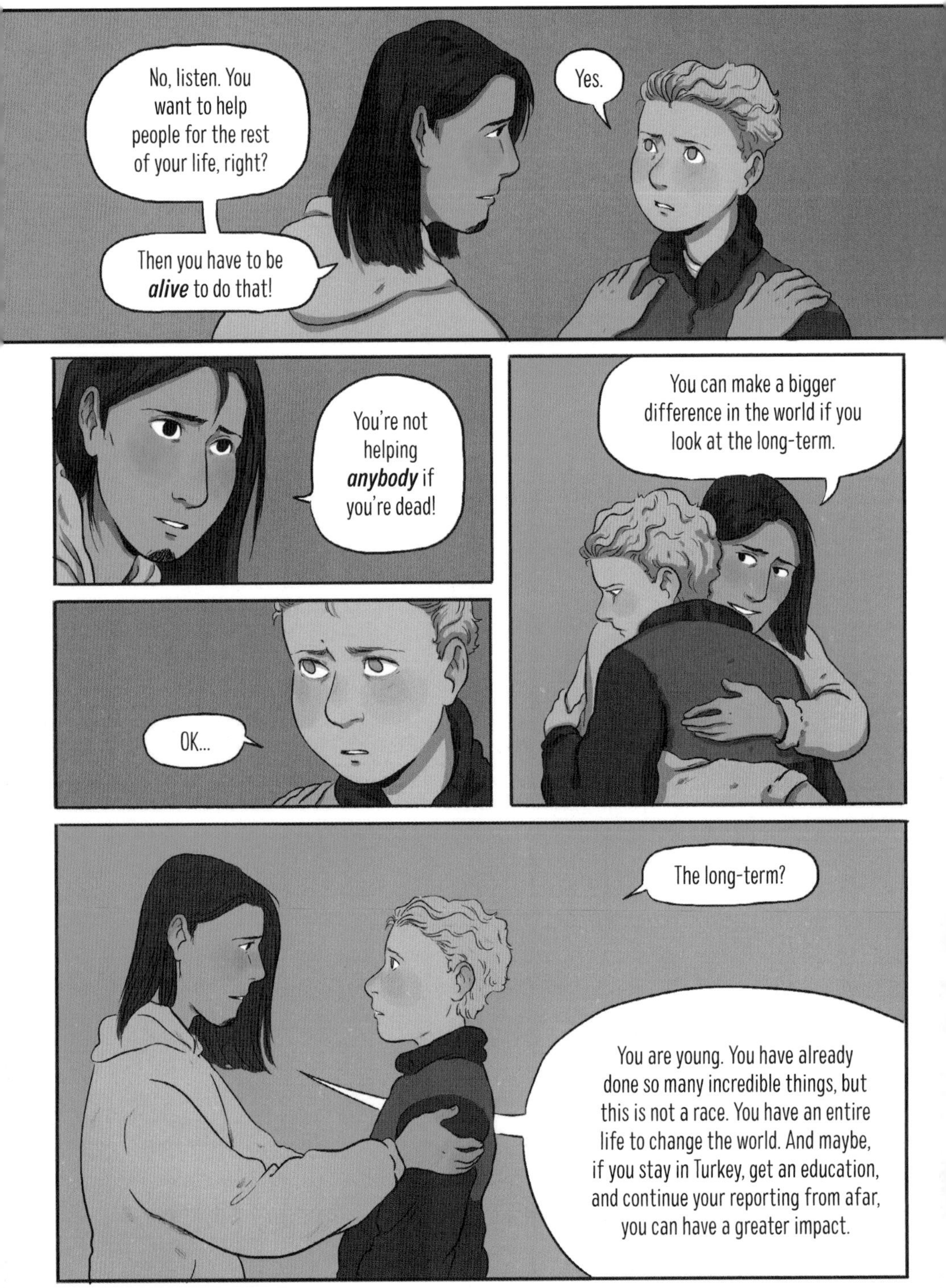
No, listen. You want to help people for the rest of your life, right?
Yes.
Then you have to be ***alive*** to do that!
You're not helping ***anybody*** if you're dead!
OK...
You can make a bigger difference in the world if you look at the long-term.
The long-term?
You are young. You have already done so many incredible things, but this is not a race. You have an entire life to change the world. And maybe, if you stay in Turkey, get an education, and continue your reporting from afar, you can have a greater impact.

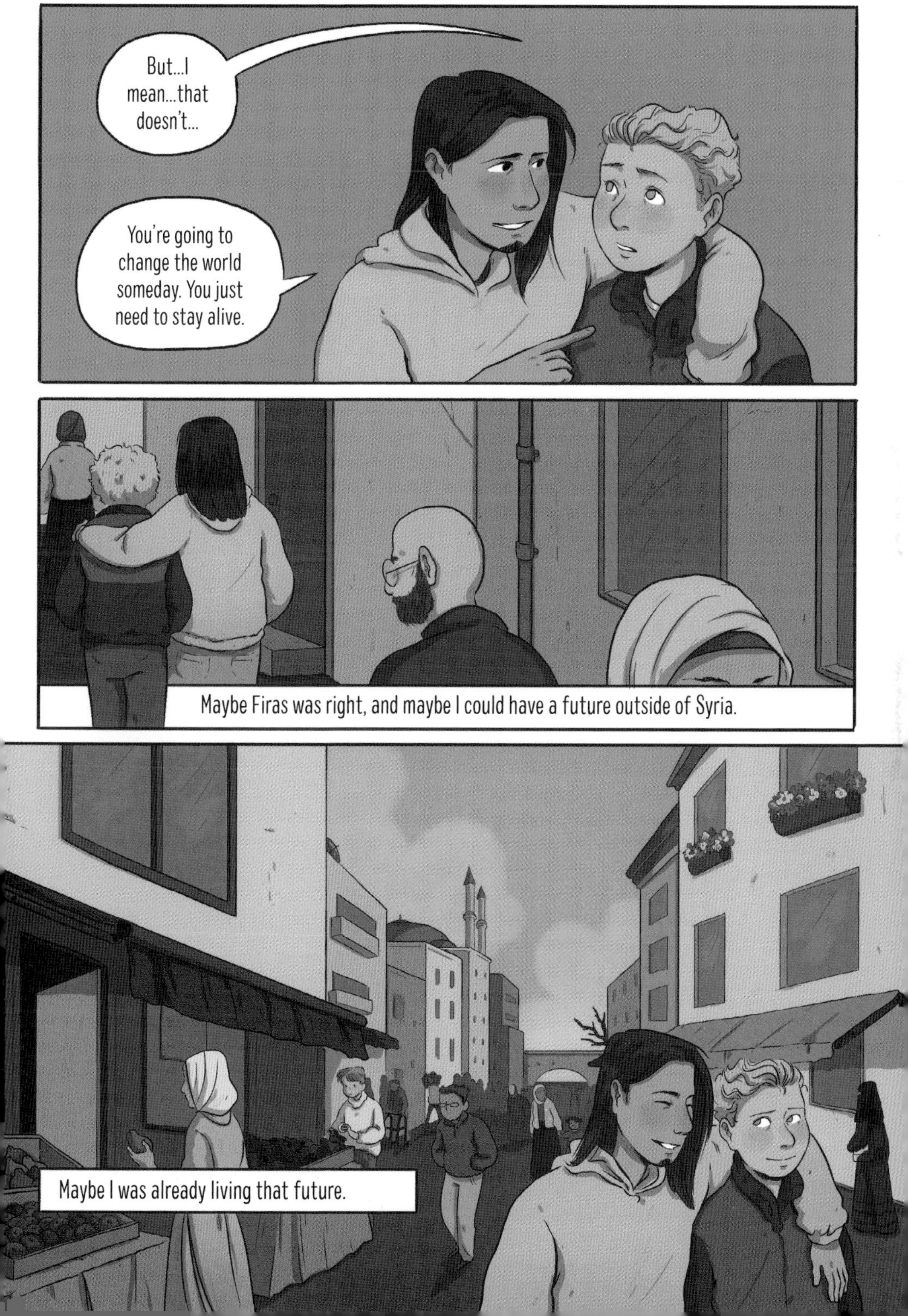
But...I mean...that doesn't...
You're going to change the world someday. You just need to stay alive.
Maybe Firas was right, and maybe I could have a future outside of Syria.
Maybe I was already living that future.

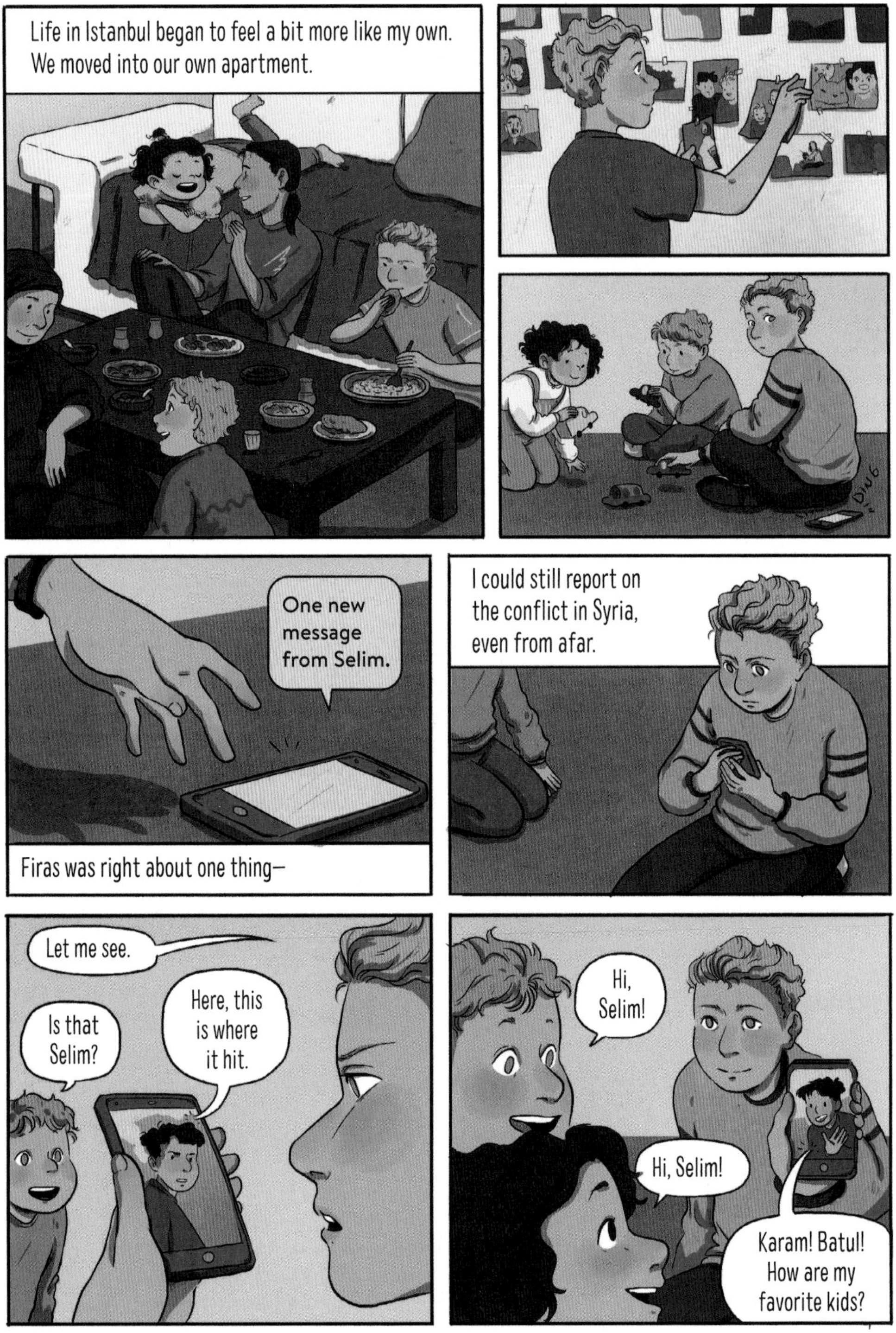

Life in Istanbul began to feel a bit more like my own. We moved into our own apartment.
DING
One new message from Selim.
Firas was right about one thing—
I could still report on the conflict in Syria, even from afar.
Let me see.
Is that Selim?
Here, this is where it hit.
Hi, Selim!
Hi, Selim!
Karam! Batul! How are my favorite kids?

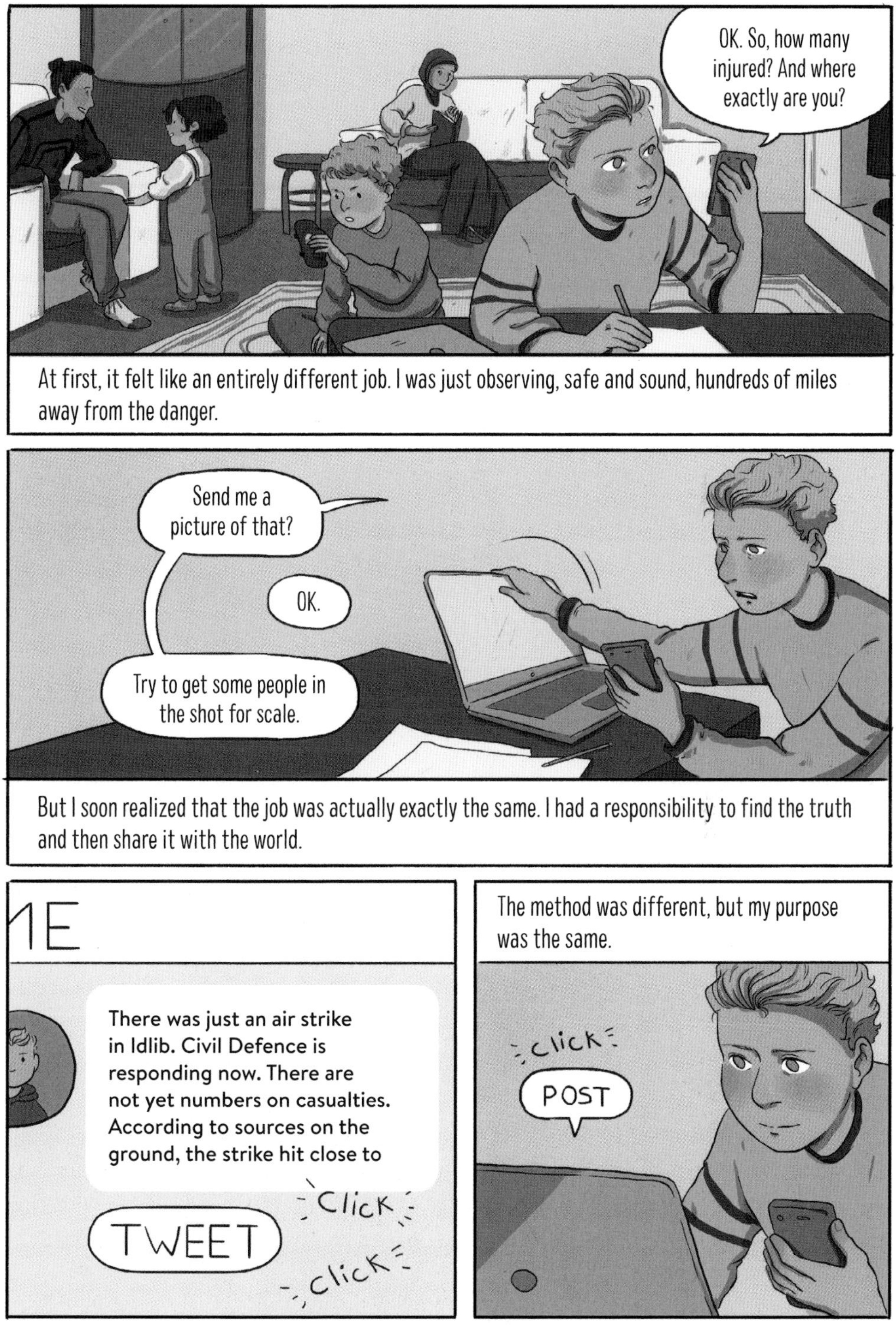
OK. So, how many injured? And where exactly are you?
At first, it felt like an entirely different job. I was just observing, safe and sound, hundreds of miles away from the danger.
Send me a picture of that?
OK.
Try to get some people in the shot for scale.
But I soon realized that the job was actually exactly the same. I had a responsibility to find the truth and then share it with the world.
There was just an air strike in Idlib. Civil Defence is responding now. There are not yet numbers on casualties. According to sources on the ground, the strike hit close to
TWEET
Click
click
The method was different, but my purpose was the same.
click
POST

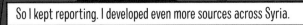

So I kept reporting. I developed even more sources across Syria.

Sorry, but...are you Muhammad Najem?

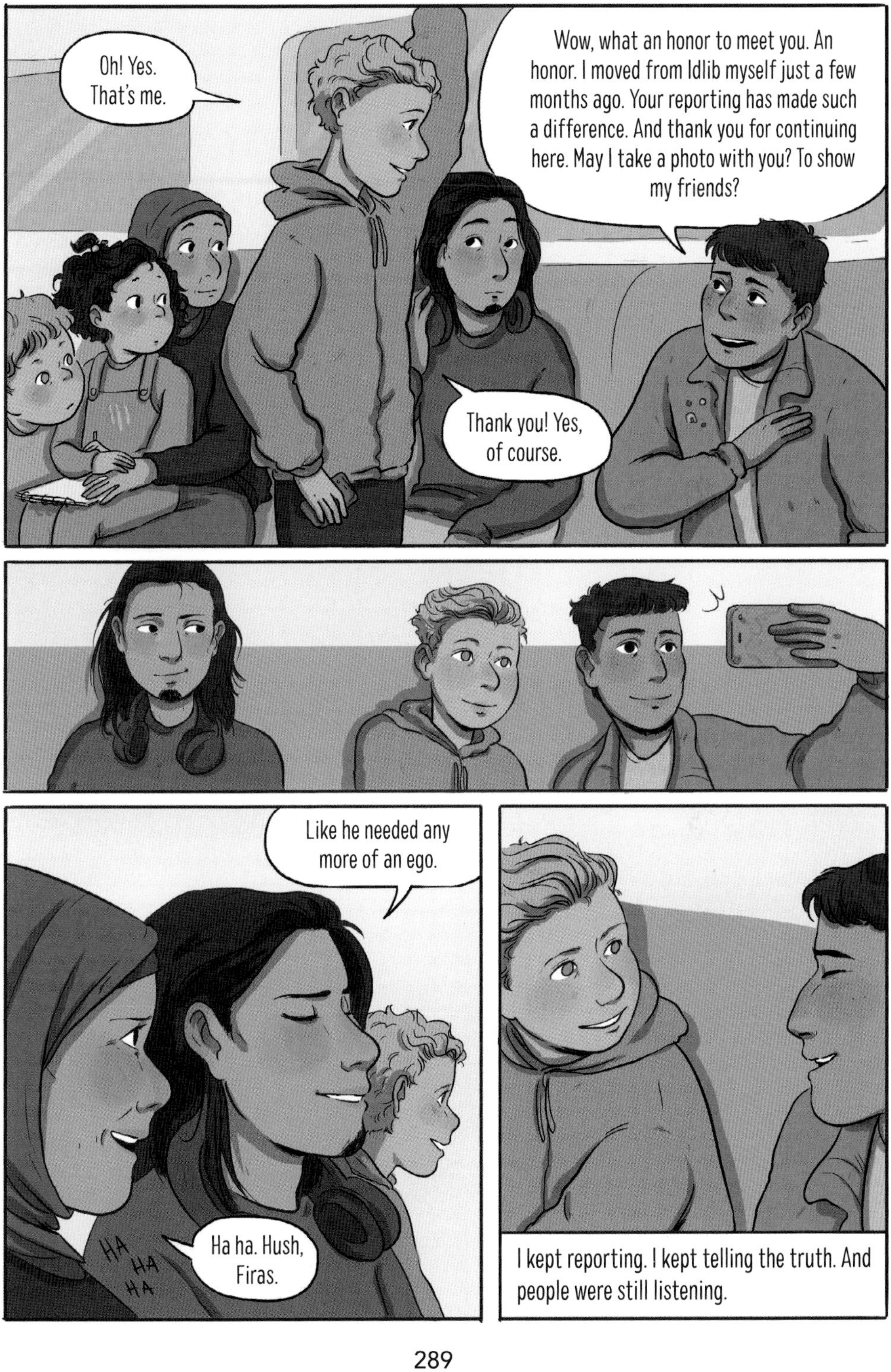
Oh! Yes. That's me.
Wow, what an honor to meet you. An honor. I moved from Idlib myself just a few months ago. Your reporting has made such a difference. And thank you for continuing here. May I take a photo with you? To show my friends?
Thank you! Yes, of course.
Like he needed any more of an ego.
HA HA HA
Ha ha. Hush, Firas.
I kept reporting. I kept telling the truth. And people were still listening.

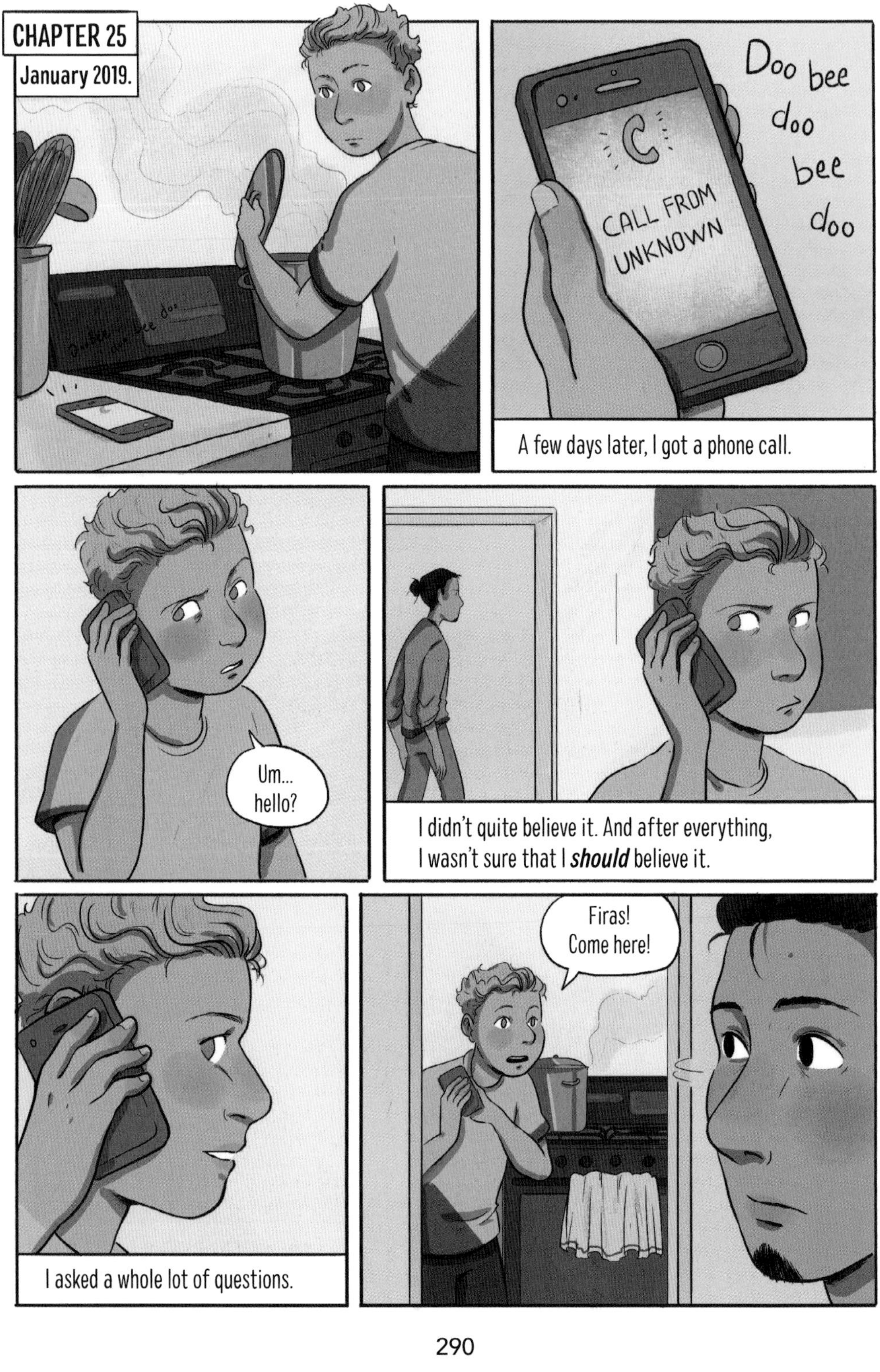
CHAPTER 25
January 2019.
Doo bee doo bee doo
CALL FROM UNKNOWN
A few days later, I got a phone call.
Um... hello?
I didn't quite believe it. And after everything, I wasn't sure that I ***should*** believe it.
I asked a whole lot of questions.
Firas! Come here!

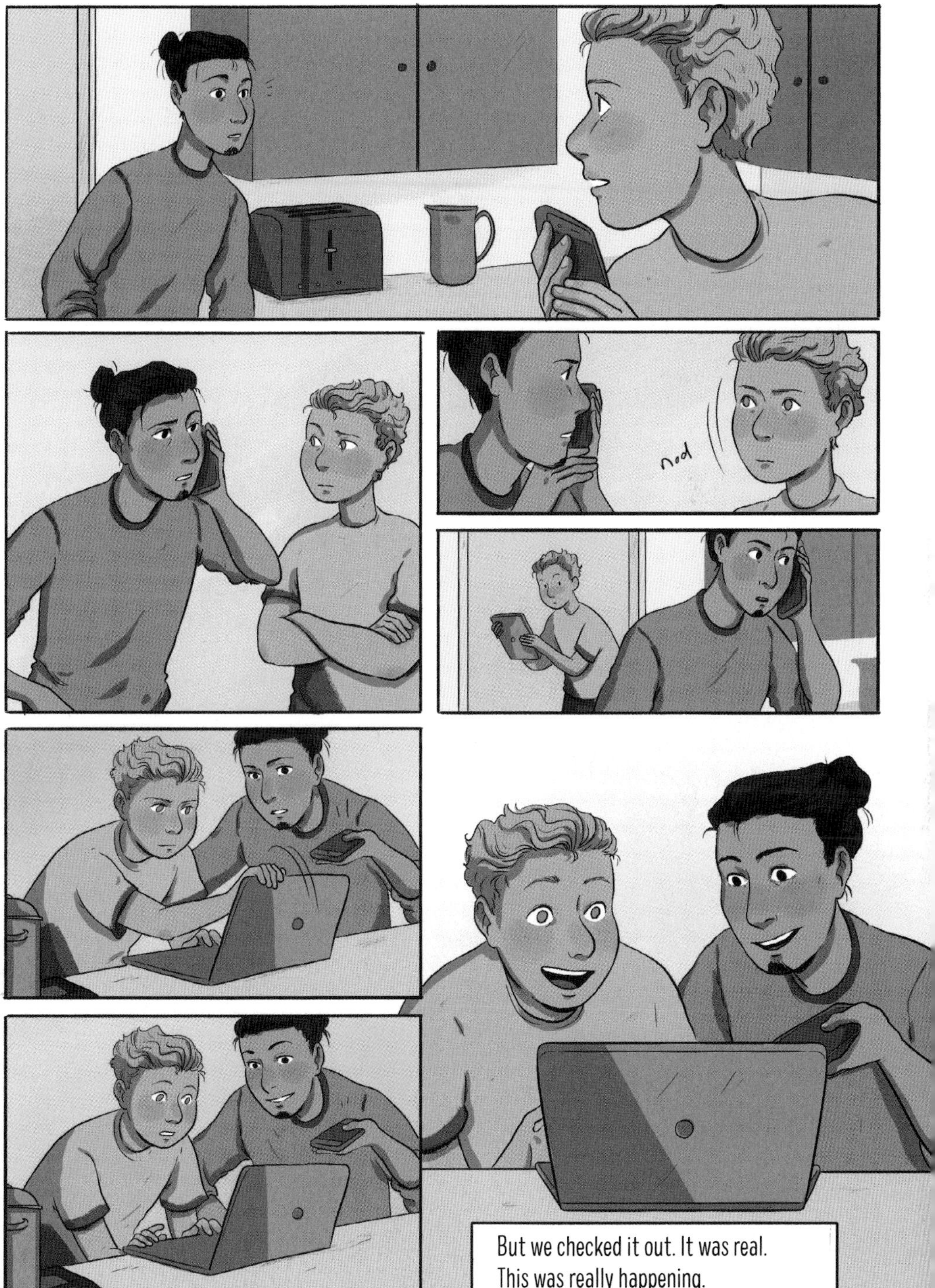
nod
But we checked it out. It was real.
This was really happening.

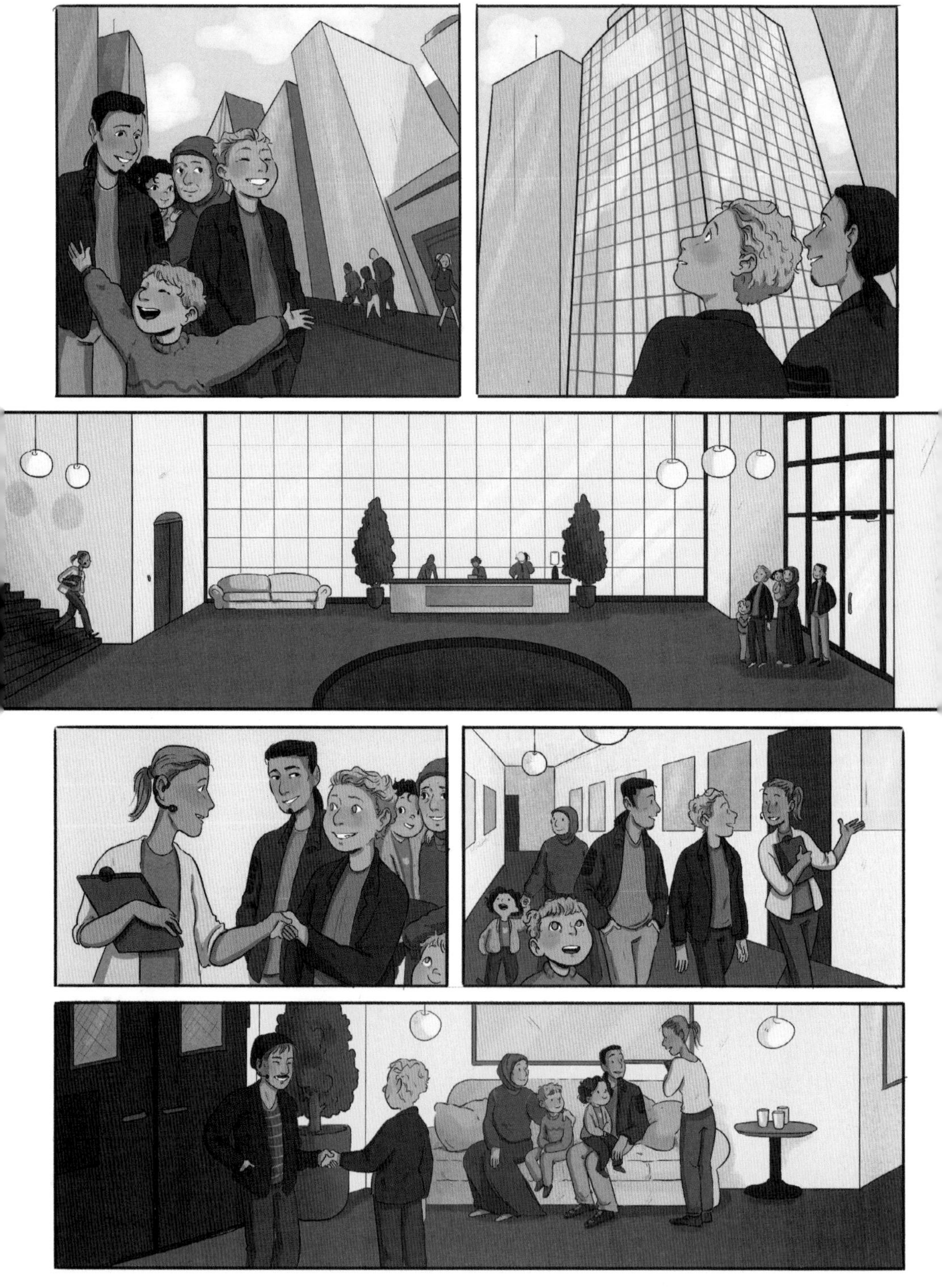

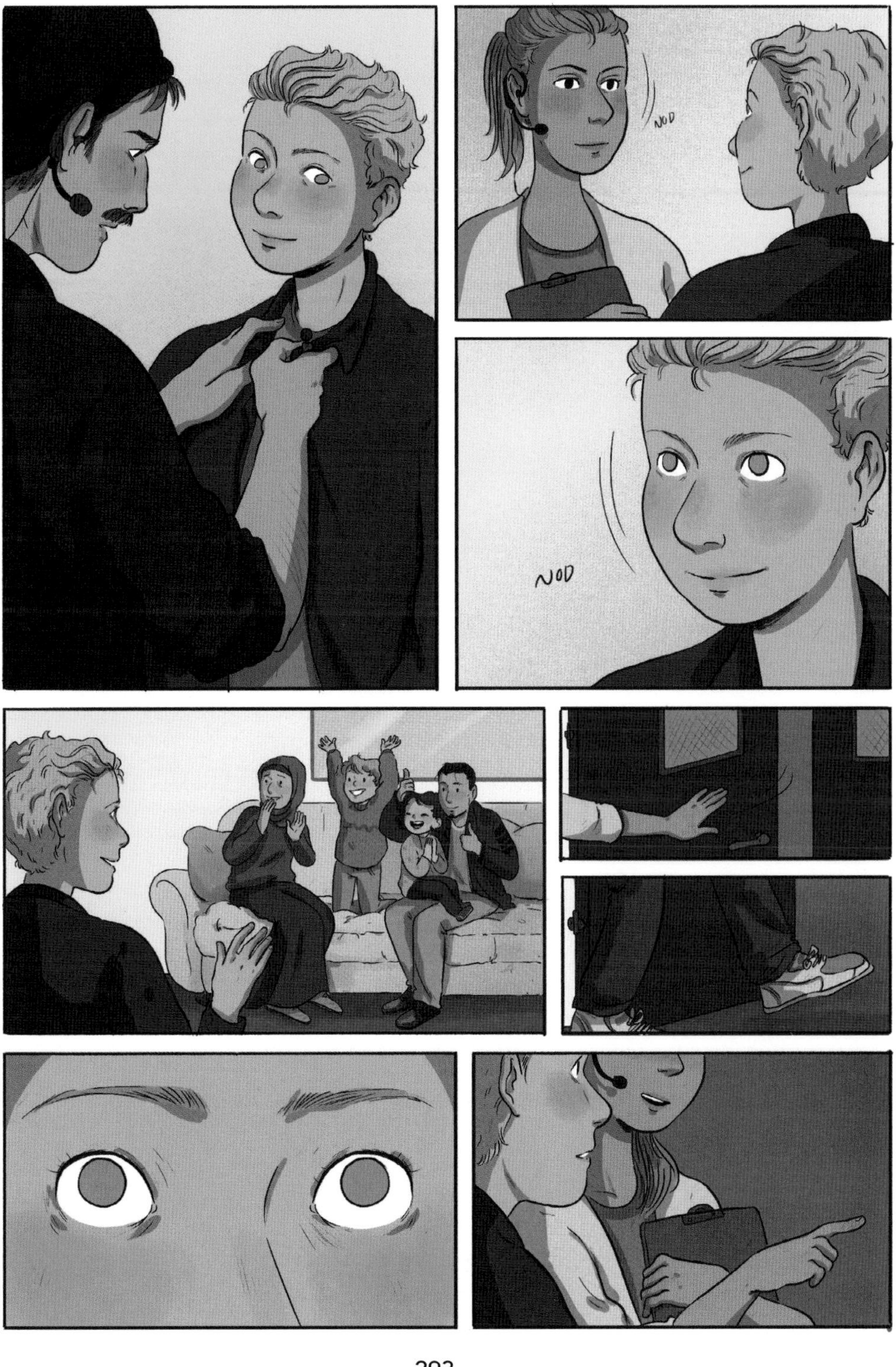
NOD
NOD

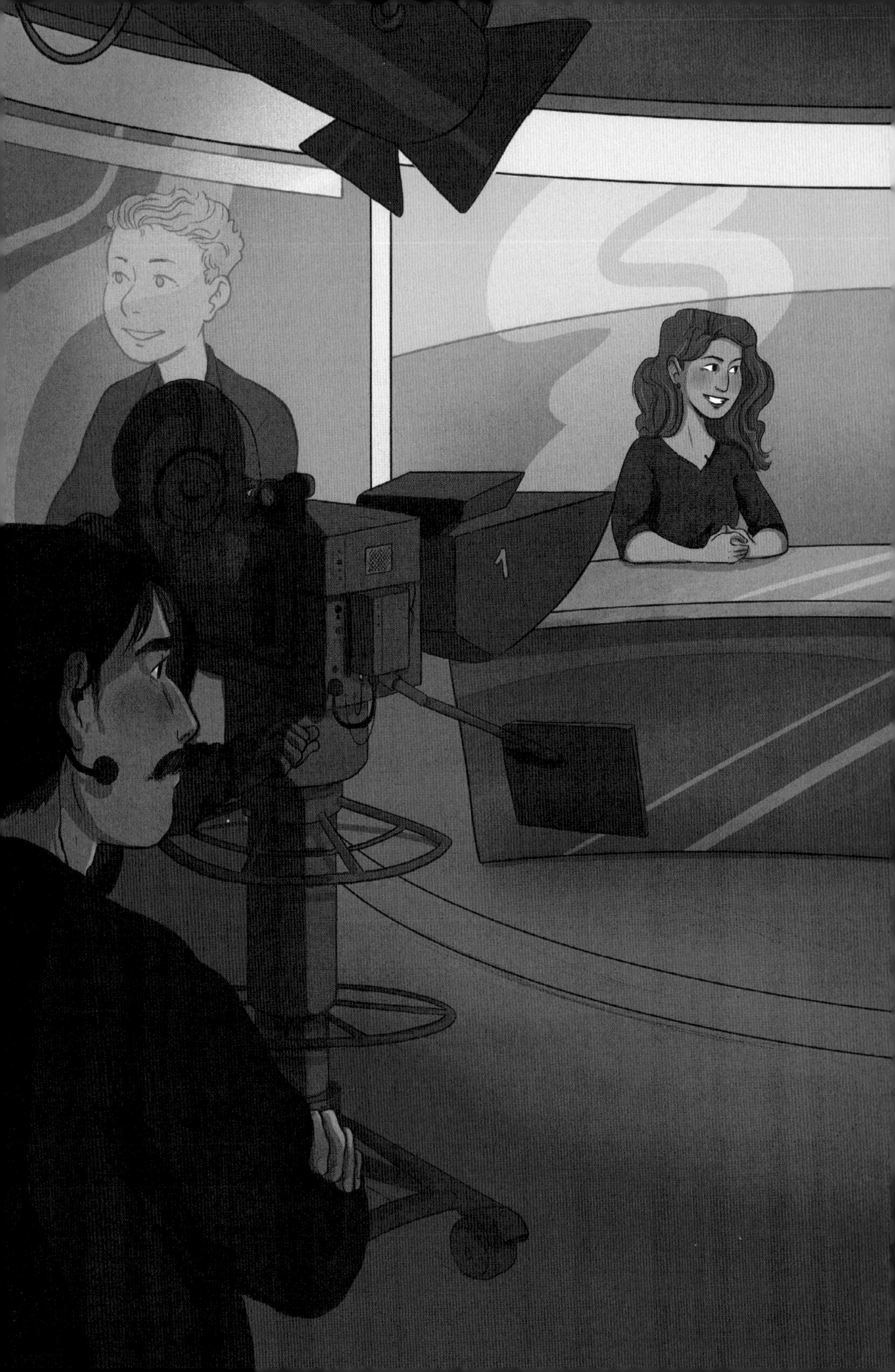
1

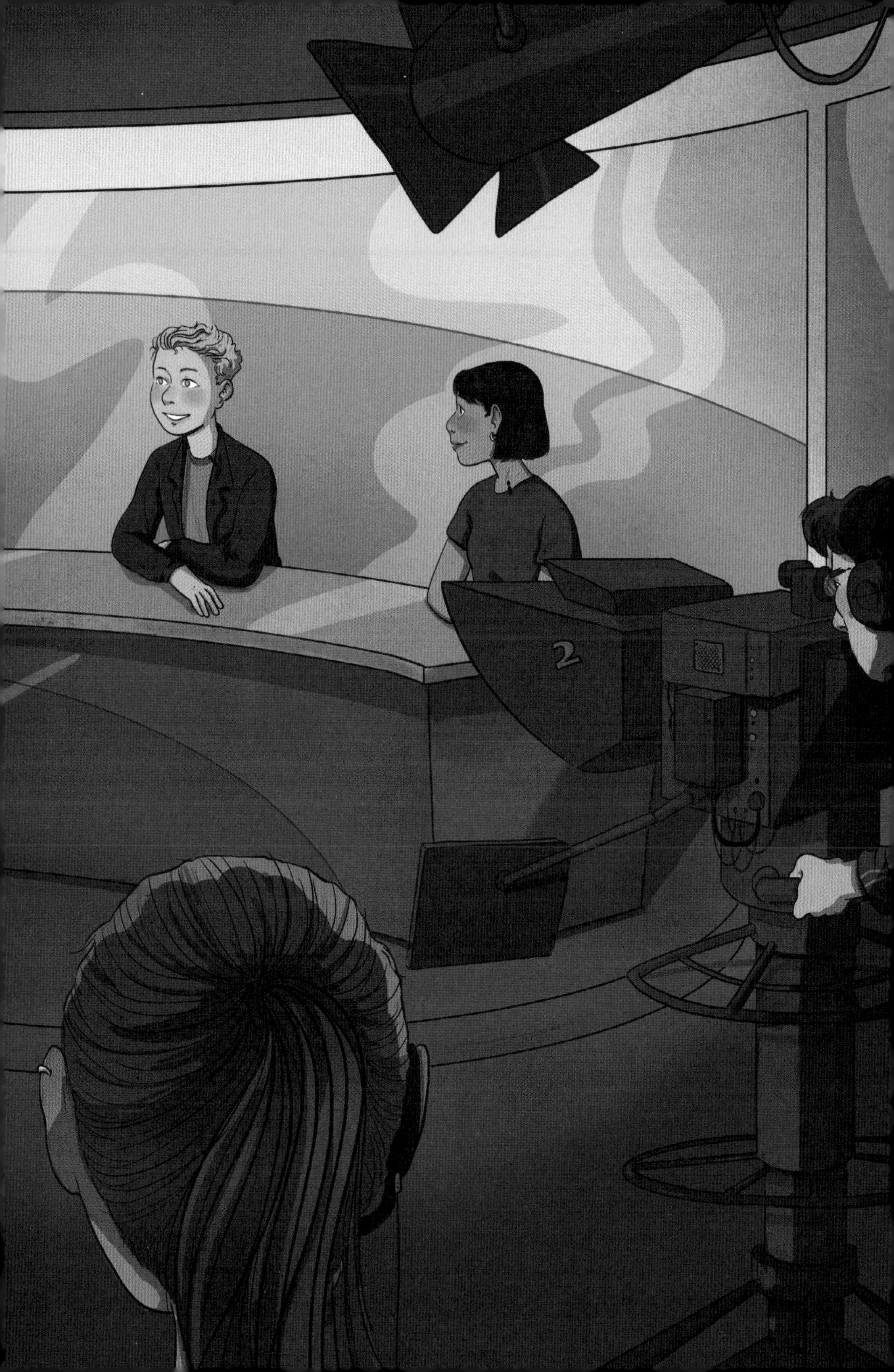
2

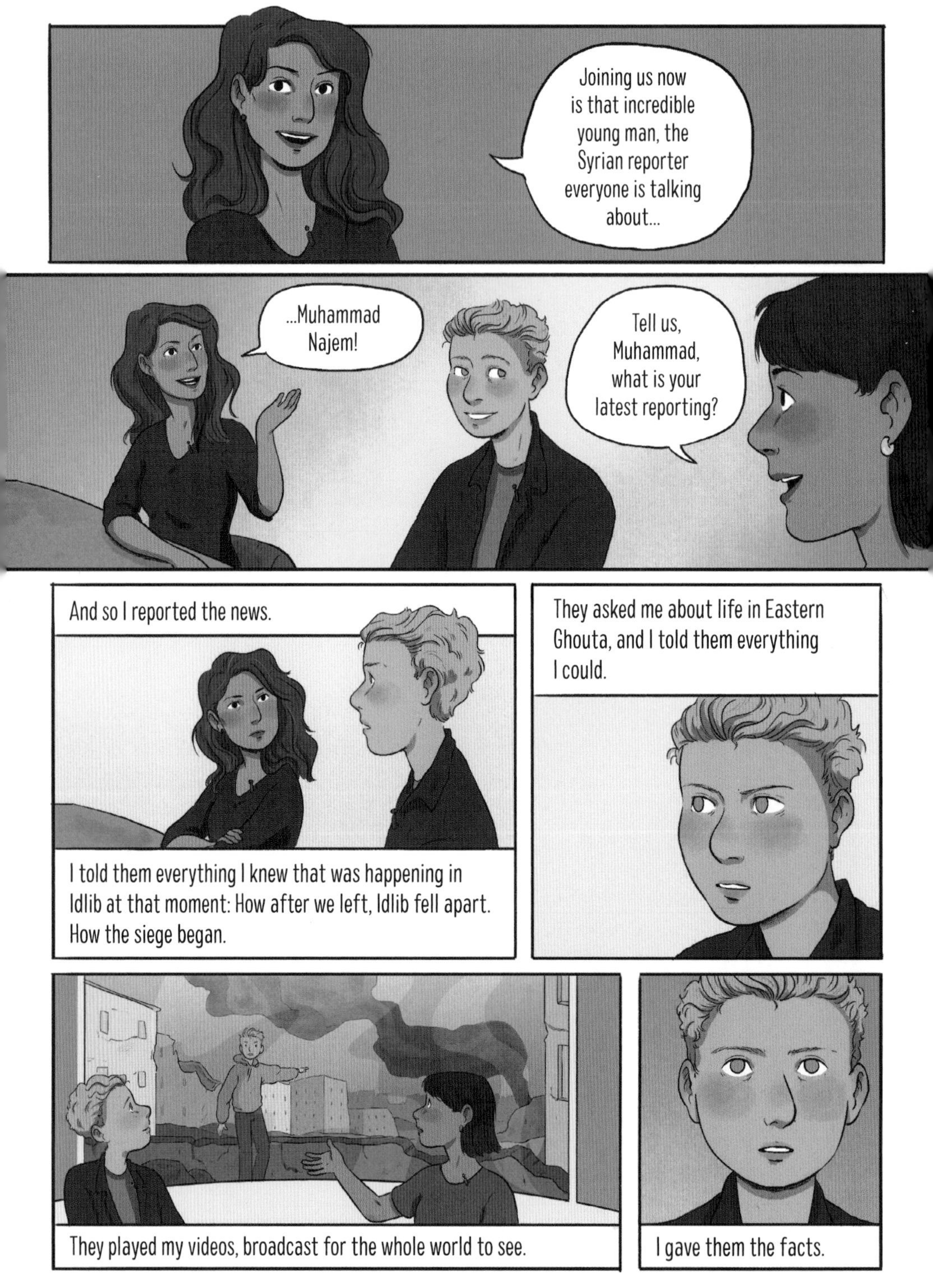
Joining us now is that incredible young man, the Syrian reporter everyone is talking about...
...Muhammad Najem!
Tell us, Muhammad, what is your latest reporting?
And so I reported the news.
I told them everything I knew that was happening in Idlib at that moment: How after we left, Idlib fell apart. How the siege began.
They asked me about life in Eastern Ghouta, and I told them everything I could.
They played my videos, broadcast for the whole world to see.
I gave them the facts.

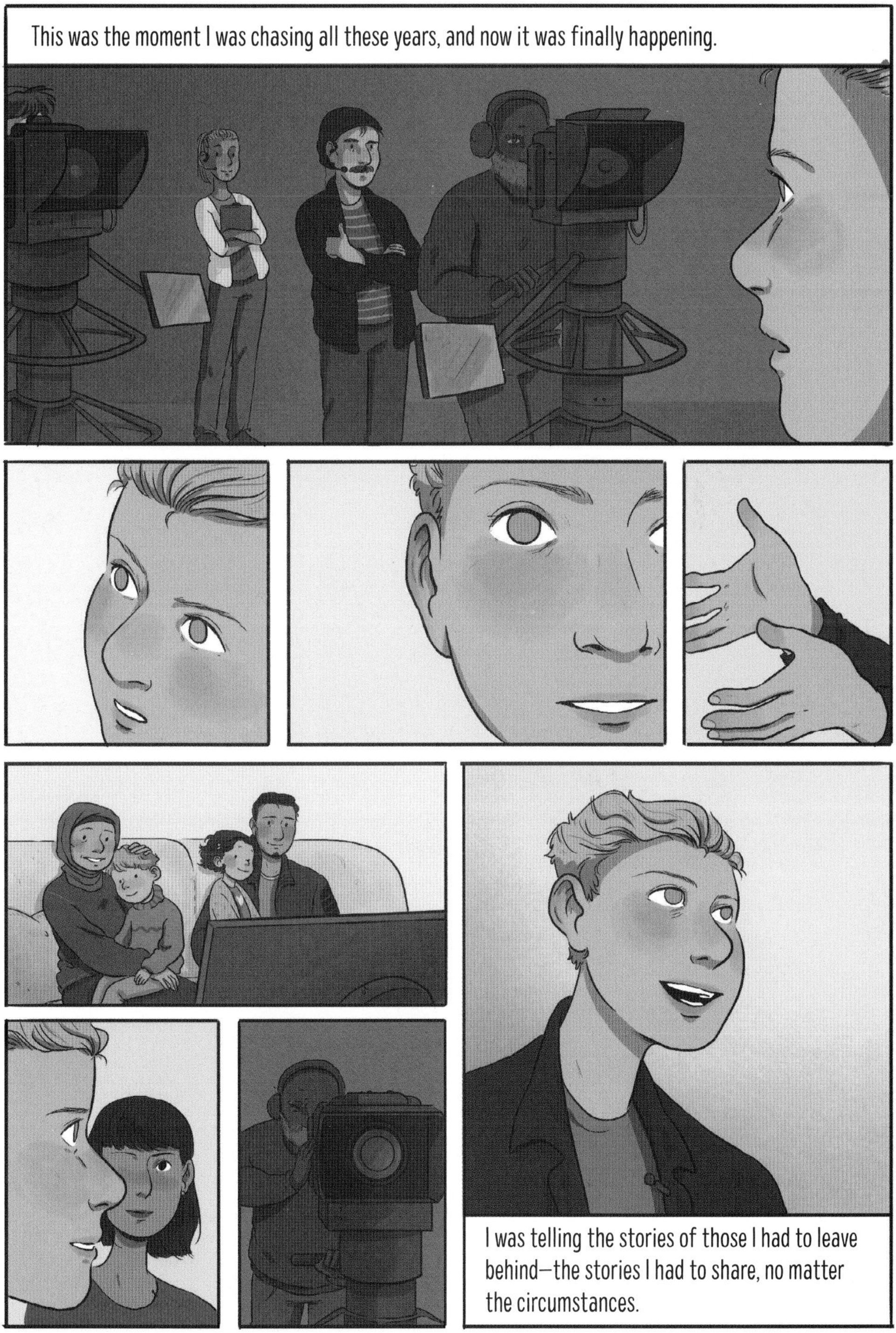

This was the moment I was chasing all these years, and now it was finally happening.
I was telling the stories of those I had to leave behind—the stories I had to share, no matter the circumstances.

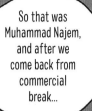
So that was Muhammad Najem, and after we come back from commercial break...

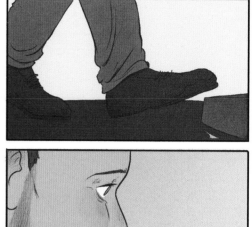
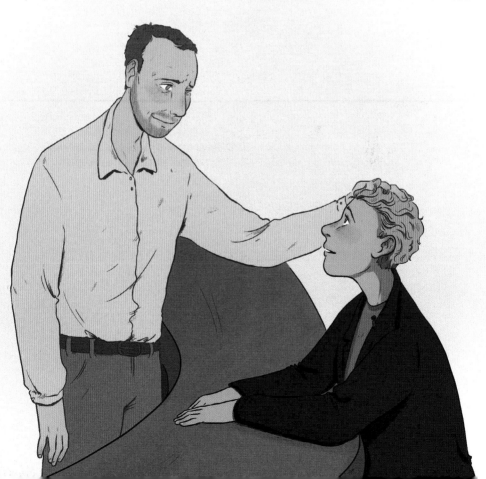

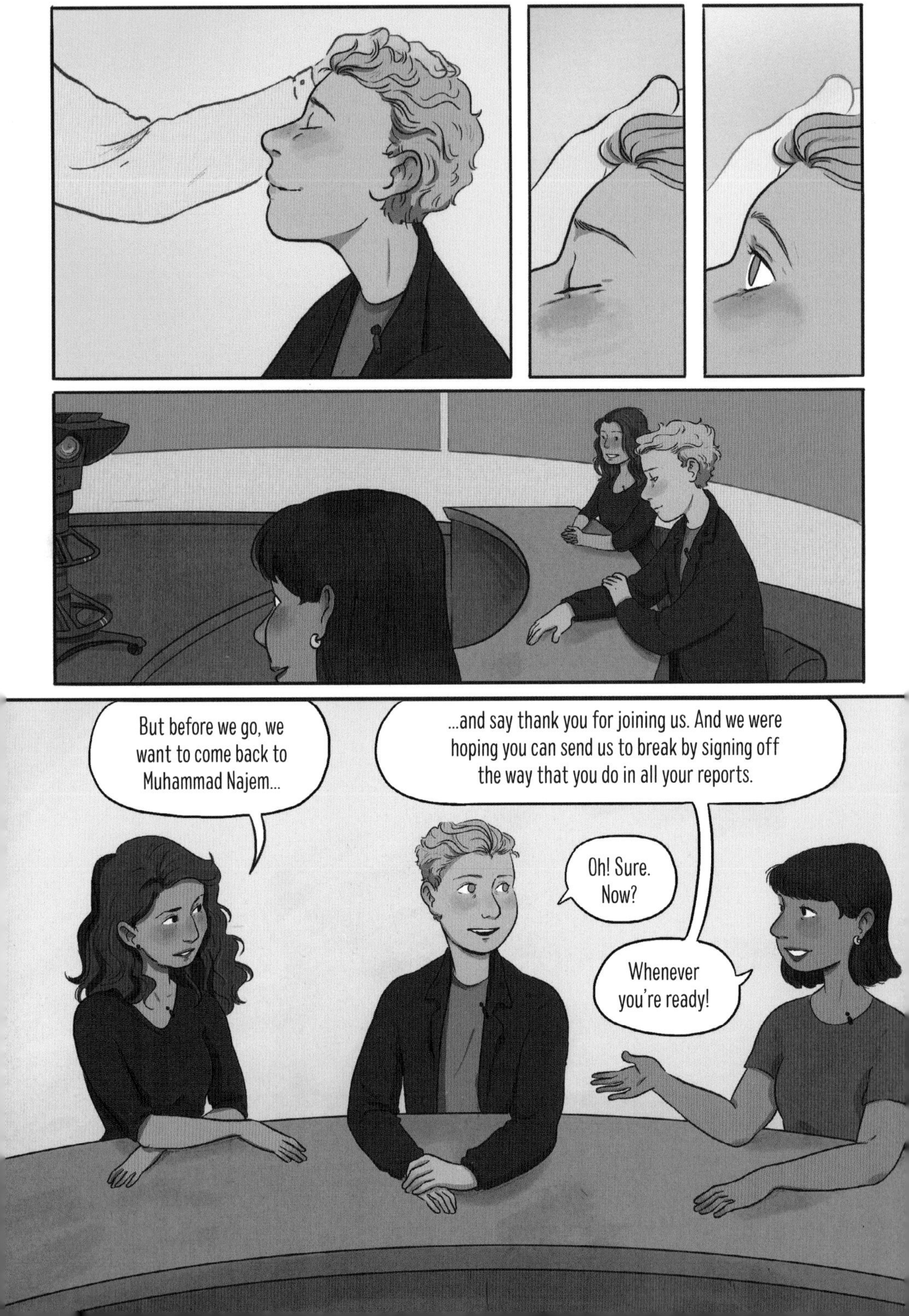
But before we go, we want to come back to Muhammad Najem...
...and say thank you for joining us. And we were hoping you can send us to break by signing off the way that you do in all your reports.
Oh! Sure. Now?
Whenever you're ready!

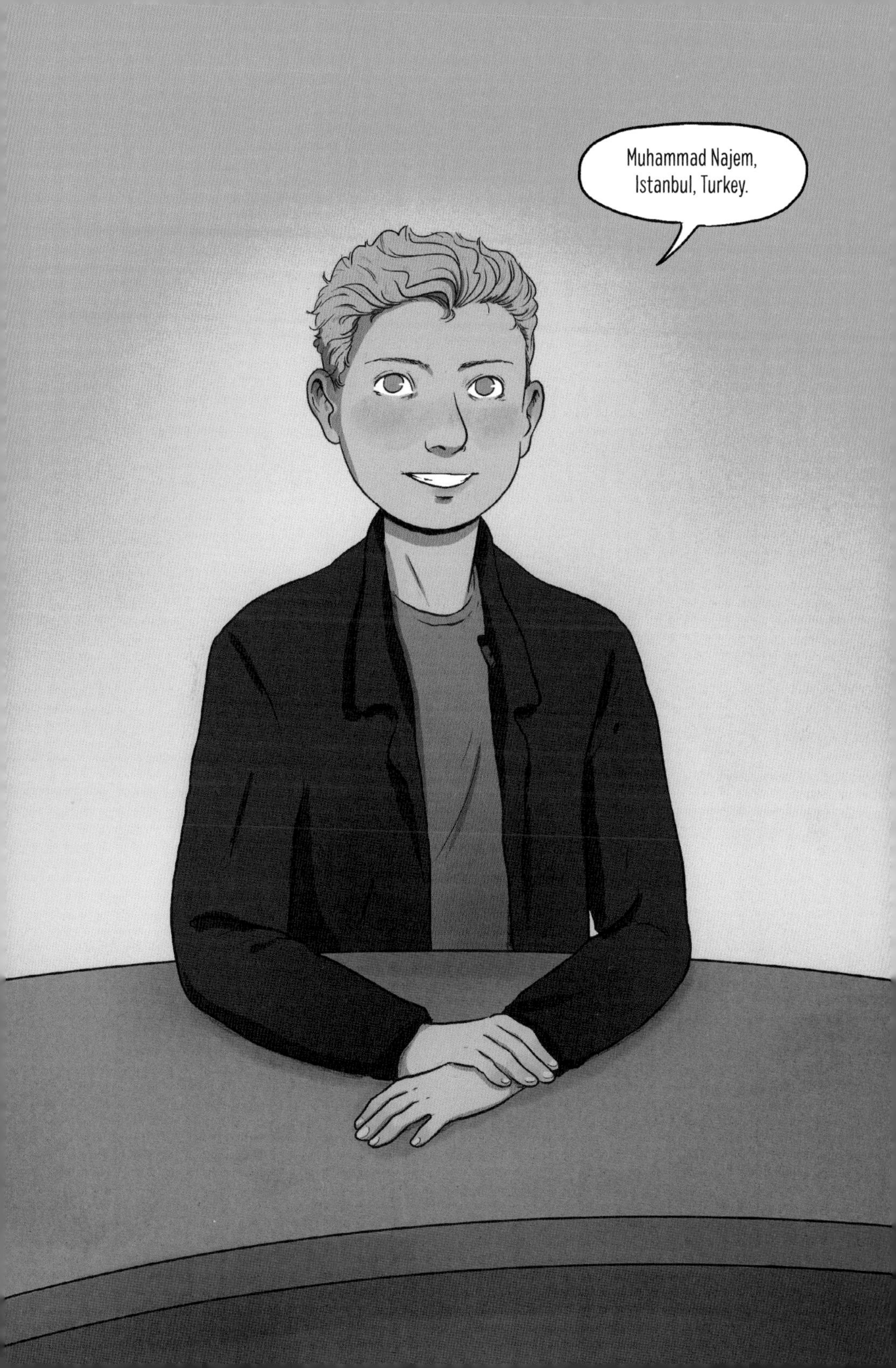
Muhammad Najem,
Istanbul, Turkey.

MUHAMMAD IN 2022, AT 19.

AFTERWORD

In the years following the events of this book, Muhammad and his family began the long work of building a new life. As of 2022, they live in Istanbul, Turkey, where Muhammad still reports on Syria and world events. He has become an advocate for refugee children around the world and has spoken with actress Angelina Jolie and for Amnesty International.

Hiba and Mourad moved to Afrin, another rebel-held area in northern Syria, where Hiba gave birth to a healthy baby boy named Rayan. In 2019, after multiple unsuccessful attempts to cross the border and join the rest of their family, Hiba, Mourad, and Rayan entered Turkey with Nora's help. They settled in Istanbul and soon had another child, a daughter named Sewar. Fadi chose to remain in Syria, where he found his life's work helping others in wartime, delivering food and vaccines to those in need.

Nora was able to visit the family in Istanbul in 2019, cementing their lifelong friendship. Muhammad proudly showed off his improved English skills, his family's cute apartment, and how to use the metro to get to Taksim Square. Hiba even taught Nora how to make her famous yebrak.

Aunt Nasrin and her family remain in Syria, as does Selim. They keep up with Muhammad and his family through video calls.

Muhammad dreams of the day he can finish his education. He would like to eventually live in the United States.

A NOTE FROM NORA

I still remember the first time I saw one of Muhammad's videos. It was January 2018, and I stumbled across his Twitter account while doing research for my MA in War Studies, in addition to working for Anderson Cooper at CNN. Muhammad looked right at me through the camera, and I instantly knew that he was special, that his words could have the power to change the world if more people heard them. I'm so grateful that my bosses at CNN, Charlie Moore and Chuck Hadad, saw the potential as well and gave me their blessing to write an article about Muhammad for CNN.com. We didn't expect much: It would just be a little online story with an accompanying video that I edited on my laptop in my spare time. We were shocked when the story went viral, but we were pleased...and then terrified.

I've struggled a lot with feeling guilty for what happened to Muhammad and his family after our CNN story put a target on their backs. Part of me wonders if Uncle Nazar would still be here today if not for the spotlight on their specific neighborhood in Eastern Ghouta. But at the same time, I do believe that Muhammad's videos and his incredible reporting would have gone viral eventually, with or without me.

We kept in touch after Muhammad and his family moved to Turkey. I was heartbroken to hear that Hiba had to stay behind in Syria. She's only two years older than I am, and we'd spoken through the course of my reporting because Muhammad was still a minor then, and I thought of her as a friend. In the winter of 2019, after trying everything possible, I was finally able to find a way to help her and her family get to Turkey. It's important to note here: I may have helped with the logistics, but the bravery to leave everything they'd ever known and start anew was all theirs.

Just a few months later, I flew to Istanbul to meet Muhammad and his family. Landing at the airport, I was honestly a little scared; I had flown halfway across the world to meet them for the first time in person! But Firas picked me up, and in a matter of minutes of getting to their apartment, we were all hugging and crying, opening gifts from the United States, drinking supersweet tea, and telling one another the stories of our lives. Firas and I are only two *months* apart in age, so we've become very close friends as well.

Today, Muhammad, Firas, Hiba, and I keep in touch through video calls, messages, and emails. I am beyond honored that they call me their extra sister and that they trust me to help tell their incredible, inspiring story to the world. I am keenly aware of how lucky I am to know this world-changing family, and hopefully now you feel the same.

HIBA'S YEBRAK

Adapted by Elle Abitante

PREP TIME: 30 minutes

COOKING TIME: 2½ hours

TOTAL TIME: 3 hours

YIELD: about 40 pieces

A NOTE FROM HIBA

Yebrak, or stuffed grape leaves, is the most popular Syrian dish and my favorite food! But I didn't always like it. When I was a kid, I refused to touch the grape leaves, instead eating just the rice mixture inside. I thought the leaves wouldn't taste good! But when I finally tasted them, I loved them so much, and I regretted all the years I'd missed out!

As a young girl, I watched my mom and aunts make yebrak, taking hours to carefully roll the grape leaves and arrange them in perfect circles at the bottoms of their pans. When I turned fifteen, I started to roll yebrak with my mom. The first time, I thought my yebrak looked okay, but when I uncovered the pot, each one had fallen apart! The pot was just full of watery rice and empty grape leaves. I learned that I hadn't rolled them tightly enough.

Soon I learned how to properly roll my yebrak and cook the dish all by myself, even adding my own secret ingredient. It turned out incredible! Now everyone in my family, including my husband, loves the amazing taste of my yebrak.

It takes a long time to prepare, but as soon as you taste it, you'll forget how tired you are! You can make it with meat or vegetables, or you can leave it plain, and all three ways are delicious. Here's how.

INGREDIENTS

2 cups white rice

1 (16-ounce) can grape leaves*

1 tablespoon olive oil

1 teaspoon salt

1 teaspoon pepper

1 teaspoon coarse or ground cumin

Juice of 1 lemon

2 cloves garlic, minced or grated

½ cup pomegranate juice

Optional: 1 pound ground lamb or beef

---

* These are usually found in the Mediterranean section of the grocery store. You can also use fresh grape leaves if you have access, but they can be hard to find in some parts of the world!

EQUIPMENT

Mixing bowl

Small saucepan

Measuring cups

Clean dish towels

Heavy-bottomed, wide-mouthed pan with a lid

Heavy pot or bowl of water (to weigh down the yebrak)

DIRECTIONS

1. Put the rice in a large mixing bowl. Rinse the rice with water, then fill the bowl with water until the water level is an inch above the rice. Let soak for 30 minutes.

2. Prepare the pomegranate sauce (my secret ingredient!). Heat the pomegranate juice in a small saucepan over medium heat. Stir often until the liquid begins to thicken, about 7 to 10 minutes. The sauce will continue to thicken as it cools—it should be the consistency of runny honey.

3. Separate and rinse the grape leaves. Then pat them dry with a clean dish towel. If using canned grape leaves, be sure to rinse them thoroughly, as the salt content is very high. When I made Nora yebrak in Istanbul, it was right after I moved from Syria and I had never used canned grape leaves, since we used fresh leaves at home. They were so salty that the yebrak was almost inedible!

4. Prepare the rice mixture. Drain the soaked rice. Then return it to the bowl and add olive oil, salt, pepper, cumin, lemon juice, garlic, and the pomegranate sauce. If using meat, add raw ground meat to the rice mixture. Stir to combine.

5. On a clean surface, lay an individual grape leaf out flat, vein-side up. With the stem facing you, spread 1 tablespoon of rice mixture in a thin line across the lower third of the leaf. Fold the bottom over the rice, tuck in the sides, and continue rolling the leaf tightly, making sure to apply gentle and even pressure. Grape leaves can be tricky to work with, so having a strong but delicate hand is very important. Try not to rip the leaves, but know that it does happen! Roll the remaining leaves.

6. After rolling the leaves, arrange the yebrak in a circular pattern on the bottom of the wide-mouthed pan, keeping the rows tight to prevent the stuffing from seeping out. If you are adding meat or vegetables, place those in the bottom of the pan first and then place the yebrak on top.

7. Place a heavy pot on top of the yebrak to prevent it from moving around during cooking.

8. Add just enough water to the pan to cover the yebrak. Bring to a boil, then simmer for 2 hours.

9. After cooking, carefully remove the yebrak from the pot and enjoy!

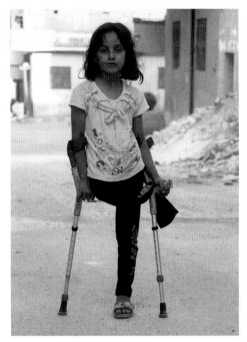

Fatima from Aleppo.

Muhammad as a toddler, in one of his first school photos.

One of Muhammad's early school photos.

Muhammad as a child.

Firas, Fadi, and Hiba.

Muhammad and the
beloved family parrot.

Muhammad plays his favorite
video game on the family
computer in their first house.

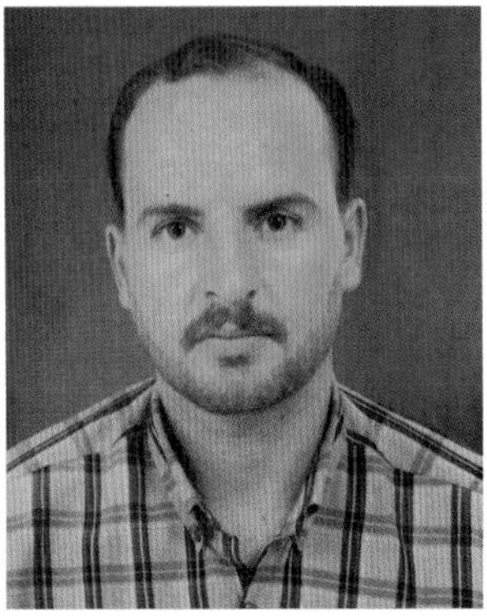

Baba's passport photo from before the war.

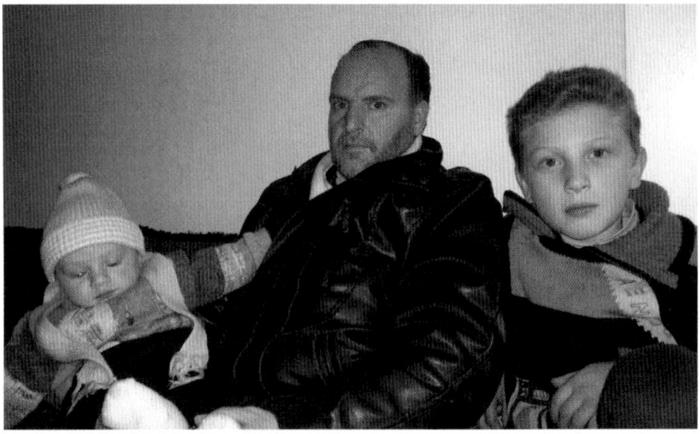

Karam, Baba, and Muhammad during the war.

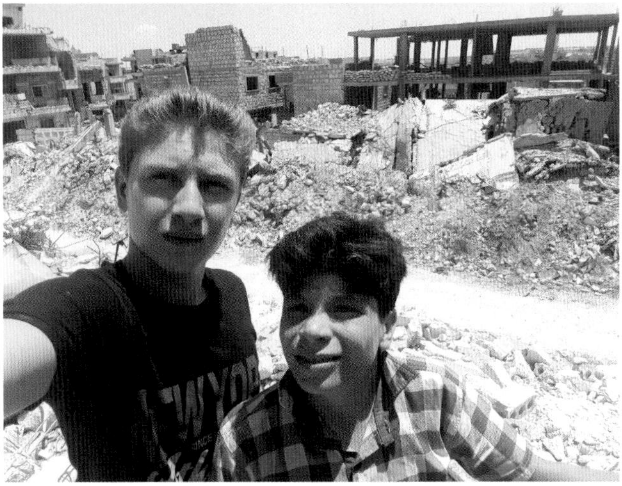

Muhammad and his best friend, Selim, before Selim was injured in an air strike.

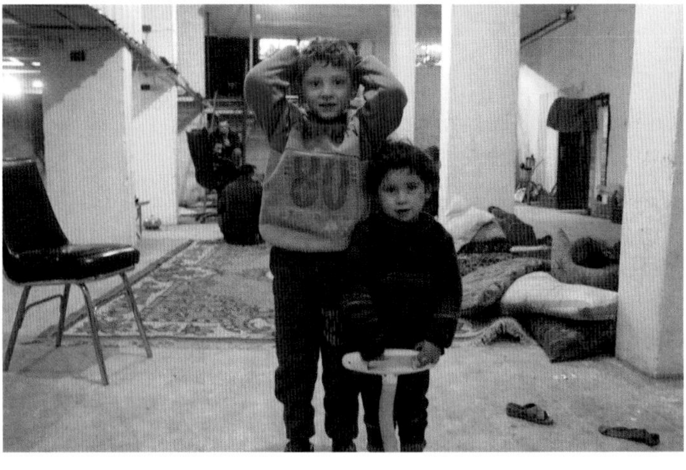

Karam and Batul in the underground shelter where the family spent most of their time with their neighbors and friends.

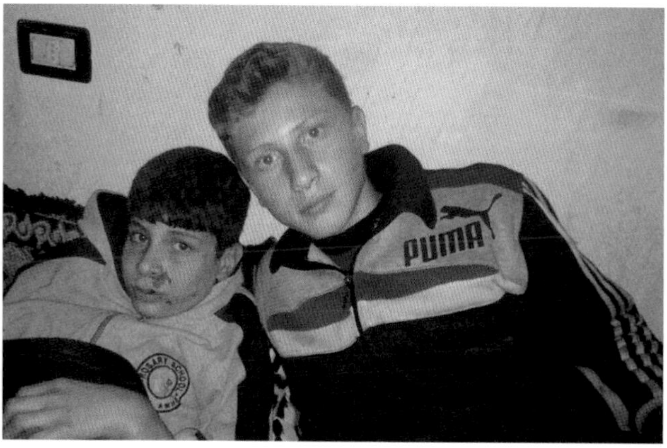
PUMA

Selim and Muhammad when Selim got out of the hospital after the air strike that injured him.

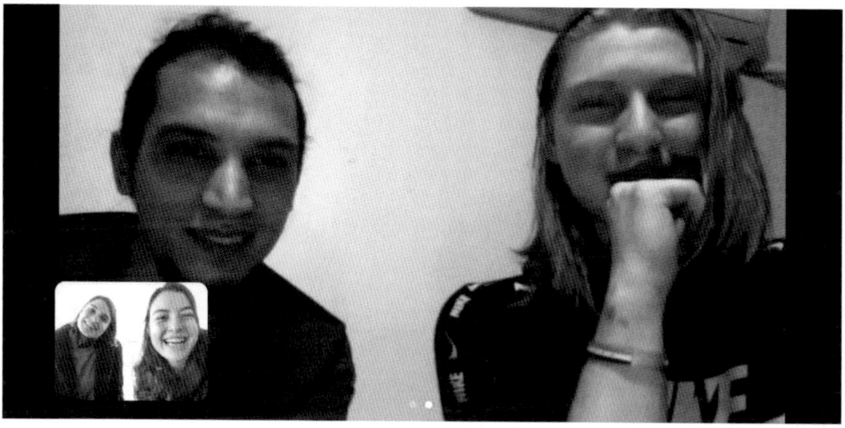

Firas and Muhammad speak with Julie and Nora (*inset*) on a video call.

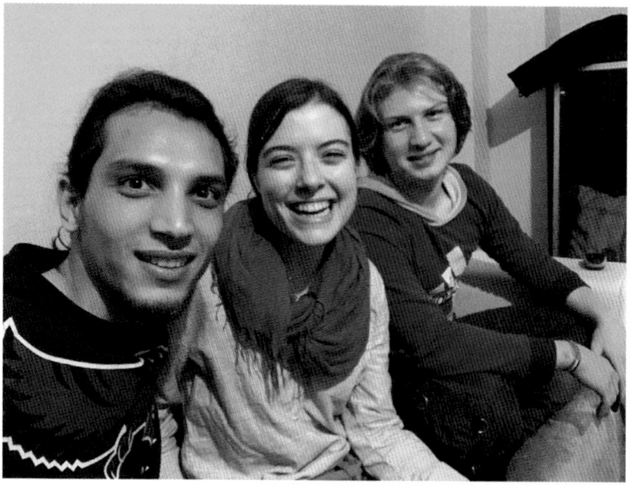

Firas, Nora, and Muhammad hang out at the family's apartment in Turkey.

Karam and Batul "help" Firas pick out photos to show Nora for book research while eating a traditional Syrian breakfast.

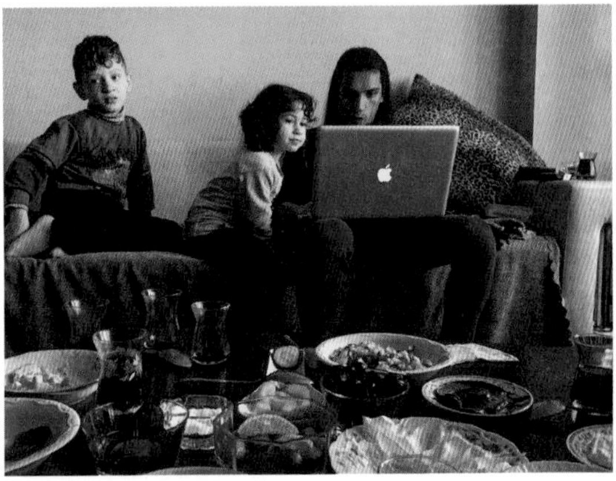

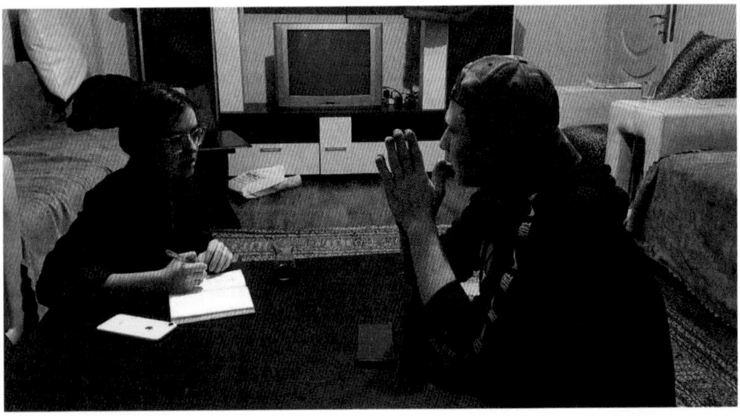

Nora interviews Muhammad for the book in Istanbul—always with tea!

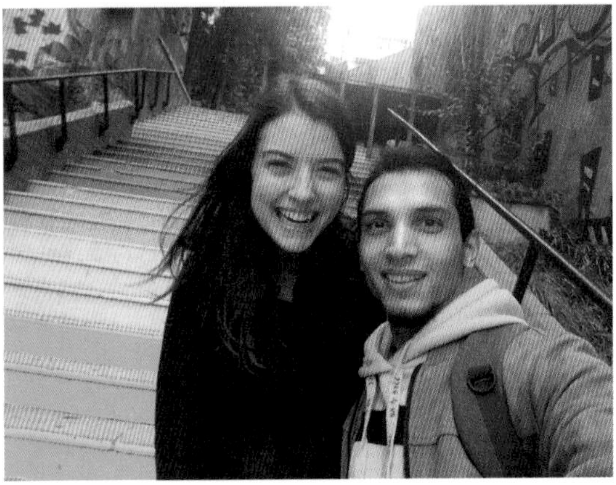

Nora and Firas sightsee in Istanbul.

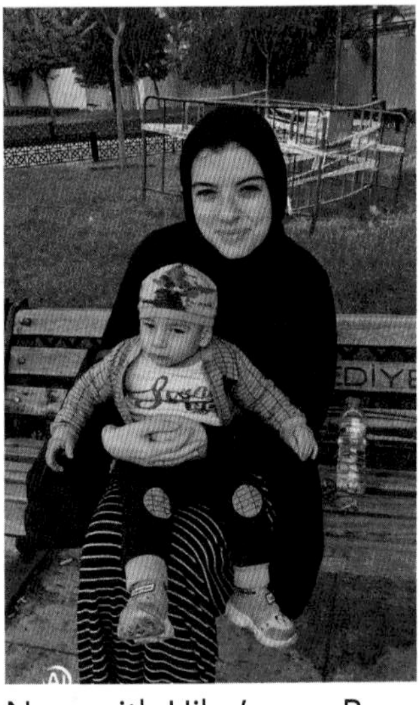

Nora with Hiba's son, Rayan, in Istanbul.